PRIVILEGE AND PROPERTY

Daniel Chodowiecki's allegorical copper plate of 1781 shows unauthorised reprinters and original publishers, respectively as highwaymen and their victims while the Goddess of Justice is asleep. The full title reads: 'Works of Darkness. A Contribution to the History of the Book Trade in Germany. Presented Allegorically for the Benefit of and as a Warning to All Honest Booksellers.' The identities of most of the characters have been identified: the bandit chief is the Austrian publisher Johann Thomas von Trattner (1717-1798) who made a fortune by reprinting books from other German-speaking territories. His victims are the publishers Friedrich Nicolai (in the centre), and Philipp Erasmus Reich (fleeing into the background). The small bat-like monster hovering overhead (a position normally reserved for angels in religious paintings!) is modelled on Gerhard van Swieten (1700-1772), an influential adviser and doctor of Maria Theresa of Austria who eased censorship regulations but encouraged the reprinting of foreign books in Austria. Nicolai's right arm extends the bat monster's line of gaze and points to the head of the Goddess Justitia, sleeping as if drugged by the poppy blossoms above her head.

Apart from a scriptural-theological aspect (equating reprints with 'works of darkness') and a more juridical one (comparing reprinting to robbery), the title, by describing the etching as a 'warning to all honest booksellers', also evokes moral principles in civil society. The 'honest' bookseller is one who does not deal in reprints. Ironically, Christian Friedrich Himburg, the Berlin publisher of the copper print was himself to be branded a pirate for a 1777 two-volume Goethe edition which in turn was soon reprinted by two other publishers: in 1778 by Schmieder in Karlsruhe and by Fleischhauer in Reutlingen.

Source: Antiquariat Voerster, Stuttgart.
For more details see: Chodowiecki's Allegory 'Works of Darkness' (1781), *Primary Sources on Copyright (1450-1900)*, www.copyrighthistory.org

Wercke der Finsternis.

oder Beytrag zur Geschichte des Buchhandels in Deutschland Allegorisch vorgestellt zum besten,
auch zur Warnung aller ehrliebenden Buchhændler.

zu finden bey C.F. Himburg in Berlin.

Ronan Deazley is Professor of Law at the University of Glasgow. He is the author of *On the Origin of the Right to Copy: Charting the Movement of Copyright Law in Eighteenth Century Britain (1695-1775)* (2004) and *Rethinking Copyright: History, Theory, Language* (2006, 2008).

Martin Kretschmer is Professor of Information Jurisprudence and Director of the Centre for Intellectual Property Policy & Management (CIPPM) at Bournemouth University, UK. His research includes a long-term project on artists' labour markets and earnings funded by the Arts Council and Collecting Societies ALCS and DACS, as well as numerous interdisciplinary studies addressing specific policy issues (funders include European Commission, Economic and Social Research Council (ESRC), and the UK Strategic Advisory Board for IP Policy).

Lionel Bently is the Herchel Smith Professor of Intellectual Property Law at the University of Cambridge, and Director of the Centre for Intellectual Property and Information Law, Cambridge. His published works include: *The Making of Modern Intellectual Property Law* (with Brad Sherman) (1999) and *Intellectual Property Law*, 3rd ed (2008).

Lionel Bently and Martin Kretschmer are joint project directors of the Arts and Humanities Research Council (AHRC) funded digital archive: *Primary Sources on Copyright (1450-1900)*, www.copyrighthistory.org.

Privilege and Property

Essays on the History of Copyright

Edited by

Ronan Deazley, Martin Kretschmer and Lionel Bently

Cambridge

OpenBook Publishers

2010

OpenBook
Publishers

Open Book Publishers CIC Ltd.,
40 Devonshire Road, Cambridge, CB1 2BL, United Kingdom
http://www.openbookpublishers.com

As with all Open Book Publishers titles, digital material and resources associated with this volume are available from our website:
http://www.openbookpublishers.com

ISBN Hardback: 978-1-906924-19-5
ISBN Paperback: 978-1-906924-18-8
ISBN Digital (pdf): 978-1-906924-20-1

Acknowledgment is made to the The Jessica E. Smith and Kevin R. Brine Charitable Trust for their generous contribution towards the preparation of this volume.

All paper used by Open Book Publishers is SFI (Sustainable Forestry Initiative), and PEFC (Programme for the Endorsement of Forest Certification Schemes) Certified.

Printed in the United Kingdom and United States by
Lightning Source for Open Book Publishers

Contents

Contributors

Isabella **Alexander** is a Newton Trust Lecturer in Law at the University of Cambridge and Beachcroft LLP Fellow in Law and Director of Studies in Law at Robinson College, Cambridge. Her publications onclude 'The Lord Chancellor, the Poets and the Courtesan: Public Morality and Copyright Law in the Early Nineteenth Century', in *Law and the City: Proceedings of the 17th British Legal History Conference* (2005) and 'Criminalising Copyright: A Story of Pirates, Publishers and Pieces of Eight' (2007) 66 *Cambridge Law Journal* 625. She is the author of *Copyright and the Public Interest in the Nineteenth Century* (2010).

Maurizio **Borghi** is a Lecturer in Intellectual Property Law at Brunel Law School, and holds a Ph.D. from Bocconi University of Milan. He studied social sciences and philosophy at the University of Milan, has been a researcher at Bocconi University and a visiting scholar at the Center for the Study of Law and Society of the University of California, Berkeley. He has authored a monograph on the history of copyright (*La manifattura del pensiero*, 2003), edited a book on digital copyright (*Proprietà digitale*, 2006, with Maria Lillà Montagnani), and translated philosophical works from German and French. He is also author of a number of articles and papers on different topics, including philosophy and copyright law.

Oren **Bracha** is an Assistant Professor of Law at the University of Texas School of Law. He received his LL.B. from the Tel-Aviv University Faculty of Law in 1998 and his S.J.D. from Harvard Law School in 2005. Bracha is a legal historian and an intellectual property law scholar who has published various articles about the history of intellectual property, copyright law, and internet law. His forthcoming book *Owning Ideas* is an intellectual history of American intellectual property law in the nineteenth century. Bracha was a law clerk for Chief Justice Aharon Barak of the Supreme Court of Israel. During his time at Harvard Law School he worked on various projects for the Berkamn Center for Internet and Society. His fields of interest and scholarship include intellectual property, cyberlaw, legal history and legal theory.

John **Feather** has been Professor of Library and Information Studies at Loughborough since 1988, having worked in publishing and librarianship before moving to Loughborough. He has served as Head of Department (1990-94, 2003-06), Dean of Education and Humanities (1994-96) and Pro-Vice Chancellor (1996-2000). He has been a Visiting Professor at UCLA, and undertaken many other international tasks for the British Council, the EU, and UNESCO among others. He was a founding Board member of AHRC, and has served on committees and advisory bodies of learned societies, professional bodies and government and international agencies. His many publications include *A History of British publishing* (2nd ed, 2006), and *Publishing, Piracy and Politics. An Historical Study of Copyright in Britain* (1994).

Stef **van Gompel** is a Ph.D. candidate at the Institute for Information Law (IViR) of the University of Amsterdam. His dissertation covers the history of, rationales for, and possible future of, the prohibition on copyright formalities (Article 5(2) Berne Convention). Before he started his Ph.D. programme, Mr Van Gompel worked at IViR, first as an intern, and later as researcher. He wrote articles on collective rights management, orphan works, and the possible term extension of related rights in sound recordings. Following this he was co-author of the study, commissioned by the European Commission, on the Recasting of copyright and related rights for the knowledge economy. Mr Van Gompel is a member of the Study Group on the History of Copyright of the Dutch copyright organisation 'Vereniging voor Auteursrecht' (VvA). His key publications include: (with M.M.M. van Eechoud, P.B. Hugenholtz et al) *Harmonizing European Copyright Law: The Challenges of Better Lawmaking*, Information Law Series 19 (Kluwer Law International, 2009); 'Unlocking the Potential of Pre-Existing Content: How to Address the Issue of Orphan Works in Europe?', 38 IIC 669 (2007); (with P.B. Hugenholtz, M.M.M. van Eechoud et al.) *The Recasting of Copyright & Related Rights for the Knowledge Economy*, report to the European Commission, DG Internal Market, November 2006.

Friedemann **Kawohl** has degrees in Music theory and Arts management and received his PhD in Musicology from Technische Universität Berlin. He has written a book on music copyright in Prussia, published in German: *Urheberrecht der Musik in Preußen* (2001). He has lectured at Bournemouth University, School of Finance & Law (2000-03), and is now a research fellow in the Centre for Intellectual Property Policy & Management, Bournemouth University (www.cippm.org.uk).

Joanna **Kostylo** received a PhD in Italian history from the University of Cambridge, King's College. A Research Fellow at the Centre of Research in the Arts, Social Sciences and Humanities at Cambridge, she also teaches for the Italian Department and works on a research project *Primary Sources on Copyright (1450-1900)* at the Faculty of Law in Cambridge. The author of 'Commonwealth of All Faiths: Republican Myth and the Italian Diaspora in Sixteenth-century Poland-Lithuania', in Friedrich and Pendzich (eds), *Citizenship and Identity in a Multi-national Commonwealth: Poland Lithuania in Context, 1569-1795* (2008), her research interests range from Renaissance and Reformation studies to the history of the book and authorship in the early modern period.

Alastair **Mann** is Lecturer in Scottish History at the University of Stirling. He is co-editor of the online resource *Records of the Parliaments of Scotland* (2007/08) (www.rps.ac.uk) and of the forthcoming *History of the Book in Scotland*, vol. 1: *Medieval to 1707* (2009). He is author of the Saltire prize win-ing *The Scottish Book Trade, 1500 to 1720* (2000) and researches and publishes widely in both book and parliamentary history. Additionally, he is currently working on a biography of James VII and II from a Scottish perspective.

Karl-Nikolaus **Peifer** is currently Director of the Institute for Media Law and Communications Law of the University of Cologne and Director of the Institute for Broadcasting Law at the University of Cologne. He stud-ied law, economics and romanic languages at the Universities of Trier, Bonn, Hamburg and Kiel. He previously held positions as a researcher at the Max-Planck-Institute for Intellectual Property Law in Munich, as an Assistant Professor in Kiel, and as a Professor of Private, Business, Media and Intellectual Property Law in Frankfurt/Oder and Bochum. Since 2003 he has been a judge at the Oberlandesgericht Hamm. His main fields of research are Intellectual Property and Media Law.

Laurent **Pfister** is Professor of the History of Law at the University of Versailles Saint-Quentin and has written extensively on intellectual prop-erty, the history of private law, and the history of copyright.

Frédéric **Rideau** is a lecturer in legal history at the Faculty of Law of the University of Poitiers. His published works include: *La formation du droit de la propriété littéraire en France et en Grande-Bretagne: Une convergence oubliée* (2004).

Mark **Rose** is Professor of English at the University of California, Santa Barbara. He has published many books on a range of subjects from Shakespeare to science fiction, including *Heroic Love: Studies in Sidney and Spenser*; *Shakespearean Design*; *Spenser's Art*; and *Alien Encounters: Anatomy of Science Fiction*. His study of the emergence of copyright in eighteenth-century Britain, *Authors and Owners: The Invention of Copyright* (1993), was a finalist for a National Book Critics' Circle Award in 1993. In addition to writing on the history of copyright, he frequently serves as a consultant and expert witness in movie and television matters involving allegations of copyright infringement.

Katie **Scott** is a graduate in the History of Art from University College, London (1980), and was a Junior Research Fellow at Christ's College, Cambridge (1983-87) before joining the staff of The Courtaud Institute of Art in 1988. She has a PhD from the University of London (1988) and has had her subsequent research funded by the Leverhulme Trust (1999) and the AHRC (2004-05). She is the author of various scholarly publications, including: 'Authorship, the Académie and the Market in Early Modern France', *Oxford Art Journal*, 21/1 (1998); 'Art and Industry – A Contradictory Union: Authors, Rights and Copyrights during the Consulat', *Journal of Design History*, 13/1 (2000); and 'Invention and Privilege in Early Modern France: The Case of Colour', in *Pratiques historiques de l'innovation et histo-ricité de l'économie des savoirs (12e-19e siècles)*, ed. Liliane Hilaire-Pérez and A.-F. Garçon (Paris, CNRS, November 2003). She is the author of the forth-coming monograph: *Becoming Property: Art, Theory and Law in the French Enlightenment*.

William **St Clair** FBA FRSL, is Senior Reseach Fellow, Institute of English Studies, School of Advanced Study, University of London. Among his recent books are *The Reading Nation in the Romantic Period* (2004) and *The Political Economy of Reading* (2005).

Introduction.
The History of Copyright History: Notes from an Emerging Discipline.

Martin Kretschmer,
   with Lionel Bently and Ronan Deazley

What is Copyright History?

History has normative force. There was no history of colonialism, gender, fashion or crime until there were contemporary demands to explain and justify certain values. During much of the twentieth century, 'copyright' history (the history of legal, particularly proprietary, mechanisms for the regulation of the reproduction and distribution of cultural products – as opposed to the history of art, literature, music, or the history of publishers and art-sellers) was not thought of as a coherent, or even necessary field of inquiry. It was a pursuit of individual often rather isolated scholars, not an urgent contribution to knowledge.[1]

This was not always so. Copyright history had been the subject of intense and sustained study during several periods in the past, in the sense that there was a common set of questions, a community of scholars who read and responded to each other's concerns, and an audience to which this history mattered. Between around 1740 and 1790 copyright history was

---

1   Examples include: L. Gieseke, *Die geschichtliche Entwicklung des deutschen Urheberrechts* [The historical development of German author right law] (Göttingen: Schwartz, 1957); Marie-Claude Dock, *Contribution historique à l'étude des droits d'auteur* (Paris: LGDJ, 1962); L.R. Patterson, *Copyright in Historical Perspective* (Nashville: Vanderbilt University Press, 1968).

elevated to an academic sub-discipline under this (sociological) definition in at least Britain, France and the German-speaking countries. William Blackstone (1723-1780), Denis Diderot (1712-1784) and Johann Stephan Pütter (1725-1807) all searched in different ways for the historical sources of a law prescribing norms of copying. Copyright history is also present in virtually every nineteenth-century jurisprudential treatment of literary property, author's rights, publisher's rights or copyright law.

Following the adoption of an international framework of treaties, most prominently with the Berne Convention of 1886, interest in copyright history appeared to wane. As Martti Koskenniemi remarks in the context of international law: 'For a functionally oriented generation, the past offered mainly problems, and few solutions.'[2] Lawyers for most of the twentieth century were functionalists, oriented towards the future.

Several fields of legal scholarship experienced a new historical turn towards the end of the twentieth century. Why did the need to understand how we got to where we are arise? For international law, the changing world order after the fall of the Berlin Wall has been suggested as an obvious stimulus. For copyright law, the renewed interest in history may be traced to the translation of Michel Foucault's 1969 essay *Qu'est-ce qu'un auteur?* which first appeared in English in the mid-seventies.[3] Poststructuralist author theory influenced literary scholars profoundly, just at a time when digitization began to pose questions of authorship and ownership. In the Anglo-American context, the landmark texts of recent copyright history are perhaps Martha Woodmansee's 'The Genius and the Copyright' (1984), turning her gaze on the aesthetic, economic and legal conditions which made enlightenment thinkers frame copyright law in the first place, and Mark Rose's 1988 article 'The Author as Proprietor', developing an argument from the case of *Donaldson v. Becket* (1774) that, historically, there was no necessary connection between author and text. Many of the questions raised by Rose and Woodmansee still pervade this volume.[4]

2   M. Koskenniemi, 'The History of International Law Today', 4 *Rechtsgeschichte* (2004), 61-6.
3   M. Foucault, 'Qu'est-ce qu'un auteur?', *Bulletin de la Société française de philosophie*, 63/3, juillet-septembre (1969), 73-104; M. Foucault, 'What is an author?' (translated by James Venit), *Partisan Review*, 42:4 (1975), 603-14; and 113-38 in D. Bouchard (ed.), D. Bouchard and S. Simon (trans.), *Language, Counter-Memory, Practice* (Ithaca, NY: Cornell University Press, 1977).
4   M. Woodmansee, 'The Genius and the Copyright: Economic and Legal Conditions of the Emergence of the "Author"', *Eighteenth-Century Studies*, 17:4 (1984), 425-48; M. Rose, 'The Author as Proprietor: Donaldson v Becket and the Genealogy of Modern Authorship', *Representations*, 23 (1988), 51-85. Copyright history was then

Given the burgeoning interest in copyright history over the last 25 years, of which the digital archive motivating this edited collection is one of several indicators,[5] this is a timely opportunity for a more fundamental historiographical challenge.[6] Historiography is meta-history, the philosophy of science of historical scholarship. As the field is maturing, how do copyright historians identify their objects of inquiry, the primary sources that matter? How do scholars offer explanations, conceptual explications, and narratives of causes and effects in the evolution of the norms of copying? Which justificatory goals are served by historical investigation?

In the funding application for the digital archive project,[7] we confidently claimed that we knew which jurisdictions, and what kind of materials mattered: 'The focus is on five countries that have shaped the modern concepts of copyright law: Italy (20 documents), France (50), the UK (50), Germany (50), and the US (20). The documents will include statutes, materials relating to legislative history, case law, tracts, and commentaries.'

Not only did we claim to know where copyright history took place, we also expressed confidence in the historical inflections that had provided the sources for the modern framework of copyright law: 'There is considerable consensus among legal scholars as to the key points in the intellectual history of copyright law: Invention of printing press (ca1450); Feudal regime of printing privileges (Venice late 15th century; imperial fairs c15-c17); Stationers' companies (Basel 1531; London 1557); First Statutes (England 1710; US 1790); Author Rights (France 1791/1793; Prussia 1837; UK 1842); Berne Convention (1886).'

The backward projection of modern nation states into historical jurisdictions (while also omitting important regional centres such as

consolidated as a law and literature field of inquiry at a 1991 conference whose proceedings were published in 1992 as a special issue of the *Cardozo Art & Entertainment Law Journal*, and then as a much cited edited volume: M. Woodmansee and P. Jaszi (eds), *The Construction of Authorship: Textual Appropriation in Law and Literature* (Durham: Duke University Press, 1994).

5   In March 2008, the digital archive *Primary Sources on Copyright (1450-1900)* was launched with a two-day conference at Stationers' Hall, London. The edited resource comprises over 550 documents / 10,000 pages, and is available at <http://www.copyrighthistory.org> (hereafter: *Primary Sources*). All contributors to this edited volume spoke at the conference, which also initiated the International Scholarly Society for the History and Theory of Intellectual Property (ISHTIP).

6   Kathy Bowrey had already posed the question in 1996: 'Who's Writing Copyright's History?', *European Intellectual Property Review*, 18, 6 (1996), 322-29.

7   Lionel Bently and Martin Kretschmer, 'Primary Sources on Copyright (1450-1900)', application for a digital resource enhancement grant to the UK Arts & Humanities Research Council AHRC (2004).

the Netherlands) may be excused by the need to explain the project to potential funders.[8] We had to convey at least confidence in the possibility of copyright history.

Our methodology then aimed to select documents for the digital archive according to three criteria:[9]

> (1) Documents that open up alternative interpretations of copyright history
>
> Particular national copyright laws have come to be associated with distinct philosophical traditions: the US and UK are said to be 'public interest'-oriented, or utilitarian; France and Germany are regarded as author-centric, reflecting deontological philosophical ideas (personality, natural rights). We are interested in documents that affirm, and contradict, these presentations. For the editorial comments on such documents, we are particularly interested in bibliographic references that evidence early occurrences of particular interpretations.
>
> [...]
>
> (2) Documents that illustrate interaction of copyright laws with commercial and aesthetic developments
>
> We are interested in documents that say something about the way in which the law reacted to, and also affected, social circumstances and practices (including technological change, commercial practices and aesthetic practices).
>
> [...]
>
> (3) Documents that evidence influences across jurisdictions
>
> Copyright histories are often told as if national systems remained hermetically sealed from one another. So we have a British history, a French history, etc. We are interested in documents that indicate influence from outside the particular nations. For example, we are interested in evidence that the Venetian privileges constituted a model for licensing systems in France, Germany, England, etc., or evidence that suggests there was no such influence (each country independently coming up with the same idea of regulation). Assuming that there was influence, we are interested in documents

---

8   Several essays in this collection offer a corrective here: Alastair Mann examines the distinct tradition of Scots Law before and after the Union with England of 1707; Stef van Gompel gives voice to the Dutch influence on the evolution of copyright formalities during the nineteenth century; Friedemann Kawohl is careful to distinguish the many principalities of the Holy Roman Empire of the German Nation; and, Maurizio Borghi discusses eighteenth-century copyright reforms within the context of the Venetian jurisdiction (Germany and Italy did not exist as unified states until 1861 (Italy) and 1871 (Germany)). The *Primary Sources* archive will be extended in the near future to other countries, such as Spain and the Netherlands.
9   Cited from the methodology section at http://www.copyrighthistory.org/htdocs/method.html

which tell us about how certain legal systems became models for others.

We are also interested in documents that indicate the development of national self-consciousness, or national images of copyright. When, where, and how did French, US, German, Italian and UK commentators start to articulate their national laws as different from those of other nations (with different histories, philosophies, functions, concepts, etc.)?

From a historiographical perspective, it appears that our main thrust was to investigate the construction of narratives around the reference points of copyright history (taken as given), but we did not confront the orthodoxy that views copyright history as the history of laws. Although we recognized that history is more than an accumulation of legal materials within the context of national jurisdictions, politics and perhaps diplomacy, we did not systematically address how inquiry could reach beyond the documents of government.[10] This is a rather fundamental methodological point, so it may be useful to illustrate the implications with an example taken from Deazley's paper in this volume.[11]

From a legal perspective, the UK's Fine Art Copyright Act of 1862 introduced copyright protection for three types of artistic work – original drawings, paintings, and photographs. Prior to the 1862 Act, only engravings were protected under the Engravers' Act of 1735. Thus, a gap persisted for almost 130 years in which engravings but not paintings and drawings were covered under UK law. As Lord Mansfield remarked (*obiter*) in *Sayre v. Moore* (1785): '[I]n the case of prints, no doubt different men may take engravings from the same picture, but one cannot copy the engravings of another.' In 1853, Roberton Blaine commented that it was still dangerous to exhibit pictures 'before they are engraved'.[12] Yet there was a lively market for works of art, and painters did command substantial reproduction fees in relation to their works.

For the empirical reality of the arts market, what should the historian identify as the relevant norm under investigation? As Deazley suggests in his commentary (pp. 294-95):

10 In the wider historical academy, the methodological turn toward documents of ordinary people ('everyday life') is associated with the French journal *Annales: économies, sociétés, civilisations* under the leadership of Fernand Braudel after 1945 (thanks to Thomas Knubben for the reference). The empirical reality of societies (rather than their leaders and documented rules) becomes the focus of historical study.

11 Ronan Deazley, 'Breaking the Mould? The Radical Nature of the Fine Arts Copyright Bill 1862', Chapter 11 in this volume.

12 R. Blaine, *On the Laws of Artistic Copyright* (London: John Murray, 1853), p. 26; also in *Primary Sources*.

When painters purported to realise payment on the right to engrave their works, upon what basis did they do so? Did it turn upon negotiating physical access to a painting to ensure a faithful reproduction of the same? Was it simply a recognised and accepted commercial convention of the printsellers' market? Or did the status of an engraving right rest upon some other legally significant construct that predated (and perhaps rendered redundant) the need for statutory protection in 1862?

In historiographical terms, the legal construction of works of art in the UK pre-1862 does not appear to match the commercial and aesthetic practices of the period. Norms and practices of copying arguably superseded the legal framework. This indicates the limits of orthodox method. Establishing forensically the meaning of concepts, within a closed circle of legal reasoning that finds persuasive authority in historical sources of law, does not suffice. 'Copyright law' needs to be understood as having been only one mechanism for the articulation of proprietary relationships: other legal norms (personal property, contract, bailment), and, more interestingly, other social norms, allowed for systems of ascription and control, flows of money, as well as the transfer and sharing of ideas and expression. Copyright history is not just another branch of positive law.[13]

In this introduction, we invite readers to take a historiographical perspective on copyright history as a discipline. We do this by suggesting a number of meta-narratives, i.e. narratives about the construction of history at various periods. We then evaluate the essays in this volume in that methodological light: how do the scholars in this collection convert sources into explanations?

A Brief Historiography of Copyright

Historical narratives of copyright were first prominently mobilized during the eighteenth century. As one would expect, this occurred when norms of reprinting and copying where contested in the context of political, economic and aesthetic shifts.

In Britain, the seminal debate interweaving strands of historical and legal argument sought to establish, or refute an author's right 'at common law' that may survive the limited copyright term of the Statute of

---

13   An important proviso: Had the 1862 Fine Art Copyright Act not occurred, the historian would not have treated painter-engraver relations as a matter of copyright. Thus, copyright law offers a lens for viewing practices that may not have resulted in law – perhaps a paradoxical outcome for a copyright historian.

Anne (1710). For example, in the so-called 'battle of the booksellers' between Scottish and London publishers, the Tonson family of publishers used a contract under which Simmons had acquired Milton's *Paradise Lost* in 1667 to seek an injunction against the Scottish printer Walker in 1739 (when the 21-year term for books already in print under the Statute of Anne had clearly expired).[14]

Under the influence of Lord Mansfield (as William Murray the counsel for Tonson in *Tonson v. Walker*), the common law historiography developed more fully in the cases of *Tonson v. Collins* (1762) and *Millar v. Taylor* (1769). As Deazley[15] puts it in his commentary on *Tonson v. Collins*: In the first extended pre-history of English copyright, Wedderburn and Blackstone (counsels for the plaintiff) 'took the judges back through the bye-laws of the Company of Stationers, the printing patent cases of the late seventeenth century, and the Licensing Act 1662; back through the various decrees of the Star Chamber, the incorporation of the Stationers, and the origins of the prerogative right to grant printing privileges; back to the very introduction of printing itself by Caxton in 1471'. In return, Thurlow and Yates (counsels for the defendant) characterized the stationers' bye-laws as 'private regulations', the letters patent were 'merely privileges', the King's prerogative had nothing to do with the present case, and the decrees of the Star Chamber were dismissed as being merely political in scope and intent.

At about the same time, Denis Diderot (commissioned by the Paris Guild) gave himself the task of 'tracing the establishment of our laws on privileges in the book trade from their origin to the present day' (p. 15).[16]

---

14   Peter Lindenbaum, 'Milton's Contract', 175-190 in Woodmansee and Jaszi (eds), p. 189: 'Simmons's copy of the contract [the original publisher of Paradise Lost, contract of April 27, 1667] seems to have been passed on to the bookseller Jacob Tonson when that marketing genius acquired the full copyright to *Paradise Lost* (in two separate steps, in 1683 and 1691). Thereafter, the contract remained, no doubt as proof of possession of the copyright, in the hands of the Tonson family until 1768, along with the manuscript of Book I of the poem. The third generation Jacob Tonson even used it as evidence in a court action to frighten off a prospective publisher of Milton's poem in 1739, well after the Copyright Act's prescribed twenty-one years had elapsed.' See injunction in *Tonson v. Walker* (5 May 1739) c 33 1753/208.
15   R. Deazley (2008), 'Commentary on Tonson v. Collins (1762)', in *Primary Sources*. Cf. R. Deazley, *On the Origin of the Right to Copy* (Oxford: Hart, 2004), 138ff.
16   Denis Diderot (1763), *Lettre historique et politique adressée à un magistrat sur le commerce de la librairie* (A historical and political letter to a magistrate on the book trade, its former and current state, its regulations, privileges, tacit permissions, censors, pedlars, the expansion of trade across the river and other subjects relating to literary laws), in *Primary Sources*; with commentary by F. Rideau. Page numbers refer to the English translation of the manuscript (trans. by Lydia Mulholland).

The first third of Diderot's extensive 1763 pamphlet *Lettre historique et politique sur le commerce de la librairie* narrates the numerous conflicts between the provincial booksellers and the Paris Guild, and various attempts by the French Parliament and Council to circumscribe the guild's monopoly.

Seventeenth-century regulations, from the incorporation of the Paris Guild in 1618 to the book trade relations of 1649 and 1665,[17] had eventually confirmed that unlimited extensions could be obtained to privileges for 'new' books, as well as through renewals of privileges for 'ancient' works. However, during the eighteenth century, persuasive arguments were made that any privilege, as a temporary monopoly, must eventually expire. In this context, Diderot's historical excursions aim to show that the privilege system should be simply understood as a system of state approval for publication (or censorship), and that the prior right lay with the author who dealt with this as a matter of contract. Diderot claims that 'the possessors of manuscripts purchased from authors may obtain permission to publish, and seek as many continuations of this permission as they wish; they may transmit their rights to others by selling them, passing them on to their heirs or abandoning them' (p. 12) – in effect a justification for a perpetual transferable copyright.

In other words, '[t]he agreement between the bookseller and the contemporary author worked in the same way then as it does now: the author approached the bookseller and offered him his work; they agreed on a price, format and other conditions. These conditions and this price were stipulated

---

17 Book trade regulations and incorporation of the Parisian book trade (1618); Book trade regulations (1649); Book trade regulation (1665); all in *Primary Sources*. For the level of detail of Diderot's narrative, see his account of the 1649 regulations (p. 10): 'To suppress these disputes between publishers which were wearying the Council and the chancellery, the magistrate verbally prohibited the guild from printing anything without letters of privilege stamped with the great seal. The guild, that is to say, the destitute party, protested; but the magistrate held firm; he even extended his verbal order to old books, and the Council, ruling, as a consequence of this order, on privileges and their continuation by letters patent of 20 December 1649, prohibited the printing of any book without a royal privilege, gave preference to the bookseller who had obtained the first letter of continuation if several had been granted, banned pirate editions, postponed requests for continuations on the expiry of privileges, restricted these requests to those to whom the privileges had originally been granted, permitted these same people to have them renewed when it seemed fit to them, and required that all letters of privilege and continuations be recorded in the guild's register, which the syndic would be obliged to present whenever it was required, so that in future one could not plead ignorance, and so that there would be no fraudulent or unforeseen competition on the obtaining of a single permission.'

in a private agreement, in which the author permanently and irreversibly ceded his work to the bookseller and to his successors in titles' (p. 8).

The leading eighteenth-century German jurisprudential commentary by Johann Stephan Pütter, *Der Büchernachdruck nach ächten Grundsätzen des Rechts* (1774),[18] devotes about two thirds of this 206-page treatise to the historical sources of the principles that should govern the issue of reprinting. The argument contains a potted history of the book trade, an account of the early privileges (Venetian, Papal, French, and Imperial, back to 1494), a discussion of the governance of the imperial trade fairs in Frankfurt and Leipzig (such as the Frankfurt *Büchercommission* of 1579), and the views of earlier thinkers. It is Pütter who elevates Martin Luther's 1525 preface admonishing unauthorized reprinters to a foundational text of German copyright discourse.[19] Pütter aimed to legitimate printing privileges provided by both the Empire and the confederate states as reaching beyond Germany's many internal borders. Pütter's justification of copyright has its roots not in Roman or Canon (church) law, but in European wide practice [*Europäische Gebräuche*].[20]

As in the British common law debate, we have an attempt to lend support to systematic reasoning from a historical perspective, although Pütter (1774, p. 118) concedes that the past may be 'darkened by prejudice' [durch Vorurtheile verdunkelt], and at variance with what he calls the 'true principles of law' [den ächten Rechtsgrundsätzen].

Diderot's letter is more overtly a political intervention, with rhetorical flourishes dominating the argument. However, the debates in Britain, France and Germany all evidence narratives that combine, in a typically eighteenth-century manner, historical explanation with justificatory concerns. The early copyright historians in Britain, France and Germany argue as if past rules, practices, statutes or court decisions may serve as normative precedents in a doctrinal sense.

---

18 *The Reprinting of Books Examined in the Light of True Principles of Law* (Göttingen, 1774), in *Primary Sources*; with commentary by F. Kawohl.
19 Pütter (1774), p. 125, cites almost in full Luther's preface to the 1525 edition of 'Interpretation of the Epistles and Gospels from Advent to Easter' [*Auslegung der Episteln und Evangelien*]. The original version is available in *Primary Sources*, with commentary by F. Kawohl. Luther characterizes unauthorized reprints as both fraud [Betrug] because they spread errors, and from economic damage with respect to labour and costs [Arbeiten und Kost].
20 Citing Adrian Beier (1634-1712), a law professor at Jena university: 'It does not follow: where there is no privilege, there is no law, no help, no sin, no punishment.' [Folgt darum nicht: wo kein Privilegium, da sey kein Recht, keine Hülfe, keine Sünde, keine Strafe. Das natürliche Recht, die Vernuft weiset einen jeden an, liegen zu lassen, was nicht sein ist.] (Pütter (1774), p. 127).

Within the constraints of this introduction, we cannot offer a historiography of 250 years of copyright historical writing since Wedderburn and Blackstone's plea in *Tonson v. Collins* (1762). The history of copyright history is yet to be written. However, we would like to invite such future research with some observations on the use of copyright history in nineteenth-century jurisprudential commentaries, and on the revival of copyright history since Foucault's intervention in 1969.

Robert Maugham (1788-1862), the first Secretary of the Law Society of England and Wales, published the first substantive explication of British copyright law in 1828.[21] In many respects, his treatment of the subject is orthodox in that he provides a reasonably exhaustive doctrinal account of the current state of the law, not just for works of literature, but also with respect to dramatic works, lectures and artistic works (engravings and sculpture). However, two of Maugham's *bête noires* dominated and shaped the structure and tenor of his treatise: the duration of copyright in literary works,[22] and the library deposit provisions.[23] Respectively, Maugham considered that limiting the duration of copyright to the statutory periods of protection was a 'monstrous injustice',[24] whereas the library deposit provisions were 'iniquitous', a 'disgrace to the country', and obnoxious to '[e]very principle of political economy'. On both issues, Maugham's 'historical view' of the law – 'from the invention of printing, to the Statute 8 Anne 1710' – was marshalled to present 'a striking proof of the of the injustice of their nature'.[25]

Whereas Maugham engaged a range of historical sources in mapping out an agenda for copyright reform, John Lowndes, who published the first

---

21   R. Maugham, *A Treatise on the Laws of Literary Property* (London: Longman, 1828), also in *Primary Sources*. Prior to Maugham, Richard Godson had published *A Practical Treatise on the Law of Patents for Inventions and of Copyright* (London, 1823). However, Maugham's treatise was the first that was concerned only with the law of copyright.

22   The term of protection for literary works was twenty-eight years from the point of publication and, if the author was alive at the end of that period, then for the residue of his natural life; *Copyright Act*, 1814, 54 Geo.III, c.156, s.4.

23   *Copyright Act*, 1814, ss.2-3, 5-7.

24   Maugham, p. 196.

25   Ibid., x. Indeed, Maugham concluded his treatise with an appendix containing a selection of 'authorities regarding the limitation of copyright and the library tax, arranged chronologically'. For example, quotations and commentary from John Milton, Thomas Carte, William Warburton, Sir Thomas Clarke, Lords Mansfield and Monboddo, Francis Hargrave, Catherine Macaulay, and others, were presented as 'statements and reasonings' confirming Maugham's arguments for extending the copyright term.

treatise (within Britain at least) specifically concerned with the history of copyright, wrote his work in support of Thomas Noon Talfourd's attempts to overhaul the copyright regime between 1837 and 1841, which efforts eventually lead to the passing of the Copyright Act in 1842.[26] Two editions of the work were published in 1840 and 1842, both of which were dedicated to Talfourd '[f]or his generous advocacy of the rights of authors'. Like Wedderburn and Blackstone, Lowndes was convinced that the concept of an author's natural right of literary property was one of long standing, and that copyright existed at common law predating the interventions of the legislature in the guise of the Statute of Anne; his treatise was an exercise in demonstrating the same. As for his 'motive in laying it before the public', he hoped 'to remove the misapprehensions which prevail with regard to this species of property, both as to its former existence, and as to the effect and the expediency of the measure proposed by Sergeant Talfourd'.[27] In this regard, Lowndes's work was overtly propagandist in both nature and intent.

The Swiss jurist Johann Kaspar Bluntschli (1808-1881) included a section on the history and nature of author's rights in his 1854 treatise on German private law (*Deutsches Privatrecht*).[28] Bluntschli constructs a sequence of four historical stages, ascending 'to ever greater perfection' in the recognition of author's rights [bildete sich zu höherer Vollendung aus] (pp. 186-190):

> a) the point of view of a *privilege* [der Standpunkt des *Privilegiums*]. Whilst the latter had before been conferred in individual cases, it was now granted universally. However, the form of a preferential concession [*Vergünstigung*] and a special right [*Ausnahmerecht*] was nevertheless retained, even though what was actually being protected was a universal right. That is, the need for protection of these rights was felt, but there was no understanding as yet of their nature.

26 For further commentary see J.J. Lowndes, *An Historical Sketch of the Law of Copyright* (1840, facsimile edition) with a new Introduction by R. Deazley (New Jersey: Law Book Exchange, 2008), pp. iii-xvii.
27 Lowndes, vii. In the preface to the first edition of his work, Lowndes wrote that 'more time and study than have been in my power to bestow, are necessary to do justice to this subject, but if, by the perusal of the following pages, the reader is convinced that such a right as that known by the name of Copyright did formerly exist at common-law, and was only taken away by a mistaken interpretation of the effect of the statute of Anne, and that the state of the present law is such as imperatively demands alteration; I shall not consider the few leisure hours I have appropriated to their composition from the severer duties of my profession, as either misspent or unprofitably employed.'
28 Johann Kaspar Bluntschli, Chapter 'On Author's Rights' [Vom Autorrecht], in *Deutsches Privatrecht* (München: 1853), in *Primary Sources* (trans. by Luis Sundkvist).

b) the point of view of a *publishing right* [der Standpunkt des *Verlagrechts*], which was often tied to the aforementioned privilege. In this consideration the interests of the publishers were uppermost and their publishing right was to be safeguarded. However, this was a most unsatisfactory approach because it failed to take into account that the authorised publisher and the unauthorised reprinter have a different right only by virtue of their different relationship to the author, and that a monopoly granted to the former without consideration for the author, merely for the sake of the priority of the commercial enterprise, lacks any proper foundation.

c) the point of view of intellectual or *literary property* [der Standpunkt des *litterarischen Eigenthums*], which is championed above all by writers, but is of no use juristically. For common parlance, which calls a person's control over his nerves, his hands, or his thoughts, ownership and applies this term to anything which belongs to the person and is peculiar to him, certainly makes sense, but it simply covers too many different kinds of circumstances for it to be of use in civil law. [...] Moreover, the author's right is also different from ownership in the sense that the former always refers back to the author as a specific individual person, from which it can never dissociate itself completely, as long as it exists as such, whereas ownership is not concerned with the individual person of the owner. [...]

d) the fourth point of view, according to which *the author's right* is seen not as a property right, but, rather, as a *personal right of the author*, as *the right of the originator* [der vierte Standpunkt, von welchem das *Autorrecht* nicht als Sachen-, sondern als ein *persönliches* Recht des Autors betrachtet wird, als *Recht des Urhebers*]. It is to the philosopher Kant[29] that the merit belongs of having been the first to clearly point to the personal nature of author's rights. In other respects, though, his exposition of the matter is immature. The French jurist Renouard,[30] in an excellent treatise on author's rights, has greatly furthered our understanding of this question, although even he concentrates too much on the property right aspect of author's rights and thus ends up describing these as a kind of privileged monopoly, albeit one that is fully deserved by the author and holds universally. This means that he too overlooks the personal nature of the author's right.

Bluntschli chastises legislators and judges, with reference to the 1774 decision of the English House of Lords (i.e. *Donaldson v. Becket*), who until recently failed to understand the historical logic in the development of author's rights.

---

29   *Editors' note:* Immanuel Kant, 'Von der Unrechtmäßigkeit des Büchernachdrucks', *Berliner Monatszeitschrift* (1785), 403-17; also in *Primary Sources*. Cf. F. Kawohl and M. Kretschmer, 'Johann Gottlieb Fichte, and the Trap of *Inhalt* (Content) and *Form*', in M. Kretschmer and A. Pratt (eds), *Copyright and the Production of Music*, special issue *Information, Communication and Society*, 12, 2 (March 2009), 41-64.
30   *Editors' note:* A.-C. Renouard, *Traité des droits d'auteur dans la littérature, les sciences et les Beaux-Arts*, vol. 1 (Paris: Jules Renouard & Co., 1838).

In the French context, Laurent Pfister, in his essay in this volume, points out several examples of the instrumentalization of history: 'In 1859, with the controversies about the duration of *droit d'auteur* in full swing, the lawyer Édouard René de Laboulaye published a number of historical sources all of which tended to affirm his particular theory of perpetual literary property.[31] Similarly, in the decades that followed, a number of French lawyers tried to consolidate the moral right by asserting that it was not only a natural right but one that had existed since the dawn of time.'[32]

A cross-jurisdictional study of the spread of the teleological story of copyright during the nineteenth century – from the dark beginnings of privileges to the full recognition of author's rights – is yet to be written.[33] Why did the ideological emphasis on authorial works coincide with an increasing industrialized mode of exploitation? One answer stems from Marxist theory that understands law as a representation of the conditions of production in capitalism. For the specific case of photography, Bernard Edelman has argued that the French courts recognized during the nineteenth century a creative, authorial contribution in photographic activity in order to enable the operation of a property logic that served the interests of capital.[34]

31   Edouard Laboulaye et Georges Guiffrey, *La propriété littéraire au xviiie siècle: Recueil de pièces et de documents* (Paris, 1859). In contrast, some years later François Malapert published an historical study to refute Laboulaye's thesis of perpetual property: 'Histoire abrégée de la législation sur la propriété littéraire avant 1789', *Journal des économistes*, 1880, p. 252, and 1881, p. 437.

32   See, for example, Pierre Masse, *Le droit moral de l'auteur sur son œuvre littéraire ou artistique* (Paris, 1906), p. 35: 'le droit moral [...] a existé de tout temps. A Athènes et à Rome, alors que les auteurs étaient sans droit pécuniaire, le droit moral était reconnu et sanctionné, sinon par une disposition expresse de la loi, du moins par la conscience publique'. See also André Morillot, *De la protection accordée aux œuvres d'art, aux photographies aux dessins et modèles industriels et aux brevets d'invention dans l'Empire d'Allemagne* (Paris & Berlin, 1878), p. 117.

33   In the United States, copyright law resisted the continental story of non-utilitarian author's rights well into the twentieth century. Yet, here too doctrine developed that combined (in Oren Bracha's words) 'a metaphysical concept of the copyrighted work as an intellectual essence that could take many specific forms and a dominant concern for protecting the work's commercial value in all secondary markets that could be traced to it.' O. Bracha, 'Commentary on Folsom v. Marsh (1841)', in *Primary Sources*. Bracha traces this ideology in George Ticknor Curtis, *A Treatise on the Law of Copyright in Books, Dramatic, and Musical Compositions, Letters, and other Manuscripts, Engravings, and Sculpture as Enacted and Administered in England and America* (Boston: C.C. Little and J. Brown, 1847), p. 293; and Eaton S. Drone, *A Treatise on the Law of Property in Intellectual Productions in Great Britain and the United States: Embracing Copyright in Works of Literature and Art, and Playwright in Dramatic and Musical Compositions* (Boston: Little, Brown 1879), 97-98.

34   B. Edelman, *Ownership of the Image, Elements of a Marxist Theory of Law* (London:

Edelman's Marxist conception of law influenced Anglo-American writers in the Critical Legal Studies movement but has had little influence on the recent trajectory of copyright history as a discipline. As we suggested earlier, for much of the twentieth century copyright discourse was dominated by positive law in a climate where the basic settlement of the Berne Convention (that the author should have exclusive control over the full value of the works created) was applied and extended to new forms of exploitation (such as radio, television and reprography). The law looked forward to solutions, in which the proprietary model held central place,[35] not backwards to history.

Research on material which we would now consider to be an integral part of copyright history continued outside the discipline of legal scholarship: an important strand being contributions to publishing history, and in particularly the history of the Stationers' Company published on the pages of the journal *The Library*. Contributions were made by scholars of journalism (such as Frederick Siebert), librarians and bibliographers (such as Gordon Duff and Graham Pollard),[36] as well as publishers themselves, such as Edward Arber[37] and Cyprian Blagden, probably the two most significant historians of the Company.[38] Some of this historical work focused on 'copyright' as such: literary historian Harry Ransom published his influential work on the origins of the Statute of Anne,[39] while librarian Simon Nowell-Smith and historian James J. Barnes produced important work exploring the politics of international copyright relations between the United States and Great Britain in the nineteenth century.[40] The existence of this painstaking research was crucial groundwork on which recent scholars from a range of disciplines have been able to draw.[41]

Routledge, 1977 [1973]). Edelman locates the reclassification in legal doctrine (making photography capable of attracting the protection of authorship) to investments in the embryonic moving picture industry.

35   Even if copyright practice witnessed increasing levels of collective management.

36   Edward Gordon Duff received a small obituary in *The Times*, October 1, 1924; for Pollard's obituary, see *The Times*, November 16, 1976.

37   Arber was not only involved in the reprinting of old texts, but also lectured at UCL and in Birmingham. For Arber's obituary, see *The Times*, November 25, 1912.

38   Blagden spent much of his career at Longman's and was a liveryman of the Stationers' Company. For Blagden's obituary, see *The Times*, December 4, 1962, p. 15.

39   Ransom's PhD focused on the literary property debates, and in 1956 he published *The First Copyright Statute* (Austin: University of Texas Press).

40   Simon Nowell-Smith, *International Copyright Law and the Publisher in the Reign of Queen Victoria* (Oxford, Clarendon Press, 1968); James J. Barnes, *Authors, Publishers and Politicians: The Quest for an Anglo-American Copyright Agreement, 1815-1854* (London: Routledge & Kegan Paul, 1974).

41   In Germany, the trade body of publishers and booksellers (*Börsenverein*,

In the Marxist and poststructuralist intellectual debates of 1960s France, it was the concept of authorship (in the analysis of Roland Barthes and Michel Foucault) that became the subject of historical study. In English-speaking discourse, Foucaultian arguments about the 'author function' as a set of beliefs governing the production, circulation and consumption of texts gained wide currency among literary scholars. Foucault's concern was with the genealogy of 'authorship', understood as an ideological construction through which responsibility for texts had come to be allocated, culture organized, and the proliferation of meaning controlled. Foucault's key observation was that, historically speaking, the attribution of authors to texts/ascription of texts to authors was a relatively recent phenomenon, and one on which practices had (and continued) to vary as between 'scientific' and 'non-scientific' texts. In an attempt to explain this, Foucault not only linked the genealogy of authorship historically to the legal system of censorship, but also identified an important shift in the history of authorship, that from responsibility to ownership.[42] From around 1800, he claimed, a new conception of authorship emerged, that of the 'author-as-proprietor'. It was this insight that led (it seems) Woodmansee and Rose to begin their seminal studies of copyright history in eighteenth- and early nineteenth-century England and Germany.[43]

For copyright lawyers, it was probably the advent of digitization that motivated a turn to history as a strategy for understanding what copyright was intended to do, how it has functioned, and for paths that we could now take. Simultaneously, expansion in higher education, and burgeoning interest in the field of 'intellectual property' (fed by assumptions of its growing economic importance in the developed world), led to the appointment of a new generation of (copyright) scholars looking for research projects. Digital sampling,[44] computer programming,[45] and the production

---

founded in 1825) sponsored a project on the history of the book trade since 1876. Its historical committee published between 1886 and 1913 Friedrich Kapp's and Johann Goldfriedrich's influential four-volume *Geschichte des Deutschen Buchhandels*.

42　Foucault (1969). Kathy Bowrey points out, amusingly, that during the 1980s and 1990s, it became almost *de rigueur* to cite Foucault in the opening lines of academic essays on copyright theory, as if to confirm the Foucaultian ideological compulsion to identify authorship (Bowrey (1996), p. 323).

43　Woodmansee (1984); Rose (1988).

44　G. Born and D. Hesmondhalgh (eds), *Western Music and Its Others: Difference, Appropriation and Representation in Music* (Berkeley: University of California Press, 2000); K. McLeod 'How copyright law changed Hip Hop: an interview with Public Enemy's Chuck D and Hanks Shoklee', *Stay Free Magazine* (2002).

45　Richard Stallman pioneered an open approach to software development and

of databases,[46] prompted interrogation of legal notions of 'authorship', 'originality' and 'work', and raised doubts about the appropriateness of proprietary models of regulation. Foucault's genealogy of authorship offered a vital pointer towards understanding the underlying logics and epistemic underpinnings of the institutions and practices of copyright that legal commentators during the twentieth century had pretty much taken for granted.[47]

Of course, not all contributions to the new copyright history sprang from the appropriation of poststructuralist ideas (in translation). Foucault had little influence on the work of certain English and Continental

---

distribution in the GNU Project, launched in 1984 in order to develop a complete Unix-like operating system (GNU is a recursive acronym for 'GNU's Not Unix'). In 1988, Stallman issued the first version of the General Public License (GPL) forcing derivatives of GNU software to keep their source code free from proprietary claims. The GPL has been described as the constitution of the Free Software/Open Source movement, and is probably the single most important expression of discomfort with proprietary understandings of authorship in the field of computer programming. M. Kretschmer, 'Software as Text and Machine', *The Journal of Information, Law and Technology (JILT)*, 1 (2003), 1-24: http://www2.warwick.ac.uk/fac/soc/law/elj/jilt/2003_1/kretschmer/ [accessed 13/3/2010]

46   Jane Ginsburg's historical exploration of copyright law in revolutionary France and the United States was published almost simultaneously with her examination of the legal protection of compilations, a year before the United States Supreme Court decision in *Feist Publications v. Rural Telephone Service Co.* 499 US 340 (1991). The *Feist* decision, and the authorial ideology that the decision expressed, were a key focus for US copyright scholarship. J. Ginsburg, 'A tale of two copyrights: literary property in revolutionary France and America, *Tulane Law Review* 64 (1990), 991-1031; J. Ginsburg, 'Creation and Commercial Value: Copyright Protection of Works of Information', *Columbia Law Review*, 90, 7 (1990), 1865-1938.

47   Peter Jaszi excavated the legal refractions of the 'romantic' ideology of authorship further into the nineteenth and twentieth centuries ('Toward a Theory of Copyright: The Metamorphoses of Authorship', *Duke Law Journal* (1991), 455-502); James Boyle explored how that same ideology informed legal fields beyond copyright – such as blackmail, traditional knowledge, and genetic material (*Shamans, Software, and Spleens: Law and the Construction of the Information Society*, Cambridge, MA: Harvard University Press, 1996); Brad Sherman and Lionel Bently sought to highlight how conceptions of creativity were implicated in the categories and structures of intellectual property that 'crystallized' in the mid-nineteenth century (in Britain) and drew attention to a range of different narratives in copyright history, such as those of national tradition, and colonialism, which warranted further investigation (*The Making of Modern Intellectual Property Law: The British Experience, 1760-1911* (Cambridge: Cambridge University Press, 1999)). Other examples of the early infiltration of copyright law academe by authorship theory can be found in B. Sherman and A. Strowel (eds), *Of Authors and Origins: Essays on Copyright Law* (Oxford: Clarendon Press, 1994).

scholars, such as Feather, Cornish, Seville, Kawohl or Pfister.[48] Reviewing the range of contributors to this volume and their methodological base offers an opportunity to examine the state of the discipline.

Methodology in this volume

The historical treatises of the eighteenth century analysed the legal character of privileges as antecedents of a general law regulating reprinting: Were privileges an encroachment on common rights or liberties, were they necessarily limited in term, could they extend across borders, did they permit or rely on certain rights of the author? As we have seen during our brief historiographical sketch, many jurisprudential commentaries have continued to view privileges as part of a continuous line that eventually led to the recognition of authorship and copyright law proper.

In the first essay of this collection ('From Gunpowder to Print: The Common Origins of Copyright and Patent'), Joanna Kostylo, a cultural historian, steps out of this trajectory. Kostylo explores the instruments of Renaissance letter patents on their own terms, locating them in the 'very material world of craftsmanship and mechanical inventions' (p. 22). According to Kostylo, the history of copyright 'must be explored from a wider perspective of contemporary arts, crafts, music, painting and print making, as well as the aesthetic theories of Italian humanism that influenced these various disciplines' (ibid.). It follows that the primary source material that concerns the historian may be as much rich social material (for example about the transmission of knowledge in guilds) as proto-legal material (such as the Venetian printing privilege for Johannes of Spyer of 1469). Here the historiography of copyright is at its most fluent.

The subsequent essays mostly return again to law (and its immediate context) as the object of study, although there are certain exceptions, such as Mark Rose's ambitious reading of Habermas's theory of the public

---

48   John Feather, 'The Book Trade in Politics: The Making of the Copyright Act of 1710', *Publishing History*, 8 (1980), 19-44; W.R. Cornish, 'Authors in Law', *Modern Law Review*, 58, 1 (1995), 1-16; Catherine Seville, *Literary Copyright Reform in Early Victorian England* (Cambridge: Cambridge University Press, 1999); Laurent Pfister, *L'auteur, propriétaire de son œuvre?: La formation du droit d'auteur du XVIe siècle à la loi de 1957* (Strasburg PhD thesis, 1999); Friedemann Kawohl, *Urheberrecht der Musik in Preußen 1820-1840* (Tutzing: Hans Schneider, 2002). In the German-speaking countries, a historical society of copyright jurists *Arbeitskreis Geschichte des Urheberrechts* (drawing on the research of Gieseke, Rehbinder, Vogel and Wadle) has held regular bi-annual meetings for several decades.

sphere into a single English seventeenth-century text (Milton's *Areopagitica*), or Katie Scott's account of the contribution of the visual arts, and in particular maps, to establishing property claims in seventeenth- and eighteenth-century France.

It is not surprising that the focus of investigation tends to narrow as the analysis progresses through time, and a body of jurisprudence is becoming known as copyright law in its various incarnations – such as literary property, *droit d'auteur* or *Verlagsrecht* (publishers' right). This steers the historian's selection of primary sources towards decisions by courts and documents of the legislature.

It is important to note that this is not necessarily a disciplinary choice. Legal historians, cultural historians, economic historians, art historians, book and literary historians, music historians, or intellectual historians may, or may not, differ in their selection of objects. The same materials may serve different explanations, depending on explanatory goals and methods used.

The type of objects covered in this collection include specific narrow legal interventions, for example, on performing rights in the UK (Alexander), publishing contracts in Prussia (Kawohl), perpetual copyright in Venice (Borghi), artistic property in France (Rideau) and the UK (Deazley), as well as wider surveys on the customs of the publishing trade (Feather), freedom of commercial exploitation under Scots law (Mann), the regulation of the printing press in the North American colonies (Bracha), the concept of the author in the French privilege system (Pfister), or formalities in nineteenth-century Europe (van Gompel). Some essays even attempt to spin threads through several centuries, for example on the personality interests of the author (Peifer), and on the political economy hidden in metaphors of intellectual property (St Clair).

Following an identification of the *objects* of investigation, a second set of observations relate to the *goals* of historical analysis. Here we may distinguish among the contributions to this volume:

(i) Papers making claims about national identity and influence:

Peifer (dislodging the Anglo-American influence on recent scholarship in favour of a pre-eminent and preferable German tradition); Mann (making the case for Scotland's importance and influence within British copyright's 'pre-history'); Kawohl (making the case for a particularly German jurisprudence that pre-empts/disrupts the significance of the 1791 and 1793 French decrees within the civil law tradition);

(ii) Papers making claims about disciplinary relevance:

Scott (the contribution that visual art made in the formulation of contemporary copyright, which itself makes claims about the importance of being able to 'read' the visual); Feather (locating copyright history within a broader (more important?) history of publishing);

(iii) Papers seeking to challenge existing (dominant) narratives:

Kostylo (on the significance of industrial privileges in the formation of the authorial ego and the intangible work); Bracha (on the typical presumptions about 'copyright' in colonial America, and in turn problematizing the role of the author – and author-ideology – in the formation of early American copyright jurisprudence); Pfister (presenting a more nuanced historical account of conceptions of the author and the work – as well as the relationship between the two – than has typically been the case in existing scholarship about the history of copyright in France);

(iv) Papers drawing upon history with a view to interrogating contemporary policy:

St Clair (a critical understanding of the use of metaphor in obfuscating historical and current debates); Alexander (the importance of exploring mistakes that may have been made in the past with a view to future policy, and invoking history to unsettle current perceptions about the naturalness or inevitability of the contemporary regime); Pfister (the instrumentalization of history, and its continuing relevance for contemporary debate); Borghi (on the importance and value of evidence-based policy); van Gompel (in seeking to ameliorate the perceived conflict between the existence of certain copyright formalities and the *droit d'auteur* tradition).

Lastly, and perhaps most controversially, we would like to offer an interpretation of the *methods* used in the essays. How are primary sources converted into explanations? A 'legal positivist' analysis of copyright law as part of an institutionalized system of social recognition will seek explanations immanent to law.[49] At the other end of the spectrum, copyright law may be explained by technological, economic, political, social or aesthetic factors, i.e. explanations outside law.

In this collection, grand theories, such as the 'romantic author hypothesis' (explaining the rise of author's rights at the end of the eighteenth century from an aesthetics of genius), theories about the 'public domain' (conceiving of copyright as a regulatory mechanism for the benefits of learning), or teleological stories about the ascent of copyright laws from privileges to

---

49 H.L.A. Hart, *The Concept of Law* (Oxford: Clarendon Press, 1994 [1961]).

authorial consciousness are being challenged by micro-studies that bring a wider range of methods to bear on a wider range of sources. This is a sign of disciplinary evolution. There may be no grand pattern that explains the development of copyright laws across all societies, yet carefully sustained work on primary materials may discover new narratives for new social conditions, aware of one of the central paradoxes of legal theory: that law is both a set of rules and a discourse about what these rules should be.

John Milton, in his 1644 *Areopagitica* speech *For the Liberty of Unlicensed Printing*, accuses parliament of having been deceived by the 'fraud of some old patentees and monopolizers in the trade of bookselling' (i.e. the Stationers' Company): 'Truth and understanding are not such wares as to be monopolized and traded in by tickets and statutes and standards. We must not think to make a staple commodity of all the knowledge in the land, to mark and license it like our broadcloth and our woolpacks.'[50] Today, we still struggle to relate norms of communication and norms of transaction (as copyright law forces us to do). That is why copyright history matters.

---

50   Cited in Mark Rose's essay in this volume. Rose makes a complex causal argument about the role of a bourgeois public sphere in the collapse of traditional press controls, enabling the recognition of authorship in the Statute of Anne (1710). The public sphere (in the sense of Habermas) is an early modern political force that emanated in new civic institutions of conversation and exchange, such as coffee houses, newspapers and clubs: Jürgen Habermas, *The Structural Transformation of the Public Sphere: An Inquiry into a Category of Bourgeois Society*, trans. by Thomas Burger (Cambridge, MA: The MIT Press, 1991 [*Strukturwandel der Öffentlichkeit*, 1962]).

1. From Gunpowder to Print: The Common Origins of Copyright and Patent

Joanna Kostylo

> In Venice, as I heard, and in many places beyond the sea, they reward and cherish every man that brings in any new art or mystery whereby the people may be set to work.
>
> Sir Thomas Smyth, *Discourse on the Common Weal of this Realm of England* (1581)

The history of intellectual property has been subject to much revision in recent years. It no longer appears to be the domain of legal studies alone but has become a focus of inquiry across diverse fields and disciplines. Most of this work has focused on copyright, while the history of patents remains largely unexplored by this burgeoning area of cross-disciplinary studies. This is partially due to the traditional legal taxonomy which distinguishes sharply between these two institutions, a taxonomy which took root from the eighteenth century onwards.[1] This paper challenges this distinction by exploring some early developments and cross-fertilisation between these two fields.

A closer look at the historical relationship between copyright and patents reveals the common origins of these two institutions. Before exploring these common origins however it is important to make a distinction between modern intellectual property law and the ancient system of

1 The most important international treaties which sanctioned this modern differentiation between copyright and patent were the 1883 Paris Convention for the Protection of Industrial Property and the 1886 Berne Convention for the Protection of Literary and Artistic Works. J.H. Reichmann, 'Legal Hybrids between the Patent and Copyright Paradigms', *Columbia Law Review*, 94 (1994), 2432-558; S. Ricketson, *The Berne Convention for the Protection of Literary and Artistic Works: 1886-1986* (London: Centre for Commercial Law Studies, Queen Mary, 1987).

privileges. In contrast to modern copyright and patent, early privileges were conceived as a form of municipal favour (*gratiae*) and an exception to the law (*priva lex*) rather than the recognition of the author's inherent rights. Such *privilegia* took various forms, from exclusive monopolies permitting the inventors or introducers of a new technology the right to exploit their trade or engage in other productive activity, to printing privileges bestowing the publishers or authors with the exclusive rights to print and sell a work. These two types of privileges would later be identified as patents for inventions and proto-copyrights respectively but in the early stage of their development there was little differentiation between the two. This original lack of differentiation can be explained by two factors: legal (institutional) and cultural (ideological). In legal terms, the early printing privileges and grants for mechanical inventions were virtually indistinguishable: they had not developed separate bureaucratic regimes and both continued to rely on the same mechanism of ad-hoc discretionary privileges. They were both awarded on the same basis, in order to offer protection from competition and secure returns on an initial investment. On the cultural and intellectual level, this convergence could be explained by the manner in which the subject matter of copyright protection initially developed, focusing first on the material realm of printing technology before it expanded to less material objects of protection. These developments have their roots in Renaissance Italy.

The Renaissance period is a particularly interesting moment in the history of intellectual property, since many developments – technological, economic, institutional, legal, cultural, intellectual, and ideological – had converged in this period to produce a unique environment in which new attitudes towards authorship, intellectual production and ownership would evolve. Paradoxically, as this article will argue, these new attitudes towards creative production did not spring from the immaterial realm of ideas and books but from the very material world of craftsmanship and mechanical inventions. Similarly, the history of authorship is not exclusively concerned with authors and readers of texts but must be explored from a wider perspective of contemporary arts, crafts, music, painting and print making, as well as the aesthetic theories of Italian humanism that influenced these various disciplines. This article brings together these various strands of research to identify the diverse ways in which the rhetoric of authorship developed in different contexts and within specific modes of production.[2]

---

2   This article is based on a series of documents and accompanying commentaries

The First Printing Monopolies in Europe

Several lines in the genealogy of copyright have been traced to fifteenth century Venice – the home of the first printing privileges. The earliest and most famous patent was a five-year monopoly granted on 18 September 1469 to a German print master Johannes of Speyer to establish a press and foster printing within the Venetian Republic.[3] Although this monopoly has been hailed as the first known patent pioneering a long tradition of granting printing privileges in Europe, Speyer's monopoly does not appear as something new or exceptional in the economic life and legal tradition of Venice. Ever since the thirteenth century, the Venetians led Europe in their efforts to attract foreign expertise by granting monopoly rights to immigrants who brought with them new skills and techniques to the city. When Speyer reached Venice, the city had already become a vibrant centre of innovation and technology and, while the Venetians may not have been the first to introduce print in Italy, they were quick to recognise the importance of the new craft. Thus when a skilled German master appeared before the Venetian Collegio and promised to introduce a new faster and cheaper way of producing books the councillors did not pass on the opportunity to secure his services. They were careful to stress that 'such an innovation, unique and particular to our age and entirely unknown to those ancients, must be supported and nourished with all our goodwill and resources'. They considered that 'his art of printing' was 'something to be expanded rather than something to be abandoned', and granted Speyer an extensive monopoly over the entire art of printing for five years in Venice and its dominions – measures, they explained, that had been adopted for years in supporting other and much smaller enterprises. The councillors, therefore, made little distinction between Speyer's petition to operate a printing press and other requests for a concession to exercise a new enterprise or to work

relating to the history of printing privileges in Venice which can be found on the *Primary Sources* website www.copyrighthistory.org.

3   ASV, Collegio, Notatorio, reg. 19 (1467-1473), fol. 55 verso. This document has been transcribed and published several times; see: Rinaldo Fulin, 'Documenti per servire alla storia della tipografia veneziana', Archivio Veneto, 23 (1882), 84-212, 390-405; Carlo Castellani, *La stampa in Venezia dalla sua origine alla morte di Aldo Manuzio Seniore*. Ragionamento storico di Carlo Castellani prefetto della Biblioteca di San Marco. Con appendice di documenti in parte inediti. Presentazione de Giorgio E. Ferrari. (Trieste: Edizioni LINT, 1973), p. 69; and Horatio Fortini Brown, *The Venetian Printing Press 1469-1800: An Historical Study Based upon Documents for the Most Part Hitherto Unpublished* (London: John C. Nimmo, 1891), pp. 6-7. See also J. Kostylo, 'Johannes of Speyer's Printing Monopoly (1469)', in *Primary Sources*.

a new invention, requests which were regularly submitted to the various magistracies of the Venetian state.[4]

Indeed, throughout the fifteenth and sixteenth centuries the Venetian government received in excess of a thousand petitions from experts in various fields: makers of soap, of gunpowder and saltpetre, of glass, tanners, miners, metallurgists and civil engineers.[5] These petitions cover every imaginable subject, from devices for draining marshes to windmills and poisons, or culinary experiments such as special kinds of lasagne in an Apulian style and new types of dumplings filled with meat and fish.[6] In this regard, Speyer's monopoly appears to have been simply the application of a familiar administrative mechanism for granting monopolies that had already been at work in Venice for some considerable time. These ad hoc privileges were instituted to offer fixed-term exclusive monopolies to

---

4   In fact, by granting such an extensive monopoly, the councilors failed to anticipate the potential impact of this new way of producing books. Speyer's privilege was revoked a few months later, after his death, but had the monopoly remained in force for the entire five years it would have prevented other printers from establishing their presses in the city and, arguably, Venice would have never become the fastest-growing publishing industry in Europe. Even this short period during which the monopoly was in effect must have deterred some printers from moving to Venice. In 1470 about a dozen new printers opened shop in Rome and elsewhere in Italy, while only Nicolas Jenson and Christopher Valdarfer did so in Venice. Brown claims that the monopoly was never intended to be stringently binding but was more in the nature of a diploma of merit. Brown, pp. 52-3. See also: Carlo Castellani, *I privilegi di stampa e la proprietà letteraria in Venezia: Dalla introduzione della stampa nella città fin verso la fine del secolo XVIII* (Venezia: Stabilimento Tipo-Litografico Fratelli Visentini, 1888), p. 5; and Leonardas V. Gerulaitis, *Printing and Publishing in fifteenth-century Venice* (Chicago: American Library Association, 1976), pp. 21, 34.
5   Between 1474 and 1500, the Senate alone issued 33 monopolies, which number grew to 116 during the first half of the sixteenth century, and to 461 in the next half century, totaling 577 for the entire period of 1501-1600; see Roberto Berveglieri, *Inventori stranieri a Venezia (1474-1788): Importazione di tecnologia e circolazione di tecnici artigiani inventori* (Venice: Istituto Veneto di Scienze Lettere e Arti, 1995), pp. 21-2. This data, however, is not entirely accurate as the documentation regarding patents is now irretrievably lost in that some registers of the Provveditori di Comune are missing. In the course of the fifteenth and sixteenth centuries, a substantial number of immigrants from Germany, the Netherlands and other Italian states were able to obtain monopolies as importers of a new art or invention.
6   See for example the patent granted to Alvise di Valentin di Bossi on 2 May 1587 for 'lasagne tirate a forza de mani sottilissime senza alcun edificio stagiarini et macaroni alla pugliese fatti di pasta', or the patent granted to Alessandro Tornimben and Gerolamo Prevaglio for 'pastizzi fatti de diverse sorti di paste lavorati con ogni sorte de carnami et uzzelami, sì di grasso come dim agro, con pesce et senza'. ASV, PC, b. 16, reg. 31, f. 79r-v. Quoted from Luca Molà, *The Silk Industry of Renaissance Venice* (Baltimore, London: Johns Hopkins University Press, 2000), p. 375.

inventors and entrepreneurs initiating new technologies or products, and would later be identified as patents for inventions.

Speyer's monopoly was hardly distinguishable from the industrial privileges typically granted by the Venetian government in that it was awarded over an exercise of a new technological innovation rather than the works printed as a result of the same, as would be the case with later printing privileges. This grant was therefore part of the general framework of governmental support for, and regulation of, industry. That is, the world of the press developed as an industry governed by the same rules as other trades exercised in Venice and, initially, press products were not distinguished from other industrial products. Books were treated in more or less the same way as any other piece of merchandise: they were valued by weight at the customs just like any commodity and they were used as a barter payment to purchase wine, oil, flour and other industrial products. Indeed, the invention of the printing press itself could be seen as an adaptation of the wine or olive press, or any of the other industrial devices that used the technique of a screw press.

However, in contrast to other medieval crafts, this new art of printing developed outside the guild structure, and therefore in the absence of any administrative body regulating the control and operation of that particular trade. In fact, the Venetians did not organise the printing and publishing trade into a closed corporation until 1549. So, for the first eighty years of printing in Venice, printing privileges continued to be granted sporadically and on an ad hoc basis.[7] Thus, any early differentiation between industrial monopolies and proto-copyrights that might be attributable to the existence of a well-organised guild dedicated to regulating the operation of the

---

7   This can be compared with the situation in early modern England in which, prior to the formal incorporation of the Stationers' Company in 1557, the Scriveners' Guild had operated to regulate various aspects of the book trade (the writing of legal texts, illumination of manuscripts, bookbinding and bookselling) since 1403. The establishment of the Stationers' Company, and its relationship with the government of the day, occupies a particularly important place in the history of the development of copyright in early modern England. It has been argued that the tension between these two parallel systems of press regulation – the printing privileges based on the royal prerogative (the Crown) and the Stationers' Hall system, based on the by-laws of the guild – was largely responsible for the development of statutory copyright which, in turn, led to the passing of the *Statute of Anne*. For this interpretation see: Joseph Loewenstein, *The Author's Due: Printing and the Prehistory of Copyright* (Chicago: University of Chicago Press, 2002), p. 30; and Mark Rose, *Authors and Owners: The Invention of Copyright* (London: Harvard University Press, 1993), pp. 12-16.

book trade did not take place in early modern Venice. Moreover, even after the chartering of the Venetian Guild of Printers and Booksellers in 1549, the guild failed to develop a separate bureaucratic regime and the regulation of the trade continued to rely upon these ad hoc discretionary measures, following the traditional form of industrial privileges dispensed by the Venetian government in a variety of economic fields.[8]

There was also convergence between book privileges and privileges for mechanical inventions during this period in relation to the sphere of protected subject matter. Many of the early book-related privileges were granted for innovations in printing technology and type-design, as with the case of the monopolies granted to Aldus Manutius between 1496 and 1502 for the italic typeface and the new systems of printing Greek, or the privileges for an improved method of printing music introduced by Ottaviano Petrucci (in 1498) and the chiaroscuro technique introduced by the printmaker Ugo da Carpi (in 1516).[9] These privileges were concerned with printing technology, techniques of production, book layout, type of fonts and other material aspects of the book. This type of privilege was therefore conceptually very close to those regulating monopolies for mechanical inventions or processes of production. For example, the privileges of Aldus Manutius concerning his cursive type and the pocket-size book format were granted on the basis of how a text looked rather than what it said. They aimed to protect him from the unauthorised imitation of the format, type and ornament of imprints rather than the appropriation of the actual text itself. In 1501, Manutius launched his series of classic authors in octavo, employing a new cursive type which later came to be called italic. The innovation proved epochal in regard to both the reduced format, permitting a price reduction and the introduction of italic, which would eventually overshadow the international gothic type. Aldus Manutius was fully aware of the revolution his editions of classics in octavo format and italic type were ushering onto the book market. He wrote to the humanist Marino Sanudo,

8   In the preamble of the 1549 Decree chartering the Guild, the Venetian Council of Ten complained about the lack of regulation of the trade of printing: '[T]here is no one who represents the aforesaid art, nor who is responsible for it, so it happens that everyone does as he pleases amidst extreme disorder and confusion'; ASV, CX, Comuni, reg. 18, 18 Gennaio 1548 (m.v.). However, the establishment of the Guild did not restore order within the trade nor standardize or improve its copyright procedures. In fact, the Guild was not granted the exclusive control over published works until 1603 when it finally secured the right to grant and register copyrights. The Decree is reproduced with an accompanying commentary in J. Kostylo, 'Decree Establishing the Venetian Guild of Printers and Booksellers', in *Primary Sources*.
9   All these privileges are cited in Fulin, pp. 84-212.

in a dedication of his edition of Horace (1501), that such a pocket-sized book could be read at leisure, encouraging him to read his books whenever he was free from political engagements. Similarly, he suggested to captain Bartolomeo d'Alviano that he could take such small-format books to the battlefield.

Aldus's remarkable success quickly attracted the attention of competitors who counterfeited his books in cheap and hastily produced editions in Venice, Brescia, and Lyon. In his Warning Against Lyonnais Counterfeiters (1503), Aldus denounced the printers of Lyon, whose imitations of his Virgil, Horace, and other ancient classics: 'deceived unwary buyers both with the similarity of the letters and the format of the volume very similar to my own, so that they were tricked to believe that the books have been printed under my care in Venice'. He complained that all counterfeited editions were forgeries of the poorest quality: '[t]he lettering, upon closer inspection, betrays a certain Frenchiness'; 'in the same way upper case letters are misshapen'. Moreover, they were produced on foul paper, 'with [a] strange odour', and with many errors.[10]

In protecting his innovative editions of classics, Aldus was primarily concerned with the physical appearance of the work – the format and the accuracy of its presentation – rather than with its intellectual content or with the authorship of the same. It is understandable that in the case of well-known texts which had already been published many times, only a new font or format could qualify for privilege protection. Deciding the question as to what was worthy of protection was complicated at a time when privileges were granted for translations, abridgments, editions of the ancient authors and classics or for the Latin grammars, law books, catechisms and almanacs – in other words, for the categories of works which underwent continuous revision and improvement, works that could not be attributed to any individual author.[11] A well-known text could be

10   This document was discovered by the Abbé Mercier de S. Léger in a Greek manuscript of the Bibliothèque Nationale in Paris with several of Aldus's advertising circulars; BN, Ms. Gr. 3064, c. 85. It has been reprinted by: Antoine-Auguste Renouard, *Annales de l'Imprimerie des Alde, ou histoire des trios Manuce et de leurs editions* (Paris: Renouard, 1803), II, pp. 207-11; and, Ambroise Firmin Didot, *Alde Manuce et l'hellénisme à Venise* (Paris: D'Ambroise Firmin-Didot, 1875), pp. 187-226.

11   The early presses often focused on the production of the same popular titles. For example, Cicero's *De officiis* were printed in Venice between 1465-82 seven times, while in Rome three times, Milan five times, Naples two times, and in Brescia Parma and Turin once, not to mention numerous editions of Paris, Cologne, and Mainz. By 1476 17 editions, and by 1482 28 editions, had come on the market. There were also numerous reprints of Sallust, Virgil, Lucans or other standard titles such as the

abridged, lengthened, or refurbished (corrected) and reclaimed as new. In a petition of 1 March 1533, for example, the editor Marcangelo Accursio emphasised that he corrected his edition of 'Arumiano Marcellino' in 'five thousand places' and refurbished the work with several new additions.[12] While some printers resorted to evasive tactics of making minor alterations and additions and claiming that the work was 'new', others applied for privileges in derogation of the earlier claims. In 1502, for example, Andrea Torresani asked for a privilege for all the work of Scotus, Aquinas, Origen, Savonarola and other authors emphasising that he wished to obtain the privilege 'despite the concession' ('non obstante concessione') which must have already been claimed on these authors by others.[13] Sometimes, even the magistrates themselves did not know whether a book had been given a privilege before, or if it was still in effect, and granted a new concession without taking into account previous privilege holders. This is why they often added to the new privileges the clause 'dummodo aliis pro simillibus libris prius concessum non fuerit' or 'cum conditione, quod nulli antea fuerit concessum hoc idem'.[14] In order to cut down on these practices, the Venetian Senate issued a series of decrees which made more stringent rules for obtaining privileges. A Decree of 1517 revoked all existing privileges and established the principle of the public domain for all the books already in print ('libri comuni').[15] Subsequent provisions of 1534 and 1537 set out further restrictions, limiting the duration of the privileges to ten years and reiterating that only works which had not been previously published as a whole qualified as new. This new privilege regime put pressure on the printers to seek new publishable material and oriented the market towards

---

Confessionale of Antoninus Florentinus, the *De civitate dei* of St. Augustine, the *Biblia Latina*, the *Imitatio Christi*, among many others. Rudolf Hirsch, *Printing, Selling and Reading, 1450-1550* (Wiesbaden: Harrasowitz, 1967), p. 44.

12   ASV, Senato Terra, reg. 14, fol. 110, 1 March 1533.

13   Fulin, p. 150, nr 128.

14   For examples see: Fulin, nr 31, 33, 124,153, 161, 162, 169; Castellani, *La stampa*, p. 17.

15   This Decree is reproduced with an accompanying commentary in J. Kostylo, 'Venetian Decree on Press Affairs (1517)', in *Primary Sources*. 'Libri comuni' were those texts for which privileges could no longer be requested and which were considered a common patrimony of all publishers. These included classical Greek and Latin texts, liturgical and juridical works, dictionaries and grammars. See: Marino Zorzi, 'La produzione e la circolazione del libro', in *Storia di Venezia dale origini alla caduta della Serenissima, 7: La Venezia barocca*, ed. by Gino Benzoni and Gaetano Cozzi (Rome: Istituto dell'Enciclopedia Italiana, 1998), pp. 921-85 (p. 967); Angela Nuovo and Christian Coppens, *I Giolito e la stampa nell'Italia del XVI secolo* (Genève: Droz, 2005), p. 213.

'new' and 'original' works. With this shift towards contemporary texts and author-centred works, the question of protecting the content of the book, rather than its format, font or novelty of edition, began to gain greater weight. Boundaries of protection expanded beyond the sphere of verbatim reproduction in order to avoid evasions by additions, compilations and mutilations of the actual text. Similarly, verbatim reproductions, disguised in a different format or font, were no longer permissible. In his petition to the Venetian Senate, the celebrated poet Ludovico Ariosto explicitly specified that the text of his Orlando Furioso for which he was granted a privilege could not be reproduced in the same size or made larger or smaller. Nor could it be copied by employing a different type. He emphasised that it was not permissible:

> [T]o print or to put to print my work, by using any other font, neither in a grand folio size, nor in the smallest one, without the explicit license and concession of me, Ludovico Ariosto, the author of the aforementioned work.[16]

One consequence of the expansion of the protected subject matter from printing technologies to specific texts was the practice of granting printing privileges not just to printers and publishers but also directly to the authors. The privileges granted to Marc'Antonio Sabellico for the publication of his history of Venice, *Decades rerum Venetarum* (1486), and to Pietro Tomai of Ravenna for his work *Phoenix* (1492) on the art of improving the memory, set a precedent for granting these authorial privileges. Thereafter, writers began to make applications for privileges to the Venetian state on a regular basis.[17] Indeed, over the next thirty-four years, 254 privileges were granted, of which 79 (or, approximately thirty percent) were given to authors,[18] editors, commentators and translators of original works.[19]

It might be tempting to think that this practice of granting privileges directly to authors reflected a growing recognition of 'authorial rights', one

---

16   ASV, Notatorio Collegio, reg. 18, c.23r, 25 October, 1515.
17   Although Sabellico's privilege is often referred to as the Venetian precursor of copyright, the main body of book privileges dates from the privilege granted to Pietro Tomai of Ravenna on 3 January 1492. These privileges are reproduced in Fulin, p. 102, nr 3, 4. On the historical context of Sabellico's privilege see Ruth Chavasse, 'The first known author's copyright, September 1486, in the context of a humanist career', *Bulletin of the John Rylands University Library of Manchester*, 69 (1986-7), 11-37.
18   In particular, 49 cases involved a grant to the author of a work (as opposed to the editor or translator of the same).
19   According to the privileges recorded by Rinaldo Fulin for the years 1469-1526 ('Documenti').

that would lead to a new way of conceptualising the literary work – that is, in more abstract and immaterial terms than was the case for industrial products. However, there exists no such linear progression in this regard. In fact, many early developments in this field moved in exactly the opposite direction.[20]

First, in applying for privileges, early authors were not necessarily making any aesthetic or moral claims in relation to their works, but were instead simply displaying entrepreneurial acumen in seeking to capitalise on the emerging book market. Moreover, if in the early years of printing, authors took an active part in the publication of their own texts by securing privileges and coming to contractual agreements with the printers, with the expansion of the book market and the eventual establishment of the Guild of Printers and Booksellers these practices became increasingly unusual as professional interests began to dominate the trade. After 1549, the exclusionary politics of the guild towards non-members gradually obviated the ability of individual authors to claim privileges and retain control over their own texts. In short, authors found it difficult to control the commercial and artistic exploitation of their own work.

It was however in the course of this struggle that authors themselves began to consider the nature of the rights they enjoyed in their work, and so to express ideas about the author's relationship with his work. Initially, though, this understanding was far removed from any notion of the text as a particular category of 'intellectual' property that extended beyond the act of publication. While some outstanding writers such as Ariosto, Erasmus, Marsilio Ficino, Pietro Bembo or Torquato Tasso were certainly aware of the intellectual value of their work and spoke of the authorial 'honour', artistic 'fame' and 'paternity' of their work, alluding therefore to less material aspects of the bond that linked authors with their work, the extent to which they felt entitled to claim 'property rights' in these immaterial aspects is not clear. For example, a famous Venetian poet Pietro Bembo took an active part in the legal control and protection of the artistic integrity of his texts but he never applied for privileges himself. These applications were always made by others: his younger brother Carlo, the printer Aldus Manutius, his

---

20   Drawing on the critique of authorship scholarship developed by David Saunders, I tend to agree that there was no pattern, no single historical axis along which legal and aesthetic developments progressed towards one coherent goal. David Saunders, 'Approaches to the Historical Relations of the Legal and the Aesthetic', *New Literary History*, 23 (1992), 505-21.

secretary and friend Cola Bruno, his nephew Giovan Mateo Bembo.[21] This is perhaps because Bembo would have never considered coming down from the pedestal of his artistic rank and getting involved in detailed negotiations with the mercenary world of printers and book sellers.[22]

In order to safeguard their rights against professional producers, authors were often compelled to rely upon the same arguments as the publishers themselves: the physical labour expended, the high costs of production, and the other practicalities involved in the material production of books. In justifying their grants, they employed the same language found in industrial monopolies, emphasising the economic risks and public benefits involved, as well as the novelty and usefulness of their 'invention'. In fact, the contemporary term *inventio* did not discriminate between industrial and literary inventions.[23] Any distinctive sense of their product as a particular category of commodity – as a work of mind – appears to have been absent from these documents, as the authors hoped to concretise the property in the physical object of the manuscript for which they could claim a familiar trade privilege protection – a protection based upon the principle of protecting economic interests in material goods. From this point of view, book privileges were still largely tied to the material product of the printing press and conceptualised as a traditional trade privilege of the publisher extended to an author. Instead, the way in which the protected work came to be conceptualised in more abstract and intangible terms – that is, as a product of mind – can be explained by reference to the world of artisanship and crafts.

Medieval Guilds and Corporate Ownership of Knowledge

One of the greatest centres of trade and production during the Renaissance period was Venice. Already by 1600, Italian historians looked back to fifteenth century Venice as the most prosperous of European cities. In 1605 Giovanni Botero wrote:

21 Brian Richardson, 'From scribal publication to print publication: Pietro Bembo's Rime, 1529-1535', *Modern Language Review*, 95 (2000), 684-95.

22 On contemporary humanist attitudes towards printing see Brian Richardson, *Printing, Writers and Readers in Renaissance Italy* (Cambridge: Cambridge University Press, 1999), p. 79.

23 This term was used for example in the privilege granted to Pietro Tomai of Ravenna in 1492, for the new the art of improving the memory he 'invented'; Fulin, 102, nr 4. See also: Fulin, 204, nr 246.

> There is such a variety of things here [in Venice], pertaining both to
> man's well-being and to his pleasure, that, just as Italy is a compendium of
> all Europe, because all the things that are scattered through the other parts
> are happily concentrated in her, even so Venice may be called a summary of
> the universe, because there is nothing originating in any far-off country but
> it is found in abundance in this city.[24]

Several developments contributed to the economic success of the Venetian
Republic: its thriving commerce with the East and transalpine Europe, the
rapid expansion of artisan crafts and industry, the development of merchant and artisanal guilds and the rise of material culture and capitalistic mercantilism.[25] These in turn provided the essential environment in
which proprietary attitudes towards artisan artefacts and the specialised
knowledge required for their production could develop. These attitudes
were manifest in two related phenomena: the emergence of widespread
craft secrecy to protect craft knowledge from theft within the guild system,
and the development of the privilege as a form of limited monopoly for
inventions and craft processes granted to individuals. The former, which
will be considered within this section, emerged as an aspect of medieval
urban economic policies associated with the collective, corporate ownership of the guilds. The latter, which will be addressed in the next section,
substantially built upon the older corporate protectionism of the guilds
but also eroded it by offering monopolies to individual craftsmen for new
inventions and processes that could no longer be claimed by corporate
institutions to be part of artisanal 'mysteries'. The clash between these two
cultures – traditional guild monopolies and the new individualised form
of industrial property – contributed to the emancipation of the individual
author-inventor and the emergent notion of original authorship.

The institutions devoted to guarding trade secrets were the guilds
(arti).[26] The guilds developed and used various mechanisms in order to

---

24   Giovanni Botero, *Le relazioni universali* (Paris, 1605), in *Venice: A Documentary
History, 1450-1630*, ed. by D. Chambers and B. Pullan (Oxford: Oxford University
Press, 1992), pp. 167-8.
25   Fernand Braudel, *The Mediterranean and the Mediterranean World in the Age of
Philip II*, trans. from the French by Siân Reynolds (London: Collins, 1984), p. 128.
Braudel's claim that Venice, as the cradle of modern capitalism, which 'from the
very first raised all the problems of the relations between Capital, Labour and the
State relations' might be overstated. Nevertheless, with its corporatist structures
and thriving economy, attracting artisans and entrepreneurs of various sorts, Venice was the centre in which these capitalist transformations were well pronounced.
26   Venice had numerous *arti* which had regulated the conduct of various professions and trades since the Middle Ages. Each of these *arti* had its own charter and

protect these trade secrets and traditional techniques inherited from the past: most technical and craft knowledge was transmitted orally through apprenticeship and under secrecy oaths; the guilds restricted the movement of workers to prevent them from disseminating this 'tacit' knowledge of their trades abroad; and, the guilds also sought to place limits upon the initiative of individual entrepreneurs by keeping workshops small, forcing artisans to work on only a single project at a time, and by taxing individual masters for hiring additional assistants. Such mechanisms were intended to keep any single interest from breaking out of the guild system.

By the mid thirteenth century, there was already a fairly organised guild structure in Venice and contemporary craftsmen were willing to introduce, develop and practice their skills under the protection and control of these guilds. With the lucrative sales and demand for Venetian products, however, many Venetian artisans were tempted to leave the guild framework and establish their workshops independently. To protect Venetian specialties, the city and the guilds started introducing rigid regulations on the various trades.

This can be illustrated with the example of the guild of Vetrai in Venice, who were very protective of their glass making techniques. Venetian glass products were valued and sold profitably throughout the continent but the export of the craft itself, that is, of information concerning the craft processes and the practice of the craft, was strictly forbidden. Such knowledge was perceived as communal property to be used strictly for the benefit of the Venetian commune and the guild. As early as 1271, guild capitularies warned that 'anyone of the aforementioned art who will have gone out beyond Venice with the aim of practicing the said art' would pay a fine. In 1295, the Great Council deplored the loss of glassmaking secrets to the competition abroad and lamented that 'furnaces had multiplied at Treviso, at Vicenza, at Padua, at Mantua, at Ferrara, at Ancona and Bologna'. The Council ruled that glassworkers who left Venice to work outside would be banished from the guild and forbidden to work in Venice again.[27]

---

legislation regarding fees, contracts, working conditions, training apprentices and setting standards of the working techniques. See Richard Mackenney, *Tradesmen and Traders: The World of the Guilds in Venice and Europe, c. 1250-c. 1650* (London: Croom Helm, 1987).

27   *I capitolari delle arti veneziane sottoposte alla Giustizia e poi alla Giustizia vecchia dalle origini al 1330*, 3 vols, ed. by Giovanni Monticolo and Enrico Besta (Rome, 1905-14), 2, p. 66, nr 8; 2, p. 79, nr 51; 2, pp. 88-9, nr 80. Such regulations were continued throughout the fourteenth and fifteenth centuries. See for example: ASV, Archivio Podestà di Murano, b. 211; Consiglio dei Dieci, parti comuni, b. 1020, Inquisitori

The possibility of the flight of artisans with the consequent diffusion of their techniques was a problem that had haunted the Venetian government for centuries, despite increasingly severe penalties for artisans caught jeopardising the Venetian monopoly, penalties which could include death.[28] Such extreme remedies, however, were not unique to Venice. In Genoa, the city most injured by artisan emigration, the authorities offered in 1529 a reward up to two hundred ducats to anyone who killed a fugitive artisan. Similarly, Lucca had been offering a bounty for the murder of emigrant workers since 1314, and Florence punished transgressors by beheading.[29]

These draconian measures, designed to prevent the movement of workers, illustrate how contemporary governments and guilds placed great value on specialised expertise and knowledge and sought to protect it from individualistic entrepreneurial challenges. According to Pamela Long, this culture of corporate protectionism produced a unique environment in which a basic awareness that craft processes and knowledge constituted intangible property, property which could be protected and owned, was allowed to develop: 'In promoting attitudes of ownership toward intangible property – craft knowledge and processes as distinct from material products – the guilds developed the concept of 'intellectual property' without ever calling it that.'[30]

alle arti, b. 3; and, M. Miani, D. Resini, and F. Lamon, *L'arte dei maestri vetrai di Murano* (Venice: Matteo Editore, 1984), ch 3, pp. 108-18. On Venetian glassmakers in general, see: A. Gasparetto, *Il vetro di Murano dalle origini ad oggi* (Venice: Neri Pozza Editore, 1956); Luigi Zecchin, *Vetri e vetrai di Murano*, 3 vols (Venezia: Arsenale Editrice, 1987-90); and, Luigi Zecchin, 'Il segreto dei vetrai murnaesi del Quattrocento,' *Rivista della Stazione Sperimentale del Vetro*, 11, 4 (1981), 167-72. The silk industry sought to maintain control over traditional procedures by similar methods; Molà, *The Silk Industry*.

28   In fact, it is largely due to the emigration of these entrepreneurs that the knowledge of Venetian crafts and the use of industrial patents spread across Europe. For instance, the first industrial patent in France was awarded in 1551 to a migrant from the Venetian jurisdiction, Theseus Mutio, for the production of glass 'according to the manner of Venice.' Early patents were issued to Venetian glassmakers also in Antwerp, Germany, and England. See: Giulio Mandich, 'Venetian Patents (1450-1550)', *Journal of the Patent Office Society*, 30, 3 (1948), 166-224 (p. 206); Maximilian Frumkin, 'Early History of Patents for Invention', *Transaction of the Newcomen Society*, 26 (1947-9), 47-56 (pp. 50-4); Jeremy Phillips, 'The English Patent as a Reward for Invention: the Importation of an Idea', *Journal of Legal History*, 3, 1 (1982), 71-9; and G. Doorman, *Patents for Inventions in the Netherlands during the 16th and 18th Centuries* (Amsterdam: Netherlands Patent Board, 1942), pp. 12-13.

29   Molà, p. 43.

30   Pamela O. Long, 'Invention, Authorship, 'Intellectual Property' and the Origin of Patents: Notes toward a Conceptual History', *Technology and Culture*, 32, 4 (1991), 846-84 (p. 870).

Such a claim, however, must be treated with some caution, for these possessive and mercantilist attitudes towards trade secrets cannot be equated with the proprietary models of modern intellectual property law. The question is whether the contemporary guilds were concerned with keeping the craftsmen for the sake of their labour and skills, or whether they were attempting to protect expertise and knowledge as a valuable commodity understood in more abstract immaterial terms. Moreover, we must bear in mind that the proprietary attitudes of the guilds were closely tied to the notion of corporate ownership and were developed within the context of protecting communal and guild interests, quite apart from the notion of individual authorship. Craft knowledge was not generally linked to individual owners or to innovation; rather it was understood as a corporate resource – part of the governance structure of the guild's communal activities which were controlled by the government. In a similar way, the process of writing and producing books in the early years was perceived as a collective and collaborative enterprise.[31] The development which encouraged the separation of the notion of individual authorship from communal corporate ownership was the emergence of the industrial patent system.

The Statute of 1474 and the Venetian Privilege System

No matter how severe the punitive guild regulations were in attempting to restrict the emigration and entrepreneurial initiative of individual workers, their effectiveness was mitigated by the simultaneous development of the legal incentives designed to lure skilled professionals, or an entire industry, into other cities and states. While the guilds' monopolies often sought to constrain the freedom to import foreign goods or expertise, the use of individual privileges provided short-term exclusive rights to inventors and entrepreneurs initiating new technologies or products in order to revitalise native industry. Contemporary states might have been pressured into such 'modernising' policies in order to adapt to contemporary innovations and to ward off foreign competition.[32] Princes, city councils and popes in Rome,

---

31   On the continuing importance of the collective, corporate and collaborative aspects of writing and producing books see: Roger Chartier, *The Order of Books: Readers, Authors, and Libraries in Europe between the Fourteenth and Eighteenth Centuries* (Cambridge: Polity, 1994), pp. 9-10; and, H.J. Chaytor, *From Script to Print: An Introduction to Medieval Literature* (Cambridge: Cambridge University Press, 1945), pp. 115-37.
32   Traditionally, economic historians saw the guilds as essentially conservative institutions inclined to reject any kind of innovation and individual initiative. For

all sought to attract new technologies and trades by guaranteeing legal, fis-
cal, and social benefits to any artisan or merchant willing to move to the
new city. These benefits ranged from the rights to immigrate and settle in
the city, the cancellation of debts, granting immunity from prosecution for
criminal offences, or, in the case of those holding papal office, even the
promise of an absolution from specific sins. Venice itself was one of the
first states to develop and benefit from such a system. As early as 1272,
the Venetian government provided that 'any one who comes to Venice to
exercise the trade of a wool weaver shall receive a house to live in and to
exercise said trade, at Murano, Torcello or in the country, free from cost
for ten years'.[33] Initially, these public appeals were meant to attract entire
crafts from abroad but they also provided incentive to local entrepreneurs
by offering individual monopolies to those who undertook to introduce a
new device or practice a new skill in the city.

Of course, one of the most famous legislative initiatives in this regard is
the Statute of 19 March 1474. The Statute elaborated that the greatness of
Venice had attracted numerous individuals 'who have most clever minds,
capable of devising and inventing all kinds of ingenious contrivances' and
who sought to test their skills and inventions in the city. In order to freely
exercise their talents these men needed a fundamental incentive: the certainty that no one could copy and use their inventions with impunity. And
therefore 'should it be legislated that the works and contrivances invented
by such men could not be copied and made by others'. The Statute also
provided that monopolies might be granted for 'any new and ingenious
device, not previously made', as long as it was useful and beneficial to the
community. In addition, it required that each inventor had to register his
discovery at a state office (Provveditori di Comun). In return, no one within
the Venetian territory could make a similar device for ten years without
the consent and licence of the inventor and if anyone infringed the law,
they were to pay one hundred ducats and the device might be immediately
destroyed.[34]

---

a recent critique of this essentially Marxist interpretation see *Guilds, Innovation and
the European Economy, 1500-1800*, ed. by S.R. Epstein and M. Prak (Cambridge: Cambridge University Press, 2008). Francesca Trivellato's essay on the Venetian silk and
glass trades, for example, demonstrates how these guilds were able to adapt to an
evolving market through collective invention and competitiveness within the guild
itself: 'Guilds, Technology, and Economic Change in Early Modern Venice', ibid.,
pp. 199-231.

33　　Mandich, 'Venetian patents (1450-1550)', p. 171.

34　　For the text of this Statute and further discussion see J. Kostylo, 'Venetian Stat-

For a long time this Statute has been celebrated as the first comprehensive law which provided a statutory basis for the Venetian privilege system. It has been argued that, for the first time, an attempt had been made to apply general rules to the granting of a patent rather than conferring ad hoc favours (*gratiae*) in response to individual petitions. Now, apparently, 'every inventor enjoyed some [...] substantive right, arising from the very fact of his invention and not merely a privilege granted on the basis of some state policy'.[35] In the most recent scholarship of this persuasion, the Statute has been portrayed as the earliest instance of the constitutionalization of patent law which inaugurated 'the first modern patent system'.[36] In 'Constitutionalizing Patents: From Venice to Philadelphia', Craig Allen Nard argues that the practice of granting ad hoc individual monopolies by the state as a reward to inventors was replaced in Venice by a more durable general patent law because of the 'republican' structure of the Venetian government which prevented the organisation of factions and interest groups thus undermining the stability of such ad hoc bargains. Arguably, in addition to overstating the significance of the 1474 Statute, this interpretation oversimplifies the relations between patrician elites, the citizen bureaucracy and the *popolo* members of the guilds in favour of a public choice explanation for the enactment of the Statute of 1474 and other important episodes in the history of patents.[37]

There are various reasons for being sceptical about the interpretation presented by Nard and others. In the first place, the Statute of 1474 did not introduce any new principles but functioned primarily as a codification of

ute on Industrial Brevets (1474)', in *Primary Sources*. See also Giulgio Mandich, 'Le privative industriali veneziane (1450-1550)', *Rivista del diritto commerciale e del diritto generale delle obbligazioni*, 34 (September-October 1936), 511-47 (pp. 518-9); Frumkin, 'Early History of Patents for Invention'; and more recently, Molà, p. 187.

35   Mandich, 'Venetian Patents (1450-1550), p. 180.

36   Craig Allen Nard, 'Constitutionalizing Patents: From Venice to Philadelphia', *Review of Law & Economic*, 2 (2006), 224-321.

37   Nard's interpretation is characteristic of much of the American scholarship in the tradition of Bugbee, Prager, Frumkin and others. According to Prager, for example, in 'most places the patent system was adopted almost exactly as developed in Venice [...] all of the basic rules developed in Venice were preserved in the subsequent systems'; Frank D. Prager 'A History of Intellectual Property from 1545 to 1787', *Journal of the Patent Office Society*, 26, 11 (1944), 711-60 (p. 720). See also: B.W. Bugbee, *Genesis of American Patent and Copyright Law* (Washington, DC: Public Affairs Press, 1967), 23; M. Frumkin, 'The origins of patents', *Journal of the Patent Office Society*, 27, 3 (1945), 143-9; and, Christopher May, 'The Venetian Moment: New Technologies, Legal Innovation and the Institutional Origins of Intellectual Property', *Prometheus*, 20 (2002), 159-79 (p. 162).

previous customs.[38] It neither fostered any universal privilege regime nor marked the beginnings of the modern patent system. It was itself essentially an ad hoc measure rather than a premeditated institutional shift from individual grants to a bureaucratised system. Moreover, it neither committed the executive to enforce it, nor did it instigate any further legal developments in this field. Neither do we find any specific appeals to this Statute by any individuals subsequently petitioning for protection. In short, the Statute should be best understood as a declaratory instrument codifying existing general principles and customs of granting patent rights for innovations in Venice.

However, neither can one speak of this Statute as purely accidental. It has to be placed within the context of many similar public appeals which aimed to attract foreign expertise and innovation in order to adapt to an increasingly competitive market. Such provisions were becoming one of the characteristic instruments of international economic competition. Arguably, another historical factor that might have prompted the emergence of this law was the extraordinary success of printing itself. The introduction of the press by Speyer five years earlier, in 1469, demonstrated the financial benefits of attracting technical innovations to the city. In very little time, printing became one of the most important economic activities of Venice, alongside the silk manufacturing and glass making industries. However, as previously noted, unlike these industries the practice of printing was not incorporated within the guild structure until 1549. Neither was there any general regulation which would deal with the printing industry as a whole.[39] That is, it can be argued that the rapid expansion and economic success of the printing industry combined with the absence of any regulatory procedures encouraged the Venetian authorities to issue a more general provision which would, in turn, further stimulate an influx of new technologies as well as standardise licensing procedures. Such a reading also supports the argument that there was no strict separation between industrial and printing monopolies during this period, and suggests the existence of a continuing dialogue between the two.

The real significance of the 1474 Statute however lies in the fact that it

---

38   On the previous development of patents and related issues see Mandich, 'Primi riconoscimenti veneziani', pp. 116-55.
39   The first general law regulating the printing trade was not passed until 1517. Beforehand, the trade was left virtually uncontrolled. On the significance of this law see J. Kostylo, 'Commentary on the Venetian Senate's Decree on Press Affairs (1517)', in *Primary Sources*.

focuses on protecting and rewarding individual inventors, in contrast to the monopolies reserved to guilds which were concerned with the effective control of the market as opposed to providing reward or compensation for innovation. That is, the Statute can be understood as an instance of municipal protectionism favouring individual rather than a corporate form of property. Unlike the guild monopolies, which were perpetual in duration, the Statute limited the available term of protection to ten years. And although we do not find any specific appeals to this Statute on the part of individual petitioners, it may be that this law encouraged the further use of state monopolies by individual inventors.[40] While these grants were exceptions from the guild monopolies, conferring favour on foreigners and non-members, they could also protect petitioners from the local constraints of guilds engaged in related production and jealous of their economic rights. When, in 1297, the Venetians sought to stimulate the invention of new medicines, they passed a law which provided that 'if any physician wished to make any of his own medicine in secret, he may be empowered to make it [...] and all guild members may swear not to interject themselves into the above mentioned [matter]'.[41] Such judicial decisions served to facilitate innovation and foster public interests rather than private rights of individuals. Nevertheless, in the long term, these individual grants and laws eroded the jurisdiction of the guilds and provided a formal legal mechanism by which individual entrepreneurs could challenge the corporative monopolies of the guilds. That is, in an incidental but significant way, these grants became important vehicles for individualisation of authorial rights.

From Corporate *Ars* to Individual *Ingenium*: Filippo Brunelleschi and the Humanist Synthesis of Theory and Practice

The effort of the guilds to monopolise and control trade secrets was designed to restrict the personal initiative of individual entrepreneurs and compel contemporary craftsmen to practice their skills under protection and control of those guilds. Ironically, these monopolistic attitudes increased the awareness of the commercial value of craft knowledge and heightened the level of intra-guild competitiveness and mercantilism among the artisans themselves. Venetian records of stolen glassmaking recipes reveal

40 Berveglieri, *Inventori stranieri a Venezia*.
41 Long, 'Invention', p. 876.

these attitudes. A fifteenth-century glassmaker, Giorgio Ballarin, for example, stole the recipes for 'various colours mixed in glass' from the famous Venetian inventor of crystal, Angelo Barovier. He then gave the recipes to Angelo's rival, his future father-in-law, and subsequently became one of the leading glassmakers of Murano.[42] Moreover, with the emergence of privileges for inventions, more entrepreneurial individuals would sometimes break out of the guild system by securing individualised patent protection of the state. The most conspicuous instance of this is the Florentine architect and engineer Filippo Brunelleschi.

Trained as a goldsmith, Brunelleschi matriculated as a master in the silk guild (which also trained the goldsmiths) in Florence in 1404. He also became a member of the *Opera del Duomo*, the committee that supervised the construction of the Florentine cathedral at the time. Brunelleschi designed and built the dome using improved scaffolds and without rigid, wooden centring or formwork. He also designed his own hoisting crane and other machines which secured cheaper, more secure and faster delivery of the building materials. This method of building without centring had never been applied on such a gigantic scale; probably it was altogether unknown to the Florentine masters. In fact, the committee for the construction of the cathedral dome refused to follow Brunelleschi's innovative methods and continued to follow the more traditional approach of his rival and co-supervisor of the construction, Lorenzo Ghiberti, instead.

Brunelleschi's tenuous relationship with the Dome Committee and his conflicts with his rivals and other guildsmen are well known.[43] In the course of his notorious dispute with the woodworkers and stoneworkers' guild he was jailed for eleven days. He refused to join the guild and sought to

---

42   This story comes from the fifteenth-century account written by a monk Gian Antonio, in honour of his master Paolo de Pergola, 'the first author and inventor of various colours mixed in glass' who taught his secrets to Angelo Barovier one of his pupils. A transcription of this account appears in Emanuele Antonio Cicogna, *Delle inscrizioni veneziane*, vol. 6, pt. 1 (1852; repr. Bologna: Forni Editore, 1970), pp. 466-71 (p. 467). See also Pamela Long, *Openness, Secrecy, Authorship: Technical Arts and the Culture of Knowledge from Antiquity to the Renaissance* (Baltimore: Johns Hopkins University Press, 2001), pp. 91-2.

43   Many details of Brunelleschi's life are known from the biography written in the 1480s by his younger contemporary Antonio di Tuccio Manetti, *The Life of Brunelleschi*, ed. by Howard Saalman (University Park and London: Pennsylvania State University Press, 1970); and Giorgio Vasari, *Le vite de più eccellenti architetti, pittori & scultori italiani, da Cimabue insino a tempi nostri* (Florence: Giunti, 1550), Seconda parte, pp. 301-26, esp. pp. 301-2, for his conflict with the guild and Ghiberti. Architecture and sculpture, along with masonry and carpentry were monopolized and regulated by the Guild of the Masters of Stone and Wood.

reassert his individual authority as an architect and constructor. He argued that he alone was the author ('autore') and inventor of his construction methods and devices and refused to disclose them to other guildsmen.[44] Moreover, he contested the guild's claims to the ownership of his own inventions by applying himself for privileges.

In 1421, he applied to the Florentine commune for a privilege on a cargo boat that he had invented to improve the shipping of the building materials for the dome construction along the Arno River. In his petition, Brunelleschi described himself as 'a man of the most perspicacious intellect, both of industry, and of admirable invention'. He claimed that the newly invented ship could haul loads more cheaply and that it would provide further benefits to merchants and others. But he refused 'to make such machine available to the public in order that the fruit of his genius and skill may not be reaped by another without his will and consent'. If he could enjoy 'some prerogative' concerning his invention, he 'would open up what he [wa]s hiding and would disclose it to all'. A monopoly would allow the matter to be brought to light for the benefit of Brunelleschi and everyone else. Following his request, the state of Florence granted him a three-year exclusive right to build and use on Florentine waters a new ship or other device for transporting goods on waters; any 'new or newly shaped machine would be burned'. [45]

This broad range of rights conferred on Brunelleschi outside of the monopolistic strictures of the guilds is emblematic of the growing recognition that the medieval monopoly system associated with the guilds no longer sufficed to promote the economy of the state. In the new realities of the advancement of industrial technologies and a more aggressive commercial exploitation of inventions, it was the emerging privilege system that would foster innovation, technological change and entrepreneurship. Characteristically, Brunelleschi himself suggested that such a privilege would foster innovation and provide incentive for his further work. As he

---

44   Ibid., p. 302. He also claimed and obtained a complete refund for his material and labour costs, and an additional 100 florins for the invention as such, which was previously considered by a special commission of the Dome Authority. A similar bonus was given to him for the structural dome design itself.

45   Long, *Openness, Secrecy, Authorship*, p. 97. Brunelleschi's patent has been celebrated by many scholars, although, contrary to recent claims by Prager or Frumkin, it was by no means the first. For a translation and discussion of this document, see Frank D. Prager, 'Brunelleschi's Patent', *Journal of the Patent Office Society*, 28 (February 1946), 109-35. For the original see *Carteggio inedito d'artisti dei secoli XIV, XV, XVI*, 3 vols, ed. by Giovanni Gaye (Florence: Giuseppe Molini, 1839), 1, pp. 547-9.

put it, he would be motivated 'to higher pursuits, and would ascend to more subtle investigations'.[46]

Brunelleschi's refusal to work within the guild structure illustrates the emergence of more possessive attitudes towards craft knowledge among individual inventors, and their increasing concern to protect their knowledge and work from unauthorised dissemination. Traditionally, guilds provided such protection but once individualist assumptions about inventions collided with the corporatist interests of the guilds, individual entrepreneurs began to look for some alternative ways of protecting their knowledge. Writing in secret codes such as Leonardo da Vinci's mirror writing might have provided one possible solution.[47] Another was the use of single privileges for inventions. Motivated by his confidence in his own technical expertise and a deep concern to protect it, it is no surprise that Brunelleschi used both. His advice on secrecy and limited disclosure as remedy for the theft of ingenious inventions was recorded by his contemporary, Mariano Taccola, the Sienese author of books on machines:

> Do not share your inventions with many, share them only with a few who understand and love the sciences. To disclose too much of one's inventions and achievements is one and the same thing as to give up the fruit of one's ingenuity. Many are ready when listening to the inventor, to belittle and deny his achievements, so that he will no longer be heard in honourable places, but after some months or a year they use the inventor's words, in speech or writing or design. They boldly call themselves the inventors of the thing that they first condemned and attribute the glory of another to themselves.[48]

In addition to the availability of patents, there were also other ideological factors that exerted transforming pressures on the collective corporate identity of the guilds. According to Frank Prager, Brunelleschi was 'an outstanding exponent of the rising era of individualism' which challenged the feudal oligarchy of the guilds.[49] There is no doubt that Brunelleschi was exceptional in many ways. Born to a well-placed family of lawyers, he enjoyed a better education and higher social status than most artisans. Yet Brunelleschi was also fundamentally a product of his own time. His new

---

46   Ibid. (author's own translation of the original document).
47   Martin Kemp, *Leonardo da Vinci: The Marvellous Works of Nature and Man* (London: Dent, 1981).
48   Frank D. Prager, 'A Manuscript of Taccola, Quoting Brunelleschi, on Problems of Inventors and Builders', *Proceedings of the American Philosophical Society*, 112 (June 1968), 131-49. Quoted from Long, 'Invention', p. 879.
49   Prager, 'Brunelleschi's Patent', p. 114.

approaches to creativity, ingenuity and individual authorship were deeply rooted in the rhetorical programmes and aesthetic theories of Renaissance humanism, which placed an increased value on knowledge, learning and individual genius.

Today, historians of the Renaissance are uncomfortable with Jacob Burckhardt's claims about the Renaissance cult of individualism.[50] They have noted that these new constructions of individual identity were at every step held back by widespread collaborative processes and the continuing importance of collective (corporate) identity in Renaissance Florence, Venice and elsewhere. Yet Burckhardt does have a point about the 'rebirth' of arts and the rising status of individual artists. One of the long-lasting effects of Renaissance humanism was the elevation of certain arts, most importantly painting, sculpture, and architecture, to the status of liberal, 'fine' arts. This in turn contributed to the rising status of creators and inventors such as Leonardo da Vinci and Brunelleschi among many others celebrated in Giorgio Vassari's famous *Lives of the most excellent Italian architects, painters, and sculpturers*. Painters and other artists also contributed to this view. Albrecht Dürer's presentation of himself in his Christ-like image as a consummate godlike artist epitomises this trend.[51] Not incidentally, according to Vasari's account, he took legal action against the Venetian print maker Marc'Antonio Raimondi who had been copying Dürer's woodcuts from the *Life of the Virgin* series, and succeeded in preventing Raimondi from using his name and monogram on his works.[52] It is plausible that Vasari's story about this lawsuit actually took place since Raimondi omitted the famous monogram from his later copies of Dürer. What is interesting in this case is the fact that the Venetian Senate allowed Dürer's prints to be copied, but required that neither his name nor his monogram appear on the copies. In the context of contemporary art theory and the Renaissance culture of learning by imitation, the reproduction of the 'masters' was widespread and unproblematic.[53] But not the reproduction of the artist's personal sign which suggested the artist's personal presence in the making of a particular

50   Jacob Burckhard, *The Civilization of the Renaissance in Italy* (Harmondsworth: Penguin, 1990), pp. 81-5.
51   Joseph Leo Koerner, *Moment of Self-Portraiture in German Renaissance Art* (Chicago: University of Chicago Press, 1993), pp. 34-51.
52   Vasari recorded Dürer's complaint to the Venetian Senate in *Vita di Marcantonio Bolognese, e d'altri intagliatori di stampe, primo volume della terza parte Delle vite de' piu eccelenti pittori, scultori e architettori*, 2nd ed. (Florence: Giunti, 1568), pp. 294-9.
53   Lisa Pon, *Raphael, Dürer, and Marcantonio Raimondi: Copying and the Italian Renaissance Print* (New Haven and London: Yale University Press, 2004).

work of art, understood as a unique object created by a seemingly irreplaceable individual. It could be argued that while the Venetian legal system did not consider the copying of Dürer's prints to be illegal, at the same time, it offered protection for something much more subtle and immaterial – not the image but its expression and the artist's individual style (*maniera*) – an acknowledgement of Dürer's generative powers.

This new way of thinking about the metaphysical aspects of the artist's labour was derived in part from the humanist debates over the nature of technical knowledge. One important development in Renaissance humanism was the proliferation of humanist writings on the mechanical arts, not only on visual arts such as architecture, painting, and sculpture, but on topics such as gunpowder artillery and on machines of various kinds. This literature, the work of university-educated men who turned their hand to technical matters, and of the workshop-trained artisans who took pen in hand to write treatises, narrowed the gap between the cultures of learning and artisanal craft production. It blurred the distinction between theory and practice, transforming certain forms of crafts and constructive arts into written, discursive disciplines which came to be treated as forms of 'knowledge' rather than mechanical skill.[54] This new way of thinking about craft knowledge helped to separate the notion of invention from the immanent specific machine and resulted in a new definition of the author's work as a product of the mind.

This new definition of the invention as distinct from its material fabrication is evident in the work of Leon Battista Alberti whose writings influenced learned culture of the fifteenth and sixteenth centuries. Alberti dedicated one version of his treatise on painting *De picture* to none other than Brunelleschi. He praised Brunelleschi for his 'feat of engineering' and emphasised that the architect is not a carpenter, alluding to his notorious clashes with the woodworkers' guild, but an artist 'who by sure and wonderful reason and method devises in his mind and realises in construction whatever is needed'. Alberti, like Brunelleschi, clearly conceived architecture as a discipline involving (intellectual) design emanating from the mind of an individual creator who can then disclose his invention and realise it in (practical) engineering.[55]

---

54   Long, *Openness, Secrecy, Authorship*, p. 104.
55   Leon Battista Alberti, *De picture*, in *Opere volgari*, ed. by Cecil Grayson (Bari: Laterza, 1973), 3, pp. 7-107. For the Latin text and English translation see *'On Painting' and 'On Sculpture': The Latin texts of 'De pictura' and 'De statua'*, ed. and trans. by Cecil Grayson (London: Phaidon, 1972), pp. 34-5. See Long, *Openness, Secrecy,*

Another contemporary treatise which conveys a similar sense of distinction between the tangible and the intangible aspects of the work is the *Trattato* written in the 1470s by the Sienese engineer and writer Francesco di Giorgio. Francesco began his career as a workshop artisan before becoming a widely respected architect and military engineer. At the same time, he was an aspiring humanist who translated Vitruvius and composed a series of treatises on architecture, fortification and military engineering. Paraphrasing Vitruvius, Francesco emphasised in his *Trattato* that competence in conceptual realms must take precedence over practical skills. Architecture, he argues, 'is only a subtle image, conceived in the mind that becomes manifest in the work'. Such a work of the mind cannot easily be grasped because 'ingenuity consists more in the mind and in the intellect of the creator than in writing or design'.[56] Having recognised that the work of the mind is distinct from material objects, Francesco also emphasised the need to safeguard it. He condemned those who usurped the works of others and attributed these works to themselves, comparing them to crows dressed in the feathers of the peacock. He admitted that he had translated 'most authentic books' and credited Vitruvius with authorship, yet he also insisted that his writings were filled with his own original contributions: 'inventions of my own weak skill'.[57]

It is difficult to measure the cultural impact of this expansion of literature on the mechanical arts in the fifteenth century but it was around this time that inventions began to be conceptualised in terms of ideas. Brunelleschi construed his devices as material manifestations of immaterial genius and his petitions for privileges contain new forms of justifications and claims, couched in the vocabulary of individual genius and mental labour. Moreover, this emerging class of author-inventors introduced more

---

Authorship, p. 124. For Alberti see Franco Borsi, *Leon Battista Alberti* (Milano: Electa, 1975). For Alberti's relationship to Brunelleschi see Christine Smith, *Architecture in the Culture of Early Humanism: Ethics, Aesthetics, and Eloquence, 1400-1470* (Oxford: Oxford University Press, 1992), pp. 19-39.

56   '[È] solo una sottile immaginazione concetta in nella mente la quale in nell'op[e]ra si manifesta.' '[L]o ingegno consiste più in nella mente e in nello inteletto dell'architettore che in iscrittura o disegno, e molte cose accade in fatto le quali l'architetto overo op[e]ratore mai pensò' [*sic*]. Francesco di Giorgio, *Trattati di architettura ingegneria e arte militare*, 3 vols, ed. by C. Maltese (Milan: Edizioni il Polifilo, 1967), 1, 36. Autograph manuscript in British Library Codex 197 B21 [MS Harley 3281]. See: Giustina Scaglia's annotated transcription in *Il "Vitruvio Magliabechiano" di Francesco di Giorgio Martini*, Documenti inediti di cultura Toscana, 6 (Florence: Edizioni Gonnelli, 1985), pp. 43-50; Long, *Openness, Secrecy, Authorship*, p. 135.

57   Ibid., p. 136.

mercantilist approaches to the world of ideas and the culture of authorship. The fact that they came from the artisan's world – the world of material things, ownership and reward – is significant, for they were able to associate their intellectual effort with material application and so began to place a commercial value on the exploitation of their ideas.

Author-inventors and the Press: The Rise of Professional Writers

An increased appreciation for the technical arts and spread of humanism furnished a growing supply of technical manuals and treatises explaining craft techniques and other artisanal 'secrets'. But this growing demand for practical literature was also a response to the realities of a changing book market, as early interest in religious subjects and ancient classics began to flag and shifted to new areas, including science, medicine and technology. Since the market for books was new and almost entirely unregulated, many were encouraged to reap the rewards of technical authorship. The early recruits into the industry included craftsmen, engineers, merchants, painters, and physicians – a mosaic of the Renaissance petite bourgeoisie. Whether working for wages as in-house authors or free-lancing and dependent on patronage, these obscure but prolific literary producers signalled the emergence of a new class of professional writers making a career out of a new printing technology. Their background, combining commercial and scholarly experience, ideally prepared them for the role of cultural brokers mediating within a shifting space of a printing house where academic, 'popular' and craft influences and traditions converged.[58] Operating within an emphatically mercantilist value system, which encouraged the ideology of 'possessive authorship', they illustrate how an ideology stemming from the material world of contemporary crafts could be extended into the realm of literary production.[59] As soon as they took pen in hand to elaborate upon their technical skills and inventions in writing, they undertook also a new

---

58   On the early modern interaction between the world of scholarship and craftsmanship see Elisabeth Eisenstein, *The Printing Press as an Agent of Change: Communications and Cultural Transformations in Early-Modern Europe*, 2 vols (Cambridge: Cambridge University Press, 1979), 2, pp. 520-635; Cesare Vasoli, 'A proposito di scienza e technica nel Cinquecento', in *Profezia e ragione: Studi sulla cultura del Cinquecento e del Seicento* (Naples: Morano Editore, 1974), pp. 479-505.
59   The concept of 'possessive authorship' was coined by Joseph Loewenstein, *The Author's Due*.

craft of professional writing and sought reward for their new skill.

The rewards of technical authorship are particularly evident in the careers of early publisher-physicians in Venice, who took advantage of Venice's flourishing book market and privilege system to capitalise on the secrets of their trade by publishing medical advice for the 'common man'. These works, ranging from theoretical treatises to recipe books and surgery manuals, written in vernacular and intended for a more general non-specialist audience were often submitted by the physicians themselves who put forward all sorts of extravagant claims to obtain a privilege in relation to the same. In 1498, for example, Democrito Terracina claimed that the Arabic and Armenian medicinal tracts which he intended to publish were to foster scientific knowledge and public health. To print these books would be 'of utility to the Christian republic, and the exaltation of the faith, and the augmentation of the natural sciences, as well as medicine, in the conservation of the health of the soul and bodies of many and all faithful Christians'.[60] Another example is the 1509 privilege granted to a Venetian physician Pietro de Mainardi for the publication of his compendium containing remedies against pestilence.[61]

This convergence between scholarship, craftsmanship and business acumen was brought into sharper focus by the practice of publishing technical manuals by professionals of specialised trades writing for other professionals. Traditionally, technical and craft knowledge was transmitted orally through apprenticeship systems or handed down through families, from one generation to the next. With the advancement of craft technologies and the expansion of trade investment, however, such modes of transmission no longer seemed sufficient and artisans, entrepreneurs and investors began to rely on printed industrial manuals in order to learn a trade. Changing technologies pressured craftsmen to acquire new skills, many of which they could gain or improve by reading books, while their wealthy and literate but inexperienced patrons wanted to learn how to maximize the profitability of their investments.

The printing of books of techniques may have codified well-known practices, but they also posed the question of how to 'safely' reveal previously

---

60   '[P]er utilità della republica christiana, et exaltation de la fede, et augmento de la scientia naturale, et ancor de la medicina, per conservation de la salute de le anime et corpi de molti et infiniti fidel[i] christiani' [*sic*]; Fulin, p. 134, nr 82.

61   *Remedia praeservativa ab epidemia*; Fulin, p. 173, nr 178. Exceptionally, Mainardi was granted a shorter one-year privilege (usually privileges were granted for five or ten years) because of the common interest in public health which would benefit from an open transmission of such a work.

concealed techniques to a wider audience while protecting ideas and inventions from facile borrowings. This need for protection would become even clearer once the newly patented inventions began to be supplemented with technical manuals and advertised in print. In 1588, a successful Jewish businessman, Maggino Gabrielli, who obtained several patents from Venice, Florence, the Pope, and the King of Spain for his revolutionary methods of increasing the silk harvest, took the momentous decision to reveal all the intimate details of his inventions in print. He published his *Dialogues on the Useful Inventions for Silk* in Rome with the papal privilege.[62] Gabrielli's decision to reveal all the secrets in his possession might seem puzzling, considering the numerous privileges with which he jealously guarded his inventions. Indeed, in his second dialogue he informs his readers that the content of the inventions had been kept secret until now because he was waiting to receive all the privileges requested from the Italian princes. Once the last monopoly was obtained however he applied for a printing privilege to publish a book which would advertise and praise the qualities of his inventions.

It is clear that Gabrielli sought to capitalise on his inventions by lucrative sales of his book as well as the returns from his industrial investments, and that he used his Dialogues to disseminate and sell his inventions in Italy and 'beyond the Alps'. His book was also to serve as an instruction manual for the prospective buyers of the new devices. In fact, he intended to create a wide network of agents who would advertise and sell his products at the fairs, who 'will publicly sell both these books of mine, so that everyone might use them in the silk craft, and all sorts of contrivances and instruments that are needed to carefully tend the little worms, and they will be given at such a low price and for such a good bargain that everyone will profit from buying them'. At the same time, while selling these books, his agents were to read aloud the privileges granted by the various princes, to inform the buyers that no one was permitted to reproduce the new inventions on his own or buy them from anyone else. Moreover, the authenticity of the products would be guaranteed by the application of special identification marks.[63]

The practice of revealing protected industrial secrets in published manuals became a well-established method of demonstrating the advantages

---

62   *Dialoghi di M. Magino Gabrielli Hebreo Venetiano sopra l'utili sue inventioni circa la seta, Con privilegio, In Roma, Per gli Heredi di Giovanni Giolitti, 1558. Con licenza de' Superiori.* For a more detailed discussion of Gabrielli see Molà, pp. 204-14.
63   Ibid., p. 209.

and feasibility of patented inventions. Combined with printing, such practices expanded the reach of available technical knowledge but also contributed to a process by which proprietary attitudes towards knowledge and the idea of protected production migrated from the world of industrial monopolies to the realm of book protection. The question of how to disclose technical details of an invention without jeopardising an inventor's economic interests brought into focus the possibilities of a limited transmission and authorial control of such information under the existing printing privilege system, resulting in expanded industrial as well as printing monopoly coverage for works and knowledge that were technological in nature. Such practices further confirm the lack of any meaningful distinction between the industrial monopoly and the printing privilege that was characteristic of this time.

In conclusion, it can be said that the practice of granting industrial privileges in early modern Italy constituted an important arena in which new attitudes and models relating to authorship and property developed. These developments shaped the social and philosophical definitions of intellectual property that prefigured its legal definition and application in the copyright tradition of later periods. These views were first evident within the culture of industrial capitalism and craftsmanship. But they were also influenced by the aesthetic theories of the Renaissance humanism and had emerged from the tension-riddled relationship between collective (corporate) *ars* and individualistic *ingenium*.

The example of fifteenth-sixteenth century Venice suggests that the paradigm of proto-copyright protection was partly formulated on the model of protected industrial production and that the concept of possessive authorship developed first with regard to material inventions before it was applied to writing. Another consequence of this convergence between proto-patent and proto-copyright was an increased appreciation for the intellectual labour and the distinction between tangible and intangible aspects of the author's work. Two different strands of development can be identified in this regard. While in the realm of literary production writers were clinging to the solid and material aspects of their production and the physical object of the manuscript, which helped to concretise the property in terms of material good, in the world of crafts and mechanical inventions the humanist synthesis of theory and practice was pulling in exactly the opposite direction, supplying a much more abstract, broad and fluid concept of the artisan/artist's work. Here, I have suggested that a particular group of fifteenth and sixteenth century professionals – artisans, inventors and technical authors – made an important contribution to such a viewpoint. They conceptualised their work in terms of a mixed hybrid form, partly material and partly immaterial, seeking to establish the differentiation and abstraction of authorship from artisanal fabrication and mechanical reproduction.

Paradoxically, these efforts to liberate artistic ingenuity from artisanal fabrication, and the growing recognition that mechanical and artistic inventions were unique objects made by individuals of genius, gained in importance precisely when new cheap means of mass production became available. As Terry Eagleton has observed, the representation of the artist as a transcendent genius was born 'just when the artist is becoming debased to a petty commodity producer'.[64] It was precisely within the battlefield of these conflicting material interests of artisanal reproduction and individualistic artistic commitments that the distinction between tangible and intangible aspects of the work was forged – long before it came to be recognised by copyright law.

---

64   Terry Eagleton, *The Ideology of the Aesthetics* (Oxford: Blackwell, 1990), pp. 64-5. See also Rose, p. 120.

2. 'A Mongrel of Early Modern Copyright': Scotland in European Perspective

Alastair J. Mann

The copyright history of Scotland is generally seen to be a post-1710 phenomenon.[1] English and European commentators, but also Scottish, have been guilty of this somewhat lazy approach. Scottish historians of copyright, such as they are, have however lauded the role of Scottish judges in the evolution of British copyright law in the eighteenth century. The significance of Scottish legal traditions and theory over the interpretation of copyright, helped lead, it is asserted, to the final judgment of the House of Lords in 1774. Certainly this interest in the 'battle of the booksellers' has encouraged an output focusing on the eighteenth century.[2] Not all though

1   For a general survey of Scotland see: Alastair J. Mann, *The Scottish Book Trade 1500 to 1720: Print Commerce and Print Control in Early Modern Scotland* (Edinburgh: Tuckwell Press, 2000), chapter 4; and Alastair J. Mann, 'Scottish Copyright Before the Statute of 1710', *Juridical Review* (2000), 11-25. The only previous survey is W.J. Couper, 'Copyright in Scotland before 1709', *Records of the Glasgow Bibliographical Society*, 9 (1931), 42-57; but see also Dr. John Lee, *Memorial for the Bible Societies in Scotland* (Edinburgh: Edinburgh Bible Society, 1824), *passim*. John Feather's comprehensive, *Publishing, Piracy and Politics: An Historical Study of Copyright in Britain* (London: Mansell, 1994) does not consider Scotland before the eighteenth century.
2   For Scottish accounts of the 'bookseller war' of 1746-1774 see: Warren McDougall, 'Copyright Litigation in the Court of Session, 1738-1749 and the Rise of the Scottish Book Trade', *Edinburgh Bibliographical Society*, 5 (1987), 2-31; Richard B. Sher, 'Corporatism and Consensus in the Late Eighteenth-century Book Trade: The Edinburgh Booksellers' Society in Comparative perspective', *Book History*, 1 (1998), 32-93; Richard S. Tompson, 'Scottish Judges and the Birth of British Copyright', *Juridical Review* (1992), 18-42; Hector L. MacQueen, *Copyright, Competition and Industrial Design*, 2nd edn, Hume Papers on Public Policy, III, 2 (Edinburgh: Edinburgh University Press, 1995), pp. 1-6. For English accounts see John Feather, 'The Publishers and the Pirates: British Copyright Law in Theory and Practice, 1710-1775',

are convinced of the significance of copyright liberalisation. Recently in Richard Sher's excellent volume *The Enlightenment and the Book* (2006), a study of Scottish authors and publishing in the Enlightenment, he states that the 'Impact of Lords copyright decision [of 1774] should not be exaggerated' and that trade expanded regardless of copyright.[3] However, this takes no allowance of an early modern and perhaps 'mongrel' tradition of copyright in Scotland which profoundly influenced attitudes to intellectual property, encouraged freedom of commercial exploitation and was a precursor to a surprisingly robust Scottish Enlightenment.

Since the medieval conflict, the Scottish Wars of Independence, Scots students went to Europe not England to learn law and so became conversant with the law of Rome, in tandem with Scotland's own legal codes as confirmed in *Regium Majestatum*, a Glanville-based Scottish legal manual in wide-spread use by the late medieval period. Even when law become a subject for study in Scotland, firstly at King's College, Aberdeen in the sixteenth century, the tradition remained that students were educated abroad, especially in Holland, and notably in Leiden or Utrecht. By the time Edinburgh introduced its first chair of law in 1707, rather obvious timing given the assertion of legal independence in spite of Anglo-Scottish parliamentary union the same year, a traditional Scottish approach to the law was well-established. Scots Law, before and after the Union, had developed along typical Continental lines: owing more to Roman and civic law and natural justice and not so much to precedent and custom. Scots Law, in theory at least, was grounded on social law and the test of evident utility. Furthermore, it showed some passion for codification, from James Dalrymple, 1st Viscount Stair's *Institutions of the Law of Scotland* of 1681 to George Joseph Bell's *Principles of the Law of Scotland* of 1829.[4] How did this impact upon attitudes to intellectual property? In short, a balance was struck between public interest and private right which limited the duration and scope of copyright.

Typically in sixteenth and seventeenth century Scotland licensees obtained the right to 'print, reprint, vend, sell and import' but not

---

Publishing History, 22 (1987), 5-32; John Feather, *A History of British Book Publishing* (London: Croom Helm, 1988), pp. 76-83; and John Feather, *Publishing, Piracy and Politics*, pp. 64-96. Also of use is A.W. Pollard, 'Some Notes on the History of English Copyright', *Library*, 4, 3 (1922), 97-114.

3 Richard B. Sher, *The Enlightenment and the Book: Scottish Authors & Their Publishers in Eighteenth-Century Britain, Ireland & America* (Chicago: University of Chicago Press, 2006), pp. 25-8.

4 See Mann, *Scottish Book Trade*, pp. 96-7.

specifically 'to copy'. In Scotland copyright for individual books originated directly from patents granted by the Crown there being no Stationers' Company to whom the registration and assertion of individual copyrights could be devolved. Scottish book licences were granted by the Crown's representatives for a limited number of years, either a specific period or the lifetime of the licence holder, and after the 1590s this was extended to include heirs and successors. The first Scottish licence for an individual title sustaining the rights of heirs was John Gibson's licence to import a Psalms edition from Middelburg in 1599.[5] Therefore, like France, Spain and the Low Countries but unlike England, Scottish practice rejected the notion of perpetual copyright as simply 'unreasonable'.

'Reasonableness' was an important test for legal interpretation of book law in Scotland. For example, when in June 1614 the printer-publisher Andrew Hart purchased from King James VI and I exclusive rights to commission printing overseas for import into Scotland, the Scottish Privy Council then delivered one of the most significant judgments in Scottish book history. Although Hart came armed with a letter from the King demanding confirmation of his rights, the Council rejected the privilege entirely. The words of the judgment provide a dramatic illustration of executive views about the licensing of the press, which would, in the 1670s and 1680s, be reflected in the opinions of the Scottish Parliament:

> The freedom, liberty and privilege of printing, importing and selling of all such books and volumes which are allowed and not forbidden ought to be free to all His Majesty's subjects and not conferred and given to any one person without great hurt and prejudice to the country, because every such private freedom, liberty and privilege is not only a monopoly of evil consequence and example, but will give occasion to alter and raise, heighten and change the prices of all books and volumes at the appetite and discretion of the person and persons in whose favour the privilege shall happen to be conferred, and for this reason the said Lords ordain the gift and privilege purchased by the said Andrew Hart from the king to be halted, and in no way to be passed or expedited.[6]

The concept of 'reasonableness' is illustrated in other cases. After Agnes Campbell, Scotland's wealthiest early modern printer, inherited from her husband Andrew Anderson the royal patent of King's Printer in 1676, she strived to protect her privileges. However, when in autumn 1681 she printed

5   Registrum Secreti Sigilli, [PS], National Archives of Scotland [NAS], PS.1 .71, 47r printed in Lee, appendix xii; see Mann, 'Scottish Copyright', p. 12.
6   *Register of the Privy Council of Scotland* [RPCS], 1, 10, pp. 827-8. Text modernised by the author.

an edition of the acts of Parliament, not unreasonably given the royal patent, she was challenged before the Privy Council by the printer David Lindsay and partners who had acquired the right to print parliamentary acts by licence of the Clerk Register, the chief government administrator with responsibility for statute printing. The Privy Council confirmed Lindsay's right, and ordered the burning of Campbell's stock. Her appeal to the Court of Session in the winter of 1682-83 failed and her argument, that 'one press [was] sufficient' for official documents, was seen by the investigating committee as acting, like her old patent, 'to restrain the liberty of printing too much'. The case was, nonetheless, a temporary setback for Campbell who proved one of the most successful litigants in early book history.[7]

After the 1603 Union of the Crowns notions of copyright in Scotland and England continued to develop along different lines. In early modern England two forms of copyright co-existed – firstly, the 'printing patent' granted by the sovereign, and secondly, after 1557, the Stationers' copyright, in essence the former public and latter private.[8] But the transfer and purchase of private copyrights between Stationers' guild members from the 1580s encouraged a monopoly grip on copyrights by a small group of copyholders. This trend intensified when in 1603 James VI and I gifted to the Stationers' Company the valuable patents granted to John and Richard Day, for primers and psalters, and to James Roberts and Richard Watkins, for almanacs and prognostications. These transfers, with unintended consequences, became the legal basis for the 'English Stock', and thereafter began the frantic buying and selling of copyholding within the Stationers' Company, and the accumulation of patents into even fewer hands. King James's intentions were to free-up privileges in response to general fears

---

7 John Lauder of Fountainhall, *Historical Notices of Scottish Affairs*, 2 vols. (Edinburgh: Constable, 1848), I, p. 311; *RPCS*, 3, 7, p. 257. Registrum magni sigilli [*RMS*] Register of the Great Seal of Scotland manuscript registers, C3/10. no. 343. For the appeal, which was concluded in January 1683, see: John Lauder of Fountainhall, *The Decisions of the Lords of Council and Session from June 6th 1678 to July 30th 1712*, 2 vols. (Edinburgh: Hamilton and Balfour, 1759-61), I, p. 205; and Lauder, *Historical Notices*, I, p. 393. For a summary see Alastair J. Mann, '"Some Property is Theft": Copyright Law and Illegal Activity in Early Modern Scotland', in *Against the Law: Crime, Sharp Practice and the Control of Print*, ed. by Robin Myers, Michael Harris and Giles Mandelbrote (London: British Library, 2004), pp. 44-6.

8 Mark Rose, *Authors and Owners: The Invention of Copyright* (London: Harvard University Press, 1993), pp. 11-2; Lyman Ray Patterson, *Copyright in Historical Perspective* (Nashville: Vanderbilt University Press, 1968), pp. 78-113. For general summaries see Pollard, 'Notes on the History of Copyright in England'; Feather, *History of British Publishing*; and Cyprian Blagden, *The Stationers' Company, 1403-1959* (London: Allen and Unwin, 1960), *passim*.

over monopoly trading. But when subsequently the English Statute of Monopolies (1624) limited to fixed periods patents in inventions and industrial processes, books were exempted.[9] In Scotland, meanwhile, the duration of copyright deliberately shadowed that of manufacturing patents. Although the Statute of Monopolies did not apply in Scotland, James VI encouraged the Scottish Privy Council to set up a commission of grievances over monopolies in May 1623, and in 1641 the Scottish Parliament reviewed some major monopolies 'because of the great hurt' suffered by all, and 'patents purchased for the benefit of particular persons in prejudice of the public' were ended. However, books were not on the agenda in Scotland in 1623 or 1641 as they were already subject to limitations, and yet the judgment of 1614 appears to be linked to some monopoly concerns.[10] In due course limited copyright in Scotland helped in 1710 to ease British statutory copyright back into line with that for industrial patents north and south of the Border.

It is important, however, not to exaggerate the difference between England and Scotland over copyright. Licences granted by the English Crown, or the 'printing patent', which initially pre-date the Stationers' copyright, continued throughout the early modern period. The first of these, granted in 1512 by Henry VIII to John Rastell, was to print *Progymnasmata* by Thomas Linacre. In Scotland the first royal patent was that general gift, for statutes, histories, chronicles and the like, given by James IV to Scotland's first printers Walter Chepman and Andro Myllar in 1507, and although this was directed mainly at printing Bishop William Elphinstone's breviary the *Breviarium Aberdonense* (1510), it was clearly not a patent for a single act of publication. The first such Scottish example was the patent granted to Thomas Davidson in 1541 to print for six years the acts of the Scottish Parliament. These Scottish examples correspond to the two types of prerogative patent operating in England, the Chepman and Myllar licence – 'general', for life and containing generic classes of books, and the Davidson variety – 'particular' and limited in time, in England typically to licences

---

9   21 James I c.3. For an account of the general monopoly controversy see Christine MacLeod, *Inventing the Industrial Revolution: The English Patent System, 1660-1800* (Cambridge: Cambridge University Press, 1988), pp. 10-19; Rose, pp. 45-7; Patterson, pp. 86-7; Mann, 'Copyright and Illegal Activity', pp. 33-4.

10   *RPCS*, 1, 13, pp. 219-22, 240, and 299-302; K.M. Brown *et al*, *The Records of the Parliaments of Scotland [RPS]*, http://www.rps.ac.uk (St Andrews: University of St Andrews, 2007), *RPS*, 1641/8/192 [accessed 30 October 2008]; Mann, 'Copyright and Illegal Activity', p. 34. The monopolies abolished in Scotland in 1641 included those for tobacco, leather, pearling and armoury.

of seven to ten years.[11] It is clear then that before the Stationers' Company the practicalities of copyright in England and Scotland were pretty similar. Nonetheless, while it muddied the waters that the Stationers' Company made the impractical acquisition in 1632 of the Scottish King's Printer patent, before they withdrew back to London in 1670, Anglo-Scottish divergence became the common trend.[12]

Before 1710 Scottish copyright depended on government patents sustained by royal prerogative. The Privy Council was the main licensing authority in this period, although until around 1610 copyright licences for particular titles were confirmed via patents that passed the Scottish Privy Seal, in which royal gifts of appointments, pensions and private monopolies were confirmed, and occasionally thereafter where the king had a specific personal interest. This is seen, for example, in the 1616 privilege granted to James Primrose to print the 'catechism' *God and the King*, a liturgical work composed for, and probably in consultation with, King James himself. Subsequently, the surviving registers of the Privy Council reveal that almost all book licences were enacted and recorded in decreta registers (private business) from the 1670s, with only national publishing concerns, such as David Wedderburne's twenty-one year licence for a new national grammar in 1632, the winner of a national 'battle of the grammars' competition, being considered public business for recording in the Council's acta registers.[13]

Copyright was not merely conveyed by central government however and some patents had local origins. Unlike London, Edinburgh never reached a condition of regulatory supremacy, in spite of brief attempts by the royal printer Andrew Anderson to establish an Edinburgh society in the early 1670s.[14] So, although printing did not commence in Aberdeen,

---

11   Patterson, pp. 86-7; *Registrum Secreti Sigilli regum Scotorum: Register of the Privy Seal of Scotland* (printed series) [*RSS*], 1, p. 223 no. 1546; and R. Dickson and J.P. Edmond, *Annals of Scottish Printing: From the Introduction of the Art in 1507 to the Beginning of the Seventeenth Century* (1890; repr. Amsterdam: Gerard Th. Van Heusden, 1975), pp. 7-8; NAS, PS.1.3, 129; *RSS*, 2, p. 653, no. 4335.

12   Blagden, pp. 138-45; Mann, *Scottish Book Trade*, p. 117. A wide historiography exists on the Stationers' Company but see especially *The Stationers' Company and the Book Trade, 1550-1990*, ed. by Robin Myers and Michael Harris (Winchester: St Pauls, 1997); and Robin Myers, *The Stationers' Company Archive: An Account of the Records, 1554-1984* (Winchester: St Pauls, 1990).

13   NAS, PS.1.85, 245r-247v and *RPCS*, 1, 10, pp. 534-8; *RPCS*, 2, 4, pp. 168-9 and 500-1; NAS. Manuscript Privy Council Registers, PC. 2.24. 319 v; Mann, 'Scottish Copyright', p. 15.

14   Mann, *Scottish Book Trade*, pp. 17-18, 115, and 120; Mann, 'Copyright and Illegal

Glasgow and Dundee until 1622, 1638 and 1703 respectively, no central-ised limitation was placed on the proliferation of presses, and royal burghs were by their medieval charters authorised to license all commercial activ-ity, including presses. After the Restoration the 'printing burghs' gave local copyright protection for a variety of burgh almanacs, diurnals, newssheets and newspapers, such as Aberdeen Town Council's licensing and protec-tion of the *Aberdeen Almanac* from the 1660s.[15]

The Scottish Parliament itself sometimes licensed prestigious or national publishing activity. As with the government, it mostly acted over censor-ship, but it also ratified the general gifts to king's printers, and authorised national texts, such as the *Directory of Public Worship* introduced by the Covenanters in 1645. Worthy law texts could also be granted copyrights by Parliament. In 1633, in the presence of Charles I, Parliament agreed that Robert, son to Thomas Craig, should be licensed for twenty-one years to print in three volumes his father's great treatise on Scottish land law *Jus Feudale*. A committee appointed to oversee the printing was headed by Charles I's Lord Advocate, Thomas Hope of Craighall, himself a signifi-cant published jurist. This publishing venture was of long duration. Since Craig's death in 1608 the Privy Council and Parliament had recommended publication of Craig's writings to King James but to no avail. Hope and his committee also failed to make progress and, while manuscript versions of *Jus Feudale* circulated, the first printing did not appear until the Edinburgh edition of 1655.[16]

Copyright term is crucial to the potential for commercial exploitation of literary property. The extent and width of the right granted and the sanctions or compensation for breach are also vital. One of the clear indi-cators that Scottish early modern copyright was significant is seen in the standardised terms and conditions that developed during the seventeenth century. As we have seen, English copyright tended to extend for seven to ten years under the 'printing patent', and in perpetuity where registered

---

Activity', p. 44.

15   *Extracts from the Records of the Burgh of Aberdeen*, ed. by John Stuart, 2 vols. (Edinburgh: Scottish Burgh Record Society, 1871-2), 1, pp. 245-6; Aberdeen Coun-cil Records, lv, f. 66-7; and J.P. Edmond, *The Aberdeen Printers, 1620 to 1736*, 4 vols. (Aberdeen: J & J.P. Edmond & Spark, 1884) 4, p. xiv; Mann, *Scottish Book Trade*, pp. 102-3.

16   *RPS*, 1645/1/65 (6 February 1645); *RPS*, 1633/6/65 (28 June 1633) [accessed 30 October 2008]; Mann, *Scottish Book Trade*, p. 50; *States Papers and Miscellaneous Cor-respondence of Thomas Earl of Melrose*, ed. by James Maidment, 2 vols. (Edinburgh: Abbotsford Club, 1837), 1, pp. 43-4 and 84-5.

with the Stationers' Company. Although short-term renewals were generally available, contemporary German, French and Italian publishers were
often granted short licences of less than five years duration. Conventionally,
Dutch copyright was for longer periods of fifteen to twenty-five years.[17]
Comparisons with Scotland are of interest. By 1670, whether the licence
holder was an author, printer or licensee, the standard term of copyright
for particular works in Scotland had become nineteen years. The origin of
this term is obscure, though it was a common Scottish period for leases,
appointments and commercial monopolies. Generally, therefore, copyright
terms in Scotland approximated to those of the Dutch and not the English
or French. Scotland's copyright terms could, however, extend from as little as six years to the thirty-one years in the case of James VI's grant to
Sir William Alexander for the Psalms in metre in 1627. Nevertheless, the
logic for long or short licences was fairly consistent. Reprints, without the
novelty of 'newness' and so seen as inferior intellectual property, were
granted shorter copyright durations. The standard term for reprints was
eleven years from the 1670s. Thus in 1671 the Edinburgh printers George
Swintoun and James Glen were granted eleven year licences to reprint
thirty-seven sermons by the minister Andrew Gray. Fully revised editions
received a full term copyright, as with James Kirkwood's new editions of
his grammar and vocabulary published in the1690s (see figure 1).[18]

Essentially, the breadth of right conveyed changed very little throughout
this period. Rights of assignees were recognised in the earliest individual
copyright patents, and heirs were first mentioned in those granted to the
king's bookbinder John Gibson in 1599, and were ever-present in copyrights
granted from the 1630s. The first private copyright given to an author, that
given to William Niddrie in 1559 to produce a range of education books,
granted to him 'his factouris and assignais, to have onlie the prenting of
the saidis volumes' and that no subjects, printers and booksellers could 'tak
upoun hand to prent, sell, caus be prentit or sald [them] within this realm'.

17   Lucien Febvre and Henri-Jean Martin, *The Coming of the Book: the Impact of Printing, 1450-1800*, trans. from the French by David Gerard, ed. by Geoffrey Nowell-
Smith and David Wootton (London: N.L.B, 1976), p. 241; Elizabeth Armstrong,
Before Copyright, The French Book-privilege System, 1498-1526 (Cambridge: Cambridge University Press, 1990), pp. 16-17; P.G. Hoftijzer, *Engelse boekverkopers bij de
beurs: De geschiedenis van de Amsterdamse boekhandels Bruyning en Swart* (Amsterdam:
APA-Holland University Press, 1987), p. 108. By 1700 the typical French licence had
extended to ten years.
18   NAS, PS. 1, 100, 305; *RPCS*, 3, 3, p. 306; *RPCS*, 3, 4, p. 292 and 5, p. 268; NAS,
PC, 2, 26, 47 v; Mann, *Scottish Book Trade*, pp. 104-14.

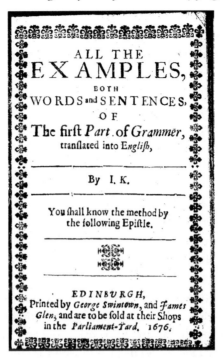

ALL THE
EXAMPLES,
BOTH
WORDS and SENTENCES,
OF
The firſt *Part* of *Grammer,*
tranſlated into E*ngliſh,*

By I. K.

You ſhall know the method by
the following Epiſtle.

EDINBURGH,
Printed by *George Swintown,* and *James
Glen,* and are to be ſold at their Shops
in the *Parliament-Yard.* 1676.

Fig. 1: Title page of the first part of James Kirkwood's successful grammar, first published in 1676, and printed by Swinton and Glen, but reissued as a revised edition with full copyright in 1695. Such works were both uncontroversial but highly profitable copyright properties.

There is no evidence of book patents that granted export rights. Alexander Arbuthnet and Thomas Bassandyne's licence of 1576, for Scotland's first domestic Bible printing, was the first to forbid other book traders to import competing editions, and by the middle of the seventeenth century this was a conventional stipulation regardless of the likelihood of foreign imports. Indeed, odd and sometimes contradictory exclusions appeared in certain copyrights. In the valuable copyright for the works of George Buchanan awarded to George Mosman in 1699, exemptions were made for editions 'already printing and imported'. This sensible qualification contrasts with the 1686 generic monopoly for prognostications awarded to James VII and II's 'household printer' James Watson, the elder, who, somewhat absurdly, was given rights over and above almanacs already in print.[19] The most

---

19   NAS, PS, 1.75, 127; *RSS*, 5, 1, pp. 143-4, no. 658; *RSS*, 7, p. 94, no. 642; NAS, PC, 2, 27, 252 v; Lee, p. 146; *RPCS*, 3, 12, pp. 460-1; Fountainhall, *Decisions*, 1, p. 424. For a listing of the multi-title patents obtained by Gibson and Niddrie see Mann, *Scottish Book Trade*, pp. 236-9.

comprehensive protections were given to copyright on official business. Meanwhile, the policing of copyright was at the behest of the copy holder. Customs officials had an important role in censorship but not over copyright. This generally placed the advantage with the wealthier, royal printers. With the great forty-one year monopoly granted to Andrew Anderson in 1671, on his appointment as King's Printer, these powers developed a controversial nature within the trade and the courts, and especially after his widow Agnes Campbell succeeded in 1676.[20] James Watson, the younger, records in his *History of the Art of Printing* (1713), the first history of printing in the British Isles, though based on Jean de la Caille's *Historie de L'imprimerie*, that in 1688 Campbell fell 'tooth and nail' upon the Edinburgh bookseller Alexander Ogston for importing London bibles into Scotland. In fact, the multi-title patent granted a century before to the Edinburgh printer Robert Smyth in 1599 was the first to grant searching powers to a licensee.[21]

The relative effectiveness of copyright regulation in Scotland before 1710 can be seen by the details of specific publishing histories. Sir George Mackenzie of Rosehaugh, the great Scottish jurist and Lord Advocate, saw his *Institutions of the Laws of Scotland* published in 1684 followed by two 'new editions' printed in 1688 and 1699, but not sufficiently new or revised to require a re-registration of copyright. The original patent was granted to John Reid, the elder, in 1684, and declared that no other was to print 'without license from the said author'. It seems Reid and Mackenzie agreed a contract before Mackenzie's death in 1691. The edition of 1688 was also printed by Reid, but acting for the Edinburgh bookseller and burgh magistrate Thomas Brown to whom the rights had been assigned by Mackenzie. Brown then published the 'third edition' in 1699. In October 1702, with the copyright due to expire the following year, the now elderly Brown transferred the rights to his son-in-law, and specialist law bookseller John Vallange of Edinburgh. Vallange petitioned the Privy Council and obtained

20   *RPS*, 1672/6/158 (11 September 1672) [accessed 30 October 2008]. This relates to the ratification by Parliament of the Anderson patent. It was granted under the Scottish Great Seal in May 1671 but was not recorded in the register. For a detailed account of the subsequent disputes see Alastair J. Mann, 'Book Commerce, Litigation and the art of Monopoly: The Case of Agnes Campbell, Royal Printer, 1676-1712', *Scottish Economic and Social History*, 18 (1998), 132-56 (pp. 136-9).

21   James Watson, *A History of the Art of Printing* (Edinburgh: Watson, 1713), p. 16; Fountainhall, *Historical Notices*, 2, p. 866; Fountainhall, *Decisions*, 1, p. 494; NAS, PS, 1, 71, 86. For a list of the titles in Smyth's patents see Mann, *Scottish Book Trade*, pp. 239-40.

a short extension to the licence for reprint purposes.[22] Details surrounding the valuable grammar copyrights are also revealing. Copyrights in James Kirkwood's grammar *Grammatica Facilis* and vocabulary *Rhetoricae Compendium*, originally granted in 1677, were due to expire in 1696 after nineteen years, and at the end of 1695 the author submitted his new editions for copyright to be re-established.[23] These examples confirm that authors and printers understood the valuable property represented by book copyright, and maintained a close watch on expiry dates. In Scotland, nearly half of private copyrights were granted directly to authors, and those like the lawyer Sir George Mackenzie were keen to protect their intellectual property.

The most desirable monopolies available to Scottish early modern book traders were those associated with royal appointments. These provided extensive generic copyrights. Early royal appointments, unlike particular copyrights, were for life, but it was only with the appointment of Walter Finlason as King's Printer in 1628 that heirs and assignees were recognised. However, for this and subsequent appointments all royal printer gifts were for a set period of years. Co-partnerships, hereditary rights and the involvement of assignees were only possible after such positions were limited to a fixed period.[24] But the attitudes of royal printers best illustrates the proprietorial view of copyright before 1710, as it increasingly became the concern of courts and of lawyers. Even two hundred years before, courts took action to protect privileges and copyrights, as did the Scottish Privy Council in the winter of 1509-10. Following a complaint by Walter Chepman that booksellers had been illegally importing England's Salisbury 'use', the standard liturgy of England, the Council issued a warning to a group of merchants to immediately halt such trade and make way for the new Aberdeen Breviary which appeared during 1510. The legal complexities increased from the Restoration. Following the extensive monopoly powers granted to Anderson in 1671, the Privy Council and Lords of Session became bogged down in over a decade of litigation between the Anderson press and its competitors. For example, in 1677 and 1680 Anderson's widow, Agnes Campbell, prosecuted the Glasgow printer Robert Sanders, the elder,

---

22   *RPCS*, 3, 8, p. 410; NAS, PC.2.28, 235v-36r. The 1699 edition was the 1694 London edition with a cancelled title page.
23   *RPCS*, 3, 4, p. 292 and 5, p. 268; NAS, PC, 2, 26, 47v; Mann, 'Copyright and Illegal Activity', pp. 40-1.
24   NAS, PS, 1, 101, 120. For a summary of the history of the privileges of Scottish royal printers see Mann, *Scottish Book Trade*, pp. 114-22.

before the Privy Council for infringing her rights. Confiscation, a huge two thousand pound fine and a short spell in prison were Sanders's fate in 1677, although in 1680 a more lenient judgment induced only confiscation of offending stock.[25] Some government exasperation with Campbell and her excessive monopoly was building towards the Lindsay judgment of 1681.

The Privy Council took on the role of an appeal court in cases between the book trades of competing burghs. In 1682 and 1683 Robert Sanders and Agnes Campbell each produced separate counterfeit editions of the highly successful *Aberdeen Almanac*. This Aberdeen edition, with the help of the mathematicians at King's College, had become the market leader since the 1660s following its introduction by the Anglo-German printer Edward Raban in 1623. Deception came before illegality and in the 1660s and 1670s Robert Sanders in Glasgow printed various almanacs suggesting calculation by Aberdeen mathematicians, and Edinburgh editions also falsely claimed Aberdeen authority. To fight against this the Aberdeen printer John Forbes, the younger, stated in doggerel in his 1674 edition: 'No almanacks are from Aberdeen but where there Armes are to be seen', it being the habit of burgh printers to add the copyright symbol of the burgh coat-of-arms. The most infamous case then arose in 1684 in which year Forbes fumed in print: 'If Counterfit, then Hang for it!' Forbes, with the support of the magistrates of Aberdeen, prosecuted Sanders and Campbell before the Privy Council in February that year. After the case was referred to a committee it ruled in favour of Forbes and Aberdeen. He won his case in law because he was 'in use and possession of printing yeirly ane almanack as printer of the toun and coledge of Aberdein', and therefore his copyright was sustained. Aberdeen's right to signify copyright had also been breached. Sanders had attempted to forge the city arms of Aberdeen which always adorned the almanac, and therefore his offence was viewed as especially reprehensible (see figure 2). Unfortunately for Forbes the drip, drip of counterfeit editions continued over this highly profitable genre.[26]

The Court of Session also became more involved in book trade matters as by the 1680s the level of litigation grew beyond the competence of the Privy Council. Cases concerning indebtedness tended to appear before

25   For the text of Council ruling on the Salisbury case see: Dickson and Edmond, pp. 84-5; Mann, *Scottish Book Trade*, pp. 129-30. For Anderson/Campbell disputes see Mann, 'The Case of Agnes Campbell', pp. 136-43.
26   Mann, 'Copyright and Illegal Activity', pp. 47-52. The only comprehensive account of almanac printing is William R. McDonald, 'Scottish Seventeenth-Century Almanacs', *The Bibliotheck*, 4, 1, 8 (1966), 257-322.

Fig. 2: Robert Sanders's 'counterfeit' almanac *A New Prognostication* of 1684, with the fake, undamaged Aberdeen coat of arms. The correct block had a tell-tale crack. Reproduced from *Bibliographia Aberdonensis*, ed. J.F.K. Johnstone and A.W. Robertson, 2 vols. (Aberdeen: Spalding Club, 1929), 2, 452 and 485.

the burgh bailie courts, especially Edinburgh, but various matters such as apprenticeship regulation and freedom of commerce came before the Session. The main three cases from the 1670s were: *the heirs of Archibald Hislop, bookseller v. Robert Currie and Agnes Campbell* (1678-87), concerning the capacity of Currie as a bookseller in the interests of his step-children; *Robert Sanders, the younger, v. Bessie Corbett, his mother* (1694-1705), about the character and value of book printing materials inherited by Sanders; and, *Watson, the younger v. Freebairn, Baskett and Campbell* (1713-18), over the validity of co-partnership agreements over the gift of King's Printer.[27]

27   NAS, Court of Session Papers, Productions and Processes (CS) 157–66/2 (1687) and CS96/ 3-6 for inventory books for Hislop; CS138/5219 (November 1699); CS158/445 (April 1705); and W.J. Couper, 'Robert Sanders The Elder', *Records of Glasgow Bibliographical Society*, 3 (1915), 26-88 (pp. 46-9) for Sanders; CS29, box 436.1 (papers from 1713, 1715-6 before House of Lords appeal 1718) for Watson. For

Although only the last of these specifically concerned copyright, these cases helped ensure that the Lords of Session developed an expanding competency over the legal basis of the business of books, and points to the vast manuscript Session records as a vital and relatively untouched resource for researchers.

The copyright historiography of early modern Scotland is but a callow youth, and while the AHRC *Primary Sources on Copyright History* is a wonderful resource for historians of intellectual property, as yet it has no Scottish material before the Statute of Anne (1710). But there is much scope in the future for researchers of intellectual property. Acts of the Scottish Parliament, beginning with the first licensing act of 1552, the registers of the Privy Seal which record early copyrights, and Court of Session rulings all exist and require exhumation and analysis. Also, contracts exist in estate papers and amongst the volumes of deeds in the National Archives of Scotland in Edinburgh. One such agreement was that struck between Sir James Dalrymple, President of the Court of Session, and Agnes Campbell, King's Printer, in 1684 for printing Dalrymple's *Institutions of the Law of Scotland*. The contract was made just before the author made his application for copyright. The author was to deliver up his manuscript, not give it to any other printer and allow Campbell exclusive reprint rights. The printer agreed to a specific type face, as per a type specimen sheet signed by both parties, to print at the rate of six sheets per hour, and to deliver out no copies without approval. Written copies and printed copies were to be kept locked away under financial penalties if they were released. Binding and advance copy delivery instructions are indicated. Finally the printer was forced to agree that she must use the privilege, must not print the book abroad and must not sub-contract the press work to another printer. This may be an agreement between an exceptional author and the royal printer, but it reveals much of the life beneath the surface of the commercial exploitation of literary property.[28]

Lastly, and most crucially, we have the Scottish Privy Council records comprising both copyright grants and case law. The position of this body is a unique one. While the excuse for its demise was the Council's apparent failure to deal with a threatened Jacobite invasion, it died in 1708

---

details of the Watson case see Mann, 'The Case of Agnes Campbell', pp. 140-3.
28   *RPS*, A1552/2/26 (1 February 1551/2) [accessed 30 October 2008]. For 1681 agreement between Sir James Dalrymple of Stair and Agnes Campbell over the printing of Stair's *Institutions of the Law of Scotland*, see NAS, PS.3.3.336-7 and NAS, Earl of Stair Papers, GD.135, 2762, 2.

for Scottish party-political reasons more than from English post-Union attitudes. Yet the timing of this demise, between the Union of 1707 and the 1710 Statute of Anne, is fundamental. The 1710 Act is traditionally regarded as legislation that was introduced following pressure from the English book trade after decades of confusion over copyright. However, both the economic and trading consequences arising from the Union, with the free interchange of trade including books, and the end of the copyright agency in Scotland, confirm that Scottish factors were vital to the precise timing of this British legislation. What greeted English lawyers thereafter was an alternative copyright tradition that would first fuel and then help resolve Anglo-Scottish conflicts from the 1730s and 1770s. But while Scotland's copyright law before 1710 contrasted with that of its southern neighbour and exhibited Continental features, some commonalties were also evident, especially in the early years. Indeed, through the Stationers' Company, perhaps it was England not Scotland which was 'the mongrel of copyright' before the clumsy book trade engagement and marriage that was 1707 and 1710. Copyright certainly mattered to early modern Scottish printers, authors and regulators, and every bit as much as those of England. The Scottish system was sometimes idiosyncratic, but for the most part it operated well and with a liberal touch that was a foundation-stone of the Enlightenment within Scotland and beyond.

3. The Public Sphere and the Emergence of Copyright: *Areopagitica*, the Stationers' Company, and the Statute of Anne

Mark Rose[*]

Associated with the German philosopher Jürgen Habermas, the notion of the public sphere, or more precisely, the bourgeois public sphere, has become ubiquitous in eighteenth century cultural studies. Habermas has also been invoked by scholars concerned with media and democratic discourse. But so far as I know the relationship between the emergence of the public sphere and the emergence of copyright in early modern England has not been much discussed. What I want to do in this paper, then, is to explore the relationship between the Habermasian public sphere and the inauguration of modern copyright law in the Statute of Anne in 1710.[1]

[*]   This paper also appears in Volume 12 of the *Tulane Journal of Technology and Intellectual Property* (2009-10), 123-44.
1   8 Anne, c. 19. One particularly influential study that applies the concept of the public sphere to eighteenth-century culture is Michael Warner, *The Letters of the Republic: Publication and the Public Sphere in Eighteenth-Century America* (Cambridge, MA: Harvard University Press, 1990). Important discussions of media and democratic discourse that invoke Habermas include: Niva Elkin-Koren, 'Cyberlaw and Social Change: A Democratic Approach to Copyright Law in Cyberspace', *Cardozo Arts & Entertainment Law Journal*, 14 (1996), 215-95; Rosemary J. Coombe, 'Dialogic Democracy', in *The Cultural Life of Intellectual Properties* (Durham, NC: Duke University Press, 1998), pp. 248-99; and Siva Vaidhyanathan, *Copyrights and Copywrongs: The Rise of Intellectual Property and How it Threatens Creativity* (New York: New York University Press, 2001).

Habermas's concept of the emergence and transformation of the public sphere is social theory on a grand scale. The danger in taking material from such a theory and applying it to a topic like the formation of modern copyright in England is that one can find oneself unable to get beyond the level of abstraction. There are two temptations that lead in this direction. One is to become enmeshed in the theoretical debates that Habermas has inspired and thus perhaps never reach the level of concrete cultural and legal history. The other is that one may be encouraged by the abstraction and generality of Habermas's own style to pitch the discussion of English cultural and legal history at an equally abstract and general level. I propose to avoid the first temptation by keeping my description of Habermas's theory as brief as possible and by limiting my critique to one point having to do with the period in which the public sphere emerges in England. Furthermore, in order to avoid the pressure of Habermas's own tendency to abstraction, I propose to anchor my discussion of the emergence of the public sphere in a single important text, Milton's *Areopagitica*. This is a tract that Milton wrote in 1644 to protest pre-publication censorship of the press. In this well-known tract, I suggest, one can find an early sketch of the public sphere vividly realised. As for the older form of publicity that, according to Habermas, preceded the bourgeois public sphere, I propose to examine some of the features of the early modern Stationers' Company, an institution in which I believe one can find the lineaments of the social form that Habermas calls 'representative publicness'. Finally, I turn to the Statute of Anne itself, a document in which, I suggest, we find the bourgeois public sphere given concrete legal reality. I conclude with a brief coda in which I touch upon the complex topic that Habermas calls the 'hollowing out' of the public sphere.

Habermas and the Public Sphere

Jürgen Habermas's study of the public sphere, originally published in 1962, first appeared in English in 1989 as *The Structural Transformation of the Public Sphere: An Inquiry into a Category of Bourgeois Society.*[2] In this influential study Habermas describes the historical appearance of a new and distinctive social space which he refers to as the 'bourgeois public sphere'. Located conceptually between the private sphere of the family and the

2   Jürgen Habermas, *The Structural Transformation of the Public Sphere: An Inquiry into a Category of Bourgeois Society*, trans. by Thomas Burger (Cambridge, MA: The MIT Press, 1991).

authoritative sphere of the state, the early modern public sphere, according to Habermas, was at first a forum in which art and literature could be discussed but quickly it developed into an arena in which issues of general social concern including the actions of the state could be examined and critiqued. Habermas sees the public sphere appearing first in eighteenth century England where the modern concept of 'public opinion' as a political force developed along with such new civic institutions of conversation and exchange as coffee houses, newspapers, and clubs.

The public sphere may be conceived, Habermas says, 'as the sphere of private people coming together as a public'.[3] This form of 'publicity' – that is, 'publicity' in the sense of the condition of being public – is to be contrasted with the form that Habermas calls 'representative publicness' and that he associates with the pre-modern period.[4] In this social form, publicity was attached to the person of the noble or other authoritative figure who displayed himself publicly as an embodiment of some higher power such as the prince or the deity. 'Representative publicness' was not a social realm but something like a status attribute. The prince and the estates were not the empowered agents of the people – that is, they did not 'represent' the people in anything like the modern republican sense of representation – rather, the prince and the estates were the living embodiment of the country. To call this older social form 'representative publicness' may at first seem confusing because of our association of representation with election. But what Habermas wants to emphasise is the way authority in this social form was represented before the people – that is, demonstrated to the people – in a continuous social drama of rituals, processions, and other presentations that incorporated distinctive elements of costume, demeanour, and forms of address including such honorifics such as 'highness', 'grace', 'majesty' and 'excellence'. In order to grasp what Habermas means by 'representative publicness', think perhaps of the ritual of coronation in which the monarch, clothed in a form of dress unique to his status, presents his person to the estates in a display of majesty. Publicity in this social form operates in a manner entirely different from that in which publicity consists of private people coming together in coffee houses, concert halls, or salons to constitute themselves as a 'public'.

Sometimes the title of Habermas's study, *The Structural Transformation of the Public Sphere*, is wrongly taken to refer to the early modern development

---

3   Ibid., p. 28.
4   Ibid., p. 5.

of the bourgeois public sphere. In fact, the 'structural transformation' referred to in the title is the later process that Habermas terms the 'hollowing out' of the public sphere and that he identifies with the appearance of mass society and the social welfare state.[5] In this process, which Habermas locates in such popular social and political movements as Chartism in Britain, the basis of the public sphere as a distinctive social space independent of the state begins to erode as the state assumes regulatory and protective functions in civil society. Now, in Habermas's account, the public sphere becomes an arena of competition and struggle rather than the site of conversation and exchange. Now, too, the mass media develop and change in response to the newly formed mass publics of modern society. Instead of being sites of discussion and debate, institutions such as newspapers and mass magazines become organs of advertising and manipulation for commercial purposes. Gradually, the social foundations underlying the formation of 'public opinion' as an independent source of political authority are eroded. In this context a process that Habermas calls 'refeudalisation' occurs as both political figures and large organisations such as commercial entities display themselves before mass publics in a manner analogous to feudal rituals of authority. This 'hollowing out' of the public sphere, which Habermas sees as beginning in the nineteenth century and continuing to the present day, is the 'structural transformation' to which his title refers.

Habermas's concept of the bourgeois public sphere and its later transformation has provoked a great deal of discussion in various circles and it has been charged with being naïve and idealist in its representation of the early modern public sphere as a social space insulated from state power. Moreover, the exclusionary and all-male public space that Habermas celebrates is by no means acceptable as an ideal today. Furthermore, it is far from clear that one can speak of a single eighteenth century public sphere as opposed to multiple overlapping arenas of discussion and critique. Still, as Michael McKeon, writing in a recent issue of the interdisciplinary journal *Criticism*, devoted to Habermas, puts it, the category of the early modern public sphere has become 'indispensable to historical thinking'.[6] Habermas's theory can be challenged on historical particulars, can be

---

5   Ibid., pp. 141, 157.
6   Michael McKeon, 'Parsing Habermas's Bourgeois Sphere', *Criticism*, 46 (2004), 273-7 (p. 273). For some critical discussions of Habermas see the important collection *Habermas and the Public Sphere*, ed. by Craig Calhoun (Cambridge, MA: The MIT Press, 1992). Luke Goode, *Jürgen Habermas: Democracy and the Public Sphere* (London: Pluto Press, 2005), provides a good account of Habermas and some of the discussion he has provoked.

adapted or revised, but it has proven its usefulness because it allows us to identify important social changes that occurred in the early modern period. Therefore it cannot, I think, simply be dismissed.

One revision that must be made, however, has to do with the period to which the nascent public sphere is assigned. Habermas emphasises the economic foundations of the public sphere and therefore locates its appearance in the early eighteenth century. But in fact many of the institutions of civil exchange that Habermas cites date from the seventeenth rather than the eighteenth century. The famous coffee houses of London, for example, were born in the aftermath of the English Revolution, proliferating in the 1670s and 1680s and creating a new kind of civic space in which tradesmen and gentlemen could meet and discuss matters of public interest on an equal basis.[7] But even before the spread of the coffee houses, the English Revolution unleashed a torrent of controversial print after the Star Chamber was abolished by the Long Parliament in 1641. This was an act that dissolved the ancient partnership between the crown and the Stationers' Company, through which the English press had long been regulated. Much of the pamphleteering focused on questions of religious doctrine and church government. In the early 1640s, we must remember, religious and political debate were so intertwined as to be indistinguishable, and matters related to church government were of fundamental importance to the political and cultural future of the country. As William Haller, who has studied this explosion of print closely, remarks, the controversies of this period were 'evidence of the growing realisation by all parties of the power of public opinion, and by each of the importance of securing for itself control of that power'.[8] The principal instrument for doing this was the newly unfettered press. It is in this revolutionary context, I think, that we can see the shape of the nascent public sphere emerging, and it is in this context that Milton wrote *Areopagitica*. Interestingly, in England, unlike France and Germany, the public sphere does not, as Habermas suggested, emerge first as a forum

7   See Markman Ellis, *The Coffee House: A Cultural History* (London: Weidenfeld & Nicolson, 2004), pp. 75-6.

8   William Haller, 'Before *Areopagitica*', *PMLA: Publications of the Modern Language Association of America*, 42 (1927), 875-900 (p. 876). David Zaret, *Origins of Democratic Culture: Printing, Petitions, and the Public Sphere in Early-Modern England* (Princeton, NJ: Princeton University Press, 2000) demonstrates how the public sphere in England arose as a consequence of the impact of printing on political communication in the context of the English Revolution. Zaret emphasizes that the appearance of the public sphere was more a product of practical commercial forces than political theory. See also Zaret's important essay, 'Religion, Science, and Printing in the Public Sphere in Seventeenth-Century England', in Calhoun, pp. 212-35.

for the discussion of art and literature but directly as an arena of religious and political debate.

Areopagitica

The context in which Milton wrote *Areopagitica* is well known. In 1643 the flood of print released by the abolition of the Star Chamber led the Stationers' Company to petition parliament to reinstitute some form of press regulation both for the good of the state and the good of the stationers. Parliament responded a few months later in June 1643 by passing an ordinance re-establishing licensing under its own authority. At first Milton does not seem to have been concerned but gradually it became apparent to him as to others that vigorous and open public discussion was the prerequisite for continuing political and religious reform. What brought this point home was evidently a petition of 24 August 1644, in which the Stationers' Company demanded stricter enforcement of the printing ordinance and cited Milton himself as a transgressor. Three months later Milton responded with *Areopagitica*. This was by no means the first appeal for liberty of the press as is sometimes claimed, but it was certainly the most eloquent and it counts as an important document in both the history of the public sphere and in some respects the history of copyright as well.[9]

One reason *Areopagitica* is a powerful document is that it vividly animates the world of books, turning the production and circulation of printed texts into little dramas. As an example let me cite the famous passage in which Milton mocks the practice of licensing as an invention of

---

9   Published 24 November 1644, Milton's *Areopagitica* was anticipated by several other tracts including William Walwyn's, *The Compassionate Samaritane*, which objected to the 1643 order on the grounds that it empowered self-interested licensers to suppress 'honest men's writings'. See Haller, p. 896, who describes the context in which *Areopagitica* was written. For a suggestive discussion of Milton and Habermas see Donald L. Guss, 'Enlightenment as Process: Milton and Habermas', *PMLA: Publications of the Modern Language Association of America*, 106 (1991), 1156-69. See also David Norbrook, '*Areopagitica*, Censorship, and the Early Modern Public Sphere', in *The Administration of Aesthetics: Censorship, Political Criticism, and the Public Sphere*, ed. by Richard Burt (Minneapolis, MN: University of Minnesota Press, 1994), pp. 3-33. I have also been influenced by Francis Barker's discussion of transformation of the subject into the private citizen in *The Tremulous Private Body* (New York and London: Methuen, 1984); Abbe Blum's 'The Author's Authority: *Areopagitica* and the Labour of Licensing', in *Re-membering Milton*, ed. by Mary Nyquist and Margaret W. Ferguson (New York and London: Methuen, 1987), pp. 74-96; and Joseph Loewenstein's suggestive discussions of Milton in *The Author's Due: Printing and the Prehistory of Copyright* (Chicago, IL: The University of Chicago Press, 2002).

the counter-reformation. Here Milton portrays the title page of an officially sanctioned book with its multiple licences or imprimaturs as an Italianate piazza in which deferential worthies bow and curtsy to each other as they debate the fate of the author, a marginalised figure who stands to one side in confusion:

> Sometimes five Imprimaturs are seen together, dialoguewise, in the piazza of one titlepage, complimenting and ducking each to other with their shaven reverences, whether the author, who stands by in perplexity at the foot of his epistle, shall to the press or to the sponge. These are the pretty responsories, these are the dear antiphonies that so bewitched of late our prelates and their chaplains with the goodly echo they made; and besotted us to the gay imitation of a lordly Imprimatur...[10]

The witty metaphor of the title page as a piazza is brilliant both because of its novelty and its aptness. Publishing is here seen as an essentially social act. But the social space of this Italianate drama of servile bobbing and bowing is not the public arena of civic exchange among equals – it is not, in other words, the bourgeois public sphere – but a courtly arena of status and deference. And this arena is dominated by the clerical censors. The author is relegated to 'the foot of his epistle' – that is, the author's name does not appear on the title page but only in the front matter of the book at the foot of the dedicatory epistle. There, in Milton's conceit, the author stands by in perplexity, silently awaiting the censors' decision as to whether his work is to be published or wiped clean with a sponge.

Dramatically opposed to this Italianate courtly scene is the social space that Milton invokes in the title page of his own publication: *Areopagitica: A Speech of Mr. John Milton For the Liberty of Unlicensed Printing, To the Parliament of England* (see figure 1). Here the author's name figures prominently, the words 'Mr. John Milton' spreading from one edge of the decorative frame to the other, printed in the same large swash type face as the title, '*Areopagitica*'. The largest and boldest word on the title page, however, is 'Speech', a word that emphasises the fiction of the pamphlet as an actual address to parliament. The title, '*Areopagitica*', alludes to the Athenian court of the hill of Ares, the Areopagos, which Milton conceives as a kind of parliament, and the rhetorician Isocrates whom Milton describes in the body of the tract as he 'who from his private house wrote that discourse to the parliament of Athens that persuades them to change the form of democracy which

---

10   *John Milton: Complete Poems and Major Prose*, ed. by Merritt Y. Hughes (Indianapolis, IN: The Odyssey Press, 1957), p. 724.

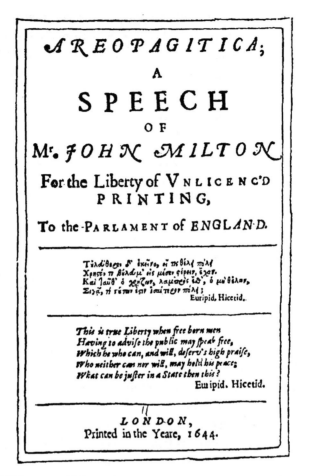

Fig. 1 Title page of John Milton's *Areopagitica,* first published in 1644.

was then established'.[11] Like Isocrates, then, Milton presents himself as a private man entering the public sphere to address the parliament and the commonwealth at large on a matter of public import. Moreover, we should note that Milton's title page bears neither the mark of the licenser – not surprising in a tract written against licensing – nor of the printer or bookseller. The consequence of omitting these names is to emphasise Milton himself as the sole authority responsible for the tract. This is related to the theme of the speech, which might either be described as a defence of 'the liberty of unlicensed printing', as the title page presents it, or, alternatively, as a protest against the indignity to which licensing subjects the author. Thus in another famous passage Milton condemns the circumstance in which

11   Ibid., p. 719.

an author 'must appear in print like a puny' – that is, a child – 'with his guardian, and his censor's hand on the back of his title to be his bail and surety that he is no idiot or seducer'. Such compelled infantilism, Milton says, 'cannot be but a dishonour and derogation to the author, to the book, to the privilege and dignity of learning'.[12] Under such circumstances, in other words, there can be no coming together of serious men to discuss public matters freely and openly.

Throughout *Areopagitica* books and authors are conflated. Books are seen as the embodiments of authors and authors are presented as living in their books. Indeed, the dominant metaphor of *Areopagitica* might be said to be the representation of books as living persons. Thus Milton acknowledges the need to keep 'a vigilant eye how books demean themselves'.

> For books are not absolutely dead things, but do contain a potency of life in them to be as active as that soul was whose progeny they are; nay, they do preserve as in a vial the purest efficacy and extraction of that living intellect that bred them. I know they are as lively and as vigorously productive as those fabulous dragon's teeth; and being sown up and down, may chance to spring up armed men.[13]

The reference to the 'fabulous dragon's teeth' invokes the myth of the hero Cadmus who, having slain a sacred dragon, sowed the ground with its teeth from which sprang a race of armed men who fought each other. It emphasises the vital, generative quality that Milton associates with the writing of books, and so, of course, does the metaphor of the brain child that Milton employs when he acknowledges that truly offensive books may be suppressed after publication. Until the institution of licensing, he says, 'books were ever as freely admitted into the world as any other birth; the issue of the brain was no more stifled than the issue of the womb'. But if a man's 'intellectual offspring' proved a monster, 'who denies that it was justly burnt, or sunk into the sea?'[14] Nonetheless, Milton urges caution even in the suppression of supposed monsters. A good book is, he says, 'the precious lifeblood of a master spirit, embalmed and treasured up on purpose to a life beyond life', and we must be wary:

> [H]ow we spill that seasoned life of man preserved and stored up in books; since we see a kind of homicide may be thus committed, sometimes a martyrdom; and if it extend to the whole impression, a kind of massacre, whereof the execution ends not in the slaying of an elemental life, but strikes

---

12 Ibid., p. 735.
13 Ibid., p. 720.
14 Ibid., p. 725.

at that ethereal and fifth essence, the breath of reason itself, slays an immortality rather than a life.[15]

I want to call attention here to the sexuality of Milton's language in his treatment of books and learning. In the early modern period, seminal fluid was believed to be a distillation of blood. Moreover, sexual and intellectual generation were thought to be parallel activities and the brain was understood to incorporate an organ parallel to the womb in which ideas were brought to term. Milton's contemporary, William Harvey, the discoverer of the circulation of the blood, believed that he had proved this parallel through his dissections of female deer.[16] Thus Milton's representation of a good book as the 'precious lifeblood of a master spirit' that has been 'embalmed and treasured up... to a life beyond life' had in its day a biological dimension that may no longer be immediately apparent. And so too does his image of a book as the 'purest efficacy and extraction' of a living intellect preserved 'as in a vial'. This train of thought, summarised in the statement that books 'do contain a potency of life in them to be as active as that soul was whose progeny they are', leads Milton from the image of the vial of living essence to the story of the dragon's teeth that transform themselves into armed warriors. As Milton's metaphors and allusions suggest, he conceives the public arena of printed discussion and debate as a social space that is also a kind of biological space, one teeming with ideas that are imagined to be in constant struggle and competition. And this sometimes confusing activity, Milton insists, is a necessary and good thing in the strenuous pursuit of truth. As he says in yet another famous passage, 'Where there is much desire to learn, there of necessity will be much arguing, much writing, many opinions; for opinion in good men is but knowledge in the making'.[17]

What I am suggesting is that *Areopagitica* is a key document in the emergence of the bourgeois public sphere in two senses. First, it is a document in which Milton, portraying himself as a private man addressing the public at large through parliament, participates in the discourse of the public sphere. Second, it is also a document that portrays both the pre-modern form of

15   Ibid., p. 720.
16   Harvey reports his experiments with deer in 'Of Conception', in *Disputationes Touching the Generation of Animals*, trans. and ed. by Gweneth Whitteridge (Oxford: Blackwell Scientific, 1981), pp. 443-53. More generally on the idea that there was thought to be a parallel between intellectual and biological generation see Mark Rose, 'Mothers and Authors: *Johnson v. Calvert* and the New Children of Our Imagination', *Critical Inquiry*, 22 (1996), 613-33 (pp. 620-2).
17   Hughes, p. 743.

publicity – here I am thinking of the satirical sketch of bobbing and bowing imprimaturs – and the vibrant arena of arguing and clashing opinions that Milton presents as a positive alternative. The Habermasian public sphere is sometimes imagined as a scene of quiet rational debate. But Milton's conception of the social space in which public opinion is formed is less serene and is in fact in some respects quite odd. I am thinking here of the biological element in his portrayal of the public sphere, his sense of the public arena as teeming with struggling life. One might imagine perhaps that Milton was a Darwinist before his time, but in fact the paradigm is biblical and religious. 'Be fruitful, and multiply'. This was the first command given to Adam and Eve and it was a crucial tenet for Milton, who, like other protestant thinkers of the period, vehemently rejected ideas of the sanctity of virginity. 'Our Maker bids increase', Milton says in *Paradise Lost*, 'who bids abstain But our Destroyer, foe to God and Man?' (IV.748-749). For Milton, then, liberty of printing was a form of Christian liberty and a principle of vitality; licensing was a dangerous and authoritarian principle of sterility.

The Early Modern Stationers' Company

In *Areopagitica*, Milton invokes the Stationers' Company in passing when he accuses parliament of having been deceived by the 'fraud of some old patentees and monopolisers in the trade of bookselling' who argued for the reinstitution of licensing. In this passage, too, Milton makes his comment about the 'just retaining of each man his several copy' (p. 749), which refers, as has often been noted, to the rights of stationers rather than of authors. For Milton copyright may have been a guild matter, but publishing in the sense of speaking in public was an affair of the author in relation to the commonwealth. But this was not the way the issue appeared in the Ordinance of 1643. There the focus was not on the author – authors were mentioned only once, along with printers, as possible producers of scandalous books – but on the Stationers' Company as the guardian of 'ancient custom'. The goal of the ordinance was to empower the Stationers' Company to suppress 'abuses' and 'disorders' dangerous to religion and government.[18]

Milton, who was undoubtedly stung by the Stationers' Company citing him as an offender in its petition for stricter enforcement of licensing, charged that the ordinance was the product of fraud and bad faith. But

---

18   *Acts and Ordinances of the Interregnum, 1642-1660*, ed. by C.H. Firth and R.S. Rait (London: H.M. Stationery Office, 1911), pp. 184-6.

while it is true that licensing was very much in the financial interests of the major figures in the company, more than deceit was involved. The early modern Stationers' Company incorporated an orientation and a stance towards the state strikingly different from Milton's. Milton was concerned with liberty and the advancement of knowledge; the company was concerned with propriety and the maintenance of order. As the controversialist Henry Parker put it in *The Humble Remonstrance of the Company of Stationers*, published in 1643 as part of the campaign for the reinstitution of licensing, the issue as the company saw it was not merely the advancement of knowledge but 'the advancement of wholesome knowledge'. Parker praised the catholic countries for their strict printing regulations – this was a touch that must have inflamed Milton – and he cited Germany and the Netherlands as examples of countries where the press was disorderly. 'It is not mere printing, but well ordered printing that merits so much favour and respect', Parker stated, and he complained about the multitude of presses that had sprung up since the abolition of the Star Chamber.[19]

In the seventeenth century, the term 'propriety' incorporated both the notion of appropriateness and of property. Consequently, as Paul Langford has noted, propriety was at once a way of looking at the world and a way of sharing it out.[20] In *The Nature of the Book*, his monumental study of how printed books achieved credibility in the early modern period, Adrian Johns analyses the structures and practices of the early modern Stationers' Company to illustrate the company's institutional commitment to order and decorum. Both dimensions of propriety were evident, for example, in the social structure of the Stationers' Company which, like that of other

---

19   [Henry Parker], *The Humble Remonstrance of the Company of Stationers* (London, 1643), sig. A1-A1ᵛ.
20   Paul Langford, *Public Life and the Propertied Englishman 1689-1798* (Oxford: Oxford University Press, 1991), pp. 4-5; cited by Adrian Johns, *The Nature of the Book: Print and Knowledge in the Making* (Chicago, IL: University of Chicago Press, 1998), p. 189. My discussion of Stationers' Company practices draws heavily on Johns' brilliant analysis of the company in *The Nature of the Book* and especially on Chapter Three, '"The Advancement of Wholesome Knowledge": The Politics of Print and the Practices of Propriety' (pp. 187-265), which adopts an anthropological approach to the early modern company. I am also indebted to Peter W.M. Blayney for useful comments made to me personally. Pending the publication of Professor Blayney's major study, the standard history of the company remains Cyprian Blagden, *The Stationers' Company: A History, 1403-1959* (London: George Allen & Unwin Ltd, 1960). For a useful discussion of the structures and practices of the London livery companies see Ian W. Archer, 'The Framework of Social Relations: The Livery Companies', *The Pursuit of Stability: Social Relations in Elizabethan London* (Cambridge: Cambridge University Press, 1991), pp. 100-48.

livery companies, was emphatically hierarchical. The most important distinction was between the freemen – those who had been admitted to the company – and the livery, the small body of elite members who had substantially greater rights, privileges, and earning potentials. Moreover, the line between the freemen and the livery was conspicuously and publicly marked. Only the livery had the right to don the impressive fur-lined gowns and satin hoods that were worn on formal occasions. The hierarchical social structure echoed that of feudal society. Likewise, as Johns notes, the governance of the company which rested in the hands of the master and a council called the 'table of assistants', echoed that in which the monarch presided over the privy council and through it governed the realm.

Propriety was also evident in the ceremonies and feasts that marked the yearly cycle of life in the company. In order to convey the flavour of these ritual occasions let me invoke one comparatively minor event, the feast held each spring by the company members who were printers by trade. We know about this feast because it was described in detail by Joseph Moxon in his seventeenth century handbook for printing known as *Moxon's Mechanick Exercises*. Held on the occasion of the annual election of four stewards to represent the printers, the feast began with a formal procession from Stationers' Hall to church led by four attendants with white staves in their hands and red and blue ribbons hung across their shoulders. After the church, the group returned to the hall for a formal meal accompanied by music. Then the ceremony of election began with the four current stewards withdrawing from the hall to a chamber from which they returned led by the company beadle. Marching in order of seniority, each steward now wore a fresh garland of leaves and carried a long white wand. Each was preceded by an attendant who carried a bowl of sugared white wine in his right hand and his staff of office in the left. Three times the procession circled the hall; then the most senior steward took his attendant's bowl, selected his successor from the assembled company, and crowning him with his garland of leaves, drank to him as 'master steward elect'. According to Moxon, there would be a great clapping of hands and drumming of feet to applaud the choice, after which the entire party would walk another round about the hall together with the newly elected steward, a ritual that was repeated three times until all four printers' stewards for the year had been elected.[21]

---

21   See *Moxon's Mechanick Exercises, 1683* (New York: DeVinne Press, 1896), pp. 363-6.

What is striking about this event is how formal and elaborately ritual-ised it was. The election was of course not an election at all in the modern sense but a ceremonial transfer of authority publicly displayed and publicly ratified with each steward responsible for the appointment of his successor, most likely on the basis of precedence and seniority. Moxon emphasises that the feast was commonly kept on or near May Day and it is interesting to note the folk elements that figure in this ceremony of renewal, including the leafy crowns and the long white wands. The printers' feast, begun in 1621, was not in fact an ancient ceremony; nonetheless, by incorporating such folk elements, the event was given an aura of antiquity. Meticulous codes of conduct, both the rules prescribed for feasts and ceremonies and the sometimes fussy rules prescribed for regular occasions such as the monthly meetings of the table of assistants were important because, as Johns puts it, they constituted 'an outward and visual guarantee of the moral propriety of proceedings'.[22] It was through the maintenance of public displays of decorum and probity that the Stationers' Company confirmed their authority and the authority of their printed productions.

Of course the reality of life in the Stationers' Company was not nearly so decorous as the description of its structures and practices suggests. At vari-ous times, as we know, the company was torn with dissension and more than once in its history unprivileged members revolted and made difficul-ties for the grandees.[23] But the point that I want to stress is precisely the appearance of propriety that the company strove to maintain. In the stately universe of the Stationers' Company with its hierarchy, and its public dis-plays of hoods and gowns, we recognise the social form that Habermas calls 'representative publicness' and that Milton mocks in his satirical invocation of curtsying imprimaturs complimenting and ducking in the piazza of an approved title page. Milton's dislike of the monopolising grandees of the Stationers' Company was echoed some years later by John Locke who also spoke disparagingly of the monopolies held by, as he called them, 'igno-rant and lazy stationers'.[24] Indeed, in later-seventeenth century progressive circles it seems to have become a form of political correctness to cast asper-sions on the grandees of the Stationers' Company, and I suspect that we,

---

22   Johns, p. 197.
23   In the 1580s, for example, John Wolfe led a revolt against privileged stationers; see Joseph Loewenstein, 'For a History of Literary Property: John Wolfe's Reforma-tion', *ELR: English Literary Renaissance*, 18 (1988), 389-412.
24   John Locke to Edward Clarke, 2 January 1693, *Correspondence of John Locke and Edward Clarke*, ed. by Benjamin Rand (Cambridge, MA: Harvard University Press, 1927), p. 366.

too, as the intellectual and cultural descendants of Milton and Locke are inclined to regard the patent and monopoly holders of the early modern Stationers' Company as retrogressive figures. My point, however, is that in looking back at the early modern Stationers' Company we must recognise that we are looking across a cultural divide. The company grandees who fought for the restoration of licensing in 1643 and who would do so again in 1695 did not see themselves as ignorant, lazy, or greedy; rather they saw themselves as the champions of order, probity, and decorum.

The Statute of Anne

Except for the brief period between the abolition of the Star Chamber and the Ordinance of 1643, and a second temporary gap after 1679, licensing in one form or another remained in effect in England from the early Tudors until 1695 when the Restoration Licensing Act of 1662 was allowed to lapse for the last and final time.[25] During the period from the Restoration through the Revolution of 1688 to the lapse of licensing in 1695 the bourgeois public sphere was actively developing in England. This was the period of the phenomenal spread of the London coffee houses. It was also the period in which clearly defined party divisions emerged and in which the English electorate, spurred by legislation that assured regular parliamentary elections, became an important force on the public scene.[26] Causality is often difficult to specify in historical matters, but perhaps the most accurate way of formulating the relationship between the bourgeois public sphere and the end of licensing is to say that the developing public sphere provided the context that enabled the collapse of traditional press controls. Open hostility to the great booksellers' monopolies provided one impetus for resistance to the continuation of licensing. Also becoming evident was the danger of having a partisan licenser in control of the press. Moreover, a third form of resistance directly echoed Milton's emphasis on the dignity of authorship and the importance of the free circulation of ideas.[27]

---

25   See Raymond Astbury, 'The Renewal of the Licensing Act in 1693 and its Lapse in 1695', *The Library*, 33 (1978), 296-322. On the general subject of licensing see Frederick Seaton Siebert, *Freedom of the Press in England, 1476-1776* (Urbana, IL: University of Illinois Press, 1952).

26   The Triennial Act (6 & 7 Will. & Mary, c.2), passed in 1694, provided for regular and frequent parliamentary elections. On the growth of the electorate and the development of political parties see J.H. Plumb, *The Origins of Political Stability, England, 1675-1725* (Boston, MA: Houghton Mifflin, 1967).

27   For the hostility to the booksellers monopolies see, for example, the objections

The active development of the public sphere provided the context for the lapse of licensing. Equally important, the collapse of press controls created a feedback loop that accelerated the further development of the public sphere. When licensing ceased on 3 May 1695, there was only one London newspaper, the official *Gazette* which published government announcements and foreign dispatches. By the end of the month, five additional papers had appeared, and within a decade there were at least nine more in London alone. These included, in addition to the *Gazette*, the *London Post*, the *English Post*, the *Post-Man*, the *Post-Boy*, the *Flying-Post*, the *Observator*, the *Review*, written by Daniel Defoe, and the *Daily Courant*. Contemporary materials suggest that by 1704 sales of newspapers – sales, not readership, which would of course be much greater – reached about 44,000 copies per week and by 1711 sales probably totalled some 70,000 copies per week.[28] Within fifteen years of the end of licensing a massive quantity of printed news and commentary was in general circulation. Moreover important politicians, Robert Harley among them, had learned to use the press to mobilise public opinion for their own purposes.[29]

The Stationers' Company together with such conservative forces as the Church of England naturally sought the restoration of licensing. Ronan Deazley counts no less than thirteen failed attempts from 1695 to 1704 to provide some form of statutory press regulation.[30] The company eventually settled for the Statute of Anne, which was enacted in the spring of 1710, and which preserved at least some elements of the structure of the trade. But whereas under the licensing regime literary property was in practice almost solely a stationers' matter, the statute gave private persons legal recognition by vesting literary property first in the author. Furthermore, it departed radically from company practices by setting limits on the term of copyright:

raised to the proposed renewal of licensing in 1695, *Journal of the House of Commons* (17 April 1695) 11: 305-6. On the continuing influence of *Areopagitica* on the licensing debate in the late seventeenth century see Ernest Sirluck, 'Areopagitica and a Forgotten Licensing Controversy', *The Review of English Studies*, n.s., 11 (1960), 260-74. At least two important tracts in the licensing controversy closely follow Milton's arguments and language. These are [Charles Blount], *Reasons Humbly Offered for the Liberty of Unlicensed Printing* (London, 1693), and [Matthew Tindal], *A Letter to a Member of Parliament* (London, 1698).

28   James R. Sutherland, 'The Circulation of Newspapers and Literary Periodicals, 1700-30', *The Library*, 15 (1934-5), 110-24.

29   See J.A. Downie, *Robert Harley and the Press* (Cambridge: Cambridge University Press, 1979).

30   Ronan Deazley, *On the Origin of the Right to Copy* (Oxford: Hart Publishing, 2004), pp. 1-29.

twenty-one years for books already in print, fourteen years for new books with the possibility of a second fourteen-year term if the author were still living at the end of the first. At the end of the term of protection a book would become open to all.

The most fundamental transformation brought about by the statute, however, relates to what it does *not* legislate; it makes no provision whatsoever for state regulation of what could or could not be published.[31] Rather than defining the purpose of a printing act as the need to maintain good order in religion and government as both the Ordinance of 1643 and the Licensing Act of 1662 had done, the Statute of Anne speaks of the liberties that abusive printers and booksellers have taken with individual authors and proprietors who have found their books and writings printed without their consent. This is a subtle but momentous change, the substitution of the individual for the state as the party in need of redress. Furthermore, instead of presenting itself as primarily an act to prevent abuses as did both the Ordinance of 1643 and the Licensing Act of 1662, the Statute of Anne presents itself as affirmative legislation designed, as the title states, for 'the encouragement of learning'. This is a phrase with a distinguished history, one that echoes, among other things, the title of Francis Bacon's *Advancement of Learning* (1605) and Milton's comment in *Areopagitica* that licensing constitutes 'the greatest discouragement and affront that can be offered to learning' (p. 735).

The purpose of licensing was to regulate and police what might be said in print, to restrain the press in the interests of good order. The stated purpose of the Statute of Anne is to stimulate study and speech, to encourage the proliferation of discourse in the public sphere. Moreover, by vesting the copyright of a printed book initially in the author rather than the printer or bookseller, the statute presents the author as the person ultimately responsible for a book. Under the old regime of licensing, the printing of a book was still in theory a kind of privilege that could be extended or not as the state decided. The statute, however, redefines copyright as a matter of right rather than privilege, an automatic grant to the author by virtue of his literary endeavour. Thus the statute gives legal reality to the public

---

31   In 'Freedom of the Press 2.0', *Georgia Law Review*, 42 (2008), 309-405, Edward Lee emphasizes another crucial lacuna in the statute; unlike the earlier printing acts, the statute makes no provision for the regulation of printing technology. Lee argues that this significant omission anticipates modern notions of press freedom, which should be understood broadly as encompassing the unregulated use of technology as well as content.

sphere, providing a regime in which individual authors, precisely as imagined by Milton, are encouraged to bring the fruits of their efforts into the public forum on no other authority but that of their reason, their learning, and their deliberation. For the traditional ideal of public order the statute substitutes the concept of private right; authors and proprietors have a right to control the printing and publishing of their own writings. And for the traditional ideal of public decorum achieved through censorship and regulation, the statute substitutes the concept of public vitality, the ideal of a public arena characterised, as Milton put it, by 'much writing' and 'many opinions'.

The 'Hollowing Out' of the Public Sphere

The old regime of licensing that empowered the Stationers' Company was a bargain between the booksellers and the state. The new regime of the Statute of Anne, as Ronan Deazley emphasises, was a three-way bargain between authors, booksellers, and the reading public.[32] Authors were given legal recognition and limited monopoly rights; booksellers were given the opportunity to purchase and exploit these monopoly rights; and the public was assured that after the lapse of the limited term of protection, the works would become free and open to all. In setting term limits the Statute of Anne thus created the literary commons that we know today as the public domain. But it was precisely the public domain that came under challenge in the period following passage of the statute. I am referring here to the eighteenth century literary property debates in which the great booksellers of London argued that the Statute of Anne was merely a supplement to an underlying common-law right of property and that the term limits had no effect on their literary properties which were properties in exactly the same sense as lands and houses. The London booksellers were countered by those who maintained that writings could not be property. The state might grant authors and their assigns a form of limited monopoly, but copyrights could not be properties in the same sense as material goods.[33] The eighteenth century debates thus exposed a tension between property and discourse – or, more precisely, between commerce and discourse – that had been implicit from at least the 1640s. We can observe this tension in nascent form in the commercial metaphors that Milton employs in *Areopagitica*, for

32   Deazley, p. 46.
33   I discuss the logic of these debates in *Authors and Owners: The Invention of Copyright* (Cambridge, MA: Harvard University Press, 1993), pp. 67-91.

example when he warns: 'Truth and understanding are not such wares as to be monopolised and traded in by tickets and statutes and standards. We must not think to make a staple commodity of all the knowledge in the land, to mark and licence it like our broadcloth and our woolpacks' (pp. 736-37). The immediate legal issues in the literary property debate were resolved in 1774 in *Donaldson v. Becket* in which the House of Lords rejected the claim that literary property was perpetual.[34] But *Donaldson* did not resolve the underlying tension between property and discourse, and this tension has been characteristic of copyright since 1710. In the first half of the nineteenth century, for example, it re-emerged in the copyright reform movement led by Thomas Talfourd in the name of the author's property right. Again the claim was made that copyrights were no less property than physical goods and that in principle the author's property right should last forever. This claim was countered by Thomas Babington Macaulay who spoke for the public interest in preserving the dissemination of knowledge. The result was a compromise: the term of copyright was re-established as forty-two years or the life of the author plus seven years, whichever was longer.[35] And the same tension has recently surfaced in the United States in *Eldred v. Ashcroft*, once again in connection with the length of the copyright term.[36] This important case concerned the constitutionality of the Copyright Term Extension Act of 1998, a revision of the copyright act that extended the basic term of protection to the life of the author plus seventy years. The petitioners argued that this extended term was effectively indistinguishable from perpetual copyright and thus violated the Constitutional clause granting Congress the right to protect copyrights for limited periods only. The US Supreme Court rejected Eldred's argument – it said that the new term of copyright might be overly long but that it was nevertheless limited – but at the same time the Court acknowledged that under some circumstances there could be a conflict between copyright and freedom of speech.

The consequences for civil conversation of treating writing simply as property would be profound. As some of the participants in the eighteenth century debates realised, such a position would allow copyright owners to regulate and limit public discussion much as state censors had done earlier.[37]

34   4 Burr 2408; *English Reports*, 98, pp. 257-62 (1774); 2 Bro PC 129; *English Reports*, 1, pp. 837-49 (1774).
35   The most complete treatment of Talfourd's movement is Catherine Seville, *Literary Copyright Reform in Early Victorian England: The Framing of the 1842 Copyright Act* (Cambridge: Cambridge University Press, 1999).
36   *Eldred v. Ashcroft*, 537 U.S. 186 (2003).
37   For example, when *Donaldson v. Becket* was debated in the House of Lords in

The US Supreme Court's acknowledgement in *Eldred* of the potential for a conflict between copyright and the First Amendment reflects the continuing concern, at least in theory, with preserving vigorous civil conversation. Nonetheless, what we have seen in the last hundred and fifty years or so is an increasing emphasis on the proprietary aspect of copyright. And this is a process that has accelerated in the United States ever since the Copyright Act revision of 1976 which, among other things, eliminated the formality of registration so that copyright is now said to adhere from the moment of creation rather than the moment of registration.[38]

The focus of eighteenth century copyright was on labour. It was the labour that an author put into a work that was the foundation of the right. Thus copyright protected against literal copying but it did not protect against adaptations such as translations because these involved additional labour. As late as 1853, a Federal court rejected Harriet Beecher Stowe's claim that a German translation of *Uncle Tom's Cabin* – the translation had been prepared for the Pennsylvanian Dutch market – infringed her copyright.[39] But in the course of the nineteenth century the focus of copyright, both in the United States and in Great Britain, shifted from a focus on labour to a focus on market value. A landmark in this shift in the US is the famous case of *Folsom v. Marsh*, decided in 1841, in which Justice Joseph Story remarked that the central issue in deciding an infringement case was not whether an entire work had been copied but whether so much had been taken that the value of the original was diminished.[40] This shift in focus, combined with the extension of copyright protection to translations and derivative works of all kinds, helps to identify, I think, a set of doctrinal transformations that relate to the process that Habermas calls the 'hollowing out' of the public sphere.[41]

1774, Lord Effingham urged the liberty of the press, pointing out that affirmation of a common-law right of literary property could provide a dangerous foundation for censorship; see *The Cases of the Appellants and Respondents in the Cause of Literary Property* (London, 1774), p. 59.

38   In an important new study of copyright in relation to the First Amendment, Neil Weinstock Netanel identifies the Copyright Act of 1976 as a turning point in American legal developments and notes the increasing tendency of US courts to treat copyright as an absolute property rather than a limited entitlement. See *Copyright's Paradox* (New York: Oxford University Press, 2008), pp. 3-12.

39   *Stowe v. Thomas*, 23 F. Cas. 201 (C.C.E.D. Pa. 1853).

40   9 F. Cas. 342 (C.C.D. Mass. 1841).

41   For important discussions of these doctrinal transformations see: Peter Jaszi, 'Toward a Theory of Copyright: Metamorphoses of Authorship', *Duke Law Journal*, 42 (1991), 455-502 (discussing how in nineteenth-century US copyright doctrine

The economic, social, and political developments that have influenced these doctrinal changes and contributed to the process of 'hollowing out' are far too complex to discuss here. As Habermas indicates, however, they have to do with the emergence in the nineteenth century of mass societies and mass markets and with the rise of very large scale commercial organisations to serve and exploit those markets. David Zaret, who has emphasised the degree to which the nascent public sphere in England was founded on commerce, challenges the pessimism that sees commercialism and modern developments in communication as responsible for the eclipse of reason in public life and the decay of the public sphere.[42] Zaret is correct, I believe, to emphasise that the explosion of print in the 1640s was a commercial as well as a political phenomenon, and to remark that commercialism itself may not be the root of modern problems. But it is not at all clear to me that his optimism about the public sphere is warranted. What he fails to take into account is the way in which changes in the fundamental contours of copyright since the eighteenth century have altered the environment of public discourse and placed new kinds of commercially grounded burdens on cultural production and civic exchange.[43]

Habermas maintains that the hollowing out of the public sphere is marked by an erosion of the distinction between public and private on which the institution of the public sphere depends. Habermas also holds that under these circumstances a process of 'refeudalisation' occurs that leads to the reappearance in modern society of social forms characteristic of the period of 'representative publicness'.[44] I note that precisely this process can be illustrated by considering the peculiar status of giant media conglomerates such as Viacom, the Walt Disney Company, or the News Corporation. Are these organisations private or public? Legally they are of course private, but in their vastness and their domination of the circulation of cultural and informational products of all kinds, they plainly have

the concept of authorship is emptied of content); Brad Sherman and Lionel Bently, *The Making of Modern Intellectual Property Law: The British Experience, 1760-1911* (Cambridge: Cambridge University Press, 1999), esp. pp. 173-204 (describing the nineteenth-century construction of the protected work as a unitary, closed object in English law); and Oren Bracha, 'The Ideology of Authorship Revisited: Authors, Markets, and Liberal Values in Early American Copyright', *Yale Law Journal*, 118 (2008), 186-271 (tracing, among other things, the shift in the focus in American doctrine from labour to market value).

42   Zaret, *Origins of Democratic Culture*, p. 275.
43   Netanel, pp. 109-53, provides a good overview of American copyright doctrine's free speech burdens.
44   Habermas, pp. 142, 195.

a public dimension as well. In fact the very concepts of public and private do not quite apply to these entities. Likewise, as we have seen, the concepts of private and public did not quite apply to the early modern Stationers' Company. The Stationers' Company was private insofar as it had its own rules and officers, but it was also public insofar as it was granted the power to regulate nearly all the printing and publishing in the realm. Chartered guilds like the Stationers' Company were the creatures of a time before the precipitation of the modern dialectic of private and public. Modern media conglomerates like Viacom collapse that dialectic producing uncanny echoes of the institutional past and raising serious questions about whether the kind of dynamic public sphere that Milton portrayed in 1644 can be sustained for the future.[45]

David Zaret's discussion of the modern public sphere fails to take account of changes in copyright doctrine. What I have left out of my discussion is of course the internet. Does the internet not provide a whole new dimension to the public sphere? Does the internet not – or, more precisely, digital technology – constitute a profound challenge to the effectiveness of copyright protection? As anyone who checks blogs even casually knows, the answer to the first question is yes. The internet has obviously changed the public sphere. But the answer to the second question, digital technology's challenge to copyright, remains unclear. As we have seen, the movie and recording industries, which are of course embedded in the giant media conglomerates, are fighting hard – and understandably so – to maintain control of their products in the context of the transformations that digital technology has wrought. The digital question is one that has political as well as legal and technological dimensions. How it will play out is anyone's guess.

---

45   I make this point in 'The Claims of Copyright: Public Purposes and Private Property', in *Media Ownership: Research and Regulation*, ed. by Ronald E. Rice (Cresskill, NJ: Hampton Press, 2008), pp. 61-76.

4. Early American Printing Privileges. The Ambivalent Origins of Authors' Copyright in America

Oren Bracha[*]

Latent in existing accounts of early American copyright is a particular version of American exceptionalism. These accounts tend to ignore the colonial period or minimise its significance to the vanishing point. It is well established that in England and the Continent copyright had a rich and complex history that extends back to the early sixteenth century. By contrast, the reader of standard American copyright history is likely to be left under the impression that, with the exception of an early isolated incident in Massachusetts, nothing interesting happened in that region until the late eighteenth century. The flipside of the coin is an overemphasis on the meteoric ascendancy of author-based copyright in the United States in the period immediately following independence. While complaints about the 'incomplete' nature of late eighteenth century American copyright abound, the current narrative depicts the appearance of modern authors' copyright in the United States almost as Athena springing out of the head of Zeus fully matured and arrayed for battle.

In this essay I wish to deny neither the differences between the European and American contexts for the development of the precursors of modern copyright nor the importance of the late eighteenth century developments in America. Instead, by providing a somewhat thicker description of American copyright's antecedents, my aim is to change the emphasis of

[*] This paper is based upon material developed for the AHRC-funded project *Primary Sources*.

the standard narrative in two ways. First, the sharp dichotomy between the early European and American experiences is weakened. In America as in Europe printing privileges developed as an organic part of the framework for governmental regulation of the printing press. While important differences in social conditions and in the patterns of governmental activity were reflected in the frequency and nature of the American printing privilege, there were still significant lines of resemblance. The American colonial privilege was a provincial and somewhat crude version of its European cousin.

Second, the emphasis of the account shifts to continuity and gradual change rather than ruptures. The late eighteenth century transition from a publisher's commercial privilege to an author's right was a gradual process. During the transitory stage the concept of authorship often played an ambivalent and problematic role in justifying and understanding copyright. I have argued elsewhere that an ideology of individual authorship played a complex, often paradoxical role, in nineteenth century copyright.[1] Authorship never had a real golden age in American copyright. The development was from hesitant use of authorship concepts together with notions and institutions still coloured by the printer's privilege to a copyright system that full-heartedly adopted authorship as its official justification while its actual institutions were shaped by the quite different demands of industrial, mass communication, market society. This essay tells the first half of this story.

The Regulation of the Printing Press in the North American British Colonies

The antecedents of what would become copyright emerged in Continental Europe and England as a governmental response to the appearance of the printing press.[2] The press was seen both as an important public resource

---

1   O. Bracha, 'The Ideology of Authorship Revisited: Authors, Markets, and Liberal Values in Early American Copyright', *Yale Law Journal*, 118 (2008), 186-271.
2   In general see: L.R. Patterson, *Copyright in Historical Perspective* (Nashville: Vanderbilt University Press, 1968); M. Rose, *Authors and Owners: The Invention of Copyright* (Cambridge, Mass.: Harvard University Press, 1993); B.W. Bugbee, *The Genesis of American Patent and Copyright Law* (Washington: Public Affairs Press, 1967), pp. 43-8; L.V. Gerulaitis, *Printing and Publishing in Fifteenth-Century Venice* (Chicago: American Library Association, 1976); J. Loewenstein, *The Author's Due: Printing and the Prehistory of Copyright* (Chicago: University of Chicago Press, 2002); E. Armstrong, *Before Copyright: The French Book-Privilege System, 1498-1526* (Cambridge:

and as posing a significant danger to established political and religious powers. Governmental reaction to it was shaped by three related purposes: suppression and censorship of content; maintaining an ordered and well regulated book trade; and public encouragement of publication projects deemed worthy or important. In the American colonies too, copyright emerged as part of a governmental response to the threat and promise of the printing press. Thus colonial printing privileges should be understood in the context of the colonial framework for regulating the press.

The first printing press in the North American British colonies arrived in Cambridge, Massachusetts at the end of 1638. The moving force behind the arrival of the press was the Reverend Jose Glover, a Puritan minister and the son of a wealthy shipping merchant family. Intensification of religious oppression in the late 1630s persuaded Glover to move. In connection to his new world business plans Glover took with him several passengers, equipment and materials, including a printing press whose type was probably made in Amsterdam, paper, and other supplies required for printing.[3] Glover's exact motivation in bringing the press to Massachusetts is unknown. However, his connections with the colony's ruling elite, his possible involvement in the founding of Harvard College and the financial help in setting up the press by 'Some Gentleman of Amsterdam'[4] – most likely Puritan or Puritan sympathisers – suggest that any commercial impulse was supplanted by other reasons. The Puritan leaders of Massachusetts Bay with their intellectual background must have perceived the potential of the press to their scholarly endeavours, to the civil authority of their government and to their religious mission. It is also possible that, in light of increasing suppression of Puritan literature during the 1630s in England and even in the Netherlands, there existed an intention to create a new Puritan publication centre in the colonies.[5]

Glover did not survive the trip and some ambiguity shrouds the question of who exactly took over the operation of the press upon its arrival.[6]

Cambridge University Press, 1990).

3   G.P. Winship, *The Cambridge Press, 1638-1692* (Portland: Southworth-Anthoensen Press, 1945), p. 9.

4   L.G. Starkey, 'The Benefactors of the Cambridge Press: A Reconsideration', *Studies in Bibliography: Papers of the Bibliographical Society of the University of Virginia,* 3 (1950), 267-70.

5   This would never happen. Whether due to its remoteness from the metropolis or the decline of the persecution of Puritans in the 1640s the Cambridge press served mainly the local needs of the colony. J.W. Tebbel, *A History of Book Publishing in the United States,* 2 vols. (New York: R.R. Bowker Co., 1972), I, p. 5.

6   Ibid., p. 7; Winship, pp. 11-15; G.E. Littlefield, *The Early Massachusetts Press,*

Harvard had a stake in the press and played an active role in its management, although the exact nature of its interest remains unclear. The fact that Reverend Henry Dunster the president of Harvard and the person who came to manage the press in its early years married Glover's widow in 1641 makes it even harder to discern the exact division of ownership and control.[7] Whatever the exact formal pattern of ownership, it is clear that both Harvard and the colony's authorities took an active role in the management and control of the press and treated it as a semi-public resource in the service of the colony.

The treatment of the press in Massachusetts Bay was influenced by the peculiar intellectual, cultural and political circumstances of the colony. However, the two main aspects of this treatment would be in play in all the other British American colonies where the printing press arrived throughout the following century. The first aspect was public patronage. The Massachusetts authorities perceived the importance of the press to both the authority of civil government and the religious and intellectual mission of the colony's elite. In a community with an unusually high percentage of university graduates,[8] as well as one that was preoccupied with maintaining religious and civil cohesion, an awareness of the importance of the press was only natural. The first known publication of the Cambridge press expressed both the religious and civic aspects of its public importance. In the *Freeman's Oath* every freeman of the colony pledged his allegiance to both religious and civil authority.[9] The Massachusetts authorities took a particular interest in sustaining the press and its operation. The General Court often made orders and provided support in regard to the operation of the press. Thus, for example, when equipment for keeping the press working or another printer was needed the Court was petitioned and it took the required measures in order to provide both.[10]

The second aspect of the treatment of the press was supervision and suppression. Alongside its public utility, the press could also be a dangerous catalyst of civil and religious dissent and unrest. To a ruling elite steeped in the English tradition of censorship and licensing this meant a need for tight regulation of the product of the press. The Massachusetts

---

1638-1711 (New York: B. Franklin, 1969), p. 101.
7   Tebbel, p. 10.
8   Ibid., p. 4.
9   Winship, pp. 18-20; R.F. Roden, *The Cambridge Press, 1638-1692* (New York: Dodd, Mead, and Company, 1903), pp. 14-17.
10   Tebbel, p. 17.

licensing legislation was the most comprehensive in the colonies as well as
the closest to being an actual licensing 'system' – a miniature, crude version
of the English licensing scheme.[11] In 1662 the General Court, in reaction
to 'irregularities & abuse to the authority of this country by the printing
presse', ordered that no copy should be printed unless licensed by two
appointed licensers.[12] The order was repealed in 1663 when it was declared
that the 'presse be at liberty'.[13] In 1664, however a comprehensive permanent licensing system was established. The new law forbade the setting up
of any press except the one in Cambridge and subjected all publications
to licensing by a special board appointed by the Court, all under threat of
forfeiture of equipment and of the liberty to exercise the trade of printing.[14]

These two aspects – patronage and regulation – were complementary.
They expressed the perception of the press as an important public resource
whose operation had to be publicly managed and regulated in order to
assure its service to the commonwealth.

When in the following decades printing gradually arrived in other
colonies,[15] authorities there exhibited various combinations of patronage
and suppression in their treatment of the press. Colonial governmental
approach to the press oscillated between viewing it as a dangerous instrument of religious heresy and political unrest, sometimes resulting in a complete ban, and the acknowledgment of such dangers accompanied by an
appreciation of the value of the press in promoting governmental purposes
or the public good. The exact mix varied. On one extreme one finds William
Berkeley, the Governor of Virginia, who in 1671 declared:

> But I thank God, there are no free schools nor printing, and I hope we
> shall not have these hundred years; for learning has brought disobedience,

11   On the English licensing system see Patterson, pp. 114-42.
12   *Records of the Governor and Company of the Massachusetts Bay in New England,*
1661-1674, ed. by N.B. Shurtleff, 5 vols. (Boston: W. White, 1853-4), IV, pt. 2, p. 62.
The two licensers were Captain Daniel Goodkin and the Reverend Jonathan Mitchel.
13   Ibid., p. 73.
14   Ibid., p. 141.
15   Virginia had a short episode with the press in 1683 which ended with a complete ban and the forced departure of the printer William Nuthead. It was reintro-
duced to Virginia only in 1730. Nuthead and his press moved to Maryland in 1685.
The press was brought to Pennsylvania in 1685 by William Bradford who moved to
New York in 1693. Connecticut received its first press in 1709 and Rhode Island in
1727. The press was first set up in South Carolina in 1731 and in North Carolina in
1749. James Parker brought the press to New Jersey in 1754. After being persecuted
in Boston Daniel Fowle moved to New Hampshire and established its first press
in 1756. In Delaware it was introduced in 1761. Georgia got its first press in 1763.
Tebbel, pp. 11-16.

and heresy, and sects into the world, and printing has divulged them, and libels against the best government. God keep us from both.[16]

Virginia followed this line. When in 1683 William Nuthead set up a press in Jamestown and printed various laws passed by the assembly, he was brought before the governor and the council that ordered him and his patron John Buckner to post bond and refrain from any other printing until instruction arrived from England.[17] Several months later such instruction arrived along with a new governor. It ordered the governor '[t]o forbid the use of any printing press upon any occasion whatever'.[18] Although the order was modified in 1690 to allow printing under special permission from the governor, the ban meant the end of printing in Virginia until 1730 when William Parks set up another press in Williamsburg.

Even where printing was not completely banned it was heavily restricted. The setting up and the operation of a press required governmental permission, which usually was not easily given. There was also prior licensing of the content of publication. In 1685 Thomas Dongan the governor of New York received instructions from England in terms that were repeated in instructions to other colonies:

And for as much a great inconvenience may arise by the liberty of printing within our province of New York, you are to provide by all necessary orders that noe person keep any press for printing, nor that any book, pamphlet or other matters whatsoever bee printed without your special leave & license first obtained.[19]

---

16   Quoted in Tebbel, p. 1.
17   L.C. Wroth, *A History of Printing in Colonial Maryland, 1686-1776* (Baltimore: Typothetae of Baltimore, 1922), pp. 1-2; H. Lehmann-Haupt, *The Book in America: A History of the Making, and Selling of Books in the United States* (New York: Bowker, 1951), p. 14; I. Thomas, *The History of Printing in America with a Biography of Printers and Account of Newspapers*, 2 vols. (Albany: J. Munsell, 1874), I, p. 551.
18   *Calendar of State Papers, Colonial Series, American and West Indies, 1681-1685*, ed. by J.W. Fortescue, 45 vols. (London: Public Records Office, 1964), XI, p. 558, instruction num. 1428 of 3 December 1683.
19   *Documents Relative to the Colonial History of the State of New York*, ed. by John R. Brodhead et al, 15 vols. (Albany: Weed, Parsons and Company, Printers, 1853-87), III, p.375. This was probably a standard phrasing of the orders that were sent to many colonies. In 1691 and 1694 the governors of Maryland received royal orders almost identical in phrasing (the 1694 instructions to Francis Nicholson read: 'And forasmuch as great inconveniences may arise by the Liberty of Printing within our Province of Maryland, you are to provide by all necessary Orders that no person use any Press for printing upon any occasion whatsoever without your special License first obtained'; quoted in Wroth, p. 18). Very similar terms were used in the 1690 instructions to Lord Francis Howard of Effingham Governor of Virginia; ibid., p. 2.

The impulse for restriction of the press was as much internal to colonial government as it was attributable to demands from England. The licensing and prior restraint limitations survived in the colonies well into the eighteenth century,[20] long after they declined in England with the lapse of the 1662 Licensing Act in 1695. The absoluteness of the licensing regimes in the colonies, however, was more a matter of theory than practice. Governmental intervention tended to be sporadic and inconsistent.[21] On the other hand, when the authorities decided to act their actions could be quite harsh. Persons who published unlicensed materials could find themselves fined, jailed or even deprived of their equipment, as William Bradford learned in 1692. Bradford ran into trouble with the Pennsylvania assembly for printing an unlicensed pamphlet by one of the factions in the religious-political skirmishes in the colony. He was arrested and his equipment was seized. It was restored to him only when the newly appointed governor of New York and Pennsylvania Benjamin Fletcher had intervened on his behalf.[22] Prior restraint of the press existed in some colonies even in the second half of the eighteenth century, although the general trend by that time was a shift toward post-publication sanctions.[23]

Alongside suppression, the colonies that did not ban the press supplied encouragement and support. There were often titles and offices such as 'public printer to the colony' which carried with them government patronage in the form of some compensation, commitment to purchase printed works, or at least the exclusive right to print some governmental documents, usually the laws of the colony. In general, government-related publications supplied the bulk of the work of many of the printers and constituted an important form of patronage.[24] Sometimes there were even land grants or convenient leases offered to printers.[25] In short, throughout

---

20   See Lehmann-Haupt, pp. 43-5; Thomas, pp. 16, 235-6.

21   See Lehmann-Haupt, p. 45.

22   See *Minutes of the Provincial Council of Pennsylvania*, ed. by Samuel Hazard, 10 vols. (Philadelphia: J. Severns, 1851-2), I, pp. 366-7. See also Tebbel, pp. 39-40. Fletcher brought Bradford to New York and recruited him for publicizing in print his recent achievements in the defense of the colony.

23   L.W. Levy, *Emergence of A Free Press* (New York: Oxford University Press, 1985), p. 32.

24   See O. Bracha, *Owning Ideas: A History of Anglo American Intellectual Property* (2005) (unpublished S.J.D. Dissertation, Harvard Law School), p. 254.

25   In 1641 the General Court of Massachusetts granted Stephen Day, the first printer of the colony, three hundred acres of land. The Court mentioned the fact that Day was the first to set up a press in the colony, but that may have been a thin cover to the fact that the grant was actually made in lieu of a business debt owed to Day by John

the colonial period, following the Massachusetts example, the press was seen as an important but dangerous public resource to be encouraged and used by the government, but also to be restricted and regulated.

Colonial Printing Privileges

The first grant of exclusive printing privileges in America took place within this general framework of colonial government's support and regulation of the press. In 1672 the bookseller John Usher made an interesting proposition to the Massachusetts colony. He offered to publish at his own expense the laws of the colony, an undertaking hitherto executed by the public authorities. John Usher's grant, which is sometimes referred to as the first American copyright, was, roughly, the equivalent of the English printing patent or continental privilege grant. It appears that the origin of the grant was a specific concern by Usher in regard to his printer, Samuel Green. Green was one of the two printers operating at the time in Massachusetts. Usher's distrust of his printer is evident in the phrasing of the General Court's order in response to his first petition in the matter:

> In ansr to the petition of John Vsher, the Court judgeth it meete to order, & be it by this Court ordered & enacted, that no printer shall print any more copies then are agreed & pajd for by the ouuner of the sajd coppie or coppies, nor shall he nor any other reprint or make sale of any of the same, wthout the sajd ouners consent, vpon the forfeiture an poenalty of treble the whole charges of printing, & paper, &c, of the whole quantity payd for by the ouner of the coppie, to the sajd ouner or his assignees.[26]

Apparently, Usher was concerned that Green would secretly make and sell extra copies of the publication, thereby undermining his market. The solution was a legislative prohibition of such an action and an exclusive vending and printing grant. A year later, in response to another petition, the General Court issued a slightly different order:

> Mr John Vsher hauing binn at the sole chardge of the impression of the the booke of lawes [...] the Court judgeth it meete to order, that for at least seven yeares, vunless he shall haue sold them all before that tjme, there shallbe no other or further impression made by any person thereof in this jurisdiction.[27]

Winthrop Jr. See: Littlefield, p. 106; Winship, p. 11. In 1658, in response to a petition of Samuel Green, the successor of Day in the position, the General Court granted him three hundred acres of land 'for his Encouragement'. Thomas, pp. 43, 52.

26   Shurtleff, IV, p. 527.
27   Ibid., p. 559.

This time the privilege of exclusivity was explicitly limited to a term of seven years. It was also restricted to the specific stock that Usher had in hand and did not cover any future reprints.

Usher's grant was similar to English printing patents that were granted by the Crown since the early sixteenth century.[28] It had nothing to do with authorship. The grant conferred a limited-duration economic privilege of exclusivity on a publisher in order to reduce his risk and encourage a specific publication. Like the printing patent it was an ad hoc discretionary grant and not part of a general legal regime. It is unclear whether Usher or the General Court modelled the privilege after the printing patent or if they were even aware of such grants in England and the continent. Be that as it may, the grant was part of a local pattern of governmental activity. Usher's grant followed the form of other privileges dispensed by colonial authorities in a variety of economic and social fields. It was no different from other Massachusetts privilege grants in the fields of manufactures or public works, such as Samuel Winslow's 1641 exclusive grant for making salt,[29] or the 1642 exclusive grant to John Glover for operating a ferry.[30] Usher's printing privilege was just another governmental encouragement to an enterprise deemed beneficial to the public good that took the common form of a legislative grant of limited-time exclusivity.

Some historians argue that the 1673 Massachusetts grant to John Usher was the only one known during the colonial period.[31] This is inaccurate. While printing privilege grants were sporadic, different variants of them were sometimes used. These grants remained isolated and case-specific occurrences. No general copyright regime, either statutory or under the common law, appeared during the colonial period. The 1710 Statute of Anne that created a general statutory copyright regime in Britain did not apply to the colonies.

The reasons for this difference between metropolis and periphery were rooted in the economic, social and cultural circumstances of the colonies. In Europe general copyright regimes developed out of cooperation between governments and the publishers' guilds rooted in an alignment of interests. The colonies had no equivalent of the English Stationers' Company. A small and unorganised book trade could not create trade-wide regulations,

---

28   In general see: J. Feather, *Publishing, Piracy and Politics: An Historical Study of Copyright in Britain* (London: Mansell, 1994), pp. 10-36; Patterson, pp. 78-113.

29   Shurtleff, IV, p. 331.

30   Ibid., II, p. 244.

31   See: Bugbee, p. 106; Lehmann-Haupt, p. 99; Tebbel, p. 46.

enforce them, and lobby government for sustained backup and support. From the point of view of colonial government a major incentive that led European governments to bestow powers on the book trade guilds was lacking in the colonies. Colonial authorities had little need for an intermediary in enforcing their censorship and licensing policies. In a colony where there were just a handful of printers and presses (often just one),[32] even if the number of potential writers and sometimes booksellers was larger, there were easily traceable targets that government could regulate effectively without any need to resort to intermediaries. Similar differences applied from the point of view of printers and booksellers. In the context of a small book trade consisting of a limited number of printers and booksellers there were probably effective alternatives to exclusive legal publishing rights for reducing the publisher's risk. Although knowledge of the exact trade practices during this period is incomplete, book historians mention two such alternative risk-reducing devices. The first was private contractual agreements among booksellers not to print each other's copies.[33] The other was an informal social norm within the trade against such behaviour, supported by what one historian has called 'an enlightened self interest'.[34] Both contractual agreements and social norms were likely to be particularly effective in the context of a small close-knit professional community with a limited number of actors. Moreover, in many cases the risk of competition was limited to the local market. In addition to the physical and economic barriers to an effective inter-colony market there were cultural barriers between the colonies. Much of what was printed in one colony – governmental documents, religious materials, and local histories – was of little relevance to the audience in other colonies. Even in cases of materials that were of general interest there were relatively effective risk-reduction mechanisms such as the offer on consignment by one bookseller or printer of materials published by another.[35]

This background explains why no parallel of the English and European guild or statutory copyright developed in the North American colonies. In the absence of guild-government cooperation no standardised entitlements akin to the Stationers' copyright could appear. In the absence of such

---

32   In 1775, a period that already saw considerable growth of the trade, there were fifty printing houses in the colonies which were about to become the United States; Thomas, p. 17.
33   Tebbel, p. 42; Lehmann-Haupt, p. 99.
34   Tebbel, p. 46. Lehmann-Haupt described it as 'a sense of mutual obligation' and as 'common decency and enlightened self-interest'; Lehmann-Haupt, p. 100.
35   Ibid., p. 101.

preexisting institutional background, sustained private demand for protection, and lobbying by a powerful organised profession no statutory scheme developed.

The same reasons account for the sporadic nature of resort to formal legislative privileges. Nevertheless, the use of legislative privileges was not limited to one singular incident in Massachusetts. Such privileges were granted occasionally as part of the general pattern of colonial regulation and encouragement of the press. For instance, in 1747 the North Carolina legislature, under the active encouragement of Governor Gabriel Johnston, decided to rectify a 'shameful condition' and publish a revised compilation of the colony's laws. In order to accomplish that goal James Davis from Virginia was persuaded to come to North Carolina and was appointed printer for the colony.[36] The legislature also enacted a statute that appointed four 'Commissioners, to Revise and Print the several Acts of Assembly in Force in this Province'.[37] In addition to a payment to the 'Commissioners' for complying and printing the laws it was ordered that they shall have 'the Benefit and Advantage of the sole Printing and Vending the Books of the said Laws, for and during the Space or Term of Five Years'.[38] The Act also provided for punishment to any person vending or importing the Law Books without a license from the Commissioners, 'their Heirs or Assigns' during the term of protection, and set a maximum price of fifteen Shillings for their sale.[39] In short, the North Carolina act followed the same scheme as John Usher's Massachusetts privilege decades earlier. It made the 'Commissioners' the publishers of the Law Book and granted them exclusive publishing and sale rights for five years.

Other colonies, instead of explicitly bestowing exclusive publishing rights, used other arrangements that accomplished the same end. In 1696 William Bladen petitioned the Maryland authorities and asked for leave to bring at his own expense a press that 'would be of great advantage to this province for printing the Laws made every session &c'.[40] The request

---

36   See G.W. Paschal, *A History of Printing in North Carolina* (Raleigh: Edwards & Broughton, 1946), pp. 4-5.

37   An Act for appointing Commissioners to Revise and Print the Laws of this Province, and for granting to his Majesty, for defraying the Charge thereof, a Duty of Wine, Rum and distilled Liquors, and Rice imported into this Province, §II, in *A Collection of all the Public Acts of Assembly, of the province of North-Carolina, now in force and use* (Newbern: James Davis, 1751), pp. 242-5.

38   Ibid., §IV.

39   Ibid., §§IV-V.

40   Wroth, p. 18.

was approved. In 1700 he further petitioned the council for 'encouragement' which resulted in a recommendation affirmed by the house that all writs, 'Bayle bonds, Letters Testamentry, Letters of Adminstration, Citacons summonses & ca'[41] regularly used should be printed. Prices were set as 'one penny or one li Tobo per peece' for some of the documents and 'Two pence or two pounds of tobbo' for others.[42] In the same year Bladen proposed to publish a compilation of Maryland laws. This was accepted by the legislature which provided that:

> Mr. Bladen according to his proposall have liberty to printe the body of the Law of this province if so his Excy shall seem meet And it is likewise unanimously resolved by this house that upon Mr. Bladen's of one Printed body of the said Laws to each respective County Court within this province for his encouragement Shall have allowed him Two Thousand pounds of tobo in each respective county as aforesaid.[43]

The net result of this arrangement was implied exclusivity and explicit subsidy to Bladen's project. Against a background rule that prohibited printing without license, the liberty to print the laws of the colony promised de facto exclusivity. Moreover, Bladen received a commitment for the purchase of a substantial number of copies for a predetermined price. Similar arrangements were used in later occurrences in Maryland[44] and in New York.[45]

Future research in the field is likely to uncover other instances of printing and publishing privileges of various kinds awarded by colonial legislatures. Even the current incomplete knowledge of this period, however, yields a rather clear picture of the colonial precursors of copyright in America. Various colonies occasionally granted on a case-specific basis different printing privileges. These privileges were granted as discretionary economic encouragements to printers or publishers and took various forms, including exclusive printing and sale rights. Like English printing patents and most European privilege grants, colonial printing grants were publishers' economic privileges and had nothing to do with authorship. They were conferred on booksellers or printers, rather than authors. The typical texts involved – most commonly compilations of the colony's

41 Ibid., p. 21.
42 Ibid.
43 Ibid., p. 23.
44 See ibid., pp. 28-9, 33-4, 49-50.
45 An Act to revise, digest & Print the Laws of this Colony [1750], 3 N.Y. Laws 832-5; An Act to revise, digest & Print the Laws of this Colony [1772], 5 N.Y. Laws, 355-7.

laws – had no easily indefinable authors in the modern sense. Nor was authorship a significant normative basis of the privilege grants that were justified in terms of the social and economic benefits to the public of a particular publishing enterprise.

A New Era: The William Billings' Privilege

Against this background of a preexisting, if somewhat sporadic, colonial practice it is not surprising that the post-independence period did not involve a total break with the past in the form of a sudden rise of fully developed authors' rights. The important changes that occurred in this time were gradual and, at first, incorporated much of the previous framework of copyright as the publisher's privilege. A look at the landmark case of the William Billings failed privilege at the very end of the colonial period is demonstrative.

In 1770 William Billings – a tanner by profession as well as a composer, a singing teacher and a choir master – was at the height of his success. He had just published his popular book of tunes, the *New England Psalm Singer*. Billings, who was working on a second edition, became aware that his popular work was about to be widely reprinted and sold, or so he said. He decided to do something about it. In November 1770 he petitioned the Massachusetts House of Representatives 'praying that he may have the exclusive Privilege of selling a Book of Church-Musick compos'd by him self, for a certain Term of Years'.[46] On 16 November a Bill to that effect was brought before the House. Further consideration of the Bill was deferred to the next session. There the matter remained until in 1772 Billings submitted another petition to the Governor, Council and House of Representatives repeating the plea that 'he might have a Patent granted him for the sole Liberty of printing a Book, by him compos'd, consisting of Psalm Tunes, Anthems & Canons'.[47] On 9 June the petition was read and Billings was permitted to bring in a Bill.[48] The Bill entitled *An Act for granting to William Billings of Boston the Sole Privilege of printing and vending a Book by him compos'd, consisting of a great variety of Psalm Tunes, Anthems and Cannons,*

---

46   *Journal of the Honorable House of Representatives* (Boston: 1770), p. 143.
47   Reproduced in R.G. Silver, 'Prologue to Copyright in America: 1772', *Papers of the Bibliographical Society of the University of Virginia*, 11 (1958), 259-62; 'William Billings' Second Petition (1772)', *Primary Sources* (hereafter: William Billings' Second Petition).
48   *Journal of the Honorable House of Representatives* (1772), p. 35.

in two Volumes[49] was read in the House of Representatives on 14 June.[50] It provided that Billings 'be and hereby is impower'd soley to print and vend his said Composition consisting of Psalm-tunes Anthems and Canons and have and receive the whole and only benefit and emolument arising therefrom for and during the full term of seven years'.[51]

This was an important landmark in American copyright history. For the first time an author rather than a printer or a bookseller applied to receive exclusive privileges in his own work and an American legislature was willing to bestow rights on an author as such. Billings' petition and Bill constituted the first appearance of the author as a legitimate claimer of rights. At the same time however the petition, the Bill and the proceedings reflected the transitional character of Billings' plea for authorial rights. Billings was neither making a general case for authors' rights nor pleading for a universal copyright regime. He was, rather, petitioning for the familiar ad hoc economic privilege that traditionally was granted to booksellers and printers. Moreover, parts of the petition justified the grant in the common terms of an enterprise useful to the public that should be encouraged. His book of tunes, Billings explained 'ha[d] been found upon Experience, to be to general Acceptance; & which composition is made much Use of in many of our Churches, & is more & more used every Day'.[52]

The petition and Bill included, however, new forms of justification and claims couched in the vocabulary of authorship and intellectual labour. Billings informed 'this Hon:ble Court that he [wa]s apprehensive that an unfair advantage was about to be taken against him, & that others [we]re endeavoring to reap the Fruits of his great Labor & Cost'.[53] The Bill referred to the fact that the book 'cost him much pains and application and ha[d] also been very expensive to him'.[54] More importantly, the proceedings were fraught with concerns about authorship and originality. The reason for the delay between the first petition in 1770 and the 1772 Bill was probably a suspicion that Billings was not the author of some of the tunes in the book.[55] Billings made a point of repeating the fact that the book was composed by

---

49   *Journal of the Honorable House of Representatives* (1772), pp. 121, 124, 134; reproduced in Silver, p. 259; 'William Billings' Printing Privilege (1772)', *Primary Sources* (hereafter: William Billings' Printing Privilege).
50   *Journal of the Honorable House of Representatives* (1772), p. 124.
51   William Billings' Printing Privilege.
52   William Billings' Second Petition.
53   Ibid.
54   William Billings' Printing Privilege.
55   Silver, p. 260.

him and pointed out that 'he [wa]s the sole Author, & should have been asham'd, to have expos'd himself by publishing any Tunes, Anthems or Canons; compos'd by Another'.[56]

Billings' petition followed the traditional form of publishers' privileges. It justified the petition in terms of specific public benefits and asked for exclusive printing rights. The novelty was that the petitioner was an author and that, for the first time in the American colonies, he based part of his case on claims of just dessert for the intellectual labour of authors.

The fate of Billings' printing privilege was tragic, at least from the point of view of the petitioner. After it was passed by the House and the Council the Bill together with a few others was vetoed by Governor Thomas Hutchinson and never came into force.[57] Hutchinson gave no reasons but it is likely that Billings was caught in the power struggle between the loyalist governor and his growingly antagonistic Assembly. Billings' friendship with the House Speaker Samuel Adams may have worsened his position in this regard.[58] Authors' rights in America would have to wait for independence.

Andrew Law's Privilege: The First Author's Privilege in America?

After the Revolution the practical and ideological centre of gravity of copyright entitlements shifted towards authors. During the first two decades of independence publishers' grants disappeared and were supplanted by grants to authors. These legislative grants were similar to colonial printing and patent grants. However, the grantees were now authors and pervading the grant practices there gradually appeared a discourse about authors' rights.

The 1781 Connecticut grant to Andrew Law is usually credited as the first author's copyright in America. However, the search for the first author's grant tends to obscure the complexity of the episode, the gradual character of the transition from publisher's copyright to authorial rights, and the ironies woven into Law's relationship with the emerging concepts of copyright and authorship. Andrew Law, born in Milford, Connecticut, was the grandson of the colony's governor Jonathan Law. He studied

---

56   William Billings' Second Petition.
57   *Journal of the Honorable House of Representatives* (1772), p. 134.
58   R. Crawford and D.P. McKay, *William Billings of Boston: Eighteenth Century Composer* (Princeton, N.J.: Princeton University Press, 1975), pp. 226-7.

divinity at Rhode Island College (later Brown University). He was ordained in 1787 but his main occupation on which he embarked years earlier was his musical career. Law taught music and singing and wrote mostly simple hymn tunes. His success and fame, however, came chiefly from compiling, arranging and publishing tunes by other composers. His printer and publisher was his brother, William Law of Cheshire, Connecticut.

Law's pioneering attempt to obtain exclusive exploitation rights may have originated in his strong awareness of the commercial aspects of his occupation. Law was a shrewd businessman who relentlessly sought ways of expanding and capitalising on his music enterprises. In the 1780s he travelled extensively throughout the country, established singing schools and promoted the use of his texts. Ever ambitious in his plans, Law contracted with young college graduate music teachers who promised to exclusively use his books or to exclusively sell them on a commission basis. Law sent several of these teacher-salesmen to the South and other rural areas in the hope of establishing a singing school movement based on his books and creating a steady stream of income.[59] These plans went sour due to, among other things, competition from cheaper and more accessible music books including those of Law's former Philadelphia associate Andrew Adgate. Law was also jealous for what he saw as his publication rights and vigilant in attempting to enforce them. In a period of three decades he was involved in numerous skirmishes and disputes over such matters.[60]

Law's Connecticut privilege was probably the result of his commercial awareness and his protective approach toward his publications. In October 1781 he petitioned the Connecticut legislature[61] explaining that 'after much application to gain a competent Degree of Knowledge in the Art of singing to qualify himself for teaching of Psalmody; he in the year 1777 made a large Collection of the best & most approved Tunes'.[62] Law further explained that publishing the collection cost him 'nearly £500,--Lawful Money' and that 'by the rapid Depreciation of the Continental Currency the three last Years he has received very little Compensation'.[63] Next came the claim of the impending violation of rights:

59   R. Sanjek, *American Popular Music and its Business: The First Four Hundred* Years, 2 vols (New York: Oxford University Press, 1988), II, pp. 5-6.
60   See I. Lowens, 'Andrew Law and the Pirates', *Journal of American Musicological Society*, 13 (1960), 206-23.
61   'Andrew Law's Petition (1781)', *Primary Sources* (hereafter: Andrew Law's Petition).
62   Ibid.
63   Ibid.

To his great Surprize he now finds that some person or persons unknown to your Memorialist who are acquainted with the Art of Engraving are making attempts to make a plate in Resemblance of that procured by your Memorialist & to strike books under the Name of your Memorialist thereby to defeat the interest of your Memorialist in his plate & in the Sale of his books.[64]

Observing that 'works of Art ought to be protected in this Country & all proper encouragement given thereto as in other Countries', Law asked for 'an exclusive patent for imprinting and vending the Tunes following for the Term of five Years'.[65]

The Connecticut legislature was duly impressed. It passed an Act[66] describing how Law 'hath with great Trouble & Expense prepared for the Press & produced to be engraved & imprinted a Collection of the best & most approved Tunes & Anthems for the Promotion of Psalmody'.[67] It awarded Law 'free & full Liberty & License [...] for the sole printing, publishing & vending the several Tunes & Anthems above-mentioned [...] for the Term of five Years'.[68] The grant enumerated by name the protected tunes and imposed a five hundred pound penalty per violation as well as 'just Damages'. Despite a somewhat obscure phrasing the grant was probably stipulated upon Law's 'printing & furnishing a sufficient number of Copies of the sd. Tunes for the use of the Inhabitants of this State at reasonable prices'.[69]

At first blush, Law's privilege seems to be a classic author's copyright. The published original creations of a composer were copied by others, which resulted in the grant of a limited-time exclusive right to publish and sell his tunes. The reality however was more complicated. To begin with, there is much confusion about the exact work that Law composed and what was copied by others. Commentators rely on Law's petition to conclude that the work was *Collection of the Best and Most Approved Tunes and Anthems for the Promotion of Psalmody*. Unfortunately, it is very probable that such a work never existed.[70] There is neither direct nor indirect evidence that it was ever created or published. The assumption that there was such a work was the

---

64 Ibid.
65 Ibid.
66 The Public Records of the State of Connecticut, 9 vols., ed. by C.J. Hoadly (Hartford: various publishers, 1894-1953), III, pp. 537-8; 'Andrew Law's Privilege (1781)', *Primary Sources*.
67 Ibid.
68 Ibid.
69 Ibid.
70 Lowens, 'Andrew Law', no. 6, p. 210. I. Lowens, 'Copyright and Andrew Law', *Papers of the Bibliographical Society of America*, 53 (1959), 150-9.

result of a bibliographical mistake by modern scholars originating from the references in Law's petition and the Connecticut Act.[71] The Connecticut legislature may have believed that Law published or intended to publish a collection encompassing all the enumerated tunes. In fact, Law published the tunes in several separate works. Moreover, significantly, Law was not the composer of the overwhelming majority of the tunes protected under his grant. As he admitted in his petition: 'Copies of some of which he purchased of the original Compilers, others he took from Books of Psalmody printed in England which were never printed in America'.[72] In other words Law copied most of his protected tunes from English publications, from manuscripts he obtained from American composers or publishers (who had no exclusive publication rights they could assign), and possibly from American published works.

In light of these facts, the question arises: in what exactly did the protection awarded by the grant consist? A modern copyright lawyer's instinctive reaction would be that Law received protection not in the individual tunes, but rather in the particular selection and arrangement of tunes embodied in his collection. This, however, was not the case. As explained, there was no actual work that constituted a collection of the works mentioned in the grant. Moreover, Law asked for protection in the 'Tunes following', and the Connecticut legislature specifically declared that the Act prohibited 'all the Subjects of this State, to reprint the same, & each & every of the sd. Tunes or Anthems, in the like, or in any other Volume, or Form whatsoever'. Thus Law received exclusive rights in the individual tunes of which he was not the author. In this respect the grant, though bestowed on an authorial figure was close to the traditional publisher's privilege. Law was simply the first one to publish those tunes in America, or so he claimed.

The extent to which Law's grant and his proprietary attitude were the exception rather than the rule is demonstrated by examining some of the instances of piracy of 'his' works. The piracy of which Law complained in his petition was probably of his 1775 *A Select Number of Plain Tunes Adapted*

---

71   The seminal bibliographical work on early American publications Charles Evans' *American Bibliography* has several references to a work entitled *Collection of the Best and Most Approved Tunes and Anthems for the Promotion of Psalmody* by Andrew Law. Lowens explains that these 'would appear to be ghosts manufactured by Evans'. See Lowens, 'Andrew Law', no. 6, p. 210. In another work Lowens explains in detail the circumstances that led to the mistake by Evans and others and to the entrenchment of the mistaken assumption that such a work existed. See Lowens, 'Copyright', pp. 158-9.
72   Andrew Law's Petition.

to Congregational Worship.[73] Although not named in the petition, the most probable culprit was John Norman, one of the few expert music engravers on the scene at that time. The book printed by Norman was his *New Collection of Psalm Tunes Adapted to Congregational Worship*, a work with a similar title, structure and engraving style to Law's *Select Number*. Twenty-three out of the fifty-one tunes in the *New Collection* were identical to those in the *Select Number*.[74] It is likely that Norman imitated Law's work, but Law's accusations may have been exaggerated. A closer look at the two works reveals that out of the twenty-three shared tunes twenty-one were old popular tunes that were published in England and America well before Law's *Select Number* and were readily accessible from other sources. Surviving copies of the *New Collection* do not support Law's petition claim that the unauthorised reprint was under his name, but the resemblance of the engraving style supports the claim of 'a plate in Resemblance of that procured by your Memorialist'.[75] This last complaint was somewhat disingenuous. The practice was not uncommon in the music publishing of the period. Indeed, the engraved title page by Joel Allen of a 1779 edition of another work by Law himself – the *Select Harmony* – was an exact copy of Henry Dawkins' design for the title page of the 1761 *Urania* by James Lyon.[76]

Law was involved in numerous other disputes over printing rights of his works, including with the famous American printer Isaiah Thomas.[77] Out of these many disputes, Law's tussle with Daniel Bayley of Newburyport, Massachusetts sheds the most light on the gradual development of proprietary attitudes toward publications. In the preface of his 1783 *Rudiments of Music* Law, referring to his earlier work, *Select Harmony*, expressed his hope 'that it w[ould] not be pirated as the other was, by those who look, not at the public good, but at their own emolument'.[78] Law most probably was aiming here at Bayley who published a collection of tunes[79] with the following text on its title page:

73   Lowens estimates that the *Select Number* may have appeared in 1775, but probably did not come out before 1777. See Lowens, 'Andrew Law', p. 208.
74   Ibid., p. 212.
75   Andrew Law's Petition.
76   See Lowens, 'Andrew Law', p. 208. Lowens reproduced the title pages of Law's *Select Harmony* and of *Urania*. Ibid., plate 1.
77   For a comprehensive survey of Law's disputes see ibid.
78   Andrew Law, *Rudiments of Music* (Cheshire, Conn.: William Law, 1783).
79   Complicating the matter is the fact that the only known copy of Bayley's collection is later than Law's *Rudiments of Music* where he deplored the piracy. Lowens explains that indirect evidence indicate the existence of a prior edition by Bayley and makes it possible to deduce its content. Lowens, 'Andrew Law', pp. 211-2.

> Select Harmony, containing in a plain and concise manner, the rules of
> singing chiefly by Andrew Law, A.B. To which are added a number of psalm
> tunes, hymns and anthems, from the best authors. With some never before
> published. Printed and Sold by Daniel Bayley, at his house in Newbury-port
> [...][80]

Forty-two out of the one hundred and forty-four tunes in Bayley's collection had appeared in Law's *Select Harmony*. Half of those were tunes for
which Law received protection in his Connecticut grant.

Legally, there was little Law could do. Bayley was printing in
Massachusetts and Law's state grant was limited to Connecticut. Law's
only remaining option was public denunciation. On November 17, 1784 he
published the following in the *Essex Journal*:

> Andrew Law informs the public, that a book entitled 'Select Harmony,
> chiefly by Andrew Law,' which is printed by Daniel Bayley of Newburyport
> is *not* chiefly, nor *any part* of it by him. The title is absolutely false. There are
> in that book ten or fifteen capital errors in a single page, and whoever pur-
> chases that book for Law's collection, will find it a very great imposition.[81]

Two weeks later Bayley published the following response in the *Essex
Journal*:

> I would inform the publick, in answer to Mr. A. Law's charge, that the
> rules for singing, laid down in my book, as to the scales, characters, and
> examples are very nearly the same with Mr. Law, excepting some few emen-
> dations – as to the music, out of 65 pieces in Mr. Law's book, I have 45 of
> them in mine, with the addition of 100 psalms and hymn tunes and anthems.
> As to the errors, let him who is without cast the first stone.[82]

A few features of this exchange are noteworthy. The first is that the focus
of the public exchange was the allegedly misleading use of Law's name,
leaving untouched the issue of copying. As mentioned, the claim that
Bayley reproduced Law's tunes raised no formal legal problem. The mar-
ginalisation of the question in the public exchange implies that it also did
not raise serious issues of propriety. Reprinting tunes published by others
was a very common practice in the music publishing business of the time.
It does not appear that anyone saw Bayley's behaviour in this respect as
particularly reprehensible. In fact, a close look at the content of Bayley's
book reveals how unusual and novel Law's later outraged reaction was to
the alleged piracy. Many of the tunes that appeared in both publications

---

80   Daniel Bayley, *Select Harmony* (Newburyport, Mass: Daniel Bayley, 1784).
81   Quoted in Lowens, 'Andrew Law', p. 212.
82   Quoted in ibid.

were published years earlier in other sources. Moreover, out of the forty-two shared tunes, sixteen, including three protected by Law's Connecticut grant, were published by Bayley himself in a 1774 book: John Stickney's, *Gentleman and Lady's Musical Companion*. This was years before Law published his *Select Harmony* and before he applied for copyright protection. Bayley used the same plates from the 1774 book to print the reprinted tunes in his new collection. In fact, it is very likely that it was Law who used tunes previously published in Bayley's very popular books in his later collections of tunes.[83]

The other issue raised in the debate was the allegedly misleading use of Law's name. Again, trying to capitalise on familiar names of authors and publishers and use them to attract customers was not an uncommon practice in the music publishing business of the time. Thus, the main thrust of Bayley's public defence of the propriety of his actions was claiming that there was nothing misleading in his book. His book, he explained, was 'chiefly by Andrew Law' because of the similarities and overlap in content between the two works. The very element that under modern copyright thought may cause Bayley's actions to look questionable was the foundation of the public justifications he offered. The entire episode, demonstrates the novel and exceptional character at the time of Law's protective attitudes as a matter of both law and propriety. It also indicates, however, that Law embodied a newly appearing possessive approach and a strong, if not always consistent or entirely good-faith, sense of entitlement toward 'his' publications.

Law's Connecticut privilege was not exactly the unambiguous author's copyright that some later accounts made it. The grant and the events surrounding it embodied the gradual nature of the change from printers' privileges to authors' rights. It marked the beginning of the shift toward authors in American copyright thinking, the emergence of a new proprietary approach to the circulation of texts, and some early legal recognition of such an approach. It also reflected the extent to which this process was gradual and replete with ambiguities, in terms of both the legal means used and the general public attitudes surrounding it.

---

83   See ibid., pp. 212-3.

State Privileges in the Age of Authors' Rights: John Ledyard's Privilege

In a period of less than a decade beginning in 1783 the United States had completed its formal transition from ad hoc publishers' privileges to a general statutory regime of authors' rights. During the 1780s, following the 1783 legislation of the first general copyright Act in America by the Connecticut legislature,[84] all states but one passed similar statutes, modelled to various degrees after the English Statute of Anne.[85] The final recognition and entrenchment of general authors' rights regimes came with the 1789 constitutional clause that empowered Congress to 'promote the Progress of Science and useful Arts, by securing for limited Times to Authors [...] the exclusive Right to their [...] Writings'[86] and the 1790 federal Copyright Act.[87] Printing privileges, however, did not instantaneously disappear. State grants persisted after the states legislated general copyright statutes and even after the creation of the federal regime. During this period several authors petitioned various state legislatures for individual privileges in their works. Noah Webster is most well-known for his journeys in search of legislative privileges for his book,[88] but other authors too petitioned for and sometimes received such grants. Authors probably kept applying for individual privileges either because they did not qualify under the general regimes, or because they hoped for better terms than the standard entitlements bestowed on them.

Like Andrew Law's privileges, other state legislative grants constituted a transitory stage between the traditional publishers' privileges and the new general regimes of authors' rights. Unlike colonial privileges, the grants were awarded to authors in their works. Equally important was the fact that for the first time arguments based on the notion of authors' rights in the fruit of their intellectual labour started to appear in the public discourse surrounding these grants. At the same time the grantees, the justifications

---

84   An Act for the Encouragement of Literature and Genius, 1783 Conn. Acts 133, available in *Acts and laws of the State of Connecticut in America* (New London, Connecticut: T. Green, printer to the Governor and Company of the State of Connecticut, 1784), p. 133.
85   See in general F. Crawford, 'Pre-Constitutional Copyright Statutes', *Bulletin of the Copyright Society of the U.S.A*, 23 (1975), 11-37.
86   The Constitution of the United States of America, Art. 1, §8, cl. 8.
87   Copyright Act 1790, 1 Stat. 124 (1790).
88   See in general O. Bracha, 'Commentary on the Connecticut Copyright Statute 1783', *Primary Sources*.

they offered, and the grants themselves often relied on tropes taken from the more traditional vocabulary. The grant was frequently described and justified not so much in terms of authorship as in terms of 'encouraging' an entrepreneur who offered a specific useful service to the public.

John Ledyard's 1783 Connecticut petition for protection is demonstrative of this ambivalent character of state grants. Ledyard was a romantic figure. In 1773 at the end of his first year at Dartmouth College he was forced to leave the institution due to financial problems. He made a dugout canoe and paddled home to Hartford, Connecticut down the Connecticut River, an event that left a lasting impression on Dartmouth.[89] Ledyard followed the common trail of young men in his position – he went to sea. In 1776 after some journeys and adventures, he joined as a mariner in the British Navy the crew of Captain James Cook's expedition. After the voyage, Ledyard was sent to America as a member of the British Navy. He deserted and returned to Hartford where he wrote his *Journal of Captain Cook's Last Voyage*. The printer and bookseller Nathaniel Patten agreed to pay him twenty guineas for the manuscript, a sum almost equal to Ledyard's entire pay for his four year journey with Cook. The fact that Ledyard wrote the account of the journey in four months and Patten's rush to publish it were reflected in the quality of the work. Nevertheless, the book was probably very popular and sold well.[90]

In January 1783 Ledyard petitioned the Connecticut legislature and asked for 'the exclusive right of publishing the said Journal or history in this State for such a term as shall be thot fit'.[91] Ledyard's petition is striking in its lack of emphasis on authorship and on authors' rights as the foundation of his claim. Following a lengthy description of his journeys, Ledyard's first plea was for patronage in the form of employment, or in the words of the petition:

> [Y]our Memorialist having lost his pecuniary assistance by his abrupt departure from the British is thereby incapacitated to move in a circle he could wish without the Assistance of his friends & the patronage & recommendations of the Government under which he was born & whose favour and esteem he hopes he has never forfeited: he therefore proposes as a matter of consideration to your Excellency and Council that he may be introduced into some immediate employment wherein he may as well be usefull to his country as himself during the War.[92]

---

89 J. Zug, *American Traveler: The Life and Adventures of John Ledyard, the Man Who Dreamed of Walking the World* (New York: Basic Books, 2005), pp. 19-20.
90 Ibid., p. 124.
91 'Petition of John Ledyard (1783)', *Primary Sources*.
92 Ibid.

This was the plea of a subject asking for state patronage in exchange for what he saw as a useful public service. The same spirit pervaded the plea for printing rights that followed. His book, he wrote, '[he thinks] will not only be meritorious in himself but may be essentially usefull to America in general but particularly to the northern States by opening a most valuable trade across the north pacific Ocean to China & the east Indies'.[93] In return for this public benefit Ledyard asked for exclusive printing rights as yet another form of patronage.

A committee appointed by the legislature to consider the petition reported that: 'in their Opinion a publication of the Memorialist Journal in his voyage round the Globe may be beneficial to this United States & to the world, & it appears reasonable & Just that the Memorialist should have an exclusive right to publish the same for a Reasonable Term'.[94] At this point, in a surprising turn of events, the committee instead of recommending an individual Bill for Ledyard suggested a general copyright statute. It observed that: 'it appears that several Gentlemen of Genius & reputation are also about to make similar Applications for the exclusive right [to] publish Works of their Respective Compositions', and recommended to 'pass a general bill, for that purpose'.[95] This recommendation resulted in the first general copyright regime in America, the Connecticut copyright statute enacted in January 1783.[96] Thus, Ledyard, together with the anonymous 'Gentlemen of Genius' supplied the trigger for the first general American copyright regime. As the legislature probably assumed that the general Act made an individual privilege redundant, Ledyard never received the grant for which he petitioned. Some accounts seem to assume that he or his publisher registered the book for protection under the state regime,[97] but there is no direct evidence of that.

The role played by Ledyard's petition in the rise of authorship-based copyright and in triggering an act specifying its purpose as the 'Encouragement of Literature and Genius' is somewhat ironic. Ledyard borrowed extensive parts of his account and straightforwardly plagiarised others. He worked with John Hawkesworth's *An Account of the Voyages Undertaken by the order of his Present Majesty for Making Discoveries in the*

---

93 Ibid.

94 'Ledyard Petition Committee Report (1783)', *Primary Sources*.

95 Ibid.

96 In general see Bracha, 'Commentary on the Connecticut Copyright Statute 1783'.

97 E.G. Gray, *The Making of John Ledyard: Empire and Ambition in the Life of a an Early American Traveler* (New Haven: Yale University Press, 2007), pp. 95-6.

Southern Hemisphere that was based on the logs of several of Cook's first voyage officers, an anonymous 1781 book about the third voyage, and probably several other publications.[98] Apart from the use of anecdotes, factual information and occasional sentences from those sources, Ledyard copied verbatim the last thirty-eight pages of his book from the 1781 anonymous publication.[99] The significant fact is that nobody seemed to care. Ledyard's biographer appears to be shocked by the 'the appalling theft'. He finds that Ledyard's behaviour was 'blatantly in violation of the copyright ethos', and even attempts to absolve him by suggesting that his publisher Patten who was left with an incomplete manuscript may have been the culprit.[100] Contemporaries were less shocked. Since the 1781 anonymous book was circulating in the United States, readers would have known of the copying, but there is no evidence that anybody, including the Connecticut legislature, was concerned. The point is exactly that the original-authorship 'copyright ethos' did not yet exist or was only in its early infancy. Ledyard was not presenting himself to the assembly as a genius creator of original ideas, but rather as an entrepreneur offering a useful service to the state. Thus, his literary borrowing was of little relevance.

Conclusion

The era of individual state printing grants that lasted until the end of the century was marked by the ambiguity and duality that characterises Law's and Ledyard's petitions. Like these two, many of the other state grants were still rooted in the colonial patterns of state patronage extended to a person who offered a useful public service.[101] On the other hand, the state grants were an important site in which the reorientation of copyright towards authorship began to appear. The grantees were now authors rather than publishers, or at least, as in the case of Ledyard and Law, held an ambiguous status in between these two categories. The public discourse

---

98   Zug, pp. 127-8.
99   Ibid.
100 Ibid., pp. 128-9.
101 Another striking example of this character of the early state privileges is Joseph Purcell's 1792 South Carolina grant for a map of the state. Purcell was in charge of producing the map, but was not necessarily the person who actually created it. The grant of exclusivity was part of his appointment to the position of state Geographer. See: *Statutes at Large of South Carolina*, 11 vols., ed. by T. Cooper (Columbia, S.C.: A.S. Johnston, 1836-73), V, pp. 219-20; 'Purcell's Printing Privilege (1792)', *Primary Sources*.

surrounding the grants and the general states' Acts sometimes triggered by individual petitions were often laced with the rhetoric of a new authorship-based ideology. The notions that state encouragement was given to authors for their original creation and that authors deserved a just reward for the expense and labour that was invested in their intellectual creation gradually appeared and took root in this discourse.

By the end of the century the practice of individual printing privileges had disappeared. The concept of copyright as an author's right in his original creation that first appeared ambivalently within this practice became the official ideology of American copyright. Episodes like Law's and Ledyard's grants would be reconceptualised as paradigmatic instances of authors' grants, and the irony and ambiguities that pervaded them would be forgotten. In the nineteenth century copyright's new official representation as authors' rights would be subverted not by the old colonial grant tradition but rather by the forces and demands of a new industrialised market society.

5. Author and Work in the French Print Privileges System: Some Milestones

Laurent Pfister*

In France, the history of literary property was born with the concept of literary property. Since the eighteenth century, those contesting the concept of literary property have endeavoured to locate it within an historical context, with both supporters and opponents developing historical narratives to bolster their particular claims. In his *Letter on the booktrade*, in 1763, Diderot devotes lengthy passages to the history of the subject in order to demonstrate its long-standing provenance.[1] In 1859, with the controversies about the duration of *droit d'auteur* in full swing, the lawyer Édouard René de Laboulaye published a number of historical sources all of which tended to affirm his particular theory of perpetual literary property.[2] Similarly, in the

* This article is based upon a paper that was delivered at the conference launching the *Primary Sources* website on 19 March 2008 (www.copyrighthistory.org). My thanks to Lionel Bently and Martin Kretschmer for their invitation to speak at that event, and to Ronan Deazley for his editorial assistance in preparing this paper for publication

1   *Lettre sur le commerce des livres* (1763). Although this text has been often published, it is interesting to read the original manuscript preserved at the Bibliothèque nationale de France (Mss. Fr. (Naf) 24232 n°3) and now published with an accompanying commentary by F. Rideau, 'Diderot's Letter on the book trade (1763)', *Primary Sources*. About the history of this text and the history presented within this text see: Jean-Yves Mollier, *Postface, Lettre sur le commerce de la librairie* (Paris: éd. Mille et une nuits, 2003); Roger Chartier, *Inscrire et effacer. Culture écrite et littérature (xɪᵉ-xvɪɪɪᵉ siècle)* (Paris: Gallimard Seuil, 2005), p. 177.

2   Edouard Laboulaye and Georges Guiffrey, *La propriété littéraire au xvɪɪɪᵉ siècle. Recueil de pièces et de documents* (Paris, 1859). In contrast, some years later François Malapert published an historical study to refute Laboulaye's thesis of perpetual property: 'Histoire abrégée de la législation sur la propriété littéraire avant 1789', *Journal des économistes* (1880), p. 252; and (1881), p. 437.

decades that followed, a number of French lawyers tried to consolidate the moral right by asserting that it was not only a natural right but one that had existed since the dawn of time.[3] In short, since the eighteenth century, the history of literary property has been subject to a process of instrumentalisation, a process which still continues today.[4]

This instrumentalisation of the history of literary property prompts two considerations. In the first place, it reminds us of the importance of returning to the primary sources concerned. On this point, the publication of *Primary Sources on Copyright (1450-1900)* can only be welcomed. It will now be much easier for interested scholars to engage critically with these primary materials, and to draw parallels and points of difference between them. Second, the instrumentalisation of history raises important questions of methodology. How do we write history? Which sources should we use? Should we prioritise some sources – such as legislation or case law – over others? What value should we place upon other, non-legal, historical sources, such as the letters, petitions, or complaints of authors? Of late, various criticisms have been levelled at the historians of the French concept of *droit d'auteur* for the teleological nature of their approach. That history, it has been argued, has been distorted by the pursuit of an end goal – the validation of both the author and of a natural *droit d'auteur*. Professor Jane Ginsburg, for example, has highlighted the mistake of reading only a part of the well-known 1791 report by Le Chapelier, the partial reading of which tending to obscure the extent to which Le Chapelier placed the public domain – and not the author – at the centre of his conception of the literary property regime.[5] David Saunders, on the other hand, proffers a more

---

3   See for example Pierre Masse, *Le droit moral de l'auteur sur son œuvre littéraire ou artistique* (Paris, 1906), p. 35: '[L]e droit moral [...] a existé de tout temps. A Athènes et à Rome, alors que les auteurs étaient sans droit pécuniaire, le droit moral était reconnu et sanctionné, sinon par une disposition expresse de la loi, du moins par la conscience publique'. See also André Morillot, *De la protection accordée aux œuvres d'art, aux photographies aux dessins et modèles industriels et aux brevets d'invention dans l'Empire d'Allemagne* (Paris – Berlin, 1878), p. 117.

4   Consider for example the deputy Patrick Bloche who, in support of the proposal for a global license that would have legalised the exchange of copyright-protected content on the internet in exchange for a fixed income, presented before the National Assembly, called upon the remarks of the 19th century lawyer Auguste-Charles Renouard in support of the proposition that 'the *droit d'auteur* is a social contract' (Assemblée Nationale, 21 December 2005, 1rst seance, pp. 8606-7).

5   Even if I don't entirely agree with her interpretation, Prof Ginsburg's study has encouraged a renewed attention as to the significance of the copyright regime during the time of the French Revolution. Jane Ginsburg, 'A Tale of two copyrights: literary property in Revolutionary France and America', *Revue Internationale du Droit*

broadly conceived critique of both the unwelcome influence of 'Romantic historicism' in shaping histories of copyright, as well as of the way in which post-structuralist accounts of authorship only serve to entrench the inevitability of the authorial figure as a precondition to the deconstruction of the same.[6] That is, if the author is dead (and let us assume that he is), then at some point he must have lived – an inescapable and natural phenomenon, independent of any artifice.

Where, then, to begin with the history of *droit d'auteur*? Despite some objections,[7] it seems reasonable to explore the origins of French literary property within the system of granting royal privileges for the protection of books – that is, so long as we remain wary of the dangers of exploring this 'sixteenth-century cultural-legal arrangement from the philosophical standpoint of the Romantic author'.[8] There are, of course, obvious parallels between these royal privileges and the rights established at the end of the eighteenth century, in that both involve exclusive rights to print and sell a work. Moreover, it's also important to appreciate that the legislation of the French revolution finds part of its inspiration in the system of granting royal privileges.[9] However, significant differences exist between the early royal privileges and *droit d'auteur* as conceived in the eighteenth century. In the first place, these early privileges were royal favours often granted to reward someone for a public utility, as opposed to giving recognition to any natural or subjective right.[10] Second – a very important point – the privilege

---

d'auteur, 147 (1991), 125. See also Carla Hesse, 'Enlightenment Epistemology and the Laws of Autorship in Revolutionary France, 1777-1793', *Representations* 30: Special issue on Law and the Order of Culture (Spring, 1990), pp. 109-37. For the text of, and a commentary upon, Le Chapelier's Report, see F. Rideau, 'Le Chapelier's report (1791)', *Primary Sources*.

6   David Saunders, 'Dropping the Subject: An Argument for a Positive History of Authorship and the Law of Copyright', in *Of Authors and Origins. Essays on Copyright law*, ed. by Brad Sherman and Alain Strowell (Oxford: Clarendon Press, 1994), p. 93.

7   See for example: Pierre Recht, *Le droit d'auteur, une nouvelle forme de propriété. Histoire et théorie* (Paris: LGDJ, 1969), p. 20; Maxime Dury, *La censure. La prédication silencieuse* (Paris: Publisud, 1995), p. 271.

8   Saunders, p. 94. See also C. Haynes, 'Reassessing "Genius" in Studies of Authorship. The State of the Discipline', *Book History*, 8 (2005), 287-320 (p. 291).

9   L. Pfister, 'L'auteur, propriétaire de son œuvre. La formation du droit d'auteur du xvie siècle à la loi de 1957' (unpublished doctoral thesis, University of Strasbourg, 1999), pp. 54-90, 483-8.

10   Ibid., pp. 50-60. See also Henri Falk, *Les privileges en librairie sous l'Ancien Régime* (Paris, 1905); Raymond Birn, 'Profit of Ideas: *Privilège en librairie* in Eighteenth-Century France', *Eighteenth Century Studies* (1970-1), 131-68; Frédéric Rideau, *La formation du droit de propriété littéraire en France et en Grande-Bretagne: une conver-*

granted was an exception to the so-called *liberté publique de l'imprimerie*.[11] This public freedom of press can be considered to be an inheritance of medieval ideas concerning the production and dissemination of knowledge,[12] as well as an antecedent of the public domain; that is, in the absence of a privilege prohibiting the unauthorised reproduction of a published work, that work was considered to fall within what we now call the public domain.[13] Third, important differences between the two forms of protection lie in the place occupied by the author in the system of privileges and also in how the work itself was understood. It is this last point that provides the particular focus of this paper. The first section considers the way in which, prior to the eighteenth century, the author enjoyed an indifferent status within the privilege system, as well as the manner in which the author's work was not conceived of as an exclusive property that would survive publication of the same (1). The second explores how and why, by the end of the *Ancien Regime*, the author came to be more fully integrated within the privilege system, as well as the way in which ideas about the author and his work – and the relationship between the two – were significantly transformed as part of that process (2).[14]

1. The Author and the Work during the Early Years of Print

Before the invention of the printing press, during the Middle Ages, texts could be freely reproduced.[15] After Gutenberg's invention, the reproduction

---

gence oubliée (Aix-Marseille: PUAM, 2004), pp. 33-60.

11   Following the expression employed in 1579 by the king's prosecutor Barnabé Brisson (*Recueil de plaidoyez notables de plusieurs anciens et fameux advocats de la Cour de Parlement ...et divers arrêts* (Paris, 1644)), p. 512, and in 1586 by the barrister Simon Marion (*Plaidoyez de M. Simon Marion, advocat en Parlement, Baron de Druy: plaidoyez second, sur l'impression des Œuvres de Sénèque, revueuës et annotées par feu Marc Antoine Muret*, Bibliothèque nationale de France, Manus. Fçs. 22071, n°28). For the text of the latter document, with an accompanying commentary, see F. Rideau, 'Simon Marion's plea on privileges (1586)', *Primary Sources*.

12   See G. Post, K. Giocarinis and R. Kay, *The Medieval Heritage of Humanistic Ideal: "scientia donum dei est, unde vendi non potest"'*, in *Traditio*, 11 (1955), especially pp. 197-210.

13   Pfister, 'L'auteur, propriétaire', pp. 123-60; Rideau, *La formation*, pp. 52-9.

14   See in particular Roger Chartier, 'Qu'est-ce qu'un auteur? Révision d'une généalogie', *Bulletin de la société de philosophie*, 94 (2000), 15.

15   For example, in 1316 the statutes of the University of Paris relating to copyists states that: 'Item nullus stationnarius denegabit exemplaria alicui etiam volenti per illus aliud exemplar facere.' *Statuta Universitatis Paris. De librariis et stationariis*, 4

of texts was protected by the granting of exclusive, but temporary, royal privileges. In France, the first of these were granted at the beginning of the sixteenth century (perhaps influenced by the Italian model) in order to combat the economic injury caused by unauthorised printing.[16] From 1566, however, the privilege system was closely linked to the censorship of texts, in that the approbation of the censor was an essential pre-condition for obtaining a privilege.[17]

Whereas, during the early years of print, many authors knew how to capitalise upon the privilege system and the operation of the book trade, authorial status (*la qualité d'auteur*) did not constitute a central element of the legal system of the *Ancien Regime* – at least, not until the middle of the eighteenth century (1.1). Moreover, during this period, while many regarded the author as owning the work that he produced, this understanding did not extend to the published work – again, an idea that would not take root until the eighteenth century (1.2).

1.1 Relative Indifference of the Legal System towards the Author

From the sixteenth century onwards, authors, or at least some authors, took an active role in the control of their works. For example, some authors concluded beneficial contracts with booksellers and printers, while others complained about the publication of their work without their consent (a manner 'of assuming rights on the writings of others' according to Erasme),[18] or about poorly produced editions of their work (which, according to Marot

---

décembre 1316, in *Chartularium Universitatis Parisiensis*, Paris, 1891, 2, p. 190.

16   In the *Epître dédicatoire* published at the beginning of *Virgile* printed by Ulrich Gering in Paris in 1478, Paul Maillet writes that: 'Certains libraires, voyant un bon livre imprimé par un autre Maître, parfaitement bien, et avec grande dépense, le contrefont aussi-tôt par une autre impression fort négligée et remplie d'un grand nombre de fautes qui coûte peu d'argent; faisant perdre au premier par cette malice, le gain légitime qu'il pouvait espérer'. About the early privilege system in France, see Elisabeth Armstrong, *Before Copyright. The French Book-privileges System. 1498-1526* (Cambridge: Cambridge University Press, 1990), p. 21.

17   The royal ordinance of Moulins (February 1566) prohibited the publication of any book without 'Our leave and permission, and letters of privilege.' Decrusy, Isambert, Jourdan, *Recueil général des anciennes lois françaises depuis l'an 420 jusqu'à la Révolution de 1789*, Paris, Belin-Leprieur, 1821-1833, 14, p. 210 (hereafter: Isambert).

18   Letter to Pierre Gillis, Fribourg-en-Brisgau, 28 January 1530; about this letter and others testimonies of Erasme's complaints, see K. Crousaz, *Erasme et le pouvoir de l'imprimerie* (Lausanne: Antipodes, 2005), pp. 89-105.

amounted to a 'tort' made to '*my honor* [...] *my person*').[19] Moreover, many individual authors obtained royal privileges to protect the exploitation of their own work. Such evidence speaks of an active role played by the author in the emergent business of the book trade – an involvement that, to some extent, reveals a consciousness of the bond that links authors with their works, of the problems caused by the ubiquity which the press conferred upon their writings,[20] as well as one that suggests a keen interest – on the part of some authors at least – in the legal control and exploitation of their work (as opposed to the myth of the author as a noble and disinterested producer of scholarly works).[21] We should, however, be careful not to over-state the apparent implications of such evidence. That is, such examples should not lead us to conclude that the protection of the author provided the primary focus of the privilege system. Indeed, the general rules of the system gave very little prominence to the author, while some proved to be positively unfavourable. And so, while some authors did, in practice, play an important role in the management and exploitation of their work, by and large the author remained an indifferent – some might say peripheral – figure within the legal system regulating the operation of the book trade.

The first French legislation to use the word 'author', in the sense of someone who composes a text, was the 1551 *Edit de Châteaubriant*, Article 8 of which prescribed all printers to ensure that 'the name of the author' appeared in the works they published.[22] From this date, it was compulsory to make public the person responsible for writing the work. Should this requirement be understood as one concerned to protect an author's right of paternity? Arguably not, in that it sits within an arsenal of rules prima-rily concerned with the censorship of the press at a time when the French monarchy was battling the oncoming tide of the Protestant Reformation. Rather, this prescription was designed to ensure that the author of a text could be more easily identified and so could be held accountable for his

---

19 Preface of the edition of *Œuvres de Clément Marot* (Lyon, 1538).

20 For example, Marot writes in the request for his privilege in 1539 that 'il se trouve de mes *œuvres courantes et disposées par tous les lieux et endroits* de ce royaume, qui sont imprimées et mises en lumière *avec impressions si impertinentes et mal ordon-nées que le plus souvent l'on y voit plus de faultes que de bons mots*' (*Catalogue des actes de François I*, Paris, 1887, 8, n° 33273). This privilege is published in P.A. Becker, 'Das Druckprivileg für Marots Werke von 1538', *Zeitschrift für französische Sprache und Litteratur*, 42 (1914), 224-5.

21 About this myth, see Alain Viala, *Naissance de l'écrivain* (Paris: éditions de Min-uit, 1985), p. 104.

22 *Edit de Châteaubriant du 27 juin 1551*, Article 8, Bibliothèque nationale de France, Manus. Fçs 22061, n 8.

writings. That is, it is a rule of penal responsibility not of protection, and one that resonates with Michel Foucault's idea that the penal appropriation of texts preceded their ownership.[23] During the *Ancien Regime* then, the legislative regime first conceptualised the author as an individual bearing public responsibilities and not one enjoying private rights.

However, authors could and did obtain rights in their works. Never at any time during the *Ancien Regime* were authors ever excluded from the granting of privileges.[24] Indeed, they were among the first subjects to petition for such privileges. In 1504, dissatisfied that the printer Michel Le Noir was printing his work, *Le vergier d'honneur*, without his consent, André de La Vigne petitioned the Parliament of Paris to prevent the printing and sale of the text; judgment was given in La Vigne's favour, and he was granted an exclusive right in his work – perhaps one of the first privileges ever granted in France.[25] During the next few years, other authors, such as Pierre Gringore and Jean Lemaire de Belge, followed La Vigne's example by seeking and securing such privileges.[26] Moreover, in the decades and centuries that followed, many others, like Marot, Rabelais, and later Descartes, continued to ask for and obtain royal privileges.[27]

And yet, if the author was not excluded from the privilege system, neither did he occupy a position of particular reverence within that system – although the privilege obtained by Ronsard in 1554 might seem to suggest otherwise. The *narratio* of Ronsard's privilege set out that 'it could give better order and fidelity of the impression of works only by the *superintendance of the author*'.[28] The pre-eminent role accorded to Ronsard in relation to the

---

23   Michel Foucault, 'Qu'est-ce qu'un auteur?', *Bulletin de la société française de philosophie* (1969), 73-104.
24   As some scholars have suggested. See for example: Jean de Borchgrave, *Evolution historique du droit d'auteur* (Bruxelles: Larcier, 1916), p. 12; G. Boytha, 'La justification de la protection des droits d'auteur à la lumière de leur développement historique', *Revue Internationale du Droit d'Auteur* (1992), 52-100 (p. 60); and, more recently, Bernard Edelman, *Le sacre de l'auteur* (Paris: Le Seuil, 2004), pp. 151-2.
25   Armstrong, p. 36-7. See also Cynthia Brown, *Poets, Patrons and Printers. Crisis of Authority in Late Medieval France* (Ithaca: Cornell University Press, 1995), p. 17.
26   See for example the privilege granted to Pierre Gringore for *Les folles entreprises* (Paris: 1505). See also the privilege granted to Eloi d'Armeval, reproduced in F. Rideau, 'Eloy d'Amerval's privilege (1507)', *Primary Sources*.
27   Indeed, authors secured privileges more frequently in the seventeenth than in the sixteenth century. According to a statistical study by Nicolas Schapira (*Un professionnel des lettres au xvii* siècle. *Valentin Conrart: une histoire sociale* (Paris: Champ Vallon, 2003), p. 126), the number of the privileges granted to the authors between 1636 and 1665 increases from 24.5 % to 43.5 %.
28   The privilege obtained by Pierre Ronsard for *Le bocage*, edited in Paris, 1554, is

production and publication of his work under this privilege was, however, the exception rather than the rule. In general authors were simply treated in the same way as was any other subject of the king. One's status as an author carried with it no entitlement to the granting of a privilege, at least not until 1777. Put another way, the granting of privileges was indifferent to the status of the petitioner, and indifferent to the fact that the petitioner was an author seeking protection of his work.

Because of this, and in the absence of a provision similar to the Venetian Decree of 1545,[29] it happened in France that works were published with a royal privilege but without the author's consent – or worse, against the author's express will. Such was the experience of the lawyer Antoine Lemaistre who, in 1651, was surprised to see that his work, *Plaidoyers*, had been published by Parisian booksellers with a royal privilege. Technically, it was possible for Lemaistre to challenge the validity of the privilege,[30] and he certainly contemplated taking such action. For Lemaistre, the royal privilege had been granted 'in violation of the order of civil society' which prohibited printing 'works of people alive without their agreement and participation'.[31] But, to my knowledge, neither Lemaistre, nor any other author, such as Molière (who was the victim of a similar misadventure concerning the unauthorised publication of the *Précieuses ridicules*),[32] ever actually challenged the granting of such privileges. That being the case, it is impossible to say what weight might have been given to the argument that a work should not be published, nor a privilege granted, without the consent of the author. What can be said, though, is that the privilege system was not established with the principal aim of protecting and securing the interests of the author.

Perhaps, however, the best evidence in support of the idea that the author played a peripheral role in the operation of the book trade at this time lies in the fact that, even if an author obtained a privilege, he was

reproduced in *Œuvres complètes* (Paris, 1930), 6, p. 3.
29   This Decree required printers to obtain the consent of the author (or his heirs) before printing and selling their work; the Decree is reproduced with an accompanying commentary in J. Kostylo, 'Venetian Decree on Author-Printer Relations (1545)', *Primary Sources*.
30   Royal privileges were granted 'sauf le droit d'autrui' meaning that if a third party suffered damage or loss because of the privilege then he or she was entitled to dispute or challenge the grant of the privilege.
31   See the *Preface* of the authorized edition of *Plaidoyers et harangues de Lemaistre* (Paris, 1659).
32   See Molière's *Preface* to the *Précieuses ridicules* (Paris, 1660), in which he writes that he had fallen 'into disgrace to see a stolen copy' of his play 'in the hands of the booksellers accompanied by a privilege'.

nevertheless marginalised by the structure and organisation of the trade itself. As Furetiere wrote in his dictionary at the end of the seventeenth century, 'the royal privileges for print are granted with the aim that the author draws some reward from his labour. But *by the event*, it's only to the advantage of the publisher'.[33] The *event* referred to was the incorporation of the Parisian booksellers and printers in 1618. Before 1618, authors would sometimes publish their own work themselves.[34] After 1618, the Parisian corporation prevented authors from interfering in the printing and sale of their own books.[35] When an author obtained a privilege, he was forced to sell it to the bookseller and could not exercise those exclusive rights himself. And while an author may well have obtained greater reward by selling a manuscript accompanied by a privilege than if he had simply sold the manuscript itself, nevertheless the incorporation of the Parisian trade ensured that the printers and booksellers were in a position to benefit most from the exploitation of such works.

During the seventeenth century, some authors did try to challenge this corporative monopoly but without success. This was particularly true of the forgotten author Le Pelletier who maintained that his privilege entitled him to print and sell his own work.[36] Calling into question the legitimacy of the corporative monopoly, he argued that writing was a form of labour by which he earned his living, and as such it should be as free as any other form of labour, such as agriculture. To prohibit authors from selling their works denied them their means of subsistence as well as diverting them from composing (new) works.[37] However, his arguments failed to convince the Royal Council and Le Pelletier was condemned in 1700 for his violation of the corporative monopoly.[38]

---

33   *Dictionnaire universel* (Rotterdam, 1690), see: 'Privilège'.

34   G. Defaux, 'Trois cas d'écrivains éditeurs dans la première moitié du xvie siècle: Marot, Rabelais, Dolet', *Travaux de littérature*, 14 (2001), pp. 91 et seq.

35   See Article 14 of *Lettres patentes du Roy pour le règlement des libraires, imprimeurs et relieurs de la ville de Paris*, Bibliothèque nationale de France, Manus. Fçs 22061, n° 69, reproduced with an accompanying commentary in F. Rideau, 'Book trade regulations and incorporation of the Parisian book trade (1618)', *Primary Sources*: 'les auteurs des livres ou correcteurs ne pourront avoir d'imprimerie ni presses, en leurs maisons ou ailleurs, *pour imprimer ou faire imprimer leurs livres, ni les vendre*, ni faire afficher, sous leurs noms ou autres'.

36   About this litigation, and for other examples, see Pfister, 'L'auteur, propriétaire', pp. 113-9.

37   'Si l'on privoit les Auteurs de la faculté de vendre eux-mêmes leurs Livres, ce seroit leur ôter les moyens de subsister' et 'les détourner de composer'. Le Pelletier's argument is reproduced in the *Mémoire pour les Imprimeurs et Libraires de Paris*, Bibliothèque nationale de France, Manus Fçs. 22067, n. 156, f. 304.

38   *Arrest du Conseil d'Etat du Roy du 27 janvier 1700*, Bibliothèque nationale de

1.2 The Incompatibility of Property and Publication

During the *Ancien Regime*, the written work was predominantly conceived of as an action – an act of speech – and not as a thing. Drawing upon Roman law principles, some lawyers regarded writing and paper as instruments of speech – a conversation *in vivo* – such that the ownership of any text lay with the owner of the paper or the parchment upon which it was written and not necessarily with the author of the same.[39] Significantly, however, other lawyers at this time expressly differentiated between the intellectual work and the material upon which that work was written. In François Hotman's commentaries upon Roman law, for example, he underlines that the stories of Virgil are not to be confused with the paper upon which they were written,[40] an idea that was developed in subsequent litigation. For example, in 1583, in challenging a privilege obtained for the *Corpus Iuris canonici*, Simon Marion, barrister for the Parisian booksellers, argued that while the work could be reduced to a physical object, it was at the same time a 'spiritual thing'; for this reason, he continued, it should not be the subject of an exclusive privilege, an argument that found favour before the Royal Council.[41] Similarly, in 1610, Jean Corbin was successful before the Parliament of Paris in suggesting that books consist 'more in science than in matter and merchandise' and must consequently be free from any taxes.[42]

France, Manus. Fçs. 22067, n. 160, f. 312.

39   See for example the observations of the sixteenth-century lawyer François Connan, drawing a distinction between painting and writing in this regard: *Commentarius Iuris civilis*, Paris, 1553, tome 1, Lib. III, cap. VI, f. 171, v. 1: 'Hoc differunt, quod pictura magis ad rerum uerarum naturaliumque similitudinem accommodatur, ut eas oculis tanquam praesentes offerat: scriptura uero fatis habet, si animi alterius cogitata nobis declaret, et nobiscum tanquam uiuo sermone colloquatur'. For a more general discussion of the comments of the medieval jurists on these various rules, see: Paola Maffei, *Tabula picta. Pittura e scrittura nel pensiero dei glossatori* (Milan: Giuffrè, 1988); Marta Madero, *Tabula picta. La peinture et l'écriture dans le droit médiéval* (Paris: éditions de l'École des Hautes Études en Sciences Sociales, 2004).

40   *Commentarius in quatuor libros institutionum iuris civilis* (Lyon, 1588), p. 125: 'praetera charta non est pars historia Liuianae, aut carminis Virgiliani: neque quum Virgilium nos habere dicimus, chartam in aliqua ipsius parte numerus'.

41   *Plaidoyez de M. Simon Marion*, Bibliothèque nationale de France, Manus. Fçs. 22071, n. 28, f. 62.

42   *Plaidoyez de Mc Jacques Corbin*, Paris, 1611, chap. CXIIII (*Du privilège des Livres et de l'Imprimerie*), p. 348 (with the decision of the Parliament of Paris from the 25 February 1610). Before Corbin, see also Cardin Le Bret, *Plaidoyers* dans *Œuvres* (Paris, 1689), p. 470, quatorzième action (*l'immunité des excellens ouvrages*), with the decision of the Parliament of Paris from June 1596.

More importantly perhaps, some explicitly sought to link the intellectual work as an object of property with the author of that work. In 1545, in a commentary upon Roman law, the lawyer François Baudouin considered that intellectual works were priceless treasures of human study and that, as a result, if an author wrote upon paper or parchment that belonged to another, then the author should be entitled to retain the work subject to providing compensation to the owner of the physical material for the cost of the same.[43] Some years later, Marion would go even farther with his well-known assertion that: 'by a common instinct, each man recognises every other to be the master of what he makes, invents, or composes. The author of a book is entirely its master'. In support of this idea, Marion developed an argument by analogy, in which the concept of the property in the work of an author finds a parallel in God's dominion over his creation:

> Even speaking in human terms of the greatness of God, and of His power over the things He made, they say that the Heavens and the Earth belong to Him, since they were created by His word, and that the day and the night are His, since He made the light and the Sun. Such that by analogy, the author of a book is entirely its master [...][44]

However remarkable Marion's plea may seem, it is important to qualify the apparent implications of it. In the first place, in this particular litigation, the author of the work – Antoine Muret – was already dead; indeed, Marion was not pleading in support of the privilege, but was instead seeking its annulment. In fact, the existence of authorial property here was an argument marshalled against the power of the State. Indeed, because divine and natural laws obliged the king to respect the property of his subjects, and, in this case, as the author had already made his work public, the king could not reserve it again to someone else by granting a privilege in relation to the same. More importantly, according to Marion, the property that an author enjoyed in his work ended with the publication of that work:

---

43   *Justiniani Institutionem seu Elementorum libri quattuor*, Paris, 1545, ad. 2, 1, 33: 'nulla pateretur ratio, eam haberi vilis charti rationem, ut vel tuarum lucubrationem inaestimabilem iacturam facere, vel eas aliis communicare cogaris [...] ergo si meum carmen, historiam vel orationem (sacrosanctas et inaestimabiles hominis studiosi divitias) in charta forte tua scripserim: satis erit me tibi tuae chartae precium solvere'.

44   *Plaidoyez de M. Simon Marion, advocat en Parlement, Baron de Druy: plaidoyez second, sur l'impression des Œuvres de Sénèque, revueuës et annotées par feu Marc Antoine Muret*, Bibliothèque nationale de France, Manus. Fçs. 22071, n. 28; see F. Rideau, 'Simon Marion's plea on privileges (1586)', *Primary Sources*. About this argument by analogy, see L. Pfister 'L'auteur, propriétaire', pp. 143-6.

that is, after publication the work can no longer be regarded as private property but rather belongs to everyone. The published work is conceived as a *gift* made to the public,[45] and only a privilege – here referred to as the 'right of patronage' – granted by the State in the name of the public, and within the context of a tacit social 'contract', can ensure remuneration in exchange for such publication.[46] This idea of a property limited by publication predominates almost until the end of the seventeenth century. In 1663, d'Aubignac writes that when the printed copies had been sold, the author or his bookseller 'does not have any more the right to prevent the use' of the work 'to all those which buy them [printed copies]; what is done cannot be undone, say our customs, and what we make print is not any more with us'. Each purchaser of a copy is an owner of work and 'can use about it with its will'.[47] And so, while some lawyers and barristers during the sixteenth and seventeenth centuries did strive to conceive of the work as a thing – and as one that belonged to the author of that work – this notion did not extend to the *published work*; that is, during this period, property and publication were considered to be incompatible.[48] It was not until the eighteenth century that the published work began to be conceived of as a property, a development that turned upon the integration of the author within the system of royal privileges.

---

45   About the appearance of this unusual rhetoric, see Natalie Zemon Davis, 'Beyond the Market: Books as Gifts in Sixteenth-century France', *Transactions of the Royal Historical Society*, 33 (1983), 69-88.

46   The author can release his book, 'granting it the liberty enjoyed by all: this may be accorded purely and simply, with no restriction of any kind, or with a reservation, by a kind of right of patronage, that no other person may print it before a certain time. Which is effectively a contract without a fixed name, mutually binding, since there is a fair obligation on both sides, the one not wishing to *give* to the public his personal property, unless the public grant him this prerogative in return […] it is ungrateful to contravene the law of benefit, and to attempt to steal from the public sphere something which the *munificence* of its creator has put there, in order to appropriate it for oneself'; 'Simon Marion's plea on privileges (1586)'.

47   *Troisième dissertation concernant le poëme dramatique en forme de remarques sur la tragédie de M. Corneille* (Paris, 1663), p. 11-2. A similar testimony is offered by Richelet who, in the same period, writes that 'an author who gives to the public his work gives it up and strips [the] property right' (*Dictionnaire de la langue française* (Paris, 1690), see: 'Plagiaire').

48   This was an idea that continued to have some currency well into the nineteenth century. Renouard, writing in 1838, considers that 'to give and retain the thought is impossible'. On the use, in the nineteenth century, of this argument concerning the incompatibility of property and publication, see Laurent Pfister, 'La propriété littéraire est-elle une propriété? Controverses sur la nature du droit d'auteur au XIXe siècle', *Revue Internationale du droit d'Auteur*, 205 (2005), 116-209.

2. The Integration of the Author within the System of Royal Privileges

How does one explain the way in which the author – a figure initially on the periphery of the privilege system – came to be regarded as the owner of his intellectual work? The most direct explanation lies in the evolution of the system itself. In this regard, it is ironic that the conceit of the author as owner of his intellectual work was an invention of the Parisian booksellers, one designed to assist them in defending their privileges against interference from both provincial competition and the State – a conceptual Trojan horse employed to secure their existing monopoly of the market. This re-imagining of the author – of the author as natural owner of his literary property – also drew upon a number of other influences, and in particular the rise of aesthetic and possessive individualism.[49] The attempt of the Parisian booksellers to redefine the author in this way, however, was not without controversy. Indeed, given the implications of this new conception of the author, it was inevitable perhaps that the provincial booksellers would seek to contest it (2.1). Nevertheless, this new conception would prove influential in shaping the reform of the privilege system in 1777 and 1778, an influence that would ultimately prove counterproductive to the best interests of the Parisian booksellers (2.2).

2.1 The Author Re-Invented

During the second half of the seventeenth century, with the support of monarchy,[50] the Parisian booksellers came to monopolise the French book trade and, in attempting to bolster their dominance of the market, they began to articulate the notion of the author as the natural owner of his intellectual work. In two reports by Aubry, a barrister for the Parisian booksellers, the author is presented as the owner of any new composition, and

---

49   In this regard, as Frédéric Rideau has demonstrated, the evolution of literary property in France has parallels with developments in England at this time (even if substantive differences between the two regimes remained); see Rideau, *La formation.*

50   See for example the *Arrêt du Conseil privé du roi* from 27 February 1665 (*Extrait des registres du Conseil Privé du Roy*, Bibliothèque nationale de France, Manus. Fçs 22071, n. 107) which confirmed that the Parisian booksellers could obtain indefinite extensions to their privileges for 'new' books (that is, books composed after the invention of printing). See F. Rideau, 'French Book Trade Regulations (1665)', *Primary Sources.*

it is from the author that the bookseller derives his rights.[51] While this idea was developed to support the arguments of the Parisian booksellers, it was also one that was justified by the increasing professionalisation of writing itself. Indeed, as Aubry noted, writing had 'so to speak, become a trade (*métier*) for earning one's living'.[52]

In 1725 this construct of the author was taken a step further. In that year, the monarchy altered its policy in relation to the book trade and commanded the revocation of all abusive privileges held by the Parisian booksellers.[53] In response, the Parisian booksellers sought to challenge this order by conflating their privileges with arguments that drew upon a theory of natural and perpetual property rights acquired from the author as owner of the work in question. This line of argument was developed by the lawyer Louis d'Héricourt in a memorandum drafted on behalf of the Parisian booksellers.[54] He argued that the work and the exclusive right to print that work were private properties, acquired naturally and originally by the author by virtue of his intellectual labour, and that the author was free to sell his work by contract such that the bookseller who bought it must 'remain perpetually owner' of that work. In this way the booksellers sought to move the author from the periphery to the centre of the legal regime regulating the production and distribution of books. In short, this new conception of authorship was being invoked by the booksellers to usurp the royal authority as the true source of rights, with the role of the privilege relegated to one of simply protecting the natural and perpetual right of literary property.

51   Aubry writes that, contrary to books that were common to all people, 'the particular sorts include all the books which have been produced for the first time in this Kingdom by the individual industry of a bookseller or by the labour of an author who cedes to the latter his work and his right, in some way which the two of them have agreed on Together'. He adds that 'books of recent composition, produced by the labour of a modern author or by the industry of a bookseller, are all the more of private right [sont de droit particulier], given that no one else, apart from that author or bookseller, could possibly claim any sort of property in them'. *Mémoire sur la contestation qui est entre les libraires de Paris et ceux de Lyon au sujet des privilèges et des continuations que le Roy accorde*, Bibliothèque nationale de France, Manus. Fçs. 22071, n. 177, also registred in 22119, n. 21; see F. Rideau, 'Memorandum on the Opposition between the Parisian and the Provincial Booksellers (1690s)', *Primary Sources*.
52   About the professionalization of letters, see Viala, pp. 270-90; Roger Chartier, 'Figures de l'auteur', in *Culture écrite et société. L'ordre des livres (xive – xviiie siècle)* (Paris: Albin Michel, 1996), p. 51.
53   *Arrêt du Conseil d'Etat portant règlement sur le fait de la librairie et imprimerie*, 10 April 1725, Bibliothèque nationale de France, Manus. Fçs. 22062, n. 41. Also reproduced in *Isambert*, 21, p. 287.
54   'Louis d'Héricourt's Memorandum (1725-1726)', *Primary Sources*.

Moreover, whereas during the seventeenth century an author's 'property' was tied to the physical manuscript, now the property in question concerned the 'text' – the work itself, distinct from the manuscript, and regardless of the fact that it had been published.[55] At the end of the seventeenth century, the French lawyer Domat had drawn this distinction between the text and the manuscript upon which it is written, asserting that the author of a text – even of a letter – should be regarded as the owner of the same.[56] But in France, as in England, it was the work of John Locke that proved decisive in influencing this conception of literary property: if the man is owner of his person and of his labour, then an author could easily be regarded as the owner of his spirit and of the fruit of his intellectual labour.[57] In addition, this theory of possessive individualism intertwined with an emergent discourse concerning the creative individual. The legitimacy of being a creator, long reserved to God,[58] and, during the Renaissance, extended to some exceptional artists,[59] was in the eighteenth century more

---

55   For example, Louis d'Héricourt writes that 'a Manuscript […] is so much the property of its Author, that it is no more permissible to deprive him of it than it is to deprive him of money, goods, or even land since, as we have observed, it is the fruit of his personal labour, which he must be at liberty to dispose of as he pleases'; elsewhere, d'Héricourt speaks about the 'property of texts'; 'Louis d'Héricourt's Memorandum (1725-1726)', *Primary Sources*. See also the bookseller Michel-Antoine David, author of the article 'Droit de copie', in Diderot and d'Alembert's *Encyclopédie ou dictionnaire raisonné des sciences, des arts et des métiers*, vol. 5: 'Droit de copie, *terme de Librairie*, c'est le droit de propriété que le libraire a sur un ouvrage littéraire, manuscrit ou imprimé'. He added: '*droit de copie*, ce qui signifie proprement *droit de propriété sur l'ouvrage* […] s'il y a *dans la nature* un effet dont la propriété ne puisse pas être disputée à celui qui la possède, ce doivent être les *productions de l'esprit*'.

56   'It is sure that the master of paper won't become *master of what is written*, even if it is a simple letter' (*Les lois civiles dans leur ordre naturel*, Paris, 1727, Liv. 3, tit. 7, section 2, art. 15, p. 298). In another abstract, Domat distinguishes between the intellectual work and the material upon which it is written (*Les quatre livres du droit public*, Liv. 1, tit. 13, in *Les lois civiles dans leur ordre naturel, le droit public et legum delectus*, 2, p. 98).

57   See for example Gerhard Luf, 'Philosophisches Strömungen in der Aufklärung und ihr Einfluss auf das Urheberrecht', in *Woher kommt das Urheberrecht und wohin geht es?*, ed. by R. Dittrich (Wien: Manz, 1988), pp. 11-2; Diethelm Klippel, 'Die Idee des geistigen Eigentums in Naturrecht und Rechtsphilosophie des 19. Jahrhunderts', in *Historische Studien zum Urheberrecht in Europa*, ed. by Elmar Wadle (Berlin: Duncker et Humblot, 1993), pp. 125-6. About Locke's writings, see Laura Moscati, 'Un *memorandum* di John Locke tra censorship e copyright', *Rivista di storia del diritto italiano*, LXXVI (2003), 69.

58   See for example Ernst Kantorowicz, 'La souveraineté de l'artiste. Note sur quelques maximes juridiques et les théories de l'art à la Renaissance', trad. L Mayali, in *Mourir pour la patrie* (Paris: Presses Universitaires de France, 1984), p. 43.

59   In particular, Dürer and da Vinci; see for example Erwin Panofsky, 'Artiste,

readily extended to all men.[60] At the same time, the concept of originality assumed a new significance as an aesthetic criterion, especially under the influence of the English writer Edward Young. Now, an author was able to give free rein to his imagination and personality.[61]

This merging of aesthetic and possessive individualism was invoked by the spokesmen of the Parisian booksellers – Diderot in 1763, and Linguet in 1774 and 1777 – to forge the modern conception of the author.[62] For Diderot, the work originated within the spirit of the man of letters, within that which makes the person an individual. And, as one's person is understood to be the first property of man, so too must an original work be considered to be the property of the author.[63] For Linguet the composition of a book was an act of 'true creation'; 'if there is a sacred and undeniable property' he asserted 'it is that of an author to his work'.[64] However, both Diderot and Linguet take care to limit the property of the author to the particular 'manner' in which an author might treat a topic or subject, thereby articulating an essential principle of intellectual property: the distinction between form and idea.[65]

Savant, Génie. Notes sur la "Renaissance-Dämmerung"', in *L'œuvre d'art et ses significations. Essais sur les arts visuels*, ed. by M. et B. Teyssèdre (Paris: Gallimard, 1993), p. 128.

60   In 1787 Ferraud notes that the verb is 'strong with the mode: everyone became [a] creator' (*Dictionnaire critique de la langue française*, Marseille, 1787-8, see : 'Créer', p. 626 b).

61   Roland Mortier, *L'originalité, une nouvelle catégorie esthétique au siècle des Lumières* (Genève: Droz, 1982), pp. 50 et seq.

62   See in particular Hesse, p. 114; Alain Strowel, 'Liberté, propriété, originalité: retour aux sources du droit d'auteur', *Journal des procès* (1994), p. 7; Chartier, 'Figures de l'auteur', p. 51; Chartier, 'Qu'est-ce qu'un auteur?', p. 14. In relation to England, see Mark Rose, *Authors and owners. The Invention of Copyright* (Cambridge: Cambridge University Press, 1993), pp. 113-27. For commentary upon Germany, see Martha Woodmansee, *The Author, Art, and the Market. Rereading the History of Aesthetics* (New York: Columbia Press, 1994), pp. 35-55.

63   'Indeed, what can a man possess, if a product of the mind, the unique fruit of his education, his study, his efforts, his time, his research, his observation; if the finest hours, the finest moments of his life; if his own thoughts, the feelings of his heart, the most precious part of himself, that part which does not perish, that which immortalises him, cannot be said to belong to him? What comparison can there be between a man, the very substance of a man, his soul, and a field, a meadow, a tree or a vine which, at the beginning of time, nature offered equally to all men, and which the individual claimed for himself only by cultivation, the first legitimate means of possession? Who has more right than the author to use his goods by giving or selling them?' *Letter on the Book Trade*, Paris (1763), Bibliothèque nationale de France, Manus. Fçs (Naf) 24232, n. 3; see 'Diderot's Letter on the Book Trade (1763)', *Primary Sources*.

64   *Mémoire sur les propriétés et les privilèges exclusifs de librairie*, B.N., Ms. Fr. 22123, n. 50, f. 224. See also the memorandum from 1777: F. Rideau, 'Linguet's memorandum (1777)', *Primary Sources*.

65   About this point, see for example L. Pfister, 'L'œuvre une forme originale. Naissance d'une définition juridique (xviiie – xixe siècles)', in *Littérature et nation*, actes du

While careful to incorporate this distinction within their conception of literary property, Diderot and Linguet were, nevertheless, presenting an argument on behalf of the Parisian booksellers in support of a property in a text lasting in perpetuity; it was one that the provincial booksellers were keen to contest. The provincial booksellers' spokesman, the lawyer Gaultier, in a very important report,[66] rejected the notion of literary property proposed by Diderot and Linguet – a view that was also shared by Condorcet.[67] Gaultier and Condorcet argued that, according to the common law, once a work was published it no longer belonged to the author or to the editor of the work but to everyone. Instead, they presented a theory of social contract in connection with a functional conception of the author. For them, every human production originates within the community of ideas upon which everyone can equally and freely draw for inspiration. According to Condorcet, 'the man of genius does not make books for the money'; Gaultier adds that a man of genius is guided by the desire to educate and instruct his fellow man. When he communicates his thoughts to society, an author does so in exchange for the goods that society has already provided for him.[68] For this contribution to public instruction he will be able to receive a reward – a privilege – but a privilege that is necessarily temporary in nature. That is, it is for the king to limit the duration of these exclusive privileges in order to preserve a public domain, a condition of competition, the free circulation of ideas, and the progress of Enlightenment.

How did the monarchy react to this debate?

2.2 The Compatibility of Property and Privilege

From the middle of the eighteenth century, the king and his ministers began to adopt a more favourable attitude to both authors and their legal

---

colloque *Le plagiat littéraire*, ed. by Hélène Maurel-Indart (2002), 245-68 (pp. 252-6).

66   Jean-François Gaultier, *Mémoire à consulter, pour les Libraires et Imprimeurs de Lyon, Rouen, Toulouse, Marseille et Nismes, concernant les privilèges de librairie et continuation d'iceux*, Bibliothèque nationale de France, Manus. Fçs. 22073, n. 144; see F. Rideau, 'Gaultier's Memorandum for the Provincial Booksellers (1776)', *Primary Sources*.

67   *Fragments sur la liberté de la presse* (1776), in *Oeuvres* (Paris: Firmin Didot, 1847), II, p. 253; see F. Rideau, 'Fragments on the Freedom of the Press (1847)', *Primary Sources*. About Condorcet's analysis see, in particular, Hesse, p. 111.

68   'Every man owes to society the tribute of his physical and intellectual abilities in exchange for that which he receives from the other individuals who comprise it. The man of genius, who communicates his ideas to society, is only returning, in exchange, the product of those ideas that he has received from society'; see 'Gaultier's memorandum for the provincial booksellers (1776)'.

situation. For example, Malesherbes, Director of the *Librairie*, suggested that writers should be free of the corporative monopoly.[69] The *inspecteur de la librairie*, Joseph d'Hémery, advocated the integration of writers within the privilege system and in particular that privileges should be granted exclusively to the authors for the duration of their life.[70] Moreover, during this time authors (and their heirs) also enjoyed some success before the royal courts. Three such examples can be given. The first concerned the dramatic author Crebillon. Prosecuted by his creditors, Crebillon argued before the Royal Council of State that the remuneration accruing from his literary works was not seizable by those creditors as it enabled him to live and encouraged him to produce new works. The Council adjudicated in his favour.[71] Some years later, in 1769, another writer, Luneau de Boisgermain, came into conflict with the Parisian booksellers. Accusing Luneau of 'meddling in the book trade', the booksellers secured an order for the confiscation of several boxes of books that Luneau had arranged to have distributed to various provincial booksellers; Luneau however was successful in having the confiscation order overturned.[72] This case is particularly important because Linguet, Luneau's barrister, co-opted the theory of literary property developed by the Parisian booksellers and turned it against the booksellers own best interests. Linguet argued that the author was the natural owner of his work and that a royal privilege was simply a confirmation of that authorial property; as a consequence, he continued, an author was free to enjoy his property as he wished, a freedom which allowed him to sell his work without regard to the booksellers' corporative monopoly.[73] In

---

69   Chrétien Guillaume de Lamoignon de Malesherbes, *Mémoires sur la librairie. Mémoires sur la liberté de la presse*, presented by Roger Chartier (Paris: Imprimerie Nationale, 1994), pp. 160-1.
70   'Nottes que j'ai remises à M. Marin pour le mettre en état de faire les siennes', Bibliothèque nationale de France, Manus. Fçs 22073, n° 85. About this memorandum, which consists of notes upon Diderot's *Letter on the book trade*, see Pfister 'L'auteur, propriétaire', pp. 290, 294-308. About the testimonies of royal officers, see also Birn, p. 155.
71   F. Rideau, 'Crébillon's Case (1749)', *Primary Sources*.
72   Jugement rendu par M. de Sartine, Lieutenant Général de Police de la Ville, Prévôté & Vicomté de Paris [...] Entre le Sieur Luneau de Boisjermain, et les Syndic & Adjoints de la Librairie & Imprimerie de Paris, Bibliothèque nationale de France: Manus. Fçs. 22073 n. 10; see F. Rideau, 'Luneau de Boisjermain's case (1770)', *Primary Sources*.
73   *Dernière réponse signifiée et consultation pour le Sieur Luneau*, Bibliothèque Nationale de France, Manus. Fçs. 22069, n° 7: 'mes pensées, le manuscrit auquel je les confie, sont encore plus à moi que ma maison ou mon champ. Ces biens par leur nature étaient susceptibles d'une jouissance indivise: la politique seule en a restreint le

the third example, from 1777, the Royal Council allotted to Fénelon's heirs a right to the works of the writer by asserting that the works are a 'good legitimately owned by the family'.[74]

In spite of these judicial pronouncements – or perhaps because of the attention that these decisions, as well as the opinions of administrators such as Malesherbes and d'Hémery, had drawn to the situation of the author – the monarchy reformed the privilege system with two decrees of the Royal Council in 1777 and 1778,[75] the interpretation of which has given rise to notable differences of opinion. Some historians, such as Carla Hesse, refuse to see in these reforms the consecration of the author's property; instead she argues that under the 1777 decree the author was simply a construction of an 'absolutist police state' – one designed to refute the concept of literary property as a natural right, while at the same time reaffirming the 'absolutist interpretation of royal law as an emanation of the king's grace alone'.[76] In my view, however, Hesse's interpretation is incorrect. I would suggest instead that these royal decrees do indeed give recognition

---

partage; mais mes idées à qui sont-elles? Qui peut sans mon consentement, prétendre en partager le domaine? [...] Y a-t-il un être au monde qui puisse en revendiquer la possession, ou la disposition exclusive, au préjudice de celui qui les a conçues et enfantées'. *Réponse signifiée pour le Sieur Luneau*, Bibliothèque Nationale de France, Manus. Fçs 22069, n. 5, p. 29: 'y a-t-il [une loi], peut-il y en avoir qui défende *à des propriétaires de se réserver l'administration de leur bien, de garder sous leurs yeux le produit de leurs récoltes, de prétendre seuls au gouvernement des fruits que leur a procuré une exploitation sage et bien entendue?* Tel est précisément le cas d'un homme de lettres en général, quand il a fait les frais de l'impression de son ouvrage. Cet ouvrage en manuscrit étoit son bien sans doute, il lui appartenoit exclusivement; quand il a été imprimé, *en vertu d'un privilège qui confirme encore cette propriété, a-t-il changé de nature?* [...] Ce livre, dont l'auteur peut se réserver la garde et la possession exclusive quand il étoit en manuscrit, il peut donc aussi le retenir dans ses mains, même après qu'il a passé sous la presse. Cette conduite ne viole pas la loi [...]. Tous usent également de la prérogative accordée par *le droit social et consacrée par les institutions civiles* d'entasser, autour d'eux, sous leur main, l'objet de leur propriété. L'auteur à cet égard ne pourroit, sans la plus cruelle injustice, être placé dans un rang différent des autres propriétaires'. About this litigation and Linguet's arguments, see Pfister, 'L'auteur, propriétaire', pp. 326-40; Rideau, *La formation*, pp. 132-4.

74   Following the expression used by the *Bureau de la Chancellerie*, an office competent to consider litigation about privileges (Archives Nationales, E. 2533, n. 241).

75   Arrêt du Conseil du 30 août 1777, portant règlement sur la durée des privilèges, *Isambert*, 25, p. 110. See also Bibliothèque nationale de France, Manus. Fçs. 22073, n. 146, reproduced with accompanying commentary in F. Rideau, 'French Decree of 30 August 1777, On the Duration of Privileges (1777)', *Primary Sources*; Arrêt du Conseil du 31 juillet 1778, portant règlement sur les privilèges en librairie et les contrefaçons, *Isambert*, 25, p. 371.

76   Hesse, pp. 113-4, 129. See also Borchgrave, pp. 22, 33, and Dury, p. 279.

to the concept of authorial property. In support of this reading, for example, consider the letter addressed to the *Académie Française* by the drafter of the decrees, Miromesnil, the Keeper of the Seal. He writes that it appeared 'fair to him to consecrate in favour of men of letters a *property* on their intellectual productions', and also 'to make them enjoy all the advantages able to encourage their talent'.[77] The property of the author here rests upon two foundations, that of natural right and utilitarianism – it is both a just reward for the labour of the author as well as an encouragement to create for the benefit of all.

Miromesnil's letter, however, does not explain why the decrees continue with the operation of the privilege system instead of formally acknowledging the absolute nature of the author's right. Influenced by physiocratic economic theory,[78] and unwilling to hand over the control of the book trade to the Parisian booksellers, the monarchy decided to confirm a perpetual property in favour of authors and their heirs, while denying that property to the booksellers. In this way, the retention of the privilege system ensured that the State also retained a measure of control over the book trade in general, while at the same time giving recognition to the primacy of an author's labour over the activities of a bookseller.[79] As regards the latter, for example, the preamble to the 1777 decree asserts that the author, on account of his labour, 'has a greater right to a more enduring favour', whereas the bookseller 'may only expect the favour granted to him to be proportional to his total expenditure and to the size of his operation'. Thereby, it seems clear that the author's right, opposite to the bookseller's favour, is a private right, founded of author's labour, recognised by the power and prior to the privilege.

The differentiation between the interests of the author and the bookseller, as well as the nature of the rights enjoyed by the author under these decrees, provides a significant contrast with the situation in England at this time. For one thing, the 1777 decree acknowledges that an author enjoys a right in his work prior to the grant of the privilege. Moreover, the author's

---

77   Letter from 19 February 1778 addressed to the *Académie française*, in Laboulaye and Guiffrey, pp. 627-8.

78   This economic theory was influenced by Locke's theory of property, and favoured the abolition of trade corporations; indeed, one year before the 1777 decree, the physiocratic minister, Turgot, had propsed in vain to have the corporations abolished. About the influence of physiocratic theory on *droit d'auteur*, see Pfister, 'L'auteur, propriétaire', p. 335.

79   See also Philippe Gaudrat, *Propriété littéraire et artistique. Droits des auteurs. Droits moraux. Théorie générale du droit moral*, Jurisclasseur, fasc. 1210, 2001, n/ 11.

right acknowledged is the property of the privilège, the *propriété de droit*, and thereby the property of the intellectual work itself.[80] Also, the duration of the author's creative labour is perpetual in nature, granted for the benefit of the author and his heirs.[81] Moreover, under the influence of the physiocrats, the right secured to the author as the owner of the work is a right to use and enjoy that work; that is, the author was entitled to 'sell that work in his own home', regardless of the corporative monopoly of the Parisian booksellers.[82]

In addition, the decree of 1778 provided that an author might contract with a bookseller to publish his work and still retain control over this work. That is, the author could delegate the printing and sale of his work to a bookseller without losing his property therein.[83] That the contracts between an author and bookseller might be regulated in this way was suggested by Linguet in his pleas for Luneau,[84] and anticipates, to a certain extent, the approach that Kant would later adopt.[85] Should, however, the author actually transfer his privilège to a bookseller then, under the 1777 decree, the duration of the privilège, as a result of that transfer, would be reduced to the life of the author.[86] Entitled only to these temporary privileges, the booksellers were relegated to the role of simple intermediary between the author and the public – the result of a concerted effort on the part of the monarchy to undermine the monopoly which the Parisian booksellers had previously held over the book trade, and to encourage increased public access to more affordable works.[87]

---

80   This recognition of author's property was subsequently confirmed by another decree of the Royal Council from 1786 in favour of musicians (expressly recognising the 'property rights' of musicians). This decree is reproduced with and accompanying commentary in F. Rideau, 'French Decree on Musical Publications (1786)', *Primary Sources*.

81   See the Preamble and Article 5 of the Arrêt du Conseil du 30 août 1777 portant règlement sur la durée des privilèges, *Isambert*, 25, p. 110.

82   Ibid.

83   Article 2 of Arrêt du Conseil du 31 juillet 1778, portant règlement sur les privilèges en librairie et les contrefaçons, *Isambert*, 25, pp. 371 et seq.

84   *Réponse signifiée pour le Sieur Luneau*, Bibliothèque Nationale de France, Manus. Fçs. 22069, n° 5, p. 14: 'Lors même que ces Marchands font imprimer ou vendent des livres en leur nom en apparence, ils ne sont encore que les représentants, les mandataires de l'homme de lettres dont ils ont acquis les droits'.

85   See for example F. Kawohl, 'Kant: On the Unlawfulness of Reprinting (1785)', *Primary Sources*.

86   Article 5 of the Arrêt du Conseil du 30 août 1777 portant règlement sur la durée des privilèges, *Isambert*, 25, p. 110.

87   Arrêt du Conseil du 30 août 1777, portant règlement sur la durée des privilèges, Preamble and Articles 1 to 4, 6 et seq. The preamble sets out that 'a regulation

3. Conclusion

Within a century, under the combined influence of various factors – legal and economic, social and cultural – the author passed from the periphery to the centre of (or at least to a very comfortable place within) the privilege system. Moreover, the idea that the intellectual work was the private property of the author, property which would survive publication, was also admitted. However, both of these developments were contested at the time, and both were vulnerable to forthcoming changes within the legal regime. In 1789, the subtle balance that the royal decrees had established between the interests of the author, the bookseller, and the public, was shattered with the abolition of the privilege system. With the Revolution, the debates on the nature and duration of literary property were revived with an even greater intensity. Extreme positions were adopted by those, on the one hand, who claimed that any property in a work ended with its publication, and by those, on the other hand, who sought to reassert the absolute control over a work formerly enjoyed by the old corporations. Between these two, more moderate proposals emerged. Panckcoucke, for example, favoured the adoption of the English *Statute of Anne*.[88] Sieyès, by contrast, advocated a property right that came to an end shortly after the author's death, and it was, in the end, the proposals of Sieyès that would be enshrined in the two laws of 19 January 1791 (concerning dramatic performances) and 19 July 1793 (concerning literary and artistic property). The combined effect of these legislative measures was to create a new legal regime, less favourable for the author than the royal decrees of 1777 and 1778, but nevertheless one that was founded upon property, as well as one that sought to strike a balance between private and general interests, between private and public property, and between the exclusive rights of the author and his beneficiaries and the freedom of the public to make use of and exploit published works.

---

restricting the duration of the exclusive rights of publishers to the period stipulated by the privilege […] would be to the advantage of the public, who may expect the cost of books to fall in consequence to a level determined by the means of the buyers'. About this, see Robert Dawson, *The French Booktrade and the 'Permission Simple' of 1777: Copyright and Public Domain* (Oxford: The Voltaire Foundation, 1992), pp. 33 et seq.

88   See *Sur l'état actuel de l'imprimerie. Lettres de M. Panckoucke à MM. Les Libraires et Imprimeurs de la Capitale*, dans le *Mercure de France*, 6 March 1790, pp. 32 et seq.

6. A Venetian Experiment on Perpetual Copyright

Maurizio Borghi

The recognition that rights pertaining to intellectual creations are of limited duration is one of the 'constitutional moments' in the making of many copyright laws at the end of the eighteenth century. In the English case of *Donaldson v. Becket* (1774) the House of Lords rejected the claim that authors were entitled to perpetual copyright in their published work, and decisively affirmed the pre-eminence of the statutory time-limited protection.[1] In France, the royal *arrêt* of 30 August 1777 on the duration of privileges established a seminal distinction between authors' absolute property right in their creations and the limited duration in the exercise of such right once it has been transferred to a publisher.[2] On the other side of the Atlantic, the principle of limited duration for rights pertaining to creations and inventions has been entrenched in the so-called 'intellectual property clause' of the Constitution of the United States, which came into effect in 1789.[3]

It was in the same period of time that the Prince of Venice approved a ruling on the art of printing.[4] It was just the last of the many attempts to improve the fortunes of a printing industry that found itself increasingly incapable of replicating the performance of its renowned past. The

---

1 See Ronan Deazley, 'Commentary on *Donaldson v. Becket* (1774)', *Primary Sources*, and the bibliography quoted therein.
2 'French Decree of 30 August 1777 on the Duration of Privileges', *Primary Sources*.
3 The constitutional clause provides that Congress shall have the power: 'To promote the Progress of Science and useful Arts, by securing *for limited Times* to Authors and Inventors the exclusive Right to their respective Writings and Discoveries' (Const. U.S. Art. 1, § 8, Cl. 8) (emphasis added). On the backgrounds of the clause, see Oren Bracha, 'Commentary on the Intellectual Property Constitutional Clause 1789', *Primary Sources*.
4 Terminazione degli Eccell. Riformatori, 30 Luglio 1780, '"Pezzana e Consorti" Case: Supporting documents, Venice (1780)', pp. 49-53, *Primary Sources*.

ruling urged 'new efficient measures and useful remedies' in order to stop the 'current disarray' and to relieve the art from the 'present state of decadence'. The root of all troubles being 'the quantity of books lying unsold on the shelves', and this in turn being the effect of 'the excessive amount of books whose privilege has expired', upon which a number of printers 'hurl themselves all at once', so that several editions of the same book flood the market fuelling 'disorder, worse quality of printing, black-market selling by unlicensed and even foreign traders': for all these reasons it was ruled that 'licence to reprint a book whose privilege has expired shall be exclusively granted to the initial owner of the privilege', whether he was the printer or the author, 'and this for as long as he should want'.[5] The ruling introduced a dramatic change in the privilege system that was in force for about three centuries in the *Serenissima* Republic and privileges became, *de facto*, perpetual.

One year later, the ruling was reaffirmed in a case adjudicated before the Senate, whereby a group of booksellers and publishers (*Pezzana e Consorti*) opposed, as claimants, representatives of the Guild as respondents.[6] The claimants' arguments against the perpetuity of privileges were dismissed, although the Senate affirmed the need to 'carefully supervise' the effects of the newly introduced system.

In 1789, less than a decade after, the ruling was eventually revoked and the system abandoned, thus restoring the previous system of twenty year non-renewable privileges. The decree amending the privilege regulation acknowledged 'abuses and harmful consequences of perpetual privileges'.[7] This was the last act of the *Serenissima* Republic on the subject of the printing press.[8]

The Venetian experiment is a remarkable example of the difficulties that lawmakers encounter when trying to accommodate the tension between monopolies in the book trade economy and freedom to use public domain resources. From a more general perspective, this ten year experience can be regarded as a legal experiment aimed at regulating the access to – and

---

5   Ibid.
6   27 Settembre 1781, reprinted in Horatio F. Brown, *The Venetian Printing Press* (New York: Putnam's Son; London: John C. Nimmo, 1891), pp. 315-6.
7   Terminazione 10 Giugno 1789, reprinted in Brown, pp. 384-8.
8   On the history of the Venetian printing press in the eighteenth century see Mario Infelise, *L'editoria veneziana nel '700* (Milano: Franco Angeli, 1991). Venice's fall occurred only seven years after the mentioned decree, as effect of Napoleon's first Italian campaign. The last doge of Venice, Ludovico Manin, was deposed on 12 May 1797 after the Peace of Leoben between France and Austria.

the extraction of economic value from – the public domain, in a phase of the history where the public domain as such revealed itself as a critical value for both the economy and society, and modes of production, distribution and the reception of books and other 'cultural products' were changing accordingly.[9] Interestingly, this experiment with perpetual protection occurred within the most evolved and experienced privilege system of the modern age, in a time when the emerging principles of the *ius naturalis* increasingly overlapped with the traditional systems of market regulation, thereby shaping most of the legal principles constituting the modern copyright system.[10]

The Legal Nature of the Book Privilege: Exceptions to Law, Regulatory Instrument or (Publishing) Contract?

The Venetian Bill of 1780 is not the one and only experiment with perpetual protection in the five century history of copyright law.[11] It is, however,

9   In the Venetian experiment the notion of 'public domain' tends to have the strict economic meaning of 'books freely reprintable'. However, some of the arguments put forward in the *Pezzana e Consorti* case suggests at the same time a broader understanding, covering aspects such as the free availability of basic knowledge for readers and scholars (see for example Pezzana's counter-petition of 28 March 1871: 'In all possible sciences and arts [...] there has always been a series of classic and original books, consecrated by time and the universal consensus of mankind and all nations. Theology, History, Medicine, all the endless arts and sciences are planted on these *foundations of indispensable books*, that is books which can be rightly called *of first necessity*.' '"Pezzana e Consorti" Case: Counter-petition and Rulings (1781)', trans. by Luis A. Sundkvist, p. 7, *Primary Sources* (emphasis added)).

10   The above mentioned French decree of 1777 can be seen as an example of this overlap and shaping. The transition of the privilege system into forms of intellectual property, that took place from the end of eighteenth / beginning of nineteenth century, represents the first 'paradigmatic change' of copyright law. For a reading of copyright history based on Kuhn's notion of 'paradigm' see Willem F. Grosheide, 'Paradigms in Copyright Law', in *Of Authors and Origins. Essays on Copyright Law*, ed. by Brad Sherman and Alain Strowel (Oxford: Clarendon Press, 1994), pp. 203-33.

11   Examples of perpetual copyright can be found in statutes of some Latin American countries at the end of the nineteenth century: Guatemala (Literary Property Act 1879, Art. 5); Mexico (Civil Code 1884, Art. 1253 – where, however, the 'right to perform in public' was limited to 30 years *post mortem auctoris*); Venezuela (Civil Code 1880, Art. 2). For details, see Ch. Lyon-Caen and Paul Delalaine, *Lois françaises et étrangères sur la propriété littéraire et artistique*, 2 vols (Paris: Cercle de la Librairie etc.; F. Pichon Éditeur, 1889), II, pp. 117, 132 and 165). Perpetual reproduction and republication rights has also been enacted in the 1927 Portuguese copyright law, before being replaced in 1966 by a life plus 70 system (see C. Trabuco, *O Direito de*

a unique case where such a solution has been effectively used in a pre-'intellectual property' regime, namely in a regulatory regime based on the ancient privilege system. For this reason, the first step of our analysis will be to contextualise the Venetian experiment within its own legal conceptuality, as determined by the very legal nature of the book-privilege.

As a first general characterisation, privilege can be described as a law introducing an *exception* to the law, namely to the benefit of an individual or class of individuals. The *Zedler* lexicon enumerates more than twenty types of *privilegium*, and explains the meaning of the word as *priva lex*: 'a law or a ruling specifically pertaining to single persons (*privus*)'.[12] Privilege is therefore:

> [A] specific right or freedom which the legislator grants to the subject citizen, exempting him from the law. Such *privilegia* can be granted by any legislative authority to any subject who submits a justified claim and who is entitled to draw a legitimate benefit from it.[13]

Accordingly, the book privilege – *privilegium impressionis operum* – bestows the publisher with the exclusive right and freedom to print a work, thereby releasing him from the competition of other publishers. The rationale for awarding such release is analogous to that underlying the granting of privileges for other productive activities, namely, to ensure protection from competitors in order to recoup the initial investment. In a popular eighteenth century business dictionary we can read that the privilege is a useful legislative instrument:

> [O]nly for those industries that require an investment that is so high, the return so uncertain and initially so modest that it is very unlikely that a single individual be willing to take on the burden – but industries whose introduction into the nation is so useful to justify a measure that, with the aim of not immediately destroying their business, temporarily protects it from its competitors.[14]

Reprodução de Obras Literárias e Artísticas no Ambiente Digital (Coimbra: Coimbra Editora, 2006), pp. 121-2). In France, a proposal for perpetual copyright was discussed by the Parliament in 1862 and eventually rejected. On this subject see the pamphlet of P.J. Proudhon, 'Les Majorats littéraires (1868)', *Primary Sources*.

12   J.H. Zedler, *Grosses vollständiges Universal-Lexikon aller Wissenschaften und Künste* (Leipzig und Halle: 1732-50), entry *Privilegien*, 29, p. 589. In Roman law *privilegium* was used sometimes as being synonymous with *ius singulare* (A. Berger, *Encyclopedic Dictionary of Roman Law* (Philadelphia, 1953), entry *Privilegium*, p. 651).

13   Zedler, 29, p. 589.

14   H. Lacombe De Prezel, *Dictionnaire du citoyen, ou abrégé historique, théorique et pratique du commerce* (Paris, 1756), entry: *privilege*.

In this text, which can be taken as exemplary of the mercantilist view of the economy,[15] three requirements are mentioned in order for a privilege to be justified: the industry that the privilege applies to must be *new,* it must require *an initially high investment,* and it must be of particular *utility* to the national economy. When such 'test' is applied to book publishing, it appears that the requirements are potentially fulfilled not only at the initial stage, when the industry as such is 'new' to the nation, but each time a new book is being published. As a matter of fact, publishing a new book is always a risky and uncertain activity, where investments are easily jeopardised by 'free riders'. For this reason, privileges are not exceptional measures for the publishing industry: rather, they represent a necessary infrastructure – at least as far as new editions are concerned.[16] In order to properly operate, such an industry needs privileges just as much as it needs paper and ink.

In this respect, the rationale justifying book privileges is not different from that which is commonly used today by mainstream economists to explain the need for intellectual property protection for 'non-excludable goods', namely: creating artificial exclusion in order to avoid free riding and enable recouping of investments. From this point of view, both the ancient privilege and the modern copyright law can be seen as systems of market regulation for goods that are not 'naturally' excludable.

The first and foremost question arising with such kind of 'exceptions to law' is: *for how long* should the exception be in force? Should the exception last forever, or should it in turn be limited in time? And, if this were the case, what would be a fair and appropriate duration of the given exception?

These questions lie at the very heart of both the ancient and the modern copyright lawmaking, and a number of arguments have been used by scholars and jurisprudence to justify time restrictions in the exercise of author's or publisher's rights.[17]

Limited duration finds its justification also within the so called 'authorship paradigm', where the earliest raison d'être of copyright law lies in the permanent link that the author establishes with his work by virtue of the

---

15   See Donald J. Harreld, 'An Education in Commerce. Transmitting Business Information in Early Modern Europe', paper presented at the XIV International Economic History Congress, Helsinki, 21-25 August 2006.

16   As we will discuss in the next paragraphs, the requirement that books must be 'new' in order to be eligible for privilege is a cornerstone in the process of codification of the Venetian privilege system (see *infra* notes 35-8 and accompanying text).

17   For an overview see Joseph P. Liu, 'Copyright and Time: A Proposal', *Michigan Law Review*, 101 (2002), 409-81 (pp. 428-52).

act of creation.[18] As an example of how civil law jurisprudence justifies the statutory limits of copyright duration, we can read the following excerpt from a classic Italian treaty on *diritto d'autore*:

> After the author has published his work, thus allowing society at large to share it, his work becomes part of human civilization, and the public appropriates it, so that it can criticise it, use it while creating new works, and so forth and so on; the later the work is published, the more influence the work exerts on civilization, the less it belongs to its author and, so to say, breaks away from him to enter the public domain.[19]

After breaking into the realm of 'human civilization' as part of it, thanks to the creative act of its author, the work takes on a life of its own, and the more it moves out into the world, the fainter becomes the echo of its creation. Although no work can completely break its original liaison with its creator, it is nonetheless true that with the passing of time such a liaison becomes weaker and changes its meaning. Indisputably, works such as Shakespeare's sonnets, Dickens's novels or Joyce's *Ulysses* belong nowadays more to humanity at large than to their respective authors or heirs. But the same principle applies to all kind of works, since, once published, they become part of a 'whole' that gradually incorporates them.[20]

A third, and perhaps more acknowledged, rationale for copyright's limited duration is the argument based on the idea of a 'contract' between the author and the society at large, the former being rewarded by the latter for the benefits he provides by giving his work to the world. Since the benefit is intrinsically limited (no author creates *ex nihilo* – so runs the argument), the reward, in terms of a temporary monopoly over certain uses of the work, must be limited in turn.

An exemplary expression of the 'contract' argument was penned by Proudhon:

> Between the author and society there is a tacit agreement, by virtue of which the author will be paid *à forfait* by means of a temporary privilege of sale. If there is a great demand for the work the author will earn a great deal.

---

18   For a comprehensive and insightful discussion of the classical 'duality' between 'marketplace norms' (typical of Anglo-Saxon copyright laws) and 'authorship norms' (inspiring continental-European laws), see Paul Geller, 'Must Copyright Be For Ever Caught between Marketplace and Authorship Norms?', in Sherman and Strowel, pp. 159-201.

19   Nicola Stolfi, *La proprietà intellettuale*, vol. II (Turin, 1911), p. 39.

20   The argument that 'the longer a work has been published, the lesser copyright protection does it deserve' inspires the proposal of Joseph Liu of adjusting the scope of copyright protection by considering time as a factor in fair use analysis (see Liu, 'Copyright and Time').

If the work is refused he will earn nothing. Let's allow him an exclusive right that lasts for 30, 40, or 60 years to cover the costs. I say that this contract is perfectly regular and fair, and that it satisfies all the needs, safeguards the rights, respects the principles, and responds to all objections.[21]

Copyright can be metaphorically described as a contract between the author and society at large. But this is, precisely, a metaphor. Copyright is not a contract that can be revoked on grounds, for example, of non-fulfilment. It is not, legally speaking, an agreement whose terms could be modified according to the quality of the work done. Paradoxically, works that disclose the most spectacular and useful knowledge, and which may have required years of study and labour, benefit from the same 'contractual terms' as the most trivial and frivolous ones.[22] In the course of the nineteenth century, copyright law has progressively entrenched the 'principle of neutrality', namely the rule that copyright arises independently of the 'merit or purpose' of a work.[23] Modern copyright can be described as a content-neutral system, whereby rights are granted unconditionally to anyone who 'authors' anything, irrespective of the worth of the creation. No substantive examination is required. The 'originality' qualification is not an absolute test of quality, but only a minimal requirement that the work actually originated from the author.[24]

By contrast, privilege is a real – not only 'metaphorical' – contract between the State and the publisher. As we will see in the next paragraphs, while detailing the Venetian system, the privilege can be understood as a true publishing contract that the State signs with a publisher on certain conditions. And this contract is not, in principle, 'content-neutral'. The duration of the privilege, as well as its scope,[25] can depend on the quality of the work. The granting and maintenance of the privilege is subject to

21   Proudhon, p. 24.

22   This 'paradox' is being incidentally discussed in many cases and treaties of the nineteenth century. For example Antonio Scialoja observed that copyright, by virtue of the idea/expression divide, tends inevitably to promote *more* the works that contribute *less* to the progress of knowledge (Antonio Scialoja, 'Relazione alla Legge 25 giugno 1865 n. 2337 sui diritti spettanti agli autori delle opere dell'ingegno', *Atti del Senato* (1864), 1136).

23   On this 'trend' towards 'a position of neutrality' towards the content of works see Geller, p. 182.

24   For an in-depth analysis of the concept of originality in copyright law see Abraham Drassinower, 'Authorship as Public Address: On the Specificity of Copyright vis-à-vis Patent and Trade Mark', *Michigan State Law Review*, I (2008), 199-232.

25   For instance the extent of sanctions and the amount of remedies that were usually provided with the privilege. See examples in Rinaldo Fulin, 'Documenti per servire alla storia della tipografia veneziana', *Archivio veneto*, XXIII (1882).

controls over quality and price. It can be revoked on many grounds, including non-use or delay of use.[26] The counterpart of the privileged publisher is not an abstract notion of 'society', but the State as such, its concrete representations and agencies, its appointed inspectors and superintendents, who permanently watch over the fulfilment of the contract. Privilege is not a title of property. It cannot be assigned or transferred. If the publisher is unable to fulfil the mandate, namely to publish the work for which the privilege was sought *in the form and at the conditions* that are specified in the privilege itself, the latter can be simply revoked. The legal nature of the privilege consists essentially of a publishing contract between the State and the printer.

It is within such a contractual-like framework that the Venetian privilege system evolved over three centuries, from the early variable-term grants to the concluding experiment with perpetual protection.

The Origins of the System in the 'Golden Age' of the Venetian Printing Press (the Fifteenth and Sixteenth Centuries)

The Venetian legislation on the privilege system was administered by the *Riformatori dello Studio di Padova*. After its institution in the early 1500s as a judiciary responsible for the reform of the University of Padua, it was then appointed in charge of all matters concerning the circulation of books and journals, which included, first and foremost, the sensitive task of censorship. Their duties covered a range of subjects, from press censorship to the governance of the book market and production in general, hence including the regulation of the privilege system. Over the years the *Riformatori* became the legal advisory body of the Republic whenever a problem concerning the printing press was on the agenda.

As to the running of the privilege system, several interventions have been recorded over the three centuries of its existence, spanning from substantial law making to dispute resolution, day-by-day administration, and even *ad personam* decisions.[27]

---

26   See *infra* the Venetian decree of 1533.
27   For a broad overview of the activity of the *Riformatori* see G.B. Salvioni, 'L'arte della stampa nel Veneto: la proprietà letteraria', *Giornale degli Economisti di Padova*, IV (1877), 191-285.

At the time the *Riformatori* took over the regulation of the press, the practice of the Venetian authorities of granting temporary monopolies over the exploitation of books or series of books had already been in place for decades.[28] The average and customary duration of these monopolies was ten years, although there are many cases of both shorter and longer privileges, as well as privileges of unspecified duration.[29] In a few cases privileges were required and granted for up to twenty or even twenty-five years.[30] The rationale justifying such differing durations is not always clear and it may be that this depended more on contingent factors than on advised policy. As a matter of fact, it is not even wholly clear what the criteria were to be applied in the granting or refusal of a privilege. In general, the authorities seemed to be orientated towards maintaining a certain proportion between the value of the book and the duration of the monopoly, and this could have justified a shorter duration – or even the refusal – of a privilege for reprints, whereas a longer privilege was usually granted to books requiring an exceptional investment (such as dictionaries, illustrated books, and editions of classics). The latter could also have been rewarded with a term extension once the privilege was expired.[31] In one particular case, a privilege of only one year was granted: it was for a booklet explaining remedies against pestilence, and it might be the case that reasons of 'public interest' had suggested the granting of such a *short* monopoly.[32]

However, such a case-by-case system soon became unsustainable in a market place that numbered around one hundred and fifty publishers, with more than a hundred new editions being launched every year. Even though privileges were sought only for a minority of highly qualified and commercially valuable books (in a range of about one in ten),[33] the lack of certainty as to the eligibility criteria and the scope of protection encouraged practices that were detrimental to the whole art. Powerful publishers accumulated privileges covering wide ranges of books, which then, by virtue of renewals or further privileges obtained from a different authority after the

---

28 The first known printing privilege granted by the Venetian authorities dates back to 1469 (see 'Johannes of Speyer's Printing Monopoly, Venice (1469)', *Primary Sources*). A comprehensive collection of requests and grants of privileges from the period 1469 to 1526 is available in Fulin, pp. 84-212.

29 Brown, pp. 236-40.

30 Fulin, n. 41, 150, 188, 189 and 206.

31 Ibid., n. 137.

32 Ibid., n. 178.

33 Between 1470 and 1500 about three thousand editions were published in Venice, while the total number of known privileged editions in the same period is 298 (data drawn from Brown).

expiration of the first grant, became *de facto* perpetual monopolies.[34]

The first known act of the *Riformatori* was a general regulation of the granting of privileges. The decree of 1 August 1517, concerning the printing trade, revoked all existing privileges and introduced a 'novelty' requirement for all works.[35] The only works eligible for a privilege were those that had never been printed before. In addition, 'blanket privileges' covering wide and even indeterminate ranges of works were disallowed. The authority of granting privileges was vested in the Senate only, requiring a two-thirds majority.

This decree was the first of a series of legislative interventions that, in the subsequent two decades, shaped the Venetian privilege system in a thorough anti-monopoly sense. In 1533 a decree introduced a further restrictive provision, whereby any privileges would become void if the book was not printed within one year from the granting of the privilege itself.[36] The one-year term could be extended in the case of voluminous works. Along with this 'use it or lose it' provision, it was affirmed that no privilege could be obtained twice for the same book.

With the *Parte* of 4 June 1537, sanctions and remedies were introduced for counterfeiters and for printers issuing books of bad quality. Most importantly, the 'novelty requirement' was reasserted and more narrowly constructed, requiring that a book should not be considered *new* 'only by virtue of few amendments and corrections'.[37] The *Parte* of 7 February 1544 settled that no book could be printed or sold in the absence of an 'authentic document' providing evidence that the author of the book in question, or his heirs apparent, granted permission to print and sell.[38] The novelty requirement, the 'use it or lose it' clause, limited duration and author's permission became the four pillars of the Venetian privilege system of the sixteenth century.

With the requirement that only previously unpublished books were eligible for privilege, the Senate aimed at two objectives. The first was to avoid double granting, which would have unduly extended the duration of the monopoly. The second, which was perhaps more important, was

---

34   Joanna Kostylo, 'Commentary on the Venetian Senate's first Decree on Press Affairs (1517)', *Primary Sources*.

35   '[Grace is conceded] *solum pro libris et operibus novis numquam antea impressis, et non pro aliis* – only for new books and works never printed before, and for none else'. 'Venetian Decree on Press Affairs, Venice (1517)', p. 2, *Primary Sources*.

36   Brown, pp. 208-9.

37   Ibid., pp. 209-10.

38   'Venetian Decree on Author-Printer Relations (1545)', *Primary Sources*.

to discourage book reprinting and to provide an incentive for investing in the production of new books. While reprints were mainly sold in the domestic market, new editions represented a true added-value for publishers operating in the international arena.[39] For this reason, in this first series of legislative acts, 'novelty' was to be interpreted as 'absolute novelty', that is, a book was considered to be new if never printed previously, *anywhere*.[40] The meaning of 'novelty' has been subject to reviews over the three centuries of the Venetian printing press. The main problem was the evaluation of books whose 'novelty' consisted merely in the addition of supplements and amendments to previous editions. The issue had been repeatedly addressed in different legislative acts, starting from the above mentioned 1537 decree, but it was not until 1753 that an examination procedure was put in place in order to assess the 'worth of supplements and amendments' in new editions of books.[41]

The purpose of the 'use it or lose it' clause was clearly to disallow the blocking effects of the monopolies. Privileges were intended to promote production, not to be mere 'intangible assets' in a publisher's portfolio. A manuscript lying unprinted on one publisher's shelves could have been successfully exploited by a competitor. The same rationale inspired the limited duration of privileges.

Harmonising Duration, Defining Novelty, Eroding the Public Domain: The Privilege System in the Seventeenth and Eighteenth Centuries

It was not until the beginning of the seventeenth century that the duration of privileges was standardised. The decree of 11 May 1603, which represents the first overall codification of the privilege system in Europe, harmonised the duration of privileges introducing a three-tier system: the duration was standardised at twenty years for books 'never printed before anywhere'; books lacking novelty but which were 'never printed before in Venice' and those 'of great value' which had been out of print for at least twenty years

---

39   Like Manuzio, Torresani, Giolito (just to mention the major ones). For a thorough history of the Italian publishers operating in the international market during the Renaissance see Angela Nuovo, *Il commercio librario nell'Italia del Rinascimento* (Milano: Franco Angeli, 2003).

40   As we will see below, this criteria has been afterwards re-designed in the seventeenth and eighteenth centuries.

41   See *infra* note 44.

were granted a privilege of ten years; finally, books 'of great value' which had been out of print for at least ten years were granted a privilege of five years. In practice, only reprints of books out of print for less than ten years were not eligible for a privilege.[42]

Table 1. Privilege Term Duration in the 1603 Part

Duration	Category of books	Scope of novelty requirement
20 years	New books	Absolute novelty
10 years	Reprints – if never printed in Venice Or	Territorial novelty
	Books 'of great value' out of print for at least 20 years	Relative novelty *plus* 'special merit' qualification
5 years	Books 'of great value' out of print for at least 10 years	

This three-tier system applied to different categories of books, and the scope of the 'novelty' requirement for eligible books was modulated accordingly. Longer privileges were granted to books meeting an 'absolute novelty' requirement, that is, books never printed before anywhere. A shorter privilege, however, was still available for books previously printed elsewhere, thus meeting a narrower 'territorial novelty' requirement. Finally, also books printed previously in Venice, but no longer in print, were eligible, according to a sort of 'relative novelty' requirement coupled with a 'special merit' qualification.

In spite of the standardisation of the duration, the Venetian privilege system maintained a logic of discrimination, to the extent that the content of the book (its 'value') was still a discriminating factor in deciding whether a book already in the public domain could be re-privileged.

Although the 1603 *Parte* unambiguously settled a 'novelty' requirement in order for a book to be privileged, thus excluding the possibility of granting a further privilege after the expiring of the initial one, it was still not clear what standard of novelty was used with respect to second 'revised' editions of books. On 15 January 1725 the judiciary felt the need to intervene to limit the practice of seeking privileges for further editions of books printed previously 'on the pretext of supplements and amendments'.[43] As a general rule, it was stated that *no privilege can be granted twice for the same*

42   'Venetian Decree on Privileges for New Books and Reprints (1603)', *Primary Sources*.
43   Brown, pp. 724-8.

book, although no guidance was given as to the meaning of the term 'same'. The rule was repeatedly asserted in 1745 and in 1753, when, as mentioned above, an appointed procedure of examination was eventually introduced, in order to assess 'the worth of supplements and amendments' in new editions of books.[44]

Uncertainty about the status of reprinted books was at the origin of most of the disputes between publishers in the eighteenth century. On 27 July 1763 the *Riformatori* issued an *ad hoc* decision declaring that a specific book was in the public domain.[45] In a petition submitted one year later by the Venetian Guild of Booksellers and Printers (30 March 1764) it was affirmed that the price of the book in question dropped from ten pounds to four pounds after the decision. The petition complained about the unfair handling of the privilege system: while some publishers had their privileges unduly extended on the grounds of 'petty supplements and amendments, of little or no importance', others suffered undue losses because the privileges on most of their backlist titles had irretrievably expired.[46] In these years the interventions of the *Riformatori* became more frequent, and were often handled in collaboration with the Venetian Guild of Booksellers and Printers. The complaint of the latter eventually led to the first main amendment of the privilege system: the *Parte* of 6 February 1765 introduced a principle according to which a number of books in the public domain where allocated to 'needy printers', that is, to printers in financial difficulties.[47] A list of one hundred and four titles, including consumer books such as ABCs, dictionaries and classics, was then appointed, and a tortuous procedure of allocation by auction was put in place. This system introduced a sort of regime of 'exceptions' to the public domain: from then on, books whose privilege had expired were in the public domain *except* if the Guild declared that they were to be included in the special list.

As to the duration of privileges, the three-tier system of twenty, ten and five years, established in the 1603 Act, remained unchanged for more than a century and a half. In 1767 the duration for new books was extended to thirty years, and that of reprints to fifteen years irrespective of the length of time they had been out of print.[48] However, only Venetian printers were eligible for these extended privileges: books printed on the *terraferma* (that is, on the

---

44   *Parte* of 26 August 1753, in Salvioni, p. 205.
45   Ibid., p. 206.
46   Ibid., p. 208.
47   Ibid., pp. 209-10.
48   *Parte* of 29 July 1767, in Brown, pp. 298-300

Venetian Republic mainland) were granted, respectively, only ten or twenty years protection. Secondly, no privilege would be granted to books whose privilege had expired, and no *terraferma* publisher could print a book in the 'public domain' when it had been previously owned by a Venetian printer.

Table 2. Privilege Term Duration in the 1767 Part

Duration	Category of books	Scope of novelty requirement
30 years (20 if printed on *terraferma*)	New books	Absolute novelty
15 years (10 if printed on *terraferma*)	Reprints, if never printed in Venice	Territorial novelty
No privilege – *terraferma* excluded	Books whose first Venetian privilege is expired	Territorial public domain

The System in the Age of Crisis: The Perpetual Privilege Experiment (the End of the Eighteenth Century)

The term extension of 1767 must be appreciated against the background of the rising conflict between the traditional publishing manufacture, based in Venice, which came under the umbrella of the Guild, and the emerging modern book industry based on the *terraferma*. In spite of the unfavourable legal conditions, compared to those enjoyed by the members of the Guild, *terraferma* publishers were by large the driving force of the Venetian publishing industry by the mid-eighteenth century.

While the traditional Venetian publishing industry was losing its leadership, not only in the international market, but also in the Italian one, a new capitalistic industry was successfully emerging in some areas of the Venetian mainland, thus balancing the increasingly weaker performances of the *matricolati* (members of the Guild).[49] One publisher in particular must be mentioned, namely Remondini of Bassano, one of the biggest publishing companies in Europe at the time. An increasing number of publishers from the city, members of the Guild, were almost exclusively working on orders from Remondini. In this way, Remondini could bypass the restrictions imposed on printers of the *terraferma* and have access to the privilege

---

49   Infelise, p. 223.

system *via* its Venetian commissioners. At the same time, Remondini and his associates were able to exploit public domain books more efficiently than other printers. By virtue of modern machinery and an efficient distribution system, Remondini was better suited than his Venetian counterparts to take advantage of mass-production. Not only were classic texts reprinted in cheap high-circulation editions, but also translations, abridgments and compilations on an extensive range of subjects were printed on a low-cost basis, thereby bringing the prices to a very low level.[50]

In 1750 Remondini was finally admitted as a member of the Guild, although he was allowed to maintain his establishment in Bassano. In this way, he was able 'to combine the double benefit of having access to the same privileges as any other publisher in the city, and also to the lower production costs of the *terraferma*'.[51]

In 1780 the head of the Guild Marcantonio Manfré submitted a petition complaining about 'a disorder which destroys all good faith and proper work in the art of printing, and undermines the revenues and business of the printing workshops and bookshops of this *Dominante*'.[52] The source of this 'disorder' was the 'proliferation of print', and this in turn was due to the excessive number of unprivileged books that 'fatten the bookstalls of colporteurs, unlicensed and unregistered sellers, not members of the Guild'. As soon as a book falls into the public domain, many printers 'take possession of it' at the same time, and as a result, a huge number of copies, usually of low quality, flood the market thus reducing the price. The argument was plain: unprivileged books fuelled the 'junk production' of the *terraferma* printers (low price for low quality), provoking a drop in prices and consequently in revenues. In order to reduce this abundance of books in circulation, the prior of the Guild suggested a radical remedy, which would have inspired an even more radical measure, the redefinition of the Venetian privilege system as was in force for almost three centuries: 'to issue a prohibition, whereby books which have been rendered common property upon expiry of their privileges may not be reprinted other than by two matriculated members of the Guild at most, namely by the first one who undertakes this task and by only one more apart from him'.

---

50 Marino Berengo, 'La crisi dell'arte della stampa veneziana alla fine del XVIII secolo', in *Studi in onore di Armando Sapori* (Milan: Istituto Editoriale Cisalpino, 1957), II, p. 1325.
51 Ibid., p. 1326.
52 'Memoriale Manfré e Compagni, 1780 in Maggio', in '"Pezzana e Consorti" Case: Supporting Documents, Venice (1780)', pp. 46-9, *Primary Sources*.

The ruling of the *Riformatori* of 30 July 1780 converted this complaint into a Bill.[53] Since the root of the troubles of the Venetian printing press was apparently the number of books available in the public domain, the legal solution was simply to eliminate the public domain as such. More accurately, the temporary privilege was replaced by a system of perpetually renewable privilege: 'Be it enacted that henceforward the first legitimate owner of a privilege, and only him, shall be entitled to seek licence for reprinting the book in question once the privilege is expired, and this for how many reprints he wants'; and the same right 'shall have, before the privilege owner, whoever he is, the author of the work in question, as it has always been done'. The public domain was hence limited to books 'abandoned' by the first privilege owner or by the author. However, any publisher could seek a ten year privilege for up to six 'abandoned' books. Moreover, a list of about a hundred books to be reserved to 'printers in financial difficulties', was maintained.[54]

The duration of privilege, as established in the 1767 Act, was amended as follows:

Table 3. Perpetually Renewable System (1767)

Duration	Category of books	Scope of novelty requirement
30 years (20 if printed on *terraferma*) – Indefinitely renewable	New books	Absolute novelty
15 years (10 if printed on *terraferma*) – Indefinitely renewable	Reprints, if never printed in Venice	Territorial novelty
10 years – Indefinitely renewable	'abandoned' books (up to 6 per publisher)	

In order for a book to fall into the public domain, it should have been 'abandoned' after the first or a subsequent privilege term *and* not be required by any publishers *or* recorded in the list of books to be used by printers in need. The public domain was, *de facto*, cancelled.

---

53 Terminazione degli Eccell. Riformatori, 30 Luglio 1780.
54 A tricky system of allocation of books between 'printers in need' was defined in a further ruling of 28 September 1780.

The *Riformatori*'s Bill, as inspired by the Guild's petition, was passed by the Senate on 9 August without any substantial amendments.[55] Such an unprecedented measure, however, was harmful for the most 'capitalistic' part of the Republic's publishing industry which relied heavily on public domain books. This part was represented not only by Remondini – who, although not mentioned in the Guild's complaint, was the real addressee of the grumbles – but also by its main competitors in the new and promising market of cheap editions. Hence, the Bill and its inspiring petition were opposed by a group of twelve publishers lead by Francesco Pezzana who submitted a counter-petition to the Senate on 28 March 1781.[56]

In the *Pezzana e Consorti* petition, many commercial arguments against the perpetual privilege were put forward. The publishing industry, it was argued, is nourished by an 'abundance of genres', while monopoly keeps prices artificially high. Moreover, monopolies discourage the circulation of books, since the owner of an exclusive right to sell has no incentive to circulate his book, and, because of the system of exchange,[57] 'by limiting the circulation of his book he destroys also that of the other'. Furthermore, the complaint stressed the importance of maintaining 'a basis of essential books' (classics and the like) in the public domain, since they represent the necessary 'infrastructure' of the book trade, and 'a monopoly over these books would deprive a business of its very basis, thus striking at the root of its trade, also making it impossible for a printer to venture into new editions'.[58]

The public domain of books, which in the Guild's petition was regarded as the source of all evils, was addressed by *Pezzana e Consorti* as the very basis of the publishing business. Granting a monopoly over this basic infrastructure would have meant depriving the whole industry of its starting material, and reducing the 'abundance of genres' which represented the basic layer which sustained the whole market place for books.

The case was discussed in due form before the Senate, and a counter-argument submitted by the Guild, replying to *Pezzana e Consorti's*

---

55   Decreto dell'Eccell. Senato, 9 Agosto 1780, in '"Pezzana e Consorti" Case: Supporting Documents, Venice (1780)', pp. 54-6, *Primary Sources*.

56   '"Pezzana e Consorti" Case: Counter-petition and Rulings (1781)', pp. 1-19, *Primary Sources*.

57   According to this system of distribution each book house (which normally functioned both as publisher and as bookseller) could keep an assorted stock of books by 'exchanging' their own books with other book houses.

58   Ibid.

arguments was heard on 20 April 1781.[59] The decision of the Senate issued on 27 September 1781 was in favour of the Guild and of the *Riformatori*'s Bill, and thus for the maintenance of the perpetual-privilege system.[60] However the Senate seemed aware that the Bill represented a major departure from the legislative trail, since it addressed an unconventional recommendation to the *Riformatori* to carefully supervise the effects of the Bill 'upon the advantage of the art of printing and upon the universal benefit of the subjects [of the Republic]'.[61]

During its nine years of life the system was assessed twice as to its effects. In 1784 a detailed report on the state of the publishing industry remarked a slight progress in the number of printing presses in activity: although there was no conclusive evidence that the improvement was due to the new privilege system, the report strongly advocated for its maintenance[62]. Apparently the positive trend was continued in the following years.[63] However, on 1 May 1789, a further review of the whole printing press concluded that the effects of the perpetual privileges were more harmful than beneficial.[64] As a consequence of this, the *Riformatori* eventually took the view of revoking the system of perpetual privileges and re-established the previous terms of thirty and twenty years for new books and reprints respectively. Acknowledging 'abuses and harmful consequences that derived from the perpetual privileges that were granted to booksellers and printers of the Guild upon every category of books', the *Riformatori* terminated all the privileges for 'common place books, such as school, religious, and other small-size books', and restored the previous twenty year system for all new books. The Senate enacted the Bill on 10 June 1789.[65]

Conclusion

The Venetian experience is not only a case concerning the duration of monopolies. It is, above all, an experiment *on* the public domain. It is an attempt at administering this *res nullius* which, unexpectedly, became a

---

59   Memoriale avversario, 20 Aprile 1781, in '"Pezzana e Consorti" Case: Counter-petition and Rulings (1781)', pp. 20-1, *Primary Sources*.
60   27 Settembre 1781, in Brown, pp. 314-5.
61   Ibid., p. 315.
62   Relazione 15 luglio 1784 (Antonio di Prata), in *Archivio di Stato di Venezia*, Rifor-matori, filza 47, c. 43-7.
63   Infelise, p. 330.
64   Brown, pp. 320-4.
65   Ibid., p. 324.

valuable resource and perhaps even *the* most sought-after raw-material for a brand new mode of production – namely, the emerging capitalistic publishing industry. In general terms, we can observe that the duration of legal monopolies over creative products becomes a burning issue whenever a technological or cultural shift transforms the public domain into a valuable resource. Or, alternatively, it increases significantly the value and the importance of the stock of creations which are not owned or controlled by anyone. Faced with such a structural changing in the mode of production, the Venetian legislator responded with a parallel changing in the legal system, which in practice extended to the whole public domain the monopoly regime that was traditionally applied only to 'new' works. Insofar as the book privilege can be described, in its legal essence, as a sort of 'publishing contract' between the State and the publisher,[66] the experiment with the perpetual privileges represented an undefined extension of the 'terms' of the contract, whereby both new books and reprints benefited from the same conditions.

The solution eventually revealed itself as either useless or even detrimental to the printing industry, and therefore was abandoned. In this U-turn, the privilege system and its underlying contractual approach revealed an unexpected virtue, namely a certain 'ductility' coupled with a safe pragmatism.[67]

Compared to the ways in which other jurisdictions, in those same years, dealt with the conflicts over the duration of monopolies,[68] the Venetian experiment represents more an ending point than a constitutional moment. It is the end of the privilege system as was in force for three centuries, and of all the world that flourished around it.

---

66   See *supra* par. 1.
67   Compare this evidence-based approach to term duration with the policy that is being adopted nowadays on the same subject. For a discussion of recent developments on the matter see Christophe Geiger, 'The Extension of the Term of Copyright and Certain Neighbouring Rights – A Never-ending Story?', *IIC* (International Review of Intellectual Property and Competition Law), 40 (2009), 78-82.
68   See *supra* notes 1-3 and accompanying text.

7. *Les formalités sont mortes, vive les formalités!* Copyright Formalities and the Reasons for their Decline in Nineteenth Century Europe

Stef van Gompel*

1. Introduction

At present, the national copyright laws of most countries do not contain copyright formalities such as the registration of copyright, the deposit of copies, the affixation of a copyright notice, and so on. This is due, in particular, to the prohibition on formalities, which was introduced into the international copyright system at the 1908 Berlin Revision of the Berne Convention for the Protection of Literary and Artistic Works.[1] This

---

*   I would like to thank P.B. Hugenholtz, J.J.C. Kabel, L. Bently, A. van Rooijen, the members of the Study group on the history of copyright of the Dutch copyright organisation *Vereniging voor Auteursrecht* and the participants of the AHRC Primary Sources on Copyright History Project Conference, which was held in London on 19-20 March 2008, for their valuable comments on an earlier draft of this chapter. Any errors are my own.

1   Art. 5(2) BC (1971), previously Art. 4(2) BC (1908), reads: 'The enjoyment and the exercise of these rights shall not be subject to any formality [...]'. Except for purely national situations, the provision prohibits contracting states from imposing formalities on authors or copyright owners. Once countries began to protect foreign works automatically, i.e. without formalities, however, it made little sense to retain the same prerequisites for domestic works. For this reason, copyright formalities

prohibition on formalities is inspired mainly by pragmatic reasoning. When international copyright protection was first explored, there was a strong desire to relieve authors from the multitude of formalities with which they needed to comply in order to secure protection in different states.[2] Apart from that, the proceedings of the various conferences that modelled the Berne Convention do not reveal any philosophical, ideological or dogmatic arguments for their abolition. Thus, the rationale behind the proscription of formalities at the international level seems to be practical rather than idealistic.[3]

In the recent debate on a possible reintroduction of copyright formalities, however, it is often suggested that the absence of formalities in copyright law is attributable, to a great extent, to the ideological foundation of copyright and authors' rights.[4] It is generally asserted, for instance, that subjecting the enjoyment or exercise of copyright to formalities undercuts the notion of copyright as springing from the act of authorship,[5] and that,

---

were gradually abolished, or reduced to a minimum, in virtually all countries. This effect has increased because of the incorporation by reference of Art. 5(2) BC (1971) in both the TRIPS Agreement (Art. 9(1) TRIPS Agreement) and the WIPO Copyright Treaty (Art. 1(4) WCT).

2   Illustrative, in this respect, is the opening speech which Numa Droz, president of the Berne conferences of 1884-86, held at the opening meeting in 1884, in *Actes de la Conférence internationale pour la protection des droits d'auteur: réunie à Berne du 8 au 19 septembre 1884* (Berne: Imprimerie K.-J. Wyss, 1884), p. 21: 'Une seconde question est celle des formalités à remplir pour la constatation du droit. Les écrivains et les artistes demandent sous ce rapport la plus grande simplification. Tel pays a conclu récemment vingt-cinq conventions pour la propriété littéraire et artistique. Si ses ressortissants doivent remplir vingt-cinq fois la formalité de l'enregistrement et du dépôt, cela devient tout ensemble fastidieux et coûteux'.

3   Nonetheless, some academics assume that the removal of formalities at the international level is strongly based on philosophical underpinnings. See for example Silke von Lewinski, *International Copyright Law and Policy* (Oxford: Oxford University Press, 2008), p. 119 (no. 5.58), and Adolf Dietz, *Copyright Law in the European Community: A Comparative Investigation of National Copyright Legislation, with Special Reference to the Provisions of the Treaty Establishing the European Economic Community* (Alphen aan den Rijn: Sijthoff & Noordhoff, 1978), p. 25 (no. 54), who believe that the rationale behind the prohibition on formalities lies in 'natural rights' theory.

4   The reintroduction of formalities has been called for, in copyright literature, inter alia, by Lawrence Lessig, *Free Culture: How Big Media Uses Technology and the Law to Lock Down Culture and Control Creativity* (New York: Penguin Press, 2004), pp. 287-90, and Christopher Sprigman, 'Reform(aliz)ing Copyright', *Stanford Law Review*, 57 (2004), 485-568; and in economic literature, inter alia, by William M. Landes and Richard A. Posner, 'Indefinitely Renewable Copyright', *University of Chicago Law Review*, 70 (2003), 471-518 and François Lévêque and Yann Ménière, *The Economics of Patents and Copyright* (Berkeley Electronic Press, 2004), p. 105.

5   See Jane C. Ginsburg, 'A Tale of Two Copyrights: Literary Property in Revolu-

similar to any other property right, authors should have property rights over their creations 'naturally', that is without compliance with formalities.[6] Because these moral claims cannot be traced back to the Berne Convention, this raises the question of whether, except for the practical reasons for prohibiting formalities at the international level, there were other – ideological or pragmatic – reasons why formalities in copyright law have generally fallen out of favour.

An investigation into the history and theory of copyright formalities in nineteenth century Europe may well unveil these reasons. Throughout the nineteenth century, the national laws of most European states subjected literary and artistic property rights to formalities of some kind. This certainly was the case in the still premature copyright or authors' rights legislation in Europe at the beginning of that century. Yet, even as the century approached its end and the copyright laws of most countries had been better developed, only a few European states had completely done away with formalities.[7] Nonetheless, there was a clear tendency among more and more countries to begin to reduce their application, or to mitigate their legal effects.

This chapter will therefore examine, from a legal-historical perspective, how formalities developed in the nineteenth century literary and artistic property laws of some European states and why their attachment to literary and artistic property rights gradually weakened in the course of the century. The states that will be discussed here are France, Germany, the Netherlands and the UK. These countries are chosen because they influenced, to a greater or lesser degree, the development of the doctrine of copyright and authors' rights in Europe. This study will focus exclusively on domestic legislation. The international protection of copyright, which started in the second part of the nineteenth century, will not be further analysed.[8] Also, the history of copyright formalities in the USA, which perhaps

---

tionary France and America', in *Of Authors and Origins: Essays on Copyright Law*, ed. by Brad Sherman and Alain Strowel (Oxford: Clarendon Press, 1994), pp. 131-58 (pp. 133-4, 147), who touches upon formalities in an attempt to demonstrate that in the period following the French Revolution, the goals and principles underlying the seemingly author-oriented French *droit d'auteur* system were similar to those of the utilitarian and society-oriented US copyright system.

6   See Lessig, pp. 250-1, who strongly rejects the idea that copyright would be 'a second-class form of property' if it were conditional on formalities.

7   See the overview in Ernst Röthlisberger, *Der interne und der internationale Schutz des Urheberrechts in den verschiedenen Ländern: Mit besonderer Berücksichtigung der Schutzfristen, Bedingungen und Förmlichkeiten* (Leipzig: Börsenverein der Deutschen Buchhändler, 1904).

8   In France, works of foreign origin were protected by the Decree of 28-30 March

can be regarded as the country of formalities par excellence, will not be considered. Since the (partial) removal of formalities in US copyright law in 1989 was based fully on making US copyright law compliant with the Berne Convention,[9] the history of formalities in the USA cannot explain why formalities have lost their significance for copyright and authors' rights. Moreover, whereas the history of US formalities has been frequently analysed in past studies, this study seeks to close the gap left by the sparse analysis of the history of formalities in nineteenth century Europe.[10]

Besides contributing to the literature on the history and theory of copyright and authors' rights, the aim of this study is to further the insight into the question of copyright formalities in general. As observed, this is particularly important in view of the increased calls for a reintroduction of copyright formalities. Because the author-centred *droit d'auteur* doctrine, which in the course of the nineteenth century was developed in continental Europe, is often seen as a great, and perhaps even unbridgeable obstacle to reintroducing formalities, it seems critical to the debate to explain whether, and to what extent, formalities were consistent with the dominant philosophies of copyright and authors' rights in Europe at different stages of the nineteenth century. This is where this study attempts to make a contribution.

For systematic reasons, this chapter will be split in two parts, covering the first and second half of the nineteenth century respectively. The first

---

1852. In the UK, international copyright protection was secured by the International Copyright Act (1844), 7 and 8 Vict., c. 12, as amended, inter alia, by the International Copyright Act (1852), 15 and 16 Vict., c. 12 and the International Copyright Act (1875), 38 and 39 Vict., c. 12. In Germany and the Netherlands, on the other hand, works of foreign origin did not receive protection unless they were (first) issued by a domestic publisher and/or printed by a domestic printing house.

9   Berne Convention Implementation Act of 31 October 1988, Pub. L. No. 100-568, 100th Cong., 2nd Sess., 102 Stat. 2853. This act became effective on 1 March 1989. In implementing the Berne Convention, however, the US government employed a minimalist approach. At present, therefore, US federal copyright law still draws heavily on copyright formalities. For works of US origin, registration is a prerequisite for initiating an infringement action. Moreover, for works of both US and foreign origin, the recovery of statutory damages and attorney's fees is limited to instances of infringement occurring after registration. See 17 U.S.C. §§ 411 and 412.

10   Although the literature on the history of copyright and authors' rights is very rich, to the author's knowledge, it does not yet contain a comparative analysis of copyright formalities in nineteenth-century Europe. Unquestionably, there are some interesting historical accounts, but they only present an overview of the state-of-the-art of formalities in national law at a given moment in time. See for example A.W. Volkmann, *Zusammenstellung der gesetzlichen Bestimmungen über das Urheber- und Verlagsrecht: Aus den Bundesbeschlüssen, den deutschen Territorialgesetzgebungen und den französischen und englischen Gesetzen* (Leipzig: Polz, 1855), pp. 132-6.

part shall begin with a short overview of formalities in the early legislation on literary and artistic property, followed by a description of their nature and legal effects. It shall be seen that while, in the UK, formalities were relatively mild, the laws in continental Europe included rather rigorous formalities. The part shall conclude by identifying the main reasons for this divide. The second part shall look at how formalities developed in the laws of the different states in the second half of the century. While, in the Netherlands and the UK, formalities were generally retained, in Germany, there was a tendency to limit their use and, in France, to soften their nature and legal effects. These tendencies will be explained on the basis of some ideological, functional and conceptual innovations that transformed copyright and authors' rights law during the nineteenth century. Furthermore, a few reasons explaining why the same developments did not occur in the Netherlands and the UK shall be given. A short conclusion shall present the main findings of this study and link them to current debate.

2. Copyright Formalities in the First Half of the Nineteenth Century

2.1 A Short Overview of Formalities in National Copyright Law

The early legislation on literary and artistic property on the European continent involved many formalities. The French decree of 19-24 July 1793, which conferred an exclusive reproduction right in 'writings of all kind' and 'productions of the *beaux arts*', included the requirement for authors of literature or engravings to deposit two copies of their work at the National Library or the Cabinet of Prints of the Republic respectively.[11] The formality of legal deposit was also contained in early Dutch copyright law,[12] and

---

11 Art. 6 of the Decree of 19-24 July 1793 on the property rights of authors of writings of all kind, of music composers, of painters and of designers. The French Decree of 13-19 January 1791 on theatrical plays, which was followed by a Decree of 30 August 1792, also included a formality. It required authors, who wished to retain a public performance right in their plays, to publicly announce this by a notice, which should be deposited with a notary and printed at the text of the play. Because the 1791 Decree was repealed by the Decree of 1 September 1793 and this formality did not reappear in later acts, however, it will not be further discussed here.
12 Art. 7(b) of the Act of the Batavian Republic of 3 June 1803; Art. 12 of the Sovereign Enactment of 24 January 1814; Art. 6(c) of the Dutch Copyright Act of 25 January 1817 ('an act establishing the rights which in the Netherlands can be exercised in relation to the printing and publication of literary and artistic works').

in the copyright laws of several German states, such as those of Bavaria, Hamburg, Holstein and Lübeck.[13]

Another formality that was commonly applied was the registration of works. In Saxony, for instance, registration on the Leipzig *Eintragsrolle* (entrance roll) was a general condition for the protection of works of literature and the arts.[14] In Prussia, on the other hand, there was no registration requirement in respect of literary and musical works. Yet, authors of a work of art needed to register a claim at the *obersten Curatorium der Künste* of the Ministry for Cultural Affairs in order to reserve an exclusive reproduction right in their works.[15] A similar rule was provided for in the state copyright law of Saxe-Weimar-Eisenach.[16]

Several laws also stipulated a notice formality of some kind. In the Netherlands, the law prescribed that the publisher's name, together with the place and date of publication, were to be imprinted on the work.[17] The Bavarian law also required works to be duly marked with the author's or publisher's name.[18] Lastly, in several copyright acts, reservation requirements were laid down for retaining specific rights, such as the translation

---

13 Art. V of the Bavarian Act of 15 April 1840 concerning the protection of property in productions of literature and the arts from publication, reproduction and reprint; Art. 11 of the Decree of Hamburg of 1847; Art. II of the Letter patent of the Chancellery (*Kanzleipatent*) of 30 November 1833, whereby a Resolution from the German Federal Assembly (*Bundesversammlung*) on the reprint of books was publicly announced and carried out, for the Duchy of Holstein; Art. 7 of the Regulation of Lübeck against reprinting, as well as for the protection of musical and dramatical works from unauthorized performance of 31 July 1841. It appears that the legal deposit was also linked to the protection of literary and artistic property in Sonderhausen and Luxemburg. In other German states, it was less commonly applied. See Johannes Franke, *Die Abgabe der Pflichtexemplare von Druckerzeugnissen: Mit besonderer Berücksichtigung Preussens und des deutschen Reiches, unter Benutzung archivalischer Quellen*, Sammlung bibliothekswissenschaftlicher Arbeiten, 3 (Berlin: A. Asher and Co., 1889), pp. 72-3.
14 Act of Saxony of 22 February 1844 concerning the protection of rights in literary works and works of the arts, and the accompanying Decree of the same date to execute this act. See also Friedemann Kawohl, *Urheberrecht der Musik in Preussen (1820 - 1840)*, Quellen und Abhandlungen zur Geschichte des Musikverlagswesens, 2 (Tutzing: Schneider, 2002), p. 276, notes 61 and 62.
15 Arts 27 and 28 of the Prussian Act of 11 June 1837 for the protection of property in works of science and the arts from reprint and reproduction.
16 Arts 27 and 28 of the Act of Saxe-Weimar-Eisenach of 11 January 1839 for the protection of property in works of science and the arts from reprint and reproduction.
17 Art. 7(a) of the Act of the Batavian Republic of 3 June 1803; Art. 5 of the Sovereign Enactment of 24 January 1814; Art. 6(b) of the Dutch Copyright Act of 25 January 1817.
18 Art. II of the Bavarian Act of 15 April 1840.

right for literary works.[19]

Similar formalities were in place in the UK. The 1710 Statute of Queen Anne, which was still in force at the beginning of the nineteenth century, contained a number of formalities. To acquire the protection afforded by the Statute of Anne, the recipient of the right was required, before publication, to enter the title of a literary work in the register book of the Stationers' Company.[20] Also, the law imposed a duty to deposit nine copies of each new book and reprint with additions, before publication, to the Stationers' Company's warehouse keeper.[21] In 1801, this number of copies was increased to eleven,[22] but lowered to five, in 1836.[23]

Other types of copyright, such as the copyright in engravings, prints and lithographs and in sculptures, models and casts, existed without registration. Nevertheless, the copyright in these works was generally subjected to a notice requirement. The 1735 Engravers' Copyright Act required the date of first publication and the name of the copyright owner to be truly engraved on each plate and printed on each print.[24] Likewise, the 1798 and the 1814 Sculpture Copyright Acts required the name of the copyright owner and the date of publication to be put on the work before it was published and exposed to sale or otherwise put forth.[25]

---

19   See for example: Art. 4(b) of the Prussian Act of 11 June 1837; Art. 4 of the Act of Hessen-Darmstadt to secure the rights of writers and publishers of 23 September 1830; Art. 4(b) of the Act of Saxe-Weimar-Eisenach of 1839; and Art. 2 of the Act of Braunschweig of 1842 for the protection of property in works of science and the arts.

20   Sec. 2 of the Act for the Encouragement of Learning (1710), 8 Anne, c. 19.

21   Ibid., Sec. 5. The copies were destined for the use of the Royal Library (later: the British Museum); the university libraries of Oxford, Cambridge and four universities in Scotland; the library of Sion College in London; and the library of the Faculty of Advocates at Edinburgh.

22   Sec. 6 of the Copyright Act (1801), 41 Geo. III, c. 107. While extending the law of copyright to Ireland, this Act required two extra copies to be deposited for the libraries of Trinity College and the King's Inns in Dublin.

23   Sec. 1 of the Copyright Act (1836), 6 and 7 Will. IV, c. 110. The reason why the number of copies was considerably reduced was to alleviate the burden for the book trade, which for long had tried to find a means of relief from the outrageous 'tax' of the deposit. See R.C. Barrington Partridge, *The History of the Legal Deposit of Books Throughout the British Empire* (London: Library Association, 1938), pp. 60-79.

24   Sec. 1 of the Engravers' Copyright Act (1735), 8 Geo. II, c. 13.

25   Sec. 1 of the Models and Busts Act (1798), 38 Geo. III, c. 71 and sec. 1 of the Sculpture Copyright Act (1814), 54 Geo. III, c. 56.

2.2 The Nature and Legal Effects of the Early Copyright Formalities

2.2.1 General Observation

The copyright formalities contained in the literary and artistic property laws of the first half of the nineteenth century differed significantly in their nature and legal effects. In general, they were either constitutive or declarative of the right. In the former capacity, formalities were initial conditions for the coming into existence of the right. They essentially operated as one-way switches between non-protection and protection: literary and artistic property rights were recognised only if the prescribed formality had been duly complied with. Therefore, the nature and legal effects of constitutive formalities were rather harsh. Works for which the prescribed formality had not been fulfilled automatically fell into the public domain. Hence, for beneficiaries of the right, this involved an assessment of whether a certain work would be commercially valuable enough to warrant protection, that is, whether the expected revenue of royalties would exceed the costs of complying with the formality.[26] Formalities of this kind thus 'imposed an initial filter separating works with significant potential commercial value for which authors desired protection from other works for which protection was irrelevant'.[27]

By contrast, the nature and legal effects of declaratory formalities were relatively soft. In general, declaratory formalities can be characterised as means for authors to acknowledge and formally claim possession of their rights. This was considered important, inter alia, as proof in court proceedings. In view of that, the penalty for non-compliance was not the defeat of rights, but the impossibility of enforcing them (or claiming other benefits).[28] Yet, one may query what the rights are worth if they are unenforceable and, in effect, without a remedy if the prescribed formalities are not fulfilled.[29]

---

26   Friedemann Kawohl and Martin Kretschmer, 'Abstraction and Registration: Conceptual Innovations and Supply Effects in Prussian and British Copyright (1820-50)', *Intellectual Property Quarterly*, 2 (2003), 209-28 (pp. 221-2).

27   Sprigman, p. 502.

28   Examples of declaratory formalities can still be found in US federal copyright law.

29   See for example John M. Kernochan, 'Comments on Discussion Bill and Commentary Prepared for the April 15 Subcommittee Meeting as a Proposed Draft of Implementing Legislation to Permit U.S. Adherence to Berne', *Columbia-VLA Journal of Law & The Arts*, 10 (1986), 693-704 (p. 703).

Failure to comply with declaratory formalities, however, did not as such prevent authors from exercising their rights (as was the case with constitutive formalities which, if not fulfilled, caused complete loss of protection). In fact, the rights could still be legally assigned, licensed, exploited, and so on. Furthermore, it will be seen that, in the course of the century, declaratory formalities were held to be curable. Any failure or imperfection in completing the formality could always be repaired before legal action was started. This significantly mitigated the – otherwise harmful – nature of these formalities.[30]

2.2.2 The Nature and Legal Effects in Practice

Interestingly, the nature and legal effects of formalities varied considerably on both sides of the Channel. While most formalities in the British copyright system were declarative rather than constitutive of the right, the opposite was true for the majority of formalities in the early-nineteenth century literary and artistic property laws in continental Europe.

The formalities contained in the laws of the Netherlands and some German states were express conditions for the coming into existence of the right. In the Netherlands, to come into possession of and claim the property right in literary works, the law stipulated a compulsory deposit of copies and required that the publisher's name, together with the place and date of publication, be indicated on these works.[31] Likewise, in Bavaria, copyright did not attach to works of literature and the arts without these works being duly marked with the author's or publisher's name.[32] Finally, in some German states, the coming into existence of literary or artistic property depended on a compulsory registration or mandatory deposit of copies.[33]

---

30   At the same time, this greatly weakened the incentives for authors to fulfil these formalities, thus undermining the effectiveness of the system. In many countries, formalities were poorly complied with.

31   Art. 6(c) of the Dutch Copyright Act of 1817. Art. 8 of the Act of the Batavian Republic of 3 June 1803 also threatened with the loss of copyright if these formalities were not fulfilled. Art. 6 of the Sovereign Enactment of 1814, however, seemingly subjected the existence of authors' rights to compliance with the legal deposit, though not with the copyright notice. See Chris Schriks, *Het kopijrecht - 16de tot 19de eeuw: Aanleidingen tot en gevolgen van boekprivileges en boekhandelsusanties, kopijrecht, verordeningen, boekenwetten en rechtspraak in het privaat-, publiek- en staatsdomein in de Nederlanden, met globale analoge ontwikkelingen in Frankrijk, Groot-Brittannië en het Heilig Roomse Rijk* (Zutphen [etc.]: Walburg Pers/Kluwer, 2004), p. 393.

32   Art. II of the Bavarian Act of 15 April 1840.

33   See for example: the Act of Saxony of 22 February 1844; Art. 11 of the Decree of Hamburg of 1847.

Other formalities were not constitutive of the property right, but only affected its exercise. In Bavaria, the legal deposit functioned as a condition to sue (*Prozeßvoraussetzung*): in legal action against counterfeiting, the receipt given upon the deposit of the copies needed to be presented as evidence before the court, otherwise the claim would be declared inadmissible.[34] In Holstein and Lübeck, on the other hand, the receipt of deposit did not serve as a condition to sue, but as legal evidence of the property and publication date of the work only.[35]

In France, the legal deposit also seemed to be designed as a condition for the institution of a copyright infringement proceeding. The law stated that failure to satisfy the deposit resulted in inadmissibility of an infringement claim before a court should an author want to file suit against a counterfeiter.[36] However, from the outset, courts repeatedly considered compliance with the deposit as constitutive of the author's property right.[37] It was ruled, for example, that an author who published a work without completing the legal deposit was without right vis-à-vis third parties who had later published and deposited the work.[38] In 1834, the Court of Cassation ruled that even though authors' rights did not exist because of the deposit, the latter at least was a formality necessary for the author to reserve its exclusive enjoyment. As the law only promised to secure the rights of those authors who had fulfilled the deposit, failure to do so would render the author's property right void.[39] Finally, it was held that the legal deposit was not merely a condition to sue. The Court of Rouen found that its purpose was

34   Art. V of the Bavarian Act of 15 April 1840.
35   Art. II of the Letter patent of the Chancellery (*Kanzleipatent*) of 30 November 1833 for the Duchy of Holstein; Art. 7 of the Regulation of Lübeck of 31 July 1841.
36   Art. 6 of the French Decree of 19-24 July 1793.
37   For the situation in France until the end of the Napoleonic era, see Ginsburg, pp. 147-8. See, more generally, Eugène Pouillet, *Traité théorique et pratique de la propriété littéraire et artistique et pratique et du droit de représentation*, ed. by Georges Maillard and Charles Claro, 3rd edn (Paris: Marchal and Billard, 1908), p. 474 (no. 434). In the first half of the nineteenth century, many courts assumed that protection could only be obtained if the formalities prescribed for acquiring the authors' rights were fulfilled. See for example French Court of Cassation, 30 January 1818, *Michaud v. Chaumerot*, Sirey (1er Sér.) 18, 1, 222 (p. 224), which found that the plaintiff had observed 'toutes les formalités prescrites pour s'en assurer la vente exclusive'.
38   See for example Royal Court of Paris, 26 November 1828, *Troupenas, Gaz. trib.* 29 November 1828, which held that the author's right could not be restored by way of a deposit subsequently made.
39   French Court of Cassation, 1 March 1834, *Thiéry v. Marchant, Dalloz* 1834, 1, 113; *Sirey* (2me Sér.) 1834, 1, 65. See also French Court of Cassation, 30 March 1838, *Dalloz* 1838, 1, 194; Imperial Court of Paris, 22 November 1853, *Escriche v. Bouret, Rosa et autres, Dalloz* 1854, 2, 161.

essentially that the author reserve an exclusive property right over his creation by formally announcing that he had not given up his exclusive right to the benefit of the public domain.[40]

By contrast, in the UK, the legal effects of formalities were fairly mild. Failure to register affected the enforcement of copyright, but not the copyright as such. According to the Statute of Anne, 'nothing in this act contained shall be construed to extend to subject any [...] person whatsoever, to the forfeitures or penalties therein mentioned, [...] unless the title to the copy of such book or books hereafter published shall, before such publication, be entered in the register book of the Company of Stationers'.[41] Also, it provided that if registration were not completed because of a refusal or negligence by the clerk, an advertisement in the Gazette would 'have the like benefit, as if such entry [...] had been duly made'.[42]

Hence, unless a work was duly registered or advertised in the Gazette, a right owner could not rely on the statutory forfeitures or penalties in a copyright infringement suit. Yet, beyond this purpose, registration was not required. In *Beckford v. Hood*,[43] the Court of King's Bench ruled that an author whose work was pirated during the statutory term of protection might maintain an action for damages against the offending party, even though the work had not been entered at Stationers' Hall. The Court found that the statutory penalties alone were an insufficient remedy for the injury of another man's civil property, as the right of action was not given to the grieved party but to a common informer, and the penalties did not attach during the full copyright term, but only during the first fourteen years.[44]

---

40   Court of Rouen, 13 December 1839, *Rivoire, Sirey* (2ᵐᵉ Sér.) 1840, 2, 74. However, the court decisions in this period were very contradictory on the nature and legal effects of legal deposit. In some judgments, it was held that authors could present their case before a court even if the deposit, though posterior to the counterfeit, had been fulfilled prior to the institution of the infringement proceeding. See for example: Criminal Court of Paris, 8 fructidor XI (26 August 1803), *Bertrandet v. Lassaulx, Sirey* (1ᵉʳ Sér.) 4, 2, 15; Royal Court of Paris, 3 July 1834, *Jazet v. Villain, Gaz. Trib.* 28 May and 4 July 1834. See also Criminal Tribunal of Paris, 18 May 1836, *L'administration des postes v. Bohain* in Étienne Blanc, *Traité de la contrefaçon en tous genres et de sa poursuite en justice*, 4th edn (Paris: Plon, 1855), p. 142; Tribunal of Paris, 10 July 1844, *Escudier v. Schonenberger* in Blanc, pp. 35-6; and Imperial Court of Paris, 8 December 1853, *Lecou v. Barba* in Blanc, pp. 38-9.

41   Sec. 2 of the Statute of Anne (1710).

42   Ibid., Sec. 3.

43   *Beckford v. Hood*, 101 *Eng. Rep.* 1164, 7 *T.R.* 620 (Court of King's Bench, 1798).

44   See, in particular, the argumentation by Justice Ashhurst (101 *Eng. Rep.* 1164 (p. 1168), 7 *T.R.* 620 (p. 628): 'The penalties to be recovered may indeed operate as a punishment upon the defender, but they afford no redress [...] for the civil injury

Therefore, the Court allowed a common law remedy to be applied, even though the work had not been registered.[45]

In the same ruling, the Court of King's Bench also confirmed the principle that statutory copyright in literary works was secured by publication independently of registration.[46] This principle was later adopted in the 1814 Copyright Act, which expressly declared that failure to register would not affect any copyright, but would only forfeit the statutory penalties.[47]

The same soft regime applied to the Statute of Anne's deposit requirement. A failure to deposit the prescribed number of copies of the work did not imperil the author's copyright, but the author would forfeit, besides the value of the copies, the sum of five pounds for every copy not delivered, plus the legal costs of suit for claiming the deposit.[48] Although in 1775 the deposit had become a condition for recovering statutory penalties (akin to the registration requirement),[49] the penalty of five pounds plus the value of the copy and the legal costs of suit as provided for in the Statute of Anne were reinstated by the Copyright Act of 1814.[50]

However, in contrast to the mild approach towards the registration and deposit for literary works, the regime for engravings, prints and lithographs was quite rigid. In the case *Newton v. Cowie*, the condition of the

sustained by the author in the loss of his just profits'). See also the argumentation by Justice Grose (101 *Eng. Rep.* 1164 (p. 1168), 7 *T.R.* 620 (pp. 628-9)).

45   This was not considered to run counter to the general principle adopted in the landmark case *Donaldson v. Beckett*, 98 *Eng. Rep.* 257, 4 *Burr.* 2408; 1 *Eng. Rep.* 837, 2 *Brown's Parl. Cases* 129 (House of Lords, 1774), where the majority of the judges held that the author's property right in a published work was confined to the copyright given to him by the statute, as opposed to a copyright at common law. The forfeitures and penalties provided for in the Statute of Anne (1710) were simply considered an additional statutory remedy, accumulative to the common law remedies that the author could generally call upon for the enforcement of his right. See the argumentation by Chief Justice Lord Kenyon (101 *Eng. Rep.* 1164 (p. 1167), 7 *T.R.* 620 (p. 627)).

46   R.F. Whale, *Copyright: Evolution, Theory and Practice* (London: Longman, 1971), p. 9. This principle had also been voiced by Lord Mansfield in the case *Tonson v. Collins*, 96 *Eng. Rep.* 180; 1 *Black. W.* 321 (Court of King's Bench, 1762). He held that registration at Stationers' Hall was necessary only to enable a grieved party to institute legal action to recover the statutory forfeitures or penalties. In his opinion, registration was not required, therefore, for enjoying statutory copyright as such (96 Eng. Rep. 180 (p. 184); 1 Black. W. 321 (p. 330)).

47   Sec. 5 of the Copyright Act (1814), 41 Geo. III, c. 107.

48   Sec. 5 of the Statute of Anne (1710).

49   The University Copyright Act (1775), 15 Geo. III, c. 53, ordered that no person would be subject to the statutory penalties unless the copies were actually delivered to the Stationers' Company's warehouse keeper.

50   Sec. 2 of the Copyright Act (1814).

Engravers' Copyright Act of 1735 of marking these types of works with the date of first publication and the name of the proprietor was formulated as a 'hard' formality. The Court of Common Pleas held this notification to be not merely directory, but conditional for the vesting of the right.[51] If the works were not marked with the name of the proprietor and date of first publication, it would be impossible for rival publishers to know whether, and against whom, they were offending.[52] This may explain the radical nature of these formalities as compared to those for literary works. On the latter, the names of the author and publisher and the year of first publication were routinely inscribed. For literary works, ownership and duration of protection were thus easier to resolve than for engravings, prints and lithographs. This appears to be the main reason why the Court decided that copyright attached to artistic works only if they were duly marked with the prescribed notice. The notice requirement laid down by the 1798 and 1814 Sculpture Copyright Acts seems to have followed the same rationale.[53]

2.3 Some Important Reasons for the Different Attitude towards Formalities

The previous section reveals that, in the first half of the century, the nature and legal effects of formalities differed noticeably between the UK and the countries on the European mainland. This difference in attitude towards formalities may perhaps seem a bit odd. However, there are various circumstances with which the divergence might be explained.

First, the formalities in early continental-European literary and artistic property legislation were clearly remnants from the old system of book privileges (or letter patents) issued by the sovereign to protect the output of the book trade. The grant of a book privilege was typically conditioned on the obligation to deposit a certain number of copies of the book,[54] to

---

51   *Newton v. Cowie*, 130 *Eng. Rep.* 759, 4 *Bing.* 234 (Court of Common Pleas, 1827). This decision was upheld in *Brooks v. Cock* (1835), 111 *Eng. Rep.* 365, 3 *AD. and E.* 138 and subsequent decisions. Previously, it had been ruled that a copyright owner could maintain an action against an infringer, even if his or her name had not been inscribed on the print. See the decision in *Roworth v. Wilkes* (1807), 170 *Eng. Rep.* 889, 1 *Camp.* 94.

52   *Newton v. Cowie* (1827), 130 *Eng. Rep.* 759 (p. 760), 4 *Bing.* 234 (pp. 236-7).

53   This follows from the phrasing of the Sculpture Copyright Acts, according to which the copyright was granted, 'provided always' (1798) or 'provided, in all and in every case' (1814), that the proprietor shall cause his or her name to be put on the work, together with the date of publication.

54   It was Francis I who introduced the legal deposit in France by the Ordinance of Montpellier of 28 December 1537. Although it first only served to enrich the royal

insert a copy of the privilege (including the licence to print from the censor) and the publisher's name and place of printing inside the book[55] and, occasionally, to make a recording of the privilege or the title of the book in a central register.[56] While the old feudal order was destructed during the French Revolution,[57] it is most likely that the early legislation on literary and artistic property in continental Europe took the principles that were in force at the end of the *Ancien Régime* as its reference point. Since the protection of literary works hitherto had been fully dependent on compliance with formalities, this influence of old feudal principles may have been a first important reason why formalities in the early continental-European authors' rights legislation were considered constitutive rather than declarative of the right.[58]

collections, it was made a formal prerequisite for the acquisition of privileges by the Royal edict of Louis XIII 7 September 1617. It would maintain this function until the end of the *Ancien Régime*. See Henri Lemaitre, *Histoire du dépôt légal: 1re partie (France)* (Paris: Picard, 1910), pp. ix-xxvii. In the Netherlands and several German states, similar systems of legal deposit were in place. See Alfred Flemming, *Das Recht der Pflichtexemplare* (München/Berlin: Beck, 1940), pp. 7-13.

55   Notice requirements of this kind could be found, inter alia, in France, in the Edict of Chateaubriant of 26 June 1551 and in the Orders of 1618, 1649, 1686 and 1723; and in Germany, in the Diets of Augsburg (1530) and Speyer (1570), the Imperial Regulation Orders (*Reichspolizeiordnungen*) of Augsburg (1548) and Frankfurt (1577) and the Imperial Edicts of 1715 and 1746. These requirements were commonly linked to censorship: the notifications enabled the authorities to better monitor the authenticity of privileges and the licences to print. For this reason, they were less commonly applied – though not completely absent – in the Dutch Republic, which was known for its liberty of thought and religion and fairly moderate censorship of books.

56   In France, both privileges and licences to print needed to be registered at the *Chambre Syndicalle* of the community of printers and book publishers of Paris. See for example the Decree of the Council of State of 13 August 1703 and Art. 106 of the Order of 28 February 1723. In Germany, the Act of Saxony concerning the mandate of the book trade of 18 December 1773 provided for a registration in a register (*Protokoll*) held at the Leipzig Books Commission. Lastly, in the Netherlands, there were some regional initiatives aimed at setting up registers. An example is the register established by Art. XII of the 'indissoluble contract' of the *Leids Collegie* of 1660.

57   On the destruction of the old feudal order during the French Revolution, see John Markoff, *The Abolition of Feudalism: Peasants, Lords, and Legislators in the French Revolution* (University Park, PA: Pennsylvania State University Press, 1996). Following the liberal ideals of the French Revolution, the Netherlands abolished the system of book privileges at the end of the eighteenth century. Germany, however, maintained the privilege system for a relatively long time. In 1856, the privileges of authors like Schiller, Goethe, Wieland and Herder were extended for the last time. They finally expired in 1867. See Schriks, p. 253.

58   See Adolphe Lacan and Charles Paulmier, *Traité de la législation et de la jurisprudence des théâtres*, 2 vols (Paris: Durand, 1853), II, p. 202 (no. 653): 'C'est dans cet

Admittedly, the early-nineteenth century British formalities were remnants from ancient times as well. Yet, book privileges played no role in their conception.[59] Instead, it was the stationers' copyright that provided the elements on which the British copyright system would later be built.[60] A condition for obtaining stationers' copyright was registration of the title of a work and the name of the copyright holder in the 'Hall Book' of the Stationers' Company.[61] Moreover, stationers were required to deposit copies at the Master of the Company.[62] Unlike privileges, which were a purely governmental grant, the stationers' copyright had a public-private character.[63] This is important, as it might be a primary reason for the fairly moderate stance towards formalities taken in the UK. At least it seems likely that, because of the public-private roots of formalities in the stationers' copyright, the framers of the Statute of Anne had little inclination to lay down very strict state-imposed formalities.

Another, perhaps more important, reason for the dissimilar position vis-à-vis formalities between the literary and artistic property right schemes

---

esprit, d'ailleurs, que nous paraît avoir été conçue la disposition de l'art. 6 de la loi de 1793. Cette loi [...] s'est inspirée des principes qui étaient en vigueur auparavant, et qui subordonnaient l'existence même du droit des auteurs à la condition préalable d'un dépôt'.

59   In England, by the end of the seventeenth century, book privileges lost their significance, when their granting had for all practical purposes come to an end. See Lyman Ray Patterson, *Copyright in Historical Perspective* (Nashville, TN: Vanderbilt University Press, 1968), pp. 78 et seq.

60   See Oren Bracha, *Owning Ideas: A History of Anglo-American Intellectual Property* (S.J.D. Dissertation, Harvard Law School, 2005), http://www.obracha.net/oi/oi.htm [accessed 1/2/2009], pp. 176 et seq.

61   It is uncertain whether registration initially was a condition for acquiring the stationers' copyright. The earlier entries in the Hall Book of the Stationers' Company appeared to be receipts for the registration fees charged only. See *A Transcript of the Registers of the Company of Stationers of London, 1554-1640 A.D.*, ed. by Edward Arber, 5 vols (London: privately printed, 1875-94; repr. Mansfield Center, CT: Martino Publishing, 2006), I, pp. xvi-xvii. As time passed by, however, registration became a legal requirement. See Patterson, pp. 59-63.

62   The free library deposit had its origin in the Bodleian Agreement of 1610. See Barrington Partridge, pp. 17 et seq. The legal deposit was made a formal requirement for obtaining a licence to print from the censor by Secs IV and XXXIII of the Star Chamber Decree of 11 July 1637; Secs III and XVI of the Press Licensing Act (1662), 13 and 14 Car. II, c. 33; and Secs II and III of the Press Licensing Act (1665), 17 Car. II, c. 4.

63   The stationers' copyright essentially was a private matter of the Stationers' Company. Yet, it was officially endorsed by the Crown when it issued the Charter of the Stationers' Company (1557), Patent Rolls, 3 and 4 Philip and Mary, part 10, membrane 46. See also Confirmation Roll (1559), 1 Elizabeth, part 4, membrane 15.

in continental Europe and the UK was the position of the author. Whereas, in the UK, at the end of eighteenth century, the notion of copyright as an author's right had been firmly established,[64] in many continental-European countries, copyright was not yet a full author's right. Even though in several countries, the law seemingly conferred a property right on the author, it was essentially the publisher who received protection (as under the old privilege system).[65] This certainly was the case in the Netherlands and some German states, where copyright protected the printed work rather than the product of the mind, and the bookseller or publisher rather than the author.[66] Since it had not yet been fully recognised that property rights were vested in the author, it certainly was not accepted that the right automatically attached upon the author's creative act. Hence, there was ample opportunity for formalities to play a determinative role. Besides, even if the law was deemed to grant property rights to authors, statutory formalities were still considered very important. In the absence of privileges, the formalities and conditions set by law were deemed critical for establishing the title of property: it was believed that, if these formalities and conditions were not fulfilled, authors could never acquire intellectual property rights.[67]

---

64   It was the case *Millar v. Taylor*, 98 *Eng. Rep.* 201, 4 *Burr.* 2303 (Court of King's Bench, 1769) in which the court firmly established the idea of the author as the creator and ultimate source of literary (and artistic) property rights. See Patterson, pp. 14-5 and 151-79. For a comprehensive account on the formation of the conception of authorship in eighteenth century Britain, see Mark Rose, *Authors and Owners: The Invention of Copyright* (Cambridge, MA: Harvard University Press, 1993).

65   Although it occurred that authors were granted book privileges, the privilege system was not primarily designed for their benefit. See F.W. Grosheide, *Auteursrecht op maat: Beschouwingen over de grondslagen van het auteursrecht in een rechtspolitieke context* (Deventer: Kluwer, 1986), p. 52.

66   Schriks, p. 424. Instead of authors' rights, the Dutch Copyright Act of 1817 and most German state copyright granted a *kopijrecht* or *Verlagsrecht*. These were typical publishers' rights, similar to the old English stationers' copyright. Their origin lay in customary law of the seventeenth and eighteenth centuries. The rights arose with the sale of a manuscript from the author to the publisher. Alongside the manuscript, the publisher was believed to have acquired the exclusive 'right to copy', i.e., to have the manuscript appear in print and to distribute it to the public. See Schriks, pp. 23 and 75-82 and in the English summary, p. 511. See also Ludwig Gieseke, *Vom Privileg zum Urheberrecht: Die Entwicklung des Urheberrechts in Deutschland bis 1845* (Göttingen: Schwartz, 1995), pp. 93 et seq. However, not all German state copyright acts granted a *Verlagsrecht*. The Prussian Act of 1837, for instance, assumed protection of authors' rights instead of the old publishers' *Verlagsrecht*.

67   See for example the plea held by Mr. D. Donker Curtius at the hearing of the Dutch Supreme Court on 2 June 1840: 'dat als men een eigendom wil scheppen, men er ook kenmerken aan moet geven, welke zijn als de voorwaarden, waaronder het alleen kan worden geëerbiedigd. [...] De wet [...], wil voortaan geene privile-

Even in France, which in the second half of the nineteenth century became the cradle of the author's right (*droit d'auteur*), copyright was not consistently perceived as a right inherent to the author.[68] The theory that the literary and artistic property rights in a work belonged to the author 'naturally' because of the personal bond between the work and its creator, for example, had not entirely infiltrated the French legal order. It seems that, at the time, this idea was still overshadowed by the ideology that authors' rights were based on a social contract.[69] The idea was that, upon publication, the author dispossessed himself of his work and all the rights in the work, including the exploitation rights, passed to the public. In return, the author had a private claim against society, which allowed him to demand remuneration for the exploitation of the work. The supporters of this theory believed that this claim took the form of a privilege granted by the legislator on behalf of the public.[70] This is particularly evident from an 1841 report drawn up for the French government which unambiguously stated: '*La jouissance garantie aux auteurs n'est point un droit* naturel, *mais un* privilege *resultant d'un* octroi bénévole *de la loi*'.[71] This report illustrates that,

---

giën meer en erkent geen kopy-regt, dan aan hem, die aan de voorwaarden, welke zij stelt, heeft voldaan', in *Het letterkundig eigendomsregt in Nederland: Wetten, trak-taten, regtspraak. Benevens de wetgeving op de drukpers in Nederland en Nederlandsch Indië*, 2 vols ('s-Gravenhage: Belinfante, 1865-7), II (1867), 109-25 (p. 117). This statement was upheld by the decision of the Dutch Supreme Court, 8 September 1840, *Johannes Noman en Zn. v. Staat der Nederlanden*, in *Het letterkundig eigendomsregt in Nederland*, II (1867), pp. 132-4. See also the argumentation by Serjeant-at-law Wilde in the case *Newton v. Cowie* (1827), 130 *Eng. Rep.* 759 (p. 760), 4 *Bing.* 234 (p. 236): 'The statutes having given a monopoly, it is essential to the title of the party who claims the monopoly, that he comply with all the conditions attached to it'.

68   See Ginsburg, p. 157.

69   See Laurent Pfister, 'La propriété littéraire est-elle une propriété? Controverses sur la nature du droit d'auteur au XIXème siècle', *Revue Internationale du Droit d'Auteur*, 205 (2005), 116-209, describing the two leading currents of thought on the nature of authors' rights in nineteenth-century France, i.e. the theory of authors' rights as a social contract (supported by Augustin-Charles Renouard, Edouard Calmels, Louis Wolowski, Léonce de Lavergne, Pierre-Joseph Proudhon, Charles Demolombe and others) and the theory of authors' rights as property rights (supported by Joseph Marie Portalis, Auguste Marie, Edouard Laboulaye, Eugène Pouillet and others).

70   Pfister, pp. 136-7, 144-5 and 148-9. In Germany, there also was a tendency to revert back to the privilege system to explain the position of the author as benefi-ciary of intellectual property rights. See Diethelm Klippel, 'Die Idee des geistiges Eigentums in Naturrecht und Rechtsphilosophie des 19. Jahrhunderts', in *Histori-sche Studien zum Urheberrecht in Europa: Entwicklungslinien und Grundfragen*, ed. by Elmar Wadle, Schriften zur europäischen Rechts- und Verfassungsgeschichte, 10 (Berlin: Duncker & Humblot, 1993), pp. 121-38 (p. 133).

71   Édouard Romberg, *Compte rendu des travaux du Congrès de la propriété littéraire*

at the time, authors were considered beneficiaries of the right not because they had a natural right in their intellectual creations, but because they were granted a right by virtue of the statute. Thus, where copyright was deemed a statutory grant,[72] a greater importance may have been attached to copyright formalities.[73]

Lastly, as Ginsburg has clearly demonstrated in her inspiring 'A Tale of Two Copyrights', the French copyright law of 1793 was not just motivated by authors' personal claims of rights in their intellectual works, but also by concerns of public welfare and social utility.[74] In general, it was thought that the rights and interests of authors needed to be established in accordance with those of the public domain. Gastambide, for example, held the opinion that the primary objective of legal deposit was neither to establish *prima facie* evidence of the ownership of a work, nor to enrich national libraries (further discussed below). He found that its purpose was principally to enable authors to inform the public about their intention as to whether or not they would want to enjoy and exercise their rights. While abstaining from depositing, he believed, authors gave evidence of a voluntary abandonment of their property rights to the public domain.[75] He therefore argued that the moment a work was published, it needed to be deposited or else it would be in the public domain. If authors were allowed

et artistique, 2 vols (Bruxelles/Leipzig: Flatau, 1859), I, p. 68.

72   In the UK, copyright in published works was also limited to the statutory terms and conditions. Nevertheless, because registration was a condition to claim statutory remedies only, common law remedies could still be called upon during the statutory term, even without a prior registration.

73   In this respect, an interesting comparison can be made with the United States of America where the Supreme Court in the famous case of *Wheaton v. Peters*, 33 U.S. (8 Pet.) 591 (1834) held that in passing the Federal Copyright Act of 1790, Congress 'instead of sanctioning an existing right, as contended for, created it' (pp. 657-61). These considerations formed the basis for a strict construction of the Act and the formalities contained therein. Where the copyright in published works was believed to exist only by virtue of the Act, the Court ruled that 'when the legislature are about to vest an exclusive right in an author, [...] they have the power to prescribe the conditions on which such right shall be enjoyed; and that no one can avail himself of such right who does not substantially comply with the requisitions of the law' (pp. 663-4). As a corollary, the Court held that copyright came into being only if the mandatory conditions of the Copyright Act had in fact been complied with.

74   Ginsburg, pp. 143 et seq.

75   Gastambide argued that by dedicating the work to the public domain, the author would satisfy himself with the advantages of a honourable publicity. Such thoughts were not uncommon at the time. It appears that several commentators found that 'writers and authors should not be guided by the reckless pursuit of profit and money' but should rather feel rewarded by the glory and honour of the public. See Pfister, pp. 128-9.

to perform the deposit at a later stage, this would oppose the presumed intention of authors abandoning their property rights and destroy the rights devoted to the public domain.[76]

There were also commentators who followed the opposite line of thought. Renouard, for instance, did not consider the absence of deposit to constitute evidence of the author's consent to his work entering the public domain: '*Dire que l'auteur est censé [...] avoir personnellement contracté avec le domaine public, et avoir stipulé l'abandon de ses droits, c'est une exagération inadmissible*'.[77] He reasoned that, if legal deposit was interpreted as involving the absolute loss of rights in case of disobedience, this was a transgression of the law. The law did not declare the author's right void in case of absence of deposit; it only extinguished the possibility of litigation.[78] Accordingly, Renouard considered the formality of legal deposit to be declarative rather than constitutive of authors' rights. In his opinion, neither the text nor the spirit of the law would justify another interpretation.[79] This reasoning would foreshadow the developments in the second half of the nineteenth century, although the constitutive nature of formalities would, at that time, be rejected on other, more philosophical, grounds.

---

76   Adrien-Joseph Gastambide, *Traité théorique et pratique des contrefaçons en tous genres* (Paris: Legrand and Descauriet, 1837), pp. 150 et seq (no. 124-5). See also Lacan and Paulmier, II, pp. 201-2 (no. 653), arguing that if the simultaneity of deposit and publication were given up, the existence of authors' rights could only be established arbitrarily and retroactively, thus causing legal uncertainty for third parties relying on the supposition that works not deposited are dedicated to the public domain. In their view, this would be '*un piège que la loi ne peut comporter, et qu'une sage jurisprudence ne peut admettre*'. In support of their opinions, both Gastambide and Lacan and Paulmier used examples of industrial property rights (industrial designs; patents), which for their coming into existence also depended on formalities (deposit of a sample; patent application).

77   See Augustin-Charles Renouard, *Traité des droits d'auteurs, dans la littérature, les sciences et les beaux-arts*, 2 vols (Paris: Renouard, 1838-9), II (1839), p. 374 (no. 218), underscoring that the negligence that consisted in omitting the deposit was often ascribable to the publisher rather than the author.

78   See Renouard, II (1839), pp. 374-5 (no. 218), who considered the legal deposit to be nothing but a law enforcement measure and a tax established in the interest of libraries.

79   Thus, Renouard based himself primarily on the text of the law. This is consistent with the positivist character of the social contract theory. See Pfister, pp. 150-1. Alfred Nion, *Droits civils des auteurs, artistes et inventeurs* (Paris: Joubert, 1846), pp. 128-9 and Blanc, pp. 140-1 also relied strongly on the text of the law. Nevertheless, these last two commentators rejected the idea of legal deposit being constitutive of literary or artistic property rights because they believed that authors' rights were born with the creation of the work.

3. Copyright Formalities in the Second Half of the Nineteenth Century

In the second half of the century, the different formalities were generally maintained. Yet, a few important developments can be witnessed, which, at least in some of the countries that we consider here, caused a fundamental change of perspective vis-à-vis copyright formalities. In this section, a number of key developments shall be identified. But first, the question of how copyright formalities evolved in the laws of the various countries examined shall be considered.

3.1 The Development of Formalities in National Copyright Law

While in the second half of the nineteenth century formalities were continued in the national laws on literary and artistic property in virtually all countries, the attitude towards formalities changed radically. In several continental-European states, the nature of formalities softened. There was a growing belief that the *existence* of literary and artistic property rights should not depend on compliance with formalities. In France, for example, the deposit formality was not as strictly construed as had previously been the case. From the mid-century onwards, courts increasingly ruled that this formality was not a condition for the coming into being of authors' rights.[80] They began to see the legal deposit purely as a law enforcement measure or a tax established in the interest of literature and the arts. Therefore, they held that an omission to deposit was not to be regarded as an abandonment of authors' rights in the interest of the public domain.[81] Moreover, they found that authors could satisfy the deposit at any time which they deemed appropriate for taking advantage of their rights: claims were admissible in court as long as the deposit was fulfilled before legal action against a counterfeiter was started.[82] Thus, there was broad consensus that the legal deposit was not constitutive, but only declarative of authors' rights. This

---

80 Pouillet, pp. 473-4 (no. 433).
81 Civil Tribunal of the Seine, 21 November 1866, *Franck, Pataille* 1866, 394.
82 Tribunal of Paris, 10 July 1844, *Escudier v. Schonenberger* in Blanc, pp. 35-6; Civil Tribunal of the Seine, 21 November 1866, *Franck, Pataille* 1866, 394; Court of Paris, 28 March 1883, *Roussin et Duvoir v. Arpé, Pataille* 1884, 84; Civil Tribunal of the Seine, 14 December 1887, *Enoch et autres v. Bruant et autres, Pataille* 1890, 59; Court of Pau, 31 May 1878 and 6 December 1878, *Latour v. Cazaux, Dalloz* 1880, 2, 80; Court of Paris, 12 June 1885, *Decauville, Pataille* 1886, 129; Court of Paris, 25 March 1903, *Bernier v. Desvignes, Pataille* 1904, 93.

opinion also became prevalent in French legal doctrine.[83]

The notion that authors' rights should exist independently from formalities was taken even further by the German legislator. The Federal Copyright Acts of 1870 and 1876,[84] which were adopted after the unification of Germany,[85] were based on the assumption that formalities needed to be avoided as much as possible and could only be justified to the extent that a true public need existed.[86] Except for photographs, the protection of which depended on the indication of the name and place of residence of the photographer or publisher and the year of first publication on each copy of the work,[87] no formalities were required for the coming into existence of authors' rights. The German legislator only required a registration of certain facts for which it believed adequate public knowledge should exist to enable users to determine whether a particular work was still subject to protection or could yet be freely used.[88]

---

83   See for example: E. Delalande, *Étude sur la propriété littéraire et artistique* (Paris: Marescq Aîné, 1880), p. 123; R. Garraud, *Traité théorique et pratique du droit pénal français*, 2nd edn, 5 vols (Paris: Larose et Forcel, 1888-94), V, pp. 554-5 (no. 530); Léon Poinsard, *Études de droit international conventionnel* (Paris: Librairie Cotillon, 1894), p. 491; Gustave Huard, *Traité de la propriété intellectuelle*, 2 vols (Paris: Marchal and Billard, 1903), I, pp. 94-5; Pouillet, pp. 471-3 (no. 432).

84   Act concerning the authors' rights in writings, illustrations, musical compositions and dramatic works of 11 June 1870; Act concerning the authors' rights in works of the visual arts of 9 January 1876; Act concerning the protection of photographs from unauthorized reproduction of 10 January 1876.

85   Art. 4(6) of the Constitution of the North German Confederation of 26 July 1867 instructed the government to draft national copyright legislation. This resulted in the Federal Copyright Act of 1870. In 1871, this Act was also made applicable to the southern German states which had united with the North German Confederation and together formed the German Empire. Later, the Federal Copyright Acts of 1876 were established.

86   Robert Fischer, *Gesetz, betreffend das Urheberrecht an Schriftwerken, Abbildungen, musikalischen Kompositionen und dramatischen Werken vom 11. Juni 1870* (Gera: Griesbach, 1870), pp. 33-4; Otto Dambach, *Die Gesetzgebung des Norddeutschen Bundes betreffend das Urheberrecht an Schriftwerken, Abbildungen, musikalischen Kompositionen und dramatischen Werken* (Berlin: Enslin, 1871), pp. 205-7.

87   Art. 5 of the Act concerning the protection of photographs of 1876. An inaccurate or incomplete notification caused the loss of protection from unauthorized reproduction. See R. Klostermann, *Das Urheberrecht an Schrift- und Kunstwerken, Abbildungen, Compositionen, Photographien, Mustern und Modellen nach deutschem und internationalem Rechte* (Berlin: Vahlen, 1876), p. 190.

88   See Fischer, p. 33; Dambach, p. 207; Oscar Wächter, *Das Autorrecht nach dem gemeinen deutschen Recht* (Stuttgart: Enke, 1875), p. 136. The registration included (a) the reservation of the translation right for literary or dramatic works (which was subject to statutory maximum terms); (b) the names of authors of anonymous or pseudonymous works that were revealed before the term of protection for these works ended (which caused the works to be protected longer); and (c) the titles of works that were still pro-

In other countries, on the other hand, the nature of formalities remained largely unchanged. In the Netherlands, for example, the formality of legal deposit – which was fully maintained under the 1881 Copyright Act – continued to be constitutive by nature.[89] Although the Dutch legislator had underscored that authors' rights arose with the act of creation and not with the act of deposit,[90] any failure to deliver the copies within one month after publication would signify forfeiture of the rights.[91] This resulted in a somewhat remarkable situation, whereby, while in theory the formality of legal deposit was not constitutive for the author's right, in practice, the rights perished and the work fell into the public domain, if the deposit was not fulfilled within one month. Any failure to deposit, therefore, meant that the exercise of authors' rights would be impossible and, in all probability, the rights themselves would not actually come into existence.[92]

Likewise, in the UK, the formalities of the first half of the century were all maintained and their nature and legal effects remained unaffected. Thus, for literary works, the 1842 Copyright Act laid down a registration and a deposit requirement. The latter requirement was left completely unchanged. Like before, failure to deposit involved a fine, but the copyright was not forfeited as a result.[93] In contrast to registration under the earlier British copyright laws, however, the 1842 Copyright Act made registration a technical condition to *any* suit for infringement of law or in equity, thus avoiding the previous distinction between statutory and common law remedies. At the same time, the rule was maintained 'that the omission to make such entry shall not affect the copyright in any book'.[94] Failure to register only affected the right to sue in respect of a copyright infringement. Nonetheless, the courts held that, once registration was effected, authors

---

tected under a privilege issued before the Federal Copyright Acts of 1870 and 1876 took effect. See Arts 6, 11, 52 and 60 of the Federal Copyright Act of 1870; Arts 9 and 19 of the Federal Act concerning the authors' rights in works of the visual arts of 1876.

89   Art. 10 of the Dutch Copyright Act of 1881.
90   See for example the Explanatory Memorandum and the Memorandum in Reply, in *Auteurswet 1881: Parlementaire geschiedenis wet 1881 - ontwerp 1884* (Zutphen: Walburg Pers, 2006), pp. 94-6.
91   This rule was based on the assumption that the author did not want to avail himself of his rights, if the copies were not delivered within the first month of publication. See for example: J.D. Veegens, *Het auteursrecht volgens de Nederlandsche wetgeving* ('s-Gravenhage: Belinfante, 1895), p. 119; Johannes van de Kasteele, *Het auteursrecht in Nederland* (Leiden: Somerwil, 1885), p. 159.
92   See: Veegens, pp. 119-20; Van de Kasteele, p. 160.
93   Secs 6 to 10 of the Copyright Act (1842), 5 and 6 Vict. c. 45.
94   Ibid., Sec. 24.

could proceed even in respect of infringements made before the registration date. In view of that, there was no need to register until a violation
occurred. As long as authors had registered before issuing the writ, their
cases were admissible before a court.[95] Apart from the registration of copyrights, the 1842 Copyright Act also opened the possibility for registering
assignments and licensing agreements.[96] This was an absolute novelty in
comparison with the earlier British copyright laws.

In contrast to literary works, registration became compulsory for the
vesting of copyright in paintings, drawings and photographs. The Fine Art
Copyright Act of 1862 provided that, until registration, the copyright owners of these works were not entitled to the benefits of this Act. Furthermore,
no action would be sustainable and no penalty would be recoverable in
respect of 'anything done before registration'.[97] Yet, this latter rule was
weakly interpreted. It was held that after the registering of a drawing, damages could be obtained for the illegitimate sale of copies of that drawing,
even if these copies were made prior to the registration date.[98]

Lastly, for engravings, prints and lithographs and for sculptures, models and casts, the rule remained in place that copyright attached only if
these works were marked with the notice prescribed by the 1735 Engravers'
Copyright Act and the 1814 Sculpture Copyright Act.

In addition, and this concerns a development that can be witnessed in
most of the countries under consideration, the latter part of the nineteenth
century also saw the introduction of new formalities. As will be demonstrated later, these new formalities were established in response to an
extended protection granted to authors. In order to retain a public performance right in musical compositions or dramatic (musical) works,[99] a transla-

---

95 See for example *Goubard v. Wallace*, 36 L.T. (n.s.) 704, W.N. 130 (1877) and *Warne
v. Lawrence*, 54 L.T. 371, 34 W.R. 452 (1886). Especially this latter decision displayed
a case of an extremely late registration: the entrance in the register was made earlier
in the day on which the plaintiff had issued the writ.
96 Sec. 11 of the Copyright Act (1842).
97 Sec. 4 of the Fine Arts Copyright Act (1862). It followed from Sec. 1 of the Fine
Arts Copyright Act (1862) that when a painting, drawing, or negative of a photograph was first sold or disposed of, this sale or disposition also needed to be
accompanied by a written agreement between the artist and purchaser as to whom
the copyright would belong, otherwise the copyright in the painting, drawing, or
photograph would be lost altogether. See Thomas Edward Scrutton, *The Law of
Copyright*, 4th edn (London: Clowes, 1903), pp. 192-3.
98 *Tuck v. Priester*, 19 Q.B.D. 629 (Court of Appeal, 1887).
99 See for example: Art. 50 of the German Federal Copyright Act of 1870; Art. 12
of the Dutch Copyright Act of 1881; Sec. 1 of the British Copyright (Musical Compositions) Act (1882), 45 and 46 Vict., c. 40. Although not expressly stated by the

tion right in literary works[100] or a reproduction right in (short) articles, in newspapers or periodicals,[101] the legislature in several countries began to require that authors mark all copies of these works with an explicit notice of reservation. Hence, authors could claim specific rights that they did not previously enjoy, but only if they attached a prescribed notice to all copies of their works. Therefore, these new formalities are sometimes referred to as 'specifying formalities'.[102] Systematically, they can be grouped in neither the category of constitutive nor of declaratory formalities. While the latter types of formalities have general application and thus relate to authors' rights as a whole, specifying formalities only affect the enjoyment of the particular type of right to which they pertain. Hence, failure to comply with these formalities did not cause entire works to enter the public domain, as did constitutive formalities, but only rendered a specific right void. Further in the chapter it will be explained why, concurrently with the removal or softening of constitutive and declaratory formalities, new specifying formalities were adopted.

Ultimately, in the early twentieth century, we observe the end of copyright formalities in the European states under discussion. In Germany, all statutory formalities were abolished even before this was required by the Berne Convention (that is, for literary and musical works, in 1901 and, for artistic works and photographs, in 1907).[103] Following the introduction of the prohibition on formalities in the Berne Convention in 1908, the British and Dutch lawmakers also decided to eliminate all domestic copyright formalities.[104] France, however, remained an exceptional case. It retained the legal deposit as a prerequisite to suit until 1925.[105]

---

latter Act, it was held in *Fuller v. Blackpool Winter Gardens* [1895], 2 Q.B. 429 (Court of Appeal, 1895), that the failure to print the notice of reservation prevented the copyright owner, or his assignee, from asserting the public performance right.

100 See for example: Art. 6(c) of the German Federal Copyright Act of 1870; Art. 5(b) of the Dutch Copyright Act of 1881. A notice of reservation to retain a right to make translations in literary works was also prescribed by several earlier German state copyright acts.

101 See for example: Art. 7(b) of the German Federal Copyright Act of 1870; Art. 7 of the Dutch Copyright Act of 1881.

102 See Kawohl and Kretschmer, pp. 221 et seq, who introduced the term 'registration as specification'.

103 Act concerning the copyright in literary and musical works of 19 June 1901, *RGBl.* 1901, 227; Act concerning the copyright in artistic works and photographs of 9 January 1907, *RGBl.* 1907, 7.

104 See, for the UK, the Copyright Act (1911), 1 and 2 Geo. V, c. 46 and, for the Netherlands, the Act of 23 September 1912 containing new regulation for copyright, *Stb.* 1912, 308.

105 By the Act of 19 May 1925, *Journal Officiel*, 27 May 1925 the French legisla-

3.2 Some Important Reasons for the Change of Perspective Vis-à-vis Formalities

The preceding section demonstrates that, while the Netherlands and the UK retained formalities on almost the exact same level as in the first half of the century, formalities began to be perceived differently and their nature and legal effects softened in France and Germany. At the same time, the second half of the century also saw the introduction of new formalities. This raises several questions. What caused the change of perspective towards formalities in France and Germany? Why were formalities nevertheless continued in these countries? And what was the reason for the introduction of new sets of formalities? It will be seen that these questions are closely related to some ideological, functional and conceptual innovations in nineteenth century copyright law.[106] These innovations, upon which this section will touch, concern (i) the increased focus on the person of the author and the corresponding idea that the author's creation is the ultimate source from which copyright emerged, (ii) the growing idea that for a good functioning of the copyright system formalities are not necessary per se; and (iii) the awkwardness of formalities in the context of the new concept of abstract authored works and some newly protected categories of works. The reason why these innovations exerted little influence in the Netherlands and the UK shall be explained below.

3.2.1 The Increased Person-oriented Nature of Authors' Rights

In the course of the nineteenth century, the position of authors on the European mainland had gradually become stronger. This was attributable, in particular, to an increased belief that the person of the creator was the very foundation of the property in the work.[107] In France, the idea that the

---

tor finally disconnected the legal deposit requirement from French authors' rights legislation. Previously, in Tribunal de Commerce de la Seine, 13 November 1913, *Magalhaès et Moniz v. Muroz Escamoz*, in *Le Droit d'Auteur*, 27 (1914), pp. 38-40, it was already ruled that legal deposit was not required for foreign works for which protection was claimed under the Berne Convention, as this was inconsistent with the Berne prohibition on formalities.

106   See Brad Sherman and Lionel Bently, *The Making of Modern Intellectual Property Law: The British Experience, 1760-1911* (Cambridge: Cambridge University Press, 1999), who draw a general distinction between 'pre-modern' and 'modern' intellectual property law, the transformation of which, at least in the UK, took place around the middle part of the nineteenth century.

107   Pfister calls this a process of '*personalising* literary and artistic property', which was particularly fruitful for the development of the French *droit d'auteur*. This pro-

creation of a work was a service which the author rendered to society, in return for which society assured the author certain exclusive rights, faded. Instead, the justification for the protection of authors' rights was increasingly found to exist in their identification as property rights. Expanding on the theory of 'intellectual property' developed in the eighteenth century under the influence of natural law,[108] and in particular on John Locke's labour theory, holding that man has a natural right to property which exists in his own person and which he originally acquires by appropriating the commons through his labour,[109] the proponents of the theory of literary and artistic property emphasised the inextricable bond between the work and the person of its creator.[110] By regarding the person of the creator as 'the natural law basis of literary and artistic property',[111] they believed

cess was a prelude to and preceded the recognition of the authors' moral right. As a consequence, '"the person-oriented nature of *droit d'auteur*" was not "discovered" by Morillot in the 1870s when he framed the notion of the moral right'. See Pfister, pp. 126-7 and 152-3.

108   On the evolution of the theory of intellectual property ('*geistigen Eigentum*') in eighteenth-century Germany, see Gieseke, pp. 115 et seq. This theory also found support in France. Already in 1725, Louis d'Héricourt pleaded that the author should be recognized as the owner of the work he created. D'Héricourt did not question the ownership of the tangible work, but found that the author deserved to be accepted as a proprietor of a work because of the act of intellectual creation. See the text of his *Mémoire* in Éd. Laboulaye and G. Guiffrey, *La propriété littéraire au XVIIIe siècle: Recueil de pièces et de documents* (Paris: L. Hachette, 1859), pp. 21-40.

109   John Locke, *Two Treatises of Government* (London, 1690), pp. 245-6 (Sec. 27). Locke's labour theory appears to have been quite popular among nineteenth-century liberal thinkers in France. See for example Nion, pp. 127-8: 'Nous avons déjà eu l'occasion de déclarer que pour nous le principe de la propriété littéraire et artistique était le travail de l'auteur, la création. De même avons-nous dit, que l'homme qui le premier s'est emparé d'un champ n'ayant jusqu'alors appartenu à personne, se l'est approprié en le cultivant, de même celui qui s'empare des idées tombées dans le domaine public et les marque de cachet de sa personnalité en en composant un ouvrage, devient propriétaire de ce produit de son activité'.

110   For instance, during the parliamentary debates of 1839, Joseph Marie Portalis maintained that the author's right constituted a 'propriété par nature, par essence, par indivision, par indivisibilité de l'objet et du sujet'. In 1879, Eugène Pouillet affirmed that the author's work consisted 'dans une création, c'est-à-dire dans la production d'une chose qui n'existait pas auparavant et qui est tellement personnelle qu'elle forme comme une partie [de son auteur]'. The quotations are taken from Pfister, pp. 156-7 and 158-9.

111   Pfister, pp. 158-9. Ibid., pp. 124-5 and 156-7: 'For the proponents of literary and artistic property, the work was all the more its creator's own as it proceeded immediately from an original and natural property of man: his person'. Authors' rights were increasingly perceived as a natural right. In a case involving the operas of Verdi, for example, the French Court of Cassation fully acknowledged that authors' rights derived from natural law. See French Court of Cassation, 14 Decem-

that authors' rights emanated directly from the quality of the authors' own intellectual creations.[112] The law was seen as merely recognising the existence, and regulating the exercise, of authors' rights.[113] This idea also became widespread among German academics and intellectuals. As in France, authors' rights were progressively regarded more as rights of intellectual property (*'geistigen Eigentum'*).[114] The foundation of authors' rights was seen to reside in the very nature of things: '*Der Mensch hat […] ein aus seinem "Urrecht" entspringendes "ursprüngliche(s) Recht auf die Erzeugnisse seiner Geistes- und Körperkräfte"'.*[115] Hence, it was not the laws that created authors' rights: these rights were believed to have always existed in the legal conscience of men.[116]

In parallel, another theory evolved in Germany which gave even more prominence to the person of the author as creator of his work. This was the personality theory, which was based largely on the philosophies of Kant and Fichte. Kant regarded authors' rights not as property rights, but as personal rights. In his view, books are not just material objects capable of being owned, but also means through which authors speak to their readers.[117] Kant believed that it is a man's innate right to communicate his thoughts to the public. Therefore, authors should be vested with some right to control when, how and by whom these thoughts, as expressed in their writings, are

---

ber 1857, *Verdi et Blanchet* v. *Calzado*, *Dalloz* 1858, 1, 161: 'Attendu que si la propriété des œuvres littéraires, musicales et artistiques dérive du droit naturel […]' (p. 164). See also Blanc, p. 139: 'la propriété littéraire était une création […] du droit naturel et des gens'.

112   See Blanc, p. 138: 'La propriété, c'est-à-dire la qualité d'auteur […]'.

113   See Imperial Court of Paris, 8 December 1853, *Lecou v. Barba* in Blanc, pp. 38-9: 'Considérant que la création d'une œuvre littéraire ou artistique constitue au profit de son auteur une propriété dont le fondement se trouve dans le droit naturel et des gens, mais dont l'exploitation est réglementée par le droit civil'.

114   German natural law and legal philosophy assumed a fairly broad concept of property, included property of physical goods, property of the human body and property of man-made commodities. See Klippel, pp. 126 et seq. Intellectual property thus was also generally accepted, as it constituted '*durch Arbeit mit der Persönlichkeit verbundene geistige Eigentum*' (ibid., p. 135). Here again, we see the influence of the labour theory of Locke.

115   Klippel, p. 125.

116   See Francis J. Kase, *Copyright Thought in Continental Europe: Its Development, Legal Theories and Philosophy* (South Hackensack: Rothman, 1967), p. 8, who concludes that under the theory of authors' rights as intellectual property rights, '[copyright] is thus a natural right growing out of natural law'.

117   I. Kant, 'Von der Unrechtmäßigkeit des Büchernachdrucks', *Berlinische Monatsschrift*, 5 (1785), pp. 403-17, in *Primary Sources*, p. 406: 'In einem Buche als Schrift redet der Autor zu seinem Leser […]'.

publicly disseminated. Kant thus recognised that, in parallel to a property right in the book as a physical object (*'ius in re'*), authors have an innate right vested in their own person (*'ius personalissimum'*).[118] This idea was expanded by Fichte who, instead of two forms of existence, differentiated between three, that is, (1) the book as a tangible object, to which the normal rules of property apply; (2) the thoughts or ideas in the book, which cannot be exclusively owned, but are the common property of all; and (3) the form of these thoughts or ideas, that is, the way in which they are expressed in the book (the combination with which they appear, their phrasing, their wording, and so forth), which is the inalienable and exclusive property of the author.[119] This last differentiation between freely usable content and the protected form of the author's thoughts and ideas provided an even stronger justification for copyright to be vested in the author. It assured protection not only against a straightforward reproduction of the author's writings, but against any taking of the personal and unique form in which the author had expressed his thoughts or ideas. Thus, this new abstract concept linked everything done to the work back to the personality of the author.[120] This laid the groundwork for a few German scholars to develop the theory of a largely personal author's right.[121] By accentuating the per-

---

118   Kant, p. 416: 'Der Autor und der Eigenthümer des Exemplars können beide mit gleichem Rechte von demselben sagen: es ist mein Buch! aber in verschiedenem Sinne. Der erstere nimmt das Buch als Schrift oder Rede; der zweite bloß als das stumme Instrument der Überbringung der Rede an ihn oder das Publicum, d. i. als Exemplar. Dieses Recht des Verfassers ist aber kein Recht in der Sache, nämlich dem Exemplar (denn der Eigenthümer kann es vor des Verfassers Augen verbrennen), sondern ein angebornes Recht in seiner eignen Person, nämlich zu verhindern, daß ein anderer ihn nicht ohne seine Einwilligung zum Publicum reden lasse [...]'.
119   J.G. Fichte, 'Beweis der Unrechtmäßigkeit des Büchernachdrucks: Ein Räsonnement und eine Fabel', *Berlinische Monatsschrift*, 21 (1793), pp. 447 et seq, in *Primary Sources*.
120   Friedemann Kawohl and Martin Kretschmer, 'Johann Gottlieb Fichte, and the Trap of *Inhalt* (Content) and *Form*: An Information Perspective on Music Copyright', *Information, Communication & Society* (special issue on *Copyright, and the Production of Music*, ed. by Martin Kretschmer and Andy C. Pratt), 12 (2009), 205-28 (pp. 210-6).
121   See Johann Caspar Bluntschli, *Deutsches Privatrecht*, 2 vols (Munich: Literarisch-artistische Anstalt, 1853-54), I (1853), pp. 191-2: 'Das Werk als Geistesproduct gehört zunächst dem Autor an, der es erzeugt hat, [...] als eine Offenbarung und ein Ausdruck seines persönlichen Geistes. Zwischen Autor und Werk besteht ein natürlicher Zusammenhang, wie zwischen Schöpfer und Geschöpf, und jener hat ein natürliches Recht, dass dieses Verhältnis geachtet werde'; and p. 186: 'Heutzutage gehört das Autorrecht zu den allgemein anerkannten menschlichen Rechten'. See also Otto Gierke, *Deutsches Privatrecht*, 3 vols (Leipzig: Duncker & Humblot, 1895-1917), I (1895), p. 756: 'Das Urheberecht ist ein Persönlichkeitsrecht, dessen Gegenstand ein Geisteswerk als Bestandtheil der eignen Persönlichkeitssphäre bildet'.

sonal element in the author's creation, they claimed that authors' rights arise directly from the authorship of a work.[122] Hence, they considered these rights to come into being through the very act of creation ('*die geistige Schöpfungsthat*') and through the act of creation alone.[123]

This had some important consequences for the way in which formalities were perceived. In general, the idea that authors' rights were born with the creation of a work did not correspond with the notion of formalities being constitutive of these rights. Moreover, as the legitimation of protection was seen in the very nature of the author's personal creation, it was considered unreasonable that authors could lose protection due to a failure in the process of completing a formality. This was especially the case if the failure was not attributable to the author (for example, if the formality could also be legally complied with by the publisher),[124] if a formality was not fulfilled because of the intricacy and costs involved (for instance, if the facilities where the formality must be completed were located too far away) or if it concerned mere technical failures (for example, innocent mistakes or late submissions of applications).[125] In the nineteenth century, it was not uncommon for authors to lose protection as a result of any of these practicalities.

Accordingly, there was a growing consensus that the *existence* of authors' rights should not be conditional on formalities and that failure to comply with formalities should never be the occasion of a defeat of authors' rights. In France, it was argued, both in jurisprudence and legal doctrine, that legal deposit was neither constitutive of nor formed the legal basis for literary or artistic property.[126] Decisions appeared in which it was ruled that authors' rights emerged with the creation of a work and that legal deposit was a formality necessary for the exercise of their rights only.[127] Courts also held

---

122   See Bluntschli, p. 199: '[Das Autorrecht] entsteht aus der Urheberschaft [...]'; and Gierke, p. 755: 'durch die Schöpfung eines Geisteswerkes [entsteht] in der Person seines Schöpfers ein gutes Recht'.

123   Gierke, pp. 766, 787-8: 'Das Urheberrecht entsteht durch die geistige Schöpfungsthat, [...] wird unmittelbar durch die Schöpfungsthat begründet [und] wird nur durch geistige Schöpfungsthat begründet'.

124   This was the case, for example, with respect to the legal deposit requirement in France.

125   See for example Henri Louis de Beaufort, *Het auteursrecht in het Nederlandsche en Internationale recht* (Utrecht: Den Boer, 1909; repr. Amsterdam: Buma, 1993), p. 263.

126   See Blanc, p. 137: 'Le dépôt ne constitue pas la propriété, et n'en est pas le point de départ'.

127   See for example Tribunal of Paris, 10 July 1844, *Escudier v. Schonenberger*, in Blanc, pp. 35-6.

that even if a counterfeiter deposited a work before the author did, the author's right would remain unharmed, since this right found its origin in the creation of the work and not in the deposit.[128] Thus, authors' rights were believed to appear directly, automatically and exclusively with the creation of a work.[129] This also became the general opinion in Germany and other continental-European states.[130] Moreover, the idea that authors' rights came into being independently of formalities figured prominently at both the 1858 International Conference on Literary and Artistic Property in Brussels[131] and the 1878 International Conference on Artistic Property in Paris.[132]

At the same time, however, it was acknowledged that the protection of literary and artistic works was not unconditional, but should always be established in accordance with the public interest and societal order. In 1857, the French Court of Cassation ruled that the *exercise* of authors' rights could always be restricted if that would be in the interest of the public.[133] This was equally the case for all other property rights.[134] Proprietors of real property, for example, were also obliged to sacrifice a portion of their rights if the public interest so required, for instance, for the exploitation of (mineral)

---

128   See for example Court of Paris, 12 June 1863, *Mayer et Pierson, Pataille* 1863, 225.
129   See Blanc, p. 138: 'Ce droit découle directement, nécessairement et exclusive-ment du fait de la conception et de la création de l'œuvre. La propriété [...] est antérieure au dépôt et le précède. Il y a plus, elle en est indépendante et peut exister même en son absence [...]'. See also Nion, p. 129.
130   See for example Klostermann, pp. 103 et seq and 185 et seq: 'die Erwerbung des Urheberrechts [erfolgt] durch die Hervorbringung des Geisteswerkes und [ist] nicht an die Erfüllung von Förmlichkeiten gebunden'.
131   See Resolution, part II, no. 7: 'Il n'y a pas lieu d'astreindre les auteurs d'ouvrages de littérature ou d'art à certaines formalités, à raison de leur droit. [...] [Leur] inob-servation ne peut et ne doit jamais entraîner la déchéance du droit'; and Resolution, part IV, no. 4: 'Des formalités particulières ne doivent pas être exigées pour les oeu-vres d'art, pas plus que pour les productions littéraires, comme condition absolue de l'acquisition et de la conservation de la propriété', in Romberg, I, pp. 175-8.
132   See Resolution no. 7: 'L'auteur d'une œuvre d'art ne doit être astreint à aucune formalité pour assurer son droit', in *Congrès International de la Propriété Artistique: Tenu à Paris du 18 au 21 septembre 1878* (Paris: Imprimerie Nationale, 1879), pp. 115-7.
133   French Court of Cassation, 14 December 1857, *Verdi et Blanchet* v. *Calzado, Dal-loz* 1858, 1, 161: 'Que des considérations d'ordre et d'interêt public ont dû deter-miner le législateur à en régler et modifier l'exercice' (p. 164).
134   See Art. XVII of the Declaration of the Rights of Man and of the Citizen of 1789, which speaks of property as 'an inviolable and sacred right, that no one shall be deprived of except where the public interest, legally defined, shall evidently require it [...]'.

resources or for road construction.[135] Likewise, because of their cultural importance and social utility, it was deemed completely normal that authors' rights at a certain moment would enter the public domain, and thus were of a limited duration, and that their exercise could be subject to particular formalities.[136] In Germany and other continental-European states the laws were based on a comparable 'balancing act' between the protection of authors, on the one hand, and the interest of the public, on the other hand.[137]

Thus, while literary and artistic property was believed to *exist* independently of formalities, there was a general understanding that the *exercise* of authors' rights could always be restricted if that were to be in the public's interest.[138] This explains to a great extent why, despite the increased person-oriented nature of authors' rights and the ensuing belief that authors' rights were born with the creation of a work, formalities were nevertheless continued. In France in particular, formalities were thought to fulfil some important functions for the exercise of authors' rights. This does not seem to be at odds with the labour theory and natural rights approaches underlying the theory of literary and artistic property, which focus on the acquisition of property rights and thus on their enjoyment (that is, the existence of the rights) rather than their exercise.[139] As long as they left the title of ownership of works unharmed, formalities were not believed to contradict the literary and artistic property theory on which authors' rights were based.[140]

---

135   See Étienne Blanc at the 1858 International Conference in Brussels, in Romberg, I, p. 69.

136   See the very interesting debate on the duration of the literary and artistic property rights at the 1858 International Conference in Brussels in Romberg, I, pp. 69 et seq and 95 et seq. In this debate, a clear appraisal of the interests of authors and the public domain was made.

137   See for example: Bluntschi, p. 193 ; Gierke, p. 755 ; and Klippel, p. 135.

138   See Resolution, part II, no. 7: 'Si des formalités particulières peuvent être utiles, soit comme mesure d'administration et d'ordre, soit comme moyen de constater et de prouver le droit de propriété [...]'; and Resolution, part IV, no. 4: 'dans un cas comme dans l'autre, des formalités peuvent être désirables comme mesure d'ordre et pour faciliter l'exercice régulier du droit' of the 1858 International Conference on Literary and Artistic Property in Brussels in Romberg, I, pp. 175-8.

139   For the late nineteenth century French legal terminology of the 'enjoyment' and 'exercise' of a property right, see Marcel Planiol, *Traité élémentaire de droit civil: conforme au programme officiel des facultés de droit*, 5th edn, 3 vols (Paris: Pichon etc., 1908-10), I (1908), p. 161 (no. 431): 'Avoir la jouissance du droit de propriété, c'est avoir l'aptitude nécessaire pour devenir propriétaire' (referring basically to the acquisition of the right and thus to the title of property); and: 'en avoir l'exercice [du droit de propriété], c'est pouvoir user de son droit de propriété' (referring to the ability to use the right, i.e. to legally enforce it, assign it, license it, etc.).

140   In general, all limitations to authors' rights were considered permissible by

3.2.2 The Functions of Copyright Formalities

In the nineteenth century, copyright formalities were thought valuable for a variety of reasons. They were considered to play an important role, both within the copyright system (internal functions) and without the copyright system (external functions). In general, this approbation of formalities fits the general mind-set of this period. At the time it seems that formalities, and registration in particular, were seen as a panacea that could cure nearly all problems, at least those concerning title and assurances of property.[141] Moreover, because of technological and administrative innovations in the earlier nineteenth century, such as the improvement of the postal services and transport infrastructures, registration had become much easier.[142] In the UK and elsewhere, this prompted a great interest in different types of registries, those for land, deeds and mortgages,[143] and for designs, patents and trade marks,[144] probably being the most noteworthy examples. Registration was thus assumed to be good. This may well explain the continuation of formalities in nineteenth century copyright law.[145]

3.2.2.1 Internal Functions

Within the copyright system, formalities performed several key functions. First, they fulfilled an imperative evidentiary function.[146] In France, for

the proponents of literary and artistic property, provided that they did not affect the authors' title of ownership and thus the property rights in their works, during the statutorily prescribed terms of protection. See Pfister, pp. 166-7.

141   See for example J.E.R. de Villiers, *The History of the Legislation Concerning Real and Personal Property in England during the Reign of Queen Victoria* (London: C.J. Clay and Sons, 1901), p. 11, who mentions that, in 1830, the UK Real Property Commissioners found compulsory registration of real property '[the] great and sovereign remedy [...] to cure all evils; to render titles secure, fraud impossible, and loss of deeds harmless'.

142   See Lionel Bently, 'Requiem for Registration? Reflections on the History of the UK Registered Designs System', in *The Prehistory and Development of Intellectual Property Systems*, ed. by Alison Firth, Perspectives on Intellectual Property Series, 1 (London: Sweet & Maxwell, 1997), pp. 1-46 (p. 35).

143   See A.W.B. Simpson, *A History of the Land Law*, 2nd edn (Oxford: Clarendon Press, 1986), pp. 280-3.

144   Systems of registration were introduced by the Designs Registration Act (1839), 2 Vict., c. 17, the Patent Law Amendment Act (1852), 15 and 16 Vict., c. 83 and the Trade Marks Act (1875), 38 and 39 Vict., c. 91.

145   See Bently, pp. 34 and 35 (note 38), quoting one commentator who assumed that registration in the Fine Arts Copyright Act (1862) was nothing but a knee-jerk response to the alleged cure-all effect of registration.

146   See Sherman and Bently, p. 184, emphasizing the role of registration in establishing proof and authenticity in the nineteenth-century copyright registration sys-

example, the receipt that was given upon deposit constituted *prima facie* proof of the property right on the work deposited.[147] Although always subject to be rebutted by other evidence,[148] legal deposit was an important means of proving the anteriority of authorship and, thus, the priority of a claim to the title.[149] Moreover, because of the legal deposit, the authenticity of a work could easily be resolved. An identical function was attached to the legal deposit in several German states.[150] Equally, in the UK, the facts stated in an entry of registration gave a legal presumption in favour of the registered person. This concerned not only initial ownership. Ever since transfers of ownership could be entered on the registers, they served as *prima facie* evidence of the ownership, assignment or licensing of the right.[151] As a result, because of the evidentiary weight attached to formalities, they were capable of assisting in providing low-cost and quick resolution of disputes.[152]

Second, formalities fulfilled an important publicity function. The registration requirements in the various British copyright acts, for example, served 'as notice and warning to the public' not to infringe ignorantly another man's literary or artistic property.[153] This would establish legal certainty and, in addition, facilitate the regular exercise of rights. The idea was that the copyright owner of a work, as well as the identity and

tem in the UK.

147   See Art. 9 of the French Ordinance of 24 October 1814.

148   See for example: French Court of Cassation, 19 March 1858, *Hache et Pepin-Lehaulleur v. Goupil*, Dalloz 1858, 1, 190; Court of Paris, 29 November 1869, *Placet v. Yvon*, Dalloz 1871, 2, 59.

149   See Blanc, pp. 137-8, who speaks of a 'presumption of paternity' in favour of the depositor.

150   See for example: Art. II of the Letter patent of the Chancellery (*Kanzleipatent*) of 30 November 1833 for the Duchy of Holstein; Art. V of the Bavarian Act of 15 April 1840; Art. 7 of the Regulation of Lübeck of 31 July 1841.

151   In case of an unsettled dispute on the ownership of a work, however, courts could order that an entry was worthless as evidence at trial. See for example: *Chappell v. Purday*, 152 *Eng. Rep.* 1214, 12 M. and W. 303 (1843); *Ex parte Davidson*, 118 *Eng. Rep.* 884, 2 El. and Bl. 577 (1853).

152   See Bently, p. 33, who indicates that this was the main reason for the Select Committee on Arts and their Connection with Manufactures (1836) to propose a registration system in respect of designs.

153   The Statute of Anne (1710), for instance, stated explicitly that registration should prevent that people 'through ignorance offend against this act.' See also the argumentation by Lord Kenyon in *Beckford v. Hood* (1798), 101 *Eng. Rep.* 1164 (p. 1167), 7 *T.R.* 620 (p. 627): 'there was good reason for requiring an entry to be made at Stationers' Hall, which was to serve as notice and warning to the public, that they might not ignorantly incur the forfeitures or penalties before enacted against such as pirated the works of others'.

boundaries of the property right, should easily be ascertainable if permission was sought for the (re)utilisation of that work.[154] For that reason, it was commonly ordered that the register book be open for public inspection 'at all seasonable and convenient times'.[155] By enabling the title of ownership and the identity of the work to be established before (re)utilising that work, registration was to provide prospective users with adequate legal certainty.[156] After the law had opened the possibility for registering assignments and licensing agreements and formalised the layout of the registration scheme, the identity and whereabouts of the owner of a copyright could be better scrutinised.[157] The same functions of publicity and legal certainty were connected to the various notification requirements. This is perfectly illustrated by the British case *Newton v. Cowie*, where it was held that 'for the protection of the public, it is most material that the day of publication of the print [as well as the name of the right owner] should appear, otherwise it is impossible for a rival publisher to know whether he offends or not'.[158] Other formalities served as important indicators for the public to know whether the author had reserved a certain right,[159] or simply, whether the author had fulfilled a certain formality and, thus, if the formality was constitutive of the right, whether authors' rights attached to the work.[160] The latter function was displayed visibly in the Dutch Copyright Act of

---

154   Sherman and Bently, p. 185.

155   See for example Sec. 2 of the Statute of Anne (1710).

156   See for example Catherine Seville, *Literary Copyright Reform in Early Victorian England: The Framing of the 1842 Copyright Act* (Cambridge: Cambridge University Press, 1999), p. 237, note 38.

157   Sec. 13, plus appendix, of the Copyright Act (1842). An entry should include the title of a book, the date of first publication and the names and places of residence of the publisher and copyright owner (or assignee). Although a small error could be fatal to the registration, any inaccuracy could be repaired by a later entrance. See *Low v. Routledge* (1865-6), LR 1 Ch. App. 42 (Court of Appeal in Chancery, 1865).

158   *Newton v. Cowie* (1827), 130 *Eng. Rep.* 759 (p. 760), 4 *Bing.* 234 (pp. 236-7).

159   An example is the translation right in respect of literary works.

160   In the Netherlands, for example, Art. 14 of the Sovereign Enactment of 1814 and Art. 6(c) of the Copyright Act of 1817 required a listing of deposited works in the *Staatscourant* (the Government Gazette), but only if the deposit was carried out in conformity with the law. Likewise, in France, an advertisement of deposit was typically inserted in the *Journal de la librairie*. In the German state Lübeck, Art. 7 of the Regulation of 31 July 1841 required each copy of a work to be marked by a notice that the deposit had been complied with, together with the day and year of delivery of the copies. Finally, in the UK, Sec. 3 of the Statute of Anne (1710) provided that if the registration was not completed because of a refusal or negligence by the clerk, an advertisement in the Gazette would 'have the like benefit, as if such entry [...] had been duly made'.

1881, which required a public registration and monthly publication in the Government Gazette of all deposited works.[161] This allowed anyone to ascertain whether a work had been duly deposited and, therefore, assuming that it met the originality standard, was copyright protected or had entered the public domain.[162]

Third, formalities were considered an important instrument for establishing the duration of protection of works in those cases where the law laid down a fixed term.[163] This was the case, for example, in the UK where fixed terms, to be calculated from the date of first publication, were prescribed in respect of both artistic and literary works.[164] Hence, without some visible evidence of the date of first publication, either on the work itself or in a public register, it was almost impossible to ascertain when the term of protection commenced and, thus, when the copyright in a work expired.[165] This was equally the case in a few German states where the terms of protection were calculated from the date of first publication and where the receipt of deposit, besides a presumption of the title of ownership, provided proof of the publication date of works.[166] Lastly, in the Netherlands, the relation between formalities and the duration of protection also became an issue when, in 1881, the legislator moved away from a term of protection *post mortem auctoris* and changed it for a fixed term, which was also calculated from the officially recorded date indicated on the receipt of deposit.[167]

---

161   Art. 11 of the Dutch Copyright Act of 1881.

162   See: Veegens, p. 125; De Beaufort, pp. 265 et seq.

163   De Beaufort, pp. 257-8; F.W.J.G. Snijder van Wissenkerke, *Het auteursrecht in Nederland: Auteurswet 1912 en herziene Berner Conventie* (Gouda: Van Goor Zonen, 1913), p. 59.

164   The Engravers' Copyright Act (1735) laid down a copyright term of fourteen years from publication, which was extended to twenty-eight years by the Engravers' Copyright Act (1766). Under the 1798 and 1814 Sculpture Copyright Acts, the term was fourteen years from publication (1798) plus an additional fourteen years if the author was still living after the initial term (1814). The Fine Arts Copyright Act (1862) stipulated a term of the author's life plus seven years. For literary works, the Statute of Anne (1710) fixed the copyright term at fourteen years plus an additional fourteen years if the author survived the first term. The Copyright Acts of 1814 and 1842 increased the term of protection to twenty-eight years or 'the residue of his natural life' if the author survived this term and forty-two years or the life of the author plus seven years if that proved to be the longer.

165   *Report of the Royal Commission on Copyright* [C.2036], XXIV (London: HMSO, 1878), p. xxiii (para. 134).

166   See for example: Art. II of the Letter patent of the Chancellery (*Kanzleipatent*) of 30 November 1833 for the Duchy of Holstein; Art. 7 of the Regulation of Lübeck of 31 July 1841.

167   While Art. 3 of the Dutch Copyright Act of 25 January 1817 laid down a copy-

By the end of the century, however, the importance of formalities for the internal operation of the copyright system had gradually weakened. First, formalities were increasingly replaced with legal presumptions. In Germany, for example, the Copyright Act of 1870 laid down a general presumption of authorship, stipulating that without proof to the contrary, the person who was named as author on the work was deemed to be the actual author.[168] This was considered to give authors greater latitude for the assertion of their rights.[169] While legal presumptions were less onerous for authors, they were believed to achieve generally the same outcome as formalities.[170] As a consequence, formalities started to lose out to legal presumptions. This was clearly manifested in the Berne Convention, which contained legal presumptions of authorship from its early inception.[171] Second, formalities increasingly lost their significance for the calculation of the term of protection as the duration of copyright became increasingly linked to the author's lifespan. In France, the term of protection being that of the life of the author plus a limited period thereafter already existed since the revolutionary decrees of 1791 and 1793.[172] In Germany, a term of protection *post mortem auctoris* was also adopted in the Copyright Act of 1870.[173] Later, a term based on the author's life plus a fixed term thereafter would become the standard in the Berne Convention as well.[174] Following

right term of twenty years after the author's death, Art. 13 of the Dutch Copyright Act of 1881 prescribed a term of fifty years from publication. If the author outlived the term of fifty years, the copyright term would extend to the remainder of his life.

168   Art. 28 of the Federal Copyright Act of 1870.

169   See Dr. Dambach, in *Actes de la Conférence internationale réunie à Berne 1884*, p. 36.

170   See: Fischer, pp. 33-4; Dambach, pp. 205-9. Since most formalities established *prima facie* evidence only, legal certainty could equally be established by a set of legal presumptions. Because the facts recorded by these formalities usually were not verified *ex ante*, their correctness could always be contested. In principle, therefore, these formalities only proved that a fact was recorded at a certain time.

171   See Art. 11 BC (1886). Nowadays, legal presumptions of authorship are contained in Art. 15 BC (1971).

172   The decrees of 1791 and 1793 fixed the term of protection at the life of the author plus five and ten years, respectively. In 1810, the latter term was extended, for the author's widow, to her lifetime and, for his children, to twenty years after the author's death. Finally, in 1866, a term of protection of life plus fifty years was adopted.

173   Art. 8 of the Federal Copyright Act of 1870 set the term at thirty years after the author's death. The same term was adopted in the German Federal Act concerning the authors' rights in works of the visual arts of 1876.

174   While the 1886 Berne Convention set no minimum term of protection, Art. 7 BC (1908) laid down a term of the life of the author plus 50 years. Yet, this term was not mandatory and contracting states with a shorter term were permitted to retain

this, the UK and the Netherlands also stopped calculating the term of protection from the date of publication.[175]

Nonetheless, several legal commentators and practitioners maintained that formalities were important for the internal functioning of literary and artistic property rights. French lawyers, especially, were convinced of the necessity of formalities for facilitating the regular exercise of rights.[176] Even in 1878, when in Germany the laws had already contained legal presumptions for a number of years, Pataille, *avocat* at the Court of Appeals in Paris, argued that there were good reasons to subject the exercise of authors' rights to formalities. In infringement suits he had experienced many problems in proving priority of authorship, especially where works of small authors were concerned.[177] Therefore, Pataille believed that it was in the authors' own interest to complete a formality enabling them to provide evidence of their property rights in court.[178] In addition, formalities were still considered an important means of enhancing publicity and legal certainty. Thus, formalities were thought to play a key role in ensuring an appropriate balance between the protection of authors' rights and the public interest. This may well explain why, in France, the legislator persisted until 1925 in requiring legal deposit as a condition to suit.

---

their existing terms. Ultimately, in 1948, the term of the life of the author plus 50 years was made mandatory for all contracting states. See also the current Art. 7(1) BC (1971).

175   The 'life plus 50' term was introduced into British law for the first time by the Copyright Act of 1911. In the Netherlands, the same term was adopted in the Copyright Act 1912.

176   At the 1858 International Conference on Literary and Artistic Property in Brussels, the importance of formalities for the exercise of rights was emphasized, inter alia, by Étienne Blanc, *avocat* at the Imperial Court in Paris. See Romberg, I, p. 210. The same was done by Jules Pataille, *avocat* at the Court of Appeals in Paris, at the 1878 International Conference on Artistic Property in Paris. See *Congrès International de la Propriété Artistique*, pp. 53 et seq. For an account from Germany, see the *Mémoire* of Prof. Warnkönig and Dr O. Wächter in response of the questions proposed by the 1858 Committee of Organization, in Romberg, I, pp. 268-74 (p. 269).

177   See Jules Pataille in *Congrès International de la Propriété Artistique*, p. 53, where he stated that in four out of five lawsuits which he had to plea, he had great difficulties in proving anteriority.

178   *Congrès International de la Propriété Artistique*, pp. 53 et seq. In general, Pataille did not seem to have any problem with copyright formalities. He questioned: why should authors not register the birth of their works like a father will declare his child and have it registered on the Registry of Births, Deaths and Marriages? Ibid., p. 54.

3.2.2.2 External Functions

Except for internal functions, formalities also performed a few key roles outside the copyright system. The legal deposit of copies, for example, undoubtedly was also designed to enrich the collections of national libraries. Accordingly, as part of a general social-cultural programme aimed at creating a national cultural depositary, the legal deposit fulfilled an important goal of general utility.[179] In addition, formalities played a role in economic procedure. The registers of copyright, for instance, may have also operated as trade registers and, thus, as instruments for the economic ordering of the market for books or other protected subject matter.[180] Finally, formalities were sometimes used as an instrument of governmental control. Although this was especially the case in the old book privilege system, when censorship and formalities commonly went hand in hand,[181] the nineteenth century also witnessed a few occasions where the two were tied up together. In France, for example, Napoleon reinstated in 1810 the legal deposit as a measure of administrative monitoring.[182] He demanded that every publisher deposit five copies of each printed work,[183] one of which

---

179   Lemaitre, pp. xxxvii-xxxviii.

180   It is likely that this function was attached to the registration in Saxony, where the early literary (and artistic) property legislation was still primarily aimed at protecting the Leipzig book trade. See Kawohl, pp. 24-5. The registers in the old system of stationers' copyright in England played a similar role: as indexes for ascertaining who owned the rights for which book, the registers at the same time provided important evidence of the segmentation of the book market among the different publishers.

181   See for example: Ulrich Eisenhardt, *Die kaiserliche Aufsicht über Buchdruck, Buchhandel und Presse im Heiligen Römischen Reich Deutscher Nation (1496-1806): Ein Beitrag zur Geschichte der Bücher- und Pressezensur*, Studien und Quellen zur Geschichte des deutschen Verfassungsrechts, 3 (Karlsruhe: Müller, 1970); Cyndia Susan Clegg, *Press censorship in Elizabethan England* (Cambridge: Cambridge University Press, 1997).

182   Art. 48 of the Imperial Decree of 5 February 1810 containing regulations for the printing and the book trade.

183   Interestingly, while Art. 6 of the 1793 French Decree placed the duty to deposit on the author, the Decree of 5 February 1810 makes the publisher responsible for depositing. Yet, this must be understood correctly. In theory, the publisher's obligation was separate from that of the author. Both were equally responsible for performing the duty imposed on them. This also manifests itself in the legal consequences of non-compliance. For authors, an omission to deposit resulted in the inadmissibility of their claims before a court. For publishers, it gave rise to a fine and confiscation of the copies that were not deposited. In practice, however, it was unnecessary for both the publisher and author to deposit. A deposit carried out by the publisher exempted the author from his obligation. See Pouillet, pp. 465-6 (no. 425). Consequently, the deposit performed by the printer was sufficient to ensure

was meant for censorship control.[184] This lasted until 1829, when Martignac, the French Minister of the Interior, abandoned the idea of legal deposit as a measure of state censorship.[185] Equally, in the second half of the century, the British applied formalities as an instrument of imperial surveillance of colonial literature. Following the 1857 uprising in India, for instance, they issued the 1867 Press and Registration of Books Act, which required publishers, within one month after publication, to submit three copies of every book to the local government, along with information regarding the book and the payment of a small fee.[186] Publishers who failed to comply with these formalities could be confronted with severe fines and imprisonment. In addition, non-compliance resulted in the inability to acquire copyright protection under the domestic Indian Act of 1847.[187]

In essence, however, the different purposes for which formalities, in the above cases, were used, concerned clear external matters. While linked to the copyright system, the belief grew that they could be regulated as well, separately from one another. This was the case, first of all, with censorship rules. After the fierce struggle for freedom of the press during the French Revolution, press regulation and authors' rights protection generally developed in two distinct directions during the nineteenth century. The instances where the two were connected became increasingly sporadic.[188] The same

the preservation of the author's rights. See the rulings of the Court of Cassation of 1 March 1834, *Thiéry v. Marchant, Dalloz* 1834, 1, 113 ; *Sirey* (2ᵐᵉ Sér.) 1834, 1, 65; of 20 August 1852, *Bourret et Morel v. Escriche de Ortéga, Dalloz* 1852, 1, 335; and of 6 November 1872, *Garnier v. Lévy, Dalloz* 1874, 1, 493. But see Court of Cassation, 30 June 1832, *Noël et Chapsal v. Simon, Dalloz* 1832, 1, 289, ruling in the opposite direction.

184   Art. 4 of the Ordinance of 24 October 1814. See Lemaitre, pp. xxxvi-xxxvii.

185   Art. 1 of the Ordinance of 9 January 1828.

186   Act no. XXV of 22 March 1867, An Act for the Regulation of Printing-Presses and Newspapers, for the Preservation of Copies of Books Printed in British India, and for the Registration of Such Books. The aim was to register any relevant piece of information that could be harmful for the political situation in India and to create annual statistical reports on the state of colonial literature. See Robert Darnton, 'Book Production in British India, 1850-1900', *Book History*, 5 (2002), 239-62.

187   Act no. XX of 1847, An Act for the Encouragement of Learning in the Territories Subject to the Government of the East India Company. See Lionel Bently, 'Copyright, Translations, and Relations Between Britain and India in the Nineteenth and Early Twentieth Centuries', *Chicago-Kent Law Review*, 82 (2007), 1181-240 (pp. 1183-5, notes 8 and 11).

188   In many European countries, the link between censorship and copyright loosened after the French Revolution and disappeared entirely during the nineteenth century. See for example Ludwig Gieseke, 'Zensur und Nachdruckschutz in deutschen Staaten in den Jahren nach 1800', in *Historische Studien zum Urheberrecht in Europa*, pp. 21-31, who marks the year 1835 as the date on which the two finally

was true of national cultural depositaries. If states wished to enrich their national libraries, there was no need to establish a legal deposit formality inside the copyright framework. They could also create a system of legal deposit without depending authors' rights upon it.[189] Finally, to the degree that copyright registers also functioned as trade registers, more and more alternative sources from which data about the economic ordering of the market could be deduced, began to appear, including general book trade indexes (which were voluntarily continued) and national and international bibliographic information systems.[190] In general, these sources proved much more accurate than copyright registers, which were often incomplete, especially if the existence of copyright did not rely on the act of registration.

3.2.3 Some Important Conceptual Innovations and Transformations

Lastly, the second half of the nineteenth century saw some important conceptual innovations in copyright and authors' rights law which also affected the notion of copyright formalities. Throughout the century the scope of protection was significantly extended. More and more new categories of works found protection under copyright law. This included subject matter like sculptures, paintings, drawings and photographs. In addition, protection became independent from the specific mode or form of expression of a work. Instead of mere printed matter (such as books, maps, charts, journals and sheet music) or pre-fixed works of art (such as drawings, paintings, sculptures and engravings), protection was conferred on works *qua abstractum*; that is, the protection of authors' rights in literary

---

separated in Germany.

189   This was, for example, the critique that some people expressed regarding the continuation of the legal deposit as a condition to suit in France. See Ernst Röthlisberger, 'Gesamtüberblick über die Vorgänge auf urheberrechtlichem Gebiete in den Jahren 1904, 1905 und 1906', *Börsenblatt für den Deutschen Buchhandel*, 74 (1907), 1688-91 (p. 1689): 'An dieser Einrichtung der Pflichtexemplare, die ganz gut als presspolizeiliche oder bibliothekarische massregel neben dem Schutz des Autorrechts bestehen kann, aber auf diesen absolut keinen Einfluss ausüben sollte, wird beständig herumgedoktert, ohne nennenswerten Erfolg'.

190   A noteworthy example was the 'Universal Bibliographic Repertory' which in 1895 was set up by the *Institut International de Bibliographie* (IIB), in 1932 renamed to *Féderation Internationale de Documentation* (FID). This database, which by 1912 contained nearly nine million entries, was considered to render an invaluable service. See *Actes de la Conférence de l'Union internationale pour la protection des oeuvres littéraires et artistiques: réunie à Paris du 15 avril au 4 mai 1896* (Berne: Bureau international de l'Union, 1897), p. 178.

and artistic works was severed from the physical object in which they were embodied or manifested.[191] This gave even more prominence to the intangible character of copyright protected works. Moreover, it finally led to the recognition of copyright protection of the multiple ways in which a work could be exploited. Instead of being granted a mere right to print and reprint, which had been the essence of copyright hitherto, authors were increasingly conferred exclusive rights of reproduction (in a broad sense), of public performance and, occasionally, of making translations and adaptations.[192] These transformations seem to have had a great impact on the development of copyright formalities.

First, in respect of the increased focus on the intangible, formalities may, on the one hand, have been thought valuable to provide some sense of legal certainty. From the late eighteenth century onwards, when, at least in the UK, the idea of property in the intangible had been firmly established, the idea that a property right could exist solely in the intangible had raised many concerns.[193] One of the most prominent concerns was that it was difficult to manage and shape the limits of intangible property.[194] Formalities may well have contributed to alleviating such concerns. As Bently concludes in respect of the nineteenth century design registration scheme in the UK: 'A registration system operated as a functional equivalent of possession of title deeds − fixing ownership in and marking boundaries of a particular asset. Registration thus made the whole idea of intangible property much less threatening'.[195] Hence, by making more explicit the intangible assets which formed the subject matter of protection, formalities may have played a key role in rationalising this strange concept of intangible property.[196]

---

191   Kawohl and Kretschmer, pp. 214 et seq.

192   For example, under the Prussian act of 1837, restricted acts did not only include the simple reprinting, publication and distribution of writings (Arts 2 and 9), but also the transcription of lectures and sermons (Art. 3), the translation of writings for which the translation right was reserved by a notice (Art. 4), the adaptation or rearrangement of musical compositions (Art. 20), the creation of derivative works of drawings, paintings or sculptures (Art. 23) and the public performance of dramatic and musical works (Art. 32).

193   See John Feather, 'The Publishers and the Pirates: British Copyright Law in Theory and Practice, 1710-1775,' *Publishing History*, 22 (1987), 5-32 (p. 25), who states, in respect of the 1774 decision in *Donaldson v. Beckett*: 'Despite all the distrust of the idea of incorporeal property, such property was now deemed to exist'.

194   For a comprehensive account of the various concerns raised, see Sherman and Bently, pp. 19-42.

195   Bently, pp. 35-6. See also Sherman and Bently, pp. 182-3.

196   Arguments of this kind were voiced as late as 1878. See *Report of the Royal Commission on Copyright*, p. xxiii (para. 136): 'copyright is a species of incorporeal

On the other hand, the abstraction implicit in the new notion of authors' rights contradicted with formalities to a large extent. As Kawohl and Kretschmer have explained, formalities like registration, deposit and notice undermine the presumption that works merit protection *qua abstractum*: 'If the emerging rationale of copyright derives from the character of abstract, identical authored works (as opposed to the earlier incentive in the creation or dissemination of useful products), protection should coincide with the moment of creation'.[197] Also, abstract work identities are not easily captured in formalities, especially if they are not fixed in some tangible medium.[198] It is hard to imagine the registration of a performed musical work or the deposit of an oral lecture, speech or sermon (not to think of marking these works with a notice of some kind).[199] Hence, there was some tension between the abstraction and existing formalities.[200]

In addition, formalities did not fit easily with each and every new category of works. In particular for works of art, such as sculptures, paintings, drawings and photographs, registration and deposit proved very difficult. For this reason, representatives of artists and photographers campaigned strongly against these formalities,[201] arguing that the situation in relation to artistic works was different from that of literary works.[202] Unlike the

---

property, of which some visible evidence is desirable'.

197   Kawohl and Kretschmer, p. 221.

198   Although fixation was not an express condition in the early British Copyright Acts, protection was granted only in respect of published works, which implied their fixation in a tangible medium. According to the current Sec. 3(2) UK Copyright, Designs and Patents Act 1988 (c. 48), on the other hand, 'copyright does not subsist in a literary, dramatic or musical work unless and until it is recorded, in writing or otherwise'.

199   J. Heemskerk Az., *Voordragten over den eigendom van voortbrengselen van den geest*, 2nd edn (Amsterdam: Beerendonk, 1869; repr. Amsterdam: De Kloof, 2000, with introduction by R.J.Q. Klomp), pp. 81-2.

200   Furthermore, there is the practical difficulty of when a formality would need to be completed for securing the protection in an abstract work which only has been performed or publicly recited. This problem is illustrated by Sec. 5 of the Lecturers Copyright Act (1835), 5 and 6 Will. IV, c. 65, where copyright protection was denied for oral lectures, unless a specific formality was fulfilled. This formality consisted in a two days' previous notice in writing to be given to two justices living within five miles of the place where the lecture would be held.

201   See the interesting debates regarding the necessity of formalities to ensure the protection of artistic property rights, in *Congrès International de la Propriété Artistique*, pp. 52-9. In respect of the registration of artistic works in the UK, see also *Minutes of the Evidence Taken before the Royal Commission on Copyright* in *Parliamentary Papers* 1878 [C.2036-1], XXIV, questions 3957-4035 (pp. 212-8).

202   This was particularly the case for artistic works that were not reproducible *ad infinitum* (like paintings, drawings and sculpture). Yet, for works which were

situation with design, patent and trade mark rights, the registration or deposit of which depended on a representative description or a sample of the protected object rather than the object itself, in the case of copyright, it was considered elementary to reproduce the intangible work in its full physical appearance. In an attempt to identify the object of protection, all characteristic – subjective and original – elements that made the work eligible for protection needed to be captured.[203] However, artistic works did not lend themselves easily to reproduction. A description of the essence of artistic works was hard to give.[204] Moreover, even if a simple registration of the description of the work could be produced, it was questioned whether this would adequately provide *prima facie* evidence of the property: in the absence of a deposit of the work (or a photograph or sketch thereof), would it not give rise to problems if a similar description had been registered by another person?[205] Lastly, if artistic works were technically reproducible, it would be inapt to demand the deposit of a replica, since the cost of reproduction would often be prohibitively high.

Yet, even for literary works, for which reproduction was technically easier, reproduction costs could present too much of a barrier to performing the legal deposit, especially where a special or limited edition of the work was concerned.[206] Moreover, registration and deposit of literary works often proved unsatisfactory for accurately defining the nature and limits of the intangible property. Consequently, where it proved increasingly problematic to define *ex ante* the essence and the boundaries of literary and artistic property via formalities, it was left more and more to the legislature to find legal techniques to enable the identification of works, and to the courts to

---

intended to be reproduced (like engravings, prints and photographs), there was less resistance against formalities. See Jules Pataille in *Congrès International de la Propriété Artistique*, p. 53 and, for the UK, *Report of the Royal Commission on Copyright*, p. xxvi (para. 157).

203   Sherman and Bently, pp. 183 et seq.

204   See for example the remark on this point by Mr Meissonier, president of the 1878 International Conference on Artistic Property in Paris, in: *Congrès International de la Propriété Artistique*, p. 56. Others, however, questioned the impracticability of registration for artistic works. See for example the response by Eugène Pouillet, ibid., pp. 56-7.

205   See Allexandre Beaume, *avocat* at the Paris Court, in *Congrès International de la Propriété Artistique*, p. 58.

206   In addition, for those copyright owners holding large catalogues of rights for works with low individual value (for example, musical scores), formalities like registration and deposit often also appeared too costly and impracticable. See Lord Thring, quoted by Lord Monkswell (24 April 1899) in Sherman and Bently, p. 183 (note 38).

demarcate the nature of works *ex post*.[207] In this respect, copyright varied considerably from other intellectual property rights, the documents of registration of which became increasingly more important for establishing the property status.[208] For these latter types of rights, this seems to have also been more essential than for copyright. Due to the very personal nature of literary and artistic works, the chances of *Doppelschöpfung* (that is, the coincidental parallel and independent creation of two or more unique or highly similar works by two or more different authors) are very small, at least if compared with designs and patents law.[209] Thus, while for other intellectual property rights, systems of registration were deemed of great importance for establishing priority and avoiding difficulties of proof regarding independent production,[210] formalities seemed less indispensable for an efficient protection of authors' rights.[211]

Accordingly, while copyright law 'moved from the concrete to the abstract',[212] many of the old formalities started to lose their significance. At the same time, however, new formalities were introduced in response to the extended protection of the various modes of exploitation of abstract authored works. While copyright used to grant exclusivity regarding the printing or reprinting of works in their original manifestation only, with the new conception of abstract authored works, the scope of protection was extended and copyright began to include the rights of making translations and adaptations, public performance and recitation.[213] Still, there were great concerns about the economic implications of these previously unprotected acts being brought under the scope of protection. Therefore, national legislators often began to impose specifying formalities as threshold requirements. Before authors received protection for these new forms

---

207   Sherman and Bently, p. 192.
208   Ibid., pp. 185 et seq.
209   J.J. Wijnstroom and J.L.A. Peremans, *Het auteursrecht* (Zwolle: Tjeenk Willink, 1930), pp. 16-17.
210   Bently, pp. 38, 41.
211   The possibility to prove the author's identity by means other than formalities was stressed by John Leighton, a British artist, at the 1878 International Conference on Artistic Property in Paris. He maintained that registration was redundant because the author of a work could always be recognized by experts, either by his writing, his drawing, his brushstroke, or the manner of painting. See *Congrès International de la Propriété Artistique*, p. 57.
212   See Sherman and Bently, pp. 55 et seq, for an account of how 'the law [...] moved from the concrete to the abstract' due to the 'shift from the surface of the text to the essence of the creation'.
213   Kawohl and Kretschmer, pp. 214 et seq.

of exploitation, they were repeatedly required to mark their works with an explicit notice of reservation (as discussed above).[214] This is intended to uphold the balance between the limited exclusivity granted to authors and the common interest in the public domain. As the general attitude towards formalities changed and the Berne Convention adopted the principle of no formalities, many specifying formalities were abolished as well. However, some continued to exist and, even today, can still be found in the copyright law of various countries.[215]

3.3 The Absence of Concomitant Developments in the Netherlands and the UK

Before concluding the chapter, a final note should be made about why the Netherlands and the UK retained formalities on a more consistent and ongoing basis and, consequently, why the above innovations exerted little influence in these two countries. In the Netherlands, the second part of the nineteenth century was characterised by a pragmatic rather than ideological thinking on copyright law. It was generally believed that there was no higher legal principle which forced the state to secure the rights of authors to the fruits of their labour.[216] Instead, there was general accord that the law should grant authors certain exclusive rights solely in the public interest: protection was needed to ensure that authors continued creating works.[217] Dutch copyright law thus appears to be one of opportunity rather than of deliberate, principled choices.[218] This also fits the spirit of the time, which

---

214   Kawohl and Kretschmer, p. 221, argue that the early copyright registration in Prussian and British copyright already needs to be considered as 'an indicator of political and economic uneasiness about the [extended] locus of protection, regarding both subject matter and exclusive rights provided'.

215   See for example the reservation requirement in respect of the exclusive reproduction right for newspaper articles, which is expressly allowed by Art. 10bis(1) BC (1971) and which can be found for example in Art. 49 of the present German Copyright and Neighbouring Rights Act 1965 and in Art. 15(1) of the current Dutch Copyright Act.

216   See Mr. J. Fresemann Viëtor in *Handelingen der Nederlandsche Juristen-Vereeniging*, 1877, 8, 2 vols ('s-Gravenhage: Belinfante, 1877), I, 34-49 (p. 44): 'er is geen rechtsbeginsel dat den Staat kan nopen schrijvers en kunstenaars de rechten van hun arbeid te verzekeren. Zij kunnen daarop geen rechten doen gelden'.

217   *Handelingen der Nederlandsche Juristen-Vereeniging*, 1877, II, 69-71 (p. 71): 'dat in het algemeen belang door de wet een recht tot uitsluitende reproductie moet worden gegeven' (voted in favour by 36 votes to 10).

218   See Herman Cohen Jehoram, 'Urheberrecht: eine Sache des Rechts oder der Opportunität? Eine alte, aber unvollendete Debatte in den Niederlanden', in *Historische Studien zum Urheberrecht in Europa*, pp. 115-20.

portrayed a general resistance against another intellectual property right: the patent right. There was a growing belief that for small countries with open economies, the net benefits of granting property in inventions were few and that free trade in inventions should prevail.[219] This 'patent controversy' led to the abolition of the Dutch patent system for over forty years (1869-1910).[220] Against this backdrop, it becomes evident that the time was not yet ripe for a major liberal reform of Dutch copyright law.[221]

Likewise, in the UK, little reform of domestic copyright law took place in the second half of the century. While the need for reform and consolidating legislation was widely recognised, it would take until 1911 before copyright law was modernised and codified in a single Act.[222] This delay in the reorganisation of British domestic copyright law seems to have been caused primarily by imperial and colonial matters, which made it increasingly difficult to maintain uniformity of copyright law throughout the British Empire.[223] During a general review of the British copyright law between 1875 and 1878, a Royal Commission on Copyright made quite a number of recommendations for reform,[224] including the idea of making registration compulsory for literary works, publicly performed dramatic works and musical compositions that were not printed or published, works of fine art (not including paintings and drawings) and engravings, prints and photographs.[225] Although these recommendations found their way into a number of bills,[226] these attempts to revise British copyright law all proved unsuccessful.[227]

---

219   Eric Schiff, *Industrialization Without National Patents: The Netherlands, 1869-1912; Switzerland, 1850-1907* (Princeton, N.J.: Princeton University Press, 1971).

220   Fritz Machlup and Edith Penrose, 'The Patent Controversy in the Nineteenth Century', *Journal of Economic History*, 10 (1950), 1-29.

221   On the contrary, with reference to the abolishment of the Dutch patent system, voices were raised to do away with Dutch copyright law altogether. See for example Mr. S. Katz, quoted in De Beaufort, p. 75.

222   Bently, p. 3.

223   See Sherman and Bently, pp. 136-7, describing how imperial and colonial affairs generally resulted in inactivity on the part of the British legislator.

224   *Report of the Royal Commission on Copyright* [C.2036], XXIV (London: HMSO, 1878).

225   Ibid., pp. xxii-xxvi (paras 128-59). Note that not all recommendations received the unanimous support of all Commissioners. In respect of the recommendation for compulsory registration, see in particular the Dissent from the Report of the Commissioners as to Paragraphs 153 and 154, respecting the Registration of Books, by Mr. Anthony Trollope (pp. lix-lx); and the Note appended to the signature of Mr. Frederick Richard Daldy (p. lx).

226   See Sherman and Bently, p. 136 (note 32).

227   See Benjamin Kaplan, 'The Registration of Copyright', Study no. 17 (August

Despite the initial inactivity on the part of the Dutch and British lawmakers, the principle of no formalities was accepted without much resistance when the two countries had to change their domestic copyright law to allow adherence to the revised 1908 Berne Convention. While the Convention prohibited imposing formalities on authors of foreign works only, the Netherlands and the UK chose to abolish formalities even as to domestic works.[228] In the UK, for example, the standing registration requirements were characterised as 'anomalous, uncertain, and productive of great disadvantage and annoyance to authors with little or no advantage to the public'.[229] In addition, it appears that in both countries, formalities were poorly complied with. In the Netherlands, few books were in fact being deposited,[230] and in the UK, entries were not generally made and few books were registered until the copyright had been infringed.[231] This was not uncommon in the late nineteenth and early twentieth centuries, as

1958), in *Studies on copyright - Arthur Fisher Memorial Edition* (South Hackensack, NJ: Rothman, 1963), 325-91 (p. 333).

228   There are obvious reasons for contracting states not just to abolish formalities for foreign works, but to grant unconditional protection to all works, irrespective of their origin. Besides the clear and understandable antipathy to grant foreign authors more rights than domestic authors, it would make little sense to require national authors to continue with formalities, because they could always choose to publish their works in another Berne Union country which had eliminated formalities. This would allow them to claim protection in their own country under the Berne Convention without the need to comply with the own domestic formalities. See Stephen P. Ladas, *The International Protection of Literary and Artistic Property*, 2 vols. (New York: Macmillan, 1938), I, p. 275.

229   *Report of the Committee on the Law of Copyright* [Cd.4976] (London: HMSO, 1909), p. 12. Only one of the 16 members of the committee expressed a dissenting opinion. See the Note appended to the Signature of Mr. E. Trevor Ll. Williams, ibid., pp. 32-5 (pp. 32-3).

230   See § 2 of the 1912 Parliamentary Report of the Dutch Lower Chamber (Memorandum in Reply) in L. de Vries, *Parlementaire geschiedenis van de Auteurswet 1912, zoals sedertdien gewijzigd*, loose-leaf, 3 vols. (Den Haag: Sdu, 1989), III, 6-10 (p. 9). See also Snijder van Wissenkerke, p. 58.

231   Evidence taken before the Royal Commission on Copyright of 1875-8 reveals that the practical incentive to register was weak. See *Minutes of the Evidence taken before the Royal Commission on Copyright*, questions 340 (p. 21), 1958-9 (p. 97) and 5501-2 (p. 301); and *Report of the Royal Commission on Copyright*, p. xxiii (para. 133). See also Justice North in *Cate v. Devon & Exeter Constitutional Newspaper Co.* (1889) LR 40 Ch. D. 500 (Chancery Division, 1889), p. 506: 'It is well known that registration is only necessary as a condition precedent to suing; and the almost universal practice on the part of large publishers notoriously is that they do not register until just on the eve of taking some proceeding: then they take care to register their copyright, and sue upon it'.

other examples show.[232] As a result, it seems that in the Netherlands and the UK, at the time of their removal, formalities were not really embraced as essential and critical features of copyright law.

4. Evaluation and Conclusion

The evolution of formalities in nineteenth century Europe is one of steady decline. Literary and artistic property generally developed from a system based fully on formalities at the dawn of the century, to a system with much less reliance on formalities at the end of the century. Besides reasons of intricacy and expense, we saw that the connection between formalities and literary and artistic property rights gradually weakened because of ideological, functional and conceptual innovations that changed the contours of copyright and authors' rights law.

Unsurprisingly, the decreasing reliance on copyright formalities is attributable, to a great extent, to the development of the authors' rights doctrine in France and Germany. Unlike the situation in the first half of the century, when literary and artistic property rights were often perceived as publishers' rights or as 'privileges' granted by the legislator by virtue of a social contract, in the middle part of the century, it became well established that the foundation of copyright existed solely in the quality of the author's personal creation. Under the influence of natural property and personality rights theories, copyright was believed to automatically arise with the author's creation. This proved fatal for constitutive formalities. They were either removed altogether (Germany) or were held to be merely declarative of the right (France).

However, the general decline of formalities cannot be explained by ideological changes alone. Despite the general mind-set shifting in favour of automatic protection, there was no absolute resistance against copyright formalities. Overall, they were still believed to fulfil a few important functions in relation to the exercise of authors' rights. In France in particular, formalities were thought valuable for proving priority of authorship, enhancing publicity and establishing legal certainty. This explains why the legal

232   In Italy, for example, it was calculated that, between 1887 and 1891, only 5.5 per cent of all published literary works had actually been deposited. See 'La question des formalités en Italie', *Le Droit d'Auteur*, 10 (1897), 63-6 (p. 65). Also in France, while the number of copies deposited was fairly high (ranging from 17,000 literary works in 1884 to 21,700 literary works in 1908), there were constant complaints that for many works, the copies deposited were incomplete or in bad condition, or that no copies were deposited at all. See Lemaitre, pp. l-liv.

deposit was continued as a declaratory formality. Furthermore, in order to uphold the balance between authors' rights and the public interest, specifying formalities were increasingly imposed as threshold requirements in reply to an extended protection for new forms of exploitation. Both of these formalities are consistent with the - at that time widely accepted and prevalent - idea that while authors' rights should well be secured, this must always be done with due regard for the public interest.

Nevertheless, by the close of the century, these formalities also began to lose their practical significance. This was caused by some key conceptual changes. First, copyright formalities did not fit well with the new concept of abstract authored works. Because formalities were typically connected with the outside appearance of a work, they were incapable of capturing the essence of the author's expression in order to define the nature and limits of protection. Moreover, formalities could not be fulfilled unless a work was fixed in a tangible medium. This clashed with the idea that authors' rights exist in a work irrespective of the mode or form of its expression. Also, for some newly protected categories of works, completing formalities proved either immensely difficult or overly costly. In addition, formalities were rendered ever more redundant by the availability of alternative legal techniques for establishing authorship (for instance, legal presumptions), by the calculation of the term of protection *post mortem auctoris* and by the idea that, to the extent that formalities fulfilled external functions, they could also be imposed outside the copyright framework. Lastly, it appears that the registration and deposit systems of the late nineteenth century were very inefficiently organised and, in fact, poorly complied with. Therefore, there may have been little inclination to retain these formalities.

These observations are particularly relevant to the present debate. They at least show that, from a historical perspective, a formality-free protection of copyright and authors' rights must not be thought of as a 'sacred cow', as copyright lawyers – especially those in the continental-European *droit d'auteur* tradition – currently are often inclined to do. From a principled point of view, there is no real conflict between formalities and the natural rights theory underlying the authors' rights doctrine. This theory by no means dictates the absolute removal of copyright formalities, but merely opposes the reliance on formalities as prerequisites for the coming into existence of the right. Furthermore, the various pragmatic reasons that added to the growing irrelevance of formalities in the nineteenth century do not fundamentally oppose formalities either. Rather, they must be understood in their historical context. In the present digital age, many of the nineteenth century concerns over formalities appear to no longer exist or, at least, may be easier to overcome. Today, registration and deposit can be organised quite efficiently and made applicable to virtually any type of work. This is due to modern digital reproduction technologies, which allow a work to be easily and cost-effectively reproduced verbatim so as to capture its distinctive – subjective and original – features. Many practical objections against formalities therefore no longer apply in the current digital networked environment.

Finally, it seems that there is another important lesson to learn from the nineteenth century conception of copyright and authors' rights. The whole nineteenth century is characterised by the constant will to establish a fair balance between the protection of authors' rights and the public interest. This is precisely what the present calls for a reintroduction of formalities aim to achieve. In current copyright law, the balance has generally tipped too far in favour of protecting the author. Formalities are believed to help with restoring this copyright imbalance. The history of formalities in nineteenth century Europe reveals that formalities can indeed play an important role in this respect. From their historical roots, copyright and authors' rights certainly were not absolute and unconditional rights. Their exercise could always be restricted, or made subject to formalities, if the societal order or the public interest so required.

8. The Berlin Publisher Friedrich Nicolai and the Reprinting Sections of the Prussian Statute Book of 1794

Friedemann Kawohl[*]

1. Introduction

In the eighteenth century, the Holy Roman Empire consisted of hundreds of mostly small, German-speaking principalities or lands. Trading across these borders posed particular challenges to the book market. The War of the Austrian Succession in the 1740s weakened the power of the Habsburg dynasty which had provided the Emperor for centuries. The Viennese censorship regime was bound to book privileges individually bestowed on publishers and authors. The privilege fees also offered a continuous stream of income for the Treasury, and the Austrian trade balance benefited from domestic reprints of books that their original North German publishers had failed to privilege within the Empire. Thus initiatives for the establishment of a modern copyright system did not originate in Austria but rather in Saxony, where the book industry was strong, and in Prussia, which generally began to take over political leadership from Austria.

The vivid German debate on the legitimacy of reprinting started around 1770, and was dominated by academics rather than publishers, professional novelists or playwrights. The German copyright discourse was framed as an attempt to empower authors to verify their contribution to public discourse rather than simply to extract the best royalty share. Protection was

* This paper is based upon material developed for the AHRC-funded project: *Primary Sources*.

justified for an individual expression of a person rather than as a Lockean fruit of the author's labour. The philosophers of German Idealism, such Kant, Fichte and Hegel, based their copyright theories on these concepts of person and personality.

The reprinting sections of the Prussian Statute Book of 1794 reflect this 'personalistic' view of copyright which still shapes contemporary debate in Germany today.[1] Even the publisher Friedrich Nicolai's intervention that eventually removed the section that had returned the right to second editions to the author, was based on such a personalistic concept. Nicolai's intervention was not only resulting from a 'pro domo' argument of the successful publisher. A writer himself and a leading proponent of the Enlightenment in Prussia (Berliner Aufklärung), Nicolai was disillusioned with modern practices of writing and translating novels that made 'scholarship a craft' and 'book-writing a trade', as he had put it in a novel of 1773.[2]

Analysing the reprinting sections of the Prussian Statute Book, a specific German attitude towards author's rights can be identified. Despite the strong influence of French law in the early nineteenth century, German idealistic philosophy lingers in the tacit assumption that author's rights have to meet the needs of academic authors rather than those of somewhat contemptible paid hacks.

2. Book Privileges and the General Ban of Reprinting in 1766

Prussia experienced a flourishing of the book trade during the reign of Frederick II 'the Great' so that after Leipzig, Berlin rose to be the second most important centre of German publishing. Despite, or rather perhaps, because of the well-known fact that Frederick preferred to write and read exclusively in French and was not interested in German literature, censorship in Prussia was more liberal than in Saxony and other German states. For example, the publisher Richter, who was based in Altenburg (a small

---

1   See for example the 2009 Heidelberg appeal against open access publishing, and Google's digital library class action settlement in particular http://wiki.okfn. org/german-oa-debate [accessed 1/3/2010]. German authors are indignant not only because German law in general does not allow any 'class action' to pass over individual rights, but even more, because authors – including academic authors – regard themselves as individuals rather than members of a professional group.

2   The satirical novel *The Life and Opinions of Sebaldus Nothanker* (*Das Leben und die Meinungen des Herrn Magister Sebaldus Nothanker*) was first published in 1773; an English translation by Thomas Dutton was published in 1798.

duchy adjoining Saxony), arranged for his books to be printed in Prussia 'because', as he wrote to his colleague Nicolai in Berlin, 'I know that they are not so strict in your city'.[3]

Frederick II, adopting a classically mercantilist attitude in his famous *Testament politique* of 1752,[4] explained the benefits of fostering reprinting as follows:

> One can encourage the printing-offices – though this does involve a considerable outlay – both by [raising the level of] paper consumption and by [supporting] a branch of industry which doesn't seem to have occurred to the North yet: I mean reprinting. If a publisher buys just one copy of a book and then reprints it, he will thereby be saving his fellow-citizens from the need of having to send their money abroad, since they can acquire the desired work at home. As a result, all valuable books that are printed anywhere effectively become manuscripts for our publishers. But all this, of course, requires advances from the part of the government, and it is this which has until now prevented me from pushing forward this sphere of enterprise as vigorously as I would have liked.[5]

Prussia under Frederick II, however, never actively fostered a reprinting industry, as was the case in Austria at that time.[6] 'The Prussian government', in Pamela E. Selwyn's words:

> [W]as generally quite willing to intervene with foreign powers on behalf of Prussian publishers whose books had been pirated. When Prussian publishers themselves engaged in pirating, however, the authorities, like those elsewhere, seem to have turned a blind eye [...] At least in the 1750s

3 Letter of 24 November 1776, quoted from the Berlin Staatsbibliothek archive by Pamela E. Selwyn, *Everyday Life in the German Book Trade: Friedrich Nicolai as Bookseller and Publisher in the Age of Enlightenment* (Pennsylvania: Pennsylvania University Press, 2000), p. 184.

4 Selwyn, p. 185, with reference to *Acta Borussia*, vol. 9 (Berlin: Paul Parey, 1904-26), p. 355.

5 'Man kann die Druckereien fördern, was einen beträchtlichen Posten ausmacht, sowohl durch den Papierverbrauch wie durch den Gewerbszweig, an den der Norden noch nicht gedacht hat: ich meine den Nachdruck. Mit einem einzigen Exemplar, das der Buchhändler kauft und von neuem druckt, erspart er es den Mitbürgern, ihr Geld ins Ausland zu schicken, denn sie können das Buch im Lande bekommen. Dadurch werden alle guten Bücher, die irgendwo gedruckt werden, zu Manuskripten für unsere Buchhändler. Aber das alles erfordert Vorschüsse von Seiten der Regierung, und das hat mich bisher verhindert, es so energisch zu betreiben, wie ich gewünscht hätte'. The German translation is quoted from *Die Werke Friedrichs des Großen: in deutscher Übersetzung*, ed. by Gustav Berthold Volz, (Berlin: Hobbing, 1913-4), VII, p. 139. Online version available at: http://friedrich.uni-trier.de/volz/7/139/pageturn/ [accessed 1/3/2010]. Translation by Luis A. Sundkvist.

6 F. Kawohl, 'Commentary on the Austrian Statutes on Censorship and Printing (1781)', *Primary Sources*.

and 1760s, the Prussian government had the lamentable habit of bestowing privileges on local publishers for only slightly altered versions of already privileged works, and alteration in such cases could mean a mere change of format from quarto to octavo. What mattered was the lower price of the new edition, which was easy enough to manage when one did not have to pay the author and used smaller type and cheaper paper. This was a seemingly contradictory policy, reducing as it did the value of Prussian privileges.[7]

The notion of combating piracy with piracy, as set forth by the Leipzig publishers' cartel of 1765[8] was common practice, even if only at an informal level:

> In 1776, when the bookseller Brönner in Frankfurt am Main argued that the local town council should not pursue the pirate publisher of Friedrich Nicolai's novel *Sebaldus Nothanker*, he cited the lack of assistance he had received in Prussia when the notorious pirate Daniel Christoph Hechtel had reprinted seven of his books. But Nicolai, himself a Prussian publisher, was no safer from Hechtel's activities. The latter reprinted Moses Mendelssohn's *Phädon* and Thomas Abbt's *Vom Verdienste*. Cura's French grammar, the most frequently pirated of all of Nicolai's publications, was also reprinted by a Prussian, L.G. Faber, in Halle. The edition was confiscated, to be sure, but Faber was never required to pay the fine stipulated in Nicolai's general privilege.[9]

On 9 January 1765, the Berlin-based publisher Johann Pauli was granted a privilege for publishing Gellert's works within the Prussian lands. Reprinting and the selling of reprints were punishable by a fine of fifty thaler. Pauli's application was facilitated by general tensions between Prussia and Saxony as a result of the Seven Years' War (1756-1763) and by the fact that Gellert's original Saxon publishers did not accept payment in Prussian currency, but insisted on French louis-d'or. The privilege was granted to Pauli despite the fact that three years earlier, on 30 January 1762, the Leipzig publisher Reich had received a Prussian privilege for the exclusive sale of his edition of Gellert's works within the Prussian lands.[10]

---

7   Selwyn, p. 185, with reference to Arthur Georgi, *Die Entwicklung des Berliner Buchhandels bis zur Begründung des Börsenvereins der deutschen Buchhändler 1825* (Berlin: Paul Parey, 1926).

8   F. Kawohl, 'Commentary on Philipp Erasmus Reich and the Leipzig Publishers' Cartel (1765)', *Primary Sources*.

9   Selwyn, p. 184, with reference to letters held in the Berlin Staatsbibliothek archive.

10   Scans of the title-pages of original and reprint copies of Gellert's *Collected Works*, bearing references to Electoral Saxon, Royal Prussian and Imperial privileges serve as an apt illustration of this conflict and are published as 'Reich v. Pauli (1765)', *Primary Sources*.

Pauli not only sold his editions within Prussia, but also offered them for sale at the Leipzig fair, thus causing trouble with his Leipzig colleagues, Reich and Fritsch. However, Prussian officials declared the Leipzig publishers' cartel – of which Reich had been elected Secretary – to be an organisation of 'publishers, some of them even natives of Prussia, who have the impudence to contest His Royal Majesty's right to grant privileges'[11] and suggested summarily that Prussian publishers and booksellers henceforth be forbidden from joining the Association. Reich, though, was well-informed about the situation in Prussia thanks to the Berlin publisher Christian Friedrich Voß, who was a member of the Association, and he explained his view on Pauli's reprints in a letter to Jean-Baptiste de Boyer, Marquis d'Argens, a French philosopher who at the time was effectively acting as Lord Chamberlain to Frederick the Great. Moreover, Reich himself had successfully applied for a Prussian privilege in 1762, as was noted above. As a result, on 21 August 1766 a decree banning reprints was issued by the Berlin Chief Constable Karl David Kircheisen in the presence of all the Berlin publishers, who were summoned to the town hall for this purpose. Within just a month the Prussian Cabinet Order of 28 November 1766[12] was promulgated. Despite the general ban on reprints instituted by the Order, Pauli was nevertheless able to perpetuate his pirate edition of Gellert's works on the grounds of his Royal privilege.

The Prussian Cabinet Order of 28 November 1766 has been regarded as the first document 'generally declaring the principle of illegality of reprinting for the Prussian lands'.[13] The Prussian king (the document is signed by Frederick the Great himself) declares that he has had the Charter of the Leipzig publishers' cartel examined, and that he has ordered Councillor Karl David Kircheisen to announce to all local publishers a general ban on the reprinting of any publications. The Cabinet Order was thus a reaction to both the establishment of the publishers' cartel and to the dispute between Pauli and Reich.

11   '[E]s unverschämt ist, wenn Buchhändler, die zum Theil einheimisch sind, Ew. K. Maj. das Recht, ein Privilegium auszugeben, bestreiten'; Friedrich Hermann Meyer, 'Reformbestrebungen im achtzehnten Jahrhundert', *Archiv für Geschichte des Deutschen Buchhandels*, 12 (1889), 201-300 (p. 242). Some more details can be found in Johann Goldfriedrich, *Geschichte des Deutschen Buchhandels vom Beginn der klassischen Periode bis zum Beginn der Fremdherrschaft (1740-1804)*, (Leipzig: Verlag des Börsenvereins, 1909), III, p. 30.
12   The German text and an English translation is published as 'Prussian Cabinet Order (1766)', *Primary Sources*.
13   'Hiermit war das Princip der Unstatthaftigkeit des Nachdrucks überhaupt für die preußischen Staaten festgestellt'; Meyer, p. 246.

The situation now was, however, far from unambiguous. The Cabinet Order had been confined to the 'local' ('hiesigen'), that is, Berlin-based publishers, and Pauli's privilege for his cheap edition of Gellert's works was not revoked. Pauli thus felt at liberty to continue his reprinting activities, and he even went as far as to pirate books brought out by other Berlin publishers like Christian Friedrich Voß and Haude & Spener. A number of Berlin publishers led by Voß requested on 21 April 1767 'a general prohibition of reprinting of published books across all lands of His Majesty the King of Prussia',[14] whether or not they were privileged, and no matter whether they were of domestic or foreign origin. Furthermore, it was explicitly demanded that Pauli be threatened with punishment if he continued to bring out reprints. The requested extension to cover foreign productions may also have been a consequence of the Leipzig publishers' cartel. After Voß, Haude & Spener, Rüdiger, Mylius and Stahlbaum were contractually obliged to refrain from reprinting Saxon productions, it was in their interest to prevent local competitors from congesting their home market with cheap reprints, so that customers would come to their own bookshops to buy the original copies they had imported from Leipzig.

3. The Proposed Abolition of Privileges and the Long Journey from the First Draft to the Enactment of the Statute Book

The Prussian Statute Book (or ALR) was an all-encompassing legal compilation consisting of 19, 194 detailed single provisions. The multitude of details was intended to prevent any arbitrariness on the part of the judges. In addition to civil law provisions, the Statute Book also comprised commercial law, penal law, church law, administrative law, and constitutional law aspects, so it was considerably more than just a 'Prussian Civil Code', as the ALR is sometimes referred to in English literature. The ALR was in force in the Prussian provinces until the enactment of the *Bürgerliches Gesetzbuch* (BGB) – which, in fact, is a Civil Code – on 1 January 1900.

It is a matter of debate among legal historians as to what extent human rights were acknowledged in the ALR, and how the relevant sections in it compare with such contemporary documents as the *Virginia Declaration of Rights* (1776) and the *Declaration of the Rights of Man and of the Citizen* (1789).

---

14 '[I]n sämmtlichen Landen S. kgl. Maj. von Preußen ein General Verboth alles Nachdrucks der Verlags-Bücher'; Goldfriedrich, p. 33.

In Paragraph 83 of the preamble to the ALR we read:

> The general rights of man are based on the natural liberty whereby one may seek and promote one's own welfare without encroaching on the rights of someone else.[15]

Older literature on the subject followed the view of Hermann Conrad, who stated in 1958 that the draft version of 1791 did include 'a kind of catalogue of fundamental rights', whereas these features had been removed from the final version, partly as a result of the opposition to the French Revolution. More recent publications, however, stress that neither in the draft, nor in the final version, are individual fundamental rights explicitly stated, and that the intentions of the responsible editors Carl Gottlieb Svarez and Ernst Ferdinand Klein were in fact obstructive to the emergence of any kind of concept of a citizens' society based on liberty and equality.[16]

In contrast to the way it is understood now, eighteenth century writers on the subject of natural law regarded 'natural freedom' in the same terms as those used in the preamble to the ALR, and 'natural equality' as being confined to humans in the state of nature: 'When I am a subject, I renounce my [...] natural freedom',[17] as expressed in a 1763 treatise on natural law by Joachim Georg Darjes, who was Svarez's teacher at university. Similarly, another jurist had stated in 1721 that men 'renounced their natural equality as soon as they entered civil society'.[18]

However, a broader concept of 'equality' and (economic) 'liberty' started to gain currency when later economists and constitutional lawyers began to argue that the granting of privileges was in contravention to such principles. After the draft version was published in 1791, it was proposed that book

15   'Die allgemeinen Rechte des Menschen gründen sich auf die natürliche Freyheit, sein eignes Wohl, ohne Kränkung der Rechte eines Andern, suchen und befördern zu können'. Quoted here from Diethelm Klippel and Louis Pahlow, 'Freiheit und Absolutismus: Das allgemeine Landrecht in der Geschichte der Menschen- und Bürgerrechte', in *Reformabsolutismus und ständische Gesellschaft: Zweihundert Jahre Preußisches Allgemeines Landrecht*, ed. by Günter Birtsch and Dietmar Willoweit (Berlin: Duncker & Humblot, 1998), pp. 215-53.

16   See the discussion in Klippel and Pahlow, p. 217.

17   '[B]in ich ein Unterthan, so renuncire ich [...] meiner natürlichen Freyheit'. Joachim Georg Darjes, *Discours*, quoted in Diethelm Klippel, 'Das Privileg im Naturrecht des 18. und 19. Jahrhunderts', in *Das Privileg im europäischen Vergleich*, ed. by Barbara Dölemeyer and Heinz Mohnhaupt (Frankfurt: Klostermann, 1997), pp. 329-46 (p. 335).

18   '[Die Menschen hätten] durch Eintretung in die bürgerliche Gesellschaft ihrer natürlichen Freiheit renunciiret'. Johann Salomo Brunnquell, *Eröffnete Gednken von dem allgemeinen Staats-Rechte und dessen höchst-nützlichen Excolirung* (Jena, 1721), p. 38. Quoted in Klippel, p. 335.

privileges be abolished altogether, since 'it is rather odd that something which goes without saying according to all natural rights should first have to be obtained through the grant of a sovereign privilege'.[19] The unnamed commentator, who may or may not have been a member of the Prussian administration, apparently felt that privileges, being exemptions, would dilute the universality of the all-encompassing body of law, rather than taking the view that these exemptions constituted a restriction of the general principles of freedom and equality. The anonymous comment, however, with its mercantilist and absolutist view on privileges as admissible means of controlling the economy, does fit into the natural law tradition which was still prevalent in Germany at the time. It was not before 1800 that a younger generation of German lawyers began to raise objections, such as that 'any privilege is reprehensible also from the cosmopolitan point of view',[20] and that: 'The purpose of the association of the State is to preserve our private rights. Privileges, however, nullify the primal right of equality between men'.[21]

Svarez's co-editor Christoph Goßler agreed to the principal objection raised by the unnamed commentator, but argued that '[although the objection] does seem to be significant, it will, however, be difficult to satisfy those who have been benefiting so far from the issuing of such privileges'.[22]

Concerns over sufficient security and due process, as well as the fear of complaints from the privileged publishers, eventually led to the privilege system being preserved in general, including also the protection of books imported into Prussia from other German states.[23] It continued to remain in

---

19   '[E]s bleibt immer auffallend, daß erst durch ein landesherrliches Privilegium etwas erlangt werden soll, was sich nach allen natürlichen Rechten von selbst versteht'. *Extractus monitorum*, quoted in Robert Voigtländer, 'Das Verlagsrecht im Preußischen Landrecht und der Einfluß von Friedrich Nicolai darauf', *Archiv für Geschichte des Deutschen Buchwesens*, (1898), 4-66 (p. 46).
20   '[E]in jedes Privilegium auch in kosmopolitischer Rücksicht verwerflich'. Karl Salomo Zachariä, *Über die Erziehung des Menschengeschlechts duch den Staat* (Leipzig, 1802), p. 242. Quoted in Klippel, p. 339.
21   'Der Zweck der Staatsverbindung ist die Erhaltung unserer Privatrechte. Privilegien aber heben das Urrecht der Gleichheit auf'. Daniel Christoph Reidenitz, *Naturrecht* (Königsberg, 1803), p. 158. Quoted in Klippel, p. 339.
22   'Scheint erheblich, nur wird es schwer seyn, diejenigen zu befrieden, welche bisher von Ausfertigung solcher Privilegien Vortheil gehabt haben'. Svarez's marginal notes to the *Extractus monitorum*. Quoted in Voigtländer, p. 47.
23   After Frederick II died on 17 August 1786, his successor Frederick William II ordered the participation of the Estates in the lawmaking process. The concerns that they raised helped to ensure that the privileges of the nobility were preserved. For a general discussion on the treatment of privileges in the Prussian Statute Book,

place even after the considerably more advanced Prussian Copyright Act of 1837[24] until it was formally dropped in §. 71.1 of the Copyright Act of 1870.[25]

The Prussian Statute Book came into force on 1 July 1794 as the *Allgemeines Landrecht für die Preußischen Staaten* (ALR) after fourteen years of preparations and discussions, and after the sudden withdrawal of a completed version which had been published in 1791 as the *Allgemeines Gesetzbuch für die Preußischen Staaten* (AGB).

Frederick II had commissioned the project in 1780 and entrusted general responsibility for it to the Chancellor Johann Heinrich Carmer, who shortly afterwards appointed Svarez and, in 1781, Klein as his assistants.[26] The first draft of the copyright provisions was presented by Klein, but Svarez arranged for, and oversaw, further discussions, in which he introduced several amendments before the final version was produced. Carmer, Svarez and Klein were all close to Enlightenment circles in Berlin. In 1781 Klein was among the founders of the Society of Friends of the Enlightenment ('Gesellschaft von Freunden der Aufklärung'), a semi-clandestine literary organisation which outsiders generally referred to as the 'Mittwochsgesellschaft' (that is, the 'Wednesday Society'). Among its members were the school inspector Friedrich Gedicke and the head of the Royal Library Johann Erich Biester, who were co-editors of the *Berlinische Monatsschrift*, a leading journal of the German Enlightenment, which published the notable essays on reprinting by Immanuel Kant[27] and Johann Gottlieb Fichte.[28] Other members included Svarez and the publisher and

---

see Heinz Mohnhaupt, 'Privilegien und gemeines Wohl im ALR', in *200 Jahre Allgemeines Landrecht für die Preußischen Staaten*, ed. by Barbara Dölemeyer and Heinz Mohnhaupt (Frankfurt: Klostermann, 1994), pp. 105-44.

24   'Prussian Copyright Act (1837)', *Primary Sources*.

25   'Copyright Act for the German Empire (1870)', *Primary Sources*.

26   Carmer presided over the team as a whole, in which Svarez had more of a leading role than Klein, although the latter is regarded by Adolf Stölzel, *Carl Gottlieb Svarez* (Berlin, 1885), p. 171, quoted in Michael Kleensang, *Das Konzept der bürgerlichen Gesellschaft bei Ernst Ferdinand Klein* (Frankfurt: Klostermann, 1998), p. 21, to have been 'almost on a par with Svarez' in terms of the contribution he made to the Statute Book. Klein had practised as a solicitor after studies in Halle, and in his later years he raised his voice against the threatening constraints imposed by the government on solicitors, which he rejected as a 'destruction of civil liberties' ('Vernichtung der bürgerlichen Freiheit'). Quoted in Kleensang, p. 18.

27   'Kant: On the Unlawfulness of Reprinting (1785)', *Primary Sources*.

28   'Fichte: Proof of the Unlawfulness of Reprinting (1793)', *Primary Sources*. On Fichte's article see also F. Kawohl and M. Kretschmer, 'Johann Gottlieb Fichte, and the trap of Inhalt (Content) and Form: An information perspective on music copyright', *Information, Communication & Society*, 12 (2009), 205-28.

author Friedrich Nicolai, who successfully lobbied for significant changes to the latest draft of the copyright provisions.

The (first) completed version of the Statute Book, then called *Allgemeines Gesetzbuch für die Preußischen Staaten*, was approved by Frederick William II (who had succeeded his uncle Frederick II in 1786 as the fourth king of Prussia) in a Cabinet Order of 31 December 1789, and went into print in the spring of 1790, 'so that in the meanwhile the public might acquaint itself with the regulations to which it would henceforth have to conform its actions'.[29] But only a few weeks before it was to come into force on 1 June 1792, the enactment was suspended by a Cabinet Order of Frederick William II on 18 April. The reason, as explained in a review of 1810 by Svarez's later co-editor Goßler, was that the 'liberal and humanistic princi- ples, included by the express will of Frederick II, relating to the monarch's executive power and regalia, as well as to religion, the nobility and their manorial rights ran contrary to the interests of the party which was then at the peak of its influence both in government and the court.[30] Furthermore, the new king was anxious to dispel any possible associations with the effects of the French Revolution – associations made, for example, in an anonymous article which appeared in a Thuringian journal and stated that:

> [A]lmost all of the so vigorously decried seventeen articles of the French Declaration of Human Rights are, in fact, to be found [either] in the Prussian Statute Book, sometimes in quite similar wording, albeit in a scattered fashion and chiefly in those places where [these articles] could be applied directly, and that the legislator 'had acted in accordance with the spirit of these forever inalienable rights'.[31]

The changes from the *Allgemeines Gesetzbuch* to the ALR of 1794 concerned mainly constitutional issues such as, for example, an amendment to Section 6 of the preamble, which in its original form, according to its opponents,

---

29   '[D]as Publicum sich inzwischen mit den Vorschriften, wornach es künftig seine Handlungen einrichten soll, bekannt machen könne'. Quoted in Andreas Schwennicke, *Die Entstehung der Einleitung des Preussischen Allgemeinen Landrechts von 1794* (Klostermann: Frankfurt, 1993), p. 48.
30   Goßler, quoted in Schwennicke, p. 49.
31   '[D]ie meisten von den 17 so verschrienen Artikeln der Französischen Erklä- rung der Menschrechte, zum Theil in sehr ähnlichen Ausdrücken, entweder wirk- lich in dem Preußischen Gesetzbuche, nur zerstreut und an den Stellen, wo eine unmittelbare Anwendung davon gemacht werden konnte [...] diesen ewig unver- äußerlichen Rechten gemäß gehandelt habe'. From the anonymous article 'Etwas über die neue preußische Gesetzgebung und die Französische Revolution', *Deut- sche Zeitung* (Gotha), ed. by Rudolf Zacharias Becker (1791), pp. 797-811. Quoted in Schwennicke, p. 51.

had specified 'that a sovereign order was to have no validity in matters still awaiting the outcome of a lawsuit'.[32] The mystically-inclined king also insisted on replacing the original title of the body of legislation – 'Statute Book' – with 'Landrecht' ('National Law'), so as to awaken associations with the medieval 'Laws of the Land' ('Landrechte') that existed in the various territories of the Holy Roman Empire. On 4 January 1794, Carmer announced the execution of the king's orders and handed over to Frederick William II the new Statute Book, now entitled *Allgemeines Landrecht für die Preußischen Staaten* ('General National Law for the Prussian States').

Apart from a slightly different wording, the copyright provisions, as they stood at the end of 1790, went unchanged into the ALR. This means that the possibility of any influence from the famous French copyright acts of 1791 and 1793[33] can be excluded. To what extent the editors of the Prussian Statute Book were influenced by earlier French decrees is, however, open to further research. As Laurent Pfister has shown in this collection, the French decree of 1779 enabled authors to contract with their publishers for a restricted period of time to retain control over their works.

The list below presents the various drafts and proposals for Prussian copyright legislation in chronological order:

1780   A new body of law commissioned by Frederick II.

1786-87   First draft worked out and presented by Klein. First amendment by Svarez, discussed within the Prussian administration and leading to further proposals from Scherer.

1787   Second amendment by Svarez, published on 20 December.[34] A general discussion on this draft was encouraged. Famous jurists, such as Pütter,[35] as well as the general public, were invited to offer comments and criticisms on the draft. Fifty-two expert opinions, most of them favourable, were received by the editors.[36]

1787-88   *Extractus monitorum* which provided in a two-column format excerpts from the invited comments and proposals regarding

---

32   '[D]aß ein landesherrlicher Befehl in Sachen, worüber ein Prozeß schwebt, nicht gelten soll'. Schwennicke, p. 58.

33   'French Literary and Artistic Property Act (1793)', *Primary Sources*.

34   *Entwurf eines Allgemeinen Gesetzbuchs für die preußischen Staten*, ed. by Johann Heinrich Kasimir Carmer (Berlin: Decker, 1784-8).

35   On Pütter's contribution to eighteenth-century copyright discourse see F. Kawohl, 'Commentary on J.S. Pütter: The Reprinting of Books (1774)', *Primary Sources*.

36   *Allgemeines Landrecht für die Preussischen Staaten von 1794*, ed. by Hans Hatten-hauer (Neuwied: Luchterhand, 1970), p. 9.

the criticised points (Lat. 'monita') on the right, and comments by the assistant editor Goßler on the left.

1788 [37]   Svarez's *Revisio Monitorum*, i.e. a detailed revision of the criticised points.

1789-90   Completion of Svarez's manuscript of the *Allgemeines Gesetzbuch*.

1790   Letter of Friedrich Nicolai dated 6 December. Substantial changes incorporated into the manuscript by Svarez, in response to Nicolai's objections.

1791   20 March Publication of the *Allgemeines Gesetzbuch für die Preußischen Staaten* proposed to come into force on 1 June 1792.

1792   18 April withdrawal of the *Allgemeines Gesetzbuch*.

1794   4 January. Enactment of the *Allgemeines Landrecht für die Preußischen Staaten* ('General National Law for the Prussian States').

4. Klein's Draft Version and Svarez's Amendments

The ALR included copyright provision in both its penal law and civil law sections. Since the system of book privileges had not yet been abandoned with the enactment of the ALR, the penal law provisions stipulated fines for violations of such privileges.[38] The first draft of the copyright provisions within the civil law sections appeared in the chapter 'On rights to objects' ('Vom Sachenrechte'), as part of the sub-chapter 'On other kinds of contracts' ('Von ungenannten Verträgen'). The original heading 'On publishers' property' was crossed out and replaced by the words 'On publishing contracts', written in the same hand as the original text. Martin Löhnig has suggested that Klein 'thereby wanted to ensure the validity of the principles being applied in this system [of legislation] to the realm of publishing right',[39] and to justify the subsumption of copyright provisions under the sub-chapter 'On other kinds of contracts'. Klein's draft, however, was

---

37   The last entry in Svarez's manuscript of the "revisio monitorum" dates from mid-1788. Schwennicke, p. 43.

38   On the penal law sections see F. Kawohl, 'Commentary on the Reprinting Provisions in the Prussian Statute Book (1794)', *Primary Sources*.

39   '[W]ollte Klein dadurch eine bessere systematische Einordung der Normen in das Vertragsrecht gewährleisten'. Martin Löhnig, 'Der Schutz des geistigen Eigentums von Autoren im Preußischen Landrecht von 1794', *Zeitschrift für Neuere Rechtsgeschichte (ZNR)*, 29 (2008), 197–214. In this recent publication Löhnig has provided details from the original files in the possession of the 'Geheimes Staatsarchiv Preußischer Kulturbesitz' in Berlin.

the only one in which the term 'property' was used at all (in §. 80): subsequently this term was avoided by the editors. This original draft consisted of just ten sections:

§. 78. A publishing right entitles one to reproduce a work by means of printing.

§. 79. Without the consent of the author or his heirs, nobody can, as a rule, acquire a publishing right.

§. 80. Once a publishing right has been ceded, it remains the property of the person who has acquired it.

§. 81. Reprinters are to be subject to a fine of 100 ducats, and the copies they have printed are to be destroyed.

§. 82. Translations of already published books are to be treated as new works.

§. 83. A privilege can be applied for by those wishing to bring out new editions of foreign authors whose publishers visit the Leipzig or Frankfurt fairs.

§. 84. New editions of works by older authors from whom, or from whose heirs, no publisher has acquired a publishing right, are permitted.

§. 85. Simple reprints of editions which appeared less than thirty years ago are not allowed.

§. 86. If someone wishes to arrange for annotations to the works of still living writers to be published, then these annotations must be printed separately.

§. 87. Such annotations may be incorporated into the work itself only with the consent of the author and his publisher.[40]

---

40 '§. 78. Das Verlagsrecht besteht in der Befugnis, eine Schrift durch den Druck zu vervielfältigen. §. 79. Ohne Einwilligung des Schriftstellers oder seiner Erben kann in der Regel niemand das Verlagsrecht erlangen. §. 80. Das einmal abgetretene Verlagsrecht bleibt Eigenthum dessen, der solches an sich gebracht hat. §. 81. Der Nachdrucker wird mit einer Strafe von 100 Ducaten belegt, und die von ihm gedruckten Exemplarien sollen vernichtet werden. §. 82. Übersetzungen schon gedruckter Bücher sind als neue Werke anzusehen. §. 83. Zu neuen Ausgaben ausländischer Schriftsteller, deren Verleger die Leipziger oder Frankfurther Messe besuchen, kann ein Privilegium nachgesucht werden. §. 84. Neue Ausgaben alter Schriftsteller, von denen oder deren Erben kein Buchhändler ein Verlagsrecht erlangt hat, sind erlaubt. §. 85. Unerlaubt sind bloße Nachdrücke von solchen Ausgaben, welche noch nicht 30 Jahre alt sind. §. 86. Wenn jemand Anmerkungen zu den Werken noch lebender Schriftsteller drucken lassen will, so müssen solche besonders abgedruckt werden. §. 87 Dem Werke selbst dürfen sie nur mit Einwilligung des Verfassers und seines Verlegers beigefügt werden'. Voigtländer, pp. 37-8. Translation by Luis A. Sundkvist.

Most decisive features were already covered in this first draft. Only a publisher's property in the publication right is acknowledged, albeit conditional on the 'consent of the author or his heirs'. The draft was in accordance with Pütter's[41] concept of a publisher's property based on a contract for the acquisition of the manuscript, and also with Klein's own general view of property, which was informed by Pufendorf and Grotius rather than by Locke, in the sense of regarding property as a 'natural freedom' rather than as a consequence of the 'labour' exerted by an individual.[42] Within such a Grotian framework it made sense that no intellectual property existed at all before a publishing contract was agreed on. (In a more modern approach, based on the Lockean labour theory, an intellectual property would result from the author's or publisher's labour, but not from a mere contract). On the other hand, in Klein's draft, the author (or his heirs) did have to give his (or their) consent, in order for this creation of a publisher's property to be valid in the first place, and, moreover, the author, together with his publisher, retained the right to consent to, or reject, annotated reprints of his work.[43]

The effect of Svarez's first set of additions and amendments in 1787, was to restrict the rights of the publishers in favour of the authors (although his proposals were eventually cut back substantially as a result of the publisher Nicolai's objections). The publisher's right, according to Svarez's revision of the draft, was to be confined to the first edition (§. 715 – see also the table below), and a publisher wishing to bring out a new edition had to ask for the consent of the author or the latter's heirs (§. 716). On the other hand, the author could exercise his right to publish an amended edition with another publisher only after the first edition had sold out (§. 718), or, alternatively, if he himself was prepared to buy up all remaining copies of the first edition still in stock (§. 719).

The question arose as to whether these restrictions were still not sufficiently favourable to authors, and Sebastian Anton Scherer,[44] a member of

41 'Pütter: The Reprinting of Books (1774)', *Primary Sources*.
42 See Kleensang, p. 81ff., who refers to Ernst Ferdinand Klein, *Grundsätze der natürlichen Rechtswissenschaft* (Halle: Hemmerde & Schwetschke, 1797).
43 Löhnig, p. 200, has indicated that Klein's draft did not adopt proposals on author's property that had been advanced in recent monographs by Johann Jakob Cella, 'Vom Büchernachdruck' (one of the essays included in *Johann Jakob Cella's frymützige Aufsätze* (Ansbach, 1784)), and by Martin Ehlers, *Über die Unzulässigkeit des Büchernachdrucks* (Dessau/Leipzig, 1784).
44 Scherer, one of the older officials on the legislation committee (he died around 1791), was appointed to the rank of *Justizrat* in 1750. According to Schwennicke, p. 25, he was the director of the deputation responsible for justice matters in the leg-

the legislation committee, proposed to have the first publisher's exclusive right limited to just two years. From Svarez's marginal notes to his first amended draft we know about Scherer's proposal and what Svarez had to say about it:

> Mr Scherer is of the opinion that the publisher should not be able to prevent the author from undertaking a second, enlarged and improved, edition, as long as the publisher of the first edition has had sufficient time to sell [all] copies of this edition. [Mr Scherer suggests that] the condition of sufficient time is met if the publisher has been able to present the book in question at the Leipzig fair for two years in succession. This space of time, though, would probably be too brief for large and expensive works. The principles adopted here earlier [that is, that the author had to wait until the first edition had been successfully marketed] would indeed hinder the propagation of scholarship and tie down the author too much, for the availability of a [suitable] publisher [for a new edition] is something that is beyond his control [and, therefore, forcing him to not undertake anything until the first edition is sold off could ruin his chances of publishing an improved version of his work].[45]

Svarez suggested the following modification to Scherer's proposal for limiting the first publisher's exclusive right (with which he essentially agreed): 'In cases of doubt, if no longer or shorter period has been specified [contractually], the publishing right is to be effective for only twenty years'.[46] However, neither Scherer's limitation to two years, nor Svarez's twenty-year term were eventually adopted in the print draft which served as the basis for further discussions.

Scherer, appointed a *Justizrat* (a rank equivalent to King's Counsel) in 1750, was older than both Svarez and Klein and belonged to a generation unaccustomed to the concept of professional authorship. Therefore, his radical proposal in favouring the author's rights seems quite startling. It

---

islation committee.

45 'Herr Scherer meint, der Verleger könne den Schriftsteller nicht hindern, eine zweyte, vermehrte und verbesserte Auflage zu machen, wenn nur der Verleger der ersten Auflage hinreichend Zeit zu Debitirung derselben gehabt hat. Diese Zeit könne dahin bestimmt werden, wenn er das Buch 2 Jahre hindurch auf die Leipziger Messe hat mitnehmen können.

Diese Zeit dürfte wohl auf große und kostbare Werke zu kurz seyn. Die hier angenommenen Grundsätze hindern die Ausbreitung der Wissenschaft, und binden den Schriftsteller zu sehr, welcher den Verleger nicht controllieren kann'. Quoted in Voigtländer, p. 39. Translation by Luis A. Sundkvist. This provision, however, was not enacted.

46 'In dubio, wenn keine längere und kürzere Zeit bestimmt worden, gilt das Verlagsrecht nur auf 20 Jahre'. Quoted in Voigtländer, p. 39.

may, in fact, have been motivated by a case he had been involved in ten years previously,[47] when the poet Friedrich Gottlieb Klopstock applied for a Prussian privilege in a letter of 1 May 1778, addressed to the Minister of Justice Ernst Friedemann Baron von Münchhausen. The letter was undersigned by Klopstock, but had been drafted on the author's behalf by the already mentioned librarian Johann Erich Biester, who at the time was working as secretary to the Prussian Minister of Education Karl Abraham Baron von Zedlitz.

Klopstock had intended to publish his great religious epic *Der Messias* ('The Messiah') on a subscription basis, hoping that he would receive a Prussian privilege for this. However, Carl Hermann Hemmerde in Halle, who had published earlier editions of the first cantos of the epic, claimed to have an unlimited publishing right to *Der Messias*, allegedly based on a contract with the author. Klopstock protested that such a provision had not been part of his publishing contract with Hemmerde, which was, moreover, for just one edition. As can be seen from a note written into the margin of the original letter, Münchhausen passed it on to Scherer, instructing him to arrange for Hemmerde to be interrogated on the case by the magistrate in Halle. Eventually the Prussian privilege was refused on the grounds that Klopstock had not been able to come to terms with Hemmerde.

Scherer, and probably also the main editors of the Statute Book, had at least a basic knowledge of that case, in which one of the most famous German authors of the age had been tied down by a contract with a dodgy publisher, who had only come to an agreement with the author after publishing an unauthorised version and who had refused to pay him adequately.[48] *Klopstock v. Hemmerde* may also have induced Svarez to add those provisions confining the publisher's right to the first edition (§§. 715f. of the published draft, see the table below).

In Klein's draft the author, after concluding the publishing contract for a limited thirty-year term, only retained the exclusive right of giving or withholding his consent to annotated reprints of his works. In Svarez's revised version, however, the author kept a much more important right: for now the publisher was obliged to obtain the author's consent for every new edition. This substantial amendment was maintained, albeit attenuated after Nicolai's objections, right through to the final enactment.[49]

---

47   The following details of the case are taken from, *Klopstocks Briefe 1776-1782*, ed. by Helmut Riege (Berlin: de Gruyter, 1982).
48   Goldfriedrich, p. 455.
49   Svarez's published draft included some other provisions which were appropri-

As members of the 'Mittwochsgesellschaft' it is almost certain that Klein and Svarez attentively read the *Berlinische Monatsschrift*, edited by their fellow club members Biester and Gedicke, and in which Kant's essay on reprinting[50] had been originally published. Kant's ideas are not directly visible in the ALR, but it is possible that Svarez's decision to provide authors with an exclusive right to new editions may have been inspired by Kant's notion of the work as a speech to the public. True, Svarez did not actually adopt Kant's concept of a personal, unalienable right vested in the author, but, like the great philosopher, he did also refrain from invoking any concept of intellectual property. When the assistant editor Goßler argued that the relationship between author and publisher was covered entirely by the theory of sales and purchase, Svarez protested:

The relationship between an author and his publisher can in no way be considered in terms of the theory of sales and purchase. The ownership of the work itself, in as far as it is an intellectual product, is not transferred to the publisher at all: rather, the latter merely acquires the distribution right [to the work], that is, the right to reproduce the work by means of printing [and to sell these copies].[51]

Thus, Svarez, like Kant, refrained from introducing any notion of intellectual property as such. But whereas Kant had described the publisher's function as that of 'conducting business in the name of another person',[52] Svarez proceeded from the assumption that the publisher acquires not a property right to the work, but, rather, a licence to reproduce it.

5. The Publisher Friedrich Nicolai's Views on Authors and Translators

Friedrich Nicolai was one of the most important publishers in eighteenth

---

ate for reinforcing the author's right with regard to his publisher. In view of the fact that publishers often tried to secure twenty-year privileges for certain editions, Svarez argued that such a possibility had to be obviated: 'The publisher cannot solicit a privilege to the author's detriment' ('Zum Nachtheil der Rechte des Schriftstellers kann der Verleger kein Privilegium nachsuchen'). Quoted in Voigtländer, p. 41.

50   'Kant: On the Unlawfulness of Reprinting (1785)', *Primary Sources.*
51   '[Es] kann das Verhältniß zwischen Schriftsteller und Verleger unmöglich nach der Theorie von Kauf und Verkauf beurtheilt werden. Das Eigenthum der Schrift selbst, in so fern sie Geistesprodukt ist, geht keineswegs auf den Verleger über; er erwirbt blos das Verkaufsrecht i.e. die Befugniß, die Schrift durch Druck zu vervielfältigen'. Quoted in Voigtländer, p. 48f. Translation by Luis A. Sundkvist.
52   'Kant: On the Unlawfulness of Reprinting (1785)', *Primary Sources.*

century Berlin. Since his opinion on Svarez's draft had a decisive effect in causing substantial changes to the ALR provisions which favoured publishers as opposed to authors, it is worth considering his attitude towards contemporary authors and their profession as such. The views which Nicolai put into the mouth of the hero of a satirical novel he published in 1773 (discussed below), were to some extent re-iterated in the letter which he sent to the editors of the Statute Book.

Nicolai was educated at a boarding school in Halle, a stronghold of austere protestantism (Pietism), and in later years he showed an aversion to all kinds of religious fundamentalism. After an apprenticeship as a bookseller he took over his father's bookshop in Berlin, in 1759. The reprinting of original English literature was amongst his earliest enterprises as a publisher:

> In the early 1760s, he conceived the grandiose plan of reprinting the best works of English literature to make them available at lower prices than the expensive imports. Although the project began and ended with the ten-volume *Works* of Alexander Pope (1762-64), since few Germans could read English in the 1760s, it was a highly innovative idea that won Nicolai praise at that time.[53]

More lucrative were his review journals: the weekly *Briefe, die neueste Literatur betreffend* ('Letters Concerning the Latest Literature') 1759-65; the *Bibliothek der schönen Wissenschaften und der freyen Künste* ('Library of Fine Arts'), 1757-60; and his most important periodical, the *Allgemeine deutsche Bibliothek* ('German General Library', 1765-92, which reached an all-time circulation high during the 1770s, with more than 2,500 copies being printed of each issue.

Nicolai was a major publisher and editor, but he also won acclaim as an author. His satirical novel *The Life and Opinions of Sebaldus Nothanker* ('Das Leben und die Meinungen des Herrn Magister Sebaldus Nothanker') was first published in 1773.[54] In Chapter 2 of the second volume Nicolai gives some interesting details on the book market. Here it is worth taking a closer look at Nicolai's satirical remarks on 'works for hire' and on the market for translations, since these were the two areas of the Prussian copyright legislation which were substantially amended in the light of Nicolai's proposals in December 1790.

In this novel the aspiring author Sebaldus travels to the Leipzig fair, where he is initiated into the real workings of the book market during a

---

53   Selwyn, p. 31.
54   An English translation by Thomas Dutton was published in 1798. All the passages from the novel quoted here have been translated by Luis A. Sundkvist.

conversation he has with an old proof-reader, 'who knew everything there was to know about the publishers' and authors' business'.[55] Sebaldus's naively high esteem for authors as scholars 'eager to communicate useful knowledge to the world and to promote truth and wisdom'[56] is rectified by the proof-reader:

> What the authors want is to give the publisher as few sheets of manuscript as possible for as much money as they can get out of him. The publisher, for his part, wants to purchase as many quires [an old printer's measure for 23-25 sheets] as possible for as small a sum as possible, and then to sell [the work] at the highest conceivable price. Authors are keen on expending the least possible time, effort, thought, and skill on their books, yet with the hope of reaping as much glory, reward, and promotion as possible.[57]

In the proof-reader's view, many authors worked like hired day-labourers:

> There are quite a few publishers around who commission their authors to write works which they think will sell easily: *Stories, Novels, Murder Mysteries, Trustworthy Accounts* [...] of things which one hasn't seen [!], *Proofs* [...] of things which one doesn't believe in, *Reflections* [...] on things which one doesn't understand. To produce such books, a publisher has no need of authors who have made a name for themselves: what he needs are simply scribblers who can fill sheets of paper by the ell. In fact, I know a publisher who has up to ten or twelve such authors sitting at a long table in his house, and to each of them he assigns the task that he must complete so as to earn his daily wages.[58]

---

55   'Er kannte alle Vorfälle des Verleger und Autorgewerbes.' Quoted from the fourth, amended edition of Friedrich Nicolai, *Leben und Meinungen des Herrn Magisters Sebaldus Nothanker* (Berlin: Nicolai, 1799). Available online at: http://books. google.de/books?id=JDsJAAAAQAAJ&printsec=titlepage [accessed 1/3/2010], p. 91.
56   'Der will der Welt nützliche Kenntnisse mittheilen, der will Wahrheit und Weisheit befördern'. Ibid., p. 101.
57   'Der Autor will gern dem Verleger so wenig Bogen Manuskript als möglich, für so viel Geld als möglich ist, überliefern. Der Verleger will gern so viele Alphabete als möglich, so wohlfeil als möglich einhandeln, und so theuer als möglich verkaufen. Der Autor will gern so wenig Zeit, Mühe, Überlegung und Geschicklichkeit an sein Buch wenden, und doch so viel Ruhm, Belohnung, Beförderung, von der Welt einärndten, als möglich'. Ibid., pp. 102-3.
58   'Da ist mehr als ein Buchhändler, der seinen Autoren aufträgt was er für verkäuflich hält: *Geschichte, Romanen, Mordgeschichte, zuverläßige Nachrichten,* von Dingen die man nicht gesehen hat, *Beweise,* von Dingen die man nicht glaubt, *Gedanken,* von Sachen die man nicht versteht. Zu solchen Büchern bedarf der Verleger keine Autoren, die einen Namen haben, sondern solche die nach der Elle arbeiten. Ich kenne einen der in seinem Hause an einem langen Tische zehn bis zwölf Autoren sitzen hat, und jedem sein Pensum fürs Tagelohn abzuarbeiten giebt'. Ibid., pp. 108-9.

And after reflecting on the consequences of the traditional barter trade between publishers – namely, 'that the publisher who has the worst books stands to gain most by it because he will easily obtain something better in exchange'[59] – the proof-reader goes on to explain how the 'translation factories' worked. To Sebaldus's objection, '[b]ut surely translations are not like garments that can be woven on a loom!', the proof-reader retorts:

> And yet, you know, they are manufactured almost in the same way: it is just that, as with the stitching of socks, you only have to use your hands and not your feet as well, as is the case when weaving. And I assure you, Sir, that the army is not stricter in the orders it sets for the punctual supply and delivery of shirts and socks for its soldiers than the publishers are with regard to the supply of translations of French works, since in these factories such translations are considered to be the meanest, but also the most marketable wares.[60]

Some translators even tried to pass off their translations as original works by cutting the initial and final sections! According to the old proof-reader, translators were even more dependent on publishers, agents, and commissioners than original authors. Furthermore, when a publisher needs some quires to barter at a book fair:

> [H]e will look through all new, as yet unpublished books and choose that whose title appeals to him most. And once he has found a suitable labourer for the task (which isn't that difficult, in fact) – one who is able to get through three quires of text by the time of the next fair – he and that translator will haggle with each other over [the fee for translating] the poor Frenchman or Englishman, just like two butchers wrangling over an ox or whether to be slaughtered, taking into account the reputation [of the author who is to be translated] or sometimes even just calculating the price per weight [that is, the quantity of text]. The one who has sold at the highest possible price or purchased as cheaply as possible imagines that he has pulled off a bargain. After that, the translator takes home the poor victim and either slaughters it himself or entrusts this to someone else.
>
> *Sebaldus*: To someone else? What do you mean by that?
>
> *The proof-reader*: Ah, that's what I meant when I compared the whole thing to a factory process. You see, there are certain famous persons who

---

59   '[D]aß also der Verleger am besten daran ist, der die schlechtesten Bücher hat, weil er leicht etwas bessers bekommt'. Ibid., p. 110.
60   'Und doch werden sie beynahe eben so verfertigt, nur daß man, wie bey Strümpfen, bloß die Hände dazu nöthig hat, und nicht wie bey der Leinwand, auch die Füße. Auch versichere ich Sie, daß keine Lieferung von Hemden und Strümpfen für die Armee genauer bedungen wird, und richtiger auf den Tag muß abgeliefert werden, als eine Uebersetzung aus dem Französischen, denn dies wird in diesen Manufacturen für die gemeinste, aber auch für die gangbarste Waare geachtet'. Ibid., pp. 111-2.

undertake translations on a large scale – rather like an Irish caterer responsible for supplying salt meat to a fleet of Spanish ships – and who do this by allotting them to their various 'sub-translators'. These famous individuals are the first to hear about all new translatable books that have appeared in France, Italy, and England, just like a broker in Amsterdam will be the first to find out about the arrival of Dutch East India Company ships at the port of Texel [Tessel]. All booksellers in need of translations turn to the services of these persons, who, in their turn, know what tasks are most suited to each of their labourers and how much their wages are to be rated. They pass on the work to the industrious ones and punish those who are slack by withholding from them their protection; the only work they do themselves is perhaps to correct any faults in the translations they have ordered, or simply just to varnish them with their illustrious names. For entrepreneurs of this kind are usually very good at penning prefaces. They also know very well how much effort exactly has to be put into each type of translation, and what means they have to use, so that their translations are praised far and wide and the public expresses its gratitude to the worthy man who has thus done so much for the German scholarly world.[61]

Like his friends and collaborators Moses Mendelssohn and Lessing, Nicolai was full of enthusiasm for the Enlightenment ideals of learning and

61   '[S]o sucht er unter allen neuen noch unübersetzten Büchern von drey Alphabeten dasjenige aus, dessen Titel ihm am besten gefällt. Ist sodann ein Arbeiter gefunden (welches eben nicht schwer ist) der noch drey Alphabete bis zur nächsten Messe übernehmen kann, so handeln sie über den armen Franzosen oder Engländer, wie zwey Schlächter über einen Ochsen oder Hammel, nach dem Ansehen, oder auch nach dem Gewichte. Wer am theuersten verkauft, oder am wohlfeilsten eingekauft hat, glaubt, er habe den besten Handel gemacht. Nun schleppt der Übersetzer das Schlachtopfer nach Hause und tödtet es entweder selbst, oder läßt es durch den zweyten oder dritten Mann tödten.
Seb. Durch den zweyten oder dritten Mann? Wie ist das zu verstehen?
Mag. Das ist eben das Manufakturmäßige der Sache. Sie müssen wissen, es giebt berühmte Leute, welche die Uebersetzungen im Großen entrepreniren, wie ein irländischer Lieferant das Pökelfleisch für ein Spanisches Geschwader, und die sie hernach wieder an ihre Unterübersetzer austheilen. Diese Leute erhalten von allen neuen übersetzbaren Büchern in Frankreich, Italien und England die erste Nachricht, wie ein Mäkler in Amsterdam Nachricht von Ankunft der Ostindischen Schiffe im Texel hat. Alle übersetzungsbedüftige Buchhändler wenden sich an sie, und sie kennen wieder jeden ihrer Arbeiter, wozu er zu gebrauchen ist, und wie hoch er im Preise stehet. Sie wenden den Fleißigen Arbeit zu, bestrafen die Säumigen mit Entziehung ihrer Protection, märzen die Fehler ihrer Uebersetzungen aus, oder bemänteln sie mit ihrem vornehmen Namen; denn mehrentheils sind Entrepreneure von dieser Art stark im Vorredenschreiben. Sie wissen auch genau,wie viel Fleiß an jede Art der Uebersetzung zu wenden nöthig ist, und welche Mittel anzuwenden sind, damit ihre Uebersetzungen allenthalben angepriesen, und dem berühmten Manne öffentlich gedanket werde, der die deutsche gelehrte Welt damit hat beglücken wollen'. Ibid., pp. 114-6.

diffusing knowledge. He sought to improve the literary tastes and style of Germany's reading public and authors by acquainting them with foreign literature, and he certainly did not rejoice in the situation described by the old proof-reader, which is, of course, not free of a certain degree of satirical exaggeration. However, when Nicolai in 1790 suggested some final amendments to the copyright provisions of the Statute Book, he appears to have adopted the proof-reader's view on indentured authors and translators. The astonished question of the naïve Sebaldus, 'You call scholarship a craft? Book-writing a trade?' ('Gelehrsamkeit ein Handwerk? Bücherschreiben ein Gewerbe?'), does in fact reflect the pragmatic view of a publisher as seasoned and hardened as Nicolai was.

6. A Commented Synopsis of Svarez's Draft and the Enacted Provisions

The publishers and their interests were one of the focal points of the Prussian copyright provisions of 1794. As discussed above, Svarez's amendments to Klein's draft had given stronger rights to authors with regard to their publishers. Some of these changes, however, were not incorporated into the enacted Statute. Decisive arguments were brought forward in a memorandum by Friedrich Nicolai dated 6 December 1790. Over forty-five pages he set forth his objections to almost every section of the published draft and concluded by proposing a completely new one.[62] There is no extant evidence that Nicolai had actually been invited to submit his opinion,[63] and it is not clear either why it came so late. Bearing in mind that Nicolai published a law journal (*Annalen der Gesetzgebung und Rechtsgelehrsamkeit in den preussischen Staaten*, 1788-1809),[64] that his bookshop was the best-stocked in Berlin in terms of law books, and that he regularly attended the 'Mittwochsgesellschaft' where he met Klein and Svarez, the introductory sentence to his memorandum seems implausible: 'It is only quite recently that I found out that something concerning the publishing right of book-sellers has been specified in the draft of the new Statute Book'.[65] Moreover,

---

62   *Materialien zum ALR*, GStA PK 1. HA Rep. 84, Abt. XVI, Nr. 7, vol. 71, fol. 106-151. The printed version is in Voigtländer, pp. 5-37.

63   Löhnig, p. 207.

64   Annalen der Gesetzgebung und Rechtsgelehrsamkeit in den preussischen Staaten (1788-1809). Available online at: http://www.ub.uni-bielefeld.de/diglib/aufklaerung/index.htm [accessed 1/3/2010].

65   'Ich habe nicht lange erst erfahren daß über das Verlagsrecht der Buchhändler

one cannot help asking why Svarez agreed so readily to incorporate such substantial changes into his most recent draft, which had been the result of long discussions and a lot of work.

We have no answer to this question, but we can demonstrate the impact of Nicolai's petition by comparing nine key provisions in the enacted Statute Book (ALR) with how these were formulated (if at all) in the printed draft version of 1790.[66]

6.1 Copyright Comprises the Exclusive Right to Sell Copies

Svarez's definition of copyright (or publishing right, 'Verlagsrecht') entailed just the right to exclusively copy a work, whereas the ALR also added an exclusive right of sale, in order to prevent authors from selling self-published editions alongside (and in competition with) the editions of their appointed publishers. The extra second half of the sentence followed Nicolai's proposal word for word

Svarez	ALR
§. 712. Copyright consists in the right to reproduce a work by means of printing.	§. 996. Copyright consists in the right to reproduce a written work by means of printing, and to sell it exclusively at fairs, to the booksellers, or otherwise.

6.2 First Owner of Copyright

According to Svarez (§. 713), the publisher's copyright could be acquired *only* with the consent of the author, whereas in the ALR (§. 998) this is just referred to as something that happens *generally* or *as a rule* ('in der Regel'), since exemptions for works undertaken merely for payment are included further on in §§. 1021f. Nicolai had objected that there were 'very many works where it is the publisher who has the original idea, and who makes use of the writer merely as an instrument for the realisation of his idea'.[67]

---

etwas in dem Entwurfe des neuen Gesetzbuches verordnet ist'. Quoted in Voigtländer, p. 5.

66 The provisions in Svarez's 1790 draft are taken from Voigtländer, pp. 40-2. Translation by Luis A. Sundkvist. The German original can be accessed *Primary Sources*.

67 '[S]ehr viele Schriften, wo der Verleger selbst eine Idee hat, und zu dieser Idee sich des Schriftstellers nur als eines Werkzeuges bedient'. Quoted in Voigtländer, p. 11.

He explained at great length that publishers needed to be awarded directly an exclusive copyright for journals, almanacs and travel guides, whose structure and content they have planned and overseen.

Svarez	ALR
§. 713. Without the consent of the author or his heirs, it is impossible to acquire the copyright to a work. §. 714. Publishing contracts are, like all other contracts, to be drawn up in writing.	§. 998. As a rule, a bookseller can acquire the copyright only by making a written contract with the author.

6.3 Written and Oral Contracts

Publishing contracts had always to be set out in writing according to Svarez (§. 714), whereas the ALR did allow oral agreements, these being binding only with respect to the fee, but not with regard to the agreed number of copies. Later commentators of the Prussian Statute Book have argued that the formula 'in der Regel' ('as a rule') in §. 998 meant that an oral contract was regarded as sufficient when the fee due to the author did not exceed fifty thaler.[68] As for his remarks on §. 714 of Svarez's draft, Nicolai does not mince his words when expounding his views on the majority of contemporary authors. In fact, the views expressed here turn out to be even more critical than those which the old proof-reader had shared with Sebaldus Nothanker in the satirical novel of 1773:

> It will be very difficult to persuade most scholars to subject themselves to such formalities, especially if they are renowned authors. A great deal of writers are slovenly in business matters and often very stubborn. Some of them also like to keep a back-door open for themselves, if they receive advance payments etc. The writer is in a far better position to force the publisher into a written contract than the other way round, and I can confidently say that it is ten times more likely that, where publication and payment are concerned, the publishers should suffer an injustice from the part of the writers than the other way round. If one wishes to consider the transaction

---

68   Friedrich Wilhelm Ludwig Bornemann, *Systematische Darstellung des Preußischen Civilrechts mit Benutzung der Materialien des Allgemeinen Landrechts*, 2nd ed. (Berlin: Jonas Verlagsbuchhandlung, 1843), III, p. 198. Available online at: http://dlib-pr.mpier.mpg.de/m/kleioc/0010/exec/bigpage/%22110810_00000204%22 [accessed 1/3/2010], with reference to Gustav Alexander Bielitz, *Commentar zum Allgemeinen Landrecht für die preußischen Staaten* (1823-30).

between a writer and his publisher in its true light, then all one has to do is to bear in mind that true scholars are the smallest minority amongst all those who delve in writing. For, unfortunately, writing has become a profession like any other. An overwhelming majority of 'authors' simply want to make a living out of their writing. Therefore, they will do everything to fill whole sheets of manuscript, regardless of quality, and to then sell these for the highest possible price, so that they can spend the rest of their days in idleness and financial freedom of mind. It would be very much better both for the State and for the true progress of literature if most of these persons either prepared themselves adequately so that they could serve the State as officials, or if they simply did manual labour of some kind. The publishers, on the other hand, are valuable citizens of the State who have to undertake various enterprises, since otherwise they would not be able to carry on their business.[69]

Nicolai's two-pronged argument is very insidious and crafty, since he not only asserts that writers are not interested in written contracts anyway because they are 'slovenly', 'stubborn', and prone to deceitful actions; but he even claims that, even if they were interested in entering formal contracts, they would not be worthy of any such protection because of their idleness and – in contrast to the publishers! – uselessness to the State.

---

69 'Die meisten Gelehrten sind sehr schwer zu dergleichen Förmlichkeiten zu bringen, besonders wenn es berühmte Schriftsteller sind. Sehr viele Schriftsteller sind unordentlich in Geschäften und oft auch eigensinnig. Manche mögen auch gern eine Hinterthür offenhalten, wenn sie Vorschüsse bekommen und dergl. Der Schriftsteller kann weit eher den Buchhalter [*sic.*] zu einem schriftlichen Contract zwingen als umgekehrt, und ich weiß gewiß zehn Fälle gegen einen, wo über den Verlag und über die Bezahlung, den Buchhändlern von Schriftstellern Unrecht gethan worden als umgekehrt. Wenn man das Geschäft zwischen Schriftsteller und Buchhändler in seinem rechten Lichte betrachten will, so muß man sich nur lebhaft vorstellen, daß der wahren Gelehrten, welche schreiben, der allerwenigste Theil sind. Die Schriftstellerey ist leider ein Gewerbe geworden. Ein großer Theil der Schriftsteller will sich vom Schreiben nähren. Sie suchen also alles hervor, um Bogen voll zu schreiben, sie zu dem höchsten Preise auszubringen, und davon in Müßiggang und Independenz zu leben. Es wäre für den Staate und für den wahren Fortgang der Litteratur sehr viel besser, wenn der größte Theil dieser Leute entweder sich geschickt machte, dem Staate in Aemtern zu dienen, oder wenn sie Handarbeit thäten. Die Buchhändler hingegen sind nützliche Bürger des Staates, die Unternehmungen machen müssen: sonst können sie ihr Gewerbe nicht treiben'. Quoted in Voigtländer, p. 10.

Svarez	ALR
No corresponding provisions.	§. 999. If such a written contract has not been made, but the manuscript has been delivered by the writer, then an oral agreement will be treated as binding, as far as the fee promised to the author is concerned, but in every other respect the circumstances of the two parties are to be judged solely according to the statutory provisions.

6.4 Transfer of Copyright for Only One Edition

The general restriction of publishing contracts to the first edition, as envisaged by Svarez, is maintained in the ALR, but modifications to this stipulation are now made possible if agreed contractually. The author's right to decide whether a new edition could be undertaken by the first publisher was inheritable according to Svarez, whereas §. 1020 allows for the possibility of a clause in the contract excluding the author's heirs from this right.

Svarez	ALR
§. 715. The copyright, as a rule, applies only to the first edition of a work. §. 716. If the publisher wishes to arrange for a new edition, he must come to terms about this with the author or his heirs.	§. 1016. On the other hand, the copyright, as a rule, unless otherwise agreed in the written contract, extends only to the first edition of the work, including any subsequent volumes and sequels. §. 1017. Thus, the first publisher can never undertake a new edition without having made a new contract about this with the author. §. 1020. The author's right whereby no new edition may be undertaken without his being consulted beforehand, is transferred – unless otherwise explicitly stipulated in writing – to his heirs.

6.5 Works Undertaken Solely for Payment

As part of his annotations to §. 713, Nicolai proposed the possibility of a direct acquisition of copyright by publishers who commission writers for a specific task. This original publisher's right is effectively a precursor of the 'works made for hire' provision within the United States Copyright Act of 1976. With regard to translations, Nicolai even suggested that the publishers of these should in general be awarded a full original copyright:

> In the case of translations one can assume that they have been carried out by order of the publisher, unless a literary contract has been drawn up to the contrary [that is, a contract like those normally concluded with authors of original literary works].[70]

The ALR followed Nicolai's proposal on the whole, but did not predetermine a general publisher's copyright for translations. The Prussian Copyright Act of 1837, on the other hand, completely refrained from any such 'works made for hire' provisions, in contrast to the relevant section of the Baden Civil Code (1809) and the 1846 Austrian Law for the protection of literary property.

Svarez	ALR
No corresponding provisions.	§. 1021. The abovementioned restrictions of the copyright in favour of the author shall not apply if the bookseller has entrusted a writer with the task of preparing a work based on an idea that he, the bookseller, had conceived, and if the writer takes on this task without making any specific reservation in written form; or where the bookseller has engaged several authors to work together on the execution of such an idea. §. 1022. In such cases the full copyright belongs to the bookseller from the very start, and the author(s) cannot claim any right to subsequent impressions and editions beyond what has been explicitly reserved for them in the written contract.

---

70 'Von Übersetzungen wird präsumirt, daß sie auf den Auftrag des Verlegers gemacht sind, wofern nicht ein schriftstellerischer Contrakt das Gegentheil besagt'. Quoted in Voigtländer, p. 27.

6.6 Transfer of Copyright Limited to a Certain Number of Copies

The author's right to contractually limit the number of copies would have been exercised by all authors under the system of obligatory written contracts envisaged by Svarez. The ALR, however, as we have seen, did not explicitly prescribe such contracts, and as a result only those authors who were skilled negotiators would have known that they had to insist on the publisher drawing up a formal written contract, which would allow them to limit the number of copies.

Svarez	ALR
§. 717. The publisher is not allowed to print off more copies of the work than the number specified in the contract.	§. 1013. If the publishing contract does not specify the number of copies of the first impression, then the publisher is entitled to arrange subsequent new impressions without the explicit consent of the author. §. 1014. If, however, the number has been specified, then the publisher wishing to undertake a re-impression must come to terms about this with the author or his heirs. §. 1015. If the parties involved are unable to come to an understanding about this, then half of the fee paid for the first impression/edition is to be taken as a standard.

6.7 Author's Obligation to Buy Remaining Copies

As a consequence of the general restriction of publishing contracts to only the first edition, the author is obliged to buy any unsold remaining copies of the latter, in order to compensate the publisher for his losses. The author's liability to pay the 'Buchhändler-Preis' (the retail price minus the bookseller's discount), as stipulated in §. 1019 of the ALR, rather than the acquisition price, however, was a very tough hurdle to clear for authors – all the more so in those cases when the number of copies of the first edition was not limited; and the first publisher would always try to keep enough copies in stock (especially of bestsellers).

It is worth following in some detail the discussion generated by §. 719 of the draft, since it was in this very provision that the counterbalance of the author's bargaining power *vis-à-vis* his publisher was defined. F.W.L. Bornemann[71] interpreted §. 719 of the draft as an obligation for the author to pay the retail price, a provision that he claimed had been criticised in some of the opinions received by the editors, and which was therefore subsequently modified by Svarez in favour of the author. However, Voigtländer's excerpts from the files are quite clear in this respect: the author's obligation to pay the retail price was first proposed in one of the external opinions and recorded in the *Extractus monitorum*. The assistant editor Goßler's reply to this was as follows:

> It would be better [if the author paid] a reimbursement of the received fee (and defrayed the publisher's printing costs). This would mean that an author wanting to improve his work would not be so dependant on his [first] publisher.[72]

Nicolai had also suggested that an author who wished to collaborate with another publisher to produce an amended edition ought to pay the retail price. However, if the author insisted on a new edition and the first publisher was willing to bring this out as well, then the author had to pay, by way of compensation, a sum just ten percent above the publisher's acquisition price, and the latter would keep the remaining copies as waste-paper ('Makulatur').

In his *Revisio monitorum* Svarez agreed with a number of the opinions received which argued that §. 719 would:

> [P]ut the author far too much at the mercy of his publisher, especially if the number of copies was not stipulated in the first contract. Thus, it would be more sensible to lay down the following: that the writer can undertake a new edition once the publisher, through sales of the first edition, has recouped his outlay on the latter, as well as the fee he paid to the author plus regular interests; and that if the author is willing to pay any outstanding sum [on the debit side of the publisher's balance], the publisher has no right of objection.[73]

---

71   Bornemann, p. 200.

72   'Besser ware wohl die Zurückgabe des erhaltenen Honorarii (und die Ersetzung der Kosten des Druckes). Dann hängt auch ein Verfasser, der sein Werk verbessern will, nicht so sehr vom Verleger ab'. Quoted in Voigtländer, p. 44.

73   '[D]en Schriftsteller zu sehr in die Discretion des Verlegers setze; zumal wenn im ersten Kontrakt die Zahl der Exemplarien nicht bestimmt ist. Es dürfte daher rathsamer sein festzusetzen: daß der Schriftsteller alsdann eine neue Ausgabe veranstalten könne, wenn der Verleger aus dem Debit der ersten Ausgabe, seine Ausgabe incl. des Honorarii nebst kaufmännischen Zinsen herausgebracht hat, und daß

Obviously both Goßler and Svarez had originally envisaged a reimbursement of the publisher's expenses, rather than an obligation to pay the retail price when an author wanted to bail out of the publishing contract. The wholesale price stipulated by the ALR was thus a compromise with the objections received by the editors.

Svarez	ALR
§. 718. On the other hand, the author, too, is not allowed to undertake a second edition for as long as copies of the first edition are still available, and until he has come to terms about this with his previous publisher. §. 719. If the number of copies has not been specified in the contract, the author must, before proceeding with a new edition, buy all copies of the first, or come to terms about this with his previous publisher.	§. 1018. But the author, too, cannot undertake a new edition until the first publisher has sold [all copies of] the impressions legitimately carried out by him in accordance with §. 1013 and §. 1014. §. 1019. If the author and bookseller are unable to come to terms regarding a new edition, then the former, should he wish to publish such a new edition with another publisher, must first of all buy up from the first publisher, all copies of the first edition still in stock, paying him the retail price of these in cash.

6.8 Copyright Term for Publishers, Not Authors

Svarez's draft appears to have limited the publisher's, but not the author's, exclusive right to a twenty year term post publication. Svarez's final manuscript had even confined the term to just ten years for works costing less than one thaler.[74] Nicolai's proposal was for an eternal publisher's copyright, albeit not without providing a fair remuneration for the author's 'immediate heirs' (spouse and children):

> So long as the author and his immediate heirs are still alive, the publisher must come to fair and reasonable terms with them as far as new editions are concerned. After their death the copyright remains in the possession of the current publisher [that is, the one who had produced the latest edition].[75]

This procedure serves as a neat demonstration of how eighteenth century

---

wenn der Schriftsteller soviel als daran etwa noch fehlet, vergüten will, dem Verleger kein *ius contradicendi* zustehe'. Quoted in Voigtländer, p. 50.

74   §. 999 of the 'Letzter Entwurf'. Ibid., p. 61.

75   'So lange der Verfasser und seine nächsten Erben leben, muß sich der Verleger wegen neuer Auflagen mit ihnen auf billige Weise abfinden. Nach derselben Ableben bleibt das Verlagsrecht der bisherigen Verlagshandlung eigen'. Ibid., p. 29.

German publishers strategically conceded certain rights to the authors, in order to eventually secure further rights for themselves. In support of his proposal Nicolai also claimed that this had been the custom so far in Germany, Holland and France. Nicolai's proposal was not adopted as such in the final version of the ALR, but, all the same, the provision in Svarez's original draft restricting the publisher's exclusive copyright to twenty years was dropped.

Svarez	ALR
§. 720. All these restrictions on the author (§§. 718, 719), however, do not apply if the first edition appeared twenty or more years earlier, and if no longer duration of the copyright was agreed on beforehand in the contract.	*Deleted without substitution*

6.9 Perpetual Copyright for Publishers, Not Authors

In contrast to the United Kingdom after *Donaldson v. Becket* (1774),[76] there was no agreed standard within the German lands as to how long a publisher's copyright could be exercised for. Pütter had claimed in 1774:

> [T]hat every legitimately acquired copyright persists, as long as the publishing house which had carried out the original publication continues to be run, by heirs or other successors, using the same or also a new trade name.[77]

Nicolai, though he did not refer to Pütter, made a similar observation:

> Hitherto it has been standard practice in all countries that after an author's death, if it should unexpectedly be the case that further new editions of his works are to be produced, the copyright is always retained by the previous publisher [that is, the one who had brought out the latest new edition].[78]

Svarez's draft had, albeit ambiguously, limited the publisher's right to those

---

76   *Donaldson* v. *Becket* (1774), *Primary Sources.*
77   '[B]leibt ein jedes einmal rechtmäßig erworbenes Verlagsrecht, solange irgend die Buchhandlung, die den Verlag ursprünglich übernommen hat, von Erben oder anderen Nachfolgern unter eben demselben oder unter verändertem Namen fortgesetzt wird'. 'Pütter: The Reprinting of Books (1774)', p. 73f., *Primary Sources.*
78   'Es ist bisher in allen Ländern allgemeine Observanz, daß nach dem Tode der Schriftsteller, wenn einmahl der seltne Fall eintritt, daß nach dem ihrem Tode noch neue Auflagen ihrer Schriften gemacht werden, das Verlagsrecht allemahl den vorigen Verlegern bleibt'. Quoted in Voigtländer, p. 34.

publishers ('Buchhändler'), not publishing houses ('Buchhandlungen'), who had acquired their copyright directly from the authors or their heirs. According to §. 716, the author's right to give or withhold his approval for new editions was inheritable without any explicit restrictions as to the term of validity or the grade of kinship. The great length at which Nicolai dwelt on this point in his letter,[79] suggests how important this matter was for him, and eventually he did succeed in completely overturning the intention of the original draft: the ALR includes a restriction whereby the author's right can be transferred only to his children and extends the right of the publisher – who in Svarez's draft needed to have personally acquired his right from the author or his heirs – to a perpetual right of the 'publishing house', which, for all extents and purposes, may well have bought its copyright from anybody..

Svarez	ALR
§. 725. It is permitted to reprint new editions of works by a deceased author, to which any copyright acquired previously by a publisher, either from the author himself or his heirs, has expired.	§. 1029. If there is no publishing house left which has a copyright to the new edition of a book, and the author's right according to §. 1020 has also expired, then anyone is entitled to undertake a new edition of the work. §. 1030. However, if in such a case any of the author's children are still alive, the new publisher must make arrangements with them regarding the edition which he wishes to undertake. §. 1031. Moreover, all the conditions that are stipulated for new works are to apply to the relationship between this new publisher and the writer who prepares the new edition for publication. §. 1032. The reprinting of such editions, too, is forbidden where those very same circumstances apply, under which the reprinting of a new work, in accordance with the above regulations, is not allowed.

79   Ibid., pp. 30-5.

7. Conclusion

The copyright sections of the Prussian Statute Book were the first detailed reprinting regulations to be enacted in any of the German lands. Older provisions in Saxony or in other parts of the Holy Roman Empire had always pointed to the application of a privilege as the appropriate form of protection. The English Statute of Anne may have been the first act to make a general provision on reprinting that could be described as a copyright law; the Prussian Statute Book (ALR) probably was the first code of legislation to centre on the publishing contract.[80]

Captioned as 'Publishing Contracts' and embedded within the sections concerning provisions on contracts in general, the copyright provisions did not bestow any intellectual *property* (in the truest sense of the word) on the author or publisher. The right to exclusively reproduce and sell books (§. 996) is not originally vested in the author and then transferred to the publisher. This is the most obvious difference to the provisions in the Statute of Anne and to the French legislation of 1791 and 1793, and its adaptations in Baden in 1806 and in the Prussian copyright act of 1837.

The legal title here rather does not exist at all before the publishing contract is entered into. §. 996 specifies the publishing right ('Verlagsrecht') as 'authority' ('permit' or 'competence') – thus a literal translation of 'Befugnis' – to reproduce and sell. This 'authority' can only be acquired by a publisher from the author (§. 998). However, aside from the property in the physical manuscript, there is no such 'authority' vested in the author without a publishing contract.

Compared to the absolutist police state model which informed the Saxon Statutes of 1773,[81] the Prussian provisions were formulated within a framework of private law, acknowledging the publishers' private property and thus suitable for encouraging a capitalist market for books and other printed matter. However, the editors' principal intention of completely replacing the privilege system with a general and unconditional ban on reprinting was not fully achieved. For even when the ALR was in force, book privileges still continued, for many more years, to be issued and regarded as a stronger form of protection.

---

80   'Die erste Gesetzgebung überhaupt, die über bloße Nachdrucksverbote hinaus eine umfassende Regelung des Verlagsrechts enthält'; Löhnig, p. 197. A similar point is made by Vogel, p. 89.
81   'Saxonian Statute (1773)', *Primary Sources*.

In modern German legal parlance the kind of copyright provisions implemented by the ALR are referred to as 'publisher's right' ('Verlagsrecht') as distinct from the general term 'author's rights' ('Urheberrecht'). Looking back at these provisions from the perspective of modern German copyright discourse, we can say that the author does not sell the copyright per se to the publisher: rather, he retains his author's right – which is not conceived as a *property* right – and transfers only a clearly demarcated right to exploit the work for the specific publication of a certain number of copies. Thus, the non-transferability of author's rights within the German nineteenth and twentieth century tradition had its origins in the ALR provisions.

9. Nineteenth Century Controversies Relating to the Protection of Artistic Property in France

Frédéric Rideau[*]

Introduction

During the second-half of the eighteenth century, the Parisian booksellers, like their counterparts in London who were waging a 'battle' against the Scottish book trade, sought to defend their monopolies on books against their provincial rivals by justifying them on Lockean property grounds.[1] In France, most of the fundamental concepts of the author's right had in fact been discussed with regard to literary productions, and a perpetual property right was ultimately secured to the author by the Royal Decrees of 30 August 1777. To a certain extent, the king himself recognised, following Louis d'Héricourt, that privileges could bear a different nature when granted to secure the author's peculiar labour.[2] Although the question of artistic property had hardly been addressed in these disputes, Louis XVI also chose the same year to clarify the position of artists: in a declaration

---

[*] The author would like to sincerely thank Lionel Bently for his help in the preparation of this paper, as well as Luis Sundkvist and Ronan Deazley.

[1] For an account of the arguments exchanged see for example 'Gaultier's Memorandum for the Provincial Booksellers (1776)', *Primary Sources*. On the other hand, for a typical *jus naturalis* argument see for example 'Linguet's Memorandum (1777)', *Primary Sources*. The landmark British decision of *Millar v. Taylor* (1769), 4 Burr. 2303, should also be consulted in this context; see 'Millar v. Taylor (1769)', *Primary Sources*.

[2] On this see: 'Louis d'Héricourt's Memorandum (1725-1726)', *Primary Sources* ; 'French Decree of 30 August 1777, on the Duration of Privileges (1777)', *Primary Sources*.

of 15 May 1777, the king recognised the freedom of artists to create as well as their exclusive rights in those creations, emphasising that the arts of painting and sculpture 'should be perfectly analogous to Literature, the Sciences & other liberal arts, especially architecture; in such a manner that those wishing the above said arts of this kind should not, under any pretext, be troubled or bothered by any corporation or guild'.[3] In addition, all counterfeiting, be it by engraving or by casting, without the author's consent, was to be punished according to Article 8 of the Declaration. Now clearly linked, before 1789, with literary property, the next step towards the recognition of artistic property was for it to be consecrated and secured by a single statute, a legislative development which occurred in the wake of the first years of the Revolution, following the abolition of privileges in August 1789. The revolutionary legal recognition of the author's property would first take place with the legislation of 13-19 January 1791 concerning dramatic performances, before the subsequent legislation of 19-24 July 1793 recognised the author's right of property in his literary and artistic works, thus supposedly bringing to an end the long debates of the eighteenth century concerning booksellers' privileges and their monopolies. As in 1777, trying, without much parliamentary discussion, to reconcile a natural property right with the public interest, the Act of 1793 indeed declared the author's ownership of his work to be the form of property which was least open to contestation – although, paradoxically, this property was drastically limited in duration (to the author's life and for a further ten years after the author's death).[4]

As it happened, although it was to be the main copyright legislation for decades, the statute contained a mere seven articles, and many matters, concerning the object of the newly secured property, were left unclear.[5] Some attempt was made to add clarification to the Act through the establishment of a commission mainly devoted to the question of literary property, set up in the final months of 1825 under the presidency of the Viscount Sosthène de La Rochefoucauld and made up of several eminent jurists and

---

3 'Royal Declaration on Sculpture and Painting (1777)', *Primary Sources*. Translation by Katie Scott. An up-to-date history of artistic property in France still remains to be written; Vaunois' valuable study dates from the nineteenth century: A. Vaunois, *La condition et les droits d'auteur des artistes jusqu'à la Révolution* (Paris, 1892).
4 'French Literary and Artistic Property Act (1793)', *Primary Sources*.
5 One might contrast the very different approach to legislation in the United Kingdom where particular types of artistic work were protected under separate statutes, each with relatively detailed provisions on the threshold of protection and rights conferred.

statesmen, which was assigned the task of preparing a draft for new legislation.[6] However, the commission became side-tracked by the question of the duration of copyright, a matter which thereafter dominated parliamentary reform initiatives (for example, in 1841), until the term was extended to fifty years *post mortem auctoris* in 1866. In the absence of more general reform, therefore, in the field of artistic property, as in literary property, the interpretations given to the Act by the courts and commentators proved critical throughout the nineteenth century. The judges, obviously, but also key figures and commentators including chief prosecutor Philippe-Antoine Merlin,[7] Augustin-Charles Renouard,[8] Etienne Blanc,[9] Eugène Pouillet[10] and Claude Couhin[11], were called upon to engage with the complex task of defining what constitutes an 'artistic work', its general definition and its threshold of protection, as well as determining the relationship between the artist and the owner of a painting, sculpture or engraving, and the scope of protection.

Definition of an Artistic Work

Article 1 of the 1793 Act acknowledged that it was necessary to protect the 'Authors of writings of any kind, composers of music, painters and draughtsmen who shall cause paintings and drawings to be engraved'. The courts, throughout the nineteenth century, would have to decide what did and what did not encompass writings 'of any kind', a general expression that seemed firstly to contrast, within the same article, with the subsequent restricted list relating to the field of artistic creations. In fact, some very

---

6   The complete works of this commission is available online: 'Minutes of the 1825-1826 Commission (1826)', *Primary Sources*. Some discussion was directly concerned with artistic property and in particular the analogy between literary and artistic property, and the necessity for any new legislation to uphold a similar duration in these two comparable fields (see in particular pp. 314 and 331 for the proposed bill). For further details, see F. Rideau, 'Commentary on the Minutes of the 1825-1826 Commission (1826)', *Primary Sources*.

7   See in particular Philippe-Antoine Merlin, 'Contrefaçon', in *Répertoire universel et raisonné de jurisprudence*, 5th ed., vol. 5 (Paris, 1825); see also 'Merlin on Counterfeiting (1825)', *Primary Sources*.

8   A.C. Renouard, *Traité des droits d'auteurs, dans la littérature, les sciences et les Beaux-Arts*, vol. 2 (Paris, 1839).

9   E. Blanc, *Traité de la Contrefaçon*, 4th ed. (Paris, 1855).

10   Especially the last edition of his treatise in the nineteenth century: E. Pouillet, *Traité théorique et pratique de la propriété littéraire et artistique et du droit de représentation*, 2nd ed. (Paris, 1894).

11   C. Couhin, *La propriété industrielle, artistique et littéraire*, vol. 2 (Paris, 1898).

limited assistance in this task had been provided by the legislature which laconically, in Article 7, conferred concurrently a ten year period of protection on the heirs of authors of 'works of literature or of engravings, or of any other production of the mind or of genius within the domain of the fine arts'.[12]

The first judicial general clarifications were given at the beginning of the nineteenth century. Sculpture, for example, was surprisingly not explicitly mentioned in Article 1 (or Article 7).[13] In 1814, in the landmark *Romagnesi* case, the Supreme Court (*Cour de Cassation*) had to determine whether the conviction of the *Demoiselle* Gabrielle Robin of counterfeiting Romagnesi's bust of King Louis XVIII was lawful.[14] It was argued that Romagnesi had failed to deposit copies of the bust in accordance with Article 6 of the 1793 Act, which had some consequences on the implementation of the property right, and, more significantly, it was argued that sculptures were not protected by that legislation. The judges followed Merlin's conclusions, which relied on Article 3 of the statute, to rule against Robin.[15] Article 3 required Officers of the Peace to confiscate 'for the benefit of the authors, composers, painters, draughtsmen and others concerned [...] all copies of publications which ha[d] been printed or engraved without the formal written permission of their authors'. The reference to 'authors, composers of music, painters, draughtsmen and others' could be interpreted as implicitly including sculptors: these 'others' could only have been added, as the famous chief prosecutor Merlin put it, to benefit 'all the artists in general'.[16] Along with the general dispositions of the *Code pénal*, the Court was also reinforced in this interpretation by Article 7, relating to 'any other production of the mind or of genius', which – according to Merlin – could only complete and corroborate Article 3.[17] Affirming Robin's conviction for counterfeiting, the Court held moreover that the deposit of such sculptures had never been regarded as necessary under Article 6 to implement the property right they conveyed: the Act only obliged the authors of printed and engraved works to deposit copies of these works at the Royal Library.

---

12 'French Literary and Artistic Property Act (1793)', *Primary Sources*.
13 On this point, see F. Rideau, 'Commentary on the Court of Cassation on Sculptures (1814)', *Primary Sources*.
14 *Robin v. Romagnesi*, *Cour de Cassation*, 17 November 1814, Sirey 1812-1814.1.630-1; see 'Court of Cassation on Sculptures (1814)', *Primary Sources*.
15 Merlin, p. 286.
16 Ibid.
17 Ibid., p. 287. Merlin also relied on Article 425 of the *Code Pénal* of 1810, which also mentioned 'or of any other production'.

Such general terms had therefore to allow other forms of production of the mind or of genius to be protected under the 1793 Act. In particular, the revolutionary legislation, obviously, had not foreseen the question of photographic productions. The *Cour de Cassation*, in November 1862, finally ruled against an absolute exclusion of photography under the 1793 Act.[18]

Threshold of Protection

A second, and more difficult question, concerned more specifically the threshold criterion to be satisfied before a work might be regarded as protected. In the field of artistic works, the problem arose in particular in relation to sculptures that reproduced existing works (what we would now refer to as works in the public domain) or natural artefacts, and especially those that involved mechanical processes, such as miniaturisation.

In the context of literary works, the *Cour de Cassation* had rendered an important ruling on 2 December 1814, to the effect that compilations, as a matter of principle, were not excluded from protection under the 1793 regulations. However, the judges indicated that the threshold of protection could not be reduced to a bare quantitative 'savoir faire', a form dictated by necessity (for example, in literary compilations, the arrangement of extracts in chronological order or dictated by the nature of the texts), the mere activity of 'research', and so on. Indeed, the supreme judges asserted the legitimacy of applying the protection of the 1793 Act to collections, compilations and other works of this kind, but only where these works had 'in their execution' required 'discerning taste, learned selection, mental labour' and 'intelligence'. In short, the work had to reveal in its form 'conceptions' that were 'proper' to its author (*conceptions qui lui ont été propres*).[19] Decided again under the influence of Merlin, and because of the general, albeit ambiguous, formulation of the 1793 statute, this minimal requirement was supposed to apply and to provide a guideline to all 'productions of the mind or of genius', that is to artistic productions and in particular to sculptures.[20]

---

18   *Betbéder and Schwalbé v. Mayer and Pierson, Cour de Cassation,* 28 November 1862, Dalloz 1863.1.52; see 'Court of Cassation on Photography (1862)', *Primary Sources.*
19   *Leclerc v. Villeprend and Brunet, Cour de Cassation,* 2 December 1814, Sirey 1812-1814.1.637; see 'Court of Cassation on Compilations (1814)', *Primary Sources.*
20   In fact, a creation that had to be 'proper' to its author could reveal at the same time an objective and subjective definition of the work. Merlin had indeed referred at the time to compilations whose construction could resemble 'noble palaces', genuine 'creations', reflecting, in a way, their author's personality. On this ambiguity,

In the light of this holding, a sculpture created by purely manual and technical reproduction such as casting could readily be excluded from the protection of the 1793 statute, and this line was soon taken by some courts. For example, in 1834, the *Tribunal Correctionnel* of the Seine held that the death-mask of Napoleon, made by his doctor Antomarchi, was not protected under the Act: the process of capturing, by means of taking a cast (from a person's face) could not establish an exclusive right. The judges indicated that if one were to compare the product of a purely manual operation to the work that a sculptor has produced that would have amounted to extending the provisions of the law beyond what was a work of the mind or of genius.[21] Therefore, there was no infringement in taking further casts from the master mould without the consent of its original author or manufacturer. Thus, the mechanical process seems to have been perceived by the judges as incompatible with a more subjective approach to creation. The decision, however, was regarded by certain jurists as peremptory, and one that was maybe influenced by external pressures or lobbying – in particular by the Fine Arts Section of the *Institut Royal de France*. Indeed, Blanc, in his *Traité de la Contrefaçon*, recalled that for the Institute members, the 'mind or genius do not, as a matter of fact, play any role whatsoever in this purely manual operation, which is not at all difficult, since all it takes is a little bit of practice in order for one to be able to carry it out to the desired degree of perfection'.[22]

Miniatures (*réductions*) of statues also gave rise to similar questions, but not always with the same conclusions. For example, the courts had ruled in 1829 that the reduction of an antique figure with the model for a clock produced a property right: such reductions of statues could possibly display, as the judges explained in 1838, the 'talent' and the 'personal labour' of their author.[23] Again, the question was, however, more problematic when the production of the miniatures was mainly carried out by a machine. For jurists and major commentators like Pouillet and Couhin, even though the 'author' was just the operator of a machine, a categorical exclusion could

---

and the evolution of the criteria of protection, see the *Cour de Cassation's* ruling of 2 December 1814 and its commentary ('Court of Cassation on Compilations (1814)', *Primary Sources*).

21   *Correctional Tribunal* of the Seine, 10 December 1834, quoted from Pouillet, p. 102. See also Blanc, p. 296.
22   Blanc, p. 296f.
23   Court of Paris, 22 January 1829, and Court of Bordeaux, 26 May 1838, Sirey 1838.2.485-6 (cases quoted by Pouillet, p. 103).

not be justified.[24] Pouillet, for example, recalled that amongst the guild of bronze manufacturers, 'it is unanimously recognised that no confusion is possible between the various miniatures made of the same original sculpture, even if these have been manufactured by means of a similar mechanical process. A miniature made by one craftsman can always be told apart from that made by another, and no mistake is possible here'. And besides, he added, the fact that an artist or a worker operates the machine does not change the principle: unless judges become art critics, by what criteria are they effectively to distinguish between the two operators?[25]

The question was further complicated by the fact that, whilst the law was in theory supposed to secure protection for works of any kind, the criteria for protection became more explicitly subjective from the second half of the nineteenth century onwards. In February 1857, in an important case concerning the counterfeit of a sculpture, the *Cour de Cassation* ruled that 'however well-known the features of a commonplace article (*les traits d'un type commun*) may be, and in spite of the fact that tradition requires any copy to respect those features, this indispensable fidelity still leaves space for the talent of the artist, allowing him to create a work that bears a *special* character, and which becomes as such a property protected by law'.[26] In April 1861, the Court (of Appeal) of Bordeaux, in a case relating to the protection of telegraphic news, stressed the point that the work

------

24   The same debates would occur in relation to photography. Photographic productions gave rise to contradictory decisions before the lower courts from the early 1860s onwards, until the ruling of the *Cour de Cassation* of 28 November 1862 in *Betbéder and Schwalbé v. Mayer and Pierson*, Dalloz 1863.1.52 ('Court of Cassation on Photography (1863)', *Primary Sources*). Basically, it could be argued at the time that a photograph was purely a mechanical product, and was not creating anything. In fact, the intellectual and artistic labour of the photographer, if it existed, it did so mainly prior to the material execution of the photograph itself. On the contrary, the choice of the subject, the viewing angles, lighting, and so on, allowed the photographic production to be a potentially protectable subject matter. For further details, see F. Rideau, 'Commentary on the Court of Cassation on Photography (1862)', *Primary Sources*.
25   Pouillet, pp. 104-5. See also Couhin, p. 408 for whom these miniatures can imply, to a certain degree, 'a personal effort'.
26   *Fontana v. Public Attorney, Cour de Cassation*, 13 February 1857, Dalloz 1857.1.111; see 'Court of Cassation on Originality (1857)', *Primary Sources* (emphasis added). In some decisions, the word 'certain' can be noted; see for example Court of *Colmar*, 17 August 1858, which entirely confirmed the decision of *Tribunal Correctionnel* of Strasbourg, 30 January 1858, in acknowledging the protection of compilations 'on condition that they represent a certain conception of the mind, a genuine labour, a creation' (Pataille, *Annales de la propriété industrielle, artistique et littéraire*, Tome VI, 1860, p. 399).

had to carry 'in some way the imprint of the personality' of its creator.[27] In relation to photographic productions, the same expression would also be used by the Court of Paris in April 1862.[28] The word 'originality' was not employed frequently at this stage, but the expression used by the judges conclusively indicated that the 1793 Act would not protect a mere product of intellectual labour. Indeed, it has been pointed out that the multiplication of occurrences of such 'subjective' criteria, in particular the originality test, probably stemmed from a renewal of artistic awareness during this period, implying the belief that the purpose of a copyright statute was to protect works of an aesthetic or ornamental nature.[29]

Nonetheless, at the end of the nineteenth century, the situation before the courts remained the same as the one that Renouard had bitterly described in 1839: in 'artistic as in literary matters', there was still 'no correlation between the number and the seriousness of judicial debates, and the significance of the productions in question', adding to that, the 'flimsiest [were] often those that give rise to the greatest number of trials'.[30] More than fifty years later, Pouillet would still comment that 'the legislator, in carrying out an act of incontestable justice by protecting the most sacred of

---

27   Court of Bordeaux, 22 April 1861, in the decision *Havas, Bullier & Co. v. Gounouilhou*, which led to the decision of the *Cour de Cassation*, 8 August 1861, Dalloz 1862.1.137; see F. Rideau, 'Commentary on Court of Cassation on Telegraphic News (1861)', *Primary Sources*.
28   Court of Paris, 10 April 1862, in the abovementioned case of *Betbéder and Schwalbé v. Mayer and Pierson*, Dalloz 1863.1.53-4. See further F. Rideau, 'Commentary on the Court of Cassation on Photography (1862)', *Primary Sources*.
29   O. Laligant, *La Véritable condition d'application du droit d'auteur: originalité ou création?* (Aix-en-Provence: Presses Universitaires d'Aix-Marseille, 1999), who also discusses the impact of authors such as Baudelaire in the 'radicalization' of literary originality, pp. 62-5. Concerning the minimum threshold of protection of these productions, the criteria of protection would indeed evolve, in the course of the nineteenth century, from a work supposed to represent a certain investment of personal labour of the author (a labour 'proper to him', as stated by the Supreme French Court on 2 December 1814) to a work which had to bear or display some 'originality'. On this development, see in particular F. Rideau, 'Commentary on the Court of Cassation on Originality (1869)', *Primary Sources*.
30   Renouard, p. 81: 'One can hear a lot of vociferous protesting about the protection due to genius in the countless legal disputes relating to the articles produced by the manufacturers of bronze and porcelain figurines, by founders, enamellers, and the members of many other analogous professions – disputes which are after all concerned solely with industrial and mercantile interests, and which raise questions requiring the application of the existing special laws on trade marks and industrial designs'. Translation by Luis A. Sundkvist. On this question, see also K. Scott, 'Art and Industry. A Contradictory Union: Authors, Rights and Copyrights during the *Consulat*', *Journal of Design History*, 13 (2000), 1-21.

properties, has nevertheless inflicted upon the world of arts and letters an irreparable harm, for he has rendered that world fatally mercantile'.[31]

Finally, the *Cour de Cassation* chose to leave to the judges of the inferior courts a great deal of room to manoeuvre in the assessment of what was proper to the author in the artistic work. With regard to mechanical miniatures or reductions, for example, the Supreme Court upheld, in May 1862, the interpretation of the lower judges as to whether miniatures of these types could constitute, or not, an artistic work in the sense of the statute of 1793. In other words, such assessments, left to the lower courts, were necessarily independent.[32]

Corporeal and Incorporeal in an Artistic Work

The general wording of the terms of the revolutionary statute also led to some questions as to the relationship between the incorporeal property it conferred in a work of art and the corporeal ownership of the paintings, sculptures and engravings themselves. In particular, the question arose as to whether the transfer of the physical medium of the work implied that the right to have the painting or drawing engraved was also to be automatically transferred. Again, the judges would have to try to resolve this question.[33]

The *Cour de Cassation* considered the issue in a joint session of all its chambers on 27 May 1842.[34] In this case Antoine-Jean Gros had sold the painting the *Bataille des Pyramides* in 1809, and the question arose whether this transferred the right to reproduce it to the purchaser, or whether Gros could transfer the right to engrave the painting later to a M. Vallot. Following the conclusions presented by the chief prosecutor Dupin, and the viewpoint of the courts of first instance, the Court held that, in the absence of an explicit contractual reservation or clause formally stipulating the contrary on the part of the author, in accordance with the general regulations on

31   Pouillet, p. 23.
32   *Barbedienne v. Van Loqueren and Others Cour de Cassation*, 16 May 1862, Dalloz 1863.1.111 and, with regard to decisions as to whether photographic productions met the criterion that could sustain protection, see *Betbéder and Schwalbé v. Mayer and Pierson, Cour de Cassation*, 28 November 1862, Dalloz 1863.1.52.
33   For the position in the United Kingdom, at least with respect to paintings, see the essay in this collection by Ronan Deazley ('Breaking the Mould? The Radical Nature of the Fine Arts Copyright Bill 1862').
34   *Heirs of Baron Gros and Vallot v. Gavard, Cour de Cassation*, 27 May 1842, Dalloz 1842.1.297. For further details, see F. Rideau, 'Commentary on Court of Cassation on Artistic Property (1842)', *Primary Sources*.

property, the transfer of the original medium of the artistic work naturally implied the transfer of 'the full and absolute property of the sold object', that is, all its 'accessories' along 'with all the rights which are attached to it or depend on it'.[35] Indeed, according to Dupin, the artist was sufficiently protected by Article 1 of the statute. Furthermore, as he argued, any other solution would have been against the artist's own interests, since his glory could only increase as a result of the reproduction, by every means, of his work – reproductions which would in the end benefit the public interest.[36] In a way, the work seemed to be principally reduced, in the artistic field, to its original and first embodiment or medium, consequently giving its owner, by virtue of the mere fact of possession, the right to freely use and dispose of it. The judicial line was thus set for the rest of the nineteenth century.[37]

Yet the same judges had, a year earlier, maintained the exact opposite position to this – that is, that even without explicit contractual stipulation or reservation, the sale of a painting by its author did not imply the transfer of the right to reproduce it by 'a distinct art, that of engraving'.[38] Moreover, some important jurists continued to disagree strongly with the *Cour de Cassation*'s decision. For Couhin, for example, the 'transfer of the property of the original could not entail – at least in theory – the transfer of the property of the right of reproduction of the work in question', and this was particularly so 'in the transfer of the property of a painting'.[39] Thus, in Couhin's view, the 1842 ruling 'failed to appreciate, in a manifest way, the spirit and the text of the law'.[40] Indeed, he deduced from the 1793 Act that the legislators were clearly seeking to enshrine the property 'not of the paintings or the drawings themselves, but of the engravings of those paintings or drawings'.[41] There was, consequently, on the one hand, a property, a 'value', vested in the physical medium or material object of the work of art (that is, in practical terms, the 'ordinary' property of the painting itself)

---

35   Dalloz 1842.1.304.

36   Dupin also rejected the protection of the non-pecuniary interests of the original artist as a legitimate argument: see Dalloz 1842.1.303-4.

37   In fact, this had been the solution proposed in March 1841 in the literary and artistic property bill. For this document see 'Report of Lamartine and Parliamentary Debates on Literary Property (1841)', *Primary Sources*.

38   *Veuve Gros and Vallot v. Gavard, Cour de Cassation*, 23 July 1841, Dalloz 1841.1.322. For a precise presentation of the facts by the councillor Romiguières see 'Court of Cassation on Artistic Property (1841)', *Primary Sources*.

39   Couhin, pp. 410-1.

40   Ibid., p. 413.

41   And, of course, although not mentioned, derivative works of sculpture were also implied; ibid., p. 409.

and, on the other hand, the right to have reproductions of it made. In fact, the latter was also a 'value', a property, which was not secured by the general dispositions of the *Code Civil*, but rather by the 'special' law of 1793.[42] Likewise, according to Pouillet, he who 'buys an art object buys the material object, the right to possess the composition which has pleased him, whose execution has charmed him; this is, in short, a certain and specific item; nothing more'.[43] The decision of 1842 was of great significance because of the parallel judicial expansion of what amounted to the infringement of the artist's rights from the 1840s. As will be discussed below, the implication of the 1842 decision was not merely that the right to reproduce the work by the process of engraving was transferred to the purchaser of a painting, in accordance with the literal wording of Article 1 of the 1793 Act, but that the sale of the painting transferred the right to control reproduction by every process or technique which had developed subsequently. Such was the case with photography, for example. Because of this increasing diversity in the means of reproducing works of art, which additionally held out the potential for great profit, commentators such as Albert Vaunois were sceptical about it being possible to define the right of reproduction as a mere accessory of the original medium of the work.[44] Yet, the principle of the distinction of the property right in the work, that is, in its own 'conception' and its material incarnation, was only recognised conclusively in the law of 9 April 1910, which settled that 'the transfer of a work of art does not entail, unless otherwise convened, that of the right to reproduce it'.

Scope of Protection

Difficulties concerning the scope of protection stemmed once again from the interpretation of Article 1, which specified that painters and designers were to enjoy the right to reproduce their works. What would these means of reproduction be? Were they to be restricted to the literal terms of the law, that is, just to the engraving of works of the fine arts?[45]

On this question, the judges, at first, predictably remained quite hesitant to extend Article 1 far beyond its explicit letter. For example, the Court

---

42   Ibid., p. 410.
43   Pouillet, pp. 362-3.
44   A. Vaunois, *De la Propriété artistique en droit français* (Paris, 1884), pp. 293-4.
45   We should recall that engraving was the only means of reproduction explicitly mentioned (Article 1: Authors of writings of any kind, composers of music, painters and draughtsmen who shall cause paintings and drawings to be engraved).

of Paris ruled, on 3 December 1831, that the property right to a painting did not extend to 'preventing the imitation or reproduction of the original work by the techniques of another, essentially distinct art, such as sculpture' (in this case the painting had been produced in bronze). However, from the 1840s onwards, it seems that some judges became less reluctant to consider a broader definition of the work of art. Since considerable economic interests – though not only economic ones – were at stake for the artist, it seemed almost impossible to limit reproduction of the original work by the sole means of engraving.[46] On 16 February 1843, for example, the Court of Paris upheld an injunction prohibiting the reproduction, 'be it in porcelain or in bronze', of a painting without the author's consent. Similarly, on 6 February 1862, the *Tribunal* of the Seine ruled that the reproduction of 'paintings or engravings by microscopic photography, against the right of artists' was an instance of counterfeiting.[47]

The attitude of the major commentators followed roughly the same trajectory. For Renouard, at the end of the 1830s, the dematerialisation of the object of artistic and literary property, beyond the traditional distinction between idea and form, was found to be unacceptable.[48] He viewed, for example, the idea of 'counterfeiting' a painting by means of sculpture problematic, since 'these arts are essentially too different'.[49] At the end of the nineteenth century, however, authors like Pouillet and Couhin agreed on a broader interpretation of Article 1. Pouillet, for example, was a strong proponent of the principle that as soon as the reproduction 'takes place without the authorisation of the proprietor, it constitutes a violation of his property'. He added that if 'it is a painting that is affected, it does not matter whether it is reproduced by painting, drawing, engraving, photography, or even by sculpture, and then, for example, it is translated into a bas-relief'.[50]

'Translated' was, as in the literary field, to a form which was not strictly

---

46   As Couhin put it at p. 414, echoing Article 8 of the abovementioned Royal Decree of May 1777, 'there is also his [the artist's] fame to take into account, or, at any rate, his reputation. Nothing more delicate, indeed, and more complex, and often more difficult than the reproduction of a work of the intellect.'

47   These three decisions are summarized by Pouillet, pp. 555-6. The English court, at roughly the same time, held that the owner of copyright in an engraving was entitled to prohibit the making of copies by photographic means: *Gambart v. Ball* (1863) 14 CB (NS) 306.

48   This was also the question debated for literary translation. On Renouard's opinion on translations, see *Rosa v. Girardin*, Court of Rouen, 7 November 1845, Dalloz 1846.2.212; 'Court of Appeal on Translations (1845)', *Primary Sources*.

49   Renouard, pp. 88-9.

50   Pouillet, p. 551.

identical, but that remained at the same time, in some sense, similar, and was therefore a reproduction of the original work: 'what belongs to the author is the whole of his conception, that is, the special form which he has given to an action or an idea'.[51]

Conclusion

The controversies concerning the identification of the object of artistic property, resulting from the laconic text of the 1793 Act, revealed difficulties (and eventually conflicts amongst various interests) that were also being confronted in relation to literary property. For instance, the difficulties in determining precisely the scope of protection – in particular, that of identifying the intangible object of protection – also arose in relation to the question as to whether a 'translation' of a literary work was an infringement of the rights conferred by the Revolutionary legislation. As with the question of whether the making of a sculpture from a painting infringed the rights of the artist, so the question of whether the author's right extended to controlling translation required the courts and commentators to confront the distinction that had been embraced in the eighteenth century between idea and form.

However difficult the relationship between 'idea' and 'form' and the scope of protection might have been, perhaps the most controversial issue remained the question of the common threshold of protection, despite the attempts at synthesis undertaken by notable jurists such as Blanc, Couhin, and Pouillet. In this regard it is significant that, at the turn of the twentieth century, Eugéne Soleau, former president of the Association of Bronze Manufacturers, sought to put an end to the persistent contradictory decisions emanating from the courts by persuading the legislature that the statute of 1793 should be explicitly declared to apply to all works of the fine arts, even those with an industrial function or destination.[52] In many respects, throughout the nineteenth century, the judges seemed to be ineluctably caught between a rising or more explicit subjective definition of literary and artistic work and a legal indifference as to the kind of

---

51   Ibid., p. 552.
52   E. Soleau, *Rapport à la Chambre de commerce de Paris, sur la protection des dessins et modèles appliqués à l'industrie*, Annexe V (Bull. Ch. Com: Paris, 25 February 1905), extract cited by Pouillet, *Traité théorique et pratique de la propriété littéraire et artistique et du droit de représentation*, 3rd ed. (Paris, 1910), p. 105. Soleau's campaign was successful in that it led to the law of 11 March 1902.

production which could qualify for protection. As Pouillet tried to explain, the law 'does not concern itself with the importance or the beauty of the work: all it takes into account is the fact of creation. It is for this reason that the law protects to the same extent a painting by Raphael and an image produced in the Épinal factories (colourful prints sold throughout France in the nineteenth century).'[53] And, even though a precise definition was still lacking as to when a 'creation' was 'proper to its author', or bore 'the imprint of his or her personality', this did not prevent further developments grounded on this theoretical subjective link between the author and his work. The judicial consecration of *'droit moral'*, in particular, would also thus be elaborated, at the beginning of the twentieth century, within the framework of the old 1793 Act, as a right which would therefore have to be applied to all kind of literary and artistic works.[54]

---

53   See Pouillet, p. 89f.
54   *Cinquin v. Lecocq, Cour de Cassation.* 25 June 1902, Dalloz 1903.1.5; see 'Court of Cassation on Moral Rights (1902)', *Primary Sources.*

10. Maps, Views and Ornament: Visualising Property in Art and Law. The Case of Pre-modern France

Katie Scott[*]

In art, in printed images particularly, privilege, or the legal precursor of copyright in French law, derived originally from that pertaining to published texts; indeed, from the mid-seventeenth century, *intaglio* printmaking having no corporate body of its own, privilege in prints was administered by the Paris Corporation of booksellers, publishers and printers.[1] Consequently, it is habitually treated as a derivative instance of the law, as a poor relation in an expanding family of intellectual property rights. Painting, by this account, followed poetry not only as the misprision of Horace's epigrammatical phrase suggested, in mode and function, but also, when mechanically reproduced, by legal act. By the eighteenth century, however, *ut pictura, poesis*, that analogy by force of which the art theory of the sixteenth century discovered its inaugural voice, was visibly becoming an ill-fitting frame, and long before the publication of Gotthold Ephraim

* My warm thanks to Lionel Bently and Ronan Deazley for their improvements to both the content and presentation of this present essay, to Mark Rose for raising the question of reification, and to Julian Stallabrass for his suggestions for the clarification of the argument.

1 See Marianne Grivel, *Le Commerce de l'estampe à Paris au XVIIe siècle* (Geneva: Droz, 1986), pp. 83-116; Marianne Grivel, 'La Réglementation du travail des graveurs en France au XVIe siècle', in *Le Livre et l'image en France au XVIe siècle* (Paris: Presses de l'École normale supérieure, 1989), pp. 2-27.

Lessing's *Laokoon* (1766) it was widely recognised that, to quote Jean de La Fontaine, 'Les mots et les couleurs ne sont choses pareilles / Ni les yeux ne sont les oreilles' (Words and colours are not similar things / Nor are eyes ears),[2] or, to put it more prosaically, that disparity, as much as resemblance, marks the internal composition of the sphere of the aesthetic.

The case advanced here is that vision and visual art in fact made a telling contribution to the formulation of the legal forerunner of modern copyright; Claude Marin Saugrain, the first codifier of the laws of the Paris book trade, asserts, after-all, that law should forever be in sight, 'sous les yeux'.[3] The eye of the law invoked is not only and explicitly the eye of the subject (in this case, the several members of the Booksellers' Corporation) who is brought by sight to knowledge of the law and thereafter conforms to its decrees, but also, and metaphorically, an eye that invigilates and disciplines, and by that seemingly absolute power to do so constitutes the law as given and immutable.[4] By contrast, and supposing rather that the law, and the concepts that determine it, is fabricated, fabricated moreover by the accumulated involvement of a host of different worlds, it is argued below that sight and the visual played a significant part in the very constitution and subsequent evolution of privilege.

Prompted by developments in sociological theory,[5] it is suggested that 'property', the notion upon which all regimes of copyright necessarily stand, is best viewed as a 'boundary object', that is a concept or idea that balances at the intersection of a number of different discourses – in this instance, those of law, economics, politics, and aesthetics – that is, an 'object' at once both weak enough to bend to local discursive requirements *and* strong enough to keep recognisable fit and general rhetorical purpose across those

---

2   Jean de La Fontaine, 'Conte du Tableau', in *Contes et Nouvelles* (1664) quoted from Rensselaer W. Lee, *Ut Pictura Poesis: The Humanistic Theory of Painting* (New York: W.W. Norton & Co., 1967), p. 9.
3   Claude Marin Saugrain, *Code de la librairie et imprimerie de Paris ou conférence du réglement arrêté au conseil d'état du roi le 28 fevrier 1723* (Paris: Communauté de la librairie, 1744), p. viii.
4   On the iconography and ideology of the eye of the law see most fully and recently Michael Stolleis, *L'Œil de la loi. Histoire d'une métaphore*, introduced by Pierre Legendre (Paris: Mille et une nuits, 2006).
5   Especially the sociology of science; see: Susan Leigh Star and James R. Griesemer, 'Institutional Ecology, "Translations" and Boundary Objects: Amateurs and professionals in Berkeley's Museum of Vertebrate Zoology, 1907-39', *Social Studies in Science*, 19 (1989) 387-420; Joan Fujimura, 'Crafting Science: Standardized Packages, Boundary Objects, and "Translation"', in *Science as practice and culture* , ed. by A. Pickering (London: Chicago University Press, 1992), pp. 168-211.

disparate domains. Locally signifying contract (law), commodity (economics), source of authority (politics), figure or material stuff (aesthetics) and generally denoting belonging, 'property' in early modern thought by this account facilitated cooperation in the construction of a regime of legal practice without a presupposition of consensus having to be assumed. In the context of such collective construction of legal knowledge, it is not, however, what Painting claimed for herself, not her vaunted ambition to the autonomy or self-possession of the literary, made through deployment of such key figures of humanist rhetoric as idea, imagination, invention, that is at issue but rather what she disavowed: her servile, specula imitation, her apparent concreteness and materiality; that, in short, which made her works irredeemably spatial and tangible. To draw out the paradox more clearly, if Painting acceded to the protection of privilege by virtue of her liberal status, her likeness to Poetry, she made her particular contribution to law via her so-called mechanical facture, her 'literal' translations of properties in and of the natural world. Painting's 'truth', it is argued, as instanced in maps and views of town and country, effected a shift in the discursive function of property in privilege from metaphor to model, and provided an epistemological resource for negotiating the realignment of legal prerogatives and economic interests in the run up to capitalism.

The first part of this essay therefore provides an account of the 'possessive' depiction of urban and landed property in seventeenth and early eighteenth century France and draws attention to the ornamental strategies of framing, signing and posting notices by which all manner of images were brought potentially under an order of ownership. In attending in such detail to how notions of property intersected, overlapped, and worked to make and remake law, questions about interests are momentarily set aside. The 'stabilisation' of new definitions, of newly coined 'facts', to use Bruno Latour's terminology, is, however, always to the advantage of someone, or some group.[6] Thus, having described a phenomenon of reification in all but name, that is to say, 'the mental conversion of an abstract concept', the image, 'into a thing'[7] or object-in-law, the second, more speculative part considers whether reification in a specifically Marxist sense, as an ideological phenomenon, can be said to have occurred when, in the early eighteenth century, under threat of repeal, the Paris Booksellers articulated anew the basis of their exclusive privileges by substituting arguments about

6   Bruno Latour, *Science in Action: How to Follow Scientists and Engineers through Society* (Cambridge, MA: Harvard University Press, 1987), esp. pp. 208-9.
7   OED, *ad. voc.* 'reification'.

natural right for their former recognition of royal prerogative. The case was advanced in a memorandum addressed in 1725 by Louis d'Héricourt, the Booksellers' lawyer, to Fleuriau d'Armenonville, the Keeper of the Seals and the authority with ultimate responsibility for the regime of temporary monopolies called privilege that preceded modern copyright.[8] It caused such offence that the syndics of the Corporation in whose name it was written were publicly rebuked and its printer forced to flee.[9] The visual, it will be suggested, contributed significantly to the memorandum's offensiveness by a vivid figurative language, informed by the theory and the practice of imitation, as much as by John Locke's labour theory of property, and by a *trompe l'œil* naturalisation of property relations that in the interest of profit all but erased the constitutive power of the king.

* * * * *

By coincidence, the beginning of Louis XV's reign saw the first formulation of a *Code de la librairie* (1723), published in 1744 as a pocket-book compendium of the laws and rights of the Paris Corporation of booksellers, publishers and printers, including the *privilèges en librairie* or copy-privilege,[10] and the publication of Michel Félibien's *Histoire de la ville de Paris* (1725), one of a clutch of illustrated folio publications on the physical and social geography of the capital to appear in the first decades of the eighteenth century. It is a coincidence exploited here as happy because it serves usefully as a reminder that privilege, or the pre-modern manifestation of copyright, was a local and a bourgeois property regime.[11] A further, historically more legitimate connection between the two lies in

8   Louis d'Héricourt, 'Mémoire en forme de requête à M. le Garde des Sceaux rédigé par M. Louis D'Héricourt, avocat au Parlement', in *La Propriété littéraire au XVIIIe siècle. Receuil de pièces et de documents*, ed. by E. Laboulaye and G. Guiffrey (Paris: Hachette, 1859), pp. 21-40 (p. 22). Also available at 'Louis d'Héricourt's memorandum (1725-1726)', *Primary Sources*.
9   See Raymond Birn, 'The Profit of Ideas. *Privilèges en librairie* in Eighteenth-century France', *Eighteenth-Century Studies*, 4 (1971), 131-68.
10   See Giles Barber, 'French Royal Decrees Concerning the Book Trade, 1700-1789', *Australian Journal of French Studies*, 3 (1966), 312-30 (p. 314).
11   Pre-modern privilege varied in scope: the *privilège local* limited protection to within one specified city; by contrast the *privilège général* offered protection from piracy throughout the kingdom. International copyright agreements were not brokered until the nineteenth century. It was 'bourgeois' in as much as in practice it protected the commercial interests of publishers. See David T. Pottinger, *The French Book Trade in the Ancien Régime 1500-1791* (Cambridge, MA: Harvard University Press, 1958), pp. 210-23.

Fig. 1. Pierre Vallet after François Quesnel, Map of Paris, engraving, 1609
(Bibliothèque nationale de France, Paris).

the pages of the third volume of Félibien's *Histoire*, among the 'pièces justificatives', or historical proofs, where an abbreviated transcription is given of one of the earliest so-called *privilèges* in images, the 1608 copy-privilege for François Quesnel's *Map of Paris* (1609; figure 1),[12] granted

12 Michel Félibien, *Histoire de la ville de Paris*, expanded and edited by Guy-Alexis Lobineau, 5 vols (Paris: G. Desprez, 1725), 5 (*Extraits des régistres du Parlement*), p. 46: 'La ville de Paris gravée. Du XIV Avril [1608] Veues par la cour les letters paten[t]es du roy données à Paris le 4 janvier 1608, par lequel led. Seigneur permet à Fran-çois Quesnel maistre peintre à Paris, & après luy à sa femme & enfans & heritiers, de pouvoir librement tailler ou faire tailler soit en bois ou en cuivre, estamper en papier ou en quelque sorte que bon luy semblera, la ville de Paris, selon qu'il la deja faicte, & la vendre & debiter ou faire vendre et debiter, par tout le royaume, pays, terres & seigneuries de l'obeissance dud. Seigneur durant le temps & espace de dix ans continuels, à compter du jour de la premiere impression. Autres lettres en forme de relief de surannation du 8. du present mois, c. LA DICTE COUR a ordonné & ordonne que lesd. Lettres seront enrégistrés às registres d'icelle, ouy le procureur general du roy, pour y jouir par l'impetant de l'effect & contenu en icelles'.

by the Chancellerie[13] almost exactly a century after those first secured in texts.[14]

Up until the early seventeenth century, printed images, which had mostly taken the form of illustrations, such as the pull-out map in Jacques Signot's *La totale et vraye description des Gaules es Ytalies* (1515), and were for the most part published by booksellers, had found a measure of legal sanctuary in the shelter of privileges in books.[15] It was only with the changing political and economic climate of the turn of the century – with the accession of Henri IV, the end of the Wars of Religion, the rapid development of trade and industry in the ensuing peace, of the last of which the 're-invention' of *intaglio* technologies in France was a particular manifestation[16] – that printmaking expanded sufficiently to constitute a trade in its own right, and that single, sheet prints began to make an appearance, prints requiring their own means of protection from piracy. Quesnel's map was a highly ambitious print of this kind, conceived on the scale of a mural, engraved on twelve separate copper plates, the impression of which, when joined together created an image measuring some five square feet.[17] Though the hagiographic register of the map is undeniable, Henri IV, whose monuments and urban projects the map celebrates, was not, in fact, its sponsor. According to the copy-privilege, the author, Quesnel, appears

13   Archives nationals, X1A/8646 f. 201 quoted in extract in Hillary Ballon, *The Paris of Henry IV. Architecture and Urbanism* (Cambridge, MA: MIT Press, 1991), p. 346, n. 53.

14   See 'Eloy d'Amerval's Privilege (1507)', *Primary Sources*. On the early history of copyrights in France, see: Elizabeth Armstrong, *Before Copyright. The French Book-privilege System 1498-1526* (Cambridge: Cambridge University Press, 1990); and Cynthia Brown, *Poets, Patrons and Printers. Crisis of Authority in Late Medieval France* (Ithaca and London: Cornell University Press, 1995).

15   The book's full title is as follows, *La totale et vraye description de tõ les passaiges, lieux, destroictz: par lesquelz ou passer ētrer des Gaulles es Ytalies*. Pierre Gringore's *privilège* of 1516 made specific mention of the special effort of having illustrations made for his work *Les fantaisies de mère sotte*, 'pour la decoration dudit livre conformes aux matieres contenues en iceluy'. See Armstrong, p. 80.

16   See Marianne Grivel, 'Les graveurs en France au XVIe siècle', in *La Gravure française à la Renaissance à la Bibliothèque nationale de France* (Paris: Bibliothèque nationale de France, 1994-5), pp. 33-57.

17   The one surviving copy of the map is in the *Département des cartes et plans* at the Bibliothèque nationale de France (hereafter BnF). On the map, see Ballon, pp. 233-7; Jean Boutier, Jean-Yves Sarracin and Marianne Sibille, *Les plans de Paris des origins (1493) à la fin du XVIIIe siècle* (Paris: Bibliothèque nationale de France, 2002), pp. 16-17, 115-7 (no. 41); *Paris à vol d'oiseau*, ed. by Michel Le Moël (Paris: Archives Nationales, 1995). On the monumental wall map as a genre see Christian Jacob, *L'empire des cartes: Approches théoriques de la cartographie à travers l'histoire* (Paris: Albin Michel, 1992), pp. 54-6.

to have undertaken the project as a speculation and expected to find in the *privilège* a measure of security for the considerable investment of time, effort and capital he had made in the venture.

In comparison to the copy-privilege of 1507 (the first of its kind in France) for Eloy d'Amerval's *Diablerie*, described only *briefly* in the letters patent licensing the monopoly as a 'beau livre'[18] containing pleasant and profitable things on the life-style of each estate, Quesnel's copy-privilege waxed *expansively*. Following the king's salutation to his privy councillors in whose office privilege was granted and an introduction to the licensee, François Quesnel (1543-1616), no cartographer but a 'master painter in Paris [...] who has devoted himself to painting from his earliest youth as much on account of the excellence of that art which belongs to the liberal sciences as for it having been cherished by those Kings our predecessors and by us', the letters patent go on to note the nature of the original, a representation on a flat surface, 'en platte painture', of 'our good town and city of Paris' which the artist had:

> [P]ortrayed (*faire veoir*) completely differently (*tout autrement*) and with more gracefulness and truth than we have seen (*veue*) before, especially at this time when under the happy success of our reign, she has in a sense been all newly rebuilt and transformed into one of the most superb cities that one has ever seen to which task (*labeur*) the said Quesnel has brought time (*continuation*) and effort (*industrie*) such that there is not a single place in the said City which is not depicted with all its measurements and geometrical dimensions [...][19]

To all this, the letters add by recording the author's supplementary labour of having his painted depiction reproduced 'in woodcut or on copper'.

Rather than attend to 'originality' ('tout autrement') and 'labour' ('labeur', 'continuation', 'industrie'), twin values that the copy-privilege, and in its wake, modern scholarship, deem especially determining in the history of emergent copyright, I want rather to bring into focus the less immediately striking quality of sight, the play of the verbs *voir* and *faire voir* and the related scattering of possessives that subtend the claim to copy-privilege. Carol Rose has discussed the importance of vision in arguments over 'real' property claims at some length.[20] She notes the habitual, almost

---

18   'D'Amerval's privilege (1507)', *Primary Sources.*
19   Ballon, p. 346, n. 53.
20   Carol Rose, *Property and Persuasion. Essays on the History, Theory and Rhetoric of Ownership* (Oxford: Westview Press, 1994), pp. 267-304.

obsessive, recourse to objects of perception in referring to property, notwithstanding the fact that property is actually a relation between people and not one between persons and things.[21] Although it will not do to overstate the pre-modern case, since compelling arguments existed for resisting the encroachment of visual representation as proof of identity in property questions,[22] maps did, nevertheless, become a common sight in French law courts from the fifteenth century; they provided, as François de Dainville convincingly shows, an increasingly favoured source of evidence in legal cases concerned with landed property for which being able *to see* the disputed object was acknowledged as facilitating judicious rulings on matters of boundaries and rights.[23] It is, as Rose explains, precisely because the relation between litigants – in the present case, between the 'author' of the map, Quesnel, and those nameless 'others' who may wish to avail themselves of his property by means of unauthorised copies – is difficult 'to envision', that representation is called to the rescue, so to speak, to substitute things, maps, for the rights in question.[24]

In the text of Quesnel's *privilège* sight actually serves many purposes and has multiple meanings: it is the site of representation (the view of Paris), the means by which it is rendered by use of geometry and perspective, the public of spectators for whom the map is intended and the visible mark of the painter's honour and investment to be defended. But its primary

---

21   See also: Jack Goody, *Death, Property and Ancestors* (London: Tavistock Publications, 1962), pp. 284-7; Maurice Bloch, 'Property and the End of Affinity', in *Marxist Analyses and Social Anthropology*, ed. by Maurice Bloch (London: Malaby Press, 1975), pp. 203-28 (pp. 203-5); Alan Carter, *The Philosophical Foundations of Property Rights* (New York: Harvester, Wheatsheaf, 1989), esp. pp. 126-42.

22   See two important articles by Alain Pottage, 'The Measure of the Land', *The Modern Law Review*, 57 (1994), 361-84, and 'The Originality of Registration', *Oxford Journal of Legal Studies*, 15 (1995) 371-401, in which the legal trade-offs between resources of local memory and abstract professional cartography in English land law are discussed. My thanks to Lionel Bently for bringing these to my attention, too late I fear fully to have taken considered account of the range of different articulations of the relationship between property and topography in the complex history of conveyancing outline there.

23   I am grateful to Denis Ribouillou for the reference to François de Dainville, 'Les cartes et contestations au XVe siècle', *Imago Mundi*, 24 (1970), 99-121. See also Rose Mitchell, 'Maps in Sixteenth-Century English Law Courts', *Imago Mundi*, 58 (2006), 212-8. For a discussion of the different types of drawing and the particular moment at which each might be introduced to the judicial process in the not unrelated sphere of building regulations, see Robert Carvais, 'Servir la justice, l'art et la technique: le rôle des plans, dessins et croquis devant la Chambre royale des bâtiments', *Sociétés et représentations*, 18 (2004), 75-96.

24   Rose, pp. 275-8.

importance in making vivid and tangible the parameters or scope of the copy-privilege is undeniable. Moreover, the type of vision is specified; the map is realistic, a 'true' likeness, so much so indeed that what is described in the text of the copy-privilege is not so much the map, as the object of its mapping: Paris.[25] The instability of the text, the tendency of description to slip back and forth between 'graceful' sign and 'superb' referent, 'truth-ful' image and 'newly rebuilt' object, in short between the map and Paris, results in an involuntary exchange of attributes such that Henri's capital over which he exercises a possessive dominion ('*notre* bonne ville et citté') seems to lend property to the author of its representation, at the same time that conversely, the uniquely creative act of the map-maker folds back into the collective achievement of the reign's urbanisation projects, attributing them to the single shaping hand of the king. So to note the encomiastic register of the text is to recognise the part played by politics in the projec-tion of the legal idea of intellectual property as a thing justified by service.

Carol Rose speculates that the nature and terms of the property relation in any given society may in some instances be informed by the physical geography of the world out there, public and private access to particular parts of which it serves to regulate. She has in mind the 'forceful and impe-rious' landscapes of Hawaii and Chicago;[26] we would be thinking here about the equally powerful and imposing forms of the newly Bourbon capital. Eleven bridges, four squares, nineteen gates, twelve fauxbourgs and over one thousand streets are listed by Henri Sauval in evidence of the unprecedented scale of the 'new Rome' to rise-up by the mid century, a scale more powerfully registered, it seems, by the quantity of private property than by the beauty of the public monuments: from the top of the tour Saint Jacques in the immediate neighbourhood of the Grand Châtelet, the capital's principle criminal and civil court, sight was stunned by the monotony of 'this appalling (*épouvantable*) mass of six, seven and eight storey houses, one pressed up against the next, which multiply this great city as many times'.[27]

---

25   On the trope of true likeness in early modern city maps, see Lucia Nuti, 'The Perspective Plan in the Sixteenth Century: The Invention of a Representational Lan-guage', *Art Bulletin*, 76 (1994), 105-28 (pp. 107-9).

26   Rose, pp. 267-9.

27   See Henri Sauval, *Histoire et recherches des antiquités de la ville de Paris*, 3 vols, ed. by Anthony Blunt (Paris, 1724; Farnborough, Hants: Gregg International Publishers, 1969), 1, pp. 26-7. Though not published until the eighteenth century, Sauval's text was largely complete by 1654 when he successfully applied for a copy-privilege.

The bourgeois definition of property, which misidentifies it with such things, and which misconceives it as an exclusively private relation, became common usage, according to Crawford Brough Macpherson, towards the end of the seventeenth century in the vanguard of developing capitalist market economies.[28] Before then, property was understood as a legal title, generally in land, but also in offices, skills and duties; titles often both limited and shared.[29] Did maps play a part in shifting the paradigm towards the modern meaning succinctly encapsulated in 1680 by the dictionary writer, Pierre Richelet, as 'the right that belongs privately and absolutely to a person to some thing [...]'?[30] Alain Pottage's answer with respect to England is equivocal:[31] negative in the case of the large landed estates of the gentry where the ideology of contract as a relation between parties prevailed, the narratives of ownership remaining 'introspective' (his word), a matter of local memory, orally transmitted and verbally recorded, but affirmative in the case of types of land tenure which can, without much fear of contradiction, be termed bourgeois: small holdings and urban property. While the reasons for the rural first are largely pragmatic - the modest extent of surveys and the small number of disputes over boundaries to which resultant maps might potentially give rise are not ruled out on grounds of cost – the explanation for the urban second touches on issues of perception and conceptualisation. Both the greater regularity and the greater permanence of the built environment apparently flattered the association of property and topography and encouraged the substitution of visual for oral narrations of title. Moreover, urban development projects, such as the prominently marked Place royale and Place dauphine on Quesnel's map, inevitably disrupted local memory of property patterns and that loss of place made

28   See *Property. Mainstream and Critical Positions*, ed. by C.B. Macpherson (Oxford: Blackwell, 1978), pp. 1-13. Specifically in relation to France, see Thomas E. Kaiser, 'Property, Sovereignty, the Declaration of the Rights of Man and the Tradition of French Jurisprudence', in *The French Idea of Freedom and the Declaration of the Rights of 1789*, ed. by Dale Van Klee (Stanford: Stanford University Press, 1994), pp. 300-39 (pp. 301-9).

29   On property in offices see, among others: David Parker, 'Sovereignty, Absolutism and the Function of the Law in Seventeenth-Century France', *Past and Present*, 122 (1989), 36-74 (pp. 50-4); David Parker, 'Absolutism, Feudalism and Property Rights in the France of Louis XIV', *Past and Present*, 179 (2003), 60-96; on property in skills, see John Rule, 'The Property of Skill in the Period of Manufacture', in *The Historical Meanings of Work*, ed. by Patrick Joyce (Cambridge: Cambridge University Press, 1987), pp. 99-118.

30   Pierre Richelet, *Dictionnaire françois* (Geneva: J.-H Widerhold, 1680) *ad. voc.* 'propriété'.

31   Pottage, 'The Measure of the Land', esp. pp. 370-4.

recourse to the 'distanced' perspective of plans and maps predictable, if not necessarily inevitable.

Whereas the historian of law, Pottage, acknowledges the map and the view as having the potential to substitute a 'lordship of the eye' for a contractual narrative of property, a potential, he is keen to argue, long resisted, the art historian, Svetlana Alpers, denies categorically that the mapping mode, a mode which she identifies specifically with a prioritisation of surface and a corresponding concern with spatial extension at the expense of volumetric solidity, is inherently or necessarily bound to a discourse of ownership.[32] The map and the view, or 'prospect', she notes were commonplace pictorial genres in both seventeenth century Holland and seventeenth century England, though land tenure in England was feudal and in Holland not.[33] But, according to the seventeenth century etcher and mathematician, Sébastien Le Clerc, geometry, the art which is the common foundation of surveying, cartography and topography, was to be found in ancient Egypt where the particular physiology of the land forced Egyptians to invent it:

> [T]o rectify the disorder which was commonly inflicted on their landed property by the flooding of the river Nile which swept away the boundaries and erased the limits of their inheritances; thus, this science which then consisted only in surveying for the purpose of making restitution to each person to which it belonged was called the measure of the land, or Geometry.[34]

Property was, by this myth, the very condition of cartography. Thus if, we now concede, that what maps present is not, strictly speaking, 'land possessed' but 'land known in certain respects', that knowing was clearly regarded by Le Clerc and others as a kind of possessing and those 'respects' are precisely facts concerning the *physical* properties of the depicted things and places, things and places, that is, reduced by measurement to material value.[35] It is hard to avoid thinking, therefore, that at least for the generations led by John Locke to conceive of knowledge as formed by that which the senses let into the mind to be stored and accumulated like so many

---

32   Svetlana Alpers, *The Art of Describing. Dutch Art in the Seventeenth Century* (London: John Murray, 1983), pp. 119-68.

33   Ibid., pp. 148-9.

34   Sébastien Le Clerc, *Pratique de la géométrie sur le papier et le terrain* (Paris: T. Jolly, 1682), p. 2.

35   On sixteenth-century conceptions of the city in which its physical and the socio-political identities were still wholly confused, see Robert Descimon, 'Paris on the eve of Saint Bartholomew: Taxation, Privilege and Social Geography', in *Cities and Social Change in Early Modern France*, ed. by Philip Benedict (London and New York: Unwin Hyman, 1989), pp. 69-104.

'pictures' in a 'closet', for whom, that is, the mind was a place more or less stocked with objects of knowledge, maps would have been read not only as disclosing the origins of a property regime but, additionally, as affording possession in precisely that way.[36]

Quesnel's *Paris* is something of a hybrid; it amalgamates the map and the perspective picture in what is called a bird's eye view by force of the more-or-less successfully coordinated skills of painter and surveyor. On closer inspection the product is selectively treated, some parts springing up from the ground, others flatly delineated upon it. It is the latter parts, the schematically and monotonously rendered weave of the parcel-ised urban tissue composed of a mass of obliquely drawn dwellings stretching to the city walls and the patchwork of sub-urban fields and pasture that unfolds beyond, that particularly seem to distinguish Quesnel's map. The lack of discrimination and particularity of that net of shallow lines when describing fields, gardens, squares, houses, palaces and monuments invites comparison with the linear matrix that, by the early seventeenth century, was nearing perfection as 'an instrument of average purpose' in the field of reproductive print-making; its aim: to capture and render commensurate the gamut of pictorial traces from sketch to finished work and thereby turn them into commodities.[37] Likewise, the map, notwithstanding the fact that the scale is idiosyncratic, measured by the *pas de l'auteur*, the eye of the author, objectifies and abstracts the substance of the territory of Lutèce by means of a parallel process of generic hatchings and helps, seemingly, to instantiate the new property regime by making things not only visually and conceptually graspable, but also seemingly continuous and relational, that is freely and infinitely exchangeable.

Such is not to deny perspective's other role in drawing near the viewer the monuments of Henri's building campaigns – the completion of the Louvre, the spanning of the Pont Neuf across the Seine at the tip of the île de la Cité and the opening out of the place Dauphine behind, eventually to provide a frame for a royal equestrian monument on the bridge[38] – monuments that by such detailed plasticity dominate the scene, it is rather to note the presence in the map of two incompatible visions of the city: the

---

36   See *An Essay Concerning Human Understanding* (1690), ed. by Roger Woolhouse (London: Penguin, 1997), Book II, and for the analogy of the mind to a space for taking possession and storage, see esp. pp. 123, 158.
37   See William M. Ivins, *Prints and Visual Communications* (London: Routledge & Kegan Paul, 1953), pp. 71-92.
38   On Henri IV's urban projects see Ballon, chapters 1-4.

one symbolic and political, the other geographic and economic. Moreover, in the case of certain formal features, the symbolic seems to admit the possibility of transformation into the economic. Hillary Ballon has noted that the map's celebration of Henrician urban progress is articulated in the context of a visibly bounded city at a time when the capital had not only exceeded its ancient medieval ramparts but when these had become a political irrelevance, possibly even a barrier, to the Bourbon drive to unify and centralise the nation, exporting its defences to the borders of the kingdom.[39] Another way of 'reading' the map, however, is to note, not the actual walls but the bounded-ness, not defences as such, but definition. The clarity, order, fixity, solidity, seeming immutability, in short the crisp legibility that Quesnel brings via the sharpness of Pierre Vallet's burin to the depiction of Paris, are characteristics we have come to associate, on the one hand, with ideal form and, on the other, with bourgeois notions of property.

* * * * *

If built forms and their representation contributed to new ways of apprehending and valuing real estate, images may also have helped to establish the property-like status of so-called illusory estates: on the one hand, by force of rhetorical vividness, or what Quintilian calls *enargeia*[40] and, on the other, by deployment of visual marks – 'Avec Privilège du Roy', 'Cum Privilegio Regis', 'A.P.R.', 'C.P.R.' – around the boundaries of the works in question.

In contrast to book privileges, secured by reference to simple, identifying titles, print privileges often have recourse to description, both to designate a work's subject matter and, occasionally as in this instance, to play up the work's importance.[41] Thus, Quesnel's map is not only entitled a view of Paris for the sake of legal recognition, it is also qualified a marvel, a representation of the capital reformed and raised to the rank of 'the most excellent cities ever seen'.[42] The Quesnel copy-privilege is probably something of

---

39   Ibid., p. 233. Jacques Gomboust, in the address 'Aux lecteurs' of his 1652 map of the capital denounced earlier 'faux plans'and 'mauvaises représentations' in which 'L'enceinte des Murailles [est] toute corrompue. Les Courtines, flans et bastions, faux dans leurs angles et longueurs. Il y en a même d'autres imaginaires qui ne furent jamais que dans leurs Idées.'
40   Quintilian, *The Orator's Education, Books 6-8*, ed. and trans. by Donald A. Russell (Cambridge, MA: Harvard University Press, 2001), pp. 375-81.
41   On titles, see Gérard Genette, *Paratexts. Thresholds of Interpretation*, trans. by Jane E. Lewin (Cambridge: Cambridge University Press, 1997), pp. 55-103.
42   See Ballon, p. 346, n. 53.

an exception, but the fact that prints often lacked formal titles necessitated recourse to description, or to a mode of discourse that rhetoricians qualified as hypotiposis, a particularly persuasive and arresting form of discourse that conjures things as if before the reader's eyes.[43] Half a century later, Pierre Mariette obtained a copy-privilege for the *Triumphant Entry of their Majesties Louis XIV and Maria Theresa of Austria [...] into Paris* (1660), a collection commemorating the ultimate royal urban ritual in texts and images of 'all the things that were seen and occurred during our entry with the queen' into Paris, including, 'all the triumphal arches, the portals and other ornaments, the harangues addressed to us, the procession and generally all that concerned the entry'.[44] Over a century later, Pierre Jacob Gueroult du Pas was awarded a copy-privilege for 'diverse landscapes, views of the Royal Houses, and the most beautiful places in Paris and its environs',[45] Gilles Demortans for a 'Considerable Collection of views of the most beautiful spots in the Royal Houses and Gardens, mainly the fountains and great water displays at the château de Versailles',[46] and the royal engineer Roussel for a 'map of Paris, its fauxbourgs and environs with all the detail of villages, châteaux, highways, roads and others, mountains, woods, vineyards, lands, [and] meadows [...]'.[47] At a time when the arts were generally understood as arts of imitation the effect of such description, of its lists stuffed with things and of the superlative qualities of their appearance to which attention is drawn by the adjective 'beautiful', was surely experienced in its full rhetorical power. That is to acknowledge that description interrupts the flow in the letters patent by which copy-privileges were formally granted of what, by the seventeenth century, was already a highly conventionalised legal discourse in four acts (salutation, supplication, authorisation, prohibition); it punctures it with a poetic 'picture' and thereby makes tangible the resource over which

---

43   See César Chesneau, sieur Dumarsais, *Des tropes ou des différents sens* (1731; repr. Paris: Flammarion, 1988), pp. 133-4. See also, specifically in relation to law, Peter Goodrich, *Reading the Law: A Critical Introduction to Legal Methods and Techniques* (Oxford: Basil Blackwell, 1986), p.198.
44   Archives Nationales, X1A, 8662, f.12 (31/viii/1660). See George Duplessis, 'Privilège des gravures de l'Entrée du roi en 1660 accordé à Pierre Mariette', *Nouvelles archives de l'art français* (1872), 257-60.
45   BnF Ms f.f. Anisson Duperon 21949 (22/x/1708).
46   BnF Ms f.f. Anisson Duperon 21950 (30/i/1716). See also Maxime Préaud, Pierre Casselle, Marianne Grivel and Corinne Le Bitouzé, *Dictionnaire des éditeurs d'estampes à Paris sous l'ancien régime* (Paris: Promodis/Cercle de la librairie, 1987), *ad. voc.* 'Demortant'.
47   BnF Ms f.f. Anisson Duperon 21955 (18/i/1731). See also Boutier *et al*, pp. 242-5 (no. 206).

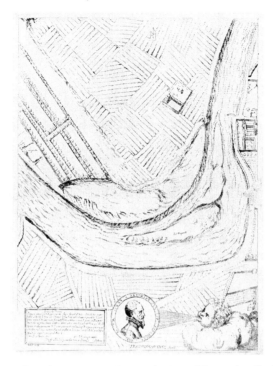

Fig. 2. Pierre Vallet after François Quesnel, Map of Paris, detail of the 'Extrait de Privilege', 1609 (Bibliothèque nationale de France, Paris).

monopoly was sought, assimilating the privilege to the thing, or rather the illusion of the thing, so that it begins to appear as an object framed by the law.

The case when looking at the location and function performed by the inscription of the privilege on the image seems, at first glance, almost exactly the reverse. Inscribed by law at either the beginning or the end of a book,[48] in the liminal space between the text and *hors-texte*, the voluntary mark of privilege in the composition or lay-out of printed images appears to belong unequivocally to the frame, that is, to the *hors-d'œuvre*.[49] In Quesnel's *Paris* it occupies, along with a profile portrait of the author and the printmaker's monogram (figure 2), the right-hand end of the lower rail, the bottom of the page, so to speak, where in a book we would conventionally expect to find it with other 'perigraphic' information, notably the name and address of the

48   Saugrain, p. 375. See also, Martin-Dominique Fertel, *La science pratique de l'imprimerie* (Saint Omer: M.D. Fertel, 1723), p. 119.

49   The reference here is, of course, to Jacques Derrida's theory of the parergon, based on a reading of Emmanuel Kant's *Critique of Judgement*. See Jacques Derrida, *The Truth in Painting*, trans. by Geoff Bennington and Ian Mcleod (Chicago and London: University of Chicago Press, 1987) pp. 15-147.

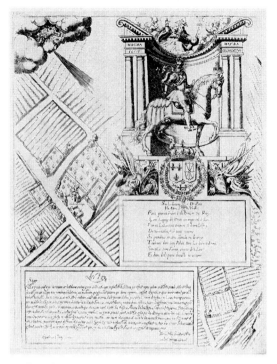

Fig. 3. Pierre Vallet after François Quesnel, Map of Paris, detail of Henri IV,
1609 (Bibliothèque nationale de France, Paris).

publisher.[50] Were it true that the inscription of privilege falls so absolutely
outside the image, that it is both formally and discursively utterly detached
from that which it serves to protect, it would seem ironically to lack force of
visual persuasion precisely there where its existence is most publicly seen.
In fact, the contours of the engraved lettering, the form of the text box and
the shape and content of word and image collectively invite relations with
the other inscriptions and decorations of the map: a liaison is yoked diago-
nally by the flow of the Seine between the portraits of the king (figure 3)
and his author-subject, a triangle of identities is caught in the circles of the
laurel wreathed coats of arms (royal and municipal) and the portrait medallion, finally, and more allusively, a connection is there to be made between
the spirit of the Law above, and her tablets of sacred text (figure 4), and the
fulfilment below of her practical reason in the extract of the privilege.[51] This

50   The term is Antoine Compagnon's from *La seconde main* (Paris: Éditions du
seuil, 1979), pp. 328-9. Significantly Compagon compares the relation of the perigraphic elements to the text proper in a book to the relation of the city walls to the
city.
51   The text box reads as follows: 'Extrait de Privilege./ Par grace et privilege du

Fig. 4. Pierre Vallet after François Quesnel, Map of Paris, detail of Faith and Law, 1609 (Bibliothèque nationale de France, Paris).

pattern of significations suggests that the copy-privilege was designed to be read, and read, moreover, as a 'discours d'escort', analogously that is, to the other 'peritextual' elements:[52] the eulogy, the royal dedication, the ode to Faith and Law and the brief 'History of the Antiquity of Paris'. Recently, Nicolas Schapira and Claire Lévy-Lelouch have explored in two remarkable essays the competitive play of voices, identities and interests articulated

Roy il est permis a François Quesnel, m. Paintre a Paris desposer en vente/ la carte de la ville de Paris, citte, universite, et fauxbourgs quil a dessigner pourtraicte et faict/ graver en planches de cuivre et sont faictes deffences a toutes personnes de graver ou faire graver/ tant en cuivre qu'en bois stampes vendre ny debiter auttre carte de la ville de Paris que celle dud/ Quesnel et ce jusques au Tems de Dix ans sur peine de confiscation de ce qui deshonnera aud/ et de cinq cens escuz damande voulons en oultre qua lextrait dudict privilege on/ adiouste scy comme a son origi-nal donne a/ Paris le 4 janvier 1608/ Par le Roy en son conseil/ Veriffié et Interiné par arrest de la cour de Parlemt'. Beneath the medallion is inscribed: 'FRANCOIS QVESNEL Inventor'.

52   The terms are Genette's from *Paratextes*. Genette distinguishes between liminal devices and conventions that mediate the relationship between text and the reader and are located inside the book or 'peritexts' (titles, dedications, prefaces, epilogues etc) and those located outside the book or 'epitexts' (advertising, reviewing etc).

by the published form of the *privilège*, noting its prestige-value for king and author in the moment of publication construed as a ritual and recognised not merely as a commercial event.[53] Presently, the concern is rather with the manner in which that duet by sovereign and subject constitutes the work as an object-in-law, and does so visually, insisting baroquely that the en-framing text be seen.

I say 'baroquely' because it is one of the paradigmatic features of the baroque that the viewer is made highly conscious of the frame, either by its obtrusive signifying or material presence, as here, or by the illusion of its erasure. In contrast, the classical frame is both unambiguously present and discrete. Jean-Claude Lebensztejn compares it to a scaffold: 'once it has helped to build the depicted space', by locating, arresting and focusing the view, 'it should', he notes, 'disappear as much as possible, so that the depicted space appears naturally self contained'.[54] Early eighteenth century views are classical in precisely this sense. In the 1720s the topographical draftsman Jacques Rigaud produced sets of printed prospects of the royal palaces, newly awakened to the rustle of courtly rural life after Philippe d'Orléans' urban Regency, for which he purchased a copy-privilege in June 1728.[55] Etched by the author after pen, ink and wash drawings,[56] the views (figure 5) are contained by a single encompassing line; the information concerning copy-privilege consigned to a separate zone, outside the space of representation. The deployment of the inscriptions within that independent under-region in a sentence like structure – 'Dessiné & Gravé par J. Rigaud',[57] on the left, followed by 'Avec Privilège du Roy'[58] on the right – effects a conjunction between 'author' and *privilège*-holder, at the same time seemingly qualifying as merely adjunctive, the relation between

53   Nicolas Schapira, 'Quand le privilège de librairie publie l'auteur', and Claire Lévy-Lelouch, 'Quand le privilège de librairie publie le roi', both in *De la publication. Entre renaissance et lumières*, ed. by Christian Jouhaud and Alain Viala (Paris: Fayard, 2002), respectively pp. 121-37, and pp. 139-59.

54   Jean-Claude Lebensztejn, 'Framing Classical Space', *Art Journal*, 47 (1988), 37-41 (p. 38). See also Meyer Schapiro, 'On Some Problems in the Semiotics of Visual Art: Field and Vehicle in Image-Signs', *Simiolus* (1972-3), pp. 11, 15.

55   BnF Ms f.f. Anisson Duperon, 21954 (30/vi/1728).

56   See, most recently on the drawings, *Jacques Rigaud, Dessinateur de Versailles*, Galerie Coatalem, rue St Honoré, Paris (14/ii-15/iii/2008), and also Charles Ginoux, *Jacques Rigaud, dessinateur et graveur marseillais* (Paris: E. Plon, Nourrit et Cie, 1898) who publishes a notarial contract (pp. 13-4) by which Rigaud is acknowledged as having advanced a loan of 16,000 *livres* at 5% in 1753, the year before his death, a considerable sum of money.

57   'Drawn & Engraved by J. Rigaud'.

58   'With the King's Privilege'.

Fig. 5. Jacques Rigaud, View of the Chapel of the Château of Versailles, etching, 1728 (British Museum, London).

Fig. 6. De Rochefort after Jean-Bernard Toro, *Nouveau Livre de Vases*, title-page, etching, 1716 (British Museum, London).

privilege and the object of its concern. Only in instances such as the prov-
ençal wood carver, Jean-Bernard Toro's designs for vases (figure 6), for
which the Paris architect Le Pas Dubuisson obtained a copy-privilege in
July 1716, instances where the formal mark of the frame is absent, does the
privilege explicitly assume a constitutive role.[59] The vases (figure 7), unlike
the views, are not autonomous or fully resolved inventions, but ideas,
improvisations, variations on a theme whose potential for re-use hangs
suspended on the page. The inscription of the copy-privilege, abbreviated
to the acronym CPR, detaches itself from the proper names on the plates to
attach itself instead to the underside of the vases, to the nominal line upon
which they stand, pressing up to the designs and marking each individually as private property.

Privilege, we can say, worked as a frame in conjunction with or in the
absence of an actual frame to demarcate and give notice of private property. Moreover, on occasion it also functioned more overtly as a strategy
of appropriation. In October 1712 and January 1713, the Italian *marchand
joaillier* Jacques-Philippe Fagniani, requested a copy-privilege, or rather the
extension of one in order to re-issue the 'œuvres' of Jacques Callot, Stefano
della Bella and Israël Silvestre whose plates he had acquired from Nicolas
Petit de Lagny, the son-in-law of the original publisher to whom they had
passed by inheritance along with the copy-privileges.[60] Copy-privileges, as
privilèges were granted for a fixed term: ten years in the case of Quesnel's
map, twelve years in the case of Rigaud's views and fifteen years in the case
of Toro's vases. Extension of privileges became common but contentious
practice during the course of the seventeenth century and were awarded
and justified on the grounds of an addition, a supplementation of the original by one fourth.[61] In the case of books this was managed by an amplifica-
tion of the length of the text, by an extension in time; Fagniani, likewise,
mounted his case for prolongation, in part, by reference to the assiduity
with which he had tracked down obscure and lost plates by his triumvirate
of artists and thereby extended their complete works.[62]

But images, unlike *œuvres*, or texts, have not the same capacity for augmentation: it is not possible to add figures, develop a landscape, multiply
still-life objects in the way you might add a chapter, footnotes, appendices

---

59   BnF Ms f.f. Anisson Duperon, 21951 (14/vii/1716).
60   BnF Ms f.f. Anisson Duperon, 21950 (22/i/1713). See also Grivel, *Le commerce*, p. 10.
61   See Saugrain, p. 361.
62   Fagnani advertised the publication of the *Receuil* by subscription in the *Mercure de France* (March 1723), pp. 561-3.

Fig. 7. Cochin after Jean-Bernard Toro, Design for a Vase, etching, 1716
(British Museum, London).

Fig. 8 Jacques Callot and Nicolas Tardieu after Gilles-Marie Oppenord,
Misères et Malheurs de la Guerre, etching, 1633 and 1713 (Bibliothèque nationale de France, Paris).

or an index. Fagniani's unorthodox solution was to augment by way of the frame. The frontispiece, which carries in addition to the names of the authors, title, place of publication and notice of *privilège*, a dedication to Philippe, duc d'Orléans, who in 1712 was still toast of court and town for his military successes in Spain, is of original, but at this stage, un-attributed design. It introduces us to the *œuvre-objet* by way of an architectural meta-phor and renders functionally redundant the original frontispiece that fol-lows. The second (figure 8), now false title page is a collage and derivative of Callot's *Misères et Malheurs de la Guerre*. That is to say, it incorporated the original title page, complete with the inscription of the 1633 *privilège*, and extends about it a frame designed by Gilles-Marie Oppenord and etched by Nicolas Tardieu whose names appear at the foot of the plate, a frame which is both a pastiche in ornament of Callot's subject-matter (though its triumphalism is in manifest contradiction to the mood of the title) and a collage of details excerpted from his work, 'bon-mots', so to speak, pasted into cartouches borne aloft by caryatids to the left and right and flanked by *putti* and ordinance at the bottom.[63] Fagniani, in his petition for extension justified his case by reference neither to labour nor to investment, but to 'enrichment', 'a new lustre'; an increase, that is, in exchange value and in property and not, as was more usually and explicitly the case in literature, in either effort or cost.

Extension of the law of copyright by analogy to new cultural domains always involves change; a challenge or revision by medium of the principles of the legal right. Art was not the passive recipient of a regime fashioned elsewhere but, by virtue precisely of its anomaly to the textual norm, a participant in shaping both the understanding of what was at stake and the terms of the discourse. In the complex of meanings assigned to property by law, economy and political power, art gave priority to its 'modern' mean-ing as absolute, private property grasped visually in the signs of physi-cal things, not the social relations that constituted those things. Moreover, artistic discourse advanced a connection between the representation of property, of ownership, and ownership by acts of representation. Roger de Piles in *Cours de peinture par principes* (1708), the single most influential art-theoretical text of the turn of the century, wrote of landscape that the painter of it is master to dispose of all things at will; that in no other genre

---

63   Other frames were designed and etched by Sebastien Le Clerc. For a highly critical response to the aesthetic effect of the frames see Edme Gersaint, *Catalogue raisonné des divers curiosités du cabinet de feu M. Quentin de Lorangère* (Paris, 1744), pp. 125-7.

is his dominion, his creative proprietorship, more evident than in the case of the view.[64] In illustration of that claim we can note that the transcription of Quesnel's *privilège* in Félibien's *History of Paris* (1725) was framed by other documented instances of property relations: by letters patent for the construction of the pont des Marchands and a contract for the alienation of parts of the clôture du Temple on one side, and by letters patent activating the construction by private lease holders of properties on royal squares on the other.[65]

* * * * *

Having analysed in some detail how a depiction of property, a visual articulation of ownership, was converted mentally into a *res* or legally constituted thing the question remaining is as follows: was the desire to see property where it was not economically determined or economically determining? Putting the question differently, what were the circumstances that occasioned the materialisation of literary and artistic work as property and whose interests did it secure? To talk of 'reification' is, of course, to invite a particular kind of answer: to engage generally with the Marxist critique of capitalism and to reach specifically for economic causes and ideological consequences.

Described abstractly in *Capital* as a double process, a dialectical relation between social being and social consciousness, specifically, between objective social relations and the subjective misapprehension of them as obtaining between things, reification for Marx, and later for Lukács, is not however a universal human propensity; on the contrary both advance a fundamentally historical theory of reification.[66] It occurs, they maintain, with the transition to market capitalism. That is, it arises in economies in which the circulation of goods creates impersonal relations of price between things exchanged rather than social relations of value between

---

64   Roger de Piles, *Cours de peinture par principes* (Paris: Jacques Estienne, 1708), p. 99.
65   Félibien, pp. 44-5, 46.
66   The starting point for Karl Marx's theory of reification is the section 'The Fetishism of Commodities and the Secret Thereof', in *Capital. A Critique of Political Economy*, vol. 1, trans. by Ben Fowles (Harmonsworth: Penguin, 1976), pp. 163-77. For Georg Lukács, see his essay, 'Reification and the Consciousness of the Proletariat', in *History and Class Consciousness*, trans. by Rodney Livingstone (London: Merlin Press, 1971), pp. 83-222. By contrast, in sociology, reification is only a modality of consciousness and has no necessary objective conditions, is not, that is, tied to any specific mode of production. See, classically, Peter Berger and Thomas Luckmann, *The Social Constitution of Reality* (Harmonsworth: Penguin, 1971), pp. 106-9.

the exchanging parties.[67] Moreover, it holds the working-class temporarily in thrall, mystifying the social relations of their exploitation as natural and therefore inescapable. Reification is thus one of a cluster of overlapping concepts, including commodification, fetishism and alienation that in Marxism collectively account for the particular form that economic relations assume in capitalism and in which the illusion of reification is necessarily rooted. There is no reification in the Marxist sense without commodification. Indeed, according to Lukács, only when commodity exchange becomes the dominant rather than the occasional mode of transaction in society does reification in the strict sense occur. To illustrate the argument he traces the path followed by traditional handicrafts in the West towards machine industry via collectives and manufacture, noting the continuous trend towards rationalisation, de-personalisation, and isolation.[68] The mood of chilly, deluded and hopeless passivity that pervades Lukács' diagnostic representation of the working-class under capitalism, and for which he re-coined the meaning of the word 'contemplation', seems in conspicuous contradiction to the active, clamorous and relatively clear-sighted narration of the relationship between masters and journeymen in Paris print-shops in the 1730s proposed by the printer Nicolas Contat in his autobiographical *Anecdotes typogaphiques* (1762); memorably so in the episode of the 'Great Cat Massacre' in which a master printer's cats were duly massacred by his apprentices.[69] And yet, in the story, the workers' sado-comic conversion of the master's wife symbolically into a thing, a cat (a cat-machine for an era when animals had no souls), occurs precisely to avenge the bourgeois', that is the master's, materialisation of the familial relations obtaining in the ideal and traditional workshop between masters, apprentices and journeymen into the modern coercion of an anonymous labour-force by capital.

Michael Sonenscher has argued that the ritual slaughter of cats by alienated apprentices made famous by Robert Darnton is only properly understood in the context of the long term restructuring of the book trade from the

---

67   The obvious point of contrast here is the case of gifts. See Natalie Zemon Davis, *The Gift in Sixteenth-Century France* (Oxford: Oxford University Press, 2000).

68   Lukács, pp. 88-9.

69   Robert Darnton, *The Great Cat Massacre and Other Episodes in French Cultural History* (Hamonsworth: Penguin, 1985), pp. 79-104. See also Nicolas Contat, *Anecdotes typographiques où l'on voit la description des coutumes, mœurs et usages singuliers des compagnons imprimeurs*, ed. by Giles Barber (Oxford: Oxford Bibliographical Society, 1980).

mid-seventeenth century.[70] In the interests of more effective censorship and absolute political control Colbert had overseen the steady concentration of the book trade in favoured shops and the integration of the several practices of printing, publishing and retailing. To give precise numbers: of the 79 shops operating 217 presses in 1666 only 51 with 195 presses remained by 1701.[71] Meanwhile, the Booksellers' statutes, radically revised in 1686, had fixed the maximum number of print-shops at 36, an anticipated further reduction never met but to which the trade remained formally committed. The Crown was not the sole beneficiary of these reforms. On the contrary, pressure to tighten controls was exerted as much from within the trade as from outside; according to Sonenscher, larger and more integrated shops facilitated the detection and proscription of piracy, and the reduction in competition improved the chances that those remaining enterprises would better survive economic down-turns.[72]

In addition to these general structural changes, the book trade instigated modifications to working practices to which, in a series of disputes from the 1660s about the length of the working day, the certification of completed tasks and the employment of disenfranchised labour, apprentices and journeymen printers vocally objected as forms of 'servitude' incompatible with their status and civil rights.[73] Indeed, opposition in 1723 to the recruitment of *alloués* (literally hands for hire, *à louer*, and actually no more than hands, because skilled neither by journeyman-ship nor by apprenticeship) was articulated by indentured printers as an opposition to the reduction of the workforce to the condition of 'slaves', to the condition, that is, of things not persons.[74] In the course of the seventeenth century the Paris book trade was, on this evidence, brought by royal will and market principle to the edge of commodity production, from which edge workers like Contat looked on and anticipated the decomposition of their 'primitive' rights and customs, the reification of labour and the subjugation of consciousness it would ultimately entail.

At the time the journeymen were taking legal action against 'enslavement', the capital's master booksellers collectively mounted a theoretical

70 Michael Sonenscher, *Work and Wages. Natural Law, Politics and the Eighteenth-Century French Trades* (Cambridge: Cambridge University Press, 1989), pp. 10-22.

71 See Henri-Jean Martin, *Print, Power, and People in Seventeenth-Century France*, trans. by David Gerard (London: Scarecrow Press, 1993), p. 481, and for the context, pp. 468-80.

72 Sonenscher, p. 15.

73 Ibid., pp. 15-6.

74 BnF Ms f.f. Anisson Duperon, 22062, f. 175; Sonenscher, p. 16.

defence of the articles concerning copy-privilege in the new 1723 *Règlement du Conseil*, that is of their incorporeal assets accumulated via the system of privilege, assets that had given them unprecedented commercial advantage over booksellers in the provinces. In the brief to Fleuriau d'Armenonville, Keeper of the Seals, the lawyer, Louis d'Héricourt, for the first time in the history of French copyright law, argues by analogy that a work of literature is a property by virtue of the labour of its author. His is a story about the reification of authorial, not artisanal labour; moreover, it seemingly puts a weapon into, rather than chains upon, the hands of the 'workers' concerned. It is, you could say, a story about the determining power of reification, to follow the account of its determined condition.

Raymond Birn has noted Héricourt's debt to John Locke's theory of the origins of private property outlined in chapter 5 of the *Second Treatise of Government* (1689).[75] Héricourt, however, inflects that debt in subtle and significant ways. Defined in the opening statement of principles as a bond (*un lien*) that effects that state of sociation to which 'men' are destined by nature, labour is according to Héricourt not so much an action as a transaction and occurs therefore not so much in the artist's workshop or writer's *cabinet* as in the market-place.[76] The register and mood of the text is pragmatic and implicitly urban by comparison to the philosophical narrative that unfolds in Locke's pastorally construed, indeed Edenic, setting.[77] Consequently, though Héricourt's case notionally acknowledges a time before property, it proceeds as if it were always already there.

The text goes on to advance two propositions: the first (that the literary text belongs absolutely and therefore in perpetuity to the author) establishing a necessary foundation for the second (that that property is transferred intact with the sale of the manuscript). Significantly, it is actually the second and secondary proposition that is elaborated at length. To be sure, at first Héricourt observes 'simply' and 'naturally' that 'a manuscript [...] is in the person of the author a good that is so absolutely his that it is no more permitted to take

---

75   See John Locke, *Second Treatise of Government*, ed. by Crawford Brough Macpherson (Indianapolis: Hackett Publishing Company, 1980), pp. 18-30, esp. §27; Birn, p. 145. There were two editions of Daniel Mazel's translation of the *Second Treatise*, one publishes at Amsterdam in 1691, the other, pertinently, in 1724 at Geneva. On the reception of Locke's thought in France, see Ross Hutchison, 'Locke in France, 1688-1734', *Studies on Voltaire and the Eighteenth Century*, 290 (1991).

76   Héricourt, p. 22. The translations of this text are my own.

77   For a discussion of God's bounty and man's subsequent and divinely sanctioned lordship of the land in the form of private property, see Matthew H. Kramer, *John Locke and the Origins of Private Property. Philosophical Explorations of Individualism, Community and Equality* (Cambridge: Cambridge University Press, 1997) pp. 93-150.

it from him than his money, his things or even his land',[78] but money, things and land represent the three categories into which property is sub-divided – specie, movable property and immovable property – and as such assume an austerely abstract and categorical value in this part of the case. By contrast, when Héricourt turns in the second to talk about the circulation of texts and manuscripts the thing-ness of a literary text is conveyed by the enumeration of multiple and categorically redundant forms of property, for instance 'land' and 'houses' (both immovable), 'furniture and other things of whatever kind they may be' (movable property, all).[79] It is indeed, in the context of commerce – in the thick of exchange and in the sweat of the accumulation of stock – that signs of property multiply and become real. They are invoked, one could say with Roger de Piles and by analogy to illusion in painting, in the 'first lines' of the proposition, in its 'foreground', in order to draw d'Armenonville's eye. '[T]hey establish (*impriment*) the first appearance of truth and contribute significantly to the persuasiveness (*à faire jouer l'artifice*) of the work and anticipate the esteem that we should have for the whole'.[80] The materiality and sensuousness of the signs of property deployed in proposition two thus retrospectively lend a vivid persuasiveness to the metaphysical condition of property abstractly enumerated in proposition one, and by force of the law of which texts were to enter most profitably into exchange.

The framing, the adornment even, of the concept of the literary work by these figures of property in Héricourt's brief, results, it seems to me, in its fetishisation. What is more, variously categorised as manuscript, textual production and literary work, the repetitious naming of the legal textual object in proposition two further betrays that state of mysterious and fascinated enthrallment by which fetishism in its original anthropological context is known: the supra-valuation of 'other' material objects in black Africa as perceived by an uncomprehending Western reason.[81] Like the fetish gold of the Akan from Guinea, much discussed at this time, Héricourt's literary-work-as-property is the embodiment of economic desire; and like that fetish gold also, it provokes a certain anxiety, a mental confusion about the exact nature of the legal entity 'discovered', a banal thing on the one hand, and on the other, an entity consecrated after all with powers to defend its possessor from danger, specifically the dangers of competition. This newly

---

78   Héricourt, pp. 23-4.
79   Ibid., p. 27.
80   De Piles, p. 111.
81   See William Pietz, 'The Problem of the Fetish, IIIa: Bosman's Guinea and the Enlightenment Theory of Fetishism', *Res*, 16 (1988), 105-23.

constituted legal textual thing is a fetish moreover, in the Marxist sense since, in proposition two, it is stripped of its uses by the discursive context of trade and reduced to a singleness and autonomy of value: exchange-value.[82]

In the process the author is eclipsed. Having been established as the origin and thus the notionally unique and absolute possessor of the text in the beginning, he is thereafter made redundant. His discursive role is exhausted by attribution. Only when Héricourt comes, in conclusion, to describe a world in which the monopoly of privileges is compromised is a social portrait briefly sketched.[83] Héricourt's author is a commodity producer, a person, that is, utterly dependent on the market for his survival. As such he differs significantly from the image of the composite author of the late-seventeenth and early-eighteenth centuries, resurrected by scholars, most notably by Alain Viala, part creature, courtier or office-holder, part entrepreneur and part disinterested genius labouring for posterity.[84] In this respect Héricourt's author corresponds more nearly to cartographers like Sanson and designers and print-makers like Jean Barbet, or Israël Silvestre, or the Perelle, that is, to graphic rather than literary authors. Thanks to the research of Mireille Patoureau we know that, notwithstanding the fact that privileges in maps were invariably licensed in the name of the cartographer, map-makers like Nicolas Sanson were rarely in a position to work independently.[85] Sanson continued in the employ of his publishers throughout his career, first Melchior Tavernier, later Pierre I and Pierre II Mariette; his financial resources remained limited, though his reputation was internationally established and his maps widely marketed and pirated abroad.[86] Likewise, Jean Barbet, as a young draftsman and counterpart of the printer *alloué*, was bedded, boarded and salaried by Tavernier to work from 5.00 am until 8.00 pm daily in the execution of architectural views.[87] Israël Silvestre was similarly marketed by a single publisher, his uncle and father-in-law, Henriet Israël, until he inherited the stock and became a publisher in turn. By contrast the Perelle, father (Gabriel) and son (Adam) hawked their talent

82   Marx, *Capital*, pp. 163-77.

83   Héricourt, pp. 28-9, 35, and 40.

84   Alain Viala, 'La triple économie du littéraire', *Studies on Voltaire and the Eighteenth Century*, 11 (2004), 19-34.

85   Nicolas Sanson, *Atlas du monde, 1665*, ed. by Mireille Pastoureau (Paris: Sand & Conti, 1988).

86   Mireille Pastoureau, 'Feuilles d'atlas', in *Cartes et figures de la terre* (Paris: Centre Geoges Pompidou, 1980), pp. 442-54 (p. 452).

87   Peter Fuhring, 'Jean Barbet's Livre d'architecture, d'autels et de *cheminées*: Drawing and Design in Seventeenth-Century France', *Burlington Magazine*, 145 (2003), 421-30.

to a number of publishers specialising in topography: Pierre Ferdinand, Jean I Le Blond, Nicolas Langlois, in addition to Henriet Israël and Pierre Mariette.[88] These were exactly the kind of authors, authors whose livelihoods depended exclusively on the market, whose careers, Héricourt anticipated, would be utterly destroyed in the event of a change in the law.

The reification of word and image by privilege in the author's name delivered profit to publishers. Rarely were authors the direct beneficiaries of its terms: the career of Jacques Rigaud who purchased his own copy-privileges and sold his own work was something of an exception. More usually the eye is merely tricked into seeing the author's right in the place of the publisher's monopoly. And, it was the scene of the latter's plight that Héricourt most eloquently described. Imagine, he asks d'Armenonville, shops, booksellers' shops, in which whole fortunes have been invested suddenly and arbitrarily stripped of the protection afforded their stock by privilege, the texts reduced to no more than the material value of the 'useless mass of paper' on which they are printed, fit only to pulp or burn; an image all the more arresting in the wake of the Law crash at the end of 1720 and the catastrophic devaluation to point zero of the paper currency, a property-standard currency as it happened.[89] To avoid a comparable collapse of the book trade, d'Armnonville is enjoined in the name of justice to turn a deaf ear to the pleas of the provinces and to continue to endorse the privileges of the Parisian patriciate. The state's role is construed as one merely of protection by maintenance of the artificial scarcity of texts and images which the legal fiction of intellectual property creates.

If such constitutive reification appears to have little in common with that critiqued by Lukács, if not by Marx, it emerged under the same economic conditions: with the formation of a literary market in France. Moreover, privilege had worked to extend the parameters of that market-place to the point that Héricourt is able persuasively to anticipate market principle as paradigmatic – the only game in town. According to Lukács such expansion is accelerated by the illusion of its inevitability in natural law;[90] in the case of copyright by the substitution of rights for privileges. That is to say, that commoditisation having obscured the social character of labour and veiled

---

88   Grivel, *Le commerce*, pp. 147-50.
89   Thomas E. Kaiser in 'Money, Despotism, and Public Opinion in Early Eighteenth-Century France: John Law and the Debate on Royal Credit', records instances where Law's paper money was condemned as fit only to burn. See *Journal of Modern History*, 63 (1991), 1-28 (p. 17).
90   Lukács, pp. 86, 94, and 169.

the human relations between, in this case, authors and publishers, behind relations among things (manuscripts and cash), a particular and contingent set of social relations becomes identified with the natural features of the physical objects (property), thereby acquiring the illusion of truth to nature, of inexorability, a condition that contributes further to the reproduction and reinforcement of existing social relations. In effect, the idea that market *places* need to be established is forgotten. Misapprehended as principle, or law, markets just are – seemingly. Such is to note with Christopher May that privilege re-formed as right falsifies or hides its historical origin and political condition under a cover; moreover, it obscures the interests served by the monopolies (temporarily) secured.[91]

In Héricourt's brief the king's hand in matters of privilege is repeatedly negated: 'it is not the privileges granted by the king [...] that make [book-sellers] into owners of the works they print [...]';[92] 'the king has no right whilst the author lives or is represented by heirs and beneficiaries; he cannot give [the work] to anyone by the favour of privilege without the consent of the person to whom the work belongs';[93] and again, 'the king having no right over the works of authors he cannot transmit them to anyone without the consent of those who are their legitimate owners'.[94] Moreover, Héricourt redoubles the erasure of the sovereign authority in privilege by a recapitulative misreading of legislation from the sixteenth century to the end of Louis XIV's reign according to which privilege is never more than an instrument of censorship first put into service by the Ordinance of Moulins in 1566.[95] He thereby denies both the statutory nature of royal justice in privilege and eliminates the historical record of its establishment. In their place he puts a right and a thing. The right, an anterior right of possession, he says, had suffered 'no compromise' at the hand of statute law; indeed with respect to authors and their cessionaries, the 'common law' had been maintained in its entirety.[96] Meanwhile, the statement, 'it is not

---

91   Christopher May, 'The Denial of History: Reification, Intellectual Property and the Lessons of the Past', *Capital and Class: Bulletin of the Conference of Socialist Economists*, 88 (2006), 33-56. According to Lukács it is the task of historical materialism to uncover that misapprehension, to undo reification and re-discover the human relations in property. See Lukács, p. 183.

92   Héricourt, p. 23.

93   Ibid., p. 24.

94   Ibid., p. 26.

95   *Ordonnance de Moulins*, February, 1566, art. 78. By contrast this ordinance is not among those recently selected by Bently and Kretschmer for inclusion in the digital archive of *Primary Sources on Copyright 1450-1900*.

96   Héricourt, pp. 24-6.

the privilege granted by the king [...] that makes [booksellers] into owners of the books they print' ends 'but only the purchase of the manuscript by which the author transmits the property to him'.[97] The manuscript, not the king, is the material thing.

In her essay 'When Privilege Publishes the King' Lévy-Lelouch argued that the compulsory publication of privileges at the beginning or end of books created a typographical and symbolic space in which the king shows himself; specifically, in which he is read performing his power of legal protection and, in his capacity as the inaugural reader, his authority majestically to guarantee the value of the works he favoured.[98] Portraiture, by this account, was the discursive mode of privilege under Louis XIV.[99] By contrast, you could say, to rewrite privilege as property Héricourt's brief selects still-life as its rhetorical register, and more particularly *trompe l'œil* or the instantiation of what de Piles defined as painting's unique capacity to make things acutely present, to trick as well as to entertain the eye.[100] To propose such an argument, one more speculative than Lévy-Lelouch's because *trompe l'œil* is neither a literary genre nor a figure of speech, its illusionism, strictly speaking, beyond the reach of text, is to hold out the possibility of a better understanding of the ideological effect of Héricourt's re-drawn definition of privilege and of the provocation it presented to d'Armenonville.

In *trompe l'œil*, perspective, rather than enfolding persons, kings, into the space and narrative of the work, rather throws forward often banal, everyday objects – books, manuscripts, letters, the paraphernalia of writing were especially favoured by the seventeenth and eighteenth century painters – into the place of the viewer-reader, making them appear real against an abstracted, vertical ground.[101] In Héricourt's brief, the author's 'fruit' obtrudes, like the grapes of Zeuxis, the paradigmatic *topos* of *trompe l'œil*.[102] His work is:

---

97   Ibid., p. 22.
98   See Lévy-Lelouch, 'Quand Privilège', pp. 146-9.
99   Lévy-Lelouch's argument is grounded on the work of Louis Marin in *Le portrait du roi* (Paris: Les Éditions de minuit, 1981) esp. the *deuxième entrée*.
100   De Piles, p. 25.
101   On *trompe l'œil* in France in the early modern period see especially Louis Marin, 'Initiation au trompe l'œil dans la théorie classique au XVIIe siècle', in *L'imitation, alienation ou source de liberté* (Paris: La Documentation françiase, 1985), pp. 181-96; *Le trompe l'œil: Plus vrai que nature?* (Bourg-en-Bresse: Monastère royal de Brou, 2005). The artists whose work yield the most thought provoking analogies are Jean-François De Le Motte and Gaspard Gresly in both of whose works books and landscape prints by the Perelle feature prominently. Ironically in the present context, both artists were working in the provinces.
102   For a discussion and examples of the trope see *Deceptions and Illusions. Five*

> [T]he fruit of his labour which is his own, and of which
> he must have the freedom to dispose of at his will.[103]

Its contours are sharply shaped by the most intimate possession and its relief effected by liberty, the law by natural force to which it detaches itself from its social moorings to circulate at will. The author's 'fruit', like Parrhasios's curtain, covers the objective circumstance of privilege and as a synecdoche for the discourse of property forestalls the need to discuss further the legitimacy of the commercial advantages it works to gain. Subjectively, it installs property as inherently pertinent. *Trompe l'œil* not only thus rivets attention, in painting it also astonishes by its dramatic reversal of values: a minor figuration of some object or property usurps the place of grandiloquent historical themes and significant human action. The king's role, his symbolic body are, as we have seen, repeatedly erased by Héricourt to make way for a thing, manuscript, a literary text. In such circumstances d'Armenonville responded instinctively as if to an act of *lèse majesté*.

Jean Baudrillard notes the 'negative pleasure' of *trompe l'œil*, its 'worrying strangeness', and the anxiety that it provokes about the metaphysical nature of the represented thing.[104] Héricourt's brief effects an analogous estrangement of privilege, transforming a once familiar commonplace, 'Avec Privilège du Roy', into something uncanny. What distinguishes *trompe l'œil* from reification as an account of that transformation is that the new discourse of copyright may be said to be installed in appearance only. Its epistemological deceit, while momentarily persuasive, is recognisable for what it is: a trick, a conceptual sleight of hand that has yet to be naturalised, 'to harden' into fact.[105] *Trompe l'œil* describes that historical moment when texts are consciously and eloquently being made into property, and before that instance of forgetting after which, as May has noted, philosophical concerns about the naturalised order of intellectual property shift and narrow to bureaucratic issues about the efficient implementation of mechanisms of control.[106]

* * * * *

Centuries of Trompe l'œil Painting, ed. by Sybille Ebert-Schifferer (Washington: National Gallery of Art, 2002-3), pp. 109-20.
103   Héricourt, p. 24.
104   Jean Baudrillard, '*Trompe l'œil*', in *Calligram: Essays in New Art History from France*, ed. by Norman Bryson (Cambridge: Cambridge University Press, 1988), pp. 53-62.
105   On the transformation of knowledge into 'facts' see Latour, pp. 174-5.
106   May, p. 44.

To conclude: the argument advanced above is that the visual contributed actively to the practice and theory of copy-privilege in France. To be precise, it is suggested that by a process of adaptation to and translation of the properties of space and tangibility that belong to art as such, and which are manifest in representation, the meaning of privilege was redefined as alluding, not to a negotiated and limited monopoly, but to an absolute property right. By addressing a dialectical question about the particular ways in which the image helped to produce the law and law came usefully to frame the image, it has been possible to show in the first part of the essay that the natural signs of western Painting, specifically the window analogy of pictorial space, were, in the provocative words of John Berger, like 'a safe, let into the wall', in which the visible was 'deposited',[107] that perspective, in short, was a property-making machine; and that, in the manner of hedges and walls, the conventional signs or marks of the law served to transform art into a bounded possession attributable to an author. If it is generally acknowledged that authors, or more especially their cessionaries, were actively trying to interest the law in their quest for better conditions of trade, it is perhaps less well recognised that the law, which tends to deny the pertinence of practices and values outside its own domain, gained in its turn from representations of property in art by force of which it crafted a new theory of privilege.

In the second part of the essay, the law, in the person of Héricourt, is staged as another interested party, attempting in turn to engineer into acceptance his definition of privilege. In a close reading of his controversial memorandum, we traced the ways he deployed visual tropes made vivid by implied illusion to preserve by logic and definition ('right' and 'property') earlier prerogatives secured by custom ('privilege'). Crucial to the construction of the new theory of privilege was the concept of property, a 'boundary object' which by seemingly enabling the articulation of statements of identity when actually no more than licensing the perpetuation of arguments by analogy, obscured the different meanings of the word in law, aesthetics, economics and politics, thereby making possible the transfer of discursive assets across incommensurate domains. Thus, while the notion of the 'boundary object' is generally used to describe and explain (sometimes uncomprehending) relations of sharing and co-operation, it by no means precludes more knowing appropriations and competition. The

---

107   John Berger, 'Past Seen from a Possible Future', in *Selected Essays and Articles. The Look of Things*, ed. by N. Stangos (Harmonsworth: Penguin, 1972), 211-20 (p. 216). My thanks to Julian Stallabrass for reference to this.

conflicts incurred by privilege becoming right are here revealed by a distanced perspective; by recourse not only to explanation at an institutional level but also to account of shifts in macro socio-economic forces. The material context of the trafficking in meanings (of property) and the reification of practices (of art) is, of course, capitalism, specifically the emergence of the literary and graphic markets, markets to the impersonal forces of fortune of which authors hazarded their works in commodity form. Intellectual property *rights* offered a means of notionally extending, and actually of securing better, commercial monopolies in fact won by privilege in pre-commercial culture. It was, however, a promise not fully or formally implemented until the passing of the *Act of the Rights of Genius* by the Convention on 19 July 1793.

Finally, illusion in the radical form of *trompe l'œil* has served to model our understanding of the historical moment when seemingly natural claims to rights of intellectual property were projected into the privilege debate. To compare Héricourt's inaugural articulation of right to the artful and ambitious representations of Zeuxis and Parrhasios, is not only to acknowledge the artificiality of the language of natural rights but also to recognise as particular and significant that moment when claims made in its name were, after the initial surprise, nevertheless seen for what they were: mere assertions, provoking assent in some, horror in others.

11. Breaking the Mould? The Radical Nature of the Fine Arts Copyright Bill 1862

Ronan Deazley[*]

Introduction

Throughout the mid to late nineteenth century the issue that came to dominate the concerns of the national copyright regime was that of international copyright relations. From the 1830s onwards, a network of bilateral copyright treaties began to mushroom throughout Europe. In 1838, Britain passed the International Copyright Act which was designed to facilitate the negotiation of such bilateral arrangements, although efforts under the 1838 legislation came to nothing as no agreements were ever concluded under the Act. After the enactment of a second International Copyright Act in 1844, however, the British government enjoyed more success in negotiating a series of bilateral treaties providing arrangements for reciprocal copyright protection. Within three years agreements had been reached with Prussia, Saxony, Brunswick, the Thuringian Union, Hanover and Oldenburg. Britain had taken its first substantive steps towards participation in a regime of international copyright protection, which regime was significantly realised with the ratification of the Berne Convention in September 1887.

Part of the reason for the government's relative success in negotiating copyright treaties after 1844, lay in the differences between the two legislative regimes designed to facilitate the same. Whereas the 1838 Act promised only protection for books published in foreign jurisdictions, the 1844

* This paper is based upon material developed for the AHRC-funded project: *Primary Sources on Copyright (1450-1900)*.

Act proffered reciprocal copyright protection for 'Books, Prints, Articles of Sculpture, and other Works of Art' as well as a performance right for 'Dramatic Pieces and Musical Compositions'.[1] Moreover, under the 1844 Act the nature of the protection that foreign works would enjoy was explicitly linked to the domestic copyright regime. So for example, the protection for foreign books was to be governed by the Copyright Amendment Act 1842, the protection for works of foreign sculpture by the Sculpture Acts, and the performance of dramatic works by the Dramatic Copyright Act 1833, and so on.[2] Thus, the range of protections available under the 1844 Act was much broader than under the 1838 regime and, in drawing explicit structural links between international protection and the domestic legislation, the later Act also ensured substantive parity as regards the protection enjoyed by both British and foreign works.

The 1844 Act however did not readily map onto existing domestic copyright law at that time. Other than prints and certain works of sculpture,[3] no other works of art currently enjoyed statutory copyright protection within the UK. In holding out the promise of reciprocal protection, not just for prints and articles of sculpture, but for 'other Works of Art' as well, the legislation clearly misrepresented the state of the domestic copyright regime. About this disjuncture between the international norm and the domestic reality, Sherman and Bently write as follows:

> [T]he image of copyright used in bilateral agreements played an important role in the development of domestic law. In particular, if we suspend our realist assumptions we see that the [international] model anticipated, possibly created, the legal reality. That is, the image of copyright law was a model *for* rather than a model *of* what it purported to represent. In effect, the laws presented during the bilateral agreements as accurate descriptions of domestic law (which they were clearly not) became real laws, real fictions.[4]

---

1   International Copyright Act 1844, 7 & 8 Vict., c.12, ss 2, 5.
2   International Copyright Act 1844, ss 3-5.
3   Engravers' Act 1735, 8 Geo. II, c.13; Engravers' Act 1766, 7 Geo. III, c.38; Engravers' Act 1777, 17 Geo. III, c.57; Models and Busts Act 1798, 38 Geo. III, c.71; Sculpture Copyright Act 1814, 54 Geo. III, c.56.
4   B. Sherman and L. Bently, *The Making of Modern Intellectual Property Law* (Cambridge: Cambridge University Press, 1999), p. 126. See also L. Bently, 'Art and the Making of Modern Copyright Law', in *Dear Images: Art, Copyright and Culture*, ed. by D. McClean and K. Schubert (London: Ridinghouse/ICA, 2002), pp. 331-51 (p. 336), in which he discusses the influence which the International Copyright Act 1844 had in creating an image of copyright as a distinct branch of the law; this image, he continues, 'became a standard or ideal which begged that the legislature pass a law to protect paintings and drawings'.

They continue that this gap between domestic and international law 'played an important role [...] in ensuring the enactment of the 1862 Fine Art Copyright Act'.[5] That is, no doubt, true. However, it is equally true that this legislative gap was not successfully addressed for nearly twenty years. How then do we account for this hiatus, and what in particular proved to be the catalyst for the move towards securing the 1862 legislation? The 1862 Act introduced copyright protection for three types of artistic work – original drawings, paintings, and photographs. By the time the Act was passed, the English market for drawings and paintings had been well-established for over one hundred years;[6] photography by contrast was a medium (and an art-form) still in its infancy, and its inclusion within the 1862 statute proved controversial, as we shall see. In relation to the former two categories however, we might equally well ask, why it was that engravings first received copyright protection in 1735,[7] why certain works of sculpture were protected in 1798,[8] and yet drawings and paintings had to wait until the mid-nineteenth century for protection at all, whether in 1844 or in 1862?

---

5   Sherman and Bently, p. 127. In a Report prepared by the Artistic Copyright Committee for the Society of Arts, designed to address the 'exceedingly defective and unjust' state of British artistic copyright law, one of the chief defects of the current law was recorded as follows: 'That our Artistic Copyright laws are unjust in their operation upon the Subjects of those foreign States who have entered into International Copyright Conventions with Her Majesty, inasmuch as such treaties are based upon the principle of reciprocity, and that while under those treaties the works of British artists first published in the British dominions are protected from piracy in within the territory of the foreign State named in any such treaty, no similar protection is afforded in the British territories in respect of the works by artists of such foreign States'; *Journal of the Society of the Arts*, 6 (1857-8), 294. See also the observation of Earl Granville on 22 May 1862, in the House of Lords, upon moving the second reading of the Bill: '[S]ome change was required in our law in order to enable us to avail ourselves of the provisions to international treaties with reference to this subject'; *Hansard*, 3rd ser., 166 (1862), 2013.
6   I. Pears, *The Discovery of Painting. The Growth of the Interest in Arts in England 1680-1768* (New Haven, Connecticut & London: Yale University Press, 1988), pp. 55-106.
7   Engravers' Act 1735, 8 Geo. II, c.13; the Act provided anyone 'who shall invent and design, engrave, etch, or work in Mezzotinto or Chiaro Oscuro, or from his own works and invention, shall cause to be designed and engraved, etched, or worked in Mezzotinto or Chiaro Oscuro, any historical or other print or prints' with a fourteen year right to print and reprint the same (s. 1).
8   Models and Busts Act 1798, 38 Geo. III, c.71.

The Working Life of an Artist

For the professional artist working in late eighteenth century Britain, there were a number of ways by which to earn a living.[9] For those painters who favoured a relatively secure (if often modest) living, commissions for portraits provided an obvious source of income.[10] For those, however, with a desire for the public notoriety and fame that sometimes came with the production of larger scale works, such as history paintings, securing commissions or individual patronage was often much more difficult.[11] Aside from commissions and sales, however, there were other ways for such artists to generate income. For instance, the successful public exhibition of a work might bring considerable reward. John Singleton Copley was a particularly adept exponent of this commercial strategy. In 1781 his *Death of Chatham* was said to have made £5000 in ticket sales alone; ten years later, when he exhibited *Floating Batteries at Gibraltar* in St James's Park he reportedly made a further £3000.[12]

In addition to the possibility of individual sales, public exhibition, and working on commission, there was also a market for reproductions of paintings and drawings that could often prove to be extremely lucrative. Reproductions of paintings generally came in one of two forms: painted replicas or prints. As regards the former, the painter himself would often produce multiple versions of a painting (often in smaller scale) depending on the success of, and demand for, the work.[13] Wendorf, for example, relates a tale about Joshua Reynolds, the first president of the Royal Academy, reproducing a painting (*Venus*) for his patron the Duke of Rutland, a similar

---

9   See: G. Reitlinger, *The Economics of Taste, The Rise and Fall of Picture Prices 1760-1960* (London: Barrie and Rockliff, 1961); and L. Lippincott, *Selling Art in Georgian England: The Rise of Arthur Pond* (New Haven and London: Yale University Press, 1983).
10   See: Lippincott, *Selling Art*; and M. Pointon, 'Portrait Painting as a Business Enterprise in London in the 1780s', *Art History*, 7 (1984), 187-205.
11   Lippincott, p. 78.
12   Reitlinger, p. 68.
13   When the Royal Academy drafted the rules pertaining to its first exhibition in 1769, it addressed this phenomenon of copies in the marketplace. The rules provided that '[n]o Picture copied from a Picture or Print, a Drawing from a Drawing; a Medal from a Medal; a Chasing from a Chasing; a Model from a Model, or any other species of Sculpture, or any Copy be admitted in the Exhibition'; quoted in Sidney C. Hutchison, *The History of the Royal Academy 1768-1968* (London: Chapman and Hall, 1968), p. 54. Similarly, when the Academy subsequently advertised for exhibitors, they were keen to stress the same: 'N.B.- No Copies'; Royal Academy Council Minutes, I, 11, quoted in ibid, p. 55.

version of which he had previously sold to the Duke of Dorset.[14] Similarly, Benjamin West, the most commercially successful artist of his generation,[15] often produced replicas. When he exhibited *The Death of General Wolfe* at the Royal Academy exhibition in 1771 the painting proved to be an instant sensation.[16] Lord Grosvenor purchased the work for £400, after which West made at least five copies, one of which he sold to the German Prince of Waldeck for £250, while another was acquired by George III for £350.[17]

The money that West received for replica paintings however was nothing by comparison with that which he received from the reproduction of his works as engravings. The engraved version of *Wolfe*, for example, was negotiated and managed by John Boydell who, by the end of the eighteenth century, had established himself as one of the leading figures in both the British and the European print market.[18] Boydell commissioned William Woollett to engrave the work and, when first published in 1777, 'it broke all records in sales and was copied by the best engravers in Paris and Vienna'.[19] Woollett earned £7000 from the *Wolfe* engraving, whereas Boydell is said to have realised over £15,000,[20] which figure accounted for only a one-third share of the profits;[21] West himself received a sum in royalties the amount of which, as Alberts notes, 'has never been revealed'.[22] With this print, Alberts continues:

> The three men created a new popularity and demand for history paintings and a vastly broadened market for prints taken from those pictures.

14   R. Wendorf, *Sir Joshua Reynolds, The Painter in Society* (Cambridge, MA: Harvard University Press, 1996), pp. 90-1.
15   Reitlinger, pp. 57, 70.
16   R.C. Alberts, *Benjamin West: A Biography* (Boston: Houghton Mifflin, 1978), p. 109.
17   Ibid. See also: H. von Erffa and A. Staley, *The Paintings of Benjamin West* (London: Yale University Press, 1986), p. 62; and D. Montagna, 'Benjamin West's The Death of General Wolfe: A Nationalist Narrative', *American Art Journal*, 13 (1981), 72-88. Roberton Blaine, writing in 1861, observed that '[i]nstances are known where artists have sold from one up to nine repetitions of their pictures!' He continued: 'Thus, for example, at the South Kensington Museum may be seen *three* pictures, called "Uncle Toby and the Widow Wadman", by a late eminent Royal Academician'. D.R. Blaine, *Suggestions on the Copyright (Works of Art) Bill* (London: Hardwicke, 1861), p. 9.
18   In general see: S.H.A. Bruntjen, *John Boydell, 1719-1804: A study of Art Patronage and Publishing in Georgian London* (New York: Garland Publishing, 1985); and W.H. Friedman, *Boydell's Shakespeare Gallery* (New York: Garland Publishing, 1967).
19   Alberts, p. 110.
20   Ibid.
21   Friedman, pp. 39-40.
22   Alberts, p. 110.

They gave the artist and the engraver a new source of income and in some measure freed them from the sole dependence on the private patron.[23]

It certainly seems to have been the case that an artist at this time could use what we might refer to as 'engraving rights' to establish his reputation and develop a wider audience,[24] while at the same time earning considerable sums of money. When the British Institution paid the unprecedented figure of £3150 for West's *Christ Healing the Sick* in 1811, they more than recouped their original investment, as well as a substantial engravers' fee, by the sale of engravings of the painting.[25] Copley made an estimated £1200 from the engravings of his *Death of Nelson* in 1806.[26] The price paid to engrave Edwin Landseer's paintings in the mid-nineteenth century outstripped the price paid for the actual paintings themselves.[27] Moreover, some artists, such as J.M.W. Turner and John Martin, rather than work in collaboration with established engravers, often took control of engraving their own works.[28] Indeed, between 1826 and 1840 Martin claimed to have made in excess of £21,000 either from royalties or in direct sales of prints of his paintings.[29]

Paintings, Drawings, and the Engravers' Acts

All of this begs the question, of course, as to the legal status of the 'engraving rights' which artists seemed to be able to capitalise upon in relation to their paintings and drawings. When painters purported to realise payment on the right to engrave their works, upon what basis did they do so? Did it turn upon negotiating physical access to a painting to ensure a faithful reproduction of the same? Was it simply a recognised and accepted

23 Ibid. See also von Effra and Staley, p. 62.
24 About West in particular, von Erffa and Staley write that, after *Wolfe*: 'Throughout the rest of the eighteenth century, reproductive prints after West's major paintings continued to appear regularly, giving his compositions an international circulation and allowing him to expand his income by appealing to a public far larger and more diffuse than they tiny fraction of it that could afford to buy large paintings. In expanding the market for works of art, the flourishing print industry encouraged and responded to popular taste, and so did painters such as West'; ibid.
25 Reitlinger, p. 70.
26 See: von Erffa and Staley, p. 63; and Reitlinger, p. 68.
27 Blaine records that whereas Landseer's painting *Peace and War* sold for £1260, the copyright for engraving the same was sold for £3150; Blaine, *Suggestions on the Copyright Bill*, p. 8.
28 See W.G. Rawlinson, *The Engraved Work of J.M.W. Turner*, vol. 1 (London: Macmillan and Co, 1908).
29 Reitlinger, p. 98; see also Bently, pp. 337-8.

commercial convention of the printsellers' market? Or did the status of an engraving right rest upon some other legally significant construct that pre-dated (and perhaps rendered redundant) the need for statutory protection in 1862? The situation is not entirely clear. In *Sayre v. Moore* (1785) for exam-ple Lord Mansfield remarked that 'in the case of prints, no doubt different men may take engravings from the same picture, but one cannot copy the engravings of another'.[30] *Sayre* concerned an action alleging the unauthor-ised reproduction of sea charts, the resolution of which Lord Mansfield considered to be 'a matter of great consequence to the country'. Within the context of a sea-faring, mercantilist nation, the implications of the decision were obvious: 'If an erroneous chart be made, God forbid it should not be corrected even in a small degree, if it thereby become more serviceable and useful for the purposes to which it is applied'. In holding for the defendant, he continued: 'This chart of the plaintiffs' is wrong in principle, inapplica-ble to navigation. The defendant therefore has been correcting errors, and not servilely copying'.[31]

A case more directly concerned with the operation of the art market was that of *De Berenger v. Wheble* (1819).[32] In *De Berenger* the plaintiff had purchased 'the privilege of engraving the prints' of two pictures by Philip Reinagle from the artist himself. The engraver who executed the prints for De Berenger also made sketches of the works 'for his own study', sketches which 'were taken from the original pictures, and had not been in any part copied from the plaintiff's engravings'. From these sketches the engraver made two further prints for the defendant who published them in his *Sporting Magazine*, upon which basis the plaintiff alleged copyright

---

30   *Sayre v. Moore* (1785) 1 East 362. About Mansfield's dictum, Blaine, writing in 1853, commented: 'Notwithstanding the very high authority of the great judge who tried that case, and the previous dictum of Lord Mansfield on the point, it may be doubted whether his direction on that occasion will stand the test of further inquiry. If it be sound, then it is obvious that the value of the copyright which an artist has in the *invention* or *design* of his picture is comparatively small; and that the enormous capital embarked in the copyright of pictures and engraving them, is placed in the greatest jeopardy; because it follows that anyone who can surreptitiously or oth-erwise gain access to a picture, either before or after it is engraved, so as to obtain sketches from, or a copy of it, may thus proceed to engrave the picture, provided he does not copy from the authorized engraving'; D.R. Blaine, *On the Laws of Artistic Copyright and their Defects* (London: Murray, 1853), pp. 25-6.
31   *Sayre v. Moore*, 362; Lord Mansfield observed: '[W]hoever has it in his inten-tion to publish a chart may take advantage of all prior publications. There is no monopoly of the subject here [...] but upon any question of this nature the jury will decide whether it be a servile imitation or not'.
32   *De Berenger v. Wheble* (1819) 2 Stark 548.

infringement in the original engravings. It was argued for the defendant that the legislation protecting engravings 'did not give any monopoly in the picture to the engraver, but left the use of it free and unrestrained to the painter who might make as many copies of it as he thought fit'. Abbott CJ agreed: 'It would destroy all competition in art to extend the monopoly to the painting itself [...] [and] in this case the defendant's engraving was made from the original picture, and not from the plaintiff's print'.[33] As with Lord Mansfield's obiter comment in *Sayre*, the decision in *De Berenger* seemed to suggest that anyone might produce copies of existing paintings and drawings without fear of reprisal from someone who had actually paid the artist for the privilege of making reproductions thereof.

And yet, painters did command substantial reproduction fees in relation to their works. One possible explanation underpinning the reality that artists regularly sold the right to engrave their paintings lay in the fact that the 'invention' and 'design' of a painting, as opposed to the painting itself, could be understood to fall within the protection of the Engravers' Act 1735. The 1735 legislation provided that every one:

> [W]ho shall invent and design, engrave, etch or work in *Mezzotinto* or *Chiaro Oscuro*, or from his own works and invention, shall cause to be designed and engraved, etched or worked in *Mezzotinto* or *Chiaro Oscuro*, any historical or other print or prints, shall have the sole right and liberty of printing and reprinting the same for the term of fourteen years, to commence from the day of first publishing the same.[34]

Although the 1735 Act had been secured by and on behalf of a group of engravers, there was nothing in principle to prevent the substance of the legislation protecting the work of other artistic communities as well. When the Engravers' Act 1766 was passed, it essentially restated the protection set out within the earlier legislation, but continued with the additional provision that:

> [A]ll and every person and persons who shall engrave, etch, or work in *Mezzotinto* or *Chiaro Oscuro*, or cause to be engraved, etched, or worked, any print, taken from any picture, drawing, model, or sculpture, either ancient or modern, shall have, and are hereby declared to have, the benefit and protection of [the 1735 Act], and this act, for the term herein after-mentioned, in like manner, as if such print had been graved or drawn from the original design of such graver, etcher, or draftsman.[35]

---

33   Ibid., pp. 548-9.
34   Engravers' Act 1735, s. 1.
35   Engravers' Act 1766, 7 Geo. III, c.38, s. 2.

Strictly speaking, this new provision did not mean that an artist could prevent an engraver from reproducing his work without prior authorisation; it simply provided that engravings produced from existing works of art (drawings, paintings, and sculptures) were to be protected as if the design of those works originated with the engraver.[36] Nevertheless, the provision implicitly lent credence to the fact that the 'invention' and 'design' of a work protected under the 1735 Act might take the form of a pre-existing painting, drawing or sketch. Roberton Blaine, writing about the 'laws of artistic copyright' in 1853 certainly considered this to be the case:

> The Engraving Acts were passed with the express object of encouraging the art of *designing* for the purposes of engraving, and *if the original design be not made public before the engraving from it be published, in accordance with the conditions imposed by the Engraving Acts*, it would seem to have been the intention of the Legislature to protect the invention of the design, as well as the authorised engraving from that design.

He continued: 'The copyright in a picture, as such, is not protected. It is merely the *design* of the picture *when coupled with engraving*, which is entitled to copyright'.[37]

In reading the legislation in this manner, Blaine was careful to stress that a work, whether a painting or otherwise, should be first engraved, and the engravings published, in accordance with the legislation, *before* the work itself was publicly exhibited; otherwise, he suggested, what protection was available in accordance with the engravers' statutes would be lost. It was dangerous, he asserted, to exhibit pictures 'before they are engraved':

> [I]f [...] as is usually the case at the present day, the picture or design be privately or publicly exhibited or otherwise published before it has been engraved, and the prints from the engraving are published, then it would seem that the design is public property; and that the work of the engraver, exclusive of the design, is alone entitled to copyright; in other words, that any one may engrave the subject provided they do not copy it from the engraving.[38]

---

36 *Newton v. Cowie* (1822) 4 Bing 234 (pp. 245-6). See also *Moon v. Broker* (1840) *The Times*, 27 June 1840, in which Moon, a printseller who had acquired 'the exclusive right of engraving and publishing copies' of a Lanseer painting (*A Distinguished Member of the Humane Society*) 'for a large pecuniary consideration, and an assignment made to him of the copyright in the engraving', secured an injunction to prevent the defendant reproducing the same by means of 'a novel and singular process, by which a copy in oil-colours was taken from the engraving in a trifling degree smaller than the original'.

37 Blaine, *On the Laws of Artistic Copyright*, p. 26.

38 Ibid., p. 27. See also Blaine's comment in the Appendix to the Report prepared

Whether exhibition of a work might compromise the protection of the design of the work in accordance with the engravers' legislation was an issue that was never brought before the courts; however, that artists considered it important to adhere to this sequence of events is borne out to some degree by the account of *Bailey v. Harrison* (1849) in *The Times* in which the plaintiff complained that his painting 'after being engraved was duly published', was reproduced without authorisation upon pocket handkerchiefs sold by the defendants.[39]

That painters, such as West, were able to command substantial fees to reproduce their works may well explain why, before the mid-nineteenth century, they felt no real need for bespoke legal protection for their craft. That is, regardless of *Sayre* and *De Berenger*, and in accordance with the established practice of the trade, painters were able to 'licence' or sell the 'right' to reproduce their work by relying upon their control over the physical access to the painting (or drawing) in conjunction with the indirect protections offered by the existing engravers' legislation. And yet, whatever protection the Engravers' Acts provided paintings and drawings in this regard, whether *de jure* or *de facto*,[40] the problem remained that this protection was tied to specific types of reproduction protected by the Engravers' Acts rather than to the original work itself. As Blaine observed in 1858, the Engravers' Acts 'give artists no copyright in their pictures, *as such*, but only for the purposes of engraving'.[41] It was clear that certain types of unauthorised use were not prohibited by the existing copyright

for the Society of Arts on artistic copyright: 'Unless a picture be engraved [...] before such a picture be publicly exhibited, no Copyright can, in my opinion, be acquired even in the design of the picture for the purposes of engraving; it is forever lost to the artist'; *Journal of the Society of Arts*, 6 (1857-8), 298.

39 *Bailey v. Harrison* (1849) *The Times*, 28 February 1849.

40 Blaine wrote about the 'practice amongst Artists as to their claims to Copyright' as follows: 'When an artist sells his picture, it seems to be generally understood that the copyright for the purpose of engraving passes with the picture to the purchaser, unless the artist at the time of the sale either verbally or in writing reserves the copyright. No case appears in the books in which this point has ever been discussed or decided, and it may well be doubted whether such a practice, which by some persons is only asserted to amount to a usage or custom, could be established in any court of law or equity in this country, even assuming that no legislative enactment existed on the subject. It is but natural justice that the artist should have the whole profits allowed by law to be derived from the invention of his picture as well as its execution. Each work he produces may be a double source of direct profit to him, first, by sale of the picture; second, by the exercise or sale of the copyright, or the exclusive right of multiplying copies of the picture by any of the various processes of engraving'; Blaine, *On the Laws of Artistic Copyright*, pp. 39-40.

41 *Journal of the Society of Arts*, 6 (1857-8), 297.

regime. In 1833, for example, John Martin sought to prevent the public exhibition of an unauthorised large scale diorama of his picture and print, *Belshazzar's Feast*. Before Shadwell VC, it was argued for Martin that 'there was no difference between selling a copy of a print, and exhibiting it for money; as, in both cases, profit was made of that which was appropriated to another'. Before even hearing the counsel for the defendant, Shadwell VC intervened: 'Exhibiting for profit is in no way analogous to selling a copy of the Plaintiff's print, but is dealing with it in a very different manner'. The engravers' legislation, he continued, 'never was intended to apply to a case where there was no intention to print, sell or publish, but to exhibit in a certain manner'; as a consequence, he concluded, 'I ought not to grant the injunction until the right has been established at law'.[42]

The Society of Arts, the International Exhibition, and the Catalyst for the Act

The initiative which ultimately resulted in the passing of the Fine Arts Copyright Act 1862 was taken by the Society for the Encouragement of Arts, Manufactures and Commerce (the Society of Arts), when on 2 December 1857 they appointed an Artistic Copyright Committee to look into 'the subject of Copyright in Works of the Fine Arts'.[43] Sir Charles Eastlake, the President of the Royal Academy, was appointed Chair; John Frederick Lewis, the President of the Society of Painters in Water Colours was appointed Deputy Chair; and Blaine, who four years previously had published his treatise *On the Laws of Artistic Copyright and their Defects*, was appointed Reporter of the Committee.[44] Reporting early in 1858, the Committee recommended that the current laws concerning copyright in artistic works should be revised and expanded. In particular the Committee suggested that the original works of painters, designers, sculptors, engravers and architects should be protected for 'the author's life, and thirty years after', and that 'works of Art of a more imitative character, and not necessarily embodying original design', such as those produced by engravers, photographers and cast makers, should also be protected for 'a like period'.[45] This

---

42   *Martin v. Wright* (1833) 6 Sim 297 (pp. 298-9).
43   *Report of the Artistic Copyright Committee to the Council* (London: Bell and Daldy, 1858). It seems that the Society was prompted to act at this time by the implications of the decision in *R v. Closs* (1858) Dears & Bell 460. For further details, see the next section: 'The 1861 Bill, the Prevention of Fraud, and the Moral Rights of the Artist'.
44   *Journal of the Society of Arts*, 6 (1857-8), 91.
45   Ibid., p. 294.

copyright term was, according to Blaine, chosen 'in accordance with the law of Prussia and all the States included in the Germanic Confederation'.[46]

On 4 June the official *Journal of the Society of Arts* reported that two petitions were about to be placed in the hands of Lord Lyndhurst, John Singleton Copley's eldest son. The first was from the Society itself, while the second was signed by the members of the Artistic Copyright Committee as well as 'a large number of gentlemen interested in the production of works of Fine Art'; both asked that the House of Lords might 'consider the grievances in question, and [...] afford such relief as [...] shall seem just and advisable'.[47] Lyndhurst, presented the petitions to the House on 26 July, and a select committee was appointed to consider the subject, but to no immediate effect.

Undeterred by the lack of success in the Lords, the Council of the Society of Arts reported in October 1859 that it would once again direct its attention to the question of artistic copyright,[48] and in May 1860, the Society's *Journal* informed its readers that the Artistic Copyright Committee, acting under the advice and guidance of Spencer Walpole, had had a meeting on 28 April with the Prime Minister, Lord Palmerston, to discuss the state of the law as regards artistic copyright.[49] No further progress was made however until 17 January 1861, when the Committee met with Sir Richard Bethell, the Attorney-General, as a result of which Bethell 'expressed his willingness to assist the Committee in settling the Bill and to take charge of it in the House of Commons and promised to urge upon Lord Palmerston the propriety of its being introduced into Parliament as a Government measure'.[50] Three months later, on 15 April, leave was given in the House of Commons to prepare and bring in a Copyright (Works of Art) Bill.[51] When Bethell introduced the Bill to the Commons, he made clear that, while the need for legislation of this kind had long been acknowledged, the plans for the forthcoming International Exhibition provided the compelling reason for Parliament to act upon the matter sooner rather than later:

> [S]ome legislation of this kind is absolutely necessary. That necessity has,
> I believe, for a long time been admitted by this House, and by the other
> House of Parliament [...] Perhaps however the House will think it necessary

46   Blaine, *Suggestions on the Copyright Bill*, p. 6 (n. 1).
47   *Journal of the Society of Arts*, 6 (1857-8), 455-6.
48   *Journal of the Society of Arts*, 7 (1858-9), 747.
49   *Journal of the Society of Arts*, 8 (1859-60), 432.
50   *Journal of the Society of the Arts*, 9 (1860-1), 136.
51   *Journal of the House of Commons*, 116 (1861), 146; see also *Hansard*, 3rd ser., 162 (1861), 543.

that even now I should state a few facts, showing the necessity that exists at present for some legislative enactment for the protection of Copyright in works of fine art. We are about to invite, within a few months, the artists of all nations to send their works of art to our approaching Exhibition; but although many nations have made great exertions to secure an International Copyright, we have not as yet, in this country, any law which would give protection to their works, which above all others are entitled to it.[52]

When a deputation from the Society met, once again, with the Prime Minister on 14 June, to impress upon him the 'justice' of the Bill, and the 'special importance of its being speedily passed', they too drew attention to both the interests of British artists as well as to those of the 'Foreign Exhibitors of Works of Fine Arts' who would be invited to the International Exhibition.[53] There is little doubt that legislation securing the interests of artists would have been introduced by the British legislature at some point throughout the late nineteenth century, if for no other reason than compliance with the Berne Convention would have mandated such protection. It is equally true, however, that the plans for the International Exhibition provided the imperative catalyst for its introduction in 1862.[54]

The 1861 Bill, the Prevention of Fraud, and the Moral Rights of the Artist

Given that the Society's Artistic Copyright Committee had produced a draft version of a Bill in May 1860, in accordance with their earlier recommendations,[55] there is every reason to believe that the Bill presented by Bethell to the Commons in April 1861 was, by and large, the work of the Copyright Committee.[56] Certainly the Bill that Bethell presented addressed

52   Quoted in Blaine, *Suggestions on the Copyright Bill*, p. 5.
53   *Journal of the Society of the Arts*, 9 (1860-1), 576, 583-4.
54   Not everyone was convinced however that the forthcoming International Exhibition provided sufficient grounds for introducing the Act at this time. A commentator for the *Athenæum*, for example, remarked as follows: 'Much has been said as to the importance of obtaining a desired act prior to the opening of the International Exhibition next May, so as to protect the works of foreign artists which will be exhibited there. This argument, it seems to us, is not of much importance, because a similar temporary act to that passed in 1851 will doubtless be obtained for the purpose of protecting from piracy persons exhibiting new inventions at the International Exhibition of 1862. Nothing, therefore, will be easier than to extend that protection to new and original works of Fine Art either by British or foreign artists'; *Athenæum*, 1 February 1862, p. 154.
55   *Journal of the Society of Arts*, 8 (1859-60), 432.
56   Indeed, when the Committee met with Bethell on 17 January 1861, it was

the various substantive recommendations which the Committee had set out in March 1858.[57] It proposed to repeal all existing legislation pertaining to works of 'fine art', and instead provide protection for new and original works of art (drawings, paintings, photographs, sculptures, engravings, and works of architecture) for the life of the author with a thirty year post mortem term;[58] moreover, anyone producing a lawful copy of any such work (for example, an authorised engraving of a work of sculpture) would also enjoy copyright in their reproduction for the same term of protection.[59] The protection provided by the Bill extended to both new and existing work,[60] and no copyright would be enjoyed in any work unless the name or monogram of the author had been in some fashion appended thereto.[61]

In addition to the various provisions dealing with copyright, however, the Bill also included a number of clauses concerning the fraudulent production and sale of works of art, designed in part to redress the decision of the court in *R v. Closs* (1857) which had been handed down on 30 November 1857,[62] just two days before the Society of Arts established the Artistic Copyright Committee. Thomas Closs, a dealer in paintings, had sold a copy of a painting by John Linnell as an original 'by means of having the name "J Linnell" painted in the corner of the picture', for which, upon indictment, he had been convicted of forgery.[63] Quashing the conviction,

resolved that sub-committees of the Artistic Copyright Committee would be appointed 'to confer with the Attorney General in settling the terms of the Bill'; *Journal of the Society of the Arts*, 9 (1860-1), 136. Moreover, at the Annual General Meeting of the Society, in June 1861, it was reported that '[t]he Bill [introduced into the Commons by Bethell] though substantially the same as that of last year, has been, under the superintendence of the Attorney General, greatly improved, and as the members are aware, has been introduced into the House of Commons as a Government Bill, and it now stands waiting for Committee'; ibid., p. 583.

57   In general see *Journal of the Society of Arts*, 6 (1857-8), 294-5.

58   1861 Bill, clause 3; in relation to works of architecture, the protection was of a limited nature, in that once the building had been constructed, then nothing in the proposed Act 'shall preclude any Person from making any Plans, Sections, Elevations, or Models of the same, or any Part thereof, and constructing any Building therefrom, provided such Plans, Sections, Elevations, or Models be made and executed, not from those of the Author of the Design thereof, but only from the said Building'; ibid.

59   Ibid.

60   1861 Bill, clause 6; this also included the work of artists who had died within ten years before the passing of the Act.

61   1861 Bill, clause 5.

62   *R v. Closs* (1858) Dears & Bell 460; see also W.A. Copinger, *The Law of Copyright in Works of Literature and Art* (London: Stevens & Haynes, 1870), p. 196.

63   The original painting had been sold by Linnell for £180; Closs sold the forgery for £130. See *Journal for the Society of Arts*, 6 (1857-8), 298.

however, Cockburn LJ explained that '[a] forgery must be of some document or writing', and continued that this case 'was merely in the nature of a mark put upon the painting with a view of identifying it, and was no more than if the painter put any other arbitrary mark as a recognition of the picture being his'.[64] In effect, Cockburn CJ decided that the offence of forgery at common law did not extend to painting an artist's name on a picture so as to pass it off as one by the original artist. Blaine, in his report to the Copyright Committee, simply remarked that '[t]he consequences of this decision, as respects the interests of artists, of the purchasers of works of Art, and the public morality, are too apparent to need any comment'.[65] The Committee recommended that various measures be adopted to protect the public against such frauds,[66] all of which were incorporated within the draft Bill, and a number of which were included in the final version of the 1862 Act.[67]

The Bill, for example, provided that no one was to fraudulently sign or affix any 'name, initials, or monogram' upon a work, nor sell, publish, or dispose of the same; moreover, no one was to 'utter, dispose of, or put off' any copy of a work (whether copyright protected or not) as having been executed by the original artist.[68] Finally, a provision was included which prevented anyone (other than the original artist) who altered an existing work in their possession from selling or publishing that work (or copies thereof) during the artist's lifetime without his or her consent.[69] The inclusion of this offence, a mid-nineteenth century forerunner to the contemporary moral right concerning the derogatory treatment of an author's work, was designed with the explicit purpose of safeguarding the reputation of an artist while he was still alive. As Bethell explained, in his capacity as Lord Chancellor Westbury, in the Lords on 22 May 1862, it was often the

---

64 *R v. Closs*, p. 466.
65 *Journal for the Society of Arts*, 6 (1857-8), 298.
66 Ibid., pp. 294-5.
67 Compare the 1861 Bill, clauses 13, 14, with the 1862 Act, s. 7.
68 1861 Bill, clause 14.
69 Ibid. This provision was included in s. 7 of the 1862 Act which provided that 'where the Author of Maker of any Painting, Drawing, or Photograph, or Negative of a Photograph, made either before or after the passing of this Act, shall have sold or otherwise parted with the Possession of such Work, if any Alteration shall afterwards be made therein by any other Person, by Addition or otherwise, no Person shall be at liberty during the Life of the Author or Maker of such Work, without his Consent, to make or knowingly to sell or publish, or offer for Sale, such Work or any Copies of such Work so altered as aforesaid, or any Part thereof, as or for the unaltered Work of such Author or Maker'.

case that paintings by 'artists of celebrity' were dealt with in such a way that 'without being actuated by petty feelings, [those artists] might naturally manifest some sensitiveness on the score of their reputation at being so treated'. He provided one such example:

> One remarkable instance was stated by Mr. Charles Landseer, the painter of a picture in which he had introduced two dogs, which had been touched up by Sir Edwin Landseer, and, as the artist himself admitted, greatly improved. This picture was sold to a dealer, who cut out the figures of the dogs, and sold them as the work of Sir Edwin Landseer; and then he filled up the hole in the original picture with two dogs painted by an inferior artist, and sold the whole picture as the work of Mr. Charles Landseer.[70]

Photography: Fine Art or Mechanical Process?

The 1861 Bill received a second reading in the Commons however the committee stage was constantly deferred such that it failed to carry in that parliamentary session.[71] In the next session, on 27 February 1862, at the request of 'a committee of artists [...] to place copyright in works of art on the same footing as that in literary works, sculptures, and engravings',[72] Roundell Palmer, the Solicitor-General, rose in the Commons and, suggesting that the law was at present 'in a very imperfect and anomalous condition', moved for leave to bring in a Bill to amend the Law relating to Copyright in Works of Fine Art.[73] This Bill differed from its predecessor in a number of respects. The most basic alteration was that the legislation was no longer framed to extend to all works of art. Instead, the existing legislation concerning engravings and works of sculpture was to be left on the statute book, and works of architecture were not to be included at all; the new Bill only proposed to provide protection for 'the author of every painting, drawing and photograph'.[74]

This Bill would of course eventually result in the 1862 Act. However, that photography was to be included within the remit of the legislation gave rise to considerable parliamentary debate.[75] In the Commons, an

---

70   *Hansard*, 3rd ser., 166 (1862), 2019.
71   See the *Journal of the House of Commons*, 116 (1861), 146, 167, 173, 181, 191, 217, 229, 235, 242, 251, 265, 268, 277, 288, 297, 319, 338, 353, 361, 374, 382, 399.
72   *Hansard*, 3rd ser., 165 (1862), 843; and *Hansard*, 3rd ser., 166 (1862), 324.
73   *Hansard*, 3rd ser., 165 (1862), 843.
74   Draft Bill, 27 February 1862, clause 1.
75   For an argument as to the influence of the emergence of commercial photography on the timing of the 1862 Act see Bently, pp. 340-3.

objection was raised as to whether 'it would be dangerous at present to include photographs' in an Act of this kind given that '[p]hotography was not a fine art, but a mechanical process'.[76] Palmer responded that while 'strictly and technically, a photograph was not in one sense to be treated as a work of fine art', nevertheless, 'very considerable expense was frequently incurred in obtaining good photographs'. He continued:

> Persons had gone to foreign countries – to the Crimea, Syria and Egypt – for the purpose of obtaining a valuable series of photographs, and had thus entailed upon themselves a large expenditure of time, labour and money. Was it just that the moment they returned home other persons should be allowed, by obtaining negatives from their positives, to enrich themselves at their expense?[77]

Behind these comments lay the interests of photographers like Francis Frith, John Thomson, Samuel Bourne, and others who had contributed, throughout the nineteenth century, to the successful establishment of a tradition of travel photography,[78] and of the art dealers who often provided these photographers with the necessary financial backing to support their work.[79] Frith, one of the founding members of the Liverpool Photographic Society, was noted for his studies of the Middle East as well as for establishing the largest photographic publishing firm in nineteenth-century Britain. During 1856 and 1860 he embarked upon three extensive expeditions, taking in Egypt and the Nile, as well as Palestine, Jerusalem and Damascus, culminating in the publication of his influential 1860 work *Egypt and Palestine Photographed and Described by Francis Frith*.[80] Having posed his rhetorical question, Palmer continued that he would not consent to exclude photographs from the Bill.[81]

---

76 *Hansard*, 3rd ser., 165 (1862), 1890-1.

77 Ibid., p. 1891.

78 G. Clarke, *The Photograph* (Oxford: Oxford University Press, 1997), p. 48.

79 In 1855, for example, Agnew's, the art dealers, commissioned Roger Fenton to travel to and take photographs of the Crimean War; after Fenton's return, Agnew's exhibited Fenton's work at the Pall Mall premises of the Society of Painters in Water Colours before publishing a selection of the photographs by subscription. For further details see Geoffrey Agnew, *Agnew's 1817-1967* (London: The Bradbury Agnew Press, 1967), 'Appendix II: Agnew's and Roger Fenton', pp. 69-76. Thanks to Elena Cooper for drawing this example to my attention.

80 *The Dictionary of Art*, ed. by J. Turner, 34 vols (London: MacMillan Publishers Ltd., 1996), XI, pp. 794-5. For more on Frith see J. Talbot, *Francis Frith* (London: Macdonald, 1985); and D. Wilson, *Francis Frith's Travels: A Photographic Journey through Victorian Britain* (London: Dent & Sons, 1985).

81 *Hansard*, 3rd ser., 165 (1862), 1891.

That was not the only objection to the inclusion of photography within the remit of the proposed legislation. When the Bill was read for the second time before the Lords, Earl Stanhope (previously Lord Mahon), who had been instrumental in securing the passage of the Copyright Act 1842,[82] voiced further misgivings. While he supported the current Bill upon the principle that 'a man should be protected in the enjoyment of his intellectual productions' whether literary or artistic, nevertheless, Stanhope considered, it exhibited 'one or two points of difficulty' especially in relation to photographs. In particular he observed that:

> It was quite possible for two or more persons to take photographs of the same scene, building, or work of art from the same spot, and under the same circumstances, and of course producing similar results; and to give a copyright in such cases [was] very likely to occasion dispute and litigation. A person, for instance, might make a photograph copy of a photograph – say of the Colisæum – originally taken by another; who could say that the copy was not the original photograph?

Under such circumstances, he continued, he could not envisage how it was practicable 'to enforce such a copyright'.[83] Bethell, now the Lord Chancellor, sought to assuage Stanhope's concerns commenting that 'the copy of a photograph might be sufficiently detected, as it would hardly be possible for two persons to produce representations of the same object under exactly the same conditions of light, position and other circumstances'.[84] As with the earlier objection, the point was ultimately conceded. When the Bill received the Royal Assent, on 29 July 1862, paintings, drawings, and photographs all enjoyed equal status under the new legislation.[85]

---

82   This operated to extend the protection of literary copyright from a bifurcated twenty-eight year term to one that was to last for 'the natural life of [the] author, and for the further term of seven years' or for forty-two years, whichever period was longer; Copyright Act 1842, 5 & 6 Vict., c.45, s. 3.

83   *Hansard*, 3rd ser., 165 (1862), 2016-7.

84   Ibid., p. 2019.

85   Section 1 set out that: 'The Author [...] of every original Painting, Drawing, and Photograph [...] shall have the sole and exclusive right of copying, engraving, reproducing, and multiplying such Painting or Drawing, and the Design thereof, or such Photograph, and the Negative thereof, by any Means and of any Size, for the term of the natural Life of the Author, and Seven years after his Death'.

Publication and Registration: The Radical Nature of the 1862 Bill

Aside from the labelling of photography as a 'fine art', there were a number of other aspects to the 1862 Bill that proved to be controversial. Indeed, the Bill, as it was first introduced into the Commons, represented a radical challenge to existing copyright doctrine and theory. On 8 March, a commentator in the influential literary magazine, the *Athenæum*, summed up the elements of that challenge as follows:

> [T]he most remarkable feature is that it disregards those three great principles upon which Parliament has legislated with respect to copyright:-
> 1. That it shall commence from the time a work is *first published*.
> 2. And, during the last twenty years, that no copyright shall be acquired by the author of a work except upon condition of its being *registered*.
> 3. Also that the work to be so registered shall be new and *original*.[86]

The question of when copyright protection was to commence was, in the Bill, bound up with the duration of the copyright term. Copyright was to last for the life of the author and seven years after his or her death, a period that was clearly modelled on the statutory term provided by the 1842 Act (and not that originally set out within the 1861 Bill).[87] The 1862 Bill differed from the 1842 Act however in that the earlier legislation also provided for a forty-two year protection from the point of first publication if that term proved longer than the seven year post-mortem period;[88] by contrast, the 1862 Bill included no such default term. In this way, the Bill represented a significant conceptual departure from the existing copyright regime. Whereas all of the existing legislation, in one way or another, specifically linked the duration of the copyright term to the moment of publication,[89]

---

86   *Athenæum*, 8 March 1862, p. 334.
87   That the duration of the copyright term should be the same as that for works protected under the 1842 Act was also in line with the recommendation which Blaine had made in his 1853 treatise *On the Laws of Artistic Copyright*.
88   Copyright Act 1842, s. 3.
89   See: Copyright Act 1842, s. 3; Sculpture Copyright Act 1814, s. 2; Models and Busts Act 1798, s. 1; Engravers' Act 1766, s. 7; Engravers' Act 1735, s. 1. There was, however, one exception in the guise of the Dramatic Literary Property Act 1833, 3 & 4 Will. IV, c.15, which provided the right to represent the work in public while the manuscript of the play remained 'not printed and published'; once published however both the copyright (in accordance with the Copyright Act 1814, 54 Geo. III, c.156, s. 4) and the representation right lasted for twenty-eight years from the day of first publication of the same and 'if the Author or Authors, or the Survivor of the Authors' was still living at the end of that time then for the remainder of his life (s. 1).

the 1862 Bill abandoned this formula; the copyright term was now to be calculated *only* by reference to the life and death of the author. Moreover, this aspect of the Bill would be retained in the final version of the 1862 Act.[90]

The other two points raised by the *Athenæum* would however be addressed as the Bill passed through Parliament. The issue of whether works should be registered under the new legislation was one that had commanded much attention amongst the Society's Artistic Copyright Committee. When they first issued their Report on the state of the law in early 1858, it noted that '[v]ery considerable discussion took place upon the point whether the *registration* of works of Art ought or ought not to be made a condition precedent to the acquisition of any Copyright therein'. The Committee decided, in the end, to recommend that no registration ought to be required, a decision which was reflected in both the 1861 Bill and the first draft of the 1862 Act. The former provided that:

> No Copyright shall be acquired in any Work of Fine Art, or in the Design thereof, until the Name or Monogram of the Author or Maker thereof shall have been legibly signed, painted, engraved, printed, stamped, or otherwise marked upon the Face or some conspicuous Part of such Work.[91]

Under the latter, even this requirement was abandoned, the Bill simply allowing for copyright protection from the point of the author's creation of the work.[92]

There were, however, a number of Committee members that considered registration to be an essential aspect of the statutory regime, and, when the Committee issued its Report in early 1858, an objection to the principle of non-registration prepared by Blaine was attached thereto. Registration, he maintained, was an established principle and practice within the existing copyright regime, both domestic and international. It provided certainty not only for the artist, but also for the purchaser of the work as well as for the public, in terms of ascertaining who owned the copyright in a work (regardless of who owned the work itself). In addition, he argued, the 'publicity of registration' assisted in providing a check on the fraudulent production and sale of works of misattributed art.[93]

Blaine reiterated and developed his thoughts on the need for registration in a pamphlet that he published after the 1861 Bill was brought before

---

90   Fine Arts Copyright Act 1862, s. 1.
91   Draft Bill, 15 April 1861, clause 5.
92   Draft Bill, 27 February 1862, clause 1.
93   *Journal of the Society of Arts*, 6 (1857-8), 296.

the Commons.[94] Part of the reason for the artists' reluctance to incorporate a system of registration within the statutory regime, he suggested, lay in the fact that registration would prevent the artists 'making repetitions' of their own work after they had sold the work on. To this end, he maintained, legislation should not only protect the authors of original works but it should also prevent the 'wrongs committed by authors of original works'.[95] This theme was also taken up by the *Athenæum*. One of '[t]he prominent mischiefs which render legislative redress essential', it suggested, was 'the misconduct of a few eminent artists, who have brought disgrace upon a noble profession';[96] it was artists of this kind, the *Athenæum* continued, who were going to 'great efforts' to 'obtain the proposed copyright without any condition for registration'.[97] On the issue of registration, it considered, the interests of the purchaser should come to the fore:

> Surely the purchasers of such valuable property are entitled to have it protected from piracy by the artist, or any other person, and especially when notorious instances have occurred where eminent English artists have sold numerous "repetitions" of their finest works without deeming it requisite to obtain any consent whatever for that purpose from the owners of the original pictures, whose property therein must necessarily have been lessened in value each time they were thus repeated.[98]

Any legislation, it argued, must make sure to protect '*all* parties interested under it [...] the artists, the purchaser of their works either when commissioned or otherwise, and the public'.[99]

When the Bill was discussed in committee in the Commons, provision was made for the registration of 'every Agreement for the Acquisition or Reservation of Copyright made upon or before the Sale of any Work of Art under this Act, and also of every subsequent Assignment of any such

---

94 By this time, Blaine had resigned from his position as the Reporter of the Society. In his 1861 pamphlet, he explained that, after a Bill had been prepared by the Copyright Committee omitting any need for registration, he made clear to the Society that he would 'advocate [his] own opinions on the Bill when it should be brought before Parliament'; Blaine, *Suggestions on the Copyright Bill*, p. 4.

95 Ibid., p. 8. He continued: 'As much of the value of a work of art depends upon its being unique, copies of it not only tend to diminish the value of the original, but likewise to cast a doubt upon its originality. Hence it is that purchasers feel deeply aggrieved by the practice of distinguished artists, in making repetitions of their works'; ibid., p. 9.

96 *Athenæum*, 8 March 1862, p. 334.

97 *Athenæum*, 29 March 1862, p. 429.

98 *Athenæum*, 1 February 1862, p. 154.

99 *Athenæum*, 31 May 1862, p. 735.

Copyright'. These transactions, unless registered at Stationers' Hall within twelve months of execution, were to be rendered null and void.[100] This arrangement, Palmer explained, had been introduced primarily 'to afford absolute protection to every purchaser of a work of art after it had left the artist's hand'.[101] When the Bill reached the House of Lords, however, this amendment was not considered sufficient.

As the Bill passed through the Lords, one of its most strident critics was Lord Overstone, an eminent and successful banker, as well as a patron of the arts whose personal collection was said to be 'distinguished above all private galleries for the finest masterpieces of the Dutch School and those works of Murillo and Claude which gave it a European reputation'.[102] In 1850, the same year in which Overstone first took his seat in the upper chamber, he was also elected a Trustee to the National Gallery. As O'Brien notes, he became, in effect, the National Gallery's spokesman in the Lords,[103] exerting an influence upon the gallery's affairs that was, in the words of one obituarist, 'always esteemed of the highest value and importance'.[104]

In relation to the registration provisions proposed in the Commons, Overstone objected on the basis that, as a result of the potential twelve-month hiatus between the sale of the copyright in a work and the registration of that sale, 'there would exist a copyright unknown to the public for the whole period of one year'.[105] An arrangement 'more inexpedient, more impolitic, and more inconsistent with justice', he considered, 'could not well have been devised'.[106] Better, in his opinion, that registration should 'accompany, if not precede, the first production of the work; otherwise copies made previous to registration, and purchased in good faith by parties ignorant of the suppressed copyright, would be liable at any moment to be seized'.[107] When the Bill came back from the Lords, the registration provision had been amended to provide that a memorandum 'of every Copyright to which any Person shall be entitled under this Act' was to be registered at Stationers' Hall, without which no action was sustainable, nor

---

100   Draft Bill, 20 March 1862, clause 4.
101   *Hansard*, 3rd ser., 166 (1862), 324.
102   'Lord Overstone and Art', *The Times*, 29 November 1883.
103   *The Correspondence of Lord Overstone*, ed. by D.P. O'Brien, 3 vols (Cambridge: Cambridge University Press, 1971), III, p. 32. For further details on Overstone's life and political career, see ibid., pp. 12-47.
104   'Lord Overstone and Art', *The Times*, 29 November 1883.
105   *Hansard*, 3rd ser., 166 (1862), 2015.
106   Ibid., p. 2094.
107   Ibid., p. 2015.

any penalty recoverable, 'in respect of anything done before Registration'.[108] On 24 July, when Palmer presented the amended Bill to the Commons, he accepted that should the amendment be objected to 'the passing of the Bill that Session would be endangered, and therefore he was prepared to ask the House to agree to them'.[109] The Commons agreed, and, five days later, the Act received the Royal Assent.[110]

Ownership, Originality, and the interests of the Art Market

That the registration system was incorporated within the final version of the 1862 Act to guard against potential 'misconduct' on the part of the artistic community, while securing the economic concerns of purchasers and publishers, is of some interest. That the legislation had to navigate and resolve these tensions was also manifest in relation to the question of ownership of the copyright in a work purchased from an artist, or produced upon commission, an issue which the 1878 Royal Commissioners' Report on Copyright would subsequently refer to as '[t]he most difficult question with relation to fine arts which we have had to consider'.[111]

When the 1861 Bill was discussed in the Commons, upon its second reading concern had been raised about the manner in which it proposed to secure the copyright in a work to the artist regardless of the fact that he

---

108   Fine Arts Copyright Act 1862, s. 4. It should be noted that this provision differed somewhat from its corresponding section in the Copyright Act 1842. Section 24 of the 1842 Act provided that 'no proprietor of copyright in any book which shall be first published after the passing of this Act shall maintain any action or suit, at law or in equity, or any summary proceeding, in respect of any infringement of such copyright, unless he shall, before commencing such action, suit, or proceeding, have caused an entry to be made, in the book of the Registry of the Stationers Company, of such book, pursuant to this Act'. That is, under the 1842 legislation, registration functioned as a prerequisite to the commencement of infringement proceedings, but did not bear upon the subsistence of copyright or upon the right to sue in respect of any infringements that occurred prior to registration. By contrast, s. 4 of the 1862 Act appeared to preclude the ability to take any form of infringement proceedings 'in respect of *anything* done before Registration' (emphasis added). Clearly, under the 1862 Act, the incentive to register the copyright in works of fine art as soon as possible was much more compelling than was the case under the statutory regime protecting literary works.

109   *Hansard*, 3rd ser., 168 (1862), 781.

110   *Journal of the House of Commons*, 117 (1862), 379.

111   Report of the Royal Commission on Copyright (1878), XXIV, C.2036, XIX.

might have sold the work to another.[112] On this point, Mr Walter, the M.P. for Berkshire, remarked that 'the effect of [the legislation] would be that any person who purchased a picture after the passing of the Act [...] would be deprived of the power of permitting any friend to copy it, or of having it engraved himself'. He continued:

> He was persuaded that very few persons would like to purchase works of art with any such conditions attached to them. The House had seen many a curious tenant-right Bill, but it appeared to him that to allow an artist, after he had sold a picture, to retain a copyright in it, and thereby to deprive the real owner of those rights which the artist originally enjoyed, was about as unreasonable a proposition as had ever been submitted to Parliament [...] He regarded [the clause] as a great infringement upon the liberty of the subject, and if he wanted to have a picture copied he should consider such an enactment as an unwarrantable interference with this right of property.[113]

When Bethell, the Attorney-General (as he was then), addressed this criticism he responded by reminding the House that anyone who wanted to do so could purchase a picture '"out and out" giving a corresponding price for it; and, if he bought the copyright, he would then hold the picture free from every description of interference'. Nevertheless, he pressed: 'If, however, he bought the picture, simply as a picture, he would then have the gratification and delight resulting from its contemplation; but was it right that he should have copies and engravings made from it, using it for a different purpose from that for which the artist sold it?'[114]

Regardless of Bethell's comments, the 1862 Bill revised the original wording of the previous Bill to provide that when any work was sold for the first time, 'the Person so selling or disposing of the same shall not retain the Copyright thereof unless it be expressly reserved to him by Agreement in Writing, signed at or before the Time of such Sale or Disposition, by the Vendee or Assignee of the Painting or Drawing'.[115] This, in the opinion of the *Athenæum*, was scarcely an improvement in that it still offered no benefit or security for the purchaser of the picture:

112   Clause 3 of the 1861 Bill provided that '[t]he Author of every Picture, Work of Sculpture, and Engraving, which shall be made, or for the first Time sold or disposed of, after the Commencement of this Act, and his Assigns, shall have the sole and exclusive Right of copyright, reproducing, and multiplying such Work, and the Design thereof, by any Means, of any Size, and for any Purpose, for the Term of the natural Life of such Author, and Thirty Years after his Death'.
113   *Hansard*, 3rd ser., 162 (1861), 1632. See also the comments of Lord Fermoy, ibid., p. 1633, and Lord Overstone (22 May 1862), *Hansard*, 3rd ser., 166 (1862), 2014.
114   *Hansard*, 3rd ser., 162 (1861), 1635.
115   Draft Bill, 27 February 1862, clause 1.

> As the section stands, it means that when an artist has acquired a copy-
> right by executing a work, that copyright is to cease, unless when he first
> sells such work his purchaser signs an agreement for the purpose of reserv-
> ing the copyright to the artist. It follows, that where an artist thus reserves
> his copyright, he will have the exclusive privilege of making as many copies
> or repetitions of his work as he pleases; – but where the purchaser declines
> to enter into such an agreement [...] then that copyright will *thereupon cease,*
> and the artist will consequently, as at present, be able to make and sell as
> many unauthorised copies and repetitions of the work as he please; the only
> difference being, that he will not have the *monopoly* for that purpose.[116]

As was the case with the provision on registration, this aspect of the Bill
was amended in the Lords. Two main changes were introduced. First, the
Act provided that, when first sold the copyright in a work would pass to
the purchaser at the same time *unless* the seller specifically retained the
copyright therein by 'agreement in writing'; this, however, was coupled
with an obligation on the part of the purchaser to secure the transfer of
copyright, by way of written agreement with the seller, before or at the time
of the sale.[117] And so, in the final version of the Act, the basic point raised
in the *Athenæum* that the copyright in a work would cease to exist in the
absence of *any* written agreement between seller and purchaser prior to or
at the point of first sale remained unaddressed.[118]

The second alteration introduced by the Lords concerned those for whom
works were made or executed 'for a good or a valuable consideration'.[119] As
was the case with the first sale of a work, an artist retained no copyright in
any work made on commission unless he or she specifically retained the
same by an agreement in writing. Unlike the situation with the first sale of
a work, however, there was no corresponding requirement that the person
commissioning the work secure the copyright in the work by way of a written agreement. That is, in the absence of any written agreement between
the two parties, there was a *presumption* that ownership of the copyright
in a work passed to the person who commissioned that work. This aspect
of the legislation was almost certainly introduced as a consequence of
Overstone's intervention on this point. He had argued in the Lords that '[i]
f a man engaged an artist to paint for him a portrait of himself or a member

---

116   *Athenæum*, 8 March 1862, p. 334.
117   Fine Arts Copyright Act 1862, s. 1.
118   On the 'surprising' nature of the legislation in this regard see for example
the comments of R. Winslow, *The Law of Artistic Copyright* (London: Clowes & Sons,
1889), p. 15.
119   Fine Arts Copyright Act 1862, s. 1.

of his family, or if he commissioned him to paint for him a picture on any given subject, the copyright of that picture ought to belong to the employer who paid for it', and that 'if Parliament were prepared to grant a copyright, it ought at once and absolutely, without necessity for negotiation or arrangement between the parties, to vest that right in the employer, and not in the artist'.[120] Overstone's intervention was also remarked upon in the *Athenæum* when it reported that he had 'presented a petition against some of its provisions on behalf of several of the most eminent publishers of illustrated books'; the report continued that '[t]hey especially complain that the measure fails to provide for the interests of *employers* of artists'.[121]

Tied to these questions of ownership and exploitation was the third of the 'great principles' upon which, in the opinion of the *Athenæum*, all previous copyright legislation was based: that any registered work should also be 'new and original'.[122] The Sculpture Act 1814 had previously established the requirement that protected works be 'new and original',[123] as had the Copyright of Designs Act 1842,[124] whose formula had also been adopted in the 1861 Bill.[125] When the first draft of the 1862 Bill came before the House, however, there was no similar requirement. As with the question of registration, this omission, for the *Athenæum* would only operate to disadvantage those purchasing works of art. Consider, for example, an artist who sold a picture without executing any written agreement in relation to the sale; in accordance with the proposed legislation, no copyright would be retained, by anyone, in that picture. 'From the fact of the words "new and original" picture being omitted', however, 'the artist may, after having sold an original picture, without retaining the copyright, instantly set up a claim to copyright in a copy or *"repetition"* of the same picture and the *design* thereof for all purpose'. That is, by ensuring that no copyright subsisted in relation to the first picture, an unscrupulous artist might produce a later identical copyright-protected work that could be relied upon to impede the ability of the person who purchased the first work to 'safely engrave or otherwise copy' the same.[126]

---

120   *Hansard*, 3ʳᵈ ser., 166 (1862), 2014, 2094.
121   *Athenæum*, 14 June 1862, p. 790.
122   *Athenæum*, 8 March 1862, p. 334.
123   Sculpture Copyright Act 1814, s. 1.
124   An Act to Consolidate and Amend the Laws Relating to the Copyright of Designs for Ornamenting Articles of Manufacture, 1842, 5 & 6 Vict., c.100.
125   Draft Bill, 15 April 1861, clause 3.
126   *Athenæum*, 5 April 1862, p. 466. The commentary continued that '[i]f repetitions of pictures are to be made, there ought to be no deception, no suppression of

This issue had also been raised in committee in the Commons when George Cavendish Bentinck, M.P. for Taunton, had asked whether 'the term "painting" in the bill applied to original paintings only, or included a copy so as to give copyright in a copy whilst there was no copyright in the original'.[127] In response, the Solicitor-General proffered that he would consider whether words 'should not be inserted to the effect that an original work being sold without copyright, no subsequent copy or repetition of the same work should be entitled to copyright';[128] no such proviso was introduced however before the Bill carried to the Lords.

Again, in the House of Lords, Overstone intervened, asking why the expression 'new and original', used in previous legislation, 'had in the present instance been carefully excluded',[129] and proposed their introduction. Although his suggestion was not followed to the letter, the final version of the Act did provide the authors of 'original' paintings, drawings and photographs with the sole and exclusive right of 'copying, engraving, reproducing, and multiplying' their work 'by any means and of any size', which protection also extended to the 'design' of both paintings and drawings, and the 'negative' of the photograph.[130] Why the existing formula that works be 'new and original' was abandoned is not clear; what is clear, though, is that the 1862 Act provided the first occasion on which the legislature introduced the requirement that works be 'original' as a threshold for copyright protection. Moreover, as was the case with the registration requirement, the inclusion of the originality threshold in the final version of the Act appeared to be principally motivated by the interests of purchasers, publishers, and the operation of the art market in general.[131]

---

the fact as to whether the object sold is original and *unique*, or a copy. The whole matter should be beyond suspicion, if a copyright is to be of any value to artists *generally* and to the public'; ibid.

127   *Hansard*, 3rd ser., 165 (1862), 1889. Similarly, a Mr Henley 'put the case of an artist selling a picture, and retaining no copyright in that picture. If the artist afterwards made a duplicate original, how would matters stand?' He continued that '[t]hey all knew that those things were often reproduced in that way, and it was difficult to determine between copies and duplicate originals. How was the second picture to stand? Was there to be copyright in it, or not?' Ibid., p. 1890.

128   Ibid.

129   *Hansard*, 3rd ser., 166 (1862), 2014.

130   Fine Arts Copyright Act 1862, s. 1; this however was subject to the proviso in s. 2 that '[n]othing herein contained shall prejudice the right of any person to copy or use any work in which there shall be no copyright, or to represent any scene or object, notwithstanding that there may be copyright in some representation of such scene or object'.

131   See also Blaine, *Suggestions on the Copyright Bill*, pp. 8-9.

Domestic Legislation and the Work of Foreign Artists

One substantive aspect of the 1862 Act remains for discussion. It concerns the question of who was entitled to the benefit of the protection of the legislation. When the Copyright Committee of the Society of Arts reported in March 1858, they noted that, in addition to the problems which the current copyright posed for British artists:

> [O]ur Artistic Copyright laws are unjust in their operation upon the Subjects of those foreign States who have entered into International Copyright Conventions with Her Majesty, inasmuch as such treaties are based upon the principle of reciprocity, and that while under those treaties the works of British artists first published in the British dominions are protected from piracy in within the territory of the foreign State named in any such treaty, no similar protection is afforded in the British territories in respect of the works by artists of such foreign States.[132]

To remedy this issue, they suggested that any Bill prepared to amend the various defects of the law, 'should likewise protect all works of Art by alien authors (whether friends or enemies), although executed or first published in any Foreign State'.[133] Like the French decree of 28 March 1852 concerning the counterfeiting of foreign works,[134] the Committee were recommending that the new legislation should be universal in its scope and effect. The 1861 Bill followed this suggestion in providing that the author of any work made 'in any place out of the British Dominions' was to be entitled to copyright protection 'whether he be a British Subject or not'.[135] No previous domestic copyright Act had ever made reference to the protection of work created (or indeed first published) *outside* the British Dominions,[136] never mind suggesting that such protection should extend to the work of foreign authors. Blaine, in his pamphlet on the 1861 Bill, described this provision as 'a liberal and noble step in the right direction'.[137]

When the first draft of the 1862 was presented to the Commons, while not as explicit as the 1861 Bill, it nevertheless provided that '[t]he author of every painting, drawing, and photograph, which shall be made [...]

---

132   *Journal of the Society of Arts*, 6 (1857-8), 294.
133   Ibid.
134   For details, see F. Rideau, 'Commentary on the International Copyright Act, Paris (1852)', *Primary Sources*.
135   Draft Bill, 15 April 1861, clause 9.
136   Except, that is, in the context of securing copyright protection for British authors in accordance with the International Copyright Acts.
137   Blaine, *Suggestions on the Copyright (Works of Art) Bill*, p. 24.

either in the British Dominions *or elsewhere'* would be entitled to copyright protection.[138] When discussing this aspect of the proposed legislation the *Athenæum*, however, was less generous than Blaine:

> [It] ignores the previous policy of Parliament in passing the International Copyright Acts; it inclines not only to British artists and photographers, but also to those of the whole world. If this measure become law, the curious and not very creditable anomaly in our legislation will exist, that a foreign author of the most trumpery "picture, drawing or photograph," made or first published out of the British dominions, will be invested with such a copyright as no foreign literary author, composer, engraver or sculptor will enjoy in respect of his works, first made or published abroad. Can these facts have been duly considered?[139]

A subsequent court might, of course, have tried to confine the scope of the legislation to the work of British subjects, in line with the sentiments expressed in decisions such as *Clementi v. Walker* (1824),[140] and *Chappell v. Purday* (1845).[141] The point, however, would not be subject to litigation, for the wording of the first section was altered in the Lords to specifically limit the operation of the legislation to an author 'being a British subject or resident within the Dominions of the Crown'.[142] This amendment, in effect, brought the legislation into line with the decision of the House of Lords in *Jeffreys v. Boosey* (1854), in which Lord Cranworth, when discussing what protection a foreign author might enjoy under British copyright legislation, had indicated that the concept of the 'British subject' could include 'all persons who are within the Queen's dominions, and who thus owe to her a temporary allegiance'.[143]

Conclusion

For many, the rationale for extending the law of copyright to the fine arts, in the guise of paintings, drawings, and photographs, was simple enough; as Bethell remarked on 6 May 1861, it was 'an attempt for the first time to do justice to the artists of this country'. '[T]he right of the author to protection had been recognised by the Legislature'; '[w]as it not just', he continued, 'to

---

138   Draft Bill, 27 February 1862, clause 1 (emphasis added).
139   *Athenæum*, 5 April 1862, p. 466.
140   *Clementi v. Walker* (1824) 2 B&C 861 (pp. 867-8, 870; *per* Bayley J).
141   *Chappell v. Purday* (1845) 14 M&W 303 (pp. 317-8; *per* Pollock CB).
142   Fine Arts Copyright Act 1862, s. 1.
143   *Jeffreys v. Boosey* (1854) 4 HLC 815 (p. 955).

extend the same protection to the artist?'[144] Similarly, in the House of Lords on 22 May 1862, Earl Stanhope, put it in the following terms:

> [T]he claims of the artist to a copyright in his works were quite as valid as those of the literary author in his; and if they at once admitted the principle that a man should be protected in the enjoyment of his intellectual productions, and if they allowed a certain period of possession to the author for his benefit before the public were put in full and free enjoyment of the work, he did not see how Parliament could refuse the same privilege to the artist as it has already been granted to the author. There was no difference in principle between a poem and a picture.[145]

And yet, what was being proposed was, by no means, a mechanistic expansion of the existing principles and doctrine of copyright law to a new category of subject-matter, that is: works of fine art. Indeed, the 1862 Bill, in its earliest incarnation, incorporated a number of elements that would have signalled a profoundly radical departure from established British copyright norms. Two aspects of the Bill stand out in this regard: the need for registration and the protection of the works of foreign authors.

When first introduced to the House of Commons, the 1862 Bill proposed that copyright protection should arise at the point of creation and that it should not be contingent upon or subject to the formality of registration. Within fifty years, of course, this proposition would become a cornerstone of the copyright system, both domestic and international. Indeed, by the 1880s, the *Athenæum* entirely abandoned its professed adherence to this 'great principle' of copyright law: 'We contend that when a right has been recognised, any formality, the performance of which is made a condition precedent to obtaining that right or to enforcing the remedy which is to protect it, is an evil'.[146] In 1862, however, that copyright works need not be registered proved too disruptive a prospect to be easily accommodated within the existing copyright framework.

Arguably more interesting, however, was the fact that, given the extent to which the need for legislation was predicated upon the existing gap between domestic law and international obligation (in the guise of the norms of the International Copyright Act 1844), the first draft of the Bill should, apparently with government approval, depart from the central

---

144   *Hansard*, 3ʳᵈ ser., 162 (1861), 1637. Similarly, as Lord Chancellor, Bethell described the introduction of the legislation as 'an act of simple justice to artists'; *Hansard*, 3ʳᵈ ser., 166 (1862), 2017.
145   Ibid, p. 2016.
146   *Athenæum*, 20 March 1886, p. 393.

principle underpinning Britain's contemporary (and continuing) attitude to international copyright relations – that is, the principle of reciprocity. Within the context of literary copyright, the courts had, for the thirty years prior to the House of Lords' decision in *Jeffreys v. Boosey* (1854), wrangled with the question as to what rights, if any, foreign authors might enjoy under British domestic copyright law. In *Jeffreys* it was decided that a foreign author had to be resident within the Empire at the time of publication if they were to enjoy copyright protection under the UK legislative regime. During that same period three International Copyright Acts had been passed to address this issue, all of which proceeded upon the basis of bilateral negotiation and reciprocal protection.[147] And yet, the 1862 Bill proposed taking the unprecedented step of abandoning both residency and reciprocity as key aspects of Britain's international copyright relations. In short, but for the intervention of the House of Lords, a British statutory measure would have embraced the same principle of universal protection that lay at the heart of the French decree of 1852. Britain, of course, would subsequently play a significant role in shaping the contours and securing the success of the Berne Convention in the mid-1880s.[148] Had the original draft of the 1862 Bill been passed without amendment, the implications this might have had for the future of the copyright regime, both domestically and internationally, might have been far-reaching indeed.

In any event, the legislation did otherwise innovate in a number of important respects. In the first place, it de-coupled the copyright term from the moment of publication, providing that the life of the author should be the sole criterion by which to calculate the duration of copyright. Second, in its section addressing the fraudulent production and sale of works of art, it provided artists with an early forerunner to the 'moral rights' currently enshrined within the Copyright, Designs and Patents Act 1988. As a result, work that artists had not produced could not be falsely attributed to them, and artists were also entitled to prevent others from altering their own work during their lifetime without their consent.[149] Third, this was the first British statute to introduce the concept of 'originality' as the standard threshold criterion for securing copyright protection.

---

147   International Copyright Act 1838; International Copyright Act 1844; International Copyright Act 1852, 15 & 16 Vict., c.12.
148   See for example the commentary and analysis in L. Bently and B. Sherman, 'Great Britain and the Signing of the Berne Convention in 1886', *Journal of the Copyright Society of the USA* (2001), 311-40.
149   Fine Arts Copyright Act 1862, s. 7.

As the discussions that surrounded the introduction of the originality requirement made clear, however, its inclusion had little to do with origination, authorship, or the conceit of the creative author-genius. Rather, for the individual who purchased both a picture and the copyright in that work, the originality threshold ensured that the artist of the work could not subsequently execute an identical repetition and claim a new, and so competing, copyright therein. Similarly, for the individual who purchased a picture without any written agreement as to the ownership of the copyright in that work (such that any copyright in the work was lost) the originality requirement would prevent the artist from relying upon a copyright-protected repetition of that work to interfere with the purchaser's commercial exploitation of the original picture. When first introduced, the 1862 Bill was, for Overstone, 'an artists' Bill, drawn up for the protection of artists only'.[150] When the Act received the Royal Assent, however, both the retention of the registration system and the requirement that works should be 'original' spoke to interests other than those of the artistic community. These aspects of the legislation were considered necessary to secure, in Overstone's words, 'the interests of the general purchasers of pictures, the interests of the publishers of illustrated works, and the interests of the public at large'.[151]

---

150   *Hansard*, 3rd ser., 166 (1862), 2014.
151   Ibid.

12. 'Neither Bolt nor Chain, Iron Safe nor Private Watchman, Can Prevent the Theft of Words': The Birth of the Performing Right in Britain

Isabella Alexander*

'Neither bolt nor chain, iron safe nor private watchman, can prevent the theft of words'.[1] In 1872, the playwright James Robinson Planché penned these words in his autobiography. Planché is not well known today – indeed his reputation was in decline during his own lifetime. However, by the time of his death in 1880 Planché had written around one hundred and eighty plays for the theatre, covering every type of dramatic genre. He was also a tireless campaigner for improvement of the theatre and the rights of dramatic authors. In 1830 he convinced the Member of Parliament and fellow-dramatist George Lamb to introduce a bill into Parliament granting copyright protection to dramatists.[2] However, the bill failed and, two years later, Edward Bulwer Lytton was more successful in convincing Parliament to pass legislation. As a result, it was to be Bulwer Lytton whose name was subsequently associated with reforming the rights of dramatists.[3]

* I am grateful to Lionel Bently and Elena Cooper for helpful comments on drafts of this paper.

1 J.R. Planché, *The Reflections and Recollections of J.R. Planché*, 2 vols (London: Tinsley Brothers, 1872), I, p. 199.
2 Ibid., p. 149.
3 Edward Lytton Bulwer changed his name to Bulwer Lytton in 1843, according

Why did dramatists need protection in the 1830s? What were the problems that Planché and Bulwer Lytton were addressing? The answer requires an excursion further back in time, and starts with the observation that the history of dramatic copyright, like that of copyright in books, is bound up with the history of censorship and monopoly powers. Censorship of the theatres stretches back to the Tudors, but the central instrument for censorship in the eighteenth and nineteenth centuries was Walpole's Stage Licensing Act of 1737.[4] This Act supported the monopolies of the two patent theatres, Drury Lane and Covent Garden, which had been granted exclusive rights to perform 'legitimate' drama by Charles II. The Stage Licensing Act required a copy of every new play to be submitted to the Lord Chamberlain, who could prohibit performance of the play if he saw fit. The powers of the Lord Chamberlain extended to the city of Westminster, which comprised the two patent theatres, as well as the Haymarket, which was granted a royal patent in 1766, and the King's Theatre. Other theatres, which grew steadily in numbers throughout the eighteenth century, were, in theory, restricted to performing plays containing singing, dancing and 'spectacles'. However, they too submitted manuscripts to the Lord Chamberlain regularly. Theatres outside the city of Westminster were subject to supplementary licensing regimes.[5]

The system of censorship and licensing, however, did not inhibit various sharp practices between rival theatres, as managers sought to obtain copies of successful plays, in order to stage them for their own profit. One popular method was to purchase a copy of the prompt book from the prompter,[6] or to send in several agents to join the audience over several nights, each tasked with recording a particular character or characters. By the 1830s, the practice had evolved to sending in shorthand writers to take down the script as it was performed.[7] In 1770, the actor and dramatist Charles Macklin, who had taken the precaution of never printing any

---

to the terms of his mother's will. In 1866 he became Baron Lytton of Knebworth. For ease and consistency he will be referred to in this paper as Bulwer Lytton. For more on Bulwer Lytton's involvement in copyright law, see C. Seville, 'Edward Bulwer Lytton Dreams of Copyright: "It might make me a rich man"', in *Victorian Literature and Finance*, ed. by F. O'Gorman (Oxford: Oxford University Press, 2007), pp. 55-72.

4   10 Geo. II c.28.

5   J.R. Stevens, *The Censorship of English Drama 1824-1901* (Cambridge: Cambridge University Press, 1980), pp. 5-7.

6   A prompter is a person who stands next to the theatre stage, but out of sight, so as to prompt the actors, should they forget their lines.

7   J.R. Stevens, *The Profession of the Playwright* (Cambridge: Cambridge University Press, 1992), p. 86.

copies of his play *Love à la Mode* and always took the copy away from the prompter, sought an injunction from the Court of Chancery against just such practices.[8] The defendants were the proprietors of a magazine called the *Court Miscellany*, rather than a rival theatre, and they published the play's first act in their magazine, promising that the second was to come in a subsequent edition. Macklin brought a bill seeking an account of profits and injunction against further publication of the first act, and the promised publication of the second. Lord Camden initially stood the case over until after the decision in *Millar v. Taylor*[9] should be given.

As is well known, the Court in *Millar v. Taylor* found that there was a common law copyright existing outside the Statute of Anne. Macklin sought to rely on this precedent, arguing that representing a play in a theatre did not amount to making a gift of it to the public, and that the defendants' publication thereof amounted to an invasion of the plaintiff's property right. The defendants, however, asserted that representing a farce on the stage gave a right to the audience to 'carry away what they could and make any use of it'.[10] Moreover, they alleged that the publication occasioned no damage to Macklin as he could still receive profits from the acting of the piece. Lord Commissioners Smythe and Bathurst rejected these arguments, finding that the printing of the play did occasion damage to the plaintiff and granted a perpetual injunction.[11]

However, the Court of the King's Bench took a different approach in the subsequent case of *Coleman v. Wathen*.[12] Colman (as it is usually spelt), was the manager of the Haymarket Theatre and had purchased the copyright of John O'Keeffe's play, *The Agreeable Surprise*. In 1793, he brought an action against Wathen, of the Richmond Theatre, for performing the piece without permission. Thomas Erskine (later Lord Chancellor), acting for the plaintiff, argued that a representation should amount to a publication within the meaning of the statute, for if it was not 'all dramatic works might be pirated with impunity'.[13] He also based his argument upon the finding in *Millar v. Taylor* that an author had a property in his works independent of the Statute of Anne. Lord Kenyon CJ did not accept this argument. By this stage, *Donaldson v. Becket*[14] had been decided by the House of Lords, and

8   *Macklin v. Richardson* (1770) Amb. 694.
9   (1760) 4 Burr. 2303.
10   (1770) Amb. 694 (p. 696).
11   Ibid., pp. 696-7.
12   5 T.R. 245.
13   Ibid., p. 245.
14   (1774) 2 Bro. P.C. 129.

the Chief Justice based his decision on this case. He noted that 'the statute for the protection of copyright only extends to prohibit the publication of the book itself by any other than the author or his lawful assignees. It was so held in the great copyright case by the House of Lords'.[15]

In his 1828 treatise on literary property, Robert Maugham suggested that the differing results in the two cases could be traced to the fact that the plaintiff in the latter case was seeking statutory penalties, rather than bringing an action for damages, with the result that he was bound by the express provisions of the Statute of Anne, which were, as penal provisions, construed strictly.[16] This seems to be borne out by the greater success of later plaintiffs in Chancery. In 1820, David Morris, also a manager of the Haymarket, obtained an injunction from Lord Eldon in respect of another of John O'Keeffe's plays, *Young Quaker*. Lord Eldon was satisfied by the production of an affidavit stating that the copyright of the play had been assigned to Morris in writing, and granted the injunction against the actress Maria Kelly and Samuel Arnold, proprietor of the English Opera House.[17] Morris was also successful in obtaining injunctions against the patent theatres for other plays by O'Keeffe.[18]

However, when the Lord Chancellor referred the case of *Murray v. Elliston* to the Court of the King's Bench, that Court found against the plaintiff.[19] This case was brought by John Murray, the publisher of Byron's *Marino Faliero*, against the manager of the Theatre Royal, Drury Lane, who was advertising a performance of the poem. Once again, counsel for the plaintiff argued that the question did not depend on the Statute of Anne, but was an invasion of Murray's property right in the poem. Counsel for the defendant relied on *Donaldson v. Becket* as deciding that the author had no remedy except that provided by the statute, as well as the authority of *Coleman v. Wathen*. The judgment of Abbott CJ, Bayley and Holroyd JJ is briefly reported as finding that the action could not be maintained for publicly acting and representing the poem.[20] It is not clear, from the report, whether they came to this conclusion because they accepted Elliston's argument that the play was an acceptable abridgment, or the argument that

15 5 T.R. 245.
16 Robert Maugham, *A Treatise on the Law of Literary Property* (London: Longman, 1828), p. 155.
17 *Morris v. Kelly* (1820) 1 Jac. & W. 481.
18 Select Committee to inquire into Laws affecting Dramatic Literature (1831-2) 7 Parliamentary Papers (679), p. 153 (hereafter: Dramatic Literature Select Committee).
19 (1822) 5 B. & Ald. 657.
20 Ibid., p. 661.

there was no 'publication' within the meaning of the Statute of Anne.

A number of defensive practices grew up in response to this uncertain situation. The managers of theatres would often buy the 'copyright' in a play from the dramatist but, rather than printing and publishing these plays, they would hoard the manuscripts, both to protect the script and as a long-term investment. Often the manuscript would be later sold to a publisher. An informal system of spying on competitors also grew up.[21] The method of remunerating authors also changed at the start of the nineteenth century. The old system which involved authors taking a share of box office takings on the 'benefit' nights (the third, sixth and ninth nights) began to give way to the more certain system of payment by a lump sum, which might include an allowance for the copyright, and might include bonus amounts on certain nights, should the play run that long.[22] However, by the 1820s and 1830s the theatres were in a general decline and this was reflected in decreasing amounts paid to authors. Reasons for the decline were variously identified as incompetent management, excessive actors' salaries, the fashion for late dinner hours, the absence of Royal encouragement and the opposition of religious sects.[23]

The fact that the surreptitious copying of plays as they were performed had become a considerable industry is illustrated by the observation of the well-known playwright Douglas Jerrold that 'Mr Kenneth, at the corner of Bow Street, will supply any gentleman with any manuscript on the lowest of terms'.[24] Planché alleged that he was given the impetus to seek reform of the law following an incident involving John Murray, lessee of the Theatre Royal in Edinburgh. According to Planché, Murray refused to pay the entirely reasonable sum of ten pounds for the privilege of staging Planché's drama *Charles XIIth* pleading poverty, and then obtained an unauthorised copy and staged that instead.[25] However, the bill that Planché convinced Lamb to introduce in 1830 was continually deferred and Lamb eventually dropped it.[26]

Interestingly, this was not the first attempt to convince the legislature to take action to protect dramatic authors. In 1814, in the course of debate concerning a bill aimed at amending the provisions regarding legal deposit,

---

21   Stevens, *The Profession of the Playwright*, pp. 86-7.
22   Ibid., pp. 25-6.
23   Ibid., p. 31, and Dramatic Literature Select Committee, p. 3.
24   Ibid., p. 157.
25   Planché, p. 148. See also Dramatic Literature Select Committee, p. 214.
26   *Parl. Deb.*, vol. 22, col. 918, 24 February 1830; *Journal of the House of Commons* (1830), LXXXVI, pp. 161, 167, 174, 222; *Parl. Deb.*, vol. 13, col. 252, 31 May 1932.

Davies Giddy, a scientist and MP for Bodmin, suddenly proposed including a clause that would protect the interests of authors in the habit of writing plays 'intended merely for the closet'.[27] Apparently, a gentleman of his acquaintance had described to him the lack of protection for dramatic authors against theatre managers putting on plays without the author's permission. It was objected that the clause was too disconnected from the rest of the bill and Giddy let the suggestion drop.

In 1832, however, the matter was taken up by Edward Bulwer Lytton. This time, the matter of dramatic copyright was raised alongside reform of theatrical London. Bulwer Lytton, a Whig radical and novelist of growing popularity, had become an MP the year before. He objected to the system of dramatic licensing and considered that the original reason for suppressing the minor theatres, namely their disorderly state during the time of Charles II, no longer existed. In his view, the system was the direct cause of deterioration in national drama.[28] Moreover, he considered the censorship powers exercised by the Lord Chamberlain over all dramatic performances to be unconstitutional.[29]

Bulwer Lytton believed that a revival in English drama would result from relieving theatres and dramatic works from the restrictions under which they operated and from conferring on dramatic authors the same rights as literary authors under copyright law. His motion to appoint a Select Committee to look into these matters was agreed to by the House of Commons, and the Committee began to take evidence on 13 June 1832. All the dramatic authors who appeared before the Select Committee were of the opinion that granting copyright protection to published plays as well as a right to consent to performances of their plays, whether published or unpublished, would benefit them and lead to an increase in the amount they were paid.[30] Moreover, they considered that granting these rights would encourage people with greater literary talents to write for the stage, instead of working on better paid periodical literature and novels.[31]

As well as being anxious to receive payment for performances of their plays, dramatists were also concerned with the effects of such unauthorised performances upon their reputations. This concern had been raised in *Murray v. Elliston* by Murray's counsel James Scarlett, who had argued

27 *Parl. Deb.*, vol. 28, col. 685, 13 July 1814.
28 *Parl. Deb.*, vol. 13, cols 239–41, 31 May 1832.
29 Ibid., col. 244.
30 Dramatic Literature Select Committee, pp. 142, 156, 176, 190, 194, 214, 227, 228.
31 Ibid., pp. 143, 157, 176.

that Byron had expressly stated that he did not want his tragedy to be performed, and claimed that the play's failure would hurt Byron's feelings as well as his fame.[32] As Douglas Jerrold put it before the Select Committee, unauthorised performances constituted a 'double injury [to authors]: in the first place, they are not paid for their pieces, and in the next place, they are represented by the skeleton of their dramas; so that, as it was emphatically said by a sufferer, the author was not only robbed but murdered'.[33] The argument was not pressed, but represents an instance of the impetus to lay claim to author's rights going beyond mere pecuniary interest.

Despite the opposition of theatre managers and proprietors to a scheme that would give authors of plays control over their performance, the Committee recommended that the authors of plays should possess the same legal rights as the authors of any other literary production, as well as the right to grant consent to performances.[34] In March 1833, Bulwer Lytton introduced a bill into Parliament to this effect.[35] Bulwer Lytton had wanted the penalty for representing a play without permission to be the sum of fifty pounds for each representation, but this was amended in the House of Commons to forty shillings.[36] With a few other small amendments the bill was passed in the House of Commons and the House of Lords made no further changes. The bill received royal assent in June 1833[37] and passed into law.[38] On the matter of censorship, the Committee's recommendations were modest: rather than abandoning the office of censor, it advocated extending the Lord Chamberlain's jurisdiction to cover the minor theatres, but removing the privileges of the patent theatres.[39] Bulwer Lytton introduced the censorship provisions in a second bill, but it was far more contentious than the dramatic copyright bill and had to be dropped.[40]

32   *The Times*, 4 May 1822, p. 3e.
33   Dramatic Literature Select Committee, p. 157.
34   Ibid., pp. 150, 209-13. The right was to last for twenty-eight years, and if the author were still alive at the end of the period, it would last for the rest of his life, just as it was for literary works under the 1814 Copyright Act.
35   Bill to amend Laws relating Dramatic Literary Property (1833) 2 Parliamentary Papers (73).
36   *Journal of the House of Commons* (1833) LXXXVIII, pp. 246, 310.
37   Ibid., p. 470.
38   3 Geo. III c.15.
39   Dramatic Literature Select Committee, pp. 3-5.
40   *Parl. Deb.*, vol. 16, cols 561-7 (12 March 1833). The bill was passed in the House of Commons but postponed twice in the Lords before being abandoned. *Parl. Deb.*, vol. 20, cols 269-277 (2 August 1833, vol. 24, cols 908-911 (27 June 1834). See also W. Nicholson, *The Struggle for a Free Stage in London* (London: Archibald Constable & Co., 1906), pp. 341-55.

Bulwer Lytton's Act sought to clarify the confusing situation that had resulted from the different approaches taken to unauthorised performances by the Courts of Chancery and Law. The statute provided that the author or assign of any 'tragedy, comedy, play, opera, farce or any other dramatic piece or entertainment' composed but not printed by the author should have the sole liberty of performing or representing the piece at any place of dramatic entertainment. The right also applied to the authors and assigns of plays printed and published within ten years before the passing of the Act and any plays printed and published after the passing of the Act. For plays that were not printed, the right granted was perpetual; for printed plays it would last for twenty-eight years and, if the author were still alive at the end of that period, for the rest of his life.[41] The penalty for breaching the Act was to be forty shillings, or the amount of benefit derived from the representation, or the loss occasioned by the plaintiff.[42]

The Dramatic Copyright Act appeared to bring dramatic authors, and their assigns, into the copyright fold, alongside the authors and publishers of printed books. However, the operation of the Act was far from straightforward. First came the question of how the new right was to be administered and enforced. In the case of printed books, there was physical evidence in existence to establish whether copyright was being observed, but a play was ephemeral, existing only at the time of its performance and leaving no trace once that was ended. A new body, the Dramatic Authors' Society, was set up to address this situation. Planché and Bulwer Lytton were, of course, members, as were many of the other leading dramatists of the day, including Douglas Jerrold, James Sheridan Knowles, Edward Fitzball, Charles Dance and Richard Brinsley Peake.[43] The Society's main aim was to facilitate the dealings of dramatic authors with the provincial theatres. The usual practice in London was for dramatists to grant a theatre the right to perform a play for a certain amount of time, or forever, but it was far harder for the dramatists to deal with the theatres outside the capital. Giving evidence before a Select Committee on theatrical licences in 1866, the Society's then secretary, Joseph Stirling Coyne, explained that the Society had been established at the suggestion and wish of the provincial managers themselves.[44] Doubt is

41   3 Will. IV c.15, s. 1.

42   3 Will. IV c.15, s. 2.

43   Stevens, *The Profession of the Playwright*, p. 175; D. Barratt, 'The Dramatic Authors' Society (1833-1883) and the Payment of English Dramatists', *Essays in English Theatre*, 7 (1988), 19-33 (pp. 21-2).

44   Select Committee to inquire into Working of Acts for Licensing and Regulating of Theatres and Places of Public Entertainment (1866) 16 Parliamentary Papers

cast on this, however, by Planché's recollection that the managers raised an outcry at the bill's introduction.[45]

The system operated by the Society changed several times throughout its fifty year life span. The Society began by asking provincial managers to send a list of the plays they had performed, which were charged on a fixed scale according to how many acts the play had and the size and location of the theatre performing it.[46] This system of uniform pricing, however, was undermined by the preferential treatment given to Sheridan Knowles, the most famous playwright of the day. Sheridan Knowles was allowed to set prohibitively high prices for his plays, his objective being to earn greater profits by acting in them himself. By the 1840s, managers could negotiate with individual dramatists for reduced rates and in the Society's list of 1840, many plays appeared at different prices to the standard ones. By 1866, the system had changed yet again, and instead of provincial managers submitting periodical lists of plays they had performed, they were required to pay a certain sum of money based upon the size of the theatre, and other factors, in return for which they could put on any play on the Society's list.[47] The London managers, however, continued to make arrangements on an individual basis.[48]

By the 1860s, however, the Society began to be affected by the growing status and prosperity of dramatic authors; ironically, the very change it had sought to achieve. A number of leading dramatists, such as Dion Boucicault, Francis Burnand, T.W. Robertson and W.S. Gilbert, left the Society, as they could obtain better remuneration by negotiating individual prices with managers. In response, the Society revised its rules by allowing members to retain rights in popular plays for a certain period before they would enter the Society's list.[49]

In addition to internal disunity, the Society faced other obstacles. Chief amongst these was non-compliance by the provincial managers, who had been accustomed to performing plays without payment and either avoided or did not understand the new system. Particularly problematic were travelling companies. In 1866, Stirling Coyne complained before the Select

(373), pp. 209-10.
45   Planché, p. 202.
46   Barratt, p. 21.
47   Ibid., pp. 21-4.
48   Royal Commission on Laws and Regulations relating to Home, Colonial and Foreign Copyrights (1878) 24 Parliamentary Papers [C.2036], p. 120 (hereafter: 'Royal Copyright Commission').
49   Barrett, pp. 26-9; Stevens, *The Profession of the Playwright*, pp. 179-80.

Committee of 'certain managers, disreputable and dishonest men, who go about from theatre to theatre, and do not pay'.[50] The same concerns were reiterated before the 1878 Copyright Commission by the current secretary, John Palgrave Simpson.[51] Both men complained that the means of recovering the penalties against such managers through the bringing of proceedings at common law was frequently ineffective, as well as expensive. The petition presented by Simpson also complained that the remedy of forty shillings was wholly inadequate to ensure compliance with the Act.[52]

Clearly, not all the parties involved understood the operations of the Society. One such example can be seen in a case that Planché brought against Hooper, the lessee of the Theatre Royal at Bath, for representing his play, *White Cat*, without permission. Counsel for Hooper argued that if he had committed an offence it was unintentional, and he had 'been drawn into his present very disagreeable situation without any fault of his own by the conduct of the Society of Dramatic Authors'.[53] Apparently, Hooper had been under the impression that as long as he sent a monthly file of the plays performed to the Society he was entitled to represent a play even without the author's consent. The Court, however, instructed the jury that if they were satisfied that the *White Cat* was a dramatic entertainment, that Planché was the author, and the play was performed without his consent, then they must find for the plaintiff, which they accordingly did. The Dramatic Authors' Society was itself hampered by its own inability to bring prosecutions to recover penalties. Simpson complained about this also before the Royal Copyright Commission, noting that the Society's application to register under the Friendly Societies Act 1875, which would allow them to sue as a body, had been rejected by the Treasury on the grounds that the Society's purposes appeared to amount to a restraint of trade.[54]

Another obstacle lay in the fact that the Act had not completely clarified the law on performances of dramatic works. Indeed, it had added new uncertainties. What was meant by a 'dramatic piece' and a 'place of dramatic entertainment'? What counted as a 'representation'? The latter question was tested in Court by Planché, who brought an action against the manager John Braham. Braham had commissioned the libretto to Weber's

50   Select Committee to inquire into Working of Acts for Licensing and Regulating of Theatres and Places of Public Entertainment (1866) 16 Parliamentary Papers (373), p. 209.
51   Royal Copyright Commission, p. 121.
52   Ibid., App. VIII, p. 354.
53   *Planché v. Hooper*, *The Times*, 19 January 1844, p. 7c.
54   Royal Copyright Commission, pp. 121-2.

opera *Oberon*, but the commissioned version used many of the same words that Planché had used in his libretto of the same piece, which had been performed at Covent Garden with Braham in the principal role. Tindal CJ held that the word 'represent' must be taken to mean 'the bringing forward on stage or place of dramatic representation' and included the singing of one or more songs from a theatrical piece.[55] Planché was ashamed to have used the Dramatic Copyright Act against a respected colleague and referred to the incident as 'one of the most disagreeable recollections of my professional life'.[56] His excuse was that he was acting at the behest of the proprietors of Covent Garden.[57]

The question of what amounted to a 'dramatic piece' was considered in *Lee v. Simpson*[58] and the Court held that the introduction to a pantomime easily fell within the meaning of the statute, despite not being mentioned specifically in the Act. More difficult issues arose in respect of musical works, which will be discussed further below. The question of what was meant by 'place of dramatic entertainment' occupied the Courts on several occasions. In *Russell v. Smith*,[59] Lord Denman CJ held that a lecture room, Crosby Hall, became a place of dramatic entertainment for the purposes of the Act when it was used for the public representation for profit of a dramatic piece. In *Wall v. Taylor; Wall v. Martin*,[60] which will be discussed in more detail below, Brett MR held that 'performing a dramatic piece makes the place where it is performed a place of dramatic entertainment'.[61] He amended this view the following year, however, in *Duck v. Bates*.[62] This case arose when an amateur dramatic club put on a free performance for the staff of St Guy's Hospital of a play called *Our Boys*. Brett MR stated that he may have been interpreted as going too far in the earlier case, as the statute clearly contemplated that there may be some place at which a piece is performed which would not breach the statute. He went on to find that domestic and private performances would not fall within the Act. It was necessary that the representation be 'public' by which was meant 'a representation to which any portion of the public are freely admitted with

---

55   *Planché v. Braham* (1837) 2 Car. & P. 68 (p. 74).
56   Planché, p. 272.
57   Ibid., pp. 270-1.
58   (1847) 3 C.B. 871.
59   [1848] 2 Q.B. 217.
60   (1882-3) L.R. 11 Q.B.D. 102.
61   Ibid., p. 108.
62   [1884] Q.B.D. 843.

or without payment'.[63] In this case, there was no such public representation and, consequently, St Guy's Hospital was not a place of dramatic entertainment. He did however note in *obiter dicta* that representations for charitable objects would fall within the Act and warned that those who went beyond the facts of the particular case might incur the statutory penalties.

Yet another problematic issue was the responsibility of the landlord, or manager, for such unauthorised performances. This was held to turn on the question of knowledge, or *mens rea*. In *Lee v. Simpson*, the defendant argued that he had purchased the play in the *bona fide* belief that he was purchasing it from the author, which was not in fact the case. Wilde CJ held that the knowledge of the person actually representing the dramatic work as to ownership was irrelevant, because 'the object of the legislature was to protect authors against the piratical invasion of their rights'[64] and the statute would altogether fail in this object if it were necessary to show that the defendant had knowledge of the plaintiff's right of property.[65] However, in *Russell v. Briant*, the same judge held that the landlord of the Horn Tavern in Kennington could not be held liable for the unauthorised performance of a dramatic piece, despite the fact that he had provided the venue, advertising and allowed tickets to be sold from the bar, on the basis that 'no one can be considered as an offender against the provisions of [the statute] [...] unless, by himself or his agent, he actually takes part in a representation which is a violation of copyright'.[66] However, in the case of *Marsh v. Conquest*,[67] the manager of a theatre who had no involvement in the performance of a play was found to be liable because he was the owner of the theatre and his son, who was in charge of the representation, was acting with his permission.

Still more fundamental and confusing was the relationship between the copyright in the printed work and the right to perform that work. Once again, Planché was involved in dealing with this issue. However, this time he was defendant to an action brought by the publisher John Cumberland.[68] In 1828, Planché had made an assignment to Cumberland of 'all right, title and interest whatsoever in the copyright' of his farce, *The Greeneyed Monster*. Prior to this assignment, Planché had granted the right to represent the piece to the Haymarket theatre and, after the passing of the Dramatic

---

63 Ibid., p. 848.
64 (1847) 3 C.B. 871 (p. 883).
65 Ibid.
66 (1849) 8 C.B. 836 (p. 848). See also *Lyon v. Knowles* (1863) 3 B. & S. 556; (1864) 5 B. & S. 751.
67 (1864) 17 C.B. (N.S.) 418.
68 *Cumberland v. Planché* (1834) 1 Ad. & E. 580; SC 3 N. & M. 537; L.J. 3 K.B. 194.

Copyright Act, Planché had allowed another theatre to perform the piece. Cumberland, however, claimed that Planché's assignment of the copyright to him meant that it was now Cumberland who had the sole liberty of representing the farce (subject to any rights of the Haymarket theatre), thereby making Planché's purported assignment an infringement of his right.

Cumberland retained Frederick Pollock as counsel, and he argued that Planché's assignment to Cumberland placed him in the same position as if he had been the author, following the Dramatic Copyright Act. Sir James Scarlett argued for Planché that the Act created a new right and could not have been assigned away by the defendant before he possessed it. He contended that the intention of the legislature was to encourage genius, and that any new privileges created must therefore have been intended to be conferred upon the author. Pollock countered that the Act's object was the protection of literary property and so an assignment of copyright must perforce carry with it the right of representation. Lord Denman CJ accepted Pollock's argument that the intention of the Act was to protect literary property and therefore an assignment of the copyright must carry with it the right of representation. He noted that this would not injure future authors, as they would merely sell their rights for a higher price.[69] This outcome was much resented by dramatic authors. In his autobiography, Edward Fitzball recalled:

> The act passed by parliament, in favour of dramatic authors, at this time, the better to allow them to meet with remuneration equal to their labour, proved highly beneficial to me; and would have been more so, had I not previously disposed of so many of my copyrights, to Mr Cumberland, who claimed upon his assignment the new privilege of nightly remuneration for dramatic pieces acted, either in town or country. This event, of course, was never contemplated by the legislature, whose intention was simply to assist literary (and too frequently necessitous) men, not publishers. However, the case was tried with Cumberland by the Authors' Society, and the judge gave it in favour of the forms. (Law but not justice).[70]

The unsatisfactory situation was amended by the 1842 Copyright Act which explicitly provided that assignment of the copyright of a book containing a dramatic piece or musical composition would not convey the right to represent that work unless entry was made in the Registry Book expressing the intention that the right of representation was conveyed.[71] That this

69   (1834) 1 Ad. & E. 580 (pp. 583-6).
70   E. Fitzball, *Thirty-five Years of a Dramatic Authors' Life*, 2 vols. (London: T.C. Newby, 1859), I, pp. 271-2.
71   5 & 6 Vict. c.45, s. 22.

provision acted to prevent an assignment of copyright from automatically conveying the right of representation, or acting, or stage right (as it was sometimes called), was confirmed in the cases of *Lacy v. Rhys*[72] and *Marsh v. Conquest*.[73]

The ongoing confusion over the relationship between the right of representation and printed copyright provided a continuing incentive for dramatic authors not to publish their plays. However, the status of unpublished works was even less clear. In 1865, Stirling Coyne brought an action against the publisher Maxwell for publishing and selling copies of Coyne's play, *The Woman in Red*.[74] Coyne had never published his works and alleged that he had a common law property in his play. The defendant argued that by giving copies of the play to the actors, Coyne had published the work and therefore, as he had not registered it, there was no copyright in it for Maxwell to infringe. Cockburn CJ appeared convinced by Coyne's argument that there was a common law right, but directed him to state the facts in the form of a special case to raise the question for the opinion of the Court.[75] In the event, it seems such a case was never brought.

It is clear that the relationship between copyright and the right of representation was not well understood in the theatrical world. However, it was not just publishers, dramatists and theatre managers who were confused. In the Digest of Copyright Law which Sir James Fitzjames Stephen had prepared prior to the Copyright Commission and which was annexed to the Report, Stephen stated, 'The exclusive right of representing or performing a dramatic piece or musical composition cannot be gained if such dramatic piece of musical composition has been printed and published as a book before the first representation thereof'. He added: 'A dramatic piece or musical composition published as a book may (it seems probable) be publicly represented without the consent of the author or his assigns'.[76]

This is an odd interpretation of section 1 of the 1833 Dramatic Copyright Act which, after providing that the author of an unpublished work should have the sole liberty of representing it, extended the same liberty to 'the Author of any such Production, printed and published within Ten Years before the passing of this Act by the Author thereof or his Assignee, or which

---

72   (1864) 4 B. & S. 873.
73   (1864) 17 C.B. (N.S.) 418. See also *Lacy v. Toole* (1867) *The Times*, 29 April 1867, p. 11c.
74   *Coyne v. Maxwell* (1865), *The Times*, 7 June 1865, p. 11a; *The Times*, 10 June 1865, p. 11a.
75   *The Times*, 10 June 1865, p. 11a.
76   Royal Copyright Commission, pp. lxxiii-lxxiv.

shall hereafter be so printed and published [...]'.[77] Moreover Stephen's view was not shared by Lord Denman who, in the unreported case of *Morton v. Shelders the Elder*, held that even though the plaintiff's play had been printed by the Dramatic Authors' Society, the plaintiff had not lost his right to consent to its performance.[78] In *Chappell v. Boosey*,[79] a case brought by Chappell against Boosey relating to the singing of a song in which Chappell owned the copyright, North J rejected Chappell's argument which relied on the statement of law in Stephen's Digest, stating he was unable to agree with that assessment of the law, and that it ignored the provisions of the 1833 Dramatic Copyright Act and the 1842 Copyright Act.[80] Nor was Stephen's view shared by T.E. Scrutton, in his treatise on copyright law.[81]

If the lawyers were unable to agree on the meaning of the statute, what chance did the general public stand, particularly given its operation was far from intuitive? As Simpson complained before the Commission, a club or society was liable to pay fees to the copyright owner for putting on an amateur dramatic performance even if they had not charged entry money. Moreover, there was no requirement to pay fees in cases where one man recited long passages from a play, but if two men recited passages together, even without costumes or scenery, they were liable to pay fees. If songs were also sung, composers could charge fees or claim the penalty.[82] These subtle distinctions in the statute's operation were not obvious and it is clear from the amount of complaints, as well as litigation generated, that those involved were tripped up time and again.

The situation was still more complex in relation to musical works, which spawned controversies of their own. Although, as mentioned above, the 1842 Copyright Act extended the operation of the 1833 Dramatic Copyright Act to cover 'musical compositions', there remained uncertainty as to whether all music, or just certain types of song, would be covered. In *Russell v. Smith*,[83] which involved the singing of a song called 'The Ship on Fire' in a lecture hall, the defendant argued that the only musical compositions

77   3 Will. IV c.15, s. 1.
78   *The Times*, 1 December 1838, p. 6d. Presumably, the distinction between this case and the earlier decision of *Cumberland v. Planché* was that in the former case there had been an assignment of copyright and none such was in evidence here.
79   (1882) 21 Ch. D. 232.
80   21 ChD 232 (p. 241).
81   T.E. Scrutton, *The Laws of Copyright* (London: William Clowes & Sons, 1883), pp. 134-5.
82   Royal Copyright Commission, p. 125.
83   (1848) 12 Q.B. 217.

intended to be protected were those composed for performance with dramatic pieces. Unfortunately, the Court did not decide on the point, as Lord Denman CJ found that the song in question was a dramatic piece because it had a dramatic subject matter and was sung with great expression. He held that the words 'dramatic piece' should be interpreted widely as any piece which 'would produce the emotions which are the purpose of the regular drama, and which constitute the entertainment of the audience'.[84]

Most music publishers were firmly of the view that only songs used in conjunction with dramatic works, or performed in theatres, music halls or as parts of operas were subject to the statutory penalties. Before the Royal Copyright Commission, John Boosey and Henry Littleton, of Novello's, argued that this was the case.[85] The composer, Arthur Sullivan was similarly of the view that the current law held that only songs sung as 'dramatic works' could be protected.[86] Thomas Chappell, however, was less sure, stating that although there had been no case on the matter, he believed that the singing of a song separately to an opera or dramatic piece would also be subject to the statute.[87]

The position of unpublished musical compositions was also unclear and, when it came before the Court, sparked debate as to whether music should be protected at all. In the case of *Clark v. Bishop*,[88] the plaintiff, a comic vocalist, had purchased a song from a composer, Elton. He sang it in music halls, after which it became very popular, but he never published it. The defendant, Bishop, printed and published the song in a one penny book of songs, whereupon the plaintiff brought an action, alleging that the song was now valueless to him. On appeal, Martin B asked the plaintiff whether he relied on the common law or the statute, to which he responded that he relied on both. With respect to the common law right, he referred to *Donaldson v. Becket* as deciding that a right in unpublished works existed in common law. With respect to the statutes, he argued that the 1842 Copyright Act did not require registration of songs.

Kemp, who was counsel for the defendant, submitted that the song could not be protected by the 1842 Act, which was intended 'to afford greater encouragement to the production of literary works *of lasting benefit to the world*', adding, 'that cannot apply to such a wretchedly worthless

---

84   Ibid., p. 236.
85   Royal Copyright Commission, pp. 102, 118.
86   Ibid., p. 114.
87   Ibid., p. 109.
88   (1872) 25 L.T. (N.S.) 908.

production as the vulgar doggerel which is the subject of the present action'.[89] He argued that there was no infringement, because by singing the song, the plaintiff had given it to the public: 'It is similar to a speech by a demagogue at Blackheath or Primrose-Hill, or by a member of Parliament to his constituents; once uttered, it is published to the whole world, and it is no infringement in a newspaper to print it'.[90] Kemp relied on Pollock CB's opinion in *Jefferys v. Boosey* that allowing copyright in non-physical objects could be easily taken too far. In that case, the Chief Baron had asked, rhetorically: 'And where is it, on principle, to stop? Why is it not to apply to a well-told anecdote or witty reply, so as to forbid the repetition without the permission of the author? And carried to its utmost extent, it would at length descend to lower and meaner objects, and include the tricks of a conjuror or the grimace of a clown'.[91] Kemp concluded by arguing that the mere singing of the song amounted to publication and because the song was unregistered there could be no action for infringement.

Martin B, dissenting, accepted the defendant's case, noting in the course of the argument, 'A man writes a song and sings it in public, and another takes down the words and publishes it. It is new to me if that is actionable'.[92] In his judgment he added that there could be no infringement because printing the words of the song would only increase its reputation and popularity.[93] The rest of the Court, however, agreed with Kelly CB, who held that the singing of a song did amount to publication, but that the song fell within the category of 'dramatic piece' and did not therefore require registration under the 1842 Copyright Act.[94] The Court of Appeal likewise held in *Boucicault v. Chatterton*,[95] following *Boucicault v. Delafield*,[96] that performance amounted to publication.[97]

The music publishers' poor understanding of the right of representation was reflected in their contractual arrangements with composers. Chappell described how he had foreseen fifteen years earlier that there might be a

---

89   Ibid., p. 910.
90   Ibid.
91   Ibid., p. 911.
92   Ibid., p. 910.
93   Ibid., p. 911.
94   Ibid.
95   (1876) 5 Ch D 267.
96   (1863) 33 L.J. 38.
97   In both cases, Dion Boucicault had first represented (but not printed) his plays in the United States of America but the operation of the International Copyright Act 1844 (7 Vict.c.12, s. 19) meant that works first published overseas could not be protected by copyright within the United Kingdom.

problem with the right of representation and began including an assignment of the performing right in his contracts. However, he noted that not all publishers had been so wise, noting 'Mr. Boosey, who is a very clever man of business, and has as large a business as anybody, has not done so'.[98] Arthur Sullivan gave evidence that the performing right had never been included in any of his publishing contracts[99] and the Rev. Bennett referred to a conversation he had had with an employee of Novello's that they did not know which songs they owned the performing rights to.[100] When Littleton, of the same firm, was asked about the difficulties of assignments, he admitted 'I have that book on Copyright by Copinger but it is very difficult to follow it'.[101]

The issue was in fact litigated in the 1878 case of *Re the Songs 'Kathleen Mavourneen' and 'Dermot Astore' ex parte Hutchins & Romer*.[102] In this case, the composer of the songs, Crouch, had assigned 'all his present and future contingent and vested copyright in the musical compositions, and the sole and exclusive right and liberty of printing and publishing the same under 5 & 6 Vict. c.45 and the Copyright Acts' to the publishers D'Almaine and McKinlay in 1843. In 1868, the executors of McKinlay had assigned to Hutchings and Romer their interest, whether copyright or otherwise 'and also of representing and performing the same'. In 1878, Crouch had assigned the 'sole liberty of performing or singing' the songs to J.F. Adams. Hutchings and Romer brought a motion to expunge Adams' subsequent entry of proprietorship in the Registry Book.

In the Queen's Bench Division, Cockburn CJ upheld the motion on the basis that Adams could not own the right of representation, as the 1842 Act did not have retrospective effect. Because the songs had been published before the Act was passed, the right of representation had already been given to the public and could not, therefore, be owned by anyone.[103] The judgment was upheld on appeal, but on a different basis.[104] The Court of Appeal found that the 1842 Act did indeed have retrospective effect, but that the outcome turned on the words used in Crouch's assignment. Accepting that *Cumberland v. Planché* was no longer good law, the Court nonetheless held that Crouch's words had been so expansive in 1843 as to pass the right of representation as well as the copyright. Consequently, Crouch had

98   Royal Copyright Commission, p. 106.
99   Ibid., p. 114.
100 Ibid., p. 116.
101 Royal Copyright Commission, p. 119.
102 [1878] L.R. 4 Q.B. 90; [1878-9] L.R. 4 Q.B. 483.
103 [1878] L.R. 4 Q.B. 90 (p. 94).
104 [1878-9] L.R. 4 Q.B. 483.

conveyed to D'Almaine and McKinlay the right of representation and could not, therefore, assign it to Adams.

One person who had quickly understood the opportunities offered by the Dramatic Copyright Act and its extension to music in 1842 was the infamous Harry Wall. Wall was married to a comic singer, Annie Adams, and it was possibly this connection which had given him the idea of setting up a business, which he called the Authors', Composers' and Artists' Copyright Protection Office, based upon the statutory penalties provided for in the 1833 and 1842 Acts. Wall's business consisted of collecting fees for unauthorised performances of songs, often by deceased composers whose assigns had given Wall power of attorney.[105] Thus, he takes his place in history as the world's first "copyright troll".[106]

The musical world was outraged by Wall's effrontery at exploiting the statutory penalties. From 1876, complaints about his activities appeared in the musical press. The first to complain was a T. Backhouse who had received a letter from Wall demanding two pounds after he held a concert at which one of the singers sang a song by Wallace.[107] The music publishers also raised the matter before the Royal Copyright Commission. Thomas Chappell said he had refused to deal with Wall when approached because he 'did not like the character of the man or the character of the proceedings',[108] later adding that such things were done by 'people who do not care anything for the work or anything else, all they want is the money they can get'.[109] John Boosey said that 'no living composer cared to employ' him[110] and Anthony Trollope spoke of a 'mercenary, vulgar, and I may say, immoral person'.[111] Evidence was also given that ladies would be discouraged from singing songs in public for fear of receiving letters from agents such as Wall demanding money.[112] Wall was clearly of a class with which the publishers did not care to mix. Born Henry Whiting, Wall had a criminal record, having been imprisoned in 1860 for eighteen months after being found guilty of unlawfully receiving property obtained under false pretence.[113]

105   Royal Copyright Commission, pp. 101, 105-6.
106   I am indebted to Lionel Bently for this apposite description of Wall's activities.
107   *The Musical Times*, 1 February 1876, p. 371. See also *The Musical Times*, 1 March 1876, pp. 394-5, 1 May 1876, p. 471.
108   Ibid., p. 106.
109   Ibid., p. 109.
110   Ibid., p. 101.
111   Ibid., p. 194.
112   Ibid., p. 115.
113   Old Bailey Proceedings Online, May 1860, trial of Henry Whiting (t18600507-491) www.oldbaileyonline [accessed 20/11/2008].

Moreover, the composers and music publishers were not convinced that charging money for performances was to their advantage. Their market revolved around sales of sheet music. The music publisher John Boosey gave evidence that the collection of fees would interfere with a composer's profits, as performance was what made music popular and stimulated sales.[114] Charles Purday likewise thought that composers should be glad to have songs sung, to make them known, and that this was also the best arrangement for publishers.[115] The composer Arthur Sullivan suggested that there should be a small fee, which in most cases composers would not collect, and no penalty for non-payment. Again, he based his views on his belief that the sale of a work depended on the popularity it acquired through performance.[116] While Sullivan supported extending the right to collect such a small fee in respect of more than just 'dramatic performances', for him the real value would lie in obtaining the power to stop his songs being sung in undesirable contexts, such as burlesques, in the street or by people with bad voices.[117] The difference between the attitudes of music composers and publishers towards the right of performance and those of dramatic authors can probably be ascribed to the strength of the market for sheet music when compared to the comparatively weak market for printed dramatic works for much of the nineteenth century.[118]

The amount of money that ought to be collected for unauthorised performances was also contentious. The 1833 Act, it may be recalled, provided that every offender would be liable for not less than forty shillings for each representation.[119] Thomas Chappell pointed out that while this might be a reasonable sum for an opera, it was excessive for the singing of a single, or even several, songs on their own. In his view, a shilling would be more appropriate.[120] This related to another objection made to Wall's mode of doing business. Rather than acting as soon as he discovered a song he owned, or for which he was the agent, was being performed, he would wait until the performance had run on for many nights, and then collect a much

114 Royal Copyright Commission, p. 102. See also the evidence of T. Chappell, ibid., p. 106.
115 Ibid., p. 193.
116 Ibid., p. 113.
117 Ibid., pp. 113-4.
118 See: Stevens, *The Profession of the Playwright*, Ch. 5; Martin R. Booth, 'Public Taste, the Playwright and the Law', in *The Revels History of Drama in English*, ed. by Clifford Leech and T.W. Craik, 8 vols. (London: Methuen & Co., 1975) VI, pp. 29-57 (p. 52).
119 3 Will. IV c.15, s. 2.
120 Royal Copyright Commission, pp. 106-7.

larger sum in respect of each performance.[121]

Related to this ongoing confusion about the different rights was a further concern. Even if the general public could be educated to realise that purchasing a printed copy of a play or piece of music did not automatically bring with it the right to perform it, how would they know to whom they should apply for permission? This question was raised before the 1878 Copyright Commission by several witnesses.[122] The Commission accepted this problem, and recommended that 'every musical composition should bear on its title page a note stating whether the right of public performance is reserved, and the name and address of the person to whom application for performance should be made'.[123] Furthermore, it recommended that instead of the penalty being automatically assessed at forty shillings, the Courts should award compensation by reference to the damage sustained.

This was the only one of the Commission's many recommendations to be enacted with any promptness, and the impetus was provided by growing complaints about Harry Wall's business and behaviour, which soon spilled into the mainstream press. An editorial in the *Times* complained that Wall gave no quarter to those arranging concerts for charitable purposes and echoed complaints before the Royal Copyright Commission as to the difficulty of ascertaining who owned the performance right.[124] As was noted before the Commission, Wall did have a list of works he was 'policing' but refused to make it available without payment.[125] Trying to address this issue, the *Musical Times* published a list of Wall's pieces that had come to their attention in December 1883 and warned vocalists and concert-givers not to sing these songs.[126]

Complaints about Wall also reached the ears of Parliament. In May 1882, Wall brought proceedings against an amateur singer, for singing 'She wore a wreath of roses', the copyright of which had been assigned to Wall, at an entertainment at a working man's club in Bishops Stortford.[127] Manisty J found for Wall, and awarded him a penalty of two pounds and costs. A week later, John Eldon Gorst, MP for Chatham, complained in Parliament that recently persons had been prosecuted for singing songs at penalty

---

121   Ibid., p.106.
122   Ibid., p. 116 (Rev. J.W. Bennett), p. 119 (Henry Littleton).
123   Ibid., p. xxviii.
124   *The Times*, 10 June 1882, p. 11g. Similar complaints were made in *The Musical Times*, 1 May 1877, pp. 214-6, 1 November 1880, p. 567, 1 December 1883, p. 684.
125   Royal Copyright Commission, p. 116.
126   *The Musical Times*, 1 December 1883, p. 684.
127   *Wall v. Harris* (unreported), *The Times*, 2 May 1882, p. 6b.

readings, and he introduced a bill to deal with the issue.[128] This bill provided that any copyright owner who wished to retain the right of performing that work should print a notice on the front of the work saying that performance could only take place with his permission.[129] Indeed, in a letter to *The Era* on 1 July 1882, Wall advocated this very solution. Defensively, but defiantly, he wrote:

> I do not (and never did) pretend to protect the interests of music, art, the public, professionals, or amateurs. I cannot, at present, afford to be so generous. I merely seek to protect and enhance my own interests – singularly selfish individual that I am. And I learn from the creators of the respective productions that they themselves would have been only too glad to have done the same, but they did not know that, or how, they could do so.[130]

In 1882, after some discussion, and amendments in both Houses of Parliament, the bill was enacted.[131] It provided that copyright owners who wished to retain the exclusive right of public performance must print a notice on the title page of every published copy stating that the right or public representation or performance was reserved. It also provided that the award of costs of any action should be in the Court's discretion.[132] As Scrutton pointed out, the Act's failure to inflict a penalty on an owner who did not print such a notice was a serious flaw, and the Act was completely ineffectual in halting Wall's activities.[133] Shortly after the bill became law, Wall brought two further actions to recover penalties for unauthorised performances.[134] In both cases, the jury found for Wall but had awarded him a mere one shilling in damages, while the Judge ordered him to pay the defendant's costs. The refusal to award the statutory penalties was based on the judge's finding that the penalties did not apply if the work was not performed in a 'place of dramatic entertainment', following *Russell v. Smith*.[135] Wall sought a new trial and, as noted above, the Queen's Bench found that any performance in public fell under the 1842 Copyright Act,

128 *Parl. Deb.*, vol. 269, col. 354, 9 May 1882.
129 A bill to amend the law relating to musical compositions (1882) 1 *Parliamentary Papers* (161), p. 571.
130 *Era*, 1 July 1887, p. 4.
131 *Parl. Deb.*, vol. 270, cols 1715-8, 20 June 1882, vol. 272, cols 428-9, 14 July 1882. 45 & 46 Vict. c.40.
132 45 & 46 Vict. c.40, ss. 1, 4.
133 Scrutton (1883), p. 160. This problem was raised, and the Act's drafting criticised, in *Fuller v. The Blackpool Winter Gardens and Pavilion Company Limited and Another* [1895] 2 Q.B. 429.
134 *Wall v. Taylor; Wall v. Martin* (1882) QBD 727.
135 Ibid., p. 728.

and there was no need to prove that it occurred in a place of dramatic entertainment. The Court awarded Wall forty shillings for each case and costs in his favour. The decisions were upheld on appeal, but reluctantly.[136] Brett MR commented that 'the action ought never to have been brought either for damages or penalties, and that it was an attempt to make money out of what had really not done the plaintiff any harm'.[137] The other judges agreed and, although the penalty award was upheld, the Court did not award costs to Wall.

Over the next few years Wall continued to bring actions, either in his own name, or in the name of the copyright owner. At one point, it was alleged that he was responsible for over seventy such actions.[138] Moreover, he seems to have spawned a number of similar operations. In the unreported case of *McGlennon v. Murphy*, for example, McGlennon told the Court that he and Wall had a reciprocal arrangement, whereby each informed the other if his songs were being sung.[139] Whilst complaints continued to be made about Wall in the press, soon the tide began to turn. Wall's actions, though much despised, had drawn attention to the issue. In January 1886, several letters were written charging the managers of theatres, and owners of copyrights, with naivety. One writer, signing himself 'The Guv'nor' wrote that managers 'are not sufficiently practical for their own interests (beyond baiting an artiste for a few shillings less than the salary paid for him) to get into their heads a little common-sense law'.[140] He proposed getting singers to sign contracts saying they would not sign any song unless they could prove that the rights had been paid for. Another letter noted that Wall had:

> [O]pened the eyes of song-writers to the fact that they are as much entitled to the protection of the law as any other of Her Majesty's liege subjects, and it therefore behoves proprietors, if only as a matter of business, to be on their guard against those unprincipled persons who would rather steal a song than pay for it, and who, knowing they are not themselves worth proceeding against, are careless of the consequences to their employers.[141]

In 1886, attempts to amend the 1882 Act began to be brought before Parliament. Addison MP brought a bill in March, and the following August, which sought to remove the fixed penalty of two pounds per infringement,

---

136   (1882-3) LR 11 QB 102 (CA).
137   Ibid., p. 108.
138   *The Times*, 4 August 1888, p. 10e.
139   *Era*, 17 July 1886, p. 8.
140   *Era*, 30 January 1886, p. 10.
141   Ibid.

but both times it was dropped. In March 1888, Addison once more introduced a bill and this time it was considered in committee and a few amendments made.[142] In the House of Commons there was no dissent as to the objectives of the bill, but the case was different in the Lords. The Secretary of the Board of Trade, the Earl of Onslow, introduced the bill as being needed to correct 'a very great abuse'.[143] By way of example, he referred to the case of a penalty being exacted from a thirteen year old girl.[144] Lord Bramwell and Lord Halsbury, the Lord Chancellor, however, opposed the bill. Lord Bramwell argued that it sought to take away from people a right which they possessed at present and for which they had paid money.[145] He further added that if he were the father of the 'dear little girl' he should have been glad to have paid what was only a just debt.[146]

Despite this opposition, the bill was eventually passed by both Houses and became law on 5 July 1888. The resulting Act provided that the penalty or damages to be awarded in cases involving unauthorised representations or performances should be in the discretion of the Court and 'reasonable', or even a nominal penalty. In addition, it provided that the costs of such actions should be in the discretion of the judge and proprietors of premises in which such unauthorised performances occurred should not be liable unless they wilfully caused or permitted the performance, knowing it to be unauthorised.[147]

1888 was a bad year for Wall. In January his son was cited for adultery in divorce proceedings. Wall appeared as witness in the case and was accused of complicity in the affair.[148] But worse was to come. In August, the Incorporated Law Society was alerted to certain irregularities in Wall's operation by counsel of one of Wall's defendants.[149] The Law Society brought an action against Wall for acting as a solicitor without being qualified to do so. He was found to have contravened section 32 of the Solicitors Act and sentenced to three months in gaol.[150] The imprisonment of Wall is

---

142 *Parl. Deb.*, vol. 324, col. 592, 6 April 1888.
143 *Parl. Deb.*, vol. 325, col. 296, 24 April 1888.
144 *Parl. Deb.*, vol. 325, col. 297, 24 April 1888.
145 *Parl. Deb.*, vol. 325, col. 298, 24 April 1888.
146 *Parl. Deb.*, vol. 325, col. 1329, 4 May 1888.
147 51 & 52 Vict. c.17, ss. 1, 2, 3.
148 *Dunn v. Dunn and Wall* and *Dunn v. Dunn* (unreported), *Lloyd's Weekly Newspaper*, 29 January 1888, p. 7.
149 *Era*, 4 August 1888, p. 8.
150 *In re a Solicitor and in re Wall, an Unqualified Person* (unreported), *The Times*, 4 August 1888, p. 10e. Wall's appeal was unsuccessful: *The Times*, 10 August 1888, p. 3c.

an appropriate point to end this story. While Wall's character, motivation and business practices may have been unsavoury to his contemporaries, it is undeniable that his actions played a significant role in revealing the economic potential of the right to perform musical works as distinct from dramatic works. At the same time, however, Wall may also have retarded the formation of a society, similar to the Dramatic Authors' Society, which could administer the performance right. Rather than embracing the opportunities opened up by the new right they had been granted, composers, music publishers and other interested parties became fixated on the Wall 'problem'. As a consequence, they convinced Parliament to pass two Acts that were not only ineffectual, but shortly to become obsolete when they conflicted with Britain's international obligations under the Berlin Revision to the Berne Convention which required the abolition of all formalities.

The story of the birth and formative years of the performance right in Britain aptly illustrates a number of the broader themes to be found in the history of copyright. One such theme is the expansion of copyright's reach beyond mere protection of the printed word. Many of today's commentators on copyright law have expressed concern about copyright's ever-increasing 'colonisation' of new territories, and the story of the origins of the performance right can be seen as an example of this. However, what is more interesting is that this was not a 'natural' expansion, nor a battle that was easily won by those seeking greater protection of their creative works. Indeed, the expansion of copyright to the spoken and sung word was contentious for much of the nineteenth century. Frequently scepticism was displayed as to whether it was both possible and desirable to protect such ephemeral and intangible things as plays and songs. It is noteworthy that it was not for one hundred and twenty years after the passing of the much vaunted 'first copyright Act' that the right to perform a work was recognised in legislation. This is in marked contrast to the situation in France, where it was a dispute between dramatists and the Comédie Française which led to the debates over literary property in France in the period 1791-3.[151] The formation of the first French society to protect the interests of dramatic authors predated this, the Société des Auteurs Dramatiques being formed in 1777.[152]

---

151   See J. Ginsburg, 'A Tale of Two Copyrights: Literary Property in Revolutionary France and America', *Tulane Law Review*, 64 (1990), 991-1031; G.S. Brown, *Literary Sociability and Literary Property in France, 1775-1793: Beaumarchais, the Société des Auteurs Dramatiques and the Comédie Française* (Aldershot, England: Ashgate, 2006); F. Rideau, 'Dramatic Copyright Act (1870)', *Primary Sources*.

152   For a history of the Société des Auteurs Dramatiques, see Brown.

The story of Wall may also serve as a timely reminder of how focussing on one particular perceived problem can lead to short-sighted and short term solutions. These points can be brought under a still more general theme of copyright's history, which is the observation that the current form of copyright is not 'natural' or 'inevitable'. Laws, not just copyright laws, frequently give this impression because of the authority they carry and their foundation in precedent. Copyright law does even more so, due to the influence of natural rights arguments. Today the right to perform a work is one of the main, if not *the* main, sources of revenue for composers and dramatists, not to mention their assigns and employers. But it is important to remember that it was not always thus, and need not have been so.

13. The Return of the Commons – Copyright History as a Common Source

Karl-Nikolaus Peifer*

Introduction

The recent history of copyright law arguably has been shaped by an Anglo-American understanding of copyright as property. The integration of intellectual property rights into the global trade system with the WTO TRIPS Agreement,[1] the WIPO Internet Treaties[2] and subsequent implementations reveal a *droit d'auteur* concept in retreat, even in the European Union. The central economic premise of the property-based approach is one of exclusivity and control. In a paradigm of scarcities, incentives can be best provided by dictating terms of use. In the digital environment, this logic has helped the publishing and entertainment industries to defend technological measures of exclusion even at the price of restricting the legitimate use of copyright limitations.[3]

*   An earlier version of this article was published under the title 'Common Access and Creative Commons – Copyright History as a Helpful Source?', *International Review of Industrial Property and Copyright Law*, 6 (2008), 679-88. This article has been included within this collection with the kind permission of the editors of the *IIC*.
1   Agreement on Trade-Related Aspects of Intellectual Property Rights (TRIPS), Annex 1C of the Marrakesh Agreement Establishing the World Trade Organization, 15 April 1994.
2   WIPO Copyright Treaty (WCT) and WIPO Performances and Phonograms Treaty (WPPT), adopted 1996. The WCT entered into force on 6 March 2002; the WPPT entered into force on 20 May 2002.
3   German courts have interpreted copyright limitations narrowly in the past, stating that exclusivity is the principle and free use the exception, see BGH (German

Contrary to the legal enforcement of the access control paradigm, the open access movement is based on a premise of knowledge dissemination. It has its recent origins in software development,[4] but grew rapidly to embrace the community of scholars and scientists. The digital archive *Primary Sources on Copyright (1450-1900)*[5] that is the catalyst of this edited volume is an example of the growing importance of such open content projects.

This chapter argues that the 'return of the commons' has a credible source in the history of copyright itself. It is the information broker that may be conceived as the heart of a copyright theory rooted in the Enlightenment.[6] In the German context, this alternative reading of copyright history, centred on the personality interests of the author, draws on the concepts of Pütter (1774), Kant (1785) and Fichte (1793),[7] and the jurisprudential tradition of Neustetel (1824), Bluntschli (1853), Gareis (1877) and Kohler (1880).[8] These texts, made available for the first time to an English speaking audience on the *Primary Sources* database, help us understand how property interest (of

Supreme Court) in BGHZ, vol. 50, p. 147 (p. 152) – Kandinsky I; vol. 116, p. 305 (p. 308); vol. 154, p. 260; with critique, however, German Constitutional Court (BVerfG), Gewerblicher Rechtsschutz und Urheberrecht (GRUR) 2001, p. 149 – Germania III. It is disputed whether copyright limitations may be set aside by contractual provisions or technical protection measures, see Schack, 'Schutz digitaler Werke vor privater Vervielfältigung – zu den Auswirkungen der Digitalisierung auf § 53 UrhG', *ZUM*, (2002), 497 (p. 502).

4   The Free Software Foundation was established in 1985: http://www.fsf.org/philosophy [accessed 2/3/2010].

5   *Primary Sources*.

6   Karl-Nikolaus Peifer, *Individualität im Zivilrecht* (Individuality in Private Law) (Tübingen: Mohr Siebeck, 2001), p. 397.

7   Johann Stephan Pütter, *Der Büchernachdruck nach ächten Grundsätzen des Rechts* (Göttingen: Vandenhoek, 1774); see 'Pütter, The Reprinting of Books', *Primary Sources*. Immanuel Kant, 'Von der Unrechtmäßigkeit des Büchernachdrucks', *Berlinische Monatsschrift*, 5 (1785), 403-17; see: 'Kant, On the Unlawfulness of Reprinting (1785)', *Primary Sources*. Johann Gottlieb Fichte, 'Beweis der Unrechtmäßigkeit des Büchernachdrucks. Ein Räsonnement und eine Parabel', *Berlinische Monatsschrift*, 21 (1793), 443-82; 'Fichte, Proof of the Unlawfulness of Reprinting (1793)', *Primary Sources*.

8   Leopold Joseph Neustetel, *Der Büchernachdruck nach Römischem Recht betrachtet* (Heidelberg: Groos, 1824), p. 30; see 'Neustetel: The Reprinting of Books (1824)', *Primary Sources*. Johann Kaspar Bluntschli, *Deutsches Privatrecht*, 2 vols (München: Literarisch-artistische Anstalt, 1853-4), I, p. 188; see 'Bluntschli: On Author's Rights (1853)', *Primary Sources*. Karl Gareis, *Das juristische Wesen der Autorrechte sowie des Firmen-und Markenschutzes* (1877), pp. 185, 187 et seq; see 'Gareis: Juridical Nature of Author's Rights (1877)', *Primary Sources*. Josef Kohler, *Das Autorrecht – eine zivilistische Abhandlung* (Jena: Fischer, 1880), p. 2; see 'Kohler: Author's Right (1880)', *Primary Sources*.

control) and individual interests (of authenticity) could drift apart during the eighteenth and nineteenth centuries. They may also offer us the kernel to a solution for the current crisis of the copyright system.

The Crisis of the Copyright System

Copyright law, as well as the entire system of Intellectual Property Rights, has fallen into a deep crisis of acceptance with respect to not only users and consumers, but creators also.

Copyright-related rights for databases and digital rights management systems have facilitated an ever increasing control not only of content expression but also of physical layers and codes.[9] The resulting pricing and distribution policies have led to a fundamental examination and critique of the role of copyright in an information society.[10] Scholars have reacted by developing many of the publishing functions which publishing houses originally fulfilled.[11] While remaining sensitive to the need to authenticate content, the proprietary logic fostered by the economic analysis of legal institutions,[12] and readily adopted by the entertainment and publishing industries, is being rejected.[13]

---

9 Lawrence Lessig, *The Future of Ideas. The Fate of the Commons in a Connected World* (New York: Random House, 2001), p. 37.

10 Reto M. Hilty, *Urheberrecht in der Informationsgesellschaft* (Copyright in the Information Age) (Zeitschrift für Urheber – und Medienrecht Sonderheft, 2003), pp. 983-1005. Rainer Kuhlen, 'Wem gehört die Information im 21. Jahrhundert?', in *Wem gehört die Information im 21. Jahrhundert?* (Who Owns Information in the 21st Century?), ed. by Thomas Dreier and Alfred Büllesbach (Köln: Schmidt, 2004), pp. 1-9.

11 Some of the examples developed at the University of Cologne are described in Karl-Nikolaus Peifer and Gudrun Gersmann, *Forschung und Lehre im Information-szeitalter – zwischen Zugangsfreiheit und Privatisierungsanreiz* (Research and Learning in the Information Age – Between Freedom of Access and Exclusivity) (Berlin: de Gruyter, 2007), p. 9.

12 Gerhard Prosi, *Ökonomische Theorie des Buches* (Economic Theory of the Book) (Düsseldorf: Bertelsmann, 1971); William M. Landes and Richard A. Posner, 'An Economic Analysis of Copyright Law', *Journal of Legal Studies*, XVIII (1989), 325-63.

13 Karl-Nikolaus Peifer, 'Urheberrechtliche Rahmenbedingungen von Open-Access-Konzepten' (Copyright Framwork for Open-Access-Concepts), in *Forschung und Lehre im Informationszeitalter*, ed. by Karl-Nikolaus Peifer and Gersmann (Berlin: de Gruyter, 2007), p. 39; see also Karl-Nikolaus Peifer, 'Zur rechtlichen Problematik des Elektronischen Publizierens' (Legal Problems of Electronic Publishing), in CLIO (Hg.), *Elektronisches Publizieren in den Geisteswissenschaften: Erfahrungen, Probleme, Perspektiven* (Berlin: CLIO, 2007), pp. 172-90. (Available online at: http://edoc. hu-berlin.de/histfor/10_I/. [accessed 2/3/2010]).

Those who tell the story of copyright law as a story of property interests will, in general, applaud any new type of protection. Those who speak of personality interests will doubt that this protection is well-suited for creators and intellectual innovations. The dichotomy of copyright as a means of appropriation and as a means of personal protection therefore lies at the heart of the history of copyright law. The 'battle of the booksellers' may be told as a story of the balance between a property function and an authenticity function. We can locate the intellectual roots of both functions in the eighteenth and the nineteenth century. They mark the division of the copyright world into the different concepts of copyright as economic incentive and *droit d'auteur*. Access to the primary sources from this time may let us begin to understand how the Western World could fall into these two factions.

I will argue that the incentive rationale has yet to discover a convincing user- and creator-friendly basis upon which to advocate an author's right. In a globalised world, the economic rationale favours exporters and may block creation. This gap may be filled by revisiting the concept of author's rights in the Kantian tradition. The publishing and entertainment industries have always used, and still use author-centric arguments to campaign for economic interests. Therefore, access to this earlier public discourse, and an understanding of the history of this discourse, is necessary to reconceive author's rights that carry public acceptance.

The Property Function and the Development of Anglo-American Copyright Law

For the Anglo-American copyright regime the basic questions are as follows: to what extent will copyright legislation incentivise the creation of new work and so benefit the public? And to what extent will the monopoly be detrimental to the public?[14] Both questions are implicit in the Copyright Clause

---

14   See the Report for the US-House of Representatives: H.R. Rep No. 222, 60th Cong. 2d Sess 7 (1909), quoted in Meville B. Nimmer and David Nimmer, *Nimmer on Copyright*, 11 vols (Matthew Bender), VIII, App. 13: 'The enactment of copyright legislation by Congress under the terms of the Constitution is not based upon any natural right that the author has in his writings, for the Supreme Court has held that such rights as he has are purely statutory rights, but upon the ground that the welfare of the public will be served and progress of science and useful arts will be promoted by securing to authors for limited periods the exclusive rights to their writings' (p. 10); 'The Constitution does not establish copyrights, but provides that Congress shall have the power to grant such rights if it thinks best. Not primarily

of the US Constitution, which itself is grounded in the development of copy-right law and the battle of the booksellers in eighteenth century England.[15] The decisive conflict to be solved at that time concerned the control of the material work, the book, in the interest of those who invested money in the fixation and distribution of the same, namely the publishers.[16] This develop-ment did not mean a negation of the author; however, the author's interest was exclusively used to legitimate the publisher's position.[17] As Mark Rose puts it, the author was made a proprietor by the Statute of Anne to legiti-mate the publisher's monopoly. Prior to the eighteenth century, privileges for individual printers, as well as for the Stationer's Company, served to foster the national printing industries.[18] However, privileges had also been used to exercise censorship and control[19] and to bring money to the Crown.[20] By combining economic and political functions through privileges and propri-etorship rules, a freedom of distribution argument developed considerable strength.[21] The Star Chamber Decree system,[22] and the regulatory regimes

for the benefit of the author, but primarily for the benefit of the public, such rights are given' (p. 11). See also the Senate Rep No. 1108, 60th Cong. 2d Sess. 7 (1909).

15   *Donaldson v. Becket* (1774) Eng. Rep. 837 (H.L.); see also '*Donaldson v. Becket* (1774)', *Primary Sources*.

16   Robert Dittrich, 'Der Werkbegriff – sinnvolle Ausdehnung oder Denaturier-ung?' (The Notion of Copyrightable work – Reasonable Extension or Denaturation), in *Woher kommt das Urheberrecht?*, ed. by Robert Dittrich (Vienna: MANZ'sche, 1988), pp. 214-37 (p. 218).

17   Mark Rose, *The Author as a Proprietor. The Invention of Copyright* (Cambridge, MA: Harvard, 1993); John Feather, 'Authors, Publishers and Politicians: The History of Copyright and the Book Trade', *European Intellectual Property Review*, 12 (1988), 377-80.

18   Richard Rogers Bowker, *Copyright: Its History and Its Law* (Boston and New York: Hougton Mifflin Company, 1912), pp. 19 et seq.

19   See: Ronan Deazley, 'Commentary on the Stationers' Charter (1557)', *Primary Sources*; Albert Osterrieth, *Geschichte des Urheberrechts in England* (Leipzig, 1895), reprinted in *UFITA*, 131 (1996), 171 (p. 192); William Cornish and David Llewelyn, *Intellectual Property: Patents, Copyright, Trade Marks and Allied Rights* (London: Sweet & Maxwell, 2007), pp. 375-8.

20   Thomas Edward Scrutton, *The Law of Copyright*, 4th ed. (London: William Clowes & Sons, 1903), pp. 10 et seq.

21   See the complaint by printer Roger Ward, in *John Day v. Roger Ward and Wil-liam Home* (1582), in *A Transcript of the Registers of the Company of Stationers of London, 1557-1640*, 5 vols, ed. by Edward Arber (London, 1875-94), II, pp. 753-69.

22   The Star Chamber Decree of 1566 prohibited the publication of any book con-trary to 'the form and meaning of any ordinance, prohibition, or commandment, contained or to be contained in any of the Statutes or Laws of the Realm, or in any Injunctions, Letters patents, or ordinances, passed or set forth, or to be passed or forth by the Queens most excellent Majesty's grant, commission, or authority'. See: Arber, I, p. 322; 'Star Chamber Decree (1566)'; 'Star Chamber Decree (1586)'; and

that replaced it,[23] prevented the development of an understanding of copyright as a natural or human right in England.[24] The Licensing Act 1662 also combined property functions with censorship interests.[25] Control in this sense did not mean authenticity but control of the content of a work. So it was that authors such as John Milton or John Locke would criticise the fact that an author's interests concerning free expression were being hindered.[26]

The very title of the Statute of Anne 1710 demonstrates the extent to which it was a reaction to the licensing statutes and decrees of the seventeenth century: it is an Act 'for the encouragement of Learning and for securing the property of copies of books to the rightful owners thereof'.[27] The rightful owners should have been the authors not the printers. The encouragement of learning is quite opposed to the control of books by censorship rules.[28] The unfortunate effect of this legislation, however, was that it interrupted the path to a common law copyright, or in continental European terms, the legal acknowledgement of personal interests of the author in his work. Birrell put it in the following strong terms: 'This well-meaning Statute spoilt all. It gave away the whole case of the British author, for, amidst all the judicial differences during the last century on copyright, there was a steady majority of judges in favour of the view that, but for the statute of Anne, an author was entitled to perpetual copyright in his published work. The right (if it ever existed) was destroyed by the Act'.[29] This view was shared by the reception of the leading case *Donaldson*

'Star Chamber Decree (1637)', all in *Primary Sources*.

23   See for example 'An Ordinance for the Regulation of Printing (1643)', *Primary Sources*.

24   Osterrieth, pp. 171, 251.

25   This is already shown by the title of the Act: An Act for Preventing Abuses in Printing Seditious, Treasonable, and Unlicensed Books and Pamphlets, and for Regulating of Printing and Printing Presses, 1662, 13 & 14 Car. II, c. 33; see 'Licensing Act (1662)', *Primary Sources*.

26   John Milton, *Areopagitica, With a Commentary by Sir Richard C. Jebb* (Cambridge: Cambridge University Press, 1918), p. 6: '[T]hat other clause of licensing books [...] will be primely to the discouragement of all learning, and the stop of truth, not only by disexercising and blunting our abilities, in what we know already, but by hindering and cropping the discovery that might be yet further made, both in religious and civil wisdom'. See also Rose, p. 32 (concerning John Locke's position).

27   An Act for the Encouragement of Learning, by Vesting the Copies of Printed Books in the Authors of Purchasers of such Copies, During the Times therein mentioned, 1710, 8 Anne, c. 19; see 'Statute of Anne (1710)', *Primary Sources*.

28   See also Rose, p. 48.

29   Augustine Birrell, *Seven Lectures on The Law and History of Copyright in Books* (London: Cassell and Company, 1899), pp. 21-2; but see Cornish and Llewelyn, p. 377, who suggest that the Statute was not intended to abridge existing rights.

v. Becket in 1774, the culmination of the debate between scholars and judges in eighteenth century Britain.[30] While the US copyright regime had initially shown sympathy for the idea of copyright as a personal right,[31] it nevertheless accepted *Donaldson* as a precedent.[32] The debate in the Anglo-American world was closed, possibly also for pragmatic reasons because the (narrow) English interpretation of copyright law served the young American nation better to give access to foreign works, than a mystification of these works as being a sacred kind of property would have done.[33]

The Authenticity Function and the Development of the *Droit d'auteur*-System

It has been said that the Statute of Anne stood in the realm of Enlightenment as opposed to a concept of copyright as a form of property being granted by principles of natural law.[34] This interpretation falsely suggests that property is given by the laws of nature while personal interests to grant and receive access have no roots in international law. However, the natural law approach has today been elevated to become a human rights approach. We no longer discuss whether national law has to accept an author's rights as something pre-existing to the state. States are moving toward a system of human rights whose protection is granted on the basis of international understanding. Such an understanding however has to do with understanding what is peculiar to the author's contribution to the process of creation. Discussion about this point was developed in the nineteenth century debates that took place in continental Europe. This discussion took place at a time when the Anglo-American concept of copyright as a matter of public

30   See the confirming judgment in *Jeffrey v. Boosey* (1854) 4 HLC 815, 10 ER 681; see also 'Jeffreys v. Boosey (1854)', *Primary Sources*.
31   See Lyman Ray Patterson, *Copyright in Historical Perspective* (Nashville: Vanderbilt University, 1968), p. 188: 'The dominant idea of copyright underlying the state statutes was the idea of copyright as an author's right'; in general, see pp. 180-96.
32   *Wheaton v. Peters*, 8 Pet. 591, 8 L.Ed. 1055 (U.S. 1834). See also: 'Wheaton v. Peters (1834)', *Primary Sources*; Howard B. Abrams, 'The Historic Foundation of American Copyright Law: Exploding the Myth of Common Law Copyright', *Wayne Law Review*, 29 (1983), 1119-91, (pp. 1178 et seq).
33   Osterrieth, pp. 103, 159. For further details see Peifer, *Individualität im Zivilrecht*, pp. 70 et seq.
34   See: Jochen Dieselhorst, *Was bringt das Urheberpersönlichkeitsrecht? Urheberpersönlichkeitsschutz im Vergleich Deutschland – USA* (Why Moral Rights? Moral Rights in Germany and the USA), (Frankfurt/Main: Lang, 1994), pp. 8 et seq; György Boytha, 'Whose Right is Copyright?', *GRUR Int.*, (1983), 379-85 (p. 380).

interest had already been shaped by the clear precedent of *Donaldson v. Becket*. In Germany, the discussion is marked by the core texts of Pütter, Kant, and Fichte. The decisive step forward in their discussion was the division of the material and the immaterial within the work. By this division it became clear that property interests as distribution interests of the publishers could be separated from the authenticity interests of authors. The understanding of copyright as a personal right of the author put a focus on the moral interest to safeguard the attribution and the integrity of the work, and to place interests under the control of the person who had authorised the publication of the work. The separation of property and authenticity interests makes it possible to separate authors' moral from publishers' proprietary interests.

From the 1990s onwards, the 'tale of two copyrights'[35] has attracted considerable attention. Post-TRIPs developments within the European Union seem to show that the *droit d'auteur* concept is in retreat. In my view, the personal right concept offers an attractive alternative to the challenges of the information society. The label 'copyright' does not indicate whose right is in question: is it the author's or the right holder's? The personal right concept is less ambiguous. This is not a solely continental idea. For example, it has been argued in *Whale on Copyright* that the negative conceptions associated with copyright may derive from the label.[36] Speaking of personal rights, on the other hand, facilitates the identification of the public with the person protected. It draws a clear dividing line between author's and neighbouring rights, and between the protection of works and the protection of physical layers and code (to use Benkler's terminology).[37] In Germany, it was Kohler who introduced the notion of 'Immaterialgüterrecht', and

---

35   Jane C. Ginsburg, 'A Tale of Two Copyrights: Literary Property in Revolutionary France and America', in *Of Authors and Origins: Essays on Copyright Law*, ed. by Brad Sherman and Alain Strowel (Oxford: Clarendon Press, 1994), pp. 131-58.

36   Jeremy Phillips, Robyn Durie and Ian Karet, *Whale on Copyright*, 5th ed. (London: Sweet & Maxwell, 1997), p. 12: 'Put in cruder terms, the author's right protects the author's message while copyright indiscriminately protects both the message and the medium by which it is disseminated'. See also Jeremy Phillips and Alison Firth, *Introduction to Intellectual Property Law*, 4th ed. (London: Butterworths, 2001), p. 128: 'The distinction [between copyright and droit d'auteur] reflects not so much a matter of terminological chance as a profound chasm between common law and civil law approaches to copyright. Common law protects a work because it can be copied with undesirable results, while civil law protects an author because he has a moral entitlement to control and exploit the product of his intellectual labour'.

37   Yochai Benkler, 'From Consumers to Users: Shifting the Deeper Structures of Regulation', *Federal Communications Law Journal*, 52 (2000), 561-79 (pp. 562-3).

Bluntschli and Gareis who separated investment or property functions from personal interests. The exclusions appropriate to these two groups of rights should differ. Norms of authenticity rather than access control will be more acceptable in an information society.[38]

Plagiarism and Integrity

Plagiarism in the terminology of author's rights is not necessarily an economically relevant offence; rather, it is an attack against personal interests. This view was already accepted in Roman law. The concept was reformed into a legally protected interest by Leopold Josef Neustetel in 1824, one of the first scholars to interpret copyright as a personality right. In ancient times plagiarism might have been interpreted as flattery, or in the middle ages as giving to the people what God has given to the author.[39] In modern terms, however, plagiarism is reaping where one has not sown. For authors standing in active competition for reputation and contracts, plagiarism might even be conceived as a business tort. First and foremost, however, it is an attack upon the authenticity function, which is not only detrimental to the interests of the author but also to the public interest. Plagiarism makes it impossible to attribute the work; it separates the work from the person responsible for it.

Under open access publishing models, scholars pay meticulous attention to correct citation, and the identification of any modifications – rightly so, because the personal author is the first and often the only authority on the authenticity of a source. Publication practices of scientific articles have cast doubt upon the importance of the single author. To proclaim the 'death of the author'[40] however is an attempt to dismantle responsibility for the work. Reading an unattributed text, for example on an on-line encyclopaedia, such as *Wikipedia*, makes it difficult to understand the ideological leanings. It makes a difference, say, if Bill Gates, Tim Berners-Lee, or an independent scholar defines the concept of software.

Apart from considerations of reputation, the attribution of the work gives the author the occasion to supervise the integrity of the work. Complaints

---

38   Friedemann Kawohl and Martin Kretschmer, 'Johann Gottlieb Fichte, and the Trap of *Inhalt* (Content) and *Form*: An information perspective on music copyright', in *Copyright and the Production of Music*, special issue of *Information, Communication and Society*, 12 (2009), 41-64.

39   Zemon Davis, 'Beyond the Market: Books as Gifts in Sixteenth-Century France', *Transactions of the Royal Historical Society*, 5th ser., 33 (1983), 69-88 (p. 87).

40   Roland Barthes, 'The Death of the Author', in *Image, Music, Text*, ed. by Stephen Heath (London: Fontana, 1977), p. 142.

about the abridgement or the mutilation of texts are age-old. Unauthorised alterations to a work were dangerous in times of censorship as authors could be held responsible for texts they had not written. In the thirteenth century *Sachsenspiegel*, a compilation of customary law and one of the first documents written in German, the author Eike von Repgow places a curse on those who dare to mutilate his text.[41] Martin Luther's 1541 *Warning to the Printers* (a preamble to his bible translation), is another famous example:

> But this I must lament about avarice, / that these greedy and rapacious pirate printers are handling our work carelessly. For, seeking only their own profit, / they don't care much about the accuracy of what they are reprinting, / and it has often happened to me / when reading their reprinted text / that I found it so full of errors / that in many places I couldn't recognise my own work / and had to correct it from scratch.[42]

Conclusion

In response to the crisis of a copyright regime that is perceived by many as a system of overprotection, shielding the investments of existing right owners, we need to recover the perspective of a personal individual right or *droit d'auteur*.[43] However, a more balanced approach to copyright, beyond the Anglo-American economic rationale, must not give rise to a new fundamentalism that criticises any critical evaluation of author interests as a violation of sacred principles of personal property.[44] A re-reading of the history

41   Ludwig Gieseke, *Vom Privileg zum Urheberrecht: Die Entwicklung des Urheberrechts in Deutschland bis 1845* (Baden-Baden: Nomos, 1995), p. 10.
42   ABer das mus ich klagen vber den Geitz / Das die geitzigen Wenste vnd reu=bische Nachdrücker mit vnser Erbeit vntrewlich vmbgehen. Denn weil sie allein jren Geitz suchen / fragen sie wenig darnach / wie recht oder falsch sie es hin nachdrücken / Vnd ist mir offt widerfaren / das ich der Nachdrücker druck gelesen / also verfelschet gefunden / das ich meine eigen Erbeit / an vielen Orten nicht gekennet / auffs newe habe müssen bessern. 'Luther's "Warning to the Printers" (1541)', *Primary Sources*. Friedemann Kawohl in his commentary on this text analyses this as a 'moral rights argument'.
43   For a review of the German reluctance to conceive copyright as an economic right, see Ansgar Ohly, 'Urheberrecht als Wirtschaftsrecht' (Copyright as Economic Law), and Haimo Schack, 'Die Rechtfertigung des Urheberrechts als Ausschließlichkeitsrecht' (Legitimation of Copyright as Exclusive Right), both in *Geistiges Eigentum: Schutzrecht oder Ausbeutungstitel?* (Intellectual Property: Protection Title or License to Exploit?), ed. by Otto Depenheuer and Karl-Nikolaus Peifer (Berlin: Springer, 2008), pp. 141-61 (Ohly), and pp. 123-40 (Schack).
44   Gerhard Schricker, then Director of the Munich Max-Planck-Institute for IP, famously castigated the first copyright green paper of the European Commisson, *Copyright and the Challenge of Technology*, as an 'Urheberrecht ohne Urheber' (droit

of author's rights in the Kantian tradition, and in the German jurisprudence of the nineteenth century, suggests that personal interests of authenticity are compatible with a more permissive conception of copyright.

First, understanding author's rights as personal rights may explain key aspects of open access distribution models that emphasise attribution and stringent norms on modifications. Secondly, defining author's rights as personal rights helps to link copyright to the creator and is widely understood by users. If we accept the conception of copyright as a personal right, many problems of overprotection within the copyright regime are cast in a new light. The protection of neighbouring rights, in contrast, will have to be analysed in economic terms only, removing the conflation of author and investment interests.

---

d'auteur sans auteur) because it dared to review economic outcomes for copyright policy. Stellungnahme der Deutschen Vereinigung für gewerblichen Rechtsschutz und Urheberrecht, *GRUR* (1989), 183; Schricker, *IIC* (1989), 466. For a critique, see Martin Kretschmer, 'Digital Copyright: The End of an era', *European Intellectual Property Review*, 25 (2003), 333-41.

14. The Significance of Copyright History for Publishing History and Historians

John Feather

> Marley was dead to begin with. There was no doubt about that.
> (Dickens, *A Christmas Carol*)

But of course there was – or there was doubt about what his 'death' actually meant. Similarly, there is no doubt that copyright is a significant issue in the publishing industry, and therefore in the history of publishing, and therefore for the publishing historian. Or is there?

In the history of copyright in Britain, it has long been accepted that one of the key sequences of events was a series of cases in the courts in England and Scotland between 1765 and 1774, culminating in *Donaldson v. Becket* in 1774.[1] It is argued that the House of Lords' decision in this case apparently settled the argument about whether common law rights overrode the limitations on rights embodied in the 1710 Copyright Act. In the course of this process, what had been essentially a trade right was transformed into an author's right.

This is of course a gross over-simplification of a complex narrative. Scholars have addressed the details of these events and their significance from many different disciplinary traditions, and with subtly different emphases in their conclusions.[2]

---

1   *Donaldson v. Becket* (1774) Hansard, 1st ser., 17 (1774), 953-1003, *Primary Sources*.
2   See Kathy Bowrey, 'Who's Writing Copyright History?', *European Intellectual Property Review*, 18, 6 (1996), 322-9, for a review of the historiography up to the time of publication.

For a legal historian:

> Copyright [...] was never simply concerned with the bookseller or the author. What emerges is that copyright [...] was primarily defined and justified in the interests of society and not the individual. A statutory phenomenon, copyright was fundamentally concerned with the reading public [...]. The pre-eminence of the common good as the organising principle upon which to found a system of copyright regulation is revealed.[3]

For the economic historian:

> The text-based culture [...] was thus simultaneously centralised, controlled, and made more uniform, in a regime of regulated printed-book production that was both financially and culturally self-reinforcing.[4]

The historian of publishing has a different perspective:

> The decision in *Donaldson v. Becket* marked a discontinuity in the history of British publishing, not only because it forced publishers to change the way in which they conducted their business, but also [...] [it] led to a new understanding of the role of the author in the book trade.[5]

An historian of bookselling acknowledges that there was long-term change, but adds that:

> [...] those booksellers who earlier defended their associations by appeal to the 1710 Copyright Act actually relied on custom and consensual practice as much as appeals to common law, property rights, and author's agreements.[6]

Despite differences of emphasis, these are essentially four ways of saying the same thing: that *Donaldson v. Becket* was a turning-point after which nothing was ever quite the same again.

But was it? There is another view. A literary historian, focussing on the emergence of the concept of the author as creator, concludes that:

> *Donaldson v. Becket* is conventionally regarded as having established the statutory basis of copyright, and of course it did. But [...] perhaps it should be simultaneously regarded as confirming the notion of the author's

---

3   Ronan Deazley, *On the Origin of the Right to Copy: Charting the Movement of Copyright Law in Eighteenth-century Britain (1695-1775)* (Oxford: Hart Publishing, 2004), p. 226.

4   William St Clair, *The Reading Nation in the Romantic Period* (Cambridge: Cambridge University Press, 2004), p. 65.

5   John Feather, *A History of British Publishing*, 2nd ed. (London: Routledge, 2006), p. 134.

6   James Raven, *The Business of Books: Booksellers and the English Book Trade 1450-1840* (New Haven and London: Yale University Press, 2007), p. 236.

common-law right.[7]

An intellectual historian who has delved deeply into book trade practices in his analysis of the Scottish Enlightenment rejects the whole notion of significant change in a complex argument to which full justice cannot be done by a brief quotation, but which is perhaps summarised in this statement:

> [A]fter 1774, the leading London bookseller-publishers continued to assert their pretended right of perpetual copyright by enforcing, to the extent that they were able to do so, the principle of 'honorary copyright' within the trade.[8]

The distinction which is being drawn here is between the apparent outcome of the legal processes and the actual practices in the book trade and the nascent publishing industry.

The 'customs of the trade' is a phrase which is sometimes still heard today in the book trade, and was certainly familiar in the late eighteenth century and for long afterwards. It was a concept which was particularly pertinent to the copyright issue, 'the literary property question' as contemporaries tended to call it, because long after the passage of the 1710 Act many bookseller-publishers continued to behave as if the only parts of the statute which were important were those of which they approved. As Ronan Deazley rightly points out in his commentary on the Act on the *Primary Sources on Copyright* website,[9] the statute is full of ill-defined terms and ambiguous language which allowed for a wide range of interpretations even if the gist of the law's intention might be thought to be clear. As a consequence, the book trade was able to argue, without straining their credibility too far, that perpetual copyright existed not only for works written and published before 1710, but also for works subsequent to that date. They therefore continued to trade in those copyrights, or shares in them, and to assume that as owners they had unique and fully protected rights. *Donaldson v. Becket* finally resolved this issue in favour of a more literal interpretation of the statute: that rights were protected only for a period of time fixed by law, and that thereafter the work was in what was to come to be called the public domain.

We need to consider why Parliament wrote the law in these terms. The

---

7   Mark Rose, *Authors and Owners: The Invention of Copyright* (Cambridge, MA: Harvard University Press, 1993), p. 112.
8   Richard B. Sher, *The Enlightenment and The Book: Scottish Authors and Their Publishers in Eighteenth-century Britain, Ireland & America* (Chicago and London: Chicago University Press, 2006), p. 20.
9   Ronan Deazley, 'Statute of Anne (1710)', *Primary Sources*.

title of the Act – 'For the Encouragement of Learning' – gives a clue which has too often been ignored or treated as a cynical whitewash designed to conceal commercial greed. For the publishers, however, and hence for the historian of the trade, the issue is a very practical one. When a publisher 'buys' a new book from an author, what exactly is being bought and sold? In the early history of the English book trade the answer to this question was reasonably clear, or would have been had it been posed. What was bought was the 'copy', a manuscript containing the text of the work, so-called because it would become the printer's 'copy' from which the compositor would work when the type was being set. With the copy, the purchaser – the printer or bookseller – acquired whatever rights might be thought to subsist in its content. In effect, the author lost all control over it, and could expect no further income. The instances in which authors secured some continuing interest in their work through letters patent or similar devices are merely the exceptions which prove the rule.

It is not my intention in this brief paper to recount the whole history of copyright in Britain. But I have started with this truncated account of a key period in its development because I think it forcefully illustrates the central argument in this paper: that an understanding of copyright – and an understanding of publishers' understanding of copyright – is essential to an understanding of publishing history as a whole.

* * * * *

It may seem self-evident to say that the business of publishers is publication, and that therefore they need works which they can publish. Sometimes, however, it is, perhaps, so self-evident that it is not apparent at all in the writings of some book trade historians. But the faults are not all on one side. Although the balance has been somewhat redressed by recent scholarship, there is a long-standing tradition of writing the history of literary authorship with little acknowledgement and less understanding of the business of putting works into print.[10] I am not now simply referring to such common myths as the alleged underpayment of Milton for *Paradise Lost* – in fact he did quite well for a long poem which did not fit the dominant literary *zeitgeist* of Restoration England – or Boswell's unfounded suggestion that Johnson was in some way ill-rewarded for his *Dictionary*, a view which

---

10   For the view of a distinguished literary scholar on this, see John Sutherland, 'Publishing History: A Hole at the Centre of Literary Sociology', *Critical Inquiry*, 14, 3 (1988), 574-89.

Johnson did not share. The problem is more deep-rooted: modern literary scholarship sometimes seems to theorise authorship to the point at which the 'author function', to use Foucault's telling phrase,[11] has become depersonalised, and is in danger of being uncoupled from the intellectual and physical act of writing. In a sense, the long established tradition of anonymous publication – arising from many cultural and political motivations – may be thought at least partly to validate such an approach by its conscious rejection of the idea of the author as an identifiable individual with a unique name.[12] But Foucault went further, and specifically identified the author-function with the creation of texts as 'objects of appropriation', and therefore with the commercialisation of authorship. In the history of English authorship, this is normally supposed to have happened in the eighteenth century, as authors looked more to the book trade and less to patrons for their support.[13] In effect, it is argued that the book trade replaced traditional patrons as the principal financial supporters of authors.[14] Although this is broadly true, the process of change was more multi-faceted than many traditional accounts would suggest, not least because there were many different channels of publication, some of which did not include the book trade at all.[15]

Whatever terminology is used – whether Foucault's language of 'appropriation' or the more ideologically neutral 'commercialisation' – it is undoubtedly the case that the profession of authorship in England was very different in 1800 from what it had been in 1700. When Scott disguised himself as 'The author of *Waverley*', he was not only protecting his reputation as a lawyer, he was also colluding with his publisher in what had become a promotional device. When Defoe had concealed his authorship of some of his political pamphlets he did so in the hope – vain as it turned out – of avoiding the pillory or worse. But while it may have been rather safer to make one's living from writing at the turn of the nineteenth century, it was not yet entirely respectable, especially for the growing band of

---

11   Michel Foucault, 'What is an Author?', in Michel Foucault, *Language Counter-Memory, Practice*, ed. and trans. by Donald F. Bouchard (Ithaca, NY: Cornell University Press, 1980), pp. 124-7.

12   Robert J. Griffin, 'Anonymity and Authorship', *New Literary History*, 30, 4 (1999), 877-95; John Mullan, *Anonymity* (London: Faber & Faber, 2008).

13   The *locus classicus* of this argument, which is still immensely influential, is A.S. Collins, *Authorship in the Days of Johnson* (London: Routledge & Kegan Paul, 1927).

14   Dustin Griffin, *Literary Patronage in England 1650-1800* (Cambridge: Cambridge University Press, 1996).

15   Sher, pp. 195-261.

women writers of fiction. But it was certainly possible. Part of the explanation for this change lies in the exploitation of the 1710 Copyright Act and
the consequences of *Donaldson v. Becket*. By recognising and exploiting the
fact that the law supported the view that an author was creating a piece
of property which could be assigned a financial value, it became possible
to move away from private to commercial patronage. A successful writer –
that is, one whose books were saleable – could therefore hope to be able to
exist on the income from his or her literary works.

Practices did not immediately change on 10 April 1710, or for some years
thereafter, but the Act provided a crucial framework within which both
publishers and authors could develop a more sophisticated understanding of the commercial transactions which took place between them. At one
end of the spectrum, this led to Alexander Pope manipulating booksellers, printers and indeed subscribers to maximise his profits from his own
works.[16] It also, however, provided the basis on which publishers could
re-assure themselves that they were obtaining a protected property, and
authors could negotiate on that basis. This is where the histories of publishing and authorship really come together. The law of copyright provides
a link between the two because it is the context within which the financial relationships between authors and publishers are defined and – most
importantly – protected. The 1710 Act marked the beginning of the provision of a statutory framework for this process; it remains my view that
it is primarily a booksellers' Act, sought by them and heavily influenced
by their commercial interests.[17] While it is true, as Ronan Deazley points
out,[18] that it did not solve all of the trade's problems, it did provide at least
a temporary solution to their immediate concern – the protection of rights
in literary property – thus giving them the confidence to buy rights from
authors, and to trade in those which they already owned.

We should not, however, confine ourselves to a narrowly legalistic
understanding of copyright. Those 'customs of the trade' that were mentioned earlier remained – and up to a point remain – as important as the
law in offering a framework for the relationships between authors and
publishers and the protection of their property. What is sometimes called

---

16   David Foxon, *Pope and the Early Eighteenth-century Book Trade* (Oxford: Clarendon Press, 1991).
17   John Feather, 'The Book Trade in Politics: The Making of the Copyright Act of
1710', *Publishing History*, 8 (1980), 34-7.
18   Deazley, 'Statute of Anne (1710)'; Deazley, *On the Origin of the Right to Copy*,
pp. 44-5.

'honorary copyright' – basically an unwritten agreement not to reprint works already published by others even when no statutory copyright subsisted – is found in Scotland and perhaps Ireland in the later eighteenth and early nineteenth centuries,[19] although it was essentially unenforceable. Such customs were not confined to Britain. In the nineteenth century, American publishers referred to the 'courtesy of the trade';[20] they meant that they would not compete with each other's reprints of British titles, ignoring the fact, as they were fully entitled to do, that in British eyes any such reprint was a piracy. The interest of this lies in the empirical recognition, even in the unrestricted and unregulated competitive ethos of nineteenth century America, that some form of protection is essential to the practice of publishing. The reason for this lies in the fundamental economics of the trade. Very few titles can genuinely sustain competition between editions; the market is too small, and the cost of making and marketing an edition proportionately too great. With rare exceptions, there is no incentive for publishers to compete at this level. It is to some extent the exceptions which have driven the development of the law. The works which were the primary focus of *Millar v. Taylor*,[21] *Donaldson v. Becket* and the other eighteenth century English and Scottish cases were the bestsellers of their day, beginning with Thomson's *Seasons* and in due course encompassing the popular steady-sellers from the seventeenth and eighteenth centuries which were the core of the reprint trade.[22] For the great majority of bookseller-publishers who were issuing single editions of new books, the law was little more than a guarantee of rights which no-one seriously sought to infringe.

With that guarantee, relationships developed within the book trade and between the publishers and the authors that determined the culture within which books were written and published. As that culture evolved from the seventeenth to the nineteenth centuries, it became increasingly commercial. It had not always been so. In the earliest days of the printed book trade in England, rights were effectively guaranteed only by grants

19   Sher, pp. 355-6; M. Pollard, *Dublin's Trade in Books 1550-1800* (Oxford: Clarendon Press, 1989), pp. 179-81.

20   Jeffrey D. Groves, 'Courtesy of the Trade', in *A History of the Book in America. Volume 3. The Industrial Book 1840-1880*, ed. by Scott E. Casper, Jeffrey D. Groves, Stephen W. Nissenbaum and M. Winship (Chapel Hill, NC: University of North Carolina Press, 2007), pp. 139-48.

21   *Millar v. Taylor* (1769) 4 Burr. 2303.

22   On this very important dimension of the trade, see: St. Clair, pp. 122-39; and Thomas F. Bonnell, *The Most Disreputable Trade: Publishing the Classics of English Poetry 1765-1810* (Oxford: Oxford University Press, 2008), especially chapters 4 and 5.

from the Crown. The practical manifestations of this were to be found both in letters patent which protected individual titles or authors – which occasionally continued to be sought even after 1710 – and, most importantly, in the grants of rights in certain classes of books which were brought together as the English Stock of the Stationers' Company at the very beginning of the seventeenth century.[23] The patent rights in their various manifestations are not quite an alternative history of copyright,[24] but they certainly represent a different tradition from that which is embodied in the development of commercial rights which was eventually to be formalised in the 1710 Act and its successors. All of these rights ultimately derived from the assumption that the Crown had the right to licence any work published in the kingdom – a well established legal principle[25] – but the ways in which they developed were very different.

It is not always remembered that just a year after *Donaldson v. Becket*, Common Pleas determined that the English Stock's monopoly of almanac publishing was also unlawful.[26] In a sense, this was a far greater break with the past than the end of the alleged common-law copyrights, for the patents went back deep into the history of the trade, several decades before commercial rights began to develop in the mid-1560s. Taking all of this together, however, it is clear that there were significant changes in the English book trade in the last three decades of the eighteenth century. Those changes, which are a pivotal point in the history of the trade as a whole and of publishing in particular, cannot be understood without an understanding of the chain of events which fundamentally transformed the contemporary understanding of the nature of the investments which publishers had made, and were continuing to make, in rights.

The development of copyright in Britain has been essentially pragmatic. *Donaldson v. Becket* facilitated the further evolution of a more entrepreneurial

23   Cyprian Blagden, 'The English Stock of the Stationers' Company: An Account of its Origins', *The Library*, 5th ser., 10 (1955), 163-85.
24   Arnold Hunt, 'Book Trade Patents, 1603-40', in *The Book Trade and its Customers 1450-1900*, ed. by Arnold Hunt, Giles Mandelbrote and Alison Shell (Winchester: St Pauls Bibliographies, 1997), pp. 27-54.
25   See for example Cyndia Susan Clegg, *Press Censorship in Elizabethan England* (Cambridge: Cambridge University Press, 1997), pp. 6-14. For the views of a legal historian, see H. Tomás Gómez-Arostegui, 'What Copyright History Teaches us About Copyright Injunctions and the Inadequate-remedy-at-law Requirement', *Southern California Law Review*, 81 (2008), 1197-280 (pp. 1213-5).
26   *Stationers' Company v. Carnan* (1775) 2 W. Bl. 1004. See also: Ronan Deazley, 'Stationers' Company v. Carnan (1775)', *Primary Sources*; Cyprian Blagden, 'Thomas Carnan and the Almanack Monopoly', *Studies in Bibliography*, 14 (1961), 23-43.

approach to publishing, but it did so only because that was already developing in the commercial world. The *Stationers' Company v. Carnan* – the almanac case – merely confirmed the recognition of a new commercial environment.[27] It was increasingly necessary to justify the existence of copyright in the face of the rapid evolution of free trade economic theories following the publication of the first edition of Smith's *Wealth of Nations* in the same year as *The Company of Stationers v. Carnan*. Perpetual copyright was beyond recall. Yet the book trade's tendency to favour cartels remained strong. Instead, the publishers and authors built an alliance to promote and defend laws which were in their mutual interest. When we look beyond 1774, and to the legislation which was eventually to displace the 1710 Act, we find that the authors increasingly take centre stage. The 1814 Copyright Act is the first piece of British legislation which explicitly acknowledges the role of the author, by linking the term of copyright to his or her lifetime.[28] The same principle was embodied in the Act of 1842 which also introduced the concept of *post mortem* protection. Subsequent legislation, up to and including the 1988 Act, has continued to link copyright protection to the life and death of the author, while simultaneously running hard to keep up with the rapid development of a multiplicity of manifestations other than the printed word in which the author's works can appear. From the development of performance rights in the early nineteenth century, to the music industry's current travails, a combination of cultural fashion and technological development has forced the law of copyright to remain a dynamic entity undergoing continuous change.

For publishing historians, the impact of changes in the law and practice of copyright on the dynamic change which characterises the development of the British book trade between about 1780 and about 1820 is inseparable from the story which we are telling and trying to explain. The same is true – albeit to a lesser extent – at some other times. Occasionally, copyright issues break the surface, and at various points in the history of British publishing it is the dominant theme for the historian as it was for contemporaries. But for much of the time, it lies dormant or submerged, embodying a series of assumptions about how business can be effectively transacted, how commercial and cultural relationships can be defined and how products can be made and marketed. It is in those less tangible spheres that there lies its deeper significance for the historian of the trade.

27 Ibid.
28 See John Feather, *Publishing, Piracy and Politics. An Historical Study of Copyright in Britain* (London: Mansell, 1994), pp. 122-48.

15. Metaphors of Intellectual Property

William St Clair*

In this essay, I discuss the main metaphors within which intellectual property has historically been conceptualised, presented, and debated in England; in the United Kingdom of Great Britain (1707); the United Kingdom of Great Britain and Ireland (1801); and the United Kingdom of Great Britain and Northern Ireland (1922). The law and practice of intellectual property were different in Scotland and Ireland before they became constituent parts of the United Kingdom, and practice in Scotland continued to differ from practice in England for around a century after a statutory copyright regime for the whole of the United Kingdom of Great Britain was established by the British Act of Queen Anne in 1710.[1]

Since we now have over five hundred years of experience, we can discern the trajectories, the gradual shifts, and the sharp turning points. We can appreciate the development in the ways in which intellectual property has been discussed that have brought us to the discursive conjuncture at which we find ourselves today. We are thereby enabled, I suggest, to approach the policy choices that we face today with a fuller, more open, and more critical understanding.

My remarks refer mainly to printed books, the main media by which complex forms of knowledge were constituted and disseminated for the

* I should like to record my thanks to Lionel Bently, Ronan Deazley, Paulina Kewes, Irmgard Maassen, Jenny Mander, Paul Mora, Douglas Paine, Aysha Pollnitz, Barbara Ravelhofer, Mark Rose, Emma Rothschild, John St Clair, the participants in seminars arranged by Lionel Bently and his colleagues at the Cambridge Centre for Intellectual Property Law (CIPIL), and others who offered comments at various stages of discussion and preparation.

1 An Act for the Encouragement of Learning by Vesting the Copies of Printed Books in the Authors or Purchasers of such Copies, during the Times therein mentioned 1710, 8 Anne, c.19.

first four hundred years.[2] But they apply also to engravings and other forms of reproducible pictures inscribed in, and carried by, the materiality of paper and ink or electronic media, over which, incidentally, the intellectual property regime, both in law and in practice, has historically been different. To avoid unnecessary clutter, I will use 'books' to include all kinds of printed matter, and 'reading' to include all the many ways of engaging with, 'consuming', the verbal and visual texts.

I leave aside paternity, brain child, fruits of the brain, creativity, and other metaphors that have been mainly deployed in discussing authorship, on which Mark Rose has written, and who has come to many of the same conclusions as I offer here.[3] I refer only incidentally to external and internal controls on the textual content of print with which intellectual property regimes have historically been closely associated. And, although I use the present-day vocabulary of 'intellectual property', rather than the words used in the past (privilege, charter, letters patent, license, literary property, and so on) I do not wish to imply that 'intellectual property' is necessarily the best way of conceptualising or analysing the practice either as it was operated in the past or now. Instead, I suggest, we should regard 'intellectual property' as the metaphor that happens to be currently dominant, and be alert to its historical genesis, to its rhetorical tendencies, and to its strengths and limitations as an instrument of analysis.

* * * * *

I begin with three points that have not always, in my experience, been given sufficient attention.

First, we cannot recover the history of intellectual property from the history of the law of intellectual property. Many intellectual property practices have been operated for long periods in contravention of the law. For example, we find English, although not Scottish, publishers conducting their businesses as if perpetual intellectual property was lawful long after the 1710 statute had declared unambiguously that copyright existed for fourteen years 'and no longer'.[4] The English publishers managed to continue

---

2   After 1900 the uniqueness of print as a medium able to carry complex texts across time and distance began to be challenged by radio and film.

3   Mark Rose, 'Copyright and Its Metaphors', *UCLA Law Review*, 50 (2002), 1-16. Rose makes many of the same points – mainly for later periods – and comes to the same conclusions about the enduring power of what he calls 'the unconscious of copyright'. I am grateful to him for drawing his article to my attention and for many useful subsequent conversations.

4   Discussed, and the effects of the regime evaluated, with quantification, by Wil-

the illegal practices for a time even after the 1774 judicial decision of the House of Lords (acting as supreme court for civil cases in Great Britain) had formally confirmed that the law was what it was plainly stated to be in the statute, and the gradual ending of the practice was due more to economic forces than to legal challenge.[5]

We also find examples of intellectual property regimes operating without any basis in law. The 1862 statute on artistic copyright, for example, begins with the words 'Whereas by Law as now established, the Authors of Paintings, Drawings and Photographs have no Copyright in such their works', but the record shows that, in practice, for at least half a century before the passing of that act, artists had been able to exercise a *de facto* copyright, and to obtain large sums from engravers and print sellers in return for extra-statutory exclusive rights to make and sell prints of their paintings.[6] And there were other business practices, such as pre-emption rights when intellectual property rights were sold at closed sales among groups of members of the industry, which although not formally part of any copyright regime, reinforced its main economic features and made it harder for outsiders to exercise their statutory and other legal rights.[7]

Many historic intellectual property practices were not set out in any publicly accessible form, and are only known from mentions in private documents, for example, denying opportunities to quote.[8] And there were other

liam St Clair, *The Reading Nation in the Romantic Period* (Cambridge: Cambridge University Press, 2004), especially chapters 2, 3, 5, 6 and 7. A brief summary of the main findings of that book is available, under Creative Commons, in the 2005 John Coffin Memorial lecture, published by the Institute of English Studies, School of Advanced Study, University of London: http://ies.sas.ac.uk/Publications/johncoffin/stclair.pdf [accessed 26/2/2010].

5   Examples of intellectual property in titles that had passed into the public domain continuing informally as 'the customs of the trade' even after 1774 are noted in St Clair, p. 113. A recently published documented example is the illegal contract by John Murray, the publisher of Byron's *Childe Harold's Pilgrimage, A Romaunt* (London: Murray, 1812) in which he claimed the 'entire and perpetual copy right'. *The Letters of John Murray to Lord Byron*, ed. by Andrew Nicholson (Liverpool: Liverpool University Press, 2007), p. 6.

6   The opening words of the Fine Arts Copyright Act 1862, 25 & 26 Vict., c.63, are reprinted in Reginald Winslow, *The Law of Artistic Copyright* (London: William Clowes, 1889), p. 101. As an example of the operation of extra-statutory copyright, in 1829 the artist Sir David Wilkie obtained £1,200 for assigning to a print publisher 'all his copyright or right in nature of copyright of his painting "The Chelsea Pensioners"'. British Library Additional Manuscripts 46,140 (a file that contains other examples).

7   For pre-emption rights, a classic feature of cartels, in the historic British book industry see St Clair, pp. 94-6.

8   Discussed in St Clair, chapter 4 and elsewhere.

intellectual property practices, including some which determined which texts were made available to large constituencies of readers in England for over two hundred years, whose existence is only known from observed economic behaviour recovered from the archival record.[9]

Secondly, histories of the law of intellectual property, even if we were to include the illegal and extra-legal components of the regimes, cannot take us to the real-world consequences. Without information from outside, we can say little about the nature of the printed books that were produced, prohibited, or discouraged by the regimes. Nor, without information from outside, can we take a view, other than in the most general and speculative terms, on the effects of the operation of the regimes on the nature of the texts, or on incentives, production, prices, access, or timing of access. Histories of the law cannot take us to reading, to the construction and diffusion of knowledge, the competition for the allegiance of minds, the rise and fall of ideas, or to the mental states that resulted from the reading (and viewing) of the texts that were historically made available as consequences of the regimes.

Thirdly, we cannot derive the real-world consequences of intellectual property regimes from histories of public, political, and judicial arguments about intellectual property. Only if we collect and analyse information from outside can we evaluate the extent to which the arguments offered in debate may have achieved their rhetorical purpose, and changes in opinion, law, practice, economic and business behaviour, and ultimately reading and mentalities, may have occurred as a result.[10]

If we regard texts, books, and reading as a literary system, within a wider cultural system, most discussions of the history of intellectual property have, I would say, been concentrated on one of the factors that governed the inputs to the system (law) to the neglect of the others (practice). Less attention has been given to the outputs of the system, (the nature, prices, quantities, and sales of the printed texts produced, prohibited or discouraged), or to the outcomes (the mental states that resulted from the reading of the texts made available under the regimes). Indeed, of the three main currently offered justifications for intellectual property – natural rights, a

---

9   A striking example is the clampdown on abridgements, anthologies, and adaptations of existing printed texts the English book industry introduced around 1600 with the aim of protecting the prices of the main texts. Discussed in St Clair, chapter 4.

10   Examples, with quantification, of the effects on prices, production, access, and so on, of the 1774 judicial decision and of nineteenth century copyright acts are given in St Clair, *Reading Nation*.

public expression of gratitude to authors, and incentives to useful innovation, only the third admits consequences as a legitimate element in the debate.[11]

This lack of attention to – or rather historical withdrawal of attention from – the consequences of intellectual property regimes, and attempts to suggest that they are irrelevant, or need not be considered, has occurred despite the fact that, since the British statutory regime was established in 1710, every single statute has been publicly presented and justified by claims about the consequences it was intended to bring about. For example, in the eighteenth century, we have acts 'for the encouragement of learning', 'for the encouragement of the arts of designing, engraving and etching', 'for the advancement of useful learning and other purposes of education', and so on. Amending statutes refer back to earlier statutes that make claims about intended consequences. The long-lived 1842 Copyright Act, which repealed the 1710 Statute of Anne, was more explicit and more restrictive in its stated objectives than its predecessor, being described in the ambit as an act 'to afford greater encouragement to the production of literary works of lasting benefit to the world'.[12]

* * * * *

It would be possible to arrange the metaphors in a rough chronological parade, but they merged, co-existed, and overlapped in time. Most continued to be deployed and retained rhetorical power long after other ways of thinking had apparently taken their place or had overlaid them, and some ancient metaphors are still frequently deployed today. I arrange them in accordance with the primary ideas with which the metaphorical comparison is made – although, as with all language, they too were often metaphors, sometimes dead. We should not expect the metaphors to be internally consistent, although the more they are, the greater their potential rhetorical power.

Metaphorical conceptualisations should not, in my view, be regarded as mere ornamental embellishments to other ways of thinking that some

---

11   Lionel Bently and Brad Sherman, *Intellectual Property Law*, 2nd edn (Oxford: Oxford University Press, 2004).

12   Quoted from the Copyright Act 1842, 5 & 6 Vict., c.45, by John Shortt, *The Law Relating to Works of Literature and Art: Embracing the Law of Copyright* (London: Horace Cox, 1871), p. 636. This wording, to be found in other publications of the time, confirms that the 'learning' which the statute of Anne was intended to encourage was the production and print publication of learned books, what today would be called research, not 'learning' in the sense of what today would be called education.

may regard as more securely founded, or as intellectually more coherent.[13] Metaphors have been intrinsic to the way in which intellectual property has historically been analysed, understood, presented, and enforced not only by authors, publishers, pamphleteers, and other participants in the book industry, but by governments, parliaments, lawyers, judges, and courts. The history of decision-making too is replete with metaphors, often mixed, that were deployed alongside, and intermixed with, arguments based on legal concepts. They are part of the history of the nexus of ideas that have historically surrounded and shaped both law and practice through to the present day, and may have been at least as influential on the real-world course of events as legal theory or jurisprudence.[14]

Commonwealth

The first set of ideas I wish to discuss is the notion of a 'commonwealth', a well-run polity in which the interests of citizens are reconciled both as individuals and as members of participating institutions, and who together contribute to the well-being – the common weal – of the whole. During the early centuries of intellectual property, notions of a well-run commonwealth were applied to the intellectual and economic as well as to the political and religious domains. One of the main school teaching texts that was sold for a hundred years after 1600 was called *Wits Commonwealth* – 'wit' here meaning knowledge.

---

13 A point also made by Rose, p. 3: 'Metaphors are not just ornamental; they structure the way we think about matters and they have consequences'.
14 A point also made by Rose, p. 16: 'We cannot simply escape from these metaphors because we cannot escape from history and from ourselves'. One of the most influential speeches in the debates of 1774 is replete with the metaphors discussed in the present article: 'all our learning will be locked up in the hands of the Tonsons and Lintots of the age, [the intellectual property owners] who will set what price upon it their avarice chuses to demand, till the public become as much their slaves as their own hackney compilers are'. But 'Knowledge and science are not things to be bound in such cobweb chains; when once the bird is out of the cage – volat irrevocabile – Ireland, Scotland, America [offshore publishers], will afford her shelter'. Speech of Lord Camden of February 22 1774, *The Parliamentary History of England, from the Earliest Period to the Year 1803. From which last-mentioned Epoch it is continued downwards in the Work entitled, 'The Parliamentary Debates'*, vol. 17 (London, 1813), col. 997. In an important judgment of 2001, one of the judges in the British House of Lords, acting as supreme court, resorted to an ancient agricultural metaphor: 'No-one else may for a season reap what the copyright owner has sown.' Quoted by Ronan Deazley, *Rethinking Copyright, History, Theory, Language* (Cheltenham: Edward Elgar, 2006), p. 3.

During that time, much economic production was formally assigned to chartered guilds that were established as formal monopolies. But, as part of the claim that 'the commonwealth' promoted and protected the interests of all citizens, these monopolies were normally closely regulated, both internally and externally. And that regulation applied to the monopoly that is today called intellectual property. Price controls, and arrangements for enforcement, penalties, and remedies against excessive prices, were intrinsic to the institutions of intellectual property, both formally in law and in practice, from its earliest days. An English statute of 1534, for example, was devoted to the control of book prices, with arrangements for complaints, redress, and penalties.[15] And action to secure compliance was taken by the state as well as by individuals and corporations. For example the English Government in 1632, considering a dispute between the rival book industries of London and Cambridge, threatened to take book pricing into its direct control, as internal price regulation was not working. The Government required, as part of allowing the privilege to continue, 'first that all bookes printed and to bee printed shoulde be sould at reasonable and fitt prizes otherwise the forme of the Statute to be put in execution. wch is for setting a rate as which euerie booke shoulde bee solde for that the prizes of bookes in respect of the many privilidges are of late times extreamely raised'.[16]

Price controls, which are seldom mentioned in modern accounts of the history of copyright, were actively enforced in the early centuries, remained on the British statute book until 1739, and were taken into the law of the newly independent United States in 1787.[17] Excessive book prices were commonly described as 'abuses', the same word as was commonly used for infringements both of the monopoly rights to copy and of the controls on textual content.

---

15   Quoted in St Clair, p. 457 from A. Luders *et al*, *Statutes of the Realm* (1810-28), iii, p. 456.

16   W.W. Greg, *A Companion to Arber* (Oxford: Clarendon Press, 1967), p. 185.

17   Summarised in St Clair, p. 457. An example of enforcement in William A. Jackson, *Records of the Court of the Stationers' Company 1602 to 1640* (London, 1957), p. 2. Price controls are not mentioned by Brad Sherman and Lionel Bently, *The Making of Modern Intellectual Property Law* (Cambridge: Cambridge University Press, 1999); or by Lionel Bently and Brad Sherman, *Intellectual Property Law*; and only once and incidentally by Ronan Deazley, *On the Origin of the Right to Copy: Charting the Movement of Copyright Law in Eighteenth-Century Britain (1695-1775)* (Oxford: Hart Publishing, 2004), p. 108, as something smuggled into a bill whose main purpose was to forbid the importation of offshore reprints of English language books. For a note on the early American legislation that included provision for redress against excessive book prices see St Clair, p. 488.

Many of the numerous recorded complaints about prices came from within the industry and concerned the state-conferred class monopolies, 'patents', to publish English language bibles, almanacs, school books, and law books. It was simple for the state and for industry insiders, by calculating the margin between the manufacturing costs and the prices set by producers, to measure the degree of price exploitation, as is done in modern price control and monopoly regulatory systems. But the record shows that participants also understood the monopoly intrinsic to copyright as such, and were able, for example, to calculate the net present financial value of the economic rent available to be taken from a future stream of income – a calculation which both the state and the industry had to make when monopoly rights were being franchised, and which members of the industry performed regularly and frequently, many times in every year until 1774 and later, whenever the monopoly copying and selling rights in other texts were inherited, sold, or otherwise transferred, second hand, between members participating in the pre-emption conjurations.[18]

The effects of intellectual property regimes on the consumer interest were understood, discussed, and in sometimes measured.[19] In 1614, for example, in a complaint about the excessive prices charged by patentees, the excluded members of the industry noted that 'his Majesties Subjects in general are abused by their exactions'.[20] Another member of the industry, in declaring in 1641, that monopolies 'robbed the commonwealth', called for international as well as local free trade in all the texts composed, compiled, or translated long ago, including English-language bibles. Another writer declared that it was 'a great injury that stationers have copies for ever. It should suffice that they should enjoy them for 5, 10, 15 years. Otherwise they never reprint them and by this means many good books are suppressed or perish altogether' – an observation about one damaging effect of long or perpetual intellectual property – the dog-in-the-manger effect – which is shown by the historical record to have frequently occurred.[21]

In the early eighteenth century, before the 1710 act came into force, Henry Hills, who printed a range of old and new texts (mainly publicly

---

18   There are many examples in [Michael Sparke], *Scintilla, or A light broken into darke warehouses* (1641).

19   See examples in *Scintilla*.

20   *A Transcript of the Registers of the Company of Stationers of London 1554-1640*, 5 vols, ed. by E. Arber (London, 1875), iv, p. 526.

21   Samuel Hartlib, quoted in *Cambridge History of the Book in Britain* (Cambridge: Cambridge University Press, 2002), IV, p. 315. For examples of the dog-in-the-manger effect see St Clair, pp. 52, 365 and 392.

delivered sermons) at cheap prices, so infuriated his colleagues by printing the words 'for the benefit of the poor' on his title pages that one declared that he should be whipped through the streets of London with a bundle of his cheap books bound to his back, and a notice hung round his neck 'for the benefit of the poor'.[22] Whether the London crowds would have appreciated the sarcasm we can only guess. It has historically always been hard for the book industry to persuade its customers, or the public, that high prices are for their own benefit. This has been especially the case when the texts were composed long before the copying occurred, the authors were long dead, the prices at which the books were monopolistically sold were far above the manufacturing cost, and there were firms keen to supply them more cheaply.

Monopoly-and-regulation, we can say in summary, was the central official discourse, and the central public justification, of the law, institutions, and practices of intellectual property during the first two and a half centuries of its existence. This political economy way of conceptualising and understanding intellectual property, which regards its effects on texts, production, prices, access, and so on, as its main purpose, long predates the language of private property rights whose rhetorical tendency is to present effects and consequences as incidental, and to try to exclude them from a legitimate place in the argument.

The political economy language of monopoly-and-regulation-in-the-public-interest continued to be heard after the private property metaphor was first formally institutionalised (with accompanying price controls) in the statute of 1710. In a pamphlet of 1735, for example, when the public domain of out of copyright texts established by the act of 1710 ought already to have come into being, after the expiry of the transitional provisions, attempts to thwart its intended effects were described as 'a perpetual Monopoly, a Thing deservedly Odious in the Eye of the Law, a Discouragement to Leaning, no Benefit to Authors, but a general Tax on the Publick'.[23] And although private property rights gradually became

---

22   Quoted by Richmond P. Bond, 'The Pirate and the *Tatler*', *The Library*, 18, 4 (1963), 257-74. The phrase 'For the Benefit of the Poor' occurs on the title page of, for example, Philip Bisse, *A Sermon preach'd at the Anniversary Meeting of the Sons of the Clergy in the Cathedral Church of St Paul on Thursday December the 2nd* (1709). Hills's catalogue, printed with that text, lists numerous other delivered sermons by churchmen, published at lower than normal prices as the hiatus in the law [between 1695 and 1710] at that time permitted.

23   Quoted by A.S. Collins, *Authorship in the Days of Johnson* (London: Holden, 1927), p. 72, from a pamphlet in the British Library BL 357.c.2.

the dominant metaphor, the previous claim that intellectual property had been established to advance the wider aims of the polity as a whole was not entirely pushed aside. Late in the nineteenth century, for example, law professionals still described copyright as a 'privilege designed to secure the aims of the community'.[24]

Metaphors of the body

The second range of ideas I wish to discuss is closely related to notions of the well-ordered commonwealth, the metaphor of the polity as a human body.

The commonwealth, when conceptualised as a body, had a 'head', normally the monarch, who in early modern political/ecclesiastical states such as England, claimed to derive his or her authority from the Christian god.[25] Most of the formal documents declare that the power was granted down from the 'sacred' monarch, and therefore that they too had divine as well as political legitimacy. The monarch was said to be the giver and ultimate owner of all land and of all industries, including the book industry. As one pamphleteer wrote in 1664, 'That Printing belongs to your Majesty, in Your publique and private Capacity, as Supream Magistrate, and as Proprietor I do with all boldness affirm'[26]

In the bodily commonwealth the different classes of society are regarded as organs or members – most are feet. Intellectual property owners, 'patentees', are hands. The state is a body politic, but so are the guilds, other bodies corporate, 'corporations', within the larger body.[27] The bodily metaphor could be used to support intellectual property institutions, noting, for example the risks that, without them, worthwhile works would be 'strangled in the womb' or 'never conceived at all'.[28] The laws and customs that governed the print industry, including intellectual property, could be presented as performing a range of bodily functions in the commonwealth,

---

24 For example, Thomas Edward Scrutton, *The Laws of Copyright* (London: 1883), p. 8.
25 See, especially, David George Hale, *The Body Politic: A Political Metaphor in Renaissance English Literature* (The Hague: Mouton, 1971).
26 Richard Atkyns, *Original and Growth of Printing* (London: Printed by John Streater, for the Author, 1664), Bi. Discussed by Jody Greene, *The Trouble with Ownership: Literary Property and Authorial Liability in England, 1660-1730* (Philadelphia: University of Pennsylvania Press, 2005), p. 30.
27 Example in Greg, p. 202.
28 Arber, i, p. 587.

for example, vivifying (male), giving birth (female), and nursing (female).[29] The printing press itself was often imagined in gendered terms, with its different parts metaphored on parts of the body, tongues, shoulders, male block, female block. Indeed the manuals for printers almost say that works of print are born as result of the coupling of human bodies with the machine. One writer declared that when there was disorder in the commonwealth the physical 'tumults' were the masculine manifestation, the printing and dispersing of the books that led to the tumults were the feminine, reflecting the fact that the women and girls who played a large part in book manufacture and distribution shared the responsibility.[30]

But mostly the bodily metaphor was deployed in support of restrictions at each stage of publication. The burning of books, for example, was compared with legal infanticide. '[In the past] Books were as freely admitted into the World as any other birth; the issue of the Brain was no more stifled than the issue of the womb: No envious Juncto [Junta] sate cross-legg'd over the Nativity of any Man's Intellectual Off-spring; but if it is proved a Monster, who denies but that it was justly burnt?'[31] Even the practice of making abridgements, long a point of contestation within the industry, was presented in bodily terms. To abridge was to 'rake through the Entrails of many a good old Author, with a Violation worse than any could be offered to his Tomb'.[32] As late as 1839, the author Thomas Hood, petitioning Parliament in favour of a bill to introduce a longer copyright, declared that 'when your petitioner shall be dead and buried, he might with as much propriety and decency have his body snatched as his literary remains'.[33]

The rhetorical tendency of the bodily metaphor is to make political and commercial practices appear 'natural', familiar, and therefore more understandable and more readily acceptable. As Rose noted, 'the issue is not truth so much as persuasion. A persuasive solution is one that works because it tells us what we already know'.[34] The rhetorical tendency was also to require that argument should be conducted within the limitations of the metaphor, and it usually was. Those who disliked ecclesiastical censorship,

---

29   Examples from *The Importance of the Liberty of the Press* (1748), p. 8.

30   Discussed by Lisa Maruca, *The Work of Print, Authorship and the English Text Trades 1660-1760* (Seattle: Helman, 2007).

31   *Reasons humbly offered for the Liberty of Unlicens'd Printing . . . In a Letter from a Gentleman in the Country, to a Member of Parliament* (London, 1692), p. 4.

32   Ibid.

33   Quoted by Catherine Seville, *Literary Copyright Reform in Early Victorian England* (Cambridge: Cambridge University Press, 1999), p. 192.

34   Rose, p. 10.

for example, might not dare to criticise censorship face on, but they could call the current bishops 'rotten members'.[35] Production and pricing decisions, are, by this rhetoric, presented not as the actions of economic agents, but as matters already settled by 'nature'. Within the bodily metaphor, to attempt to negotiate is therefore to rebel. As one author wrote of the patentees, '[t]he monarch as head gives power to the hand, the hand oppresseth the foot, the foot riseth up against the head'.[36]

Throughout the print era there has been an influential constituency that is hostile to the reading of books as such, mainly on the grounds that if uneducated persons are introduced to new ideas, they are liable to become discontented with the role to which they are assigned by society.[37] In its many attempts to control reading by limiting the size of the printing industry and bringing it under state control, it was to the metaphors of the body that the early modern political/ecclesiastical state turned for its justifications and its metaphors. 'Printing is like a good Dish of Meat, which moderately eaten of, turns to the Nourishment and health of the Body; but immoderately, to Surfeits and Sicknesses'.[38] And since excessive reading leads to 'disorder' both in the political and the individual body, it causes more deaths than guns. 'Twenty dye of Surfeits, for one that is starved for want of Meat'.[39]

Rameses's Library at Thebes in Egypt is said to have been inscribed with the words 'medicine for the soul'. The same thought can still be read above the library in the monastery on Patmos. That aspect of the bodily metaphor is not only ancient but rhetorically powerful and enduring. As one author wrote in 1624, a stationer was entrusted to supply the needs of the soul, and, like an apothecary who supplied the needs of the body, he was under an obligation not to sell any thing harmful.[40] The point had been made in almost exactly the same words in a speech to Parliament forty years earlier. Just as inspectors burned defective medicaments, this speaker advised his colleagues, let us take care in dealing with books 'because the poticaryes drugs do but poison ye body but the prynyers druggs do, poyson ye soule'.[41]

---

35   Roger L'Estrange, *Considerations and Proposals in Order to the Regulation of the Press* (1663), p. 15, quoting a pamphlet of 1660.
36   Quoted by Hale, p. 74.
37   Discussed in St Clair, especially pp. 11-2, 109-10 and 308-12.
38   Atkyns, p. Bii.
39   Ibid., p. C7.
40   Richard S. Tompson, 'Scottish Judges and the Birth of British Copyright', *The Juridical Review*, 37 (1992), 18-42 (p. 34).
41   Quoted from the original transcript by Greg, p. 144.

Metaphors of the bodily commonwealth imply that 'disorder' in one part of the body may affect the health of the whole.[42] In a royal decree of 1576 printed texts unwelcome to the English government were 'euill and corrupt limmes, which for lacke of speedie remedie may infect more of the body'.[43] Unauthorised texts were 'pestiferous' or 'pestilential', spreading 'infection'. 'Disorder', a word that was used interchangeably with 'abuse', included all texts that offended against the health of the body politic, there being little distinction in the use of either word between intellectual property disorder and textual disorder.[44] Sometimes the persons who infringed copyright were themselves called 'disordered'.[45] And often, in this epidemiological metaphor of the literary system, the sources of the plagues were conceived of as 'vermin', hard to catch, and sometimes able to spread diseases invisibly through the air. In the words of Roger L'Estrange the official English state censor at the end of the seventeenth century, disorderly books 'lie lurking in the dark, like poisonous serpents, stinging what falls within their reach, and blowing about their venom'.[46]

The bodily metaphor encourages metaphors of medical intervention. For example, the commonwealth could not thrive 'so long as such horrid Monstrosities and gibbous excrescences are suffered to remain and tumour in that disorderly and confused body'.[47] Or 'a little wound, or contusion neglected, will soon mortifie and corrupt itself to an immedicable Gangraen'.[48] And, in accordance with the metaphor, drastic action was often in fact taken. William Tyndale, whose translation of the western bible into English published offshore in the Netherlands, was condemned by the then English monarch as 'pestilential', and Tyndale was in due course judicially put to death by burning. Nor should we think of this as an aberration. There are numerous examples of members of the printed book industry being judicially put to death, often by burning, or being judicially

---

42 James Raven, *The Business of Books 1450-1850* (New Haven: Yale University Press, 2007), p. 62, quotes an ecclesiastical court using the cognates 'misorder and abusion' about the book industry, no date given.

43 Arber, i, p. 474.

44 Arber, i, p. xxvii. From his comprehensive work on the Stationers' Company registers, court records, and other primary documents over many years, Edward Arber concluded that the 'disorder' with which the Stationers were most concerned were 'trade control and copyright' [intellectual property] rather than 'religious or political power' [censorship and self-censorship of texts].

45 Examples in Arber, ii, pp. 772, 778-9.

46 Quoted by Jody Greene, p. 28.

47 *The London Printers Lamentation* (London, 1660), p. 4.

48 Ibid., p. 3.

dismembered or facially disfigured, for publishing offences – practices that, in the case of printed texts that challenged the legitimacy of the government, continued even after the 1710 statute.[49]

Many political and ecclesiastical leaders, including Sir Thomas More, not only defended but occasionally relished the practice of burning the authors and translators, as well as the books, of which they disapproved, as a means of ridding the body of 'poison'.[50] And again this should not be regarded as an aberration. Part of the justificatory superstructure of the rights of monarchs, as set out, for example, by Sir Robert Filmer, was that the monarch had absolute sovereignty over the bodies of his or her subjects, and had a legal right to 'sell, castrate, or use their persons as he pleases'.[51]

In the nineteenth century, we still frequently find the bodily poison metaphor employed against low book prices as such, often by churchmen, who, like their predecessors, feared that widening access to reading would affect the competition for the allegiance of minds in which they were engaged. As one wrote: 'An appetite for information being created, it required to be satisfied, and if not supplied with wholesome food, was sure to feed on offal and poison'.[52] When, by a quirk in the law, Byron's long epic satire *Don Juan* became easily available in vast quantities at cheap prices, lawyers and churchmen replayed the ancient metaphors.[53] 'The blast of the desert, at once breathing pestilence into the hearts, and scorching with a fatal death-blight, the minds of myriads', wrote one.[54] 'Fatal, unutterably fatal has been the influence of [...] Byron to many thousands of youthful readers'.[55] Another writer noted that 'under seemingly playful covering

49   An example from 1720 of a printer being judicially put to death for a publishing offence in St Clair, p. 88.
50   Discussed with particular reference to reading by James Simpson, *Burning to Read* (Cambridge, MA: Harvard University Press, 2007). In *The Answer to a Poisoned Book* (1534) More describes his opponents as 'the contagion [that] crepeth forth and corrupteth further, in the manner of a corrupt cancer', a risk that was also run by the 'leech that fasting cometh very near and long sitteth by the sick man busy about to cure him', quoted by Simpson, p. 270.
51   Quoted from *Patriarchia* (1660) by Catherine Gallagher, *Nobody's Story* (Berkeley: University of California Press, 1974), p. 79.
52   George Chandler [a high ranking churchman], *An Introductory Lecture delivered at the Commencement of the Second Session of the Chichester Literary and Philosophical Society* (Chichester, 1832), p. 19.
53   For the cheap editions of *Don Juan* that poured through a gap in the intellectual property regime see St Clair, chapter 16, quantified in Appendix 12.
54   *A Course of Lectures to Young Men ... Delivered in Glasgow, by Ministers of Various Denominations* (Glasgow, 1842), p. 142.
55   St Clair, p. 334.

are hidden words more poisonous than the tongues of serpents'. 'Young people should understand that to touch his volumes is like embracing a beautiful woman infected with the plague'. 'Books contain a deadly and secret poison', warned the churchman, Joel Hawes; '[m]any a young man has been destroyed by reading a single volume' – although evidently not Hawes himself.[56]

The bodily health and sickness metaphor, which appears to be one of the most ancient and most culturally fixed, turns out to have historically been adapted to the dominant public health concerns at the times when it was deployed. In the early modern period ideas derived from reading are presented as infection spreading plagues silently through the air. By Victorian times, the comparison was with female prostitutes and venereal disease.

After the act of 1710, although the metaphors favoured by the early modern theocratic state withered away, they are still occasionally heard. In the debates of 1774, for example, the newly invented 'literary property' was described as 'sacred'.[57] Meanwhile the bodily metaphor that had been invented to make the theocratic state appear familiar, continued independently. When, for example, as was quickly recognised, the private property metaphor collided with the wider political discourse of 'property' and 'liberty' as set out by Locke and others, it was to the bodily metaphors that they returned. As one writer argued: 'If a Man, for instance, writes a Book, or Sheet of Paper, with as much labour and Pains as one can imagine an Author to take, and he may not be allowed to print and publish it, for his own profit, without an *Imprimatur*, why then the Man's Property is invaded?' The answer was that an author had no more right to sell whatever he wrote than a butcher had a right to sell rotten meat, a vintner to adulterate his wines, or an apothecary to put on sale medicines that had not been prescribed by licensed medical doctors.[58]

One feature of the body metaphor continues strongly in our own day. The alliance between the printed book industry and the pharmaceutical industry can be traced back to the sixteenth century. The two industries shared – and share – many economic characteristics: both were regulated; centralised in their production; and they shared distribution networks and retail outlets. They also employed the same rhetorics and metaphors, a

56   Joel Hawes, *Lectures to Young Men on the Formation of Character ... with an Additional Lecture on Reading* (London, 1829), p. 156.
57   Tompson, p. 34.
58   *Arguments Relating to a Restraint upon the Press ... in a Letter to a Bencher from a Young Gentleman of the Temple* (London, 1712), p. 21.

tradition that continues. In current debates, the pharmaceutical industry, like the word and image text copying industries, aims to keep intellectual property conceptualised as a private property right that should be enforced by the state irrespective of its effects rather than as an instrument of public policy whose consequential benefits and disbenefits can be evaluated not only clinically but in political economy terms of incentives, prices, access, timing of access, and real-world outcomes.

Disguise

Metaphors of the body were frequently applied to what is now called plagiarism.[59] Robert Greene described his younger contemporary Shakespeare as 'an upstart crow beautified with our feathers'.[60] It was a double trope, feathers being associated not only with hats that could give false impression of a man's status, but with quill pens.[61] And indeed Shakespeare was, in modern terms a plagiarist on a vast scale, whole passages of *Antony and Cleopatra*, to take just one example, being line by line versifications of prose historical works on which he drew.

And practices that would later be conceptualised as infringements of copyright, were seen as deception. In 1559, for example, a member of the industry was fined twenty pence 'for pryntinge of halfe a Reame of ballettes [ballads] of a nother mans Copy by waye of Desceate'.[62] Or as disguise. For example, 'under colour of their patents' (1585), 'under colour of the former impression' (1626), 'by colour of an unlawful and enforced entry in the Stationers' register'.[63] I have not been able to discover where this metaphor

---

59   The main scholarly works on the historical genesis and development of notions of plagiarism are those written or edited by Paulina Kewes, *Authorship and Appropriation: Writing for the Stage in England 1660-1710* (Oxford: Oxford University Press, 1998), and *Plagiarism in Early Modern England* (London: Palgrave, 2003). But, so far have our metaphors changed since the time about which Kewes writes that I hesitate to quote. The publisher's page of the latter volume declares, that 'no paragraph of this publication may be reproduced, copied, or transmitted save with written permission'. The use of the archaism 'save' implies that the requirement is an ancient one. The publisher goes on to threaten that: 'Any person who does any unauthorised act in relation to this publication may be liable to criminal prosecution and civil claims for damages'.

60   Robert Greene, *Groatsworth of Wit* (London, 1592).

61   Sir Thomas Browne, 'To plume ourselves with others' feathers', quoted by Christopher Ricks in Kewes, p. 31. Another example, Lauder's accusation of Milton, discussed by Richard Terry in Kewes, p. 186.

62   Arber, i, p. 101.

63   Greg, pp. 73, 123; *London Printers Lamentation*, p. 8.

originated. Maybe from heraldry or from ships flying false colours? But it held its power, and it occurs in the Bill of Rights that forms part of the Constitution of the United States. But the disguise metaphor too could be rhetorically turned. Lord Thurlow noted in 1774 that the book industry had until recently been unconcerned with the financial interests of authors, and only introduced them 'to give a colourful face to their monopoly', an observation that is validated by the historical record.[64]

A variation was the metaphor of counterfeit. A copy of a piece of printed material made without the permission of the first publisher were described as 'base' or 'false', presumably on the analogy of forgery or fake coins, even although no element of deception had to be present. The metaphor was employed with success by William Hogarth and his colleagues when they promoted a bill that prevented print-sellers from having their engravings copied by others. The copiest, they argued to parliament, 'does not indeed steal the very Paper, (which if he did, tho' it is of no great a Value, he knows he should suffer for it) he steals from him every Thing that made that Paper valuable, and reaps an Advantage which he has no more Right to than He, who counterfeits a Note of Hand, has to the Money he receives by it'.[65]

Gardens

Another common set of metaphors came from horticulture, agriculture, and apiculture. An anthology is, by etymological definition a selection of flowers, and the words used for printed collections of selections from previously printed texts maintained ancient associations with gardens – garland, arbour, bower, garnish. Printed collections were also presented as honey sucked from the sweetest flowers, brought together to form a literary equivalent of the ideal commonwealth maintained by bees in a hive with a queen bee as its head. But these metaphors too were easy to reverse. Authors or booksellers who made reputations or money by appropriating other people's words were drones.[66] And so were patentees with their mysterious business practices.

> [...] those Drones, that fly about in mists

---

64 Quoted by Tompson, p. 32.
65 Quoted by D. Hunter, 'Copyright Protection for Engravings and Maps in Eighteenth-Century Britain', *The Library*, 6th ser., 9 (1987), 128-47 (p. 135), from *The Case of the Designers*, 1734/5.
66 A charge also made against the copyright infringers in the early eighteenth century. See Bond, 'The Pirate and the *Tatler*'.

Divielish *Projectors*, damn'd *Monopolists*[67]

Publishers too were metaphored as gardeners, whose task was to cultivate flowers but who, in practice, opponents declared, prevented writings from reaching readers, ('like flowers that die for lack of being refreshed and watered'). The industry's business practices, that author continued, caused them to 'miscarry', a bodily metaphor.[68] It was to similar metaphors that the Stationers' Company appealed in one of its attempts to justify the industry's monopoly privileges. Copyright, they declared in a deposition to the government, was 'a thing many wayes beneficiall to the state, and different in nature from the engrossing or Monopolizing some other Commodities into the hands of the few'. Unless the size of the industry was restricted and controlled, it would become 'like a feeld overpestred with too much stock, must needs grow indigent, and indigence must needs make it run into trespasses, and break into divers unlawful shifts; as Cattle use to do, when their pasture begins wholly to fail'.[69]

Gardens were normally presented as sanctuaries of peace but they were also bases from which swarms of insects escaped to spread plagues. Without controls on the printing presses, the monarch might be 'stung to death by the tongues of tale-bearers'.[70] Birds too could spread a plague. The commonwealth can be a 'cage of unclean birds'.[71] And they could fly out of gardens. As one writer wrote, bringing together a range of related metaphorical ideas, the human tongue, although 'but a little Member, can set the course of Nature on Fire, how much more the Quill, which is of a flying Nature in it self; and so Spiritual, that it is in all Places at the same time; and so Powerful, when it is cunningly handled, that it is the Peoples Deity'.[72]

Property

Let me now turn to metaphors of property. When in 1585 the English state granted 'a propriety', that is, an exclusive right to copy and sell a text in printed form, the right was proper to an individual, that is, it moved from public to private. But that 'propriety' continued to be officially described as

---

67   Quoted by Cyprian Blagden, *The Stationers' Company: A History* (London: Allen and Unwin, 1960), p. 131.

68   *A Letter to the Society of Booksellers* (1738), p. 44.

69   Arber, i, pp. 586-7.

70   'Epistle' in L'Estrange.

71   Hills, p. 1.

72   Atkyns, p. Bii.

a 'priviledge', that is, that it was granted for public purposes.[73] The word also reasserted the link between state-conferred economic privilege and state-enforced textual acceptability.[74] Only a proper text could qualify to be 'a proper copy'.[75] It was by turning this argument against Lord Chancellor Eldon that the unauthorised reprinters of Byron's *Don Juan* were able in the nineteenth century to bring about the largest readership of a literary work that had ever occurred until that time. And we still find traces of the same approach even in jurisdictions in which copyright is normally regarded as an absolute private property right – in some countries, for example, intellectual property rights are not accorded to texts officially regarded as pornographic.

The same verbal slide occurred with the word 'own', that was used both in the sense of owning a right to reproduce a text for sale, and in the sense of acknowledging responsibility for having produced that text – 'owning up' in modern usage. In the late seventeenth century when England had some of the tightest textual controls in its history, the prosecutors frequently asked 'do you own this book?' If the book offended the political and ecclesiastical groups then in power, the results for the 'owner' could be dire and sometimes fatal.[76]

Piracy

The language of stealing arrived in England quite suddenly at the end of the seventeenth century, and established itself as the main metaphor between the lapsing of the Licensing Act in 1695, after which, for fifteen years, until the 1710 statute, there was no statutory basis for copyright. Indeed it is striking is that before the formal link between monopoly selling rights and state textual licensing was broken in 1695, those who infringed the copying rights were seldom, if ever, accused of 'stealing'. The words most commonly used, other than variations on abuse and disorder, appear to be infringement, violation, and trespass. One publisher is said to have 'trepanned' another's copy, a notion of invasion of the body, a metaphor which contains, I suppose, some notion that the offence is

73   For example, 'such Person to whom such Entry is made, is, and always hath been reputed and taken to be the Proprietor of such Book or Copy, and ought to have the sole Printing thereof; which Privileg[e] and Interest is now of late often violated and abused'. Ordinances of 1682, Arber, i, p. 22.
74   An example in Greg, p. 35.
75   The phrase used in one case before the Stationers' Court; Jackson, p. 2.
76   Discussed with examples by Jody Greene.

intellectual?[77]

In the discussions during the years before and around 1710, which included contributions by authors, some of whom, such as Addison and Defoe, were skilled rhetoricians, we still frequently hear the old metaphors, sickness, disguise, drones that suck the honey from the working fraternity, and so on. But copyright infringements were now, for the first time, routinely equated with theft, for example, to list a few metaphors noted in the pamphlet literature of the time, with shoplifting, letter-picking, purse-cutting, highway robbery, burgling a house, plundering a hospital.[78] And piracy.[79]

The read-across from piracy to copyright may have begun from that of a sea robber who operated outside all law and could be put to death without trial. For example, it was argued in 1688 that members of ecclesiastical organisations opposed to the official English religion 'should be no more encouraged than Pyrates, and common Enemies of Mankind'.[80] But soon, as I read the record, the piracy metaphor changed to that of an interloper or a privateer – that is, to a trader who remained outside the chartered trading Company's membership and could undercut the Company's prices. This is, in fact, a precise analogy with the chartered guild of the Stationers'

---

77   [Henry Hills], *The Life of H.H. with the relation at large of what passed betwixt him and the Taylors Wife* (London: Printed by T.S., 1688), p. 54.

78   Summarised from examples quoted by Bond, and texts reprinted in *The Political and Economic Writings of Daniel Defoe*, ed. by W.R. Owens and P.N. Furbank (London: Pickering and Chatto, 2000).

79   John Fell, a bishop of Oxford, called the Stationers 'land-pirates' in 1674 for violating the university's privilege. He also attacked the Stationers' court in 1684 for 'piracie'. See Adrian Johns, *The Nature of the Book* (Chicago: Chicago University Press, 1998), p. 344, fn. 49. 'Pyrate' occurs in a document of 1697 quoted by Deazley, *On the Origin*, p. 18. We can also see the transitions within the same documents. Defoe, in his brief anonymous *An Essay on the Regulation of the Press* (London, 1704), available freely online as a Renascence Edition transcribed by Risa S. Bear, begins with metaphors of the body 'to prescribe a proper Remedy' that would provide a 'cure': [censorship] is 'cutting off the leg to cure the gout in the toe, like expelling poison with too rank a poison'; a book should not be 'damn'd in its womb'. However the author also moves to commercial and investment metaphors related to claimed outcomes: licensing would be 'a check to Learning, a prohibition of Knowledge, and [would] make Instruction Contraband'; intellectual property offences, 'some printers and booksellers printing Copies none of their own', are described as 'a most injurious piece of Violence'; and unauthorised abridgement is 'Press-Piracy', 'down-right robbing on the High-way, or cutting a purse'. Defoe also adduces the possible damage to the familial guild system, elements of which were still operating in his day: 'Nor is there a greater Abuse in any Civil Employment, than the printing of other Men's Copies, every jot as unjust as lying with their Wives, and breaking-up their Houses'.

80   *Reasons humbly offered*, p. 4.

Company which tried to bring all printers, publishers, and booksellers under its corporate jurisdiction.

One attraction of the piracy metaphor is that it caught the idea of loss of an investment, the writing of a long and useful learned work, such as the 1710 act 'for the encouragement of learning' was intended to promote, being metaphorically equated with the planning and financing of a voyage that took years to reward its investors. Addison compared the years of education and study required to write a book to the fitting out of a ship for a long hazardous voyage. 'Those few investors who have the good fortune to bring their rich wares into port are plundered by privateers under the very cannon that should protect them'.[81] Piracy at this time implied a long text.

These were the years when the English state's involvement in the transatlantic slave trade was being organised into chartered companies, and the pamphlet literature about the book industry drew its metaphors from that trade. Daniel Defoe wrote pamphlets on both, besides being the author of *Robinson Crusoe* – a much-admired literary character who, incidentally, made his fortune as a slave trader. And the arguments about the book industry of the time are full of slavery metaphors, knowledge being padlocked, authors slaves of the quill, enslaved to publishers, manumitted from one master only to be handed over to tyrannical corporations, and so on.

But the piracy metaphor was also useful to the other side. One of the first references I have found, that occurs long before the cluster at the end of the seventeenth century, is in a document prepared by the Vice Chancellor and Senate of the University of Cambridge in 1625. The occasion was the dispute with the London industry who wanted to end the University's privileged right to sell standard texts including astrological almanacs and magic prognostications, the tolerated illegitimate supernatural that continued alongside the official religion. The printed texts of these competing supernatural explanatory systems were produced in vast numbers every year with all the authority of the English state. Incidentally, I would judge that, until after 1774, most intellectual property disputes concerned breaches of the conferred monopoly to reprint astrological almanacs, the biggest and most reliably profitable sector of the historic book industry, and one which bound the political/ecclesiastical state and the industry together in a close economic/cultural alliance.[82] In the dispute of 1625, the

---

81   Quoted in St Clair, p. 89.
82   St Clair, p. 82.

University, writing in Latin, thanked the Howard family for their help in ensuring that 'our little craft was not only delivered from the fury of the pirates (I mean the London monopolists) but under Arundel as captain and pilot brought safely into harbour and propitiously made fast to land'.[83] In defence of its right to take a share of the business, the University deployed the whole panoply of common metaphors against its fellow-patentees in London – 'wicked tribe of robbers', 'Monopolists hateful to gods and men'. 'Sacrilege when the privileges of the Muses are wrested from the hands of the citizens by fraud and force', 'wresters of the law, plagues of the body politic, leeches of the state, and most artful plunderers'.[84] 'So do ye gather honey not for yourselves, ye, bees'; 'wicked and greedy gormandizers [who] did your utmost to swallow up in your gaping jaws the immunity granted to [Cambridge University]'.[85]

Another idea I offer is speculative – that the book industry's decision to describe copyright infringement as piracy may have included a fear of an alternative unregulated intellectual domain, an idea anathema both to guilds and to the political/ecclesiastical state. Although, during the slaving era, sea pirates were public enemies, they were also, despite their cruelty, admired for their equality, electing their captain, dividing their loot equally, never stealing from one another – and providing a kind of model for an alternative society and economy. Did they represent an alternative intellectual domain that would take in intellectual outcasts such as republicans and atheists?[86]

However, unlike the language of the bodily commonwealth that resulted in deaths and mutilations, the language of piracy was seldom taken seriously. For example, the industry did not proceed against the Irish offshore

---

83 Greg, p. 188.
84 Ibid.
85 Ibid., p. 189.
86 Notably in the work of the Abbé Raynal, *L'Histoire philosophique et politique des établissements et du commerce des Européens dans les deux Indes*, in which he draws on earlier writers. The first edition was published offshore in Amsterdam in 1770, to be followed by numerous editions, translations, abridgements, and piracies, 'contrefaçons'. In the 12 volume offshore edition (Geneva: Pellet, 1780) the main passage describing the customs of the 'flibustiers' or 'pirates' is in vol. v, pp. 275-319. In the less full English translation of 1811, *A Philosophical and Political History of the Settlements and Trade of the Europeans in the East and West Indies* (Edinburgh: Robertson and others, 3 volumes, 1811), the main passage is at vol. ii, p. 228. Hans Turley, *Rum, Sodomy and the Lash* (New York: New York University Press, 2001), notes that the democratic values attributed to the pirates were well known before Raynal, being noted, for example, by Defoe.

'pirates' under Irish common law. And, as the archival record shows, the London book industry often colluded with the 'piratical' practices it condemned and benefited from them. The language of piracy was largely literary knockabout, a trope as conventional as the ancient jokes about unread books being sent to the pastry cooks and the necessary houses. For centuries, the penalty for stealing, let alone for sea piracy, was death. You could be hanged for stealing a book valued at no more than a few shillings. By the beginning of the nineteenth century, the word 'pirate', meaning infringement of a state-conferred monopoly right, had become so far separated from the practice on which it was metaphored, that we find it in statute law.[87]

Until very recent years, even during the most authoritarian eras, nobody is recorded as suggesting that the penalties for theft should be applied to the money that publishers claimed that they had had 'stolen' from them by infringement of copyright. Indeed, until very recent times, the notion that unauthorised copying was morally equivalent to the crime of 'stealing' was never in practice taken seriously, and it is still at odds with public opinion. The one exception I know of in the historical record, an unsigned letter to a newspaper from 1771 when the legal/commercial dispute about perpetual intellectual property was at its most bitter. The author is referring to the Scottish printer/publishers who were exercising their rights to reprint out-of-copyright texts under the 1710 statute:

> The taking of a Volume of Tom Jones out of Mr Becket's Shop is a Felony and should the plundering the whole copy be no Offence at all? Surely a mere Embargo upon such Pirates is too mild a Punishment; they ought at least to stand in the Pillory, if not swing upon the Gallows before the Door of the Chapter Coffee house, as a Terror to piratical Booksellers, Printers, or Publishers.[88]

Landed Property

In the eighteenth century, the 'property' with which copyright was mainly metaphored shifted to land, that is, with an asset that, unlike cargos of

---

87   For example the word occurs several times in the Sculpture Copyright Act 1814, 54 Geo. III, c.56, as quoted by Shortt, p. 636.

88   From a printed letter, February 1771 'To the Printer' probably of the *Morning Advertiser* from 'a fair trader' in 'Press Cuttings on Artistic Subjects 1685-1830', National Art Library, Victoria and Albert Museum, [PP.17.G], 1, 43. *The London Printers Lamentation*, p. 6, quotes the remark in the biblical Book of Proverbs that 'He that saves a Thief from the Gallows shall first be robbed himself' but only as a part of a call for infringements not to be ignored.

ships, is not easy for pirates to steal. The talk is of 'possession' and 'title'.[89] Rights were 'trespassed on'.[90] Or 'invaded and intruded upon'.[91] Literary property was an 'occupancy'.[92] Trespass continued to be the main metaphor for plagiarism well into the nineteenth century.[93]

And we can see the attractions of the private land metaphor for the producer interest, both authors and publishers. The bodily commonwealth, harsh though it was, did imply, in theory at least, a concern for the health of every person participating in the commonwealth. But the rhetorical tendency of the land metaphor was not only to naturalise a business practice but to do so in a way that excluded as irrelevant all interests beyond those of the 'proprietor'. The landowner did not have to justify his actions to those against whom he shut his gates. Indeed he looked for 'protection' against them, a metaphor that continues. However, even at the height of the dominance of the landed estate metaphor – around 1774 – there were voices who claimed that to monopolise the ownership of texts was to damage a wider interest, a 'public utility' in the flow of invention. And with 'flow' we hear a new land metaphor, that again picks up a dominant economic concern of the times, the dredging of rivers. If knowledge is monopolised 'every article of trade, every branch of manufacture, would be affected and clogged, if not totally stopped'.[94]

It is striking that, in current discussions, even those who draw attention to damaging effects of the current long – near perpetual – copyright regimes, such as Lawrence Lessig, are reluctant to critique the discourse of 'property' as such. The potentially damaging effects with which they are mainly concerned are not the consumer interest in access to knowledge but artistic expression, that is, on the successor producer interest.[95] As was the case with its bodily predecessors, the metaphor of property has, we can say, to a large extent, succeeded in its rhetorical tendency to put the main features of the institution above or beyond question, and that it continues to do so.

89   For example in Francis Hargrave, *An Argument in Defence of Literary Property* (London, 1774).
90   Atkyns, p. E.
91   *London Printers Lamentation*, p. 6.
92   Hargrave, p. 36.
93   Especially by Wordsworth. Discussed by, for example, Tilar J. Mazzeo, *Plagiarism and Literary Property in the Romantic Period* (Philadelphia, University of Pennsylvania Press, 2007).
94   Hargrave, p. 37.
95   Lawrence Lessig, *Free Culture, How Big Media Uses Technology and the Law to Lock Down Culture and Creativity* (New York: Penguin, 2004).

Moveable Property

During the nineteenth century the property against which copyright was metaphored underwent another shift, this time from landed to moveable property. British authors, whose works were reprinted offshore in the United States, led the way in using the language of 'robbery', sometimes robbery with violence. The American reprinters were, for example, 'Rob Roy and his cattle-thieves.' [96] 'Robbers that ye are', were refrains of Dickens and Thackeray in their efforts to persuade the American state to extend copyright to works published abroad.[97] Thomas Carlyle too adopted an obsolete menacing language reminiscent of the early modern state: 'That thou belongst to a different Nation and canst steal without being certainly hanged for it, gives thee no permission to steal. Thou shalt not in any wise steal at all'.[98] It is unlikely that the political pressures – and the recent decision – to reclassify copyright infringement as a criminal rather than a civil offence could have passed the legislatures if that metaphorical shift had not occurred.

Implications

So what are the implications of this brief summary of the history of the metaphors for our understanding of the currently dominant metaphor of property? As with the bodily metaphor, we can see that the property metaphors too has shifted in accordance with the dominant concerns of the time – sea piracy, trespassing on landed estates, and theft of personal moveable property. We can also see that the forms of property on which 'intellectual' property has been metaphored have themselves changed, and in many cases are different from what they were when the comparisons first became current. The monopoly implicit in real property, for example, on which copyright continues to be metaphored has itself long been regulated by statute. The days when 'a man could do what he wills with his own', if they ever existed, have long since gone. Restrictions on the uses to which real property can be put, introduced for public policy reasons,

---

96   Quoted by Catherine Seville, *The Internationalisation of Copyright Law* (Cambridge: Cambridge University Press, 2006), p. 167.
97   Robert L. Patten, *Charles Dickens and His Publishers* (Oxford: Oxford University Press, 1978), p. 119; Jerome Meckier, *Innocent Abroad, Dickens's American Engagements* (Lexington: University of Kentucky Press, 1990), p. 73.
98   Quoted by Catherine Seville in a draft paper circulated to CIPIL from a published letter to Dickens dated 26 March 1842.

are now more comprehensive than those on intellectual property. As the authors of the standard work on land law wrote in their latest edition, an act of Parliament of 2002 marked the culmination of a long process in which '[t]he philosophical base of English land law has finally shifted from empirically defined fact to state-defined entitlement, from property as a reflection of social actuality to property as a product of state-ordered or political fact'.[99] And, with moveable property too, there is now also a large body of national and international law and regulation, much of it aimed at combating monopolistic practices or lessening the damaging effects on the interests of consumers described by Adam Smith two centuries ago.

So we have arrived at a discursive situation in which none of various forms of property on which intellectual property has historically been met-aphored can any longer act as adequate comparators. The primary idea of 'property', like its reciprocal 'piracy', has become a dead metaphor, retain-ing rhetorical power but no longer offering much explanatory or analytical value.

Essential Differences, Rivalrous and Non-rivalrous Goods

What none of the property metaphors has been able to accommodate is the fact that the differences between 'property' and 'intellectual property' are not contingent or superficial but essential, inescapable, and unignorable. If a real property, such as a ship's cargo, a landed estate, or a collection of personal moveable goods, is divided, the outcome in terms of benefit is also divided. With intellectual property, however, that is not the case. One person's level of education and knowledge does not depend upon other persons having correspondingly lower or higher levels of education and knowledge. The benefit you may receive from reading Shakespeare is not lessened if I read Shakespeare. It follows that, as soon as we admit, or rather re-admit, desired outcomes as the central purpose of the laws and institutions of intellectual property, then any analysis of the public policy choices has to give primacy to the fact that the outcomes that they are intended to promote are non-rivalrous goods.

It may be too much to expect that the metaphor of 'intellectual property' should be retired or downgraded as its predecessors have been, but when it

---

99   Kevin Gray and Susan Francis Gray, *Elements of Land Law*, 4th edn (Oxford: Oxford University Press, 2005), p. 387.

is used in public policy discussions, it is reasonable to require that, as in the past, the metaphor should adapt itself to the dominant concerns of the economy, which at the present time increasingly centre on non-rivalrous goods such as education, knowledge, and access to knowledge. And, whatever metaphors are used or adapted, we can reasonably ask that, for the purposes of analysis and policy-making, the institution is also conceptualised for what it has always been, a state-conferred and state-guaranteed monopoly right to copy and to sell a text at a monopoly price, an economic privilege bestowed by a polity with the aim of achieving certain beneficial consequences and outcomes for the members of that polity, both short term and long term.

In the United Kingdom, however, we have no arrangements for ensuring that the effects, consequences, and outcomes of the intellectual property regime are professionally evaluated against the benefits to the public that are claimed. Uniquely, for this most vital of monopolies, we have no regulator, no equivalent of Ofcom or Ofwat, no codes of practice, and no appeal tribunals, although the risks from the monopolisation of knowledge, ideas, education, and the means by which they are made available, are matters of at least as much importance as telephone charges and water bills.

Bibliography

Abrams, Howard B., 'The Historic Foundation of American Copyright Law: Exploding the Myth of Common Law Copyright', *Wayne Law Review*, 29 (1983), 1119-91.

Agnew, Geoffrey, *Agnew's 1817-1967* (London: The Bradbury Agnew Press, 1967).

Alberti, Leon Battista, *De picture, in Opere volgari*, ed. by Cecil Grayson (Bari: Laterza, 1973).

Alberts, R.C., *Benjamin West: A Biography* (Boston: Houghton Mifflin, 1978).

Alpers, Svetlana, *The Art of Describing: Dutch Art in the Seventeenth Century* (London: John Murray, 1983).

Anon., *A Letter to the Society of Booksellers* (1738).

Anon., *A Course of Lectures to Young Men ... Delivered in Glasgow, by Ministers of Various Denominations* (Glasgow, 1842).

Anon., 'Lord Overstone and Art', *The Times* (29 November 1883).

Anon., *Actes de la Conférence de l'Union internationale pour la protection des oeuvres littéraires et artistiques: réunie à Paris du 15 avril au 4 mai 1896* (Berne: Bureau international de l'Union, 1897).

Anon., *Annalen der Gesetzgebung und Rechtsgelehrsamkeit in den preussischen Staaten* (1788-1809). Available online at <http://www.ub.uni-bielefeld.de/diglib/aufklaerung/index.htm>.

Anon., *Arguments Relating to a Restraint upon the Press ... in a Letter to a Bencher from a Young Gentleman of the Temple* (London, 1712).

Anon., *The Importance of the Liberty of the Press* (1748).

Arber, Edward (ed.), *A Transcript of the Registers of the Company of Stationers of London 1554-1640*, 5 vols (London, 1875).

Archer, Ian W., 'The Framework of Social Relations: The Livery Companies', *In the Pursuit of Stability: Social Relations in Elizabethan London* (Cambridge: Cambridge University Press, 1991), 100-48.

Armstrong, Elizabeth, *Before Copyright. The French Book-privilege System 1498-1526* (Cambridge: Cambridge University Press, 1990).

Astbury, Raymond, 'The Renewal of the Licensing Act in 1693 and its Lapse in 1695', *The Library*, 33 (1978), 296-322.

Atkyns, Richard, *Original and Growth of Printing* (London: Printed by John Streater, for the Author, 1664).

[Aubry], *Mémoire sur la contestation qui est entre les libraires de Paris et ceux de Lyon au sujet des privilèges et des continuations que le Roy accorde*, Bibliothèque nationale de France, Manus. Fçs. 22071, n. 177.

Ballon, Hillary, *The Paris of Henry IV. Architecture and Urbanism* (Cambridge, MA: MIT Press, 1991).

Barber, Giles, 'French Royal Decrees Concerning the Book Trade, 1700-1789', *Australian Journal of French Studies*, 3 (1966), 312-30.

Barker, Francis, *The Tremulous Private Body* (New York and London: Methuen, 1984).

Barnes, James J., *Authors, Publishers and Politicians: The Quest for an Anglo-American Copyright Agreement, 1815-1854* (London: Routledge & Kegan Paul, 1974).

Barratt, D., 'The Dramatic Authors' Society (1833-1883) and the Payment of English Dramatists', *Essays in English Theatre*, 7 (1988), 19-33.

Barthes, Roland, 'The Death of the Author', in *Image, Music, Text*, ed. by Stephen Heath (London: Fontana, 1977).

Baudrillard, Jean, 'Trompe l'œil', in *Calligram: Essays in New Art History from France*, ed. by Norman Bryson (Cambridge: Cambridge University Press, 1988), 53-62.

Bayley, Daniel, *Select Harmony* (Newburyport, Mass: Daniel Bayley, 1784).

Beaufort, Henri Louis de, *Het auteursrecht in het Nederlandsche en Internationale recht* (Utrecht: Den Boer, 1909; repr. Amsterdam: Buma, 1993).

Becker, P.A., 'Das Druckprivileg für Marots Werke von 1538', *Zeitschrift für französische Sprache und Litteratur*, 42 (1914), 224-25.

Bell, Maureen, John Barnard, and D. F. McKenzie (eds), *Cambridge History of the Book in Britain*, Volume IV (Cambridge: Cambridge University Press, 2002).

Benkler, Yochai, 'From Consumers to Users: Shifting the Deeper Structures of Regulation', *Federal Communications Law Journal*, 52 (2000), 561-79.

Bently, Lionel, 'Art and the Making of Modern Copyright Law', in *Dear Images: Art, Copyright and Culture*, ed. by D. McClean and K. Schubert (London: Ridinghouse/ICA, 2002), 331-51.

—, 'Requiem for Registration? Reflections on the History of the UK Registered Designs System', in *The Prehistory and Development of Intellectual Property Systems*, ed. by Alison Firth, Perspectives on Intellectual Property Series, 1 (London: Sweet & Maxwell, 1997), 1-46.

—, and Brad Sherman, 'Great Britain and the Signing of the Berne Convention in 1886', *Journal of the Copyright Society of the USA* (2001), 311-40.

—, *Intellectual Property Law*, 2nd edn (Oxford: Oxford University Press, 2004).

Berengo, Marino, 'La crisi dell'arte della stampa veneziana alla fine del XVIII secolo', in *Studi in onore di Armando Sapori* (Milan: Istituto Editoriale Cisalpino, 1957), II, 1321-38.

Berger, A., *Encyclopedic Dictionary of Roman Law* (Philadelphia: American Philosophical Society, 1953).

Berger, John, 'Past Seen from a Possible Future', in *Selected Essays and Articles. The Look of Things*, ed. by N. Stangos (Harmonsworth: Penguin, 1972), 211-20.

Berger, Peter, and Thomas Luckmann, *The Social Constitution of Reality* (Harmonsworth: Penguin, 1971).

Berveglieri, Roberto, *Inventori stranieri a Venezia (1474-1788): Importazione di tecnologia e circolazione di tecnici artigiani inventori* (Venice: Istituto Veneto di Scienze Lettere e Arti, 1995).

Birn, Raymond, 'The Profit of Ideas. Privilèges en librairie in Eighteenth-century France', *Eighteenth-Century Studies*, 4 (1971), 131-68.

Birrell, Augustine, *Seven Lectures on The Law and History of Copyright in Books* (London: Cassell and Company, 1899).

Bisse, Philip, *A Sermon preach'd at the Anniversary Meeting of the Sons of the Clergy in the Cathedral Church of St Paul on Thursday December the 2nd* (1709).

Blagden, Cyprian, 'The English Stock of the Stationers' Company: An Account of its Origins', *The Library*, 5th ser., 10 (1955), 163-85.

—, 'Thomas Carnan and the Almanack Monopoly', *Studies in Bibliography*, 14 (1961), 23-43.

—, *The Stationers' Company: A History, 1403-1959* (London: George Allen & Unwin Ltd, 1960).

Blaine, D.R., *On the Laws of Artistic Copyright and their Defects* (London: Murray, 1853).

—, *Suggestions on the Copyright (Works of Art) Bill* (London: Hardwicke, 1861).

Blanc, Étienne, *Traité de la contrefaçon en tous genres et de sa poursuite en justice*, 4th edn (Paris: Plon, 1855).

Bloch, Maurice, 'Property and the End of Affinity', in *Marxist Analyses and Social Anthropology*, ed. by Maurice Bloch (London: Malaby Press, 1975), 203-28.

[Blount, Charles], *Reasons Humbly Offered for the Liberty of Unlicensed Printing* (London, 1693).

Blum, Abbe, 'The Author's Authority: *Areopagitica* and the Labour of Licensing', in *Remembering Milton*, ed. by Mary Nyquist and Margaret W. Ferguson (New York and London: Methuen, 1987), 74-96.

Bluntschli, Johann Kaspar, *Deutsches Privatrecht*, 2 vols (Munich: Literarisch-artistische Anstalt, 1853-54).

—, *Deutsches Privatrecht*, trans. Luis Sundkvist (München: 1853), *Primary Sources on Copyright (1450-1900)* <http://www.copyrighthistory.org>.

Bond, Richmond P., 'The Pirate and the *Tatler*', *The Library*, 18, 4 (1963), 257-74.

Bonnell, Thomas F., *The Most Disreputable Trade: Publishing the Classics of English Poetry 1765-1810* (Oxford: Oxford University Press, 2008).

Booth, Martin R., 'Public Taste, the Playwright and the Law', in *The Revels History of Drama in English*, ed. by Clifford Leech and T.W. Craik, 8 vols (London: Methuen & Co., 1975) VI, 29-57.

Borchgrave, Jean de, *Evolution historique du droit d'auteur* (Bruxelles: Larcier, 1916).

Born, G., and D. Hesmondhalgh (eds), *Western Music and its Others: Difference, Appropriation and Representation in Music* (Berkeley: University of California Press, 2000).

Bornemann, Friedrich Wilhelm Ludwig, *Systematische Darstellung des Preußischen Civilrechts mit Benutzung der Materialien des Allgemeinen Landrechts*, 2nd edn (Berlin: Jonas Verlagsbuchhandlung, 1843). Available online at <http://dlib-pr.mpier.mpg.de/m/kleioc/0010/exec/bigpage/%22110810_00000204%22>.

Borsi, Franco, *Leon Battista Alberti* (Milano: Electa, 1975).

Botero, Giovanni, *Le relazioni universali* (Paris, 1605), in *Venice: A Documentary History, 1450-1630*, ed. by D. Chambers and B. Pullan (Oxford: Oxford University Press, 1992), 167-8.

Bouchard, D. (ed.), *Language, Counter-Memory, Practice*, trans. D. Bouchard and S. Simon (Ithaca, NY: Cornell University Press, 1977).

Boutier, Jean, Jean-Yves Sarracin and Marianne Sibille, *Les plans de Paris des origins (1493) à la fin du XVIIIe siècle* (Paris: Bibliothèque nationale de France, 2002).

Bowker, Richard Rogers, *Copyright: Its History and its Law* (Boston and New York: Hougton Mifflin Company, 1912).

Bowrey, Kathy, 'Who's Writing Copyright History?', *European Intellectual Property Review*, 18, 6 (1996), 322-9.

Boyle, James, *Shamans, Software, and Spleens: Law and the Construction of the Information Society* (Cambridge, MA: Harvard University Press, 1996).

Boytha, G., 'La justification de la protection des droits d'auteur à la lumière de leur développement historique', *Revue Internationale du Droit d'Auteur*, (1992), 52-100.

—, 'Whose Right is Copyright?', *GRUR Int.*, (1983), 379-85.

Bracha, Oren, 'Commentary on Folsom v. Marsh (1841)', *Primary Sources on Copyright (1450-1900)* <http://www.copyrighthistory.org>.

—, 'Commentary on the Connecticut Copyright Statute 1783', *Primary Sources on Copyright (1450-1900)* <http://www.copyrighthistory.org>.

—, 'Commentary on the Intellectual Property Constitutional Clause 1789', *Primary Sources on Copyright (1450-1900)* <http://www.copyrighthistory.org>.

—, 'The Ideology of Authorship Revisited: Authors, Markets, and Liberal Values in Early American Copyright', *Yale Law Journal*, 118 (2008), 186-271.

—, *Owning Ideas: A History of Anglo-American Intellectual Property* (S.J.D. Dissertation, Harvard Law School, 2005), <http://www.obracha.net/oi/oi.htm>.

Braudel, Fernand, *The Mediterranean and the Mediterranean World in the Age of Philip II*, trans. Siân Reynolds (London: Collins, 1984).

Brisson, Barnabé, *Recueil de plaidoyez notables de plusieurs anciens et fameux advocats de la Cour de Parlement ...et divers arrêts* (Paris, 1644).

Brodhead, John R., et al. (eds), *Documents Relative to the Colonial History of the State of New York*, 15 vols (Albany: Weed, Parsons and Company, Printers, 1853-87).

Brown, Cynthia, *Poets, Patrons and Printers. Crisis of Authority in Late Medieval France* (Ithaca and London: Cornell University Press, 1995).

Brown, G.S., *Literary Sociability and Literary Property in France, 1775-1793: Beaumarchais, the Société des Auteurs Dramatiques and the Comédie Française* (Aldershot, England: Ashgate, 2006).

Brown, Horatio Fortini, *The Venetian Printing Press 1469-1800: An Historical Study Based upon Documents for the Most Part Hitherto Unpublished* (London: John C. Nimmo, 1891).

Brown, K.M., et al., *The Records of the Parliaments of Scotland [RPS]*, <http://www.rps.ac.uk> (St Andrews: University of St Andrews, 2007), *RPS*, 1641/8/192.

Bruntjen, S.H.A., *John Boydell, 1719-1804: A Study of Art Patronage and Publishing in Georgian London* (New York: Garland Publishing, 1985).

Bugbee, B.W., *The Genesis of American Patent and Copyright Law* (Washington: Public Affairs Press, 1967).

Burckhard, Jacob, *The Civilization of the Renaissance in Italy* (Harmondsworth: Penguin, 1990).

Calhoun, Craig (ed.), *Habermas and the Public Sphere* (Cambridge, MA: The MIT Press, 1992).

Carmer, Johann Heinrich Kasimir (ed.), *Entwurf eines Allgemeinen Gesetzbuchs für die preußischen Staten* (Berlin: Decker, 1784-8).

Carter, Alan, *The Philosophical Foundations of Property Rights* (New York: Harvester, Wheatsheaf, 1989).

Carvais, Robert, 'Servir la justice, l'art et la technique: le rôle des plans, dessins et croquis devant la Chambre royale des bâtiments', *Sociétés et représentations*, 18 (2004), 75-96.

Castellani, Carlo, *I privilegi di stampa e la proprietà letteraria in Venezia: Dalla introduzione della stampa nella città fin verso la fine del secolo XVIII* (Venezia: Stabilimento Tipo-Litografico Fratelli Visentini, 1888).

—, *La stampa in Venezia dalla sua origine alla morte di Aldo Manuzio Seniore. Ragionamento storico di Carlo Castellani prefetto della Biblioteca di San Marco. Con appendice di documenti in parte inediti. Presentazione de Giorgio E. Ferrari* (Trieste: Edizioni LINT, 1973).

Cella, Johann Jakob, 'Vom Büchernachdruck' (Ansbach, 1784).

Chandler, George, *An Introductory Lecture delivered at the Commencement of the Second Session of the Chichester Literary and Philosophical Society* (Chichester, 1832).

Chartier, Roger, 'Figures de l'auteur', in *Culture écrite et société. L'ordre des livres (xive – xviiie siècle)* (Paris: Albin Michel, 1996), 45-80.

—, 'Qu'est-ce qu'un auteur? Révision d'une généalogie', *Bulletin de la société de philosophie*, 94 (2000), 1-37.

—, *Inscrire et effacer. Culture écrite et littérature (xie-xviiie siècle)* (Paris: Gallimard Seuil, 2005).

—, *The Order of Books: Readers, Authors, and Libraries in Europe between the Fourteenth and Eighteenth Centuries* (Cambridge: Polity, 1994).

Chavasse, Ruth, 'The first known author's copyright, September 1486, in the context of a humanist career', *Bulletin of the John Rylands University Library of Manchester*, 69 (1986-7), 11-37.

Chaytor, H.J., *From Script to Print: An Introduction to Medieval Literature* (Cambridge: Cambridge University Press, 1945).

Cicogna, Emanuele Antonio, *Delle inscrizioni veneziane*, 6 vols (1852; repr. Bologna: Forni Editore, 1970).

Clarke, G., *The Photograph* (Oxford: Oxford University Press, 1997).

Clegg, Cyndia Susan, *Press censorship in Elizabethan England* (Cambridge: Cambridge University Press, 1997).

Collins, A.S., *Authorship in the Days of Johnson* (London: Routledge & Kegan Paul, 1927).

Compagnon, Antoine, *La seconde main* (Paris: Éditions du seuil, 1979).

Condorcet, Jean-Antoine-Nicolas de Caritat, Marquis de, 'Fragments sur la liberté de la presse' (1776), in *Œuvres de Condorcet*, 12 vols (Paris: Firmin Didot, 1847).

Connan, François, *Commentarius Iuris civilis* (Paris, 1553).

Contat, Nicolas, *Anecdotes typographiques où l'on voit la description des coutumes, mœurs et usages singuliers des compagnons imprimeurs*, ed. by Giles Barber (Oxford: Oxford Bibliographical Society, 1980).

Coombe, Rosemary J., *The Cultural Life of Intellectual Properties: Authorship, Appropriation, and the Law* (Durham, NC: Duke University Press, 1998).

Cooper, T., *Statutes at Large of South Carolina*, 11 vols (Columbia, S.C.: A.S. Johnston, 1836-73).

Coppens, Angela Nuovo and Christian, *I Giolito e la stampa nell'Italia del XVI secolo* (Genève: Droz, 2005).

Cornish, W.R., 'Authors in Law', *Modern Law Review*, 58, 1 (1995), 1-16.

—, and David Llewelyn, *Intellectual Property: Patents, Copyright, Trade Marks and Allied Rights* (London: Sweet & Maxwell, 2007).

Couhin, C., *La propriété industrielle, artistique et littéraire*, 3 vols (Paris, 1898).

Couper, W.J., 'Copyright in Scotland before 1709', *Records of the Glasgow Bibliographical Society*, 9 (1931), 42-57.

—, 'Robert Sanders The Elder', *Records of Glasgow Bibliographical Society*, 3 (1915), 26-88.

Crawford, F., 'Pre-Constitutional Copyright Statutes', *Bulletin of the Copyright Society of the U.S.A*, 23 (1975), 11-37.

Crawford, R., and D.P. McKay, *William Billings of Boston: Eighteenth Century Composer* (Princeton, N.J.: Princeton University Press, 1975).

Crousaz, K., *Erasme et le pouvoir de l'imprimerie* (Lausanne: Antipodes, 2005).

Curtis, George Ticknor, *A Treatise on the Law of Copyright in Books, Dramatic, and Musical Compositions, Letters, and other Manuscripts, Engravings, and Sculpture as Enacted and Administered in England and America* (Boston: C.C. Little and J. Brown, 1847).

Dainville, François de, 'Les cartes et contestations au XVe siècle', *Imago Mundi*, 24 (1970), 99-121.

Dambach, Otto, *Die Gesetzgebung des Norddeutschen Bundes betreffend das Urheberrecht an Schriftwerken, Abbildungen, musikalischen Kompositionen und dramatischen Werken* (Berlin: Enslin, 1871).

Darnton, Robert, *The Great Cat Massacre and Other Episodes in French Cultural History* (Hamonsworth: Penguin, 1985).

David, Michel-Antoine, 'Droit de copie', in *Encyclopédie ou dictionnaire raisonné des sciences, des arts et des métiers*, Volume 5, ed. by D. Diderot and J. le Ronde d'Alembert. Available online at <http://artflx.uchicago.edu/cgi-bin/philologic/getobject.pl?c.33:1:25.encyclopedie0110>.

Davis, Natalie Zemon, 'Beyond the Market: Books as Gifts in Sixteenth-century France', *Transactions of the Royal Historical Society*, 33 (1983), 69-88.

—, *The Gift in Sixteenth-Century France* (Oxford: Oxford University Press, 2000).

Dawson, Robert, *The French Booktrade and the 'Permission Simple' of 1777: Copyright and Public Domain* (Oxford: The Voltaire Foundation, 1992).

Deazley, Ronan, 'Commentary on *Donaldson v. Becket* (1774)', *Primary Sources on Copyright (1450-1900)* <http://www.copyrighthistory.org>.

—, 'Commentary on Stationers' Company v. Carnan (1775)', *Primary Sources on Copyright (1450-1900)* <http://www.copyrighthistory.org>.

—, 'Commentary on the Stationers' Charter (1557)', *Primary Sources on Copyright (1450-1900)* <http://www.copyrighthistory.org>.

—, 'Commentary on the Statute of Anne (1710)', *Primary Sources on Copyright (1450-1900)* <http://www.copyrighthistory.org>.

—, 'Commentary on Tonson v. Collins (1762)', *Primary Sources on Copyright (1450-1900)* <http://www.copyrighthistory.org>.

—, *On the Origin of the Right to Copy: Charting the Movement of Copyright Law in Eighteenth-century Britain (1695-1775)* (Oxford: Hart Publishing, 2004).

—, *Rethinking Copyright: History, Theory, Language* (Cheltenham: Edward Elgar, 2006).

Defaux, G., 'Trois cas d'écrivains éditeurs dans la première moitié du xviᵉ siècle: Marot, Rabelais, Dolet', *Travaux de littérature*, 14 (2001), 91-118.

Delalande, E., *Étude sur la propriété littéraire et artistique* (Paris: Marescq Aîné, 1880).

Derrida, Jacques, *The Truth in Painting*, trans. Geoff Bennington and Ian Mcleod (Chicago and London: University of Chicago Press, 1987).

Descimon, Robert, 'Paris on the eve of Saint Bartholomew: Taxation, Privilege and Social Geography', in *Cities and Social Change in Early Modern France*, ed. by Philip Benedict (London and New York: Unwin Hyman, 1989), 69-104.

Dickson, R., and J.P. Edmond, *Annals of Scottish Printing: From the Introduction of the Art in 1507 to the Beginning of the Seventeenth Century*, (1890; repr. Amsterdam: Gerard Th. Van Heusden, 1975).

Diderot, Denis, 'Lettre historique et politique adressée à un magistrat sur le commerce de la librairie, (1763)', *Primary Sources on Copyright (1450-1900)* <http://www.copyrighthistory.org>.

Dieselhorst, Jochen, *Was bringt das Urheberpersönlichkeitsrecht? Urheberpersönlichkeitsschutz im Vergleich Deutschland – USA* (Why Moral Rights? Moral Rights in Germany and the USA) (Frankfurt/Main: Lang, 1994).

Dietz, Adolf, *Copyright Law in the European Community: A Comparative Investigation of National Copyright Legislation, with Special Reference to the Provisions of the Treaty Establishing the European Economic Community* (Alphen aan den Rijn: Sijthoff & Noordhoff, 1978).

di Giorgio, Francesco, *Trattati di architettura ingegneria e arte militare*, ed. by C. Maltese, 3 vols (Milan: Edizioni il Polifilo, 1967).

Dittrich, Robert, 'Der Werkbegriff – sinnvolle Ausdehnung oder Denaturierung?' (The Notion of Copyrightable work – Reasonable Extension or Denaturation), in *Woher kommt das Urheberrecht?*, ed. by Robert Dittrich (Vienna: MANZ'sche, 1988), 214-37.

Dock, Marie-Claude, *Contribution historique à l'étude des droits d'auteur* (Paris: LGDJ, 1962).

Domat, Jean, *Les lois civiles dans leur ordre naturel* (Paris, 1727).

Doorman, G., *Patents for Inventions in the Netherlands during the 16ᵗʰ and 18ᵗʰ Centuries* (Amsterdam: Netherlands Patent Board, 1942).

Downie, J.A., *Robert Harley and the Press* (Cambridge: Cambridge University Press, 1979).

Drassinower, Abraham, 'Authorship as Public Address: On the Specificity of Copyright vis-à-vis Patent and Trade Mark', *Michigan State Law Review*, (2008), 199-232.

Drone, Eaton S., *A Treatise on the Law of Property in Intellectual Productions in Great Britain and the United States: Embracing Copyright in Works of Literature and Art, and Playwright in Dramatic and Musical Compositions* (Boston: Little, Brown 1879).

Du Marsais, César Chesneau, sieur, *Des tropes ou des différents sens* (1731; repr. Paris: Flammarion, 1988).

Duplessis, George, 'Privilège des gravures de l'Entrée du roi en 1660 accordé à Pierre Mariette', *Nouvelles archives de l'art français*, (1872), 257-60.

Dury, Maxime, *La censure. La prédication silencieuse* (Paris: Publisud, 1995).

Eagleton, Terry, *The Ideology of the Aesthetics* (Oxford: Blackwell, 1990).

Ebert-Schifferer, Sybille (ed.), *Deceptions and Illusions. Five Centuries of Trompe l'œil Painting* (Washington: National Gallery of Art, 2002-3).

Edelman, Bernard, *Le sacre de l'auteur* (Paris: Le Seuil, 2004).

—, *Ownership of the Image, Elements of a Marxist Theory of Law* (London: Routledge, 1977 [1973]).

Edmond, J.P., *The Aberdeen Printers, 1620 to 1736*, 4 vols (Aberdeen: J & J.P. Edmond & Spark, 1884).

Ehlers, Martin, *Über die Unzulässigkeit des Büchernachdrucks* (Dessau/Leipzig, 1784).

Eisenhardt, Ulrich, *Die kaiserliche Aufsicht über Buchdruck, Buchhandel und Presse im Heiligen Römischen Reich Deutscher Nation (1496-1806): Ein Beitrag zur Geschichte der Bücher- und Pressezensur*, Studien und Quellen zur Geschichte des deutschen Verfassungsrechts (Karlsruhe: Müller, 1970).

Eisenstein, Elisabeth, *The Printing Press as an Agent of Change: Communications and Cultural Transformations in Early-Modern Europe*, 2 vols (Cambridge: Cambridge University Press, 1979).

Elkin-Koren, Nina, 'Cyberlaw and Social Change: A Democratic Approach to Copyright Law in Cyberspace', *Cardozo Arts & Entertainment Law Journal*, 14 (1996), 215-95.

Ellis, Markman, *The Coffee House: A Cultural History* (London: Weidenfeld & Nicolson, 2004).

Epstein, S.R., and M. Prak (eds), *Guilds, Innovation and the European Economy, 1500-1800* (Cambridge: Cambridge University Press, 2008).

Evans, Charles Theodore, *American Bibliography ... A Chronological Dictionary of All Books, Pamphlets and Periodical Publications Printed in the United States of America from the Genesis of Printing in 1630 down to and Including the Year 1820, Etc.*, 14 vols (Privately printed: Chicago, 1903-59).

Falk, Henri, *Les privileges en librairie sous l'Ancien Régime* (Paris, 1905).

Feather, John, 'Authors, Publishers and Politicians: The History of Copyright and the Book Trade', *European Intellectual Property Review*, 12 (1988), 377-80.

—, 'The Book Trade in Politics: The Making of the Copyright Act of 1710', *Publishing History*, 8 (1980), 19-44.

—, 'The Publishers and the Pirates: British Copyright Law in Theory and Practice, 1710-1775', *Publishing History*, 22 (1987), 5-32.

—, *A History of British Book Publishing* (London: Croom Helm, 1988); 2nd edn (London: Routledge, 2006).

—, *Publishing, Piracy and Politics: An Historical Study of Copyright in Britain* (London: Mansell, 1994).

Febvre, Lucien, and Henri-Jean Martin, *The Coming of the Book: the Impact of Printing, 1450-1800*, trans. David Gerard, ed. by Geoffrey Nowell-Smith and David Wootton (London: N.L.B, 1976).

Félibien, Michel, *Histoire de la ville de Paris*, expanded and edited by Guy-Alexis Lobineau, 5 vols (Paris: G. Desprez, 1725).

Féraud, Jean François, *Dictionnaire critique de la langue française* (Marseille, 1787-8).

Fertel, Martin-Dominique, *La science pratique de l'imprimerie* (Saint Omer: M.D. Fertel, 1723).

Fichte, Johann Gottlieb, 'Beweis der Unrechtmäßigkeit des Büchernachdrucks. Ein Räsonnement und eine Parabel', *Berlinische Monatschrift*, 21 (1793), 443-82.

Firmin-Didot, Ambroise, *Alde Manuce et l'hellénisme à Venise* (Paris: D'Ambroise Firmin-Didot, 1875).

Firth, C.H., and R.S. Rait (eds), *Acts and Ordinances of the Interregnum, 1642-1660* (London: H.M. Stationery Office, 1911).

Fischer, Robert, *Gesetz, betreffend das Urheberrecht an Schriftwerken, Abbildungen, musikalischen Kompositionen und dramatischen Werken vom 11. Juni 1870* (Gera: Griesbach, 1870).

Fitzball, E., *Thirty-five Years of a Dramatic Authors' Life*, 2 vols (London: T.C. Newby, 1859).

Flemming, Alfred, *Das Recht der Pflichtexemplare* (München/Berlin: Beck, 1940).

Fortescue, J.W. (ed.), *Calendar of State Papers, Colonial Series, American and West Indies, 1681-1685*, 45 vols (London: Public Records Office, 1964).

Foucault, Michel, 'Qu'est-ce qu'un auteur?', *Bulletin de la société française de philosophie*, (1969), 73-104.

—, 'What is an Author?', trans. James Venit, *Partisan Review*, 42, 4 (1975), 603-14.

—, 'What is an Author?', in *Language Counter-Memory, Practice*, ed. and trans. Donald F. Bouchard (Ithaca, NY: Cornell University Press, 1980), 124-7.

Foxon, David, *Pope and the Early Eighteenth-century Book Trade* (Oxford: Clarendon Press, 1991).

Franke, Johannes, *Die Abgabe der Pflichtexemplare von Druckerzeugnissen: Mit besonderer Berücksichtigung Preussens und des deutschen Reiches, unter Benutzung archivalischer Quellen, Sammlung bibliothekswissenschaftlicher Arbeiten* (Berlin: A. Asher and Co., 1889).

Friedman, W.H., *Boydell's Shakespeare Gallery* (New York: Garland Publishing, 1967).

Frumkin, M., *Early History of Patents for Invention* (London: Chartered Institute of Patent Agents, 1947).

—, 'The Origins of Patents', *Journal of the Patent Office Society*, 27, 3 (1945), 143-9.

Fuhring, Peter, 'Jean Barbet's *Livre d'architecture, d'autels et de cheminées*: Drawing and Design in Seventeenth-Century France', *Burlington Magazine*, 145 (2003), 421-30.

Fujimura, Joan, 'Crafting Science: Standardized Packages, Boundary Objects, and "Translation"', in *Science as Practice and Culture*, ed. by A. Pickering (London: Chicago University Press, 1992), 168-211.

Fulin, Rinaldo, 'Documenti per servire alla storia della tipografia veneziana', *Archivio veneto*, XXIII (1882).

Gallagher, Catherine, *Nobody's Story* (Berkeley: University of California Press, 1974).

Gareis, Karl, *Das juristische Wesen der Autorrechte sowie des Firmen-und Markenschutzes* (1877).

Gareis, Karl, 'Juridical Nature of Author's Rights (1877)', *Primary Sources on Copyright (1450-1900)* <http://www.copyrighthistory.org>.

Garraud, R., *Traité théorique et pratique du droit pénal français*, 2nd edn, 5 vols (Paris: Larose et Forcel, 1888-94).

Gasparetto, A., *Il vetro di Murano dalle origini ad oggi* (Venice: Neri Pozza Editore, 1956).

Gastambide, Adrien-Joseph, *Traité théorique et pratique des contrefaçons en tous genres* (Paris: Legrand and Descauriet, 1837).

Gaudrat, Philippe, *Propriété littéraire et artistique. Droits des auteurs. Droits moraux. Théorie générale du droit moral*, Jurisclasseur, fasc. 1210, 2001, n. 11.

Gaultier, Jean-François, *Mémoire à consulter, pour les Libraires et Imprimeurs de Lyon, Rouen, Toulouse, Marseille et Nismes, concernant les privilèges de librairie et continuation d'iceux*, Bibliothèque nationale de France, Manus. Fçs. 22073, n. 144.

Gaye, Giovanni (ed.), *Carteggio inedito d'artisti dei secoli XIV, XV, XVI*, 3 vols (Florence: Giuseppe Molini, 1839).

Geiger, Christophe, 'The Extension of the Term of Copyright and Certain Neighbouring Rights – A Never-ending Story?', *IIC* (International Review of Intellectual Property and Competition Law), 40 (2009), 78-82.

Geller, Paul, 'Must Copyright Be For Ever Caught between Marketplace and Authorship Norms?', in *Of Authors and Origins: Essays on Copyright Law*, ed. by Brad Sherman and Alain Strowel (Oxford: Clarendon Press, 1994), 159-201.

Genette, Gérard, *Paratexts. Thresholds of Interpretation*, trans. Jane E. Lewin (Cambridge: Cambridge University Press, 1997).

Georgi, Arthur, *Die Entwicklung des Berliner Buchhandels bis zur Begründung des Börsenvereins der deutschen Buchhändler 1825* (Berlin: Paul Parey, 1926).

Gersaint, Edme, *Catalogue raisonné des divers curiosités du cabinet de feu M. Quentin de Lorangère* (Paris, 1744).

Gerulaitis, Leonardas V., *Printing and Publishing in fifteenth-century Venice* (Chicago: American Library Association, 1976).

Gieseke, Ludwig, 'Zensur und Nachdruckschutz in deutschen Staaten in den Jahren nach 1800', in *Historische Studien zum Urheberrecht in Europa*, ed. by E. Wadle (Berlin: Duncker & Humblot, 1993), 21-31.

—, *Die geschichtliche Entwicklung des deutschen Urheberrechts* (Göttingen: Schwartz, 1957).

—, *Vom Privileg zum Urheberrecht: Die Entwicklung des Urheberrechts in Deutschland bis 1845* (Göttingen: Schwartz, 1995).

Ginsburg, J.C., 'A Tale of Two Copyrights: Literary Property in Revolutionary France and America', *Tulane Law Review*, 64 (1990), 991-1031.

—, 'A Tale of Two Copyrights: Literary Property in Revolutionary France and America', in *Of Authors and Origins: Essays on Copyright Law*, ed. by Brad Sherman and Alain Strowel (Oxford: Clarendon Press, 1994), 131-58.

—, 'Creation and Commercial Value: Copyright Protection of Works of Information', *Columbia Law Review*, 90, 7 (1990), 1865-938.

Godson, Richard, *A Practical Treatise on the Law of Patents for Inventions and of Copyright* (London, 1823).

Goldfriedrich, Johann, *Geschichte des Deutschen Buchhandels vom Beginn der klassischen Periode bis zum Beginn der Fremdherrschaft (1740-1804)*, (Leipzig: Verlag des Börsenvereins, 1909).

Gómez-Arostegui, H. Tomás, 'What Copyright History Teaches us About Copyright Injunctions and the Inadequate-remedy-at-law Requirement', *Southern California Law Review*, 81 (2008), 1197-280.

Goode, Luke, *Jürgen Habermas: Democracy and the Public Sphere* (London: Pluto Press, 2005).

Goodrich, Peter, *Reading the Law: A Critical Introduction to Legal Methods and Techniques* (Oxford: Basil Blackwell, 1986).

Goody, Jack, *Death, Property and Ancestors* (London: Tavistock Publications, 1962).

Gray, E.G., *The Making of John Ledyard: Empire and Ambition in the Life of a an Early American Traveler* (New Haven: Yale University Press, 2007).

Gray, Kevin, and Susan Francis Gray, *Elements of Land Law*, 4th edn (Oxford: Oxford University Press, 2005).

Grayson, Cecil (ed. and trans.), *'On Painting' and 'On Sculpture': The Latin texts of 'De pictura' and 'De statua'* (London: Phaidon, 1972).

Greene, Jody, *The Trouble with Ownership: Literary Property and Authorial Liability in England, 1660-1730* (Philadelphia: University of Pennsylvania Press, 2005).

Greene, Robert, *Groatsworth of Wit* (London, 1592).

Greg, W.W., *A Companion to Arber* (Oxford: Clarendon Press, 1967).

Griffin, Dustin, *Literary Patronage in England 1650-1800* (Cambridge: Cambridge University Press, 1996).

Griffin, Robert J., 'Anonymity and Authorship', *New Literary History*, 30, 4 (1999), 877-95.

Grivel, Marianne, 'La Réglementation du travail des graveurs en France au XVIe siècle', in *Le Livre et l'image en France au XVIe siècle* (Paris: Presses de l'École normale supérieure, 1989).

—, 'Les graveurs en France au XVIe siècle', in *La Gravure française à la Renaissance à la Bibliothèque nationale de France* (Paris: Bibliothèque nationale de France, 1994-5), 33-57.

—, *Le Commerce de l'estampe à Paris au XVIIe siècle* (Geneva: Droz, 1986).

Grosheide, F. Willem, 'Paradigms in Copyright Law', in *Of Authors and Origins: Essays on Copyright Law*, ed. by Brad Sherman and Alain Strowel (Oxford: Clarendon Press, 1994), 203-33.

—, *Auteursrecht op maat: Beschouwingen over de grondslagen van het auteursrecht in een rechtspolitieke context* (Deventer: Kluwer, 1986).

Groves, Jeffrey D., 'Courtesy of the Trade', in *A History of the Book in America. Volume 3. The Industrial Book 1840-1880*, ed. by Scott E. Casper, Jeffrey D. Groves, Stephen W. Nissenbaum and M. Winship (Chapel Hill, NC: University of North Carolina Press, 2007), 139-48.

Guss, Donald L., 'Enlightenment as Process: Milton and Habermas', *PMLA: Publications of the Modern Language Association of America*, 106 (1991), 1156-69.

Habermas, Jürgen, *The Structural Transformation of the Public Sphere: An Inquiry into a Category of Bourgeois Society*, trans. Thomas Burger (Cambridge, MA: The MIT Press, 1991).

Hale, David George, *The Body Politic: A Political Metaphor in Renaissance English Literature* (The Hague: Mouton, 1971).

Haller, William, 'Before *Areopagitica*', *PMLA: Publications of the Modern Language Association of America*, 42 (1927), 875-900.

Hargrave, Francis, *An Argument in Defence of Literary Property* (London, 1774).

Harreld, Donald J., 'An Education in Commerce. Transmitting Business Information in Early Modern Europe', paper presented at the XIV International Economic History Congress, Helsinki, 21-25 August 2006.

Hart, H.L.A., *The Concept of Law* (Oxford: Clarendon Press, 1994 [1961]).

Hattenhauer, Hans (ed.), *Allgemeines Landrecht für die Preussischen Staaten von 1794* (Neuwied: Luchterhand, 1970).

Hawes, Joel, *Lectures to Young Men on the Formation of Character ... with an Additional Lecture on Reading* (London, 1829).

Haynes, C., 'Reassessing "Genius" in Studies of Authorship. The State of the Discipline', *Book History*, 8 (2005), 287-320.

Hazard, Samuel, (ed.), *Minutes of the Provincial Council of Pennsylvania*, 10 vols (Philadelphia: J. Severns, 1851-2).

Heemskerk Az., J., *Voordragten over den eigendom van voortbrengselen van den geest*, 2nd edn (Amsterdam: Beerendonk, 1869; repr. Amsterdam: De Kloof, 2000, with an introduction by R.J.Q. Klomp).

Héricourt, Louis d', 'Mémoire en forme de requête à M. le Garde des Sceaux rédigé par M. Louis D'Héricourt, avocat au Parlement', in *La Propriété littéraire au XVIIIe siècle. Receuil de pièces et de documents*, ed. by E. Laboulaye and G. Guiffrey (Paris: Hachette, 1859), 21-40.

—, 'Memorandum (1725-1726)', *Primary Sources on Copyright (1450-1900)* <http://www.copyrighthistory.org>

Hesse, Carla, 'Enlightenment Epistemology and the Laws of Autorship in Revolutionary France, 1777-1793', *Representations*, 30 (Spring, 1990), 109-37.

Hills, Henry, *The Life of H.H. with the relation at large of what passed betwixt him and the Taylors Wife* (London: Printed by T.S., 1688).

Hilty, Reto M., *Urheberrecht in der Informationsgesellschaft* (Copyright in the Information Society) (Zeitschrift für Urheber – und Medienrecht Sonderheft, 2003), 983-1005.

Hirsch, Rudolf, *Printing, Selling and Reading, 1450-1550* (Wiesbaden: Harrasowitz, 1967).

Hoadly, C.J. (ed.), *The Public Records of the State of Connecticut*, 9 vols (Hartford: various publishers, 1894-1953).

Hoftijzer, P.G., *Engelse boekverkopers bij de beurs: De geschiedenis van de Amsterdamse boekhandels Bruyning en Swart* (Amsterdam: APA-Holland University Press, 1987).

Hotman, François, *Commentarius in quatuor libros institutionum iuris civilis* (Lyon, 1588).

Huard, Gustave, *Traité de la propriété intellectuelle*, 2 vols (Paris: Marchal and Billard, 1903).

Hughes, Merritt Y. (ed.), *John Milton: Complete Poems and Major Prose* (Indianapolis, IN: The Odyssey Press, 1957).

Hunt, Arnold, 'Book Trade Patents, 1603-40', in *The Book Trade and its Customers 1450-1900*, ed. by Arnold Hunt, Giles Mandelbrote and Alison Shell (Winchester: St Pauls Bibliographies, 1997), 27-54.

Hunter, D., 'Copyright Protection for Engravings and Maps in Eighteenth-Century Britain', *The Library*, 6th ser., 9 (1987), 128-47.

Hutchison, Ross, *Locke in France, 1688-1734* (Oxford: Voltaire Foundation, 1991).

Hutchison, Sidney C., *The History of the Royal Academy 1768-1968* (London: Chapman and Hall, 1968).

Infelise, Mario, *L'editoria veneziana nel '700* (Milano: Franco Angeli, 1991).

Ivins, William M., *Prints and Visual Communications* (London: Routledge & Kegan Paul, 1953).

Jackson, William A., *Records of the Court of the Stationers' Company 1602 to 1640* (London, 1957).

Jacob, Christian, *L'empire des cartes: Approches théoriques de la cartographie à travers l'histoire* (Paris: Albin Michel, 1992).

Jaszi, Peter, 'Toward a Theory of Copyright: Metamorphoses of Authorship', *Duke Law Journal*, 42 (1991), 455-502

Jehoram, Herman Cohen, 'Urheberrecht: eine Sache des Rechts oder der Opportunität? Eine alte, aber unvollendete Debatte in den Niederlanden', in *Historische Studien zum Urheberrecht in Europa*, ed. by E. Wadle (Berlin: Duncker & Humblot, 1993), 115-20.

Johns, Adrian, *The Nature of the Book: Print and Knowledge in the Making* (Chicago, IL: University of Chicago Press, 1998).

Kaiser, Thomas E., 'Money, Despotism, and Public Opinion in Early Eighteenth-Century France: John Law and the Debate on Royal Credit', *Journal of Modern History*, 63 (1991), 1-28.

Kaiser, Thomas E., 'Property, Sovereignty, the Declaration of the Rights of Man and the Tradition of French Jurisprudence', in *The French Idea of Freedom and the Declaration of the Rights of 1789*, ed. by Dale Van Klee (Stanford: Stanford University Press, 1994), 300-39.

Kant, Immanuel, 'Von der Unrechtmäßigkeit des Büchernachdrucks', *Berliner Monatszeitschrift* (1785).

Kantorowicz, Ernst , 'La souveraineté de l'artiste. Note sur quelques maximes juridiques et les théories de l'art à la Renaissance', trad. L Mayali, in *Mourir pour la patrie* (Paris: Presses Universitaires de France, 1984).

Kaplan, Benjamin, 'The Registration of Copyright', Study no. 17 (August 1958), in *Studies on copyright - Arthur Fisher Memorial Edition* (South Hackensack, NJ: Rothman, 1963), 325-91.

Kase, Francis J., *Copyright Thought in Continental Europe: Its Development, Legal Theories and Philosophy* (South Hackensack: Rothman, 1967).

Kasteele, Johannes van de, *Het auteursrecht in Nederland* (Leiden: Somerwil, 1885).

Kawohl, F., 'Commentary on J.S. Pütter: The Reprinting of Books (1774)', *Primary Sources on Copyright (1450-1900)* <http://www.copyrighthistory.org>.

—, 'Commentary on Kant: On the Unlawfulness of Reprinting (1785)', *Primary Sources on Copyright (1450-1900)* <http://www.copyrighthistory.org>.

—, 'Commentary on Philipp Erasmus Reich and the Leipzig Publishers' Cartel (1765)', *Primary Sources on Copyright (1450-1900)* <http://www.copyrighthistory. org>.

—, 'Commentary on the Austrian Statutes on Censorship and Printing (1781)', *Primary Sources on Copyright (1450-1900)* <http://www.copyrighthistory.org>.

—, 'Commentary on the Reprinting Provisions in the Prussian Statute Book (1794)', *Primary Sources on Copyright (1450-1900)* <http://www.copyrighthistory.org>.

—, *Urheberrecht der Musik in Preußen (1820 - 1840)*, Quellen und Abhandlungen zur Geschichte des Musikverlagswesens (Tutzing: Schneider, 2002).

—, and M. Kretschmer, 'Abstraction and Registration: Conceptual Innovations and Supply Effects in Prussian and British Copyright (1820-50)', *Intellectual Property Quarterly*, 2 (2003), 209-28.

—, and M. Kretschmer, 'Johann Gottlieb Fichte, and the Trap of *Inhalt* (Content) and *Form*: An information perspective on music copyright', in *Copyright and the Production of Music*, special issue of *Information, Communication and Society*, 12 (2009), 41-64.

Kemp, Martin, *Leonardo da Vinci: The Marvellous Works of Nature and Man* (London: Dent, 1981).

Kewes, Paulina, *Authorship and Appropriation: Writing for the Stage in England 1660-1710* (Oxford: Oxford University Press, 1998).

—, *Plagiarism in Early Modern England* (London: Palgrave, 2003).

Kleensang, Michael, *Das Konzept der bürgerlichen Gesellschaft bei Ernst Ferdinand Klein* (Frankfurt: Klostermann, 1998).

Klein, Ernst Ferdinand, *Grundsätze der natürlichen Rechtswissenschaft* (Halle: Hemmerde & Schwetschke, 1797).

Klippel, Diethelm and Louis Pahlow, 'Freiheit und Absolutismus: Das allgemeine Landrecht in der Geschichte der Menschen- und Bürgerrechte', in *Reformabsolutismus und ständische Gesellschaft: Zweihundert Jahre Preußisches Allgemeines Landrecht*, ed. by Günter Birtsch and Dietmar Willoweit (Berlin: Duncker & Humblot, 1998).

—, 'Die Idee des geistigen Eigentums in Naturrecht und Rechtsphilosophie des 19. Jahrhunderts', in *Historische Studien zum Urheberrecht in Europa*, ed. by E. Wadle (Berlin: Duncker & Humblot, 1993), 121-38.

—, 'Das Privileg im Naturrecht des 18. und 19. Jahrhunderts', in *Das Privileg im europäischen Vergleich*, ed. by Barbara Dölemeyer and Heinz Mohnhaupt (Frankfurt: Klostermann, 1997), 329-46.

Klostermann, R., *Das Urheberrecht an Schrift- und Kunstwerken, Abbildungen, Compositionen, Photographien, Mustern und Modellen nach deutschem und internationalem Rechte* (Berlin: Vahlen, 1876).

Koerner, Joseph Leo, *Moment of Self-portraiture in German Renaissance Art* (Chicago: University of Chicago Press, 1993).

Kohler, Josef, *Das Autorrecht – eine zivilistische Abhandlung* (Jena: Fischer, 1880).

Koskenniemi, M., 'The History of International Law Today', 4 *Rechtsgeschichte* (2004), 61-6.

Kostylo, J., 'Commentary on Decree Establishing the Venetian Guild of Printers and Booksellers', *Primary Sources on Copyright (1450-1900)* <http://www.copyrighthistory.org>.

—, 'Commentary on Johannes of Speyer's Printing Monopoly (1469)', *Primary Sources on Copyright (1450-1900)* <http://www.copyrighthistory.org>.

—, 'Commentary on Venetian Decree on Author-Printer Relations (1545)', *Primary Sources on Copyright (1450-1900)* <http://www.copyrighthistory.org>.

—, 'Commentary on Venetian Decree on Press Affairs (1517)', *Primary Sources on Copyright (1450-1900)* <http://www.copyrighthistory.org>.

—, 'Commentary on Venetian Statute on Industrial Brevets (1474)', *Primary Sources on Copyright (1450-1900)* <http://www.copyrighthistory.org>.

Kramer, Matthew H., *John Locke and the Origins of Private Property. Philosophical Explorations of Individualism, Community and Equality* (Cambridge: Cambridge University Press, 1997).

Kretschmer, M., 'Digital Copyright: The End of an Era', *European Intellectual Property Review*, 25 (2003), 333-41.

—, 'Software as Text and Machine', *JILT* (The Journal of Information, Law and Technology), 1 (2003), 1-24. Available online at <http://www2.warwick.ac.uk/fac/soc/law/elj/jilt/2003_1/kretschmer/>.

Kuhlen, Rainer, 'Wem gehört die Information im 21. Jahrhundert?', in *Wem gehört die Information im 21. Jahrhundert?*, ed. by Thomas Dreier and Alfred Büllesbach (Köln: Schmidt, 2004), 1-9.

L'Estrange, Roger, *Considerations and Proposals in Order to the Regulation of the Press* (London, 1663).

Laboulaye, Edouard and Georges Guiffrey, *La propriété littéraire au xviii* siècle. Recueil de pièces et de documents* (Paris, 1859).

Ladas, Stephen P., *The International Protection of Literary and Artistic Property*, 2 vols (New York: Macmillan, 1938).

Laligant, O., *La Véritable condition d'application du droit d'auteur: originalité ou création?* (Aix-en-Provence: Presses Universitaires d'Aix-Marseille, 1999).

Langford, Paul, *Public Life and the Propertied Englishman 1689-1798* (Oxford: Oxford University Press, 1991).

Latour, Bruno, *Science in Action: How to Follow Scientists and Engineers through Society* (Cambridge, MA: Harvard University Press, 1987).

Lauder, John, *Historical Notices of Scottish Affairs*, 2 vols (Edinburgh: Constable, 1848).

—, *The Decisions of the Lords of Council and Session from June 6th 1678 to July 30th 1712*, 2 vols (Edinburgh: Hamilton and Balfour, 1759-61).

Law, Andrew, *Rudiments of Music* (Cheshire, Conn.: William Law, 1783).

Le Bret, Cardin, *Plaidoyers* dans *Œuvres* (Paris, 1689).

Le Clerc, Sébastien, *Pratique de la géométrie sur le papier et le terrain* (Paris: T. Jolly, 1682).

Lebensztejn, Jean-Claude, 'Framing Classical Space', *Art Journal*, 47 (1988), 37-41.

Lee, Edward, 'Freedom of the Press 2.0', *Georgia Law Review*, 42 (2008), 309-405.

Lee, John, *Memorial for the Bible Societies in Scotland* (Edinburgh: Edinburgh Bible Society, 1824).

Lee, Rensselaer W., *Ut Pictura Poesis: The Humanistic Theory of Painting* (New York: W.W. Norton & Co., 1967).

Lehmann-Haupt, H., *The Book in America: A History of the Making, and Selling of Books in the United States* (New York: Bowker, 1951).

LeMaistre, Antoine and Jean Issali, *Plaidoyers et harangues de Lemaistre* (Paris, 1659).

Lemaitre, Henri, *Histoire du dépôt légal: 1re partie (France)* (Paris: Picard, 1910).

Lessig, Lawrence, *Free Culture: How Big Media Uses Technology and the Law to Lock Down Culture and Creativity* (New York: Penguin Press, 2004).

—, *The Future of Ideas. The Fate of the Commons in a Connected World* (New York: Random House, 2001).

Lettres patentes du Roy pour le règlement des libraires, imprimeurs et relieurs de la ville de Paris, Bibliothèque nationale de France, Manus. Fçs 22061, n° 69.

Lévêque, François and Yann Ménière, *The Economics of Patents and Copyright* (Berkeley: Berkeley Electronic Press, 2004).

Levy, L.W., *Emergence of A Free Press* (New York: Oxford University Press, 1985).

Lévy-Lelouch, Claire 'Quand le privilège de librairie publie le roi', in *De la publication. Entre renaissance et lumières*, ed. by Christian Jouhaud and Alain Viala (Paris: Fayard, 2002), 139-59.

Lewinski, Silke von, *International Copyright Law and Policy* (Oxford: Oxford University Press, 2008).

Lindenbaum, Peter, 'Milton's Contract', in *The Construction of Authorship: Textual Appropriation in Law and Literature*, ed. by M. Woodmansee and P. Jaszi (Durham, NC: Duke University Press, 1994), 175-90.

Lippincott, L., *Selling Art in Georgian England: The Rise of Arthur Pond* (New Haven and London: Yale University Press, 1983).

Littlefield, G.E., *The Early Massachusetts Press, 1638-1711* (New York: B. Franklin, 1969).

Liu, Joseph P., 'Copyright and Time: A Proposal', *Michigan Law Review*, 101 (2002), 409-81.

Locke, John, *Second Treatise of Government*, ed. by Crawford Brough Macpherson (Indianapolis: Hackett Publishing Company, 1980).

—, *Two Treatises of Government* (London, 1690).

Loewenstein, Joseph, 'For a History of Literary Property: John Wolfe's Reformation', *ELR: English Literary Renaissance*, 18 (1988), 389-412.

—, *The Author's Due: Printing and the Prehistory of Copyright* (Chicago, IL: The University of Chicago Press, 2002).

Long, Pamela O., 'Invention, Authorship, 'Intellectual Property' and the Origin of Patents: Notes toward a Conceptual History', *Technology and Culture*, 32, 4 (1991), 846-84.

—, *Openness, Secrecy, Authorship: Technical Arts and the Culture of Knowledge from Antiquity to the Renaissance* (Baltimore: Johns Hopkins University Press, 2001).

Lowens, I., 'Andrew Law and the Pirates', *Journal of American Musicological Society*, 13 (1960), 206-23.

—, 'Copyright and Andrew Law', *Papers of the Bibliographical Society of America*, 53 (1959), 150-9.

Luf, Gerhard , 'Philosophisches Strömungen in der Aufklärung und ihr Einfluss auf das Urheberrecht', in *Woher kommt das Urheberrecht und wohin geht es?*, ed. by R. Dittrich (Wien: Manz, 1988).

Lukács, Georg, *History and Class Consciousness*, trans. Rodney Livingstone (London: Merlin Press, 1971).

Lyon-Caen, Ch., and Paul Delalaine, *Lois françaises et étrangères sur la propriété littéraire et artistique*, 2 vols (Paris: Cercle de la Librarie etc.; F. Pichon Éditeur, 1889).

McDonald, William R., 'Scottish Seventeenth-Century Almanacs', *The Bibliotheck*, 4, 1, 8 (1966), 257-322.

McDougall, Warren, 'Copyright Litigation in the Court of Session, 1738-1749 and the Rise of the Scottish Book Trade', *Edinburgh Bibliographical Society*, 5 (1987), 2-31.

Machlup, Fritz, and Edith Penrose, 'The Patent Controversy in the Nineteenth Century', *Journal of Economic History*, 10 (1950), 1-29.

Mackenney, Richard, *Tradesmen and Traders: The World of the Guilds in Venice and Europe, c. 1250-c. 1650* (London: Croom Helm, 1987).

McKeon, Michael, 'Parsing Habermas's Bourgeois Sphere', *Criticism*, 46 (2004), 273-7.

McLeod, K., 'How Copyright Law Changed Hip Hop: An Interview with Public Enemy's Chuck D and Hanks Shoklee', *Stay Free Magazine* (2002). Available online at <http://www.ibiblio.org/pub/electronic-publications/stay-free/archives/20/public_enemy.html >.

MacLeod, Christine, *Inventing the Industrial Revolution: The English Patent System, 1660-1800* (Cambridge: Cambridge University Press, 1988).

Macpherson, C.B. (ed.), *Property. Mainstream and Critical Positions* (Oxford: Blackwell, 1978).

MacQueen, Hector L., *Copyright, Competition and Industrial Design*, 2nd edn (Edinburgh: Edinburgh University Press, 1995).

Madero, Marta, *Tabula picta. La peinture et l'écriture dans le droit médiéval* (Paris: éditions de l'École des Hautes Études en Sciences Sociales, 2004).

Maffei, Paola, *Tabula picta. Pittura e scrittura nel pensiero dei glossatori* (Milan: Giuffrè, 1988).

Maidment, James (ed.), *States Papers and Miscellaneous Correspondence of Thomas Earl of Melrose*, 2 vols (Edinburgh: Abbotsford Club, 1837).

Malapert, François, 'Histoire abrégée de la législation sur la propriété littéraire avant 1789', *Journal des économistes*, (1881), 437-76.

Malesherbes, Chrétien Guillaume de Lamoignon de, *Mémoires sur la librairie. Mémoires sur la liberté de la presse*, presented by Roger Chartier (Paris: Imprimerie Nationale, 1994).

Mandich, Giulio, 'Le privative industriali veneziane (1450-1550)', *Rivista del diritto commerciale e del diritto generale delle obbligazioni*, 34 (September-October 1936), 511-47.

—, 'Venetian patents (1450-1550)', *Journal of the Patent Office Society*, 30, 3 (1948), 166-224.

Mann, Alastair J., '"Some Property is Theft": Copyright Law and Illegal Activity in Early Modern Scotland', in *Against the Law: Crime, Sharp Practice and the Control of Print*, ed. by Robin Myers, Michael Harris and Giles Mandelbrote (London: British Library, 2004), 31-60.

—, 'Book Commerce, Litigation and the Art of Monopoly: The Case of Agnes Campbell, Royal Printer, 1676-1712', *Scottish Economic and Social History*, 18 (1998), 132-56.

—, *The Scottish Book Trade 1500 to 1720: Print Commerce and Print Control in Early Modern Scotland* (Edinburgh: Tuckwell Press, 2000).

Marin, Louis, *Le portrait du roi* (Paris: Les Éditions de minuit, 1981).

Marion, Simon, *Plaidoyez de M. Simon Marion, advocat en Parlement, Baron de Druy: plaidoyez second, sur l'impression des Œuvres de Sénèque, revueuës et annotées par feu Marc Antoine Muret* (1586), Bibliothèque nationale de France, Manus. Fçs. 22071, n°28.

Markoff, John, *The Abolition of Feudalism: Peasants, Lords, and Legislators in the French Revolution* (University Park, PA: Pennsylvania State University Press, 1996).

Marot, Clément, *Œuvres de Clément Marot* (Lyon, 1538).

Martin, Henri-Jean, *Print, Power, and People in Seventeenth-Century France*, trans. David Gerard (London: Scarecrow Press, 1993).

Maruca, Lisa, *The Work of Print, Authorship and the English Text Trades 1660-1760* (Seattle: Helman, 2007).

Marx, Karl, 'The Fetishism of Commodities and the Secret Thereof', *Capital. A Critique of Political Economy*, trans. Ben Fowles (Harmonsworth: Penguin, 1976).

Masse, Pierre, *Le droit moral de l'auteur sur son œuvre littéraire ou artistique* (Paris, 1906).

Maugham, R., *A Treatise on the Laws of Literary Property* (London: Longman, 1828). Available online at *Primary Sources on Copyright (1450-1900)* <http://www.copyrighthistory.org>.

May, Christopher, 'The Denial of History: Reification, Intellectual Property and the Lessons of the Past', *Capital and Class: Bulletin of the Conference of Socialist Economists*, 88 (2006), 33-56.

—, 'The Venetian Moment: New Technologies, Legal Innovation and the Institutional Origins of Intellectual Property', *Prometheus*, 20 (2002), 159-79.

Mazzeo, Tilar J., *Plagiarism and Literary Property in the Romantic Period* (Philadelphia, University of Pennsylvania Press, 2007).

Meckier, Jerome, *Innocent Abroad, Dickens's American Engagements* (Lexington: University of Kentucky Press, 1990).

Merlin, Philippe-Antoine, 'Contrefaçon', in *Répertoire universel et raisonné de jurisprudence*, 5th edn, Volume 5 (Paris, 1825).

Meyer, Friedrich Hermann, 'Reformbestrebungen im achtzehnten Jahrhundert', *Archiv für Geschichte des Deutschen Buchhandels*, 12 (1889), 201-300.

Miani, M., D. Resini, and F. Lamon, *L'arte dei maestri vetrai di Murano* (Venice: Matteo Editore, 1984).

Milton, John, *Areopagitica, With a Commentary by Sir Richard C. Jebb* (Cambridge: Cambridge University Press, 1918).

Mitchell, Rose, 'Maps in Sixteenth-Century English Law Courts', *Imago Mundi*, 58 (2006), 212-8.

Moël, Michel Le (ed.), *Paris à vol d'oiseau* (Paris: Archives Nationales, 1995).

Mohnhaupt, Heinz, 'Privilegien und gemeines Wohl im ALR', in *200 Jahre Allgemeines Landrecht für die Preußischen Staaten*, ed. by Barbara Dölemeyer and Heinz Mohnhaupt (Frankfurt: Klostermann, 1994), 105-44.

Molà, Luca, *The Silk Industry of Renaissance Venice* (Baltimore, London: Johns Hopkins University Press, 2000).

Molière, *Précieuses ridicules* (Paris, 1660).

Mollier, Jean-Yves, *Postface, Lettre sur le commerce de la librairie* (Paris: éd. Mille et une nuits, 2003).

Montagna, D., 'Benjamin West's The Death of General Wolfe: A Nationalist Narrative', *American Art Journal*, 13 (1981), 72-88.

Monticolo, Giovanni, and Enrico Besta (eds), *I capitolari delle arti veneziane sottoposte alla Giustizia e poi alla Giustizia vecchia dalle origini al 1330*, 3 vols (Rome, 1905-14).

More, Thomas, *The Answer to a Poisoned Book* (1534).

Morillot, André, *De la protection accordée aux œuvres d'art, aux photographies aux dessins et modèles industriels et aux brevets d'invention dans l'Empire d'Allemagne* (Paris & Berlin, 1878).

Mortier, Roland, *L'originalité, une nouvelle catégorie esthétique au siècle des Lumières* (Genève: Droz, 1982).

Moscati, Laura, 'Un memorandum di John Locke tra censorship e copyright', *Rivista di storia del diritto italiano*, LXXVI (2003), 69.

Moxon, Joseph, *Moxon's Mechanick Exercises, 1683* (New York: DeVinne Press, 1896).

Mullan, John, *Anonymity* (London: Faber & Faber, 2008).

Myers, Robin, and Michael Harris (eds), *The Stationers' Company and the Book Trade, 1550-1990* (Winchester: St Pauls, 1997).

Myers, Robin, *The Stationers' Company Archive: An Account of the Records, 1554-1984* (Winchester: St Pauls, 1990).

Nard, Craig Allen, 'Constitutionalizing Patents: From Venice to Philadelphia', *Review of Law & Economic*, 2 (2006), 224-321.

Netanel, Neil Weinstock, *Copyright's Paradox* (New York: Oxford University Press, 2008).

Neustetel, Leopold Joseph, *Der Büchernachdruck nach Römischem Recht betrachtet* (Heidelberg: Groos, 1824). Also available online at *Primary Sources on Copyright (1450-1900)* <http://www.copyrighthistory.org>.

Nicholson, Andrew (ed.), *The Letters of John Murray to Lord Byron* (Liverpool: Liverpool University Press, 2007).

Nicholson, W., *The Struggle for a Free Stage in London* (London: Archibald Constable & Co., 1906).

Nicolai, Christoph Friedrich, *The Life and Opinions of Sebaldus Nothanker* (*Das Leben und die Meinungen des Herrn Magister Sebaldus Nothanker*) (1773), trans. Thomas Dutton (1798).

Nimmer, Meville B., and David Nimmer, *Nimmer on Copyright*, 11 vols (New York, N.Y., Matthew Bender, 1963-99).

Nion, Alfred, *Droits civils des auteurs, artistes et inventeurs* (Paris: Joubert, 1846).

Norbrook, David, '*Areopagitica*, Censorship, and the Early Modern Public Sphere', in *The Administration of Aesthetics: Censorship, Political Criticism, and the Public Sphere*, ed. by Richard Burt (Minneapolis, MN: University of Minnesota Press, 1994), 3-33.

Nowell-Smith, Simon, *International Copyright Law and the Publisher in the Reign of Queen Victoria* (Oxford: Clarendon Press, 1968).

Nuovo, Angela, *Il commercio librario nell'Italia del Rinascimento* (Milano: Franco Angeli, 2003).

Nuti, Lucia, 'The Perspective Plan in the Sixteenth Century: The Invention of a Representational Language', *Art Bulletin*, 76 (1994), 105-28.

O'Brien, D.P. (ed.), *The Correspondence of Lord Overstone*, 3 vols (Cambridge: Cambridge University Press, 1971).

Ohly, Ansgar, 'Urheberrecht als Wirtschaftsrecht' (Copyright as Economic Law), in *Geistiges Eigentum: Schutzrecht oder Ausbeutungstitel?* (Intellectual Property: Protection Title or License to Exploit?), ed. by Otto Depenheuer and Karl-Nikolaus Peifer (Berlin: Springer, 2008), 141-61.

Old Bailey Proceedings Online, May 1860, trial of Henry Whiting (t18600507-491) <http://www.oldbaileyonline.org/>.

Osterrieth, Albert, *Geschichte des Urheberrechts in England* (Leipzig, 1895), reprinted in *UFITA*, 131 (1996).

Owens, W.R., and P.N. Furbank (eds), *The Political and Economic Writings of Daniel Defoe,* (London: Pickering and Chatto, 2000).

Panofsky, Erwin , 'Artiste, Savant, Génie. Notes sur la "Renaissance-Dämmerung"', in *L'œuvre d'art et ses significations. Essais sur les arts visuels*, ed. by M. and B. Teyssèdre (Paris: Gallimard, 1993).

Parker, David, 'Absolutism, Feudalism and Property Rights in the France of Louis XIV', *Past and Present*, 179 (2003), 60-96.

Parker, David, 'Sovereignty, Absolutism and the Function of the Law in Seventeenth-Century France', *Past and Present*, 122 (1989), 36-74.

[Parker, Henry], *The Humble Remonstrance of the Company of Stationers* (London, 1643).

Paschal, G.W., *A History of Printing in North Carolina* (Raleigh: Edwards & Broughton, 1946).

Pastoureau, Mireille, 'Feuilles d'atlas', in *Cartes et figures de la terre* (Paris: Centre Geoges Pompidou, 1980), 442-54.

Patten, Robert L., *Charles Dickens and His Publishers* (Oxford: Oxford University Press, 1978).

Patterson, L.R., *Copyright in Historical Perspective* (Nashville: Vanderbilt University Press, 1968).

Paulmier, Adolphe Lacan and Charles, *Traité de la législation et de la jurisprudence des théâtres*, 2 vols (Paris: Durand, 1853).

Pears, I., *The Discovery of Painting. The Growth of the Interest in Arts in England 1680-1768* (New Haven, Connecticut & London: Yale University Press, 1988).

Peifer, Karl-Nikolaus, 'Urheberrechtliche Rahmenbedingungen von Open-Access-Konzepten' (Copyright Framwork for Open-Access-Concepts), *Forschung und Lehre im Informationszeitalter*, ed. by Karl-Nikolaus Peifer and Gersmann (Berlin: de Gruyter, 2007).

—, 'Zur rechtlichen Problematik des Elektronischen Publizierens' (Legal Problems of Electronic Publishing), in CLIO (Hg.), *Elektronisches Publizieren in den Geisteswissenschaften: Erfahrungen, Probleme, Perspektiven* (Berlin: CLIO, 2007), 172-90. Available online at <http://edoc.hu-berlin.de/histfor/10_I/>.

—, and Gudrun Gersmann, *Forschung und Lehre im Informationszeitalter – zwischen Zugangsfreiheit und Privatisierungsanreiz* (Research and Learning in the Information Age – Between Freedom of Access and Exclusivity) (Berlin: de Gruyter, 2007).

—, *Individualität im Zivilrecht* (Individuality in Private Law) (Tübingen: Mohr Siebeck, 2001).

Pfister, Laurent, 'L'auteur, propriétaire de son œuvre. La formation du droit d'auteur du xvie siècle à la loi de 1957', unpublished doctoral thesis, University of Strasbourg, 1999.

—, 'L'œuvre une forme originale. Naissance d'une définition juridique (xviiie – xixe siècles)', in *Le Plagiat Littéraire, Actes du colloque international de Tours*, ed. by Hélène Maurel-Indart (Université François-Rabelais de Tours, 2002), 245-68.

—, 'La propriété littéraire est-elle une propriété? Controverses sur la nature du droit d'auteur au XIXème siècle', *Revue Internationale du Droit d'Auteur*, 205 (2005), 116-209.

Phillips, Jeremy, 'The English Patent as a Reward for Invention: the Importation of an Idea', *Journal of Legal History*, 3, 1 (1982), 71-9.

—, and Alison Firth, *Introduction to Intellectual Property Law*, 4th edn (London: Butterworths, 2001).

—, Robyn Durie, and Ian Karet, *Whale on Copyright*, 5th edn (London: Sweet & Maxwell, 1997).

Pietz, William, 'The Problem of the Fetish, IIIa: Bosman's Guinea and the Enlightenment Theory of Fetishism', *Res*, 16 (1988), 105-23.

Piles, Roger de, *Cours de peinture par principes* (Paris: Jacques Estienne, 1708).

Planché, J.R., *The Reflections and Recollections of J.R. Planché*, 2 vols (London: Tinsley Brothers, 1872).

Planiol, Marcel, *Traité élémentaire de droit civil: conforme au programme officiel des facultés de droit*, 5th edn, 3 vols (Paris: Pichon etc., 1908-10).

Plumb, J.H., *The Origins of Political Stability, England, 1675-1725* (Boston, MA: Houghton Mifflin, 1967).

Poinsard, Léon, *Études de droit international conventionnel* (Paris: Librairie Cotillon, 1894).

Pointon, M., 'Portrait Painting as a Business Enterprise in London in the 1780s', *Art History*, 7 (1984), 187-205.

Pollard, A.W., 'Some Notes on the History of English Copyright', *Library*, 4, 3 (1922), 97-114.

Pollard, M., *Dublin's Trade in Books 1550-1800* (Oxford: Clarendon Press, 1989).

Pon, Lisa, *Raphael, Dürer, and Marcantonio Raimondi: Copying and the Italian Renaissance Print* (New Haven and London: Yale University Press, 2004).

Posner, Richard A., and William M. Landes, 'An Economic Analysis of Copyright Law', *Journal of Legal Studies*, 18 (1989), 325-63.

—, and William M. Landes, 'Indefinitely Renewable Copyright', *University of Chicago Law Review*, 70 (2003), 471-518.

Post, G., K. Giocarinis and R. Kay, 'The Medieval Heritage of Humanistic Ideal: "scientia donum dei est, unde vendi non potest"', *Traditio*, 11 (1955), 195-234.

Pottage, Alain, 'The Measure of the Land', *The Modern Law Review*, 57 (1994), 361-84.

—, 'The Originality of Registration', *Oxford Journal of Legal Studies*, 15 (1995) 371-401.

Pottinger, David T., *The French Book Trade in the Ancien Régime 1500-1791* (Cambridge, MA: Harvard University Press, 1958).

Pouillet, Eugène, *Traité théorique et pratique de la propriété littéraire et artistique et pratique et du droit de représentation*, ed. by Georges Maillard and Charles Claro, 3rd edn (Paris: Marchal and Billard, 1908).

Prager, Frank D., 'A History of Intellectual Property from 1545 to 1787', *Journal of the Patent Office Society*, 26, 11 (1944), 711-60.

—, 'A Manuscript of Taccola, Quoting Brunelleschi, on Problems of Inventors and Builders', *Proceedings of the American Philosophical Society*, 112 (June 1968), 131-49.

Prager, Frank D., 'Brunelleschi's Patent', *Journal of the Patent Office Society*, 28 (February 1946), 109-35.

Préaud, Maxime, Pierre Casselle, Marianne Grivel and Corinne Le Bitouzé, *Dictionnaire des éditeurs d'estampes à Paris sous l'ancien régime* (Paris: Promodis/ Cercle de la librairie, 1987).

Prezel, H. Lacombe de, *Dictionnaire du citoyen, ou abrégé historique, théorique et pratique du commerce* (Paris, 1756).

Primary Sources on Copyright (1450-1900) <http://www.copyrighthistory.org>.
    'An Ordinance for the Regulation of Printing (1643)'.
    'Andrew Law's Petition (1781)'.
    'Andrew Law's Privilege (1781)'.
    'Copyright Act for the German Empire (1870)'.
    'Court of Cassation on Artistic Property (1842)'.
    'Court of Cassation on Compilations (1814)'.
    'Court of Cassation on Moral Rights (1902)'.
    'Court of Cassation on Photography (1862)'.
    'D'Amerval's privilege (1507)'.
    'Diderot's Letter on the Book Trade (1763)'.
    'Eloy d'Amerval's Privilege (1507)'.

'French Decree of 30 August 1777 on the Duration of Privileges'.
'French Literary and Artistic Property Act (1793)'.
'Gaultier's Memorandum for the Provincial Booksellers (1776)'.
'Johannes of Speyer's Printing Monopoly, Venice (1469)'.
'Ledyard Petition Committee Report (1783)'.
'Linguet's Memorandum (1777)'.
'Louis d'Héricourt's Memorandum (1725-1726)'.
'"Pezzana e Consorti" Case: Counter-petition and Rulings (1781)' (trans. Luis A. Sundkvist).
'Luther's "Warning to the Printers" (1541)'.
'Memoriale Manfré e Compagni, 1780 in Maggio', in '"Pezzana e Consorti" Case: Supporting Documents, Venice (1780)'.
'Merlin on Counterfeiting (1825)'.
'Prussian Cabinet Order (1766)'.
'Prussian Copyright Act (1837)'.
'Purcell's Printing Privilege (1792)'.
'Report of Lamartine and Parliamentary Debates on Literary Property (1841)'.
'Royal Declaration on Sculpture and Painting (1777)' (trans. Katie Scott).
'Saxonian Statute (1773)'.
'Star Chamber Decree (1566)'.
'Star Chamber Decree (1586)'.
'Star Chamber Decree (1637)'.
'Statute of Anne (1710)'.
'Venetian Decree on Author-Printer Relations (1545)'.
'Venetian Decree on Press Affairs, Venice (1517)'.
'Venetian Decree on Privileges for New Books and Reprints (1603)'.
'William Billings' Printing Privilege (1772)'.
'William Billings' Second Petition (1772)'.

Printers (London), *The London Printers Lamentation, or, the Press opprest and overpresst* (London, 1660).

Prosi, Gerhard, *Ökonomische Theorie des Buches* (Economic Theory of the Book) (Düsseldorf: Bertelsmann, 1971).

Proudhon, P.J., 'Les Majorats littéraires (1868)', *Primary Sources on Copyright (1450-1900)* <http://www.copyrighthistory.org>.

[Prussian Academy of Sciences (eds)], *Acta Borussica. Denkmäler der preußischen Staatsverwaltung im 18, Jahrhundert*, 38 vols (Berlin, 1891-1936).

Pütter, Johann Stephan, *Der Büchernachdruck nach ächten Grundsätzen des Rechts* (Göttingen: Vandenhoek, 1774).

—, 'The Reprinting of Books Examined in the Light of True Principles of Law (Göttingen, 1774)', *Primary Sources on Copyright (1450-1900)* <http://www.copyrighthistory.org>.

Quintilian, *The Orator's Education, Books 6-8*, ed. and trans. Donald A. Russell (Cambridge, MA: Harvard University Press, 2001).

Rand, Benjamin (ed.), *Correspondence of John Locke and Edward Clarke* (Cambridge, MA: Harvard University Press, 1927).

Ransom, Harry H., *The First Copyright Statute* (Austin: University of Texas Press, 1956).

Raynal, Abbé, *A Philosophical and Political History of the Settlements and Trade of the Europeans in the East and West Indies*, 3 vols (Edinburgh: Robertson and others, 1811).

—, *L'Histoire philosophique et politique des établissements et du commerce des Européens dans les deux Indes* (Geneva: Pellet, 1780).

Raven, James, *The Business of Books: Booksellers and the English Book Trade 1450-1840* (New Haven and London: Yale University Press, 2007).

Rawlinson, W.G., *The Engraved Work of J.M.W. Turner*, 2 vols (London: Macmillan and Co, 1908).

Recht, Pierre, *Le droit d'auteur, une nouvelle forme de propriété. Histoire et théorie* (Paris: LGDJ, 1969).

Reichmann, J.H., 'Legal Hybrids between the Patent and Copyright Paradigms', *Columbia Law Review*, 94 (1994), 2432-558.

Reitlinger, G., *The Economics of Taste, The Rise and Fall of Picture Prices 1760-1960* (London: Barrie and Rockliff, 1961).

Renouard, Antoine-Auguste, *Annales de l'Imprimerie des Alde, ou histoire des trios Manuce et de leurs editions* (Paris: Renouard, 1803).

Renouard, Augustin-Charles, *Traité des droits d'auteurs, dans la littérature, les sciences et les beaux-arts*, 2 vols (Paris: Renouard, 1838-9).

Rice, Ronald E. (ed.), *Media Ownership: Research and Regulation* (Cresskill, NJ: Hampton Press, 2008).

—, (ed.), *Records of the Governor and Company of the Massachusetts Bay in New England, 1661-1674*, 5 vols (Boston: W. White, 1853-4).

Richardson, Brian, 'From scribal publication to print publication: Pietro Bembo's Rime, 1529-1535', *Modern Language Review*, 95 (2000), 684-95.

—, *Printing, Writers and Readers in Renaissance Italy* (Cambridge: Cambridge University Press, 1999).

Richelet, Pierre, *Dictionnaire françois* (Geneva: J.-H Widerhold, 1680).

Ricketson, S., *The Berne Convention for the Protection of Literary and Artistic Works: 1886-1986* (London: Centre for Commercial Law Studies, Queen Mary, 1987).

Rideau, F., 'Commentary on Book trade regulations and incorporation of the Parisian book trade (1618)', *Primary Sources on Copyright (1450-1900)* <http://www.copyrighthistory.org>.

—, 'Commentary on Condorcet's Fragments on the Freedom of the Press (1776)', *Primary Sources on Copyright (1450-1900)* <http://www.copyrighthistory.org>.

—, 'Commentary on Court of Cassation on Artistic Property (1842)', *Primary Sources on Copyright (1450-1900)* <http://www.copyrighthistory.org>.

—, 'Commentary on Crébillon's Case (1749)', *Primary Sources on Copyright (1450-1900)* <http://www.copyrighthistory.org>.

—, 'Commentary on Diderot's Letter on the book trade (1763)', *Primary Sources on Copyright (1450-1900)* <http://www.copyrighthistory.org>.

—, 'Commentary on Dramatic Copyright Act (1870)', *Primary Sources on Copyright (1450-1900)* <http://www.copyrighthistory.org>.

—, 'Commentary on Eloy d'Amerval's privilege (1507)', *Primary Sources on Copyright (1450-1900)* <http://www.copyrighthistory.org>.

—, 'Commentary on French Book Trade Regulations (1665)', *Primary Sources on Copyright (1450-1900)* <http://www.copyrighthistory.org>.

—, 'Commentary on French Decree of 30 August 1777, On the Duration of Privileges (1777)', *Primary Sources on Copyright (1450-1900)* <http://www.copyrighthistory.org>.

—, 'Commentary on French Decree on Musical Publications (1786)', *Primary Sources on Copyright (1450-1900)* <http://www.copyrighthistory.org>.

—, 'Commentary on Gaultier's Memorandum for the Provincial Booksellers (1776)', *Primary Sources on Copyright (1450-1900)* <http://www.copyrighthistory.org>.

—, 'Commentary on Le Chapelier's report (1791)', *Primary Sources on Copyright (1450-1900)* <http://www.copyrighthistory.org>.

—, 'Commentary on Linguet's memorandum (1777)', *Primary Sources on Copyright (1450-1900)* <http://www.copyrighthistory.org>.

—, 'Commentary on Luneau de Boisjermain's case (1770)', *Primary Sources on Copyright (1450-1900)* <http://www.copyrighthistory.org>.

—, 'Commentary on Memorandum on the Opposition between the Parisian and the Provincial Booksellers (1690s)', *Primary Sources on Copyright (1450-1900)* <http://www.copyrighthistory.org>.

—, 'Commentary on Simon Marion's plea on privileges (1586)', *Primary Sources on Copyright (1450-1900)* <http://www.copyrighthistory.org>.

—, 'Commentary on the Court of Cassation on Originality (1869)', *Primary Sources on Copyright (1450-1900)* <http://www.copyrighthistory.org>.

—, 'Commentary on the Court of Cassation on Photography (1862)', *Primary Sources on Copyright (1450-1900)* <http://www.copyrighthistory.org>.

—, 'Commentary on the Court of Cassation on Sculptures (1814)', *Primary Sources on Copyright (1450-1900)* <http://www.copyrighthistory.org>.

—, 'Commentary on the International Copyright Act, Paris (1852)', *Primary Sources on Copyright (1450-1900)* <http://www.copyrighthistory.org>.

—, 'Commentary on the Minutes of the 1825-1826 Commission (1826)', *Primary Sources on Copyright (1450-1900)* <http://www.copyrighthistory.org>.

—, *La formation du droit de propriété littéraire en France et en Grande-Bretagne: une convergence oubliée* (Aix-Marseille: PUAM, 2004).

Riege, Helmut (ed.), *Klopstocks Briefe 1776-1782* (Berlin: de Gruyter, 1982).

Roden, R.F., *The Cambridge Press, 1638-1692* (New York: Dodd, Mead, and Company, 1903).

Romberg, Édouard, *Compte rendu des travaux du Congrès de la propriété littéraire et artistique*, 2 vols (Bruxelles/Leipzig: Flatau, 1859).

Rose, Carol, *Property and Persuasion. Essays on the History, Theory and Rhetoric of Ownership* (Oxford: Westview Press, 1994).

Rose, Mark, 'Copyright and its Metaphors', *UCLA Law Review*, 50 (2002), 1-16.

—, 'Mothers and Authors: *Johnson v. Calvert* and the New Children of Our Imagination', *Critical Inquiry*, 22 (1996), 613-33.

—, 'The Author as Proprietor: Donaldson v Becket and the Genealogy of Modern Authorship', *Representations*, 23 (1988), 51-85.

—, *Authors and Owners: The Invention of Copyright* (Cambridge, MA: Harvard University Press, 1993).

Röthlisberger, Ernst, 'Gesamtüberblick über die Vorgänge auf urheberrechtlichem Gebiete in den Jahren 1904, 1905 und 1906', *Börsenblatt für den Deutschen Buchhandel*, 74 (1907), 1688-91.

—, *Der interne und der internationale Schutz des Urheberrechts in den verschiedenen Ländern: Mit besonderer Berücksichtigung der Schutzfristen, Bedingungen und Förmlichkeiten* (Leipzig: Börsenverein der Deutschen Buchhändler, 1904).

Rule, John, 'The Property of Skill in the Period of Manufacture', in *The Historical Meanings of Work*, ed. by Patrick Joyce (Cambridge: Cambridge University Press, 1987), 99-118.

Saalman, Howard (ed.), *The Life of Brunelleschi* (University Park and London: Pennsylvania State University Press, 1970).

St Clair, William, *The Reading Nation in the Romantic Period* (Cambridge: Cambridge University Press, 2004).

Salvioni, G.B., 'L'arte della stampa nel Veneto: la proprietà letteraria', *Giornale degli Economisti di Padova*, IV (1877), 191-285.

Sanjek, R., *American Popular Music and its Business: The First Four Hundred* Years, 2 vols (New York: Oxford University Press, 1988).

Sanson, Nicolas, *Atlas du monde, 1665*, ed. by Mireille Pastoureau (Paris: Sand & Conti, 1988).

Saugrain, Claude Marin, *Code de la librairie et imprimerie de Paris ou conférence du réglement arrêté au conseil d'état du roi le 28 fevrier 1723* (Paris: Communauté de la librairie, 1744).

Saunders, David, 'Approaches to the Historical Relations of the Legal and the Aesthetic', *New Literary History*, 23 (1992), 505-21.

—, 'Dropping the Subject: An Argument for a Positive History of Authorship and the Law of Copyright', in *Of Authors and Origins: Essays on Copyright law*, ed. by Brad Sherman and Alain Strowell (Oxford: Clarendon Press, 1994), 93-110.

Sauval, Henri, *Histoire et recherches des antiquités de la ville de Paris*, ed. by Anthony Blunt, 3 vols (Paris, 1724; Farnborough, Hants: Gregg International Publishers, 1969).

Scaglia, Giustina, *Il "Vitruvio Magliabechiano" di Francesco di Giorgio Martini*, Documenti inediti di cultura Toscana, 6 (Florence: Edizioni Gonnelli, 1985).

Schack, Haimo, 'Die Rechtfertigung des Urheberrechts als Ausschließlichkeitsrecht' (Legitimation of Copyright as Exclusive Right), in *Geistiges Eigentum: Schutzrecht oder Ausbeutungstitel?* (Intellectual Property: Protection Title or License to Exploit?), ed. by Otto Depenheuer and Karl-Nikolaus Peifer (Berlin: Springer, 2008), 123-40.

Schapira, Nicolas, 'Quand le privilège de librairie publie l'auteur', in *De la publication. Entre renaissance et lumières*, ed. by Christian Jouhaud and Alain Viala (Paris: Fayard, 2002), 121-37.

—, *Un professionnel des lettres au xviie siècle. Valentin Conrart: une histoire sociale* (Paris: Champ Vallon, 2003).

Schapiro, Meyer, 'On Some Problems in the Semiotics of Visual Art: Field and Vehicle in Image-Signs', *Simiolus* (1972-3), 9-19.

Schiff, Eric, *Industrialization without National Patents: The Netherlands, 1869-1912; Switzerland, 1850-1907* (Princeton, N.J.: Princeton University Press, 1971).

Schriks, Chris, *Het kopijrecht - 16de tot 19de eeuw: Aanleidingen tot en gevolgen van boekprivileges en boekhandelsusanties, kopijrecht, verordeningen, boekenwetten en rechtspraak in het privaat-, publiek- en staatsdomein in de Nederlanden, met globale analoge ontwikkelingen in Frankrijk, Groot-Brittannië en het Heilig Roomse Rijk* (Zutphen [etc.]: Walburg Pers/Kluwer, 2004).

Schwennicke, Andreas, *Die Entstehung der Einleitung des Preussischen Allgemeinen Landrechts von 1794* (Klostermann: Frankfurt, 1993).

Scialoja, Antonio, 'Relazione alla Legge 25 giugno 1865 n. 2337 sui diritti spettanti agli autori delle opere dell'ingegno', *Atti del Senato* (1864).

Scott, K., 'Art and Industry. A Contradictory Union: Authors, Rights and Copyrights during the *Consulat'*, *Journal of Design History*, 13 (2000), 1-21.

Scrutton, Thomas Edward, *The Law of Copyright* (London: William Clowes & Sons, 1883).

—, *The Law of Copyright*, 4th edn (London: William Clowes & Sons, 1903).

Selwyn, Pamela E., *Everyday Life in the German Book Trade: Friedrich Nicolai as Bookseller and Publisher in the Age of Enlightenment* (Pennsylvania: Pennsylvania University Press, 2000).

Seville, Catherine, 'Edward Bulwer Lytton Dreams of Copyright: "It might make me a rich man"', in *Victorian Literature and Finance*, ed. by F. O'Gorman (Oxford: Oxford University Press, 2007), 55-72.

Seville, Catherine, *Literary Copyright Reform in Early Victorian England: The Framing of the 1842 Copyright Act* (Cambridge: Cambridge University Press, 1999).

—, *The Internationalisation of Copyright Law: Books, Buccaneers and the Black Flag in the Nineteenth Century* (Cambridge: Cambridge University Press, 2006).

Sher, Richard B., 'Corporatism and Consensus in the Late Eighteenth–Century Book Trade: The Edinburgh Booksellers' Society in Comparative Perspective', *Book History*, 1 (1998), 32-93.

—, *The Enlightenment and The Book: Scottish Authors and Their Publishers in Eighteenth-century Britain, Ireland & America* (Chicago and London: Chicago University Press, 2006).

Sherman, Brad, and Alain Strowel (eds), *Of Authors and Origins: Essays on Copyright Law* (Oxford: Clarendon Press, 1994).

—, and Lionel Bently, *The Making of Modern Intellectual Property Law: The British Experience, 1760-1911* (Cambridge: Cambridge University Press, 1999).

Shortt, John, *The Law Relating to Works of Literature and Art: Embracing the Law of Copyright* (London: Horace Cox, 1871).

Siebert, Frederick Seaton, *Freedom of the Press in England, 1476-1776* (Urbana, IL: University of Illinois Press, 1952).

Signot, Jacques, *La totale et vraye description des Gaules es Ytalies* (1515).

Silver, R.G., 'Prologue to Copyright in America: 1772', *Papers of the Bibliographical Society of the University of Virginia*, 11 (1958), 259-62.

Simpson, A.W.B., *A History of the Land Law*, 2nd edn (Oxford: Clarendon Press, 1986).

Simpson, James, *Burning to Read* (Cambridge, MA: Harvard University Press, 2007).

Sirluck, Ernest, '*Areopagitica* and a Forgotten Licensing Controversy', *The Review of English Studies*, n.s., 11 (1960), 260-74.

Smith, Christine, *Architecture in the Culture of Early Humanism: Ethics, Aesthetics, and Eloquence, 1400-1470* (Oxford: Oxford University Press, 1992).

Soleau, E., *Rapport à la Chambre de commerce de Paris, sur la protection des dessins et modèles appliqués à l'industrie*, Annexe V (Bull. Ch. Com: Paris, 25 February 1905).

Sonenscher, Michael, *Work and Wages. Natural Law, Politics and the Eighteenth-Century French Trades* (Cambridge: Cambridge University Press, 1989).

[Sparke, Michael], *Scintilla, or A light broken into darke warehouses* (1641).

Sprigman, Christopher, 'Reform(aliz)ing Copyright', *Stanford Law Review*, 57 (2004), 485-568.

Star, Susan Leigh, and James R. Griesemer, 'Institutional Ecology, "Translations" and Boundary Objects: Amateurs and professionals in Berkeley's Museum of Vertebrate Zoology, 1907-39', *Social Studies in Science*, 19 (1989) 387-420.

Starkey, L.G., 'The Benefactors of the Cambridge Press: A Reconsideration', *Studies in Bibliography: Papers of the Bibliographical Society of the University of Virginia*, 3 (1950), 267-70.

Stevens, J.R., *The Censorship of English Drama 1824-1901* (Cambridge: Cambridge University Press, 1980).

—, *The Profession of the Playwright* (Cambridge: Cambridge University Press, 1992).

Stolfi, Nicola, *La proprietà intellettuale* (Turin: UTET, 1911).

Stolleis, Michael, *L'Œil de la loi. Histoire d'une métaphore* (Paris: Mille et une nuits, 2006).

Strowel, Alain, 'Liberté, propriété, originalité: retour aux sources du droit d'auteur', *Journal des procès*, (1994), 4-9, 12-16.

Stuart, John (ed.), *Extracts from the Records of the Burgh of Aberdeen*, 2 vols (Edinburgh: Scottish Burgh Record Society, 1871-2).

Sutherland, James R., 'The Circulation of Newspapers and Literary Periodicals, 1700-30', *The Library*, 15 (1934-5), 110-24.

Sutherland, John, 'Publishing History: A Hole at the Centre of Literary Sociology', *Critical Inquiry*, 14, 3 (1988), 574-89.

Talbot, J., *Francis Frith* (London: Macdonald, 1985).

Tebbel, J.W., *A History of Book Publishing in the United States*, 2 vols (New York: R.R. Bowker Co., 1972).

Terminazione degli Eccell. Riformatori, 30 Luglio 1780, '"Pezzana e Consorti" Case: Supporting documents, Venice (1780)', 49-53, *Primary Sources on Copyright (1450-1900)* <http://www.copyrighthistory.org>.

Thomas, Isaiah., *The History of Printing in America with a Biography of Printers and Account of Newspapers*, 2 vols (Albany: J. Munsell, 1874).

[Tindal, Matthew], *A Letter to a Member of Parliament* (London, 1698).

Tompson, Richard S., 'Scottish Judges and the Birth of British Copyright', *Juridical Review*, 37 (1992), 18-42.

Trabuco, C., *O Direito de Reprodução de Obras Literárias e Artísticas no Ambiente Digital* (Coimbra: Coimbra Editora, 2006).

Trivellato, Francesca, 'Guilds, Technology, and Economic Change in Early Modern Venice', in *Guilds, Innovation and the European Economy, 1450-1800*, ed. by S.R. Epstein and M. Prak (Cambridge: Cambridge University Press, 2008), 199-231.

Turley, Hans, *Rum, Sodomy and the Lash* (New York: New York University Press, 2001).

Turner, J. (ed.), *The Dictionary of Art*, 34 vols (London: MacMillan Publishers Ltd., 1996).

Vaidhyanathan, Siva, *Copyrights and Copywrongs: The Rise of Intellectual Property and How It Threatens Creativity* (New York: New York University Press, 2001).

Vasari, Giorgio, *Le vite de più eccellenti architetti, pittori & scultori italiani, da Cimabue insino a tempi nostri* (Florence: Giunti, 1550).

—, *Vita di Marcantonio Bolognese, e d'altri intagliatori di stampe, primo volume della terza parte Delle vite de' piu eccelenti pittori, scultori e architettori*, 2nd edn (Florence: Giunti, 1568).

Vasoli, Cesare, 'A proposito di scienza e technica nel Cinquecento', in *Profezia e ragione: Studi sulla cultura del Cinquecento e del Seicento* (Naples: Morano Editore, 1974), 479-505.

Vaunois, A., *De la Propriété artistique en droit français* (Paris, 1884).

—, *La condition et les droits d'auteur des artistes jusqu'à la Révolution* (Paris, 1892).

Veegens, J.D., *Het auteursrecht volgens de Nederlandsche wetgeving* ('s-Gravenhage: Belinfante, 1895).

Vereenigung ter bevordering van de belangen des boekhandels, Amsterdam, *Het letterkundig eigendomsregt in Nederland: Wetten, traktaten, regtspraak. Benevens de wetgeving op de drukpers in Nederland en Nederlandsch Indië*, 2 vols ('s-Gravenhage: Belinfante, 1865-7).

Viala, Alain, 'La triple économie du littéraire', *Studies on Voltaire and the Eighteenth Century*, 11 (2004), 19-34.

—, *Naissance de l'écrivain* (Paris: éditions de Minuit, 1985).

Villiers, J.E.R. de, *The history of the Legislation Concerning Real and Personal Property in England during the Reign of Queen Victoria* (London: C.J. Clay and Sons, 1901).

Volkmann, A.W. , *Zusammenstellung der gesetzlichen Bestimmungen über das Urheber- und Verlagsrecht: Aus den Bundesbeschlüssen, den deutschen Territorialgesetzgebungen und den französischen und englischen Gesetzen* (Leipzig: Polz, 1855).

Volz, Gustav Berthold (ed.), *Die Werke Friedrichs des Großen: in deutscher Übersetzung* (Berlin: Hobbing, 1913-4). Available online at <http://friedrich.uni-trier.de/>.

Von Erffa, H., and A. Staley, *The Paintings of Benjamin West* (London: Yale University Press, 1986).

Wächter, Oscar, *Das Autorrecht nach dem gemeinen deutschen Recht* (Stuttgart: Enke, 1875).

Warner, Michael, *The Letters of the Republic: Publication and the Public Sphere in Eighteenth-Century America* (Cambridge, MA: Harvard University Press, 1990).

Watson, James, *A History of the Art of Printing* (Edinburgh: Watson, 1713).

Wendorf, R., *Sir Joshua Reynolds, The Painter in Society* (Cambridge, MA: Harvard University Press, 1996).

Whale, R.F., *Copyright: Evolution, Theory and Practice* (London: Longman, 1971).

Whitteridge, Gweneth (trans. and ed.), *Disputations Touching the Generation of Animals* (Oxford: Blackwell Scientific, 1981).

Wijnstroom, J.J., and J.L.A. Peremans, *Het auteursrecht* (Zwolle: Tjeenk Willink, 1930).

Wilson, D., *Francis Frith's Travels: A Photographic Journey through Victorian Britain* (London: Dent & Sons, 1985).

Winship, G.P., *The Cambridge Press, 1638-1692* (Portland: Southworth-Anthoensen Press, 1945).

Winslow, Reginald, *The Law of Artistic Copyright* (London: William Clowes, 1889).

Woodmansee, Martha, *The Author, Art, and the Market. Rereading the History of Aesthetics* (New York: Columbia Press, 1994).

—, 'The Genius and the Copyright: Economic and Legal Conditions of the Emergence of the "Author"', *Eighteenth-Century Studies*, 17, 4 (1984), 425-48.

—, and Peter Jaszi (eds), *The Construction of Authorship: Textual Appropriation in Law and Literature* (Durham: Duke University Press, 1994).

Woolhouse, Roger (ed.), *An Essay Concerning Human Understanding* (1690) (London: Penguin, 1997).

Wroth, L.C., *A History of Printing in Colonial Maryland, 1686-1776* (Baltimore: Typothetae of Baltimore, 1922).

Zaret, David, *Origins of Democratic Culture: Printing, Petitions, and the Public Sphere in Early-Modern England* (Princeton, NJ: Princeton University Press, 2000).

Zecchin, Luigi, 'Il segreto dei vetrai murnaesi del Quattrocento,' *Rivista della Stazione Sperimentale del Vetro*, 11, 4 (1981), 167-72.

Zecchin, Luigi, *Vetri e vetrai di Murano*, 3 vols (Venezia: Arsenale Editrice, 1987-90).

Zedler, J.H., *Grosses vollständiges Universal-Lexikon aller Wissenschaften und Künste* (Leipzig und Halle: 1732-50).

Zorzi, Marino, 'La produzione e la circolazione del libro', in *Storia di Venezia dale origini alla caduta della Serenissima, 7: La Venezia barocca*, ed. by Gino Benzoni and Gaetano Cozzi (Rome: Istituto dell'Enciclopedia Italiana, 1998), 921-85.

Zug, J., *American Traveler: The Life and Adventures of John Ledyard, the Man Who Dreamed of Walking the World* (New York: Basic Books, 2005).

Index

OpenBook Publishers

Open Book Publishers is an independent community interest company (CIC) devoted to Open Access publishing. Set up and run by academics, we publish high quality, peer-reviewed monographs, collected volumes and lecture series in the humanities and social sciences.

Open Book speeds up the whole publishing process from author to reader by applying three recent technological advances: digital medium, the internet and print-on-demand. We thus offer all the advantages of digital texts (speed, searchability, updating, archival material, databases, discussion forums, and links to institutions' websites) together with those of the traditional printed medium.

All Open Book publications are available online to be read free of charge by anyone with access to the internet. During our first year of operations, our free digital editions have been accessed by people in over 120 countries, and each of our title is viewed by about ten readers every single day. Our books are thus reaching about as many people per month as many traditional - print only - titles will reach in their entire published life.

We are reliant on donations by individuals and institutions to help offset the production costs of our publications. As a CIC we do not operate for commercial profit and all donations, as with all other revenue we generate, will be used to finance new Open Access publications.

Please consider supporting Open Book Publishers. We are very happy to receive donations of any size!

For further information on how to donate to OBP, our publishing enterprise, additional digital material related to our titles or to order our books please visit our website:

www.openbookpublishers.com

or contact the Managing Director, Dr. Alessandra Tosi:
a.tosi@openbookpublishers.com

Lightning Source UK Ltd.
Milton Keynes UK
UKOW030623070312

188492UK00001B/12/P